Teacher Preparation Classroom

TEACHER PREP

MERRILL
PRENTICE HALL

See a demo at
www.prenhall.com/teacherprep/demo

Your Class. Their Careers. Our Future. Will your students be prepared?

We invite you to explore our new, innovative and engaging website and all that it has to offer you, your course, and tomorrow's educators! Preview this site today at www.prenhall.com/teacherprep/demo. Just click on "go" on the login page to begin your exploration.

Organized around the major courses pre-service teachers take, the Teacher Preparation site provides media, student/teacher artifacts, strategies, and other resources to equip your students with quality tools needed to excel in their courses and prepare them for their first classroom.

This ultimate on-line education resource will provide you and your students access to:

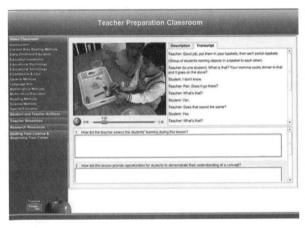

Online Video Library. More than 250 video clips—each tied to a course topic and framed by learning goals and Praxis-type questions—capture real teachers and students working in real classrooms.

Student and Teacher Artifacts. More than 200 student and teacher classroom artifacts—each tied to a course topic and framed by learning goals and application questions—provide a wealth of materials and experiences to help your students observe children's developmental learning.

Lesson Plan Builder. Offers step-by-step guidelines and lesson plan examples to support students as they learn to build high quality lesson plans.

Research Articles. Over 500 articles from ASCD's renowned journal *Educational Leadership*. The site also includes Research Navigator, a searchable database of additional educational journals.

Teaching Strategies. Over 500 research supported instructional strategies appropriate for a wide range of grade levels and content areas.

Licensure and Career Tools. Resources devoted to helping your students pass their licensure exam; learn standards, law, and public policies; plan a teaching portfolio; and survive their first year of teaching.

How to ORDER **Teacher Prep** for you and your students:
For students to receive a *Teacher Prep* Access Code with this text, instructors **must** provide a special value pack ISBN number on their textbook order form. To receive this special ISBN, please email: **Merrill.marketing@pearsoned.com** and provide the following information:
- Name and Affiliation
- Author/Title/Edition of Merrill text

Upon ordering *Teacher Prep* for their students, instructors will be given a lifetime *Teacher Prep* Access Code.

NINTH EDITION

TEACHING SECONDARY SCHOOL SCIENCE

STRATEGIES FOR DEVELOPING SCIENTIFIC LITERACY

RODGER W. BYBEE

Executive Director,
Biological Science Curriculum Study

JANET CARLSON POWELL

Associate Director,
Biological Science Curriculum Study

LESLIE W. TROWBRIDGE

Professor Emeritus of Science Education
University of Northern Colorado

PEARSON

Merrill
Prentice Hall

Upper Saddle River, New Jersey
Columbus, Ohio

Library of Congress Cataloging-in-Publication Data

Bybee, Rodger W.
  Teaching secondary school science : strategies for developing scientific literacy /
Rodger W. Bybee, Janet Carlson Powell, Leslie W. Trowbridge.—9th ed.
    p. cm.
  Trowbridge's name appears first on the earlier edition
  Includes bibliographical references and index.
  ISBN-13: 978-0-13-230450-4
  ISBN-10:   0-13-230450-3
  1. Science—Study and teaching (Secondary)—United States. 2. Science teachers—United
States. I. Carlson–Powell, Janet.
II. Trowbridge, Leslie W. III. Title.
  Q183.3.A1T76 2008
  507.1'2—dc22   2007020010

Vice President and Executive Publisher: Jeffery W. Johnston
Acquisitions Editor: Meredith D. Fossel
Production Editor: Alexandrina Benedicto Wolf
Production Coordination: Carlisle Publishing Services
Design Coordinator: Diane Lorenzo
Photo Coordinator: Maria Vonada
Cover Designer: Bryan Huber
Cover Image: Jupiter Images
Production Manager: Pamela D. Bennett
Director of Marketing: David Gesell
Marketing Coordinator: Brian Mounts

Photo Credits: Tom Watson/Merrill, p. 3; Anthony Magnacca/Merrill, pp. 10, 56, 122, 129, 160, 236, 241, 248, 313; Colleen Schneider/USDA/NRCS/Natural Resources Conservation Service, p. 27; Library of Congress, p. 40; Scott Cunningham/Merrill, pp. 54, 168, 277, 323; Rick Singer/PH College, p. 136; Pearson Learning Photo Studio, pp. 159, 199; Anne Vega/Merrill, pp. 177, 230, 326; Robert Vega/Merrill, p. 179; Maria B. Vonada/Merrill, p. 191; NASA/John F. Kennedy Space Center, p. 196; David Mager/Pearson Learning Photo Studio, p. 234; Liz Moore/Merrill, p. 264; Valerie Schultz/Merrill, p. 312; Lori Whitley/Merrill, p. 323; Kathy Kirtland/Merrill, p. 324.

This book was set in Berkeley by Carlisle Publishing Services. It was printed and bound by Bind Rite Graphics. The cover was printed by Phoenix Color Corp.

Pearson Education Ltd.
Pearson Education Singapore Pte. Ltd.
Pearson Education Canada, Ltd.
Pearson Education–Japan

Pearson Education Australia Pty., Limited
Pearson Education North Asia Ltd.
Pearson Educación de Mexico, S.A. de C.V.
Pearson Education Malaysia, Pte. Ltd.

10 9 8 7 6 5 4 3 2 1
ISBN-13: 978-0-13-230450-4
ISBN-10:   0-13-230450-3

PREFACE

Teaching Secondary School Science: Strategies for Developing Scientific Literacy, 9th Edition, addresses the needs of undergraduate preservice teachers of science. The text provides information and suggestions for teaching physical, biological, and earth sciences in the middle school and high school grades. It is also useful for graduate students whose undergraduate majors were outside the field of education, but for whom teaching middle and secondary school science is now a primary career goal. This book is also an important resource for graduate students and experienced teachers in courses concerned with assessment in science classes, curriculum development and reform, instructional problems, and current trends in science teaching. It is also a useful guide and reference in workshops and institutes for teachers emphasizing strategies for inquiry teaching. The current emphases on science education standards and inquiry are fully explained and brought to the foreground for science programs.

The ninth edition retains the strong features of previous editions: emphasis on active pupil involvement in learning, use of inquiry and investigative teaching strategies to provide experiences in gathering data to support hypotheses, discussion of advances in our understanding of how students learn science, and use of research-based instructional strategies. Based on the extensive science teaching experience of the authors, many practical examples of successful teaching strategies are provided.

The theme of developing scientific literacy among science students is stressed throughout. Suggestions for fostering the effective reading of science materials, developing the vocabulary of science, and raising the level of awareness of the interrelationships among science, technology, and society are included.

ORGANIZATION

The ninth edition encompasses eight units:

- Introduction
- Historical and Contemporary Perspectives
- Goals, Objectives, and Assessments
- Understanding the Science Curriculum
- Planning Effective Science Teaching and Programs
- Strategies for Science Teaching
- Understanding Students
- Student Teaching

These units have been reorganized not only to provide prospective secondary science teachers with the tools and resources they need to teach science effectively on a day-to-day basis, but also to develop a holistic view of science teaching, and promote enthusiasm and a desire to succeed at the tasks they encounter.

NEW AND UNIQUE FEATURES IN THIS EDITION

- **Investigating Science Teaching activities** are located at the end of each chapter and provide students an opportunity to examine various aspects of science teaching.
- **Icons highlight new integrated technology resources**. Discussions of technology have been updated and woven throughout the text, including technology margin notes that encourage students to visit the text's new website at **www.prenhall.com/teacherprep** for further research and supplemental science activities.

◆ **Guest Editorials** that showcase actual preservice and inservice science teachers illustrate concepts and provide real-world context for students.

◆ **Two resources on the Teacher Prep Website** provide additional *Teaching Science Activities* in biology, chemistry, earth sciences, physics, problem solving, science fair projects, technology, and mathematics, as well as activities for gifted students. Further, the website provides sample daily lesson plans that offer practice in using an instructional model for inquiry teaching and learning.

ACKNOWLEDGMENTS

The authors wish to acknowledge the many people who assisted in the preparation of this ninth edition of *Teaching Secondary School Science:* Patricia Bybee; our editors at Merrill/Prentice Hall—Acquisitions Editor Meredith Fossel, and Production Editor Alex Wolf; and our Project Editor at Carlisle Publishing Services, Mary Tindle. We also thank our colleagues who helped with the review process: James D. Ellis, University of Kansas; Arthur W. Friedel, Indiana Purdue University, Fort Wayne; Pamela S. Guimond, Governors State University; Terrie L. Kielborn, University of West Georgia; Janice Meyer, University of Houston Clear Lake; Janet Parker, Georgetown College; and Heather Wilson-Ashworth, Utah Valley State College.

Special recognition is given to the late Dr. Robert B. Sund, whose foresight regarding the philosophy and teaching methods in the first three editions of this text have strongly influenced subsequent editions, including this one. In particular, the current emphasis on inquiry teaching, recommended by the National Research Council in its publication, "National Science Education Standards," reflects a teaching strategy that was embodied in all of Dr. Sund's teaching and subsequently became a fundamental part of the philosophy of this book.

Brief Contents

Note: Every effort has been made to provide accurate and current Internet information in this book. However, the Internet and information posted on it are constantly changing, so it is inevitable that some of the Internet addresses listed in this textbook will change.

CONTENTS

SPECIAL FEATURES

Investigating Inquiry in the Classroom

Experiencing Ethical Analysis

GUEST EDITORIAL

Note: Every effort has been made to provide accurate and current Internet information in this book. However, the Internet and information posted on it are constantly changing, so it is inevitable that some of the Internet addresses listed in this textbook will change.

UNIT 1

INTRODUCTION

As she worked late into the night on her first lesson, Maria Romero wondered about her effectiveness as a science teacher. The next day, Ms. Romero began her lesson by asking the students to describe the genetic concepts *genes, chromosomes,* and *mutations.* Because Ms. Romero assumed students had learned these concepts in elementary school, she was surprised when they expressed a range of responses, mostly incorrect. She recognized that most students identified the terms as scientific, even biological, but that they consistently responded incorrectly. For example, students indicated that genes were different layers of skin, something in one's blood, things that indicate one's age, and a reproductive part of the body. They also thought chromosomes were either things that clogged one's arteries or plant-eating animals. Finally, they had the idea that mutations were changes that occurred as one got older, sicknesses caused by bacteria, or structures in plants.

Maria knew that elementary teachers had taught biology and even introduced some of these same ideas about genetics, but the students had little understanding of the information, and the terms had no meaning or importance to them. Maria wondered about her role in helping students develop scientific literacy, especially in connection with teaching secondary school science.

After a little research on the Internet, Ms. Romero discovered that the students displayed what contemporary learning theorists referred to as *prior conceptions* or *naive theories.* As she investigated further, she found that psychologists had proposed explanations for students' prior conceptions and the learning process. Ms. Romero discovered that the model of learning was referred to as *constructivism,* a term that expresses a dynamic and interactive view of learning. In the constructivist view of learning, students continually revise, redefine, and reorganize concepts through interactions among themselves, natural phenomena, science lessons, discussions with other individuals, and the introduction of information from other sources, such as textbooks and science teachers. Students first interpret objects and events in terms of their prior experiences, which, from the perspective of the science teacher, may be incorrect or a prior conception. In order to change the prior conceptions, someone (e.g., a teacher or another student) or an experience (e.g., observations of natural phenomena, textbooks, or laboratory experiences) has to challenge the students' prior conceptions by showing them that their current ideas are inadequate. Further, students must have time and additional experiences to reconstruct a more adequate and scientifically accurate conception.

The results of this brief review of research provided Maria with insights about teaching secondary school science and strategies for developing scientific literacy. When science teachers discover new and better ways to teach, they experience the excitement of education, and the extension of these insights to students learning science can be the most exhilarating of a teacher's career.

A life in science teaching can entail frustrations and disappointments; but it also involves satisfactions and achievements that promise to outweigh the problems. This unit introduces ideas and issues that you will have to consider as a science teacher. Ms. Romero's story about the connections between student learning and science teaching is only one of many that could be told, but more importantly, the stories reflect ones you will experience as you become a science teacher and pursue the goal of developing scientific literacy for your students.

BECOMING A SCIENCE TEACHER

If you are reading this sentence, you are in the process of becoming a science teacher. As with other important issues in your life, you no doubt struggled with this decision. While deciding, you probably gathered information on the options—you might have explored the science major, talked to friends and parents, conferred with your college advisor, and even visited your high school science teacher. With all the facts in mind, you decided to become a science teacher. Thinking all was settled, you went to work on your science major and began taking education courses. For a time, most aspects of your career choice seemed resolved. Now you are taking a course to learn about science teaching; soon you will be student teaching; in the foreseeable future, you will have your first job as a science teacher.

All of this is exciting, but now you have an entirely new set of questions about your career: "How do I teach science?", "Am I qualified to teach science?", "What do I need to know about science and technology?", "What science do I teach to middle school or high school students?", "What is science teaching like?", "What are the problems facing science teachers today?". Constantly emerging questions and concerns regarding science teaching are part of becoming a science teacher.

Some of your questions have answers; others depend on your specific talents, personality, knowledge, enthusiasm, and other important, but elusive, qualities. Obviously, we cannot answer all of these questions in this chapter or in this book, but we can provide some information and direction. We can suggest activities to help clarify your strengths and weaknesses and the realities and possibilities of science teaching. The best way you can begin is by completing Activity 1–1: How I See Myself As a Science Teacher, at the end of this chapter.

AM I QUALIFIED TO TEACH SCIENCE?

This question is difficult to answer with a simple yes or no, because of the adjective *qualified*. Traditionally, persons have qualified as science teachers by completing a set of educational requirements. Legislation passed in 2002, called "No Child Left Behind", defines highly qualified teachers as those who obtain full state certification or pass the teacher licensing examination. In addition, the law indicates that secondary teachers must demonstrate content competence through either a college major, graduate degree, or comparable coursework, or by passing a "rigorous state test" in the subject (Berry, 2002; U.S. Department of Education, 2004).

In this sense, most individuals can be qualified for teaching. A science teacher, however, must do more than fulfill a set of requirements and be able to talk about science. Certain dimensions of science teaching addressed in Activity 1–1, are identifiable in the following discussion.

Understanding Science and Technology

You should have a background in science, including both a broad general knowledge and a specific knowledge in your major. These statements may seem obvious. In today's world, however, you also will need an understanding of technology, because our society and the experiences of your students are extensively based on technology. You should be aware of the many relationships between science and technology. In the past, science teachers and textbooks presented technology as *applied science;* that is, the enterprise of science resulted in knowledge that was applied to human problems.

Although this statement still is partially accurate, in some cases scientific advances must wait until technology is developed. Technology can also be viewed as an area of study. As with science, technology also has products and processes that form the basis of study.

In addition to having scientific and technological knowledge, you should apply this knowledge in new situations, use basic science concepts to analyze problems presented by students, and synthesize knowledge so that you can answer students' questions accurately.

Understanding the Purposes of Science Teaching

Most individuals in the science education community use the term *scientific literacy* to express the major purposes of science education. The term also refers to your role in advancing individual development of students and achieving society's aspirations within the context of your classroom. Although scientific literacy expresses the highest and most admirable purposes of science teaching, as science teachers, we must be a little more concrete and practical.

What do you think the scientifically and technologically literate person should know, value, and do—as a citizen? As you think about this question, recognize that the final phrase—*as a citizen*—is an important orientation for your answer. An answer that focuses on acquiring knowledge about biology, chemistry, physics, and the earth sciences should be mediated by the question, "What is it about the knowledge from these disciplines that is important for citizens?" How do you justify that knowledge in terms of your student's future role as a citizen? What about values and skills? What

values, attitudes, and habits of mind does your teaching of science and technology help students develop?

A close connection exists between the purpose of developing scientific literacy and the various books you will encounter. Both the *National Science Education Standards* (NRC, 1996) and the *Benchmarks for Science Literacy* (AAAS, 1993) address the question of exactly what is meant by scientific literacy. We discuss these and other reports in later chapters. For now, think about the following statement on the purpose of science teaching.

> Science teaching should facilitate students' learning about science and technology as they need to understand and use them in their personal lives and as future citizens. Science teaching should sustain students' natural curiosity; develop their skills in inquiry and design; improve their scientific explanations; help them develop an understanding and use of technology; contribute to their understanding of the role, limits, and possibilities of science and technology in society; and inform the choices they must make in their personal and social lives.

Indeed this statement about science teaching is tightly packed with ideas. As you proceed through this book, we will provide many ideas for you as a science teacher.

Organizing Science Instruction

You should be well prepared, thoroughly organized, and have a clear direction in your teaching. There is no substitute for a well-prepared lesson. At one time or another, most science teachers have tried to teach without preparation. More often than not, the lesson was less than effective. As you begin organizing your science program, try to establish the "big picture" by determining your

Students should be actively engaged in science.

program for the year. You may wish to divide the year into units, and the units into coherent sequences of lessons. This simple procedure will give you an overall organization; but you require still more knowledge and skills to be an effective teacher.

Effective science teachers have a variety of instructional methods, choosing the best for each lesson. Keep in mind the following simple questions: "What do I want my students to learn?, How will I know when my students have learned?, What experience will best help my students learn?". The answers to these questions will direct you to different teaching methods. We recommend completing Activity 1–2: The What and How of Science Lessons, at the end of this chapter.

Understanding Student Learning

Imagine that you are ready to begin your first science lesson. The students are sitting at their desks, waiting for you to teach them. Do the students in front of you already understand any science concepts? The answer is probably yes. The students you will be teaching have lived 12 to 18 years. Through formal and informal experiences, the students already have developed ideas about the natural and designed world. They also have placed labels on many of the events, objects, and organisms in the world. In this regard, three points will help you: (1) Students have explanations and concepts about their world, (2) many of these concepts are inadequate when compared to scientific explanations or concepts, and (3) students' current concepts of the natural world influence what and how they learn science (Novak, 1988). David Ausubel (1963) summarized this when he wrote: "If I had to reduce all of educational psychology to just one principle, I would say this: The most important single factor influencing learning is what the learner already knows. Ascertain this and teach him accordingly."

It is interesting to note that the ideas from Novak and Ausubel have stood the test of time. In 2000, the National Research Council published a synthesis of research about how people learn. The three major points from this synthesis are as follows:

- All learners come to the classroom with prior knowledge. This knowledge must be engaged if learning is to occur.
- The facts of a discipline must be taught in the context of a larger framework so learners can understand the connections among ideas.
- All learners need practice with metacognitive skills such as setting goals and assessing their progress toward those goals.

Many science teachers approach instruction as though students are empty vessels to be filled with facts, information, and concepts about the world. This perception of how students learn generally is inaccurate. Perhaps a different metaphor is appropriate. Students have packed a suitcase for a trip, but many garments are out of fashion, inappropriate for the climate, and inadequate because the student has grown. The science teacher's task is to help students improve their "intellectual wardrobe." Students construct their explanations of the world through a personal process in which sensory data are given meaning in terms of prior knowledge. In order for learning to occur, the adequacy of students' current conceptions must be challenged, and in appropriate time and with opportunities, students can reconstruct newer and more adequate explanations. Ways to facilitate this learning process will be explored in later chapters. How is this process of learning different from what you currently understand about student learning? Review your response to Activity 1–2.

Recognizing Personal Meaning in Teaching and Learning

Imagine two middle school lessons about the life cycles of organisms. In the first lesson, the students individually read about mealworms. In the second, small groups of students each receive a container of mealworms and are asked to observe the tiny organisms. The students exclaim, "Ooh," "Ahh," "I can't touch this," "It squirmed," "Look at my worm back up!" and other utterances that indicate their feelings about the experience.

The second lesson provides an experience that is physically close, less abstract, and emotionally connected to the subject. This exercise easily could be extended into areas such as experimental design, reaction to stimuli, and the life cycle of mealworms. Both lessons convey the material; however, the second probably would be more effective in teaching the concepts, because it offers physical and psychological involvement and social interactions, all of which contribute to personal meaning for the students.

Many contemporary science curricula are inquiry oriented. For the most part, the inquiry centers on science facts and concepts; physical involvement with materials through laboratory activities provides the primary teaching method for presenting these facts and concepts. The next step in the teaching task is discovery of the personal meaning of these facts and concepts. Obviously, learning science is easier when students are interested and involved. For example, you have been motivated to read this chapter because it has some personal meaning. You are becoming a science teacher and you want to be as effective as possible. What is said in this book likely has personal meaning for you.

Personal meaning has three aspects: (1) the physical closeness of the materials, (2) the psychological interest the individual has in the materials, and (3) the social relevancy of the material or topic. To state this idea succinctly: Learning science is enhanced when students have personal involvement with materials and organisms that have some direct importance to them. Usually, science teachers have started lessons with content and assumed that personal meaning would emerge. This progression, as it turns out, may or may not occur. Science teachers engage learners by beginning with interest, motivation, and personal meaning, and structure the content on these experiences while still teaching scientific concepts.

Personalizing Science Teaching

The effective science teacher realizes the importance of interpersonal relations. An important finding in regard to helping others is that objectivity has a negative correlation with effectiveness; that is, if students are treated as objects, the teacher is less successful with students. No one becomes significant to someone else—whether student, fellow teacher, or friend—by making the other person feel insignificant. You become significant to others by treating them with integrity, sincerity, and openness (Combs, Avila, & Purkey, 1978). The best science teachers make a conscious effort to regard all students positively, to understand them as human beings, and to help them advance academically, personally, and socially. In these situations, students learn science; in fact, they probably learn more science because of the interpersonal rapport. If you become a significant person to your students, the final reward is yours.

Personalizing your relationship with students can include developing a keen understanding of the pupils, devising different tasks for different students, making individual assessments, and using varied questions or different materials and equipment. The idea of effective communication covers, in one way or another, most of the important aspects of personalizing science teaching.

Talking and listening to adolescents is a subtle and important way of recognizing their growing need for identity. It also enhances the learning relationship and increases your efficiency in facilitating their understanding of science.

Managing the Classroom and Maintaining Discipline

When beginning teachers talk about managing the classroom, they usually mean managing students in various activities of science teaching. For example: How will students form groups for laboratory? How will they handle materials and equipment safely? How do you get students to change from one type of activity to another? Such concerns are realistic, but soon you will find that most students respond to directions. Several chapters include detailed information to help you manage the classroom. Following is some initial advice:

- *Preparation will resolve many problems.* Be sure to have materials ready, know the size of groups and how you want to form them, understand your expectations for behavior and learning outcomes, and give clear and simple directions for effective classroom management.
- *Recognize the need for transition between activities.* Making a transition, for instance, from laboratory work to a class discussion, takes several minutes. Students will have to adjust to the different class structure. Plan for the transition time—it should not be long, because this is a time when some students are apt to cause a conflict. Some teachers expect the new norms of behavior to emerge instantly. A visible signal, such as turning on an overhead projector, may help complete the transition.
- *Try not to panic in nonpanic situations.* Things happen in science classrooms. We cannot tell you what they will be, only that something unexpected will happen. Our advice is to stay calm, quickly think about the situation, and act decisively on a proposed solution. If it doesn't work, try another.

The second topic of the section concerns classroom management, a concern of most teachers. Conflicts between your goals and some student behaviors are inevitable. Most management issues in science classrooms are resolved quickly and with little difficulty. We tend to refer to management issues as *conflicts* instead of *discipline problems,* because the definition—the activities or behaviors of two (or more) individuals that are incompatible—suggests that you, as a teacher, have goals, and that part of your responsibility is to achieve those goals. Avoiding or resolving educational conflicts is key to managing your classroom or maintaining discipline. It is more productive to think and act in ways to avoid or resolve conflicts than to engage in discussions of the appropriateness or fairness of rules, policies, or expectations of behavior. Chapter 20 discusses classroom management in general, and conflicts and their resolution. Following are a few initial suggestions:

- Center attention on avoiding or resolving the conflict, as opposed to defining who is right or wrong.
- Establish clear communication and agreement on the issues, rules, or expectations that define the conflict.
- Use cooperative problem solving. Because of your position as a science teacher, you have the responsibility for resolving classroom conflicts cooperatively and constructively.

Realizing Decisions Determines Effective Science Teaching

Imagine that you are about to begin a chemistry lesson on pollution. Your plan is to demonstrate how the common air pollutants sulfur dioxide (SO_2) and sulfur trioxide (SO_3) are produced when coal and oil containing sulfur are burned. You then plan to show how sulfur trioxide can react with water vapor (H_2O) to form sulfuric acid. You have some sulfuric acid on the demonstration desk so that you can show the students the corrosive power of this acid. As you begin your demonstration, you accidentally knock over the beaker containing the acid, which spills onto papers and books. Take a moment and think about the situation. What would you do?

Suppose you have just finished an activity investigating the effects of continental glaciers. You begin showing a DVD on the subject. As soon as you turn off the lights, you hear funny noises and muffled comments. You are fairly certain that Steven, the class clown, is the one making the noise. Take a moment to think about this situation. What would you do?

You could consult this textbook for answers. You could call your methods instructor or ask the science supervisor in your district for answers. You could do any number of things, most of which would help only if the same situation recurred. The one certainty in all such classroom situations is you will have to decide what to do and respond in the best way possible. Your role as a science teacher will be to combine your knowledge and perceptions of classroom situations with your understanding of the students, and then to decide on appropriate action. Many science teachers do not realize this central role of decision making. You must adapt the textbook, the curriculum, and the inquiry method to the events that occur in actual teaching situations.

Look back to the opening question, "Am I qualified to teach science?" This question still cannot be answered with a simple yes or no, but you have begun thinking about what it means to become a science teacher. How well do you understand science? How do you incorporate the purposes of science education? How are you at organizing instruction in science? What ideas do you have about student learning? Can you personalize science teaching? How can you include personal meaning as a part of science lessons? Do you realize what your role will be as manager and conflict resolver in the science classroom? These questions and many more will emerge as you continue the process of becoming a science teacher.

WHAT IS SCIENCE TEACHING REALLY LIKE?

Most individuals entering the teaching profession are concerned about daily happenings in the school. In one form or another they inquire, "What is science teaching like?" When asked to further clarify the question, they want to know what the science programs are like, what teachers talk about, what it is like actually being in front of a class, and the concerns of other science teachers. If you complete Activity 1–3: A First Lesson, at the end of this chapter, some of these questions will be answered. In addition, the next sections give glimpses into different schools, science programs, and science teachers. We have adapted these vignettes from case studies funded by the National Science Foundation (NSF) and completed as part of a larger evaluation of science education. The case studies were originally completed by individuals who spent time at different schools, observing and participating in the various activities of science teachers (Stake & Easley, 1977). Our adaptations have maintained themes from the original case studies while updating ideas, language, and issues of contemporary science teaching. Although we realize that schools, science programs, and teachers differ, the case studies present perspectives of actual science programs, glimpses of teacher conversations, and insights about science teaching.

Middle School Science Programs

This section characterizes two middle school science programs from the same science district. The district is located in central California (Western City is the name used in the case study), a region where much of the population is involved in agriculture. Due to the large African American and Hispanic American populations, student backgrounds and interests are diverse. This comparison of middle school science programs points out how differently science can be taught at the same grade level and within the same district (Serrano, 1977).

Case Study 1

Science instruction at both schools is offered at the discretion of the building principal. If the principal has no interest in science, the science program at either school will wane. As a consequence, the science program is a minimal program and only as complete and thorough as the teachers who instruct in the program. The following observations (made during site visits) tell the story.

> At Middle School I, the "science room" is almost bare. The bulletin boards have a few items about earth tacked on them. The storeroom is badly supplied with three microscopes in semioperable condition, a few unlabeled chemicals, pieces of broken glassware (thistle tubes, test tubes), a Fisher burner, and a Bunsen burner. There is no evidence of any packaged kits (such as Introductory Physical Science [IPS]) or other equipment to indicate the students have experience with hands-on materials. The desks and a few tables are available for use in the room. The principal is making a great effort to upgrade this area.

The "science room" at Middle School II is not in the same condition as the one at Middle School I. Although the walls are still relatively bare, the closets are filled with old, unused materials. Ample supplies of glassware, hardware, and chemicals normally used in a middle school science class are visible. The collection of rocks and minerals is minimal, as is the preserved animal collection. In reality, the science room is much better supplied and organized at Middle School II than at Middle School I.

The science program at Middle School II has been well established by the instructor, who has been teaching there for three years. He follows a course of study that he has developed over the years, and he continues to modify it. His counterpart at Middle School I appears to flounder in the science area. Students at Middle School I spend a considerable amount of time studying earthquakes. ("Since we live in an area that is earthquake-prone, I feel the students should spend some time studying earthquakes.") Besides earthquakes, there is not much evidence of other science topics being discussed, nor is there any evidence of students having an opportunity to get their hands on any equipment.

Because the science program at the middle school level is determined by science teachers at individual schools, these teachers use a wide range of areas and approaches. A great number of science teachers in the district are not aware of contemporary science curricula and their packaged equipment and, as a consequence, do not use them.

When asked about their major concerns regarding the science program at their respective schools, the teachers responded as follows:

Middle School I
The students lack discipline. They make little or no effort to learn. They would rather talk and delay the teaching process. They are the ones who will suffer the most.

Middle School II
The biggest problem at the school is absences. The students don't seem to care. They would much rather be somewhere else. Discipline is not as much of a problem here as is the lack of supplies and equipment. I always have to be on the lookout for equipment.

Other teachers in the same schools have voiced concern about lack of the following:

◆ Administrative support
◆ Supplies and equipment
◆ Current books
◆ Student motivation
◆ Parental interest
◆ Adequate facilities

When the science teachers were asked to describe a typical day in their science classes, they replied with this summary:

The kids come into class as soon as the bell rings. We check their homework (this is done for purposes of reinforcement). We present a short lecture (at least 20 minutes) on a given topic. We make an assignment for the following day. On Fridays, we schedule quizzes based on the last four days of work.

What are your reactions to this summary?

High School Science Programs

This case study was completed in a small city on the plains east of the Rocky Mountains. The name used for the school was Fall River (Smith, 1977).

Case Study 2

The high school science program consists of 18 courses. Despite lenient graduation requirements, enrollments are high. The courses are staffed with an impressive group of teachers, most of whom have advanced degrees in the disciplines and have attended summer programs.

The biology program has the largest enrollment and staff. All students who elect biology take a one-semester introductory course, after which they can choose one or more follow-up courses in ecology, plant structure and function, social biology, microbiology, heredity, and animal anatomy. Some students fail or opt out of biology after the introductory course. An advanced placement course in biology is also offered.

The content of the introductory course is largely the same, regardless of who teaches it. The text used is from the Biological Sciences Curriculum Study (BSCS). The instructional methods are largely lectures, laboratory investigations, review sheets, and occasional films and guest speakers. Although the BSCS text emphasizes developing students' interest and heuristic inquiry, the classroom instruction at Fall River High tends to be formal, didactic, and organized. Almost the entire text is covered. This is a large quantity of material for one semester, but it provides the background needed for the more specialized follow-up courses. In the ecology course, for example, the students review the relevant BSCS chapters and then go on to more specialized texts. They participate in simulations on DVDs designed to show the relationship between values and environmental processes. Topics covered include ecology and the law, mountain ecosystems, and the food chain. Laboratory investigations are conducted on photosynthesis and chromatography, as are field investigations in small ecosystems near the school building. The students conduct independent research on biomes.

Although the other follow-up courses are not so directly related to the environment, a strong environmental

GUEST EDITORIAL ◆ LAUREL HALL

Science Education Student
Carleton College, Northfield, Minnesota

WHO ME?! A SCIENCE TEACHER?

"Teaching science? Me? You've got to be nuts." This would have been my reaction a few months ago; however, today my response is just the opposite: Science teaching is a plausible career for me. Why the change of opinion in such a short time? The answer is simple: After seriously evaluating my interests and goals, with respect to possible careers, I found that teaching would allow me to incorporate and use more of them. The next step was to discover what education is and what methods are used. This step was achieved through a science methods course where I actually observed and participated in various teaching activities of a class at a local school. The career experience in this field has had an important positive effect on my knowledge and opinions of the educational system, besides showing me some of the realities of science teaching.

I have always been interested in helping people learn; my past working experience as a camp counselor, recreational leader, and YMCA swimming instructor and coach is evidence of this interest. However, teaching in the educational system did not appeal to me; I felt that I would become very bored with teaching the same thing to several classes year after year. Yet, with my recent finding that education was a career possibility and that many of my goals and interests could be combined with it, I began to take a new look at education and saw it as a challenge as long as I could eradicate my adolescent biases toward the educational system.

I entered the education program still unsure of what teaching science entailed. I soon found out that my preconceived biases toward the educational system, based on my own public school experiences, were not universally true. The elimination of these biases was the major factor in altering my opinion of the system. Now, instead of looking at the system as hopeless, I see myself as an agent of change: I can set an example and hope others will follow. I can challenge myself to improve, change, and alter lessons, activities, and methods to counteract any boredom in myself and in the students, and to communicate with more students.

Through a science methods course, I learned about education, the variety of methods that can be used to attain objectives, and some of the realities of teaching. From these new views, I can see that teaching can be a much tougher occupation than I had previously expected. It involves many time-consuming activities, such as developing new units, changing lesson plans, improving activities, keeping up to date on recent developments in the specific area of science, and keeping enthusiasm at a high level. Yet, it is through these same time-consuming processes that the rewards of teaching are to be found, for example: communicating with those who previously did not understand or care, introducing students to new and interesting ideas and techniques, developing within the students an enthusiasm for continued learning, and watching them develop as individuals.

consciousness pervades the entire department and has been adopted by many of the students. When asked about the principles behind the program, three teachers made the following statements:

- ◆ The purpose is to make them better citizens, help them understand the issues in society that are related to science, and help them make better decisions. For example, I ask them how the price of gas affects their driving? I don't try to impose my own view on them, but I do try to make them think.
- ◆ You can't separate our values and science anymore. When we talk about population

growth or genetics, issues come in. I tell them they should learn the material, if only so they can determine their own future.
- ◆ A person just can't be an effective citizen unless he can read and understand political issues that have scientific overtones. . . . The average citizen must have the awareness and appreciation of how his actions affect the environment and what is likely to happen, depending on the choices he makes now.

In addition to the idea of developing environmental consciousness, the teachers believe their purpose is to provide a strong and diverse academic experience that puts the students in touch with the major body of knowledge in biology and the processes used to gain the knowledge. One teacher reported, "Any systematized body of knowledge is part of the foundation of civilization. It's part of their responsibilities as citizens to be aware of it. Science has applications in all their lives." What do you think about these perspectives?

The biology program is not without its rough edges. Students in the introductory course fail in higher proportions than in other courses. Most teachers are determined to hold to their standards, however. Based on previous experience, teachers are convinced that students will take the easiest possible path, dilute the content of the course, and make the follow-up course structure impossible. The teachers believe that any student who makes the effort can pass.

Another serious problem is lack of space and facilities. The school has two well-equipped laboratories, but sometimes four sections must share them in a single class period. Therefore, the teachers have to coordinate classes so that while one section is doing lab work, the other teacher must lecture in a classroom designed for physics. No space is available for advanced laboratory preparations. They look back wistfully on the year they had a teacher's aide. "Not having the facilities lowers my interest and energy and influences what I teach. The situation has discouraged every bit of open-ended inquiry I've got. A question comes up from the class and I think of an investigation that would be related, but there we are in the physics room, so I lecture."

About 40 percent of each graduating class goes to college. A greater proportion of students follow a traditional college preparatory course of study. Most of this group take chemistry in the junior year. The chemistry classes are packed, but whether the high enrollment is due to students' scientific curiosity, the genial personality and showmanship of the teacher, or the abundance of A grades is unclear. Although some of the best students complained that the class "wasn't tough enough . . . didn't go too deep into chemistry," the instructor primarily wants them "to be interested in science and to master the basic material in the field. I feel like anybody can learn at the level I teach them. The kids who are really interested then can go off on their own and learn more."

The text *Modern Chemistry* is used, and the approach is traditional. The greatest amount of class time is spent in lectures and laboratory experiments. The laboratory areas are well equipped for a basic program, but the teacher longs for materials that would support more advanced work. The laboratories are terribly overcrowded, and the teacher worries that someone will be injured in an accident.

The physics course is taught by a man with experience and impressive credentials—advanced degrees in physics and math. His laboratory is well equipped, and under his leadership the science program has always received a healthy share of the school budget.

In answering a question about the purpose of science education, the physics teacher spoke of his own philosophy.

> In recent years, I've wondered if you could justify it. Earlier I would have said that physics was a part of cultural knowledge, something enormously practical, like all science having something philosophically to offer the public, and intellectual integrity which would carry over into politics and society.
>
> Now I don't know. We live in a technological society, so it is necessary to propagate information to some parts of the society. But for the general person in high school who will eventually go into business or become a homemaker they really don't need to know about physics, except in a very superficial way. If you want a kid to know how to change a tire, you teach him about levers. . . . I'm a good sailor and I apply my knowledge of physics, but other people are better sailors and have no physics background.
>
> That is too pessimistic. Let me state it this way. Everyone deals with nature. Every high school student knows a great deal of physics, and the teacher merely encourages him to abstract his knowledge to form more general and sometimes more useful patterns of thought. If the student can deal with ideas in the abstract, he learns this before going to college and can thereby make a sounder choice of careers. He may not do better than another competent college student, but he has had the benefit of guidance and proven academic discipline. Finally, and this is important for all ability ranges of students, a sense of being at home in the universe must be transmitted. The physical world and the technology of man must be dealt with as an important part of the total culture he is to inherit.

In addition to the more traditional track of three courses, the science program includes a great variety of offerings: astronomy, archaeology, geology, conceptual physics, electronics (less mathematical than the physics course), introduction to chemistry (a student-centered laboratory program using discovery techniques and emphasizing the process of science), and space science (a rather easy course for students who have a previous failure or little interest in science).

The science teacher responsible for several of these courses is a former geologist who runs his classes very informally, trying to structure each one around the interests and questions of the students. Environmental consciousness appears to be a strong focus in his course as well. In the course description for geology, he writes

> Our study of geology will be centered around the following concepts: Geology, the study of the earth, is essentially an environmental science. . . . Man . . . must learn to function in harmony with the earth environment. . . . Citizen roles dictate an understanding of the environmental problems confronting man, solutions to these

problems, and the responsibilities of citizens and government to work toward their solutions.

During his classes this philosophy is never far off, injected even into a presentation on the physical properties of minerals.

In his courses, perhaps more than those of others, the methods of science are given prominent attention. One of his science courses centers on the following objectives:

> Demonstrates an understanding of the process of identifying and defining a scientific problem or question to be investigated . . . of proposing a logical test of a hypothesis . . . of testing the effects of variables and controlling relevant variables . . . the ability to synthesize data from several sources to arrive at generalizations or conclusions . . . withhold judgments or conclusions until adequate information has been validated.

The following is a second view of high school science. This program is from a large high school in a major city in the Pacific Northwest. The name used to identify the school is Hardy (Welch, 1977).

> The natural science program at Hardy is strong. It is paced by an active biology program, team-taught by three full-time and one part-time teacher. Currently 472 students (93 percent of the sophomore enrollment) are enrolled in a laboratory course led by the department chairman. The classrooms are filled with science artifacts (birds, weather maps, rocks, specimens, snakes, etc.), and the spirit of the group can be portrayed by two episodes: an open session with students one day after school to discuss the implications for science of the presidential election and a weekend assault on the walls separating the three biology rooms, resulting in open portals that central administration had stalled on for nearly two years.
>
> Probably 80 percent of the class time is spent by students working on experiments, and three tracks (developed locally) are provided, depending on student ability. The course is patterned after college science courses and seems difficult for many of the students. However, teacher enthusiasm and interest seem to rub off on students, and they rate the course as very good. Marine biology, human physiology, mushrooms, and wildflowers are other courses offered as part of this strong program. Exactly which courses will be offered during a given semester depends a great deal on student interest. A college-style registration procedure is used, and if a given course doesn't fill (i.e., isn't selected by more than 25 students), then it may not be offered. Conversely, sections are added if student interest is high.
>
> During the semester following the site visit, the life science enrollment was as follows:
>
>   Biology II 250
>   Molecular Biology 29
>   Marine Biology 53
>   Wild Flowers/Edibles 34
>   Human Physiology 53

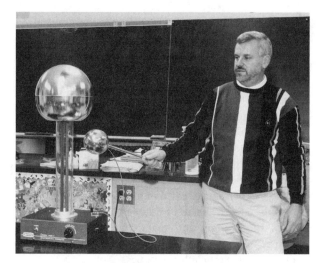

An experienced science teacher uses interesting examples of natural phenomena to engage student interest.

> Apparently, some of those students in the first semester of biology opt for more specialized courses the second semester.
>
> The first year of chemistry is currently taken by 146 students (27 percent of the junior enrollment) and is taught as a laboratory science. The five sections of chemistry are handled by the physics teacher and a chemistry teacher who also teaches biology. The course is viewed by students and teachers as primarily a college preparatory course. A third semester of general chemistry and a semester of organic chemistry are offered if enough students register for these courses.
>
> Physics may be taken in either the junior or senior year, and currently 68 students (13 percent of the senior enrollment) are enrolled. About half of the group consists of girls, which is seen by students and teachers as a result of changing female roles. Counselors, parents, and friends are changing their attitudes and beliefs that advanced science is only for boys. The course has some laboratory components, but in general is taught more like a mathematics class; that is, explain concepts, assign problems, correct problems, and discuss difficulties. This routine is interrupted occasionally by exams or experiments, but the doing of problems is predominant over the doing of science found in the other classes. The class is clearly for the academically talented, and the teacher sees no need to try to increase enrollments.
>
> An adjunct to the science program is a popular horticulture program offered in the technology education department. In a temporary building and greenhouse located about two blocks from the main building, 113 students were enrolled in environmental horticulture. The course meets the state requirements for a laboratory science, but although it is considered a strong program by the science teachers, there seems to be very little interaction between it and the rest of the science program. It has grown through the efforts of an active teacher whose academic home is technology education.

The science program is strong and surviving, but it is being subjected to many challenges: transfer of teachers, declining budgets for texts and equipment, and competition from the basics. It may be seriously affected if subjected to many more problems.

How do you respond to these descriptions of science programs? Do the descriptions align with your original perceptions?

Conversations with Science Teachers

In this section, comments from the teachers' lounge are used to point out some issues in science education. The observations are from a case study made in a greater Boston high school (Walker, 1977).

Role of the Experiment in Science Teaching

STEVE: (looking through a workbook of experiments David has been using in his class): The trouble with a lot of this stuff is that it is so obvious. Even when you have done the experiment, you only know what you knew already.

DAVID: Maybe it's obvious to you, but it isn't always obvious to these kids. To some of them maybe, but not to all of them. Sometimes they do know what is going to happen in the experiment, but they only know it vaguely; they haven't really thought it out. Like this morning we were talking about that experiment where you float a cork in water, then push an upturned glass down on top of it. They did the experiment and saw what happened. When I asked why the cork went down, one girl just said "gravity." Well, you can see what she means; it does involve gravity, but that's not an explanation of what you see happening.

STEVE: Yes, but you can't say that's exciting. Floating corks in water. I want to get these kids interested in science. I want experiments you can do that set them all off saying, "Wow! How did that happen?" Something that really challenges and excites them. (looking at the book) Finding out 20 percent of the air is oxygen, that's no challenge. Why not just tell them? You shouldn't just have to do an experiment for everybody, only if it excites them or triggers them off.

DAVID: But before you can work on these dramatic experiments they have to know scientific procedures and appreciate the methods. All this week I've been emphasizing the five stages of writing a lab report and getting them to appreciate the difference between observation and explanation. You have to do it several times, and it takes practice. And for most of them, writing a scientific report is not something they are used to doing; in fact, some of them have gotten so used to multiple-choice tests that it is an effort for them to write complete sentences.

STEVE: Maybe you are right. I think teaching them rigor and method is a useful thing to do. The danger, though, is that you end up just pacifying them. The science that is going to affect their lives isn't the five stages of writing a lab report. It is nuclear power, pollution, recombinant DNA research. Those are the things I want them to know about, and I want them to be able to pursue things for themselves, not just because they are in a course or a textbook.

Strategies and Methods of Science Teaching

CIVICS TEACHER: I feel constrained by the forty-minute period and the pressures of working in a building that is really only a heap of classrooms. I'd like to be able to get out more with the students and get to do more things.

SCIENCE TEACHER: I don't agree. I think almost the most important thing for the students to learn is the discipline of working in the classroom. When they come here at the beginning of the year, they are all up in the air and we have got to bring them down. You've got to get order and discipline before you can give it up.

CIVICS TEACHER: By this time of year [March], they should have learned some sort of classroom discipline. The problem is that enforcing it starts to become an end in itself. You begin to forget about what you are trying to teach and just think about keeping a neat, orderly class.

SCIENCE TEACHER: I don't just think of discipline as keeping an island of sanity in my class, whatever happens in the rest of the school. I don't think you can separate discipline in class from the discipline of the subject. In science especially, where you have expensive equipment and valuable things around, you have to learn certain ways of behaving, and learning those ways of behaving are [sic] part of learning the subject.

SECOND SCIENCE TEACHER: I'd like to get out of the classroom more because there are a lot of things I want to do that you can't very easily do in school. I think really the only way to get students to appreciate the significance of things like environmental pollution is to get them out of the classroom [and] looking at it.

ENGLISH TEACHER: My classroom is important to me. I can't imagine a better place for doing the kind of teaching I want to do. Going outside the classroom on some occasions might have advantages. I'd like to have students going out to interview people, for example. But what they do in the classroom (which is mainly writing) has got to remain at the center of everything else for me.

CIVICS TEACHER: Sometimes I feel limited by the expectations the students have of me as their teacher. For most of them, the range of things they will allow in a teacher is very limited, and this makes it very hard to start anything new or different. The experience I have had in the past of working a lot outside school has shown me that you can have quite a different kind of relationship with students once you get them out of the school building.

ENGLISH TEACHER: I don't want a different kind of relationship. I want to be the kind of teacher I am.

A Conclusion About Science Teaching

People in schools are conscientiously doing the jobs they have defined: tutor, scholar, but also at times, counselor, steward, custodian, and social director.

Teachers must juggle the expectations of the invisible, distant, and mostly impersonal profession of science education and the local, powerful, and relentless demands of teaching. The two roles do not necessarily conflict, but the latter usually overpowers and preempts the former.

We recommend completing Activity 1–4: An Interview with a Science Teacher.

HOW CAN YOU BECOME AN EFFECTIVE SCIENCE TEACHER?

We assume that you have the normal concerns of beginning teachers. We also assume that you are motivated to become an effective science teacher. Three things that will help reduce these concerns and increase effectiveness are preparation, time, and experience. Remember that this is only the beginning of your career as a science teacher and you cannot accomplish everything you wish, learn everything you need, or do everything you would like during the science methods course or even during the first year of teaching.

You can do something specific and immediate to help reduce your concerns and develop your effectiveness. *Be prepared.* This message is crucial. Some teachers equate preparation with knowledge of their scientific discipline. Although this is essential, preparation is key. We have mentioned some ideas, such as understanding the purposes of science teaching, organizing science instruction, understanding student learning, and managing the classroom.

Becoming an effective science teacher takes time. The corollary to time is experience. There is no substitute for the actual experience of teaching science. The one sure way that you will detect strengths and weaknesses in yourself as a teacher is through experience. You will learn more about yourself and science teaching in the first year than you can now imagine. It will not be easy, but it will be interesting and challenging. Every

day will involve you in experiences that contribute to your effectiveness. Many of these are the other topics of this book.

For now, let's look at your concerns, apprehensions, and needs concerning science teaching, by completing Activity 1–5: My Concerns, at the end of this chapter.

BECOMING A SCIENCE TEACHER: CLOSING REFLECTIONS

One premise of this book is that you can become a better science teacher. Students entering science teaching and those already in the profession are concerned about improving the quality of instruction in science and increasing student learning. Your own concerns and activities in studying this book and taking the methods course have already demonstrated your willingness to learn more about science teaching. Once you obtain a teaching position, professional development in the form of workshops, curriculum revision, and continuing education courses will be available. Participation in all of these programs indicates a desire to become a better science teacher.

A second premise is that you are the one person who best knows what is necessary for you to become an effective teacher. This is the reason for the self-evaluation exercises. Your college supervisor, methods professor, and perhaps classroom teachers also will provide you with feedback. This feedback will help, especially when you combine it with your own insights and act on the information. In other words, you have many personal choices in the process of becoming a science teacher.

The responsibility for becoming an effective science instructor is yours. Many individuals and an abundance of programs are available to aid you. Ultimately, however, you are the person who must combine all of the elements to facilitate science education for your students.

We now look at goals related to your professional growth. Becoming a science teacher means you continually demonstrate the following:

- *An adequate understanding of scientific knowledge*—This goal includes an in-depth understanding of specific disciplines, as well as a broad understanding of science in general. It also includes a comprehension of the role of science in our society.
- *An adequate understanding of scientific inquiry*—Specifically, this understanding includes the attitudes and abilities of inquiry and the application of scientific philosophies to classroom instruction.
- *An adequate awareness of educational foundations and the place of science education as a discipline in the larger realm of education*

- *An adequate understanding of and ability to use teaching methods appropriately*—This goal includes the ability to plan and organize activities for the classroom, to carry out standard classroom procedures, to use a variety of techniques and equipment in teaching science lessons, and to assess student progress.
- *Adequate interpersonal relations and an enthusiasm for working with all students*
- *The synthesis of these five goals into the practice of teaching science in the secondary school*

SUMMARY

The experience of becoming a science teacher is identifiable through the questions one asks. Here we assumed you might ask, "Am I qualified to teach science?" Although this is impossible to answer, several activities were presented, each allowing you to investigate the question. We also described several attributes essential for science teaching: understanding science, understanding students, organizing materials for science instruction, personalizing your interaction with students, recognizing personal meaning as a part of learning, managing the classroom and maintaining discipline,

and very important, realizing your own role as decision maker in the science classroom.

After discussing the first question, we turned to a second: "What is science teaching like?" To answer this we used a variety of vignettes drawn from case studies of schools from all over the country.

Next, we addressed the question of becoming an effective science teacher. The question seems to be a part of the natural sequence of questions asked by students as they enter teaching. Once the initial anxiety of becoming a science teacher is overcome, individuals turn to the problem of becoming a better teacher. Time, experience, and preparation contribute to the increasing effectiveness of the beginning teacher. One way of helping to overcome apprehension is to identify concerns and act on reducing them. We recommended completing a self-examination by responding to the question, "What are my concerns?"

The chapter ends with some goals related to the process of becoming a science teacher. The goals are summarized as demonstrating an understanding of scientific knowledge and inquiry, of science education as a discipline, and of teaching methods; forming adequate interpersonal relationships with students; and synthesizing these goals into the teaching of science in the secondary school.

INVESTIGATING SCIENCE TEACHING

ACTIVITY 1–1
HOW I SEE MYSELF AS A SCIENCE TEACHER

The statements in this exercise allow you to examine your self-perceptions as a science teacher. The exercise is designed for your personal knowledge and need not be shared with others. Read the statement and decide if you strongly agree, moderately agree, agree, are neutral, slightly disagree, moderately disagree, or strongly disagree. Then place the appropriate number in the space to the left of the statement.

Strongly agree	*Moderately agree*	*Slightly agree*	*Neutral*	*Slightly disagree*	*Moderately disagree*	*Strongly disagree*
7	6	5	4	3	2	1

_____ 1. I am well informed about science and technology.

_____ 2. Students can generally take care of themselves.

_____ 3. I identify with people.

_____ 4. My task as a science teacher is one of assisting students to learn.

_____ 5. The meaning of science and technology for our society is more important than the facts and events of science and technology.

_____ 6. Science and technology are meaningful in my personal life.

_____ 7. For the most part, other people are friendly.

_____ 8. Basically, I am an adequate science teacher.

_____ 9. I see my purpose as concerned with larger issues of science, technology, and society.

_____ 10. I try to understand how my students perceive things.

_____ 11. I have a commitment to the field of science and technology.

_____ 12. Students have their own worth and integrity.

_____ 13. I am a dependable and reliable science teacher.

_____ 14. I usually do not conceal my personal feelings and shortcomings from students.

_____ 15. Teaching science is best done by encouraging personal development of students.

_____ 16. Science and technology are essential in our society.

_____ 17. People are basically trustworthy and dependable.

_____ 18. Students generally see me as personable and likable.

_____ 19. I am personally involved with my students.

_____ 20. I am accepting of individual differences in my students.

_____ 21. My understanding of science and technology is adequate.

_____ 22. Students are important sources of personal and professional satisfaction for me.

_____ 23. As a science teacher, I am worthy of respect.

_____ 24. The process of learning science is important for our culture.

_____ 25. My orientation is toward people more than things.

The items in this list are keyed to five important dimensions of science teaching as a helping profession. If you would like to see how you perceive yourself on these dimensions, complete the following section. Add your response for the items in the left column. Divide that number by five. The result should be a number between seven and one for each of the dimensions of science teaching listed. The numbers give some indication of your self-perceptions as related to the different categories.

Items		*Average*	*Dimensions of Science Teaching*
1, 6, 11, 16, 21	÷ 5	_____	Perceptions about science subject matter
2, 7, 12, 17, 22	÷ 5	_____	Perceptions of students
3, 8, 13, 18, 23	÷ 5	_____	Perceptions of yourself as a science teacher
4, 9, 14, 19, 24	÷ 5	_____	Perceptions of your purpose as a science teacher
5, 10, 15, 20, 25	÷ 5	_____	Perceptions of the teaching task

ACTIVITY 1–2
THE WHAT AND HOW OF SCIENCE LESSONS

In this activity you are presented with a teaching situation on the left and asked to match a method from the right to achieve your teaching goal. In each case you should give a rationale for your choice of method. Complete the activity alone. Then share your responses with several other students in the class.

	What you want to accomplish—the goal	*How you would accomplish your goal—the method*		*Methods of teaching*
1.	Introduce the concept of acids and bases.	_____	a.	Bulletin board
			b.	Demonstration
2.	Clarify the effects of air pollution.	_____	c.	Discussion
			d.	Field trip
3.	Summarize the effects of erosion.	_____	e.	Video
			f.	Internet
4.	Show the interrelationships of organisms in a community.	_____	g.	CD-ROM
			h.	Guest speaker
			i.	Laboratory investigation
5.	Evaluate students' understanding of pulleys.	_____	j.	Library research
			k.	Lecture
6.	Differentiate the phylum Echinodermata from the phylum Chordata.	_____	l.	Projects
			m.	Questioning
			n.	Quiz
7.	Realize the ethical decisions involved in scientific research.	_____	o.	Analyzing data
			p.	Role playing
			q.	Presentation using video images
8.	Introduce the structure of DNA.	_____	r.	Simulation game
			s.	Television
9.	Show the dynamic qualities of weather.	_____	t.	Test
			u.	Chalkboard
10.	Expand students' understanding of the systems.	_____	v.	Computer simulation concept
			w.	Calculator (handheld)
			x.	Records
11.	Review the concept of force.	_____		
12.	Teach students to handle the microscope correctly.	_____		
13.	Outline safety procedures for the chemistry laboratory.	_____		
14.	Introduce students to careers in science.	_____		
15.	Help students understand the role of science and technology in society.	_____		

ACTIVITY 1–3
A FIRST LESSON

It is strongly recommended that you teach a short science lesson early in the methods course. Preferably, this lesson should be taught in a local science class; however, it may be taught to your peers in the methods class. An important objective of this lesson is to help you answer two questions: "Can I teach science?" and "What is science teaching like?" There is no better way to answer these questions than to actually teach a science lesson.

Here are some guidelines to help you prepare your first lesson.

1. Keep the lesson simple. Try to present a single concept, process, or skill.
2. What do you hope to accomplish by the end of the lesson? What should the students know or be able to do that they could not do before the lesson?
3. What experiences will best achieve the goals and be interesting and motivating for the students?
4. What is the most effective way to organize the materials or experiences of the lesson? What is its conceptual structure and instructional sequence?
5. Use the following format as the basis of your lesson plan.

Self-Critique of Your First Lesson

1. Rate the following:

	Poor	Fair	Good	Excellent	Comments
Voice quality and articulation	____	____	____	____	_____
Poise	____	____	____	____	_____
Adaptability and flexibility	____	____	____	____	_____
Use of English	____	____	____	____	_____
Procedure	____	____	____	____	_____
Enthusiasm	____	____	____	____	_____
Continuity	____	____	____	____	_____
Maintenance of good class control	____	____	____	____	_____
Provision for individual differences	____	____	____	____	_____
Ability to interest students	____	____	____	____	_____
Ability to involve students	____	____	____	____	_____
Ability to ask questions	____	____	____	____	_____
Ability to answer questions	____	____	____	____	_____
Use of instructional methods	____	____	____	____	_____
Provision of adequate summaries	____	____	____	____	_____
Budgeting of time	____	____	____	____	_____
Organization of the lesson	____	____	____	____	_____
Knowledge of subject	____	____	____	____	_____

2. Did you achieve your goals?

3. What were the strengths of the presentation?

4. What were the weaknesses of the presentation?

5. What would you change if you were to teach this lesson again?

ACTIVITY 1–4
AN INTERVIEW WITH A SCIENCE TEACHER

One way to find out what science teaching is like is to interview a science teacher. Tell the teacher the reason for the meeting and the general topics of discussion. If at all possible, make arrangements to observe a class period before the interview. This visit will give you some insights concerning the teacher's style and approach to science instruction. It will also provide some bases of discussion. You may wish to ask the following questions to get the conversation started.

1. What is the science program in your school?
   How many courses are offered?
   What is the enrollment in life science? Earth science? Physical science? Which textbooks are used?
   How is educational technology incorporated into each course?
   How does the science program in your school relate to the rest of the science program in the district?
   Do you offer any special science courses?
   Has the science program changed in the last five years?

2. What do you see as the important trends and issues in science teaching?
   Have enrollments in science increased? Decreased? Has the science budget increased? Decreased? How much do you use the laboratory in science teaching? Do you introduce any science-related social issues?

3. What are your concerns as a science teacher? Are your facilities adequate? Do you have materials for your program? Is student interest high? Low? Is maintaining discipline a problem?

4. What are your greatest rewards as a science teacher? Seeing students learn? Helping other people? Working with interesting and exciting colleagues? Contributing to the public's scientific literacy?

5. Why is science important?

ACTIVITY 1–5
MY CONCERNS

Listed below are several statements commonly expressed by students entering teaching. Indicate your present concern about the problem by placing an X in a space provided on the continuum: Number 1 indicates little concern, number 9 indicates a high degree of concern.

1. Developing short- and long-term purposes, goals, and objectives for science instruction
2. Understanding scientific inquiry
3. Motivating students to learn science
4. Designing programs to increase the learning of science
5. Recognizing and responding to different developmental levels of students
6. Understanding the dynamics of student groups
7. Adapting to the special needs and abilities of students
8. Designing programs for the individual needs of students
9. Knowing about science curriculum programs and instructional materials
10. Incorporating other disciplines, such as mathematics or social science, into the science program
11. Understanding and using different instructional strategies
12. Planning and organizing science activities
13. Evaluating student progress
14. Handling problems of classroom management, pupil control, and student misbehavior
15. Preparing for practice teaching
16. Budgeting time and judging the flow of science lessons
17. Handling routines such as making out reports, attendance, and keeping records
18. Lack of an adequate background in science
19. Lack of self-confidence to teach science
20. Presenting science demonstrations, questioning, and guiding student discussions
21. Adapting to the unique problems of school facilities, materials, and equipment
22. Understanding and using special school services such as counseling and testing
23. Knowing how to obtain a science teaching job
24. Understanding the place and importance of science education
25. Other concerns

These statements constitute a personal inventory of concerns. Many of them are addressed in this book and will be included as part of the methods course. Identifying and clarifying your concerns will better enable you to direct your work, study, and activities during this preparation for science teaching.

CHAPTER 7

BEGINNING YOUR INSTRUCTIONAL THEORY

This chapter introduces some practical aspects of science teaching. Chapter 1 focused on questions, such as, "Am I qualified to teach science?" and "What is science teaching like?" The questions for this chapter include: "What do I have to know in order to teach science?", "What do I have to be able to do to teach science?", and "How do I put it all together for effective science teaching?". To answer these questions, we use the idea of an *instructional theory* to help you formulate ideas about science teaching. Further, we have you begin developing an approach to science teaching.

Teaching science requires continual decision making. One way to characterize the decision-making process is through questions. How do I respond to students' misconceptions in science? The LCD projector does not work—what should I do? Where should I use this new piece of software? How can I use the Internet with my class? Is this laboratory safe? Indeed, you will have to consider many variables during the school day. Effective science teachers act efficiently and respond constructively to numerous classroom situations. Before continuing in this chapter, you should complete Activity 2–1: What Would You Do?

WHY DEVELOP AN INSTRUCTIONAL THEORY?

Scientific theories guide the research of scientists and help them develop new insights into the intricacies of nature. A theory is an effective intellectual tool that integrates many observations and helps scientists make predictions. Recall that in science, a theory is an empirically substantiated explanation of some aspect of the natural world. A theory is based on evidence and it incorporates facts, inferences, tested knowledge, and laws. Scientific theories have several fundamental attributes. They (1) guide scientific inquiries, (2) organize observations and data, (3) provide explanations for phenomena, and (4) help predict events and therefore provide direction.

An instructional theory should provide well-substantiated explanations for aspects of teaching and learning in science classrooms. Your instructional theory should be based on evidence—observations and research—not prevailing beliefs about students and teaching. As a science teacher your effectiveness can be enhanced by your ability to organize observations of students, explain behaviors, and predict what will happen as a result of your activities and actions in the classroom. Although an instructional theory may not have the power and utility of a scientific theory, it will certainly help you bring consistency to the decisions you make as a science teacher.

WHAT ARE THE FOUNDATIONS OF AN INSTRUCTIONAL THEORY?

One essential foundation is your understanding of the purposes of science education. Other foundational elements include principles of learning, motivation, development, and social psychology, as well as attitudes and values of the scientific enterprise, curriculum materials, and instructional techniques. Individual science teachers combine all of these elements in unique ways.

Guest Editorial ◆ Mary McMillan

Science Education Student
Carleton College, Northfield, Minnesota

Anticipating Student Teaching

As I anticipate my student teaching placement in the fall, I am beginning to formulate my definition of a successful teacher. The ideal teacher is organized, energetic, and confident. He or she uses subject matter as a means of helping students to develop an appreciation of themselves, others, and society. During my student teaching placement, I hope to develop the skills of an "ideal" teacher. As I work toward my goal, student teaching will have a dual purpose for me. I want to help my students appreciate their own abilities, and I hope to learn more about myself as a science teacher.

To recognize students' abilities, I will need to become acquainted with them and their interests. As I search for topics that interest them, I will hope for interesting moments and sparks of thoughtful questions. It will be necessary to appreciate diversity. Some students will have trouble with analytical skills, but they may demonstrate the ability to lead others, to communicate, or to be creative. To provide each student with the opportunity for success and enthusiasm, I will have to include a broad range of activities.

As I envision activities for students, I recognize one of the causes of my own enthusiasm. I believe that science classes provide a means of understanding the earth and its resources. Such understanding is essential if we hope to protect and improve the environment. The science courses I most enjoyed were those that increased my awareness of the environment and my perceptions of change. As a teacher, the opportunity to select materials and topics will be very important to me. I hope to teach about general principles by providing a background of specific examples. I plan to infuse a good deal of environmental education in my classes, and I hope that my enthusiasm for science will be shared.

As I try to share my interests and concerns with others, I also will be learning about myself. A cooperating teacher will probably provide both criticism and praise. Students' actions and reactions in the classroom will challenge my assumptions as well as my creativity. There will be times when I cannot select the exact subject matter I would like to teach. Unless I demonstrate my willingness to take risks and correct mistakes, however, I will not learn the ways in which I need to change. To succeed as a student teacher, I will need to be persistent, open, and energetic. I want to help others value their own abilities and, by doing so, I hope to become better acquainted with myself.

Characteristics of an Instructional Theory

In 1968, Jerome Bruner outlined the characteristics of an instructional theory in a book entitled, *Toward a Theory of Instruction*. According to Bruner, a theory of instruction is *prescriptive*. It gives direction and provides guidelines for effective instruction and enables the teacher to evaluate teaching techniques and procedures. A theory of instruction also is *normative*; it is general rather than specific. For example, a theory of instruction would give some criteria for a chemistry lesson on acids and bases but would not give specific guidelines for the lesson.

What help does a theory of instruction provide? What questions will it answer? An instructional theory has five important characteristics. It should help you specify the following:

1. *The most acceptable evidence that students have learned.* This first and most valuable aspect of an instructional theory identifies what counts as learning.
2. *The most effective experiences to enhance learning.* An instructional theory helps you answer the question, "What activities will encourage learning?"
3. *The most effective way in which knowledge can be structured to enhance learning.* An instructional theory helps you answer the question, "What is the best way to structure the knowledge and skills of my lesson?"
4. *The most effective sequence in which to present material.* An instructional theory helps you answer the question,

"How do I present the lesson so all students will develop their understandings of science?"

5. *The most effective processes for feedback and evaluation.* An instructional theory helps you answer the questions: "How and when should I give feedback?", "When should instruction be assessed?", "What is the most appropriate form to obtain and return feedback?", and "How should I modify instruction?".

One important condition for learning is *active participation by students.* Science teachers often ask, "How can I motivate students?" You will slowly accumulate ideas and activities that encourage a predisposition toward learning. Engaging the learner is difficult for even the most experienced science teacher. Consider your own response to the problems in Activity 2–1. Ideally, the problems engaged your interest. One response you could have made was the exploration of alternative solutions to the problem. Another was a curiosity concerning details of the situation. Both of these responses originated in the uncertainty and the ambiguity of the problems. There is an optimal level of uncertainty and ambiguity: too little and the problem is easily resolved; too much and there is confusion, anxiety, and lack of resolution. Part of your task as a science teacher is to help learners stay within the optimal range of their interest and curiosity.

Once you have engaged the learners, they must continue to work on the problem. To stimulate continued interest, the rewards of the exploration must be greater than the risks. Was this true with your work on the problems in Activity 2–1? Giving or receiving instruction should increase rewards and decrease risks; if such is not the case, your instruction is not as effective as it should be.

Finally, you need a direction or goal. From the alternatives provided, you were asked to resolve the classroom problems in the best way possible. The question—What would you do?—helped define the direction and goal.

A second condition for effective instruction is the *optimal structure of knowledge.* In the best cases, this condition is provided by well-designed instructional materials. The body of knowledge should be presented in a form simple enough to be understood by the learner. The fact that the material is in a textbook means that the science teacher will have to adapt the structure of knowledge to accommodate students' needs and interests.

A third condition for learning is the *optimal sequence of knowledge.* As science instruction progresses, teachers present and draw students' attention to relationships among ideas, processes, and skills. The instructional sequence should increase the probability that at each step the learner understands, transforms, and applies these ideas, processes, and skills. Here again you may encounter the problem of steps that are too small, resulting in students' boredom, or steps that are too large, resulting in frustration. In part, the purpose of your instructional theory is to help you bridge the gap between the structural and sequential logic of the curriculum and the social and psychological needs of the students.

A fourth condition is your ability to receive, respond, and give *feedback in the teaching environment.* Motivating, structuring, and sequencing of instruction are contingent on your ability to receive and respond to cues from the students. Student feedback should in turn influence your instruction and your response to student achievement.

PURPOSE, GOALS, AND OBJECTIVES

Like any journey, in science teaching you have to know where you are going. What is it that you perceive as the destination for your students? What do you see as the stops along the way to this final destination? In the first chapter, we suggested that the term *scientific literacy* expresses the destination for all students. Translating scientific literacy into concrete goals of knowledge, skills, and values of curriculum and instruction is an important process for science teachers, because the translation has to be fairly consistent with the overall purpose. Finally, the specific objectives of lessons have to be consistent with the purpose of developing scientific literacy. Separate chapters are devoted to these topics. Before continuing, complete Activity 2–2: My Aims and Preferences. You should review your responses on this investigation after completing the chapter.

The *National Science Education Standards* (NRC, 1996) also provide purpose, goals, and objectives for science teaching. They give a valuable description of your destination, and outline the territory for your travels. They do not have specific, detailed maps for the trip, so you will have to create your own maps for using curriculum, instruction, and assessment. Your instructional theory will be invaluable for this process.

LEARNING AND TEACHING

Research on student learning has long been an important factor in any teacher's instructional theory. In the 1960s and 1970s, science teachers looked to Jean Piaget's theory of cognitive development (Bybee & Sund, 1982). The research focused on two major features of Piagetian theory. First, Piaget proposed that learning occurs through an individual's interaction with the environment. This interaction is described as a student assimilating new information and ideas from various educational experiences and then accommodating the new information with previously held information. This method establishes a consistency between the individual's cognitive structure and everyday experience. Second, each individual passes through different stages of development, each characterized by the ability to perform various cognitive tasks.

The most relevant stages for science education are concrete reasoning and formal reasoning. A concrete reasoner requires tangible objects and experiences and their observable relations to reason logically. A formal reasoner can manipulate abstract ideas.

Piaget's notion of learning as an interaction with the environment has been generally supported (Luzner, 1986; Renner, Abraham, & Birnie, 1986) and, in fact, was a foundation for contemporary constructivist explanations of students' conceptual understanding and change. The concept of stages of concrete and formal reasoning, however, has been criticized and revised. Studies (Chiapetta, 1976; Renner, Grant, & Sutherland, 1978; Wavering, Perry, & Birdd, 1986) have demonstrated that, as measured by performance on cognitive tasks, the majority of secondary students are at the concrete stage of reasoning. There is also evidence that performance on such tasks is strongly influenced by context, mode, language of task presentation, and subject matter (Golbeck, 1986; Brandwein, 1979). Other studies have demonstrated that even young children are capable of abstract thought in certain situations (Chi & Koeske, 1983).

Because most secondary students engage primarily in concrete reasoning, be careful about introducing tasks that primarily require abstract thought. For example, many texts of secondary science implicitly assume that the reader can reason at the formal level. A statement about where students *are* in their reasoning ability does not, however, mean they cannot learn and develop more sophisticated levels of reasoning. Students much younger than secondary students are capable of reasoning and logical thought under certain conditions. Appropriate contexts and experiences that progress from concrete to abstract could foster the reasoning abilities necessary for understanding many science concepts.

In recent years science educators have used a model termed *constructivism* to help understand students' learning. The theoretical basis for constructivist research comes from several sources, including David Ausubel (1968). We have introduced the essence of Ausubelian theory (Ausubel, Novak, & Hanesian, 1978) earlier: A learner's prior knowledge is an important factor in determining what is learned in a given situation. L. S. Vygotsky (1968) is a second important source for constructivism. He wrote of student and teacher conceptions, and how students and teachers might use similar words to describe concepts, yet have different personal interpretations of those concepts. Vygotsky's work implies that science instruction should take into account the differences between teacher and student conceptions and should provide a great deal of student–student interaction so that learners can develop concepts from those whose understandings and interpretations are closer to their own.

Early work in constructivist research focused on identifying students' conceptions about scientific phenomena and how such conceptions differ from accepted scientific conceptions. Student conceptions have been referred to by various unfortunate labels, such as misconceptions, alternative conceptions, alternative frameworks, and naive theories. We think it is much more useful to simply recognize students' *current* conceptions and emphasize your role in changing those conceptions so they are more aligned with those recognized as scientific. Several good reviews of this research exist (Driver, Guesne, & Tiberghien, 1985; Osborne & Freyberg, 1983; Duit, 1987). We especially recommend that you review *How People Learn: Brain, Mind, Experience, and School* (Bransford, Brown, & Cocking, 2000), and *How Students Learn: Science in the Classroom* (Donovan & Bransford, 2005).

In the constructivist model, students construct knowledge by interpreting new experiences in the context of their current conceptions, experiences, episodes, and images. Students' construction of knowledge begins at an early age so that by the time they encounter formalized study of science, they have developed stable and highly personal conceptions for many natural phenomena. Given this view, one goal of your instruction must be to facilitate change in students' conceptions of the world. Researchers (Posner, Strike, Hewson, & Gerzog, 1982; Smith, Carey, & Wiser, 1985) have likened this process of conceptual change to the process by which scientific theories undergo change and restructuring. In fact, studies have demonstrated that student beliefs and conceptions often parallel early scientific theories, dating back to Aristotle and Lamarck (Caramazza, McCloskey, & Green, 1981; Champagne, Klopfer, & Gunstone, 1982; Wandersee, 1986). However, other research cautions against drawing too strong a parallel between student conceptions and the history of science, largely because student conceptions are not nearly as comprehensive as, say, Aristotelian theories.

Posner and others (1982) have proposed four conditions for conceptual change that should be recognized as you formulate your instructional theory. First, in order for students to change their conceptions of a given phenomenon, they must be *dissatisfied* with their current conception. This dissatisfaction presumably comes about through repeated exposure to experiences they cannot explain by using current conceptions. Second, the new conception must be *intelligible* in terms of prior experiences and knowledge. Third, the new conception must be *plausible* in that it can explain a number of prior experiences and observations. Finally, the new conception must be *fruitful,* opening up new areas of inquiry, primarily through predictions about future events.

Constructivist research also suggests other strategies to promote conceptual change. You should be aware that students have conceptions of the world and that they often do not differentiate concepts (Trowbridge and McDermott, 1981). Students need time to make their ideas explicit, and they should have a chance to apply their conceptions of the world in different contexts (Minstrell, 1989).

Contemporary research associated with cognitive sciences and constructivism has had an important influence on science teaching. We recommend reviewing *Learning Science and the Science of Learning,* a publication prepared specifically for science teachers (Bybee, 2002).

When considering your approach to instruction, recognize that your students may have explanations or conceptions for many objects, events, and phenomena. Stated another way, your students are not empty vessels into which you can pour scientific facts, information, and concepts. Your challenge as a science teacher is to help students realize the inadequacy of their current conceptions and provide the time and opportunity for them to construct more scientifically accurate concepts. In later chapters, we return to your role in providing linkages between students' explanations and scientific explanations.

EFFECTIVE RELATIONSHIPS WITH STUDENTS

For many years psychologists have investigated the characteristics of effective helping relationships, including teaching. Their research indicates that a teacher's perceptions of self, students, and the teaching task are critical to effective instruction.

Effective teachers perceive other people, particularly their students, as able, friendly, worthy, intrinsically motivated, dependable, and helpful. In the same manner, effective teachers see themselves as good teachers who are needed and trustworthy, and who relate well to other people.

Better teachers see themselves assisting and facilitating rather than coercing and controlling. They identify with larger issues, are personally involved with issues, problems, and other people, and view the whole process of education as important. In addition, they tend to be altruistic and self-revealing. Effective teachers see their task as helping people rather than dealing with objects; and, generally, they try to understand the perceptions and backgrounds of their students.

These studies delineated the perceptions of effective teachers. What about the students' perceptions of the science teacher? Years ago, one author conducted research on the perceptions of the ideal science teacher (Bybee, 1973; 1975; 1978). The results of these studies are summarized in Table 2–1. Note that adequate personal relations with students, and enthusiasm in working with them, consistently rank as the most important characteristics for science teachers. With only one exception, these two categories ranked first or second by all the groups studied. Although this research indicates that personal qualities are perceived as important dimensions of science instruction, knowledge, personal relations, planning, enthusiasm, and methods are all important for effective science teaching. An instructional theory should incorporate these elements, adapting them individually and *in toto* to the situation in the science classroom.

TABLE 2–1 Science Educator's Grand Mean Ranking Compared with Other Population's Data Reported by Rank

Category	Science Educators N = 172	Inservice Teachers N = 76	Preservice Elementary Majors N = 58	High School Students Average N = 44	High School Students Disadvantaged N = 106	High School Students Advantaged N = 31	Elementary School Children Grade 6 N = 25	Elementary School Children Grades 4, 5, 6 N = 18
Knowledge of subject matter	4	4	4	3	4	3	3	3
Adequate personal relations with students	1	1	1	1	1	2	1	1
Adequate planning and organization	5	5	5	4	3	4	5	4
Enthusiasm in working with students	2	2	2	2	2	1	2	2
Adequate teaching methods and class procedures	3	3	3	5	5	5	4	5

EFFECTIVE INSTRUCTION

Lee Shulman of Stanford University reported the role and development of teachers' knowledge in relation to teaching. Shulman (1986) identified three categories of content knowledge: (1) subject matter, (2) pedagogical, and (3) curricular.

For science teachers, *subject matter* is more than information and facts about a discipline. Content knowledge of a subject includes what Joseph Schwab (1966) called the "substantive and syntactic structures" of a discipline. That is, substantial knowledge is an understanding of the different ways the basic concepts and principles of a discipline are organized. What are the major conceptual schemes in your discipline? If you had to organize the information and facts of physics, chemistry, biology, or the earth sciences, what major ideas would you identify as basic structures of these disciplines? In biology, for example, one can use the levels of organization approach, studying biology from the smallest particles to larger domains, and explaining living processes in terms of molecular activities. One also can use an ecological approach in which the ecosystem is the basic level of study and individual activities are studied in terms of the systems in which they live and interact. Using either of these structures you can develop basic conceptual schemes of biology, such as energetics, genetics, diversity, and evolution.

The syntax of a discipline is the set of ways scientists establish the truth or falsehood, validity or invalidity, of new or extant knowledge claims. Science teachers' use of inquiry introduces students to the processes of obtaining new knowledge, such as observation, hypothesis, and experimentation. Students also gain the understanding that knowledge must be evaluated. By what criteria do biologists, geologists, or astronomers evaluate the worth of different theories?

Pedagogical content knowledge describes the depth and breadth of knowledge a teacher has about teaching a particular subject. Pedagogical content knowledge is the capacity to formulate and represent science in ways that make it comprehensible to learners. Examples of pedagogical knowledge include forms of representing concepts such as use of analogies, examples, illustrations, and demonstrations. Effective science teachers have a variety of ways and means of representing such ideas as ionic bonding, density, recombination of DNA, or stellar evolution.

Another dimension of pedagogical content knowledge is the understanding of what makes a concept easy or difficult for a learner to grasp. What misconceptions might students have about phenomena, such as heat and temperature, position and velocity, or living and nonliving? What preconceptions do students have for objects and events in the natural world? The science teacher's

instructional theory helps establish links between new concepts and the students' current understanding.

Next we consider *curricular knowledge*. One goal of this book is to introduce you to the many methods and materials used in science teaching. The science curriculum includes a full range of materials with which science teachers should be familiar. Materials are designed for a particular subject, at a particular level, to be used with particular students. Each discipline has its own textbooks, kinds of laboratory equipment, and educational software.

In addition to knowledge of curricular materials and how best to use them, curricular knowledge extends to science teachers' abilities to relate topics of study to the curricula their students may be studying in other disciplines.

INSTRUCTIONAL DECISIONS

The discussion of teacher knowledge as it relates to content, pedagogy, and curriculum is obviously important, even essential, but you will need more than an adequate knowledge base for your instructional theory; as we have mentioned, you will also have to make many instructional decisions. David Berliner (1984) reviewed research on teaching and provided valuable insights about these decisions, using the categories of preinstructional decisions, instructional decisions, and postinstructional decisions.

First, we introduce *preinstructional decisions*. Before you begin teaching a science lesson, be aware of the effect of certain decisions on student achievement, attitudes, and behaviors. You must make *content decisions*. What is the content of your science lesson? You must consider not only national standards and state and local standards and assessments, but also your judgments about issues, such as the effort required to teach a subject and the problems that you perceive the students will have with the subject. Finally, you must take into account the subjects you enjoy teaching. Which are the areas within your discipline that you really like? Are you excited about introducing students to the nature and history of science? Do you think it most important to have students recognize science-related social issues?

Science teaching involves groups of students. *Grouping decisions* are part of your preparation for a lesson. What is the best size of a group? How much laboratory equipment do you have? Who should (or should not) work together? Should you use cooperative groups? What criteria do you have for forming a particular group? Whether you lecture to the entire class or work in the laboratory, you will usually make grouping decisions. Even when assigning individual work on projects, experiments, and tests, a group in some sense still exists.

Finally, you will have to make *decisions about activities*. Laboratory work, for example, has specific functions; that is, it is used to achieve certain goals. In a laboratory, students may learn to design an experiment, manipulate equipment, and use computers. Operations—the rules or norms of conduct for the activity—are also important. Is it okay to be out of one's seat? What type of conversation is acceptable? What rules *must* be followed for safety reasons?

The importance of these kinds of decisions cannot be overstated. Just reading this section should make you aware of the many and varied decisions you must make *before you begin teaching even the simplest lesson*.

Next is the importance of *instructional decisions*. Once you begin teaching a lesson, numerous factors determine what your students learn. The amount of time students spend on a task—*engaged time*—is directly related to how much students will learn. Recognize that *engaged* can mean physically (hands on), mentally (minds on), or both. Although this seems obvious, the amount of engaged time varies from student to student and class to class. Be aware of the amount of time students are actually working. Engaged time is especially important for students who are under achievers and of low ability. These students will benefit most from time *on task*, but they also are the students who are most likely to be *off task*.

The *success rate* of students is related to continued achievement. Success in the early stages of learning new concepts or skills is especially important for students of low ability and those who have traditionally been unsuccessful. If students do not experience some success in the early stages of lessons, their frustration and lack of understanding can contribute to low achievement.

Decisions you make about *questioning* will also influence your teaching effectiveness. Science teachers in particular should ask many questions—questions about the natural world are the foundation of science. The first thing to consider is the cognitive level of the question. Most teachers ask low-level questions, such as: "What do the letters DNA stand for?", "What is the second law of thermodynamics?", or "What is a silicon oxygen tetrahedron?". Although questions of this nature have some benefit, remember that higher level questions facilitate thinking and learning. Questions that require students to analyze and synthesize will produce higher levels of student achievement. You could, for example, provide data in graph form and ask the students to analyze the results and form an explanation based on the evidence. Or, you could provide information from two separate but related experiments and ask students for their predictions of possible outcomes.

Another point about questioning concerns the importance of *waiting* after you have asked a question.

Research by Mary Budd Rowe (1974) confirms the importance of wait time. Longer waits (most teachers wait less than one second after asking a question) result in increases in the appropriateness, confidence, variety, and cognitive level of responses. A two- to three-second adjustment in your teaching style can result in a much higher return for you and your students.

Finally, you will make *postinstructional* decisions. Now that the lesson, unit, or semester is over, how much did the students learn? Science teachers usually arrive at an answer through the assessments, grades, and feedback given to students.

Assessment is not the central issue. In fact, we propose that planning the assessment should exactly correlate with your aims and should have been designed *before* developing the instructional sequence and providing students opportunities to learn. Although this may seem backwards, it is designing school science instruction so it is coherent (Wiggins & McTighe, 2005).

Grades motivate students to achieve; however, the overuse of grades or their use as coercion can have detrimental effects. Corrective feedback, if properly given, results in positive achievement and attitudes on the part of students. Your decisions to give praise for correct work, recognition for proper behavior, and personally neutral criticism (as opposed to sarcasm) for incorrect responses all can influence student learning.

It is easy to feel overwhelmed at the number of decisions that go into science teaching. We think the early introduction of these ideas will prepare you for the topics and activities to come. For the time being, only an awareness of these decisions is necessary.

RESEARCH ON EFFECTIVE TEACHING

Research on good teaching provides insights that may help you synthesize the ideas in this section. After reviewing the research on good teaching, Andrew Porter and Jere Brophy (1988) concluded that the concept of good teaching is changing. In the past, teachers sometimes were viewed as technicians who had to apply how-to lessons, or as weak links in the education system who had to be circumvented with a teacher-proof curriculum. Such approaches did not work. The current concept of effective teaching deals with empowering teachers. How are teachers empowered? A brief answer is through the application of research on teaching, and a longer answer involves the continuous development of an instructional theory. Our discussion assumes that student learning within science classes requires good teaching, and good teaching requires science teachers who make appropriate decisions about how to educate students.

A contemporary image of the good teacher is that of a thoughtful professional who works purposefully toward educational goals. According to Porter and Brophy (1988):

◆ Effective teachers are clear about their instructional goals. They inform their students of these goals and keep them in mind as they design lessons and communicate with students.

◆ Effective instruction provides students with strategies they can use for their own learning.

◆ Effective instruction creates learning situations in which students are expected to learn information, solve problems, and organize that information in new ways.

◆ Effective teachers continually monitor student understanding and adjust instruction accordingly.

◆ Effective teachers frequently integrate other subjects and skills into their lessons.

◆ Effective teachers design instruction so that what is learned can be used in the future.

◆ Effective teachers are thoughtful and reflective about their instruction.

Figure 2–1 summarizes these points.

Effective science teachers continually develop and improve their approach to instruction—what we call an instructional theory. The feature that mediates the instructional theory and teaching practice is decision making as it applies to different teaching situations.

METHODS OF FORMING INSTRUCTIONAL THEORY

When science teachers use the Internet, show a DVD, take a field trip, have students work in the laboratory, or guide a discussion, they are using instructional methods that they assume will develop understanding, skills,

or values relative to science and technology. The assumption underlying an instructional method is, it is the most effective, efficient, and appropriate means of facilitating learning.

In this section, we introduce a variety of teaching methods. They are listed in alphabetical order, with a brief description and guides for effective use.

Assessment

Purpose: to provide feedback to both the students and teacher about student understanding of concepts and ability to use skills

Predominant Learning Modes: visual, kinesthetic

Group Size: individual, occasionally small

Tests, quizzes, performance-based assessments, and portfolios used frequently in science classes should be

Good teaching is fundamental to effective schooling. From the studies of the Institute for Research on Teaching and from other studies conducted over the last 10 years, there is a picture of effective teachers as semiautonomous professionals who

■ are clear about their instructional goals,

■ are knowledgeable about lesson content and strategies for teaching it,

■ communicate to their students what is expected of them—and why,

■ make expert use of existing instructional materials in order to devote more time to practices that enrich and clarify lesson content,

■ teach students metacognitive strategies and give them opportunities to master them,

■ address higher- as well as lower-level cognitive objectives,

■ monitor students' understanding by offering regular and appropriate feedback,

■ integrate their instruction with that of other subject areas,

■ accept responsibility for student outcomes, and

■ are thoughtful and reflective about their practice.

FIGURE 2–1 Highlights of Research on Good Teaching (*Source:* Andrew Porter and Jere Brophy, "Synthesis of Research on Good Teaching: Insights from the Work of the Institute for Research on Teaching," *Educational Leadership* [May 1988]: 75.)

designed to provide accurate feedback concerning student progress. Appropriate and effective use of assessment includes the following:

♦ Assess the opportunities students have had to learn science.
♦ Use performance-based assessments to evaluate the processes of scientific inquiry and technological design.
♦ Provide students feedback about their understanding of concepts.
♦ Use questions and situations that require critical thinking and problem solving at different cognitive levels; that is, recall, comprehension, application, analysis, synthesis, and evaluation.

Chalkboard or Marker Board

Purpose: to illustrate, outline, or underscore ideas in written or graphic form
Predominant Learning Mode: visual
Group Size: small to large

Chalkboards or marker boards are used extensively in science classrooms. Most science teachers use the chalkboard or marker board with some skill. Here are a few helpful hints:

♦ Say what you are going to write before writing it.
♦ Use key words or concepts.
♦ Write legibly and spell correctly.
♦ Stand to the side of the material so the students can see the board and you can see the students.
♦ Erase the board before writing a new concept, idea, or diagram.

Debate

Purpose: to allow students to gain information, discuss different sides of an issue, and resolve conflicts
Predominant Learning Mode: auditory
Group Size: medium—10 to 15 students

Debate is an effective way to introduce different sides of science-related issues. The debate can continue over several days and involve several teams in various aspects of a topic. Students will have to understand information concerning their position and develop the skills of analysis and evaluation concerning their opponent's position. Here are some guidelines for using debate:

♦ Be sure the debate topic has clear pro and con sides.
♦ Use teams of three to four students per side for an issue.

♦ Set clear time limits for opening statements, rebuttals, and closing statements.
♦ Make it clear that there are to be no interruptions while a speaker has the floor.

Demonstrations

Purpose: to provide students the opportunity to see a phenomenon or event that they otherwise would not observe
Predominant Learning Modes: visual, auditory
Group Size: medium to large

Demonstrations can be used to teach concepts or skills directly, or to prepare students for work in the laboratory. Demonstrations are often used due to safety concerns or lack of equipment. The best demonstrations have a dramatic quality and usually deal with something that is puzzling to the students. Here are a few helpful hints:

♦ Present demonstrations so students can see them and hear you.
♦ Do the demonstration *before* trying it in class.
♦ Take all necessary safety precautions.
♦ Plan your demonstration so it clearly shows the intended concepts or skills.

Discussion

Purpose: to promote an exchange of information and ideas among members of a group or class
Predominant Learning Mode: auditory
Group Size: small to medium—two to eight students

Discussions are used frequently in science instruction. The teacher must plan the discussion so that information is accurate and students stay on the topic. Some suggestions follow:

♦ Think carefully about the initial questions.
♦ Prepare students for the discussion through reading or a laboratory experience.
♦ Provide a sheet of topics and/or questions that help guide the discussion.
♦ Facilitate discussions through planning, questioning, and summarizing.

Educational Software and Computers

Purpose: to allow students the opportunity to review, record, model, and acquire concepts and skills
Predominant Learning Modes: visual, auditory
Group Size: individual to small—two to four students

Examples of this technology in the science classroom include word processing, computer-assisted instruction, microcomputer-based laboratories, HyperCard, simulations, and modeling. Suggestions for use of software include the following:

- Select software aligned with the learning task.
- Use software as part of the planned instruction.

Field Trips

Purpose: to provide a learning experience that is unique and cannot be accomplished in the classroom

Predominant Learning Modes: kinesthetic, visual, auditory

Group Size: large

Field trips can be an exciting complement to the science program. They also can be a disaster. The difference between a learning experience and a disaster lies in the preparation for and appropriateness of the trip. As a science teacher, you will have to decide the appropriateness of the timing and destination of the trip in the instructional sequence. Concerning preparation, here are some guidelines:

- Take the trip yourself before making the trip with students.
- Prepare the students for the trip by informing them of the objectives, activities, and expected behaviors.
- Make sure transportation arrangements have been made and are safe and adequate.
- Confirm any prior arrangements for admission and guides at your destination.
- Obtain permission slips from parents.
- Arrange for additional adults (teachers and/or parents) to go on the trip.

Video/CD-ROM/DVD

Purpose: to present information in an interesting and efficient manner

Predominant Learning Modes: auditory, visual

Group Size: small to large

Most students are interested in video. Science teachers need to use media in a manner that will attain the established objectives. Placement of a video in the instructional sequence is critical. Following are recommendations for effective use of videos:

- Preview the video before showing it.
- Decide where the video can best fit in the curriculum.
- Prepare and distribute questions to the students.

- Identify one or two places to stop the video and have a discussion.
- Conduct a discussion after the video. You can evaluate the students' understanding of key concepts. Answer questions and make connections between the content presented and students' knowledge.

Games

Purpose: to give students an opportunity to learn in an enjoyable, stimulating manner

Predominant Learning Mode: kinesthetic

Group Size: small to medium

If used wisely, games can be valuable for developing concepts and ideas not generally conveyed by other methods. Here are some guides for using games:

- Consider the difficulty of the game.
- Consider the appropriateness of the game for your objectives.
- Provide clear rules for the game.
- Conduct pregame and postgame discussions.

Inquiry and Design

Purpose: to give students experience so they develop knowledge, skills, and values related to science (inquiry) and technology (design)

Predominant Learning Mode: kinesthetic

Group Size: individual to small

Methods related to use of inquiry and design include asking questions, using technology, designing experiments, analyzing data, formulating explanations, thinking about the relationship between evidence and explanation, and communicating explanations and methods. Here are some introductory guides:

- Select the inquiry activity that best illustrates the concepts or skills you have as objectives.
- Be sure materials are available and functional.
- Check equipment to be sure it works.
- Give clear, succinct directions including safety precautions, how to handle equipment, where to obtain materials, assignment of groups, and your expectations of conduct and reporting.

Internet

Purpose: to provide students with opportunities to gather information from a wide range of sources

Predominant Learning Mode: visual

Group Size: individual to small—two to four students

The Internet is an effective educational resource. Students can access the Internet for data and information about various topics.

- Connect use of the Internet with current activities and topics.
- Review the quality of information.

Laboratory Report

Purpose: to have students formalize their experiences and make connections between prior and present knowledge

Predominant Learning Mode: visual

Group Size: individual to small

Laboratory reports can be valuable means to bring different ideas into focus, to have students consider the context of concepts, and to reflect on the meaning of the laboratory experience. For the laboratory report to be effective, we recommend the following guidelines:

- Provide a purpose for the report.
- Outline your expectations in terms of content, length, and format.
- Have all members of groups sign the report, indicating they contributed.

Lecture and Direct Instruction

Purpose: to present a large body of information in an efficient manner

Predominant Learning Mode: auditory

Group Size: large

Lecture is used more often than it is effective, especially for middle school students. Here are some suggestions for effective lecturing:

- Use an outline and either distribute it before the lecture or place it on the overhead projector.
- Supplement the lecture with slides, overheads, or charts to illustrate concepts and ideas.
- Monitor student attention and understanding.
- Talk clearly and in a manner that identifies key points and facilitates note taking.

Oral Reports

Purpose: to allow students to demonstrate their understanding of a subject

Predominant Learning Mode: auditory

Group Size: individual to small

Oral reports are the students' equivalent of the teacher's lectures. Students—individually or in small groups—research information, organize material, and present a report. In effect, students teach other students. Here are some helpful hints:

- Presentations should align with the science program objectives.
- Allow students to report on topics of interest to them.
- Organize presentations as if they were to take place at a professional scientific meeting.
- Help students with audiovisual aids.
- Set clear time limits for the preparation and presentation of reports.
- Provide a formal evaluation in advance.

Problem Solving

Purpose: to give students experience in identifying and resolving a problem

Predominant Learning Mode: visual

Group Size: individual to small

The basic method is to place students in a situation where they must take action that is not immediately obvious. Problem solving provides opportunities for students to encounter concepts such as criteria, constraints, costs, risks, benefits, and trade-offs. Since students usually have not had much experience in problem solving, it is helpful to do some of the following:

- Identify general problems for study and resolution.
- Help students narrow their problems.
- Provide an opportunity to brainstorm possible solutions to the problem.
- Select and test reasonable solutions for the problem.
- Evaluate the tested solutions.
- Prepare a formal report using the protocol of professional papers.

Projects

Purpose: to give students knowledge, skills, and understanding related to a unique problem

Predominant Learning Mode: kinesthetic

Group Size: individual to small

Many science teachers like to have students work on projects and participate in local or regional science fairs. We believe projects are a wonderful way to give students a real sense of science. Here are some things to consider:

- Develop a list of project ideas for students.
- Provide written guidelines concerning the purpose and nature of the project and the final product.
- Provide time and assistance as the students work on their projects, particularly in locating resources.

Multimedia Projects

Purpose: to provide an opportunity to demonstrate understanding of a concept visually to a large group

Predominant Learning Mode: visual, kinesthetic

Group Size: individual to small

Multimedia techniques such as the use of slide show, hypermedia, and video clips provide means for students to put together in creative ways their ideas about a science concept. The use of computers with multimedia capabilities, including presentation software, has been shown to positively influence student achievement.[37] If considering the inclusion of multimedia projects in your classroom, consider the following:

◆ Be sure to provide options so that all students have access to appropriate technology and software, not just those with equipment at home.

◆ Provide a nontechnology alternative for completing the project so that the mechanism for demonstrating understanding doesn't overshadow the actual concept learned.

Questioning

Purpose: to stimulate thinking by engaging the learner

Predominant Learning Mode: auditory

Group Size: individual, or small, medium, and large

Questioning is a primary means teachers use to engage learners. Asking questions can be an effective and efficient means of stimulating students to think about the topic. Here are some suggestions on questioning:

◆ Use both convergent and divergent questions.

◆ Provide time for students to think about the answer.

◆ Use questions that require thinking at different levels; that is, recall, comprehension, application, analysis, synthesis, and evaluation.

Reading

Purpose: to present information that is uniform and consistent

Predominant Learning Mode: visual

Group Size: individual

Reading is central to effective instruction. Though reading should be used in science classes, it should not be the exclusive learning method. We also encourage reading of materials other than the textbook. Some guidelines follow:

◆ Use reading materials that are appropriate to the students' abilities and your program objectives.

◆ Assign a variety of readings (e.g., textbook, science books, popular magazines, and articles or tracts of historical significance).

Simulations

Purpose: to increase students' abilities to apply concepts, analyze situations, solve problems, and understand different points of view

Predominant Learning Modes: visual, auditory

Group Size: small to medium—5 to 15 students

Simulations provide teachers with a means of presenting situations, concepts, and issues in a condensed and simplified form. Simulations are especially useful for involving students in science-related social issues. Use of simulations can be enhanced by doing the following:

◆ Select a problem or issue of interest to the students.

◆ Include key issues and concepts in a realistic way.

◆ Make procedures clear, including expected behaviors, roles to be played, and time limits.

◆ Use lifelike materials and situations.

◆ Conclude the simulation with a discussion of different perceptions of the issue, how the students felt about the issue, how the conflict was resolved, and what actions might be taken in the future.

Computer-Based Learning

Purpose: to provide course content and interactive instruction in a variety of forms using the computer.

Predominant Learning Mode: visual, kinesthetic

Group size: individual, small group, whole class

Drill and practice, a repetitive approach emphasizing rote memory, was an early form of computer-based learning. Through enhanced motivation and ample practice afforded by drill-and-practice programs, learners improve their abilities to solve the type of problems presented. Software design has now gone well beyond the drill-and-practice stage; this form of computer-based learning is rarely emphasized today.

Programming advances and the use of the Internet have greatly changed the face of computer-based learning options for the science classroom. Simulations provide a computer model of the attributes, concepts, and relationships in the real world. In simulations, the student plays an active role in manipulating various factors in the computer simulation to better understand real-world phenomena. Through the variation of various factors, the computer generates creative, perhaps even impossible, environments. The computer may, for example, permit time compression by condensing large amounts of data into a short time frame or it may expand the time base to allow longer looks at changes that take place within a short time span. It can produce graphic displays of processes at work and the effects of different variable factors on the processes.

Simulations allow the effects of changes to be seen in a model before irrevocable changes are made in the real system. In this sense, minor or hypothetical risks can be taken without the cost or danger of carrying out the experiment in real life. Students using simulations are often forced to make decisions on the basis of incomplete data, and the results of these decisions can be seen quickly. This is excellent practice for the real world in which important decisions frequently need to be made on the basis of meager information.

Many examples of simulations are available for teaching secondary science. One interesting example combines the use of genetics databases and bioinformatics software to help students seek answers to questions about evolutionary relationships. Maier (2001) reports that students are able to build genetic distance matrices and phylogenetic trees based on molecular sequence data using web-based resources.

Probeware

> **Purpose:** to collect real-time data
> **Predominant Learning Mode:** kinesthetic
> **Group Size:** small

Probeware refers to equipment that can be attached to a computer or handheld device for collecting data on physical phenomena in real time, and special software for recording and displaying the results. For instance, temperature data might be collected with a temperature-sensing probe over a fixed time sequence, such as every five minutes, and the data converted into line graphs and data tables.

Powerful Microcomputer-based laboratory (MBL) tools for investigation have been available to students at the secondary level only since the mid-1980s. The Technical Education Research Center (TERC) in Cambridge, Massachusetts, has played a pivotal role in their development. Probes are available for measuring a wide variety of phenomena including the following: temperature sound, light, intensity, motion, atmospheric pressure, pH, EKG, EMG, heart rate, brain waves; humidity, wind speed, and wind direction. Commercial packages for computer-based laboratories are marketed by a variety of companies.

A goal of using probeware in your instruction should be to increase students' intuitive feel for events and to build causal links between external events and the graphs (Means, Penuel, & Padilla, 2001). Time for exploring the probes and finding out what they can tell us about the world is necessary in developing a general sense about what to expect for certain natural phenomena, such as temperature changes over time. Writing about all aspects of an experiment and telling the story of the graph is a good way to help students build correlations between the world and the graph and to reveal what students are seeing and thinking. Used in this way, computer-based laboratories represent another way to help bridge the gap between the concrete physical world and abstract conceptualizations.

This description of methods is intentionally brief; complete chapters are devoted to some of them later in this book. Use the methods described in this section in Activity 2–3: Applying the Best Method.

A FINAL NOTE

Developing your personal instructional theory will be one of the most helpful and rewarding accomplishments of your preparation for science teaching. Over time, education has fractionated, divided, and isolated many of the important components of successful teaching. Unfortunately, many teacher preparation programs emphasize these ad hoc components: "If you are well planned . . . ," "If you use this curriculum . . . ," "If you understand the students' misconceptions . . . ," and "If you know your subject . . . ." Planning, classroom procedures, methods, and subject matter are obviously important, but they are means, not ends. This educational view has shifted the emphasis of programs away from the primary and crucial variable in the classroom—the teacher. Science teachers with an adequate instructional theory have knowledge, plans, methods, and curricular materials. In addition, they have larger goals for their interaction with students and the added dimension of a personalized approach to education.

When the goals, theories, techniques, plans, and materials are combined, you are ready to interact with students. The *way* in which science teachers combine these elements and build a helping relationship with students is crucial. An instructional theory will help provide the needed direction. Science teaching is characterized by situations that require the teacher to react immediately. The creative, insightful, and prepared science teacher will effectively respond to the immediate needs of the students and school.

SUMMARY

An instructional theory will help you make predictions, explain different strategies that will enhance learning, and organize instruction. It increases instructional effectiveness by prescribing motivation, structure, sequence, and feedback.

Research indicates that knowledge of subject matter, pedagogical content knowledge, and curricular knowledge are all important to effective teaching. This knowledge can be applied to specific decisions relative to preinstruction (content, time allocation, pacing, grouping activities), instruction (engaged time, success rate, questioning), and postinstruction (tests, grades, feedback). These ideas contribute to the goal of good teaching. Characteristics of good teachers include the following:

- Clarity of instructional goals
- Knowledge of content and strategies to teach it
- Adequate communication with students
- Expert use of extant materials
- Knowledge of student needs and development
- Development of lower and higher order thinking in students
- Monitoring of student learning with appropriate feedback
- Integration of science instruction with other disciplines
- Thought and reflection about their teaching

—————————— **INVESTIGATING SCIENCE TEACHING** ——————————

ACTIVITY 2–1
WHAT WOULD YOU DO?

When you become a science teacher, you will be required to make decisions continually. An instructional theory helps you to make those decisions. This investigation directs your attention to sample situations that require decisions. It is Monday morning. You have planned a lesson examining life in pond water. Over the weekend, the heating system failed and there is no life in your pond. What would you do? (Select the answer closest to what you think you would do. Then prepare a brief justification of your answer.)

1. Omit the section on "life in a pond."
2. Tell the students to read the section in their text entitled "life in a pond."
3. Have the students find other life to examine.
4. Say nothing, ask the students to find life in the water, and when they discover that there is none, have them determine what could have happened.

Justification

As part of an environmental studies unit, the class is to examine the possibility that a local mining operation is polluting the environment. A group of parents asks you to describe your science program at the next PTA meeting. Their primary concern is that you are going to cause trouble for the community's major economic support. What would you do? (Select the answer closest to what you think you would do. Then prepare a brief justification of your answer.)

1. Decline the invitation.
2. Accept the invitation, take samples of the lesson, data sheets, and questions the students will be answering, and be prepared to explain your goals.
3. Accept the invitation on the condition that the parents come to class and complete the lesson with their sons and daughters.
4. Accept the invitation and plan the lesson in cooperation with the PTA.

Justification

You are in the middle of a class discussion. You have noticed that for 20 minutes one student has paid no attention and has also been creating a disturbance. You reprimand him. The student merely looks at you, then continues to talk and disturb the class. What would you do? (Select the answer closest to what you think you would do. Then prepare a brief justification for your answer.)

1. Demand that the student stop talking.
2. Request that the student conform to the class rules.
3. Tell the other students that you cannot expect much more from such a person (hoping that public ridicule will terminate the disruptive behavior).
4. Tell the student that "we have a problem" and we will have to work it out. Then, ask the student to leave the room temporarily.

Justification

All of the materials are ready for your first lesson in physical science. The lesson is on density. As you explain the procedures, you notice that the students are sending nonverbal messages of "Oh, no—boring!" Then, several students say, "We did this same lesson last year—the answer is $D = m/v$." What would you do? (Select the answer closest to what you think you would do. Then prepare a brief justification of your answer.)

1. Have the students describe what they did in the experiment last year.
2. Skip this lesson and go on to the next, where students apply the concepts of density.
3. Do the activity as planned and try to extend each student's understanding of density through personal discussion.
4. At the end of the investigation, have the students answer questions to see if they understand density.

Activity 2–2
My Aims and Preferences

1. What do you wish to accomplish as a science teacher?

2. Which goals do you see as important outcomes of science instruction? Rank the following in order of importance.

    _____ Develop an understanding of fundamental knowledge of science.

    _____ Develop an understanding of and an ability to use the methods of science.

    _____ Prepare students to make responsible decisions concerning science-related social issues.

    _____ Fulfill the personal needs and development of students.

    _____ Inform students about careers in science.

3. What do you think is important for effective instruction in science? Rank the following in order of importance.

    _____ Knowledge of subject matter.

    _____ Adequacy of personal relations with students.

    _____ Planning and organization of classroom procedures.

    _____ Enthusiasm in working with students.

    _____ Adequacy of teaching methods and strategies.

ACTIVITY 2–3
APPLYING THE BEST METHOD

When planning a lesson, it is important to have in mind a variety of teaching methods to complement the many classroom situations you might encounter. In this activity you meet various situations or aims of instruction, suggest a teaching method to accomplish your goal, and provide a short justification for the method you select. Your teacher may assign different situations to individuals or groups. The line to the left of the number is provided for you to indicate the suggested teaching method. The methods described in this chapter are listed below. Even if your teacher does not assign these, we recommend that you complete at least one situation in each category.

Situation	Method	Justification
Assessment		
Video/CD-ROM/DVD	Problem Solving	
Chalkboards or Marker Board	Games	Projects
Debate or Dispute Resolution	Inquiry and Design	Questioning
Demonstrations	Internet	Reading
Discussion	Laboratory Report	Simulations
Educational Software	Lecture	
Field Trip	Oral Report	

Applications

_____ 1. A student has brought to class a newspaper clipping of a current scientific event.

_____ 2. You wish to use an everyday application as a review.

_____ 3. You wish to make your course particularly functional by relating it to a "do-it-yourself" experience.

Appreciations

_____ 4. You wish to bring about the realization that we have not exhausted the unsolved problems in science. On the contrary, the more we know the more we realize how much is still to be learned.

_____ 5. You wish to develop an appreciation for the work of scientists in the past.

_____ 6. You wish to apply scientific concepts just acquired to the home situation with particular emphasis on how lack of knowledge often leads to inadequate solutions.

_____ 7. You wish to relate scientific knowledge developed in class to intelligent consumer buying.

_____ 8. You decide to try to develop an appreciation for a truly unusual scientific phenomenon.

_____ 9. You decide to try to orient the group to an appreciation for the rapid advances of scientific knowledge through consideration of what new things the text might contain for students taking the course 10 years from now.

Attitudes

_____ 10. You wish to develop the proper attitude toward thorough observation and proper interpretation of what is observed.

_____ 11. You wish to guide the group in developing a sensible attitude toward those scientific problems or situations for which there is not, as yet, a definite answer.

Demonstrations

_____ 12. A demonstration experiment has just failed to produce the desired scientific results.

_____ 13. You wish to teach the proper method to use a scientific device.

_____ 14. You wish to demonstrate how the proper problem-solving approach can be used to answer a "why does it work" type of question.

_____ 15. You wish to make the teaching of a scientific principle more functional by demonstrating several everyday applications.

_____ 16. You wish to demonstrate a new scientific principle in a simple manner that the students themselves can try out at home.

Individual Differences

_____ 17. You wish to make a genuine effort in adjusting to differences by teaching one concept so that the slowest person will understand it and the most capable one will not be bored.

_____ 18. You wish to familiarize students with new vocabulary at the beginning of a unit and convince them of the need for correct knowledge of new words.

_____ 19. You wish to emphasize the opportunities available in science careers in a manner that will appeal to students.

Knowledge

_____ 20. You wish to orient the students to the first unit of the course.

_____ 21. You wish to correct a prevalent misconception.

_____ 22. You wish to place a complex concept in a more concrete setting.

_____ 23. You wish to develop an understanding that our idea of what is "true" changes as we gain more knowledge.

_____ 24. You wish to bring about the realization that, through functional knowledge of a principle, we can group together many everyday applications.

Methods

_____ 25. You wish to emphasize the dangers of making quick decisions without enough supporting evidence.

_____ 26. You wish to use the inductive approach to teach a scientific principle.

Review

_____ 27. You wish to conduct a drill experience but at the same time use a technique that will be enjoyable for the students.

_____ 28. You wish to use an instructional game as a means of developing new learning or review, or to lend variety to the class instruction.

_____ 29. You wish to give a demonstration using "common gadgets" as a means of reviewing material previously taught.*

You may wish to share your responses with other members of the class. These situations form a good basis for discussion.

*The original list of situations was provided courtesy of Lawrence Conrey, "Instructional Techniques," unpublished work. University of Michigan, Ann Arbor.

CHAPTER 3

UNDERSTANDING SCIENCE AND SCIENTIFIC INQUIRY

This chapter serves as an introduction to the discipline of science and the processes of scientific inquiry. The next chapter, "Teaching Science as Inquiry" presents the classroom application of the ideas in this chapter. We recommend that you begin the chapter by completing Activity 3–1: Understanding Science, at the end of the chapter.

WHAT IS SCIENCE?

The simple question, "what is science," has been asked of most science teachers. The answers are as varied as the number of scientists, science teachers, and other persons who have tried to respond. You probably had to consider the question in some form as you completed the introductory activity. We will give a definition that will be expanded and clarified as our discussion progresses through the chapter.

Science is a body of knowledge about the natural world, formed by a process of continuous inquiry, and encompassing the people engaged in the scientific enterprise. The type of knowledge, the processes of inquiry, and the individuals in science all contribute in various ways to form a unique system called *science.* These factors differentiate science from other ways of knowing, such as philosophy, art, and history, which also contribute to the collective knowledge base of humans.

In the scientific subject areas, knowledge is organized within various schemes, such as the theory of evolution, atomic theory, or cell theory. The key to whether a body of knowledge should be included under the heading of science is its basis on empirical observation. If our awareness of a phenomenon is determined by use of such scientific processes as observation, measurement, experimentation, and other experimental procedures, then it is scientific knowledge. This statement is true whether the information is about an atom, flower, or child's response to stimuli.

The product of the process of inquiry is scientific knowledge. Unfortunately, it is the product—knowledge—not the process, that has characterized science teaching. Science is more than knowledge, however. Science is a human enterprise involving creativity, computational skills and strategies, curiosity, courage, and persistence, devised by individuals to discover the nature of the universe. This human investigative aspect of science is dynamic, because it evolves through the actions of persons as they penetrate the unknown. In their investigations, scientists behave differently than those in other human endeavors. For example, they formulate questions, hypothesize, design experiments, interpret data, synthesize theories, and obey rules of objectivity. These behaviors, typical of scientists at work, are called the *processes of inquiry.* They are the conditions that truly characterize science in its research role. To think of science as merely a body of organized knowledge is to conceive of it as being static. This understanding ignores the human excitement of men and women following the guidelines of scientific methodology in exploring the frontiers of knowledge. Science as a human activity is dynamic. It is what scientists do when they behave in the tradition of scientific investigation.

When scientists question, explore, and experiment, they demonstrate the inquiring nature of science.

Unfortunately, a student can learn science as a body of knowledge without understanding it as a *process* and without knowing the human qualities involved in scientific inquiry. The recorded knowledge of science is the *history* produced by men and women using scientific processes. Teachers have traditionally emphasized this product of science but have often failed to give students an understanding of the means of answering scientific questions, which is one of science education's most valuable outcomes.

The next sections describe various aspects of science, including different models of scientific inquiry. As you read the section, bear in mind that the aim of scientific investigation is new knowledge and a contribution to a body of scientific knowledge. *How* scientists gain new knowledge is central to the discussion and, in fact, defines what is valid and reliable knowledge. This aspect is that of scientific inquiry. You will also be able to clarify statements that were discussed in Activity 3–1.

UNDERSTANDING SCIENCE

Historical Perspectives and Scientific Inquiry

The sixteenth and seventeenth centuries marked the birth of empirical science. Prior to this time, explanations of the natural world were influenced by Platonism and Aristotle's deductive method. The search for truth centered on the analysis of universal ideas, with little interest in verification by experience. Either the exposition of logical inconsistencies or an appeal to the authority of Plato's and Aristotle's writings was used to solve arguments.

Francis Bacon and Rene Descartes both developed empirical methods. They maintained that there was little need to appeal to authority, for each person could find truth either through careful observation or through the power of the intellect. Descartes criticized the appeal to the authority of others. Because he could not find one person whose opinions seemed authoritative, he formed his own methods of obtaining knowledge (Descartes, 1970).

Bacon and Descartes encouraged individuals to think for themselves and described methods for discovering truths. For Bacon, the "authority" concerning the solution to problems was sensual perception, and for Descartes it was the intellect.

For Descartes (1970), the foundation of knowledge rested on clear and distinct ideas. The method for arriving at these ideas is paraphrased from his essays:

1. Accept nothing as true which is not clearly recognized to be true. Avoid prejudice in judgments and accept nothing more than is presented to the mind so clearly and distinctly that there is no doubt about the statement's truth.

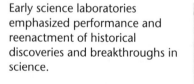

Early science laboratories emphasized performance and reenactment of historical discoveries and breakthroughs in science.

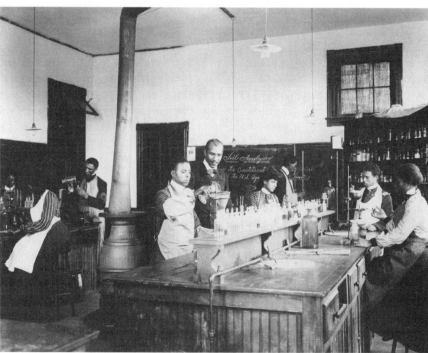

2. Divide the problems into parts for further resolution.
3. Study the objects that are simplest and easiest to understand, later raising by degrees to an order of more complex knowledge those observations which do not follow the natural sequence.
4. Make observations so complete and reviews so general that nothing is omitted.

These statements represent the initial methodology of rationalism, a philosophy that emphasizes the exercise of reason and thought as a valid basis for knowledge. Descartes' rational method centers on the scientist's mind which, through insight and induction, combined with systematic doubt, results in new knowledge. This method has been criticized by empiricists because of Descartes' metaphysical assumptions of preexisting knowledge in the mind of the scientist (Ayer, 1952).

Scientific Inquiry as Induction

Francis Bacon's method for discovering knowledge started the empiricist tradition. Bacon criticized Descartes' method in *Anticipation of the Mind* and *Interpretation of Nature* (Bacon, 1963). In these works, Bacon described two empirical methods and stated that the interpretation of nature without subjective input by the scientist is the correct scientific approach.

Unlike Descartes, Bacon's method did not involve a prior reasoning that resulted in obvious and unquestionable knowledge; rather, Bacon's method was empirical. The scientist starts with observations and forms continuously wider generalizations about the physical world. The generalizations are then checked by experiment.

The goal of Bacon's method was to discover knowledge in the world of nature, not the scientist's mind. If his methods were followed, he claimed that the truth would be discovered.

The Baconian Method of Scientific Inquiry

Observation of things and events was the first step in the Baconian method. Then, he moved inductively from specific observations to generalizations, being careful, however, not to make this jump directly. Bacon proposed experiments to guard against any "anticipation of the mind" in these observations.

At this point in Bacon's method, the scientist would deduce from a generalization, conduct an experiment, and look for confirming or refuting instances of the generalization.

> Now experiments of this kind have one admirable property and condition; they never miss or fail. For since they are applied, not for the purpose of producing any particular effect, but only of discovering the natural cause of some

effect, they answer the end equally well whichever may they turn out; for they settle the question (Bacon, 1960, p. 96).

Pointing out the importance of a negative instance of an experiment is a significant contribution of the Baconian method to scientific investigation. If a negative instance occurs during an experiment, the basic principle must be modified to include the discrepant event. Through the process of experimentation, the lesser principles develop to middle principles, and, finally, to the most general principle.

Bacon espoused the inductive method, in which facts are accumulated and slowly guide the individual to knowledge. Knowledge grows steadily from observations to axioms of increasing importance and generalization, with periodic experiments which result in verification or modification of the principle. If an experiment fails to verify the principle, then the principle is changed to account for the results. The inductive procedure, if it is correctly done, reveals natural truths or major generalizations.

Bacon pursued answers to the question, "How can one guard against and eliminate error in finding new knowledge?" or "Which method will produce verifiable knowledge?" According to Bacon, if the correct method is used and erroneous knowledge is found, the fault is with the scientist because truth exists; it doesn't change and Bacon's is the correct method for finding it. This argument leaves the observer at fault for either incorrectly using the method or allowing prejudice and bias to enter into the observations. In science classrooms this argument is simply translated to, "You made a mistake in the procedures," or "You did not record what actually happened."

Several historical examples exemplify the position of a classical Baconian method: the generalizations of planetary laws described by Johannes Kepler after tedious review of Tycho Brahe's accumulated records; Charles Darwin's accumulation of numerous observations, and the slow development of his theories on evolution.

THE ROLE OF THE SCIENTIST IN THE BACONIAN METHOD

For Bacon, knowledge existed in natural phenomena. Knowledge is real and can be observed in natural events; therefore, the role of the scientist is to find and record it. Truth is revealed with the aid of a pure mind and correct method. Assuming proper method, error results only from prejudice and/or ignorance and bias by the observer. Bacon believed that the scientist must purge the mind of anticipation, conjectures, or interpretations; scientists are not to imagine or suppose but to discover what exists in nature.

THE LOGICAL PROBLEM IN BACON'S METHOD

Human factors, such as misinterpretation of the facts and unreliable observations, are continuing problems

GUEST EDITORIAL ◆ FRANCOIS HAAS

Director, Institute of Rehabilitation
New York University, Medical College
New York, New York

DATA IN SEARCH OF A CONCEPT

At a scientific meeting I presented a study on the respiratory effects of altered upper-body position. My presentation followed the classic research protocol, i.e., the scientific method.

Hypothesis: The forward-tilted upper-body position adopted by runners aids breathing.

Method: Respiratory function was tested in both the erect and running upper-body postures.

Results: Test results improved in the running position.

Discussion: This respiratory improvement could be attributed to improved action of the muscles of the upper chest wall and neck and to changes in the geometry of the airways.

Conclusion: Runners tend, without thinking, to use an upper-body position that optimizes their respiration.

Speculation: Since people with severe chronic pulmonary diseases tend to hold the upper body in a forward-tilted position, is the consequence of this postural alteration adaptive, i.e., does it aid respiration?

Pick any professional research journal off the library shelf and open it at random. The sequence of activities in the investigation under your thumb will also follow the classic research protocol.

Most people—including scientists—would call these examples typical of scientific investigation and scientific thought. Each study followed the logical sequence of activities prescribed by the scientific method. The scientist presented his hypothesis, then the results of testing it in the laboratory, then he studied his results to see if they proved or disproved his initial hypothesis, and finally he speculated a bit on what it all means.

Does the scientific method mean that science is primarily a way of doing things, the use of a particular methodology to study a point that interests or puzzles you? Is a scientist a scientist by virtue of his consistent use of the scientific method, or do certain critical qualities of science appear only between the lines of the finished product?

My research study appears to be the result of a meticulously thought out approach to studying the runner's characteristic posture. It wasn't that at all. It evolved from a combination of logic, chance, and serendipity, sparked by the capacity to integrate nonscientific interests and experience with my professional work. Its beginnings had nothing to do with runners.

Several years before, I had taught a class on pulmonary physiology and function to master's degree students in a physical therapy program. One of my students asked me to supervise his thesis project. He was interested in the effects of the upper-body posture that characterizes patients with advanced emphysema and chronic bronchitis, the two most common pulmonary diseases. Such a patient uses his neck muscles excessively in respiration.

Because the experiment would have to be conducted after working hours, it would be virtually impossible to find patients to participate. To me a master's thesis is basically a learning exercise in conceiving and implementing a research project, so I didn't view this constraint as a problem. I suggested instead that we study healthy subjects in two neck positions, the normal and one mimicking the patients he was interested in.

Although some of the data were contrary to findings reported in the literature, we were handicapped in attempting to explain or reconcile this disparity. Previous investigators had not described their experimental neck positions sufficiently for us to know whether we had duplicated them or not. My student wrote his thesis, explaining his results as best he could. His learning experience was complete and we both forgot the project.

That fall I began running to condition myself for a winter vacation of cross-country skiing. Because I live in a large city, the area where I run is densely populated with fellow runners. I began to notice, with growing interest, that most ran with the torso tilted slightly forward and the neck stretched forward. The neck position was very similar to the one that my student and I had used in simulating a patient with severe pulmonary disease. The first time that I browsed through a collection of running publications I was struck by the photographs of world-class runners. They all ran in this posture.

I dug the student's thesis out of my file and reread it. I realized that we had ignored the torso, focusing solely on neck position. I replicated our original experiment on myself. It immediately became obvious to me that altering only the neck from the normal erect posture brought antagonistic muscles into play, thereby impeding respiration. My former student and I collaborated on a repetition of the entire study, adding the "running" posture to the two neck positions we had previously used. This time our findings agreed with the existing literature.

Our next step was to document the runners' posture, which we did by randomly photographing runners during a marathon. Then we realized that these photographs also held the key to discovering the cause behind the respiratory benefits of this posture. As we studied our collection of photographs, it became clear that the upper-chest-wall musculature shifted into a more advantageous position, improving leverage during inspiration.

The interpretation of our data raised a sequence of fundamental questions:

1. Is the characteristic runner-like posture, adapted by the pulmonary patient, an adaptive one in terms of respiration?
2. If it is, can the exhausted runner fighting for breath serve as a model for the pulmonary patient struggling for air when at rest?
3. If it is a useful model, would it mean that there is a continuum of respiratory function along which the bedridden patient, the "normal" person, and the elite marathon runner all fall, or are there qualitatively different conditions?
4. If there is such a continuum, can the methods for training marathon runners be adapted for rehabilitating the pulmonary patient?

We ended up where we began, studying the posture of the pulmonary patient, but look at the ground we covered in between and the perspective and direction our travels gave us. The dead-ended master's thesis would have gathered dust in my file cabinet if I left science behind me when I locked the laboratory door at the end of my working day. The final results of our work were translated into the classic methodological structure strictly for the purpose of professional communication.

Sometimes productive research projects really do follow these neat classical lines of development. More often they don't. Science is not just a way of doing. It is a way of seeing, a way of thinking. The scientist's curiosity is a way of life. All of the scientist's experiences are potential sources for observations. All of his observations are potential sources for progress and insight in the laboratory.

---

for Baconian methodology. A much more serious problem in his method is that of logic. The logical problem was described by David Hume in 1748. Hume was concerned with the question, "What is the nature of reasoning as related to matters of fact?" He said that "cause and effect" was the answer. Hume continued by asking, "What is the foundation of reasoning and conclusions concerning cause and effect?" Experience was his answer. Finally, and most importantly, Hume asked, "What is the foundation of the conclusions from experience?" At this point, Hume discovered the logical problems of the Baconian methodology (Hume, 1955).

Hume's criticism of the Baconian method was the logical fallacy committed in the progression from observable facts to general principles. For instance, one can observe that the sun rises every morning; therefore, one can make the generalization that the sun will rise every morning in the future. Or, all swans that one observes are white. Therefore, one can make the generalization that all swans are white. The crucial point of the logical fallacy is the induction from the facts, observed in the past, to the untested generalizations concerning the future. The sun may not rise every morning; in fact, it probably will not, albeit millions of years from now. In addition, a person may not have observed *all* swans; there may be some living swans that have not been observed, and there are swans yet unborn that may not be white. Logically, one cannot observe a few and generalize to all. Hume's critique is contained in *An Enquiry Concerning Human Understanding*.

> As to past *Experience,* it can be allowed to give direct and certain information of those precise objects only, and that precise period of time, which fell under its cognizance: but why this experience should be extended to future times, and to other objects, which for aught we know may be only in appearance similar; this is the main question on which I would insist. . . . At least, it must be acknowledged that there is a certain step taken; a process of thought, and an inference, which wants to be explained (1955, p. 125).

Hume's criticism influenced the philosophy of science by attempting to overcome the logical fallacy committed through the induction from specific observations to generalizations.

So, what did Hume suggest that scientists do to overcome these problems? Here is his proposition. First, consult experience, combine the facts of experience into effects, and then, from the effects deduce their causes. The major shift from the Baconian to Hume's method is in the interpretation of what is observed. In the Baconian method, experiences are specific instances of causes; they are grouped into axioms from which experiments are used to check the accuracy of the induction from the particular facts. On confirmation or modification of the experience, the general principles are inductively deduced.

Scientific Inquiry as Deduction

The orientation in the empiricist methods of scientific inquiry is that theories must be submitted to the test of experience to be valid. Hume and other British empiricists such as John Locke and George Berkeley influenced the development of nineteenth-century forms of empiricism, of which logical positivism has had an important influence on our understanding and approach to scientific inquiry.

Logical Positivism

As indicated earlier, the empiricists find fault with any metaphysical arguments concerning knowledge. Scientific methods cannot admit theories that cannot be tested directly by experience. The problems of science, for the logical positivists, should be confined to descriptive generalizations which can, either immediately or in the future, be directly verified by experience. There is disagreement among positivists concerning the degree to which scientific theories must be capable of observation and verification but, in general, a positivist is skeptical about scientific theories or assumptions which apparently cannot be reduced to direct experience and observation.

The Method of Logical Positivism

The first step in the method of logical positivism is the collection of data, that is, observed instances (effects) of something (cause). These data are in and of themselves meaningless until combined with other observations.

Next is the formulation of an operational definition. The observable conditions (general data, i.e., effects) are stated so that the definition can be empirically observed as either true or false, for example, "Do the words (definition) correspond to actual things or behavior?" These new observations constitute fact; they are instances of operationally defined concepts. This step establishes the concept as having meaning.

As the operational definitions are combined they produce generalizations or universal statements. Since the generalizations assert more than has been observed, they may prove to be inaccurate. Here, the role of experimentation enters. Experimental testing of the generalizations verifies their accuracy. The effects have been described, grouped, and generalized; now they are to be checked with the causes by deduction from the generalization to a specific experiment. A positive result verifies or confirms the generalization. A negative result weakens the generalization or logically refutes it. The generalization can be preserved by modifying it or by adopting new concepts.

In *Language, Truth and Logic,* Ayer (1952), a noted empiricist, discussed the principle of verification.

> The principle of verification is supposed to furnish a criterion by which it can be determined whether or not a sentence is literally meaningful. A simple way to formulate it would be to say that a sentence had literal meaning if and only if the proposition it expressed was either analytic or empirically verifiable (p. 5).

Ayer (1952) also asked the rhetorical question, "What is the criterion by which we test the validity of an empirical proposition?"

> The answer is that we test the validity of an empirical hypothesis by seeing whether it actually fulfills the function which it is designed to fulfill. And we have seen that the function of an empirical hypothesis is to enable us to anticipate experience. Accordingly, if an observation to which a given proposition is relevant conforms to our expectations, the truth of that proposition is confirmed. One cannot say that the proposition has been proved absolutely valid, because it is still possible that a future observation will discredit it. But one can say that its probability has been increased. If the observation is contrary to our expectations, then the status of the proposition is jeopardized. We may preserve it by adopting or abandoning other hypotheses; or we may consider it to have been confuted (p. 99).

Ayer's statements briefly describe the problem of verification or confirmation of a proposition or hypothesis. The strength of support for a hypothesis depends on various characteristics of the observed evidence. Variables such as quantity of supporting evidence, absence of unfavorable evidence, the variety and diversity of evidence, and the precision of the experiments contribute to the strength and validity of the initial propositions (Hempel, 1966). Note that the logic of the confirmation process is still not fully understood by philosophers (Salmon, 1973).

The positivist method of scientific inquiry is not a set of rules as described by Bacon, rather a set of rules and procedures for *stating* scientific ideas. In science teaching, this procedure has taken the form of the "scientific method," which includes:

1. Stating the problem
2. Formulating a hypothesis

3. Designing an experiment
4. Making observations
5. Recording data from the experiment
6. Confirming the hypothesis
7. Forming conclusions

These steps are the ways in which scientific information is to be reported. They are based on the logical positivist's approach to science.

The role of the scientist in the positivist system is to record the facts without bias or psychological projections, then transform them into carefully written operational definitions. These definitions are then combined to form larger generalizations and, finally, theories. The deduction arises from the generalization and a confirmation by experiment. The positivist method attempts to be valueless and neutral; its strengths are in the logical construction and the clear language used to describe the natural world.

The objectivity of science is defended by the empiricist for three reasons. First, science starts from publicly observable data that are described in language free of theoretical assumptions. Second, the generalizations or theories of science can be confirmed or refuted by comparison with experimental data. Third, the choice between theories can thus be rational, objective, and based on specifiable data. In the late 1950s and early 1960s, the ideas of empiricism were strongly criticized by other philosophers. In general, these criticisms were first, all data are value laden and have theoretical assumptions; second, theories are not confirmed or falsified through single experiments; and third, there are no value-free criteria for choice between theories (Barbour, 1974).

THE COLLECTION OF DATA

One of the first tenets of positivism to be criticized was the contention that data could be collected and described in a neutral observational language, independent of theory. This contention omitted the role of the scientist's creative imagination in the development of theories. One of the philosophers who criticized the positivist conception of theory construction was Michael Polanyi. He clearly states his position, and that of strict empiricists, concerning the collection of data in *The Study of Man* (1959).

> Natural science has been taught to regard itself as a mere description of experience, a description which can be said to explain the facts of nature only in so far as it represents individual events as instances of general features. And since such representation of the facts is supposed to be guided merely by an urge to simplify our account of them, rival explanations are professed to be merely competing descriptions between which we choose the most convenient (p. 20).

Actually, two criticisms are contained in this statement by Polanyi, the collection of data and the concept of valueless choice between rival theories. Polanyi criticized strict empiricism for eliminating the human experience as a part of the scientific enterprise and argued that elimination of the scientist's mind weakens the structure of science.

Concerning the role of the scientist in the collection of data, Polanyi centered on the mind of the scientist and argued that his creative imagination should be accepted as an important element in the growth of knowledge. He advocated a change in the ideal of knowledge. The participation of the scientist, the knower, in shaping knowledge has not recognized the true power of our cognitive abilities (Polanyi, 1964). Polanyi also advanced the idea of two kinds of knowledge, both important to science. They are explicit and tacit knowledge (Polanyi, 1967). The tacit dimension of human knowledge is an internal, preconscious conception based on the idea that we can know more than we can communicate.

Values and Science

In *Science and Human Values,* Jacob Bronowski (1965) discussed the values inherent in inquiry and the scientific enterprise. Bronowski's discussion is a step beyond a scientist's simple, individual testing of what is true or false. The growth of knowledge relies on other people; the endeavor of scientists is not exclusively an individual effort. The growth of knowledge is a community enterprise. Bronowski agrees with Polanyi concerning the tacit dimension of human understanding; however, Bronowski (1966; 1973) carries the idea a step further by asserting that our descriptions of nature are veiled by uncertainty. He differentiates between the facts of science and the activity of science. Because there are values inherent in the sciences, Bronowski (1959) argues that the activity of science is not neutral. Based on the value of truth as the goal of science, he derives other important values such as independence, freedom, and the right to dissent.

> This is why the values of science turn out to be recognizably the human values; because scientists must be men, must be fallible, and yet as men must be willing and as a society must be organized to correct their errors (Bronowski, 1975).

It is this type of reasoning that led us to include "the people" as a third part of our definition of science.

Commitment to Paradigms

Thomas Kuhn's 1970 book, *The Structure of Scientific Revolutions,* has been influential in the controversy among philosophers of science concerning the relation of observations, experiments, and theories. Kuhn's ideas were particularly influential as a counterargument to the positivist's position that theories are confirmed or falsified through single experiments and that the selection of theories is rational and objective.

The first theme of Kuhn's book is that paradigms dominate the scientific enterprise. He describes two important uses for the term *paradigm*. First, a paradigm is a "universally recognized scientific achievement that for a time provides model problems and solutions to a community of practitioners" (1970, p. viii). In this context, paradigms provide broad conceptual and methodological orientations that are founded in the "shared examples" through which individuals learn about dominating theories within scientific disciplines. The types of research questions, the metaphysical assumptions, and the types of acceptable results for working (normal) scientists are implicitly defined by the dominating scientific paradigm.

The second use of the term has a distinctly sociopsychological orientation. In a postscript written in 1969, Kuhn discussed the sociopsychological dimensions of a paradigm as a "shared commitment." He says that a paradigm "stands for the entire constellation of beliefs, values, techniques, and so on, shared by members of a given community" (1970, p. 175).

"Normal" science continues when a paradigm is not in revolution. The three types of inquiry that occur during periods of normal science are investigations into important revealing aspects of the paradigm, articulation of its various components, and verification of its theoretical predictions. Research in normal science is guided by the paradigms, that is, the scientific attempt to shape nature into forms predicted by the paradigm.

The second theme of Kuhn's (1970) book is that scientific revolutions are major shifts from one paradigm to a new one. During the period of normal science, experiments often do not verify or confirm the paradigm; thus, the results are anomalous. At first the anomalies are set aside or accommodated through ad hoc modifications of basic assumptions. As these anomalies increase, the structure of the old paradigm is rejected and replaced by the new one. This shift amounts to a scientific revolution. Kuhn also points out that the choice between two different paradigms is not determined by the normally conceived rational, objective criteria. There is much personal resistance by scientists to the new paradigms and Kuhn writes about the older generation of scientists being "converted" to the new paradigm. According to Kuhn, the paradigm shift or revolution is much more subjective than is usually presented by philosophers and scientists. This statement refers to the criticism made against the logical positivists that choice between two theories is not value free.

Kuhn mentions two other themes briefly. First, observations and experiments by scientists are paradigm dependent; and second, there is no neutral observation language. All the data observed and recorded are theory laden; that is, they are dependent on the paradigm within which the scientist is working.

Inquiry as Conjecture and Refutation

For positivists, the principle of verification seemed simple and straightforward. The only meaningful statements are operational definitions and empirical propositions verifiable by sense experience. However, one cannot verify a theory by showing that conclusions deduced from it agree with an experiment, because future experiments may conflict with the theory and other theories also may explain the present evidence. In short, verification is induction in reverse; thus, a logical fallacy is committed when universal generalizations are stated. This problem was pointed out by Karl Popper, who described a method of conjecture and refutation in science.

The inductive and deductive approaches attempt to establish valid and verifiable knowledge through correct use of a scientific method. Their basic assumption is that knowledge exists in nature; they then assume that if it is discovered through right procedures and methods, it is valid and reliable. Thus, the body of knowledge is increased. The questions asked were, "What is the best method for obtaining knowledge?" and "How do we justify our knowledge claims?" Attempts to answer these questions are found in the various methods described in this chapter. Popper changes the question; he is primarily interested in the growth of knowledge. His question then is, "How can we hope to detect and eliminate error as we accumulate knowledge (Popper, 1965, p. 25)?

Truth is still the goal of Popper's approach to scientific inquiry; however, it is a much more abstract conception than that of the other methods. For Popper, truth is beyond the scientist's reach. Science must try to approach this ideal and must also realize that accumulated knowledge is short of this highest goal.

Karl Popper's Method

Popper starts with the problem concerning the growth of knowledge. Whereas others were concerned with sources of knowledge, Popper asserts:

> Never mind the source, or the sources, from which it may spring. There are many possible sources, and I may not be aware of half of them; the origins or pedigrees have in any case little bearing on the truth (1965, p. 27).

All sources of knowledge are welcome. The problem of a scientist then is to try to determine the degree of fallibility of the knowledge. Neither observation nor intuition is reliable. Since knowledge advances mainly through modification of earlier knowledge, attempts must be made to refute the assertions. Through criticism and attempts to find error, science will continue to grow with a minimum of erroneous knowledge.

Repeated observations and experiments are tests; they are attempts to refute the original conjectures. If the results are positive, they have affirmed the hypothesis, but in Popper's method the assertion is they have failed to refute the hypothesis, so the conjecture is tentatively accepted. This assertion avoids the logical problems indicated earlier. A negative instance refutes the conjectures and provides new sources for them.

Theories are universal but not absolute explanations; they are conjectures and tentative, and subject to logical and empirical criticism (Popper, 1968). Some critics of Popper's philosophy have asked, "Is a theory not a universal statement and therefore in violation of the rules of logic?" Popper's method is not to produce theories; it is to eliminate false theories.

> Without waiting, passively, for repetitions to impress or impose regularities upon us, we actively try to impose regularities upon the world. We try to discover similarities in it, and to interpret it in terms of laws invented by us. Without waiting for premises we jump to conclusions. These may have to be discarded later, should observation show that they are wrong . . . . This was a theory of trial and error—of conjecture and refutation (1965, p. 46).

SUMMARY

Understanding science is essential in today's society. The public's understanding of science is largely influenced by its experiences in science classrooms. It is therefore important that science teachers understand science and give an accurate representation of it in their classrooms.

Science was defined as a body of knowledge, a process of inquiry, and the people involved in the scientific enterprise. Science teachers usually concentrate on the body of knowledge that forms their discipline. Students should also understand the process of scientific inquiry; the understanding should come through their experiences with the process in the science classroom. Few definitions of science include the people who are involved in the enterprise. Yet the history of science has proven, time and again, to be a history of scientists. Recognizing the individual qualities important to scientists and guarding against human shortcomings that may also influence scientific work are necessary in presenting a total picture of science.

Different models of scientific inquiry were reviewed. The accumulation of valid reliable knowledge was shown to be the aim of all the models. The models of inquiry included those of Rene Descartes and Francis Bacon, whose model used the inductive process for statements of scientific generalizations and theories. A deductive model associated with logical positivism was then reviewed. This model was reviewed for these reasons: (1) Data are value laden and have theoretical assumptions; (2) theories are not confirmed or falsified by single experiments; and (3) there are no value-free choices between competing theories. The positivists' tradition assumed the opposite for all three criticisms. The third model was one of conjecture and refutation. Instead of using experiments to verify and confirm empirical propositions, as did the positivists, this model focuses on trying to eliminate false theories.

Science teachers should understand the strengths and weaknesses, the procedures, and the logical problems of the different models of inquiry. In the science classroom there should be a balance in emphasis on science as a body of knowledge, a process, and a human enterprise.

———————— **Investigating Science Teaching** ————————

Activity 3–1
Understanding Science

Directions

1. In the blank provided in front of the statements about the scientific enterprise, indicate whether you agree (A), partially agree (PA), disagree (D), don't know (DK), or have no opinion (NO) concerning the statement.
2. Review and discuss your individual responses in a small group of three or four people. At this step, add new statements, combine, modify, or omit statements. Your group should reach agreement on the statements.
3. Compile the statements from the small groups into a class set.
4. As you read the chapter and have further class discussions, expand, modify, and/or correct the original class set of statements about the scientific enterprise.

_____   1. The goal of science is knowledge. The knowledge may originate from experiments, spiritual revelation, mystical experiences, or creative insights.

_____   2. Unexpected observations can play an important role in increasing scientific knowledge.

_____   3. Observing, classifying, predicting, and hypothesizing are examples of important skills used by scientists.

_____   4. Sometimes scientists do not find solutions to their problems.

_____   5. Observations of nature are sources of scientific information.

_____   6. Scientists believe that some unexplained events do not have causes.

_____   7. There are often several different methods of solving a single scientific problem.

_____   8. If a conflict exists between matters of empirical evidence and matters of tradition, authority and power are usually accepted.

_____   9. Some of today's scientific theories will be inadequate in the future.

_____ 10. The simplest theory that accounts for the most phenomena is the best.

_____ 11. Scientists try to improve their explanations of natural phenomena.

_____ 12. The fundamental values of science do not apply to technology since it is an application of science to human situations and must, of necessity, have either different values or no values.

_____ 13. Even though incomplete, theories are useful.

_____ 14. A basic tenet of scientific inquiry is that the universe is knowable.

_____ 15. An important result of scientific work is scientific theory.

_____ 16. Of all the goals of science, truth is the greatest.

_____ 17. Predicting and controlling future events are important uses of scientific theory.

_____ 18. Scientists should report exactly what they observe.

_____ 19. Scientists should neither question nor criticize the work of another scientist.

_____ 20. Science is a part of the society in which it exists. The goals and values of a society directly influence the existence and development of science.

_____ 21. New knowledge is more a result of skepticism, criticism, and questioning of present knowledge than it is of verifying, confirming, and strengthening present knowledge.

_____ 22. If a scientist reports his/her results precisely and truthfully, other scientists should accept the finding without skepticism.

_____ 23. Science is concerned with the formulation of general principles, theories, and laws. Processes such as hypothesizing, experimenting, and classifying are means to these ends.

_____ 24. The scientific method, that is, stating a problem, formulating a hypothesis, designing an experiment, and drawing conclusions, is central to the whole scientific enterprise. It is the exact process that scientists use in their daily work because it ensures objectivity.

_____ 25. Once a good scientific paradigm has been developed, scientists usually stick together and discourage others from finding anomalies in the paradigm.

_____ 26. The universe is ordered and it is the job of science to discover the order and specify the relationships between events.

_____ 27. Science has neither the methods nor the capability of explaining *all* of the physical world and human experience. Therefore, it should not try to do so.

_____ 28. The processes and products of science and technology must be evaluated apart from the needs and goals of society.

_____ 29. Nothing lies beyond the limits of scientific study. Therefore, scientists (and science teachers) should refrain from negative responses to the prospect of studying phenomena, no matter how weird or unusual the study.

_____ 30. Scientists should change their explanations based on new information.

_____ 31. Science is neither moral nor immoral but scientists are, so they should not speak out on controversial issues.

_____ 32. Scientists often give diverse explanations about the same observations.

_____ 33. Science starts with publicly observable data that should be described atheoretically.

_____ 34. Scientific theories are confirmed by comparison with experimental data.

_____ 35. When scientists choose between two theories, both of which explain the same natural phenomena, the choice between theories is rational, objective, and based on specifiable data.

CHAPTER 4

TEACHING SCIENCE AS INQUIRY

The idea of teaching science as inquiry has a long history in science education. There is an equally long history of confusion about what teaching science as inquiry means and, regardless of the definition, its implementation in the classroom. Publication of the *National Science Education Standards* (NRC, 1996) once again brought science as inquiry to the top of educational goals. The *Standards* answer definitional questions. Teaching science as inquiry, the *Standards* explain, requires imparting not only scientific information but also the abilities of inquiry and, more deeply, an understanding of what scientific inquiry is about. Complete Activity 4–1: What is Teaching Science as Inquiry?, at the end of this chapter. We return to a discussion of this activity later in the chapter.

HISTORICAL PERSPECTIVES AND TEACHING SCIENCE AS INQUIRY

In the United States, science itself was not valued prior to the mid-nineteenth century. "[F]aith," Charles Stedman (1987) writes, "was at least as important as empirical data and in many instances it dominated the practices of science. This faith was often a complex mixture of Christian theology, idealism, and entrenched traditions."

In the late nineteenth century, several people brought science into discussions of school and college curricula. Charles W. Eliot, president of Harvard University from 1869 to 1895, articulated the need for science and laboratory approaches in the curriculum. Louis Agassiz, also at Harvard, provided an early example of teaching science as inquiry when he had students

come to his lab and study specimens. He directed field trips to the countryside and seashore, encouraged students to make their own collections, and conducted instruction by correspondence with specimen collectors around the country (Stedman, 1987).

John Dewey and Scientific Habits of Mind

In 1909, when the presence of science in the school curriculum was bringing disagreements about what science is and thus how it should be taught, John Dewey addressed the education section of the American Association for the Advancement of Science on the topic, "Science as Subject-Matter and as Method" (Dewey, 1910). Dewey's general theme was that science teaching gave too much emphasis to the accumulation of information and not enough to science as a method of thinking and an attitude of mind: "Science teaching has suffered because science has been so frequently presented just as so much ready-made knowledge, so much subject-matter of fact and law, rather than as the effective method of inquiry into any subject-matter" (1910, p. 124).

Notice that in these passages, Dewey refers to aims that include the abilities of inquiry, the nature of science, and an understanding of a subject.

> Surely if there is any knowledge which is of most worth it is knowledge of the ways by which anything is entitled to be called knowledge instead of being mere opinion or guess work or dogma.
>
> Such knowledge never can be learned by itself; it is not information, but a mode of intelligent practice, an habitual disposition of mind. Only by taking a hand in

GUEST EDITORIAL ◆ MARIE DEL TORO
Earth Science Teacher
Fountain Valley School, Colorado Springs, Colorado

THERE'S MORE TO SCIENCE TEACHING THAN FACTS, CONCEPTS, AND MEMORIZING

Whether one has been teaching science for 10 years or 10 months, in a public or private school, or to a classroom of 50 or 5, there is the common belief that teaching is a demanding but very rewarding profession. As a new teacher, I have had my share of good and bad experiences, all of which proved very worthwhile. The purpose of this editorial is to relate some of my experiences and how they have helped me grow as a science teacher. Fountain Valley is a small college preparatory school located in Colorado Springs, Colorado. Its 220 students come from 28 states and eight foreign countries. As a result, there is a great diversity in student interests, values, and levels of academic performance. Although Fountain Valley encourages individualism, it also strives to further a community spirit. That spirit is exemplified in the following ways: Students are assigned advisers to oversee their progress both academically and socially; students and faculty eat family-style dinners twice a week; and finally, faculty live on campus, providing personal interaction between students and faculty. Although the school is small, it offers many science courses. Obviously, every student in science will not choose science as a career. The school is sensitive to that fact. As a result, Fountain Valley has developed a broad curriculum ranging from traditional one-year courses in biology and chemistry to one- and two-term electives in oceanography, geology, and anthropology. The assumption is that through a diversity of offerings, something will appeal to every student.

Teaching in a boarding school requires a great deal of time and effort. It is not enough to teach a student the basics in math or science for, as teachers in a boarding school, we are obligated to a much larger commitment. In effect, we are serving as the student's parents, and so our teaching should encourage growth in all phases of a student's cognitive, affective, and psychomotor learning. If a student is to develop into a caring, sensitive, and intellectual person, the classroom atmosphere should be conducive to attaining those goals. Like any other subject, science could be five lectures a week. However, it seems that the essence of science, learning through discovery, is lost if this method is used. As a result, the best approach to science I have found is an integration of methods such as experimentation, problem solving, reading and questions, student speeches, and field trips.

Two of my most interesting and rewarding experiences have been associated with field trips. One occurred very early in the fall during interim week. The purpose of this week is to provide students opportunities to expand their intellectual, cultural, social, and vocational horizons. I was fortunate enough to accompany another teacher and 13 students to the Oregon coast to study marine biology, rainforest ecology, and coastal geology. Before the trip I knew few of the students, but after spending a week living, eating, and talking with them, I developed a very special relationship with some students which could not have been kindled in any other environment. They have seen me in a situation outside the classroom and they know how I can act. This additional contact with students helps them realize that a teacher is a person too and not just someone whose job it is to give As and Fs. The other very rewarding experience occurred during a field trip with my geology class. After spending the afternoon driving around Colorado Springs looking at various geologic oddities, two of my students told me that they had become highly motivated about geology due to my influence. They also expressed an interest in pursuing geology in college, which is ironic considering their lack of confidence at the start of the course. A few days later, one of these students asked me if I would help with her senior independent project which, surprisingly, dealt with geology.

Reflecting on the fall term, I must say that those students advanced in their understanding of geology and, more importantly, in their outlook toward science and in their newly acquired confidence. Experiences such as these certainly make teaching worthwhile. However, it is not always that way. That is where the true challenge begins. The good student will learn regardless of the teacher and the poor student may or may not learn even with the most exciting, motivating teacher.

As a first-year teacher, my duties include teaching four courses, coaching two sports, supervising the girls' dorm one night a week and every sixth weekend, co-sponsoring the rock-climbing club, and chaperoning various trips to the school's mountain campus located in the Colorado mountains. With this spectrum of duties, I see many students other than those in my classes, and this contact is good. The hard part is in assuming so many roles: teacher, coach, disciplinarian, friend, and surrogate mother, father, brother, or sister. It must be exceedingly frustrating for a student not to know how I will react or, more importantly, how I will act in any given situation. A student rarely sees me perform all of these roles. Coaching allows me to see students in an environment outside the classroom. It is great to watch students enjoy a sport whether or not they are highly motivated in an academic situation. Sometimes students feel teachers judge them by their level of academic achievement, and so underachievers may tend to shy away from certain teachers. This attitude is rather unfortunate, for there are certain traits, just as important in life as math or science formulas, which can be instilled only in competitive sports. A student who works hard at a sport is learning a great deal about patience, sportsmanship, teamwork, and modesty, all of which are valuable and are not limited to athletics but hopefully will carry over to the classroom.

Teaching is both demanding and rewarding. It is a profession which will take as much as you are willing to give. There are always days when nothing seems to be going right, but then there are days when your students excel. If I had to start again, I would make a concerted effort to listen more intently to various students' needs and excuses; keep my expectations high, for students need to strive for more than they think they can attain; and, finally, I would make it a point to be consistent in my treatment of various classroom activities.

---

the making of knowledge, by transferring guess and opinion into belief authorized by inquiry, does one ever get a knowledge of the method of knowing (Dewey, 1910, p. 125).

Dewey emphasizes that science is a way of thinking, but goes on to note that few people seem willing to consider this approach to thinking, which gives a purpose to the teaching of science.

> But that the great majority of those who leave school have some idea of the kind of evidence required to substantiate given types of belief does not seem unreasonable. Nor is it absurd to expect that they should go forth with a lively interest in the ways in which knowledge is improved by a marked distaste for all conclusions reached in disharmony with the methods of scientific inquiry (Dewey, 1910, p. 127).

Near the conclusion, Dewey makes this powerful statement.

> One of the only two articles that remain in my creed of life is that the future of our civilization depends upon the widening spread and deepening hold of the scientific habit of mind; and that the problem of problems in our education is therefore to discover how to mature and make effective this scientific habit (p. 127).

Some 90 years ago, then, John Dewey articulated as objectives of teaching science as inquiry: developing thinking and reasoning, formulating habits of mind, learning science subjects, and understanding the processes of science. Dewey's *Logic: The Theory of Inquiry*, published in 1938, presents his stages in the scientific method: induction, deduction, mathematical logic, and empiricism. This book no doubt influenced the many science textbooks that treat the scientific method as a fixed sequence as opposed to a variety of strategies whose use depends on the question being investigated and the researchers. Discussions about the role of scientific method in science classrooms and textbooks continue in the community of science educators (Klapper, 1995; Storey & Carter, 1992).

Joseph J. Schwab

In the late 1950s and the 1960s, Joseph Schwab published articles on inquiry (or enquiry, his preferred spelling). Schwab laid the foundation for the emergence of inquiry as a prominent theme in the curriculum reform of that era (Schwab, 1958; 1960; 1966). In 1958, Schwab clarified his argument for teaching science as inquiry: "The formal reason for a change in present methods of teaching the sciences lies in the fact that science itself has changed. A new view concerning the nature of scientific inquiry now controls research." According to Schwab, scientists no longer conceived science as stable truths to be verified; they were viewing it as principles for inquiry, conceptual structures revisable in response to new evidence. Schwab distinguished between "stable" and "fluid" inquiry. These terms suggest the distinction between normal and revolutionary science as made popular by Thomas Kuhn in his classic of 1970, *The Structure of Scientific Revolutions*. Stable inquiry uses current principles to "fill a . . . blank space in a growing body of knowledge" (1966), while fluid inquiry is the invention of conceptual structures that will revolutionize science.

Schwab observed that teachers and textbooks were presenting science in a way that was inconsistent with modern science. Schwab, in 1966, found that science was being taught " . . . as a nearly unmitigated *rhetoric of conclusions* in which the current and temporary constructions of scientific knowledge are conveyed as empirical, literal, and irrevocable truths." A "rhetoric of conclusions, then, is a structure of discourse which persuades men to accept the tentative as certain, the doubtful as the undoubted, by making no mention of reasons or evidence for what it asserts, as if to say, 'this, everyone of importance knows to be true.'" The implications of Schwab's ideas were, for their time, profound. He suggested both that science should be presented as inquiry and that students should undertake inquiries.

To achieve these changes, Schwab argued in 1960, science teachers should first look to the laboratory and use these experiences to lead rather than lag behind the classroom phase of science teaching. He urged science teachers to consider three levels of openness in their laboratories. At the primary level, the materials can pose questions and describe methods of investigation that allow students to discover relationships they do not already know. Next, the laboratory manual or textbook can pose questions, but the methods and answers are left open. On the most sophisticated level, students confront phenomena without questions based in textbooks or laboratories. They are left to ask questions, gather evidence, and propose explanations based on their evidence.

Schwab also proposed an "enquiry into enquiry." Here teachers provide students with readings, reports, or books about research. They engage in discussions about the problems, data, role of technology, interpretation of data, and conclusions reached by scientists. Where possible, students should read about alternative explanations, experiments, debates about assumptions, use of evidence, and other issues of scientific inquiry.

Schwab had a tremendous influence on the original design of instructional materials—the laboratories and invitations to inquiry—for the Biological Sciences Curriculum Study (BSCS). Schwab's recommendation paid off in the late 1970s and early 1980s when educational researchers asked questions about the effectiveness of these programs. In 1984, Shymansky reported evidence supporting his conclusion that "BSCS biology is the most successful of the new high school science curricula."

F. James Rutherford and a Grounding in History and Philosophy

In 1964, F. James Rutherford observed that although in the teaching of science we are unalterably opposed to rote memorization and all for the teaching of scientific processes, critical thinking, and the inquiry method, in practice science teaching does not represent science as inquiry. Nor is it clear what teaching science as inquiry means. At times the concept is used in a way that makes inquiry part of the science content itself. At others,

authors refer to a particular technique or strategy for bringing about learning of some particular science content.

Rutherford (1964) presented the following conclusions:

◆ It is possible to gain a worthwhile understanding of science as inquiry once we recognize the necessity of considering inquiry as content and operate on the premise that the concepts of science are properly understood *only* in the context of how they were arrived at and of what further inquiry they initiated.

◆ As a corollary, it is possible to learn something of science as inquiry without having the learning process itself to follow precisely any one of the methods of inquiry used in science.

◆ The laboratory can be used to provide the student experience with some aspects or components of the investigative techniques employed in a given science, but only after the content of the experiments has been carefully analyzed for its usefulness in this regard (pp. 80–84).

In the end, Rutherford connected to teaching science as inquiry a knowledge base for doing so. Until science teachers acquire "a rather thorough grounding in the history and philosophy of the sciences they teach, this kind of understanding will elude them, in which event not much progress toward the teaching of science as inquiry can be expected" (1964, p. 84).

Project Synthesis: Inquiry Is Espoused and Not Practiced

In the late 1970s and early 1980s, the National Science Foundation supported a project that synthesized a number of national surveys, assessments, and case studies about the status of science education in the United States (Harms & Kohl, 1980; Harms & Yager, 1981). One major portion of this review centered on the role of inquiry in science teaching and was completed by Wayne Welch, Leo Klopfer, Glen Aikenhead, and James Robinson in 1981. Their analysis revealed that the science education community was using the term *inquiry* in a variety of ways, including the general categories of inquiry as content and inquiry as instructional technique, and was unclear about the term's meaning. The evidence indicated that "although teachers made positive statements about the value of inquiry, they often felt more responsible for teaching facts, 'things which show up on tests,' 'basics' and structure and the work ethic." Among the teachers surveyed, the main consideration was of inquiry as an instructional technique. For not teaching science as inquiry, not employing it for introducing the content, or not using experiences oriented to inquiry, teachers gave a number of reasons. Among them were problems managing the classroom, difficulty meeting state requirements, trouble obtaining supplies and equipment, dangers that some experiments might pose for students, and concerns about whether inquiry really worked. In conclusion, the authors reported:

> The widespread espoused support of inquiry is more simulated than real in practice. The greatest set of barriers to the teacher support of inquiry seems to be its perceived difficulty. There is legitimate confusion over the meaning of inquiry in the classroom. There is concern over discipline. There is worry about adequately preparing children for the next level of education. There are problems associated with the teachers' allegiance to teaching facts and to following the role models of the college professors (Welch et al., 1981, p. 40.)

The portion of Project Synthesis relating to biology concludes: "In short, little evidence exists that inquiry is being used" (Hurd, Bybee, Kahle, & Yager, 1980). Costenson and Lawson (1986) presented the results of their survey of biology teachers. Inquiry, some teachers claimed, takes too much time and energy. It is too slow. The reading is difficult, and the students are insufficiently mature. Experiments may put students at risk. Inquiry makes it hard to track the progress of students, and to place material in proper sequence. It violates the habits that teachers have developed, and it is expensive. The objections are similar to what Welch and his colleagues had reported. Similar results would probably be obtained for other disciplines, particularly at the secondary level. They form the substantial barriers between policies, such as that set by the *Standards* in 1996, that recommend science as inquiry and the programs exemplified in BSCS materials that incorporate into teaching science as inquiry the actual practices in science classrooms. "In our opinion," the report on biology declares:

> the previous reasons for not using inquiry are not sufficient to prevent its use. However, to implement inquiry in the classroom we see three crucial ingredients: (1) teachers must understand precisely what scientific inquiry is; (2) they must have sufficient understanding of the structure of biology itself; and (3) they must become skilled in inquiry teaching techniques (Hurd et al., 1980, p. 158).

The passage makes the important distinction between inquiry as *content* to be understood first by teachers and then by students, and inquiry as *technique* which teachers are to use to help students learn biology.

Project 2061: A Frame for Teaching Science as Inquiry

In 1985, Rutherford inaugurated Project 2061, a long-term initiative of the American Association for the Advancement of Science (AAAS) to reform K–12

education. In the initial years, the project outlined what all students should know and be able to do by the time they complete the twelfth grade. Project 2061 materials such as *Science for All Americans,* issued in 1989, and *Benchmarks for Science Literacy,* which AAAS published in 1993, have made significant statements about teaching science as inquiry. Rutherford's observations and recommendations presaged in 1964 the place Project 2061 assigns to the nature and history of science and that which it sets for habits of mind.

The lead chapter of *Science for All Americans* outlines recommendations for the nature of science and another provides recommendations for so-called historical perspectives. A chapter on habits of mind includes categories of values and attitudes, manipulation and observation, communication, and importantly, skills of critical response.

In a separate chapter on effective learning and teaching in *Science for All Americans,* the author makes the general recommendation, "Teaching should be consistent with the nature of scientific inquiry," and follows with specific advice.

- ◆ Start with questions about nature.
- ◆ Engage students actively.
- ◆ Concentrate on the collection and use of evidence.
- ◆ Provide historical perspectives.
- ◆ Insist on clear expression.
- ◆ Use a team approach.
- ◆ Do not separate knowing from finding out.
- ◆ Deemphasize the memorization of technical vocabulary. (AAAS, 1989, pp. 147–149)

Developing the abilities of sientific inquiry is an important goal of science teaching.

Benchmarks for Science Literacy (AAAS, 1993) shows specific results of learning about the nature of science, gaining historical perspectives, and acquiring good habits of mind. In addition, an excellent research base indicates what students know and are able to do relative to various benchmarks.

Project 2061 also set in place goals and specific benchmarks for teaching scientific inquiry as content. Included as well are recommendations for using teaching techniques associated with inquiry.

NATIONAL SCIENCE EDUCATION STANDARDS: INQUIRY AS CONTENT

The *National Science Education Standards* (NRC, 1996) present a contemporary statement on teaching science as inquiry. Defining what all students should know and be able to do by grade 12, and what kinds of learning experiences they need in order to achieve scientific literacy, the document reaffirms the conviction that inquiry is central to the achievement of scientific literacy.

Release of the *Standards* again brought to the forefront in the educational community the issue of teaching science as inquiry. In the *Standards,* scientific inquiry refers to several related but different things: the ways scientists study the natural world, activities of students, strategies of teaching, and outcomes that students should learn. The *Standards* provides this summary of inquiry.

> [I]nquiry is a multifaceted activity that involves making observations; posing questions; examining books and other sources of information to see what is already known; planning investigations; reviewing what is already known in light of experimental evidence; using tools to gather, analyze, and interpret data; proposing the results. Inquiry requires identification of assumptions, use of critical and logical thinking, and considerations of alternative explanations (NRC, 1996, p. 23).

The *Standards* uses the term *inquiry* in two ways. Inquiry is content, which means both what students should *understand* about scientific inquiry and the *abilities* they should develop from their experiences with scientific inquiry. The term also refers to teaching strategies and the processes of learning associated with activities oriented to inquiry.

Table 4–1 shows the standards on content in science as inquiry for grades 9 through 12.

Science as Inquiry: The Abilities

Table 4–2 presents the abilities students should attain. Note the emphasis on cognitive abilities and critical

TABLE 4–1   Content Standard for Science As Inquiry

As result of activities in grades 9-12, all students should develop

- Abilities necessary to do scientific inquiry.
- Understandings about scientific inquiry.

TABLE 4–2   Science As Inquiry: Fundamental Abilities for Grades 9-12

- Identify questions and concepts that guide scientific investigations.
- Design and conduct scientific investigations.
- Use technology and mathematics.
- Formulate and revise scientific explanations and models using logic and evidence.
- Recognize and analyze alternative explanations and models.
- Communicate and defend a scientific argument.

thinking. Without eliminating activities such as observing, inferring, and hypothesizing, this emphasis differentiates the *Standards* from traditional material that concentrates on processes.

IDENTIFY QUESTIONS AND CONCEPTS THAT GUIDE SCIENTIFIC INVESTIGATIONS

Students should formulate a testable hypothesis and demonstrate the logical connections between the scientific concepts guiding a hypothesis and the design of an experiment. They should demonstrate appropriate procedures, a knowledge base, and conceptual understanding of scientific investigations.

DESIGN AND CONDUCT SCIENTIFIC INVESTIGATIONS

Designing and conducting a scientific investigation requires introduction to the major concepts in the area being investigated, proper equipment, safety precautions, assistance with methodological problems, recommendations for use of technologies, clarification of ideas that guide the inquiry, and scientific knowledge obtained from sources other than the actual investigation. The investigation may also require student clarification of the question, method, controls, and variables; student organization and display of data; student revision of methods and explanations; and a public presentation of the results with a critical response from peers. Regardless of the scientific investigation performed, students must use evidence, apply logic, and construct an argument for their proposed explanations.

Active involvement in science
investigations help students learn.

USE TECHNOLOGY AND MATHEMATICS TO IMPROVE INVESTIGATIONS AND COMMUNICATIONS

A variety of technologies, such as hand tools, measuring instruments, and calculators, should be an integral component of scientific investigations. The use of computers for the collection, analysis, and display of data is also a part of this standard. Mathematics plays an essential role in all aspects of an inquiry. For example, measurement is used for posing questions, formulas are used for developing explanations, and charts and graphs are used for communicating results.

FORMULATE AND REVISE SCIENTIFIC EXPLANATIONS AND MODELS USING LOGIC AND EVIDENCE

Student inquiries should culminate in formulating an explanation or model. Models should be physical, conceptual, and mathematical. In the process of answering the questions, students should engage in discussions and arguments that result in the revision of their explanations. These discussions should be based on scientific knowledge, use of logic, and evidence from their investigation.

RECOGNIZE AND ANALYZE ALTERNATIVE EXPLANATIONS AND MODELS

The aspect of *standard* emphasizes the critical abilities of analyzing an argument by reviewing current scientific understanding, weighing the evidence, and examining the logic so as to decide which explanations and models are best.

COMMUNICATE AND DEFEND A SCIENTIFIC ARGUMENT

Students in school science programs should develop the abilities associated with accurate and effective

TABLE 4–3   Science As Inquiry: Fundamental Concepts for Grades 9-12

- Conceptual principles and knowledge guide scientific inquiries.
- Scientists conduct investigations for a variety of reasons including discovering new aspects of the natural world, explaining recently observed phenomena, testing conclusions of prior investigations, and making predictions of current theories.
- Scientists rely on technology to enhance the gathering and manipulation of data.
- Mathematics is essential in scientific inquiry.
- Scientific explanations must adhere to criteria, such as logical consistency, rules of evidence open to questioning and based on historical and current knowledge.
- Results of scientific inquiry—new knowledge and methods—emerge from different types of investigations and public communications among scientists.

communication. These include writing and following procedures, expressing concepts, reviewing information, summarizing data, using language appropriately, developing diagrams and charts, explaining statistical analysis, speaking clearly and logically, constructing a reasoned argument, and responding appropriately to critical comments (NRC, 1996, pp. 175–176).

Science as Inquiry: The Understandings

Table 4–3 summarizes the fundamental understandings that students should develop as a result of their science education.

CONCEPTUAL PRINCIPLES AND KNOWLEDGE GUIDE SCIENTIFIC INQUIRIES

Scientists usually inquire about how physical, living, or designed systems function. Historical and current scientific knowledge influence the design and interpretation of investigations and the evaluation of proposed explanations made by other scientists.

SCIENTISTS CONDUCT INVESTIGATIONS FOR A WIDE VARIETY OF REASONS

Scientists may, for example, wish to discover new aspects of the natural world, explain recently observed phenomena, or test the conclusions of prior investigations or the predictions of current theories.

SCIENTISTS RELY ON TECHNOLOGY TO ENHANCE THE GATHERING AND MANIPULATION OF DATA

New techniques and tools provide new evidence to guide inquiry and new methods to gather data, thereby contributing to the advance of science. The accuracy and precision of the data, and therefore the quality of the exploration, depends on the technology used.

MATHEMATICS IS ESSENTIAL IN SCIENTIFIC INQUIRY

Mathematical tools and models guide and improve the posing of questions, gathering of data, constructing of explanations, and communicating of results.

SCIENTIFIC EXPLANATIONS MUST ADHERE TO CRITERIA

A proposed explanation, for instance, must be logically consistent; it must abide by the rules of evidence; it must be open to questions and possible modification; and it must be based on historical and current scientific knowledge.

RESULTS OF SCIENTIFIC INQUIRY—NEW KNOWLEDGE AND METHODS—EMERGE FROM DIFFERENT TYPES OF INVESTIGATIONS AND PUBLIC COMMUNICATION AMONG SCIENTISTS

In communicating and defending the results of scientific inquiry, arguments must be logical and demonstrate connections between natural phenomena, investigations, and the historical body of scientific knowledge. In addition, the methods and procedures that scientists have used to obtain evidence must be clearly reported to enhance opportunities for further investigation (NRC, 1996, p. 176).

NATIONAL SCIENCE EDUCATION STANDARDS: INQUIRY AS TEACHING STRATEGIES

Let us turn to questions that emerge from the discussion of inquiry as content. How do science teachers help

---

TABLE 4–4 Science Teaching Standards

A. Teachers of science plan an inquiry-based science program for their students.
B. Teachers of science guide and facilitate learning.
C. Teachers of science engage in ongoing assessment of their teaching and of student learning.
D. Teachers of science design and manage learning environments that provide students with the time, space, and resources needed for learning science.
E. Teachers of science develop communities of science learners that reflect the intellectual rigor of scientific inquiry and the attitudes and social values conducive to science learning.
F. Teachers of science actively participate in the ongoing planning and development of the school science program.

---

students attain the abilities and understanding described in the science as inquiry standards? What do the *Standards* say about teaching?

Science Teaching Standards

The *Science Teaching Standards* (see Table 4–4) provide a comprehensive perspective for science teachers who wish to provide students with the opportunities to experience science as inquiry. The *Standards* advocate the use of diverse teaching techniques.

> Although the *Standards* emphasize inquiry, this should not be interpreted as recommending a single approach to science teaching. Teachers should use different strategies to develop the knowledge, understandings, and abilities described in the content standards. Conducting hands-on science activities does not guarantee inquiry, nor is reading about science incompatible with inquiry. Attaining the understanding and abilities described in [the prior section] cannot be achieved by any single teaching strategy or learning experience (NRC, 1996, pp. 23–24).

What Should Science Teachers Know, Value, and Do?

Science teachers should know the differences between three concepts. First is inquiry as a description of methods and processes that scientists use; next is inquiry as a set of cognitive abilities that students might develop; and last is inquiry as a constellation of teaching strategies that can facilitate learning about scientific inquiry, developing the abilities of inquiry, and understanding scientific concepts and principles.

In placing this discussion of teaching after the discussion of content, the point is that the desired outcomes—learning science as subject and science as inquiry—present the primary answer to the question, "What is teaching science as inquiry?" The very character of science as inquiry lodges in strategies for teaching inquiry.

A PRESENT-DAY PERSPECTIVE ON TEACHING SCIENCE AS INQUIRY

There is, in our view, a rich and thorough intellectual foundation for teaching science as inquiry. That foundation includes work by Bakker and Clark (1988), Moore (1993), Duschl (1994), Hatton and Plouffe (1997), and Mayr (1997).

Constructing a View of Inquiry

Our use of the initial observations of classrooms in Activity 4–1 set the context for this discussion. The questions based on those observations allowed you to think deeply about the observations and explore several issues associated with the theme of teaching science as inquiry. Returning to the observations and questions now provides an opportunity to separate inquiry as content and inquiry as teaching strategies and to establish a perspective on teaching science as inquiry.

Question 1 probes the dominant perception of teaching science as inquiry. If your view was that inquiry is primarily activity directed by students, you probably answered A. If it was using laboratory experiences to teach the subject, you probably answered B. Few teachers answer C, for most do not view understanding scientific inquiry as a primary aim of school science. Those who responded D probably explained that some elements of all three classrooms contained inquiry.

Question 2 emphasizes the conception that most secondary teachers hold of inquiry: inquiry as technique or laboratory experiences for learning science concepts. The best answer is B. In classroom 1, students had many opportunities to develop the abilities of inquiry; and students in classroom 3 developed an understanding of scientific inquiry. Neither of the two classes, however, concentrated on the subjects of science: concepts of life, earth, and physical phenomena.

Question 3 was designed to probe the idea of inquiry as teaching strategy and engage your thinking about this as a singular approach to teaching science and the implied learning outcomes for students. If you used this approach all the time, what would students learn and what would they not learn? The suggested best answer is C. The primary assumption here is that classroom experiences of inquiry alone do not guarantee understanding subjects. Teachers should make explicit connections between the experiences and the content of inquiry and subject.

Question 4 asks for a generalization about the connection between teaching strategies and learning outcomes. The suggested best response here is E, because each of the others has some basis in practical truth.

In question 5, the teacher could look at any of the responses or at them all. Response E best anticipates a theme of this essay: that science teachers must have some understanding of scientific inquiry and a variety of teaching strategies and abilities to help students learn science subjects and the content of inquiry.

Question 6 organizes the reader's thinking to other sections of this chapter. The evaluation of my success and yours lies in E and especially D.

TOWARD A STANDARDS-BASED APPROACH TO TEACHING SCIENCE AS INQUIRY

Most discussions of teaching science as inquiry begin with the assumption that inquiry is a teaching strategy. Science teachers ask, "Should I use full or partial inquiries? Should the approach be guided by the teacher or left to the student?" A standards-based perspective views the situation differently. Such a perspective begins with the educational outcomes—What is it we want students to learn?—and then identifies the best strategies to achieve the outcome. Table 4–5 provides examples of this perspective. Reading from left to right, the table asks these questions: What content do I wish students to learn? Which teaching techniques provide the best opportunities to accomplish that? What assessment strategies most align with the students' opportunities to learn and provide the best evidence of the degree to which they have done so?

In Table 4–5, we provide examples that answer questions about teaching science as inquiry. In developing the examples in this table, we tried to hold to a clear understanding of the realities of standards, schools, science teachers, and students. Science teachers must teach the basics of subjects. The content standards for physical, life, earth, and space sciences provide teachers with an excellent set of fundamental understandings that could form their educational outcomes. After identifying the educational results, teachers must consider the effective teaching strategies and recognize that we have a considerable research base for the concepts that students hold about basic science. We also have some comprehension of the processes and strategies required to bring about conceptual change (Berkheimer & Anderson, 1989; Hewson, 1984; Hewson & Hewson, 1988; Gazzetti, Snyder, Glass, & Gamas, 1993; King, 1994; Lott, 1983). The teaching strategies include a series of laboratory experiences that help students to confront current concepts and reconstruct them so they align with basic scientific concepts and principles such as those in the *Standards*. For teaching science as inquiry, a variety of educators have described methods

TABLE 4–5   Examples of Teaching and Assessment that Support Inquiry-Oriented Outcomes

Standards-Based Educational Outcomes What should students learn?	Teaching Strategies What are the techniques that will provide opportunities for students to learn?	Assessment Strategies What assessments align with the educational outcomes and teaching strategies?
Understanding Subject Matter (e.g., Motions and Forces; Matter, Energy, and Organization in Living Systems; Energy in the Earth System)	Students engage in a series of guided or structured laboratory activities that include developing some abilities to do scientific inquiry but emphasize subject matter (e.g., laws of motion, $F = ma$, etc.).	Students are given measures that assess their understanding of subject matter. These may include performance assessment in the form of a laboratory investigation, open response questions, interviews, and traditional multiple choice.
Developing Abilities Necessary to Do Scientific Inquiry (e.g., students formulate and revise scientific explanations and models using logic and evidence)	Students engage in guided or structured laboratory activities and form an explanation based on data. They present and defend their explanations using (1) scientific knowledge and (2) logic and evidence. The teacher emphasizes some inquiry abilities in the laboratory activities used for subject-matter outcomes.	Students perform a task in which they gather data and use that data as the basis for an explanation.
Developing Abilities Necessary to Do Scientific Inquiry (e.g., students have opportunities to develop all the fundamental abilities of the standard)	Students complete a full inquiry that originates with their questions about the natural world and culminates with a scientific explanation based on evidence. The teacher assists, guides, and coaches students.	Students do an inquiry without direction or coaching. The assessment rubric includes the complete list of fundamental abilities.
Developing Understandings about Scientific Inquiry (e.g., scientific explanations must adhere to criteria such as: a proposed explanation must be logically consistent; it must abide the rules of evidence; it must be open to question and possible modification; and it must be based on historical and current scientific knowledge)	The teacher could direct students to reflect on activities from several laboratory activities. Students also could read historical case studies of scientific inquiry (e.g., Darwin, Copernicus, Galileo, Lavoisier, Einstein). Discussion groups pursue questions about logic, evidence, skepticism, modification, and communication.	Students are given a brief account of a scientific discovery and asked to describe the place of logic, evidence, criticism, and modification.

compatible with standards-based approaches to teaching science as inquiry (American Chemical Society, 1997; Bingman, 1969; Connelly, Finegold, Clipsham, & Wahlstrom, 1977; Layman, Ochoa, & Heikkinen, 1996; Novak, 1963; Hofstein & Walberg, 1995).

Using investigations to learn subjects provides the first opportunities for students to develop the abilities necessary to do scientific inquiry. For teaching science concepts, a series of laboratories might encourage the use of technology and mathematics to improve investigations and communications, the formulation and revision of scientific explanations and models by use of logic and evidence, and the communication and defense of a scientific argument. Science teachers must decide for themselves, however, the appropriate abilities and make them explicit in the course of the laboratory work.

A second educational outcome, closely aligned with learning subjects, is developing *abilities* necessary to do scientific inquiry. Laboratories provide many opportunities to strengthen them. These outcomes were in the background of the discussion of subject matter; here they are in the foreground. Science teachers could indeed base the activity on content, such as motions and forces, energy in the earth's system, or the molecular basis of heredity, but they could make several of the fundamental abilities the explicit outcomes of instruction. Over time, students would have ample opportunities to develop all of them. This approach to teaching science as inquiry overlaps and complements the science teacher's effort to cultivate an understanding of science concepts. The teacher structures the series of laboratory activities and provides varying levels of direct guidance.

A further result also sharpens abilities necessary for scientific inquiry; but now students have opportunities to conduct a full inquiry, which they think of, design, complete, and report. They experience all of the fundamental abilities in a scientific inquiry appropriate to their stage of sophistication and current understanding of science. The science teacher's role is to guide and coach. The classic example of this is the science fair project.

Finally, we come to the aspect of teaching science as inquiry that is most frequently overlooked, namely, developing understandings about scientific inquiry. On the face of it, this seems like an educational outcome that would be easy to accomplish once the science teacher has decided to instruct by means of an activity or laboratory and has gained an understanding of inquiry. Numerous ways are available of having students identify, compare, synthesize, and reflect on their various experiences founded in inquiry. Case studies from the history of science provide insights about the processes of scientific inquiry. Developing students' understanding of scientific inquiry is a long-term process that can be implemented with educational activities such as are mentioned here.

Questions of time, energy, reading difficulties, risks, expenses, and the burden of the subject need not be rationalizations for not teaching science as inquiry. Nurturing the abilities of inquiry is consistent with other stated goals for science teaching, for example, critical thinking; and it complements other school subjects, among them problem solving in mathematics and design in technology. Understanding science as inquiry is a basic component of the history and nature of science itself.

THE ESSENTIAL FEATURES OF INQUIRY

To begin shifting toward a more inquiry-oriented classroom, it helps to consider five essential features identified in *Inquiry and the National Science Education Standards: A Guide for Teaching and Learning* (NRC, 2000).

1. Learner engages in scientifically oriented questions.
2. Learner gives priority to evidence in responding to questions.
3. Learner formulates explanations from evidence.
4. Learner connects explanations to scientific knowledge.
5. Learner communicates and justifies explanations.

Learner Engages in Scientifically Oriented Questions

Scientifically oriented questions center on objects, organisms, and events in the natural world; they connect to the science concepts described in the content standards. They are questions that lend themselves to empirical investigation and lead to gathering and using data to develop explanations for scientific phenomena. Scientists recognize two primary kinds of scientific questions. Existence questions probe origins and include many "why" questions: Why do objects fall toward Earth? Why do some rocks contain crystals? Why do humans have chambered hearts? Many why questions cannot be addressed by science. In addition are causal and functional questions, which probe mechanisms and include most of the "how" questions: How does sunlight help plants grow? How are crystals formed?

Students often ask why questions. In the context of school science, many of these questions can be changed into how questions and thus lend themselves to scientific inquiry. Such change narrows and sharpens the inquiry and contributes to its being scientific.

In the classroom, a question robust and fruitful enough to drive an inquiry generates a need to know in students, stimulating additional questions of how and why a phenomenon occurs. The initial question may originate from the learner, the teacher, the instructional materials, the World Wide Web, some other source, or some combination. The teacher plays a critical role in guiding the identification of questions, particularly when they come from students. Fruitful inquiries evolve from questions that are meaningful and relevant to students, but they also must be answerable by student observations and the scientific knowledge they obtain from reliable sources. The knowledge and procedures students use to answer the questions must be accessible and manageable, as well as appropriate to the students' developmental level. Skillful teachers help students focus their questions so that they can experience both interesting and productive investigations.

Learner Gives Priority to Evidence in Responding to Questions

As the *NSES* notes, science distinguishes itself from other ways of knowing through the use of empirical evidence as the basis for explanations about how the natural world works. Scientists concentrate on getting accurate data from observations of phenomena. They obtain evidence from observations and measurements taken in natural settings such as oceans, or in contrived settings such as laboratories. They use their senses; instruments, such as telescopes, to enhance their senses; and instruments that measure characteristics that humans cannot sense, such as magnetic fields. In some instances, scientists can control conditions to obtain their evidence; in other instances, they cannot control the conditions or control would distort the phenomena, so they gather data over a wide range of naturally occurring conditions and over a long enough period of time so that they can infer what the influence of different factors might be. The accuracy of the evidence gathered is verified by checking measurements, repeating the observations, or gathering different kinds of data related to the same phenomena. The evidence is subject to questioning and further investigation.

The above paragraph explains what counts as evidence in science. In their classroom inquiries, students use evidence to develop explanations for scientific phenomena. They observe plants, animals, and rocks and carefully describe their characteristics. They take measurements of temperature, distance, and time and carefully record them. They observe chemical reactions and moon phases, and chart their progress. They obtain evidence from their teacher, instructional materials, the World Wide Web, or elsewhere to "fuel" their inquiries. As the *NSES* (NRC, 1966) notes, "explanations of how the natural world changes based on myths, personal beliefs, religious values, mystical inspiration, superstition, or authority may be personally useful and socially relevant, but they are not scientific."

Learner Formulates Explanations from Evidence

Although similar to the previous feature, this aspect of inquiry emphasizes the path from evidence to explanation, rather than the criteria for and characteristics of the evidence. Scientific explanations are based on reason. They provide causes for effects and establish relationships based on evidence and logical argument. They must be consistent with experimental and observational evidence about nature. They respect rules of evidence, are open to criticism, and require the use of various cognitive processes generally associated with science—for example, classification, analysis, inference, and prediction—and general processes such as critical reasoning and logic.

Explanations are ways to learn about what is unfamiliar by relating what is observed to what is already known. So explanations go beyond current knowledge and propose new understanding. For science, this means building on the existing knowledge base. For students, this means building new ideas on their current understandings. In both cases, the result is proposed new knowledge. For example, students may use observational and other evidence to propose an explanation for the phases of the moon, for why plants die under certain conditions and thrive in others, and for the relationship of diet to health.

Learner Connects Explanations to Scientific Knowledge

Evaluation, and possible elimination or revision of explanations, is one feature that distinguishes scientific inquiry from other forms of inquiry and subsequent explanations. One can ask questions such as: "Does the evidence support the proposed explanation?", "Does the explanation adequately answer the questions?", "Are there any apparent biases or flaws in the reasoning connecting evidence and explanation?", and "Can other reasonable explanations be derived from the evidence?"

Alternative explanations may be reviewed as students engage in dialogues, compare results, or check their results with those proposed by the teacher or instructional materials. An essential component of this characteristic is ensuring that students make the connection between their results and scientific knowledge appropriate in their level of development. That is, student explanations should ultimately be consistent with currently accepted scientific knowledge.

Learner Communicates and Justifies Explanations

Scientists communicate their explanations in such a way that their results can be reproduced. This requires clear articulation of the question, procedures, evidence, and proposed explanation and a review of alternative explanations. It provides for further skeptical review and the opportunity for other scientists to use the explanation in work on new questions.

Having students share their explanations provides others the opportunity to ask questions, examine evidence, identify faulty reasoning, point out statements that go beyond the evidence, and suggest alternative explanations for the same observations. Sharing explanations can bring into question or fortify the connections students have made among the evidence, existing scientific knowledge, and their proposed explanations.

As a result, students can resolve contradictions and solidify an empirically based argument.

The Look of Inquiry

Does inquiry always look the same? Hopefully not. Think about the variations of classroom inquiry along a continuum. Sometimes the amount of self-direction by learners is high, at other times the amount of self-direction from the teacher is high. Figure 4–1 lists key features of classroom inquiry in the lefthand column. The rows across indicate variations of implementation of that feature. A reasonable goal for the science classroom that is strong in inquiry is to ensure that every student has at least one opportunity every year that would fit in column D.

As a science teacher you may have to choose instructional materials that support an inquiry-oriented classroom. Consider a means to evaluate instructional materials. BSCS, in partnership with the K–12 Alliance at WestEd, has developed the Analyzing Instructional Materials (AIM) Process. This process provides a set of tools and strategies to examine instructional materials in depth to identify evidence of conceptual flow, content accuracy, the work students do, the work teachers do, and support for assessment. (See Figure 4–2.)

Feature	less...........................learner self-direction.............................more more.................direction from teacher or material........................less			
1. Learner engages in scientifically oriented questions	Learner engages in question provided by teacher, materials, or other sources	Learner sharpens or clarifies question provided by teacher, materials, or other source	Learner selects among questions, poses new questions	Learner poses a question
2. Learner gives priority to evidence in responding to questions	Learner given data and told how to analyze	Learner given data and asked to analyze	Learner directed to collect certain data	Learner determines what constitutes evidence and collects it
3. Learner formulates explanations from evidence	Learner provided with evidence	Learner given possible ways to use evidence to formulate explanation	Learner guided in process of formulating explanations from evidence	Learner formulates explanation after summarizing evidence
4. Learner connects explanations to scientific knowledge	Learner given all connections	Learner given possible connections	Learner directed toward areas and sources of scientific knowledge	Learner independently examines other resources and forms the links to explanations
5. Learner communicates and justifies explanations	Learner given steps and procedures for communication	Learner provided broad guidelines to use to sharpen communication	Learner coached in development of communication	Learner forms reasonable and logical argument to communicate explanations

FIGURE 4–1 Essential Features of Inquiry

(*Source:* National Research Council. (2000). *Inquiry and the national science education standards: A guide for teaching and learning.* Washington, DC: National Academy Press, p. 29.)

Criteria for examining the work students do	5	3	1
Quality learning experiences: Engaging prior knowledge (HPL 1) Finding 1 from *How People Learn* (HPL 1) has implications for the design of instructional materials. To be responsive to research on learning, instructional materials should include structured strategies to elicit and challenge student preconceptions. These include strategies that encourage students to: ■ activate (think about) their current understanding of a science concept; ■ make explicit (e.g., write down) their understanding of a science concept; and ■ connect their current understandings in science to new concepts	The materials miss *few* opportunities to engage prior knowledge.	The materials miss *some* opportunities to engage prior knowledge.	The materials miss *most or all* opportunities to engage prior knowledge.
Quality learning experiences: Encouraging metacognition (HPL 3) Finding 3 from *How People Learn* (HPL 3) has implications for the design of instructional materials. To be responsive to research on learning, instructional materials should incorporate strategies that help students to: ■ recognize the goals of the chapter or unit as well as their own learning goals; ■ assess their own learning; and ■ reflect, over time, on *what* and *how* they have learned	The materials miss *few* opportunities to encourage metacognition.	The materials miss *some* opportunities to encourage metacognition.	The materials miss *most or all* opportunities to encourage metacognition.
Abilities necessary to do scientific inquiry The abilities of inquiry (from *NSES*) include: ■ asking and identifying questions and concepts to guide scientific investigation, ■ designing and conducting scientific investigations, ■ using appropriate technology and mathematics to enhance investigations, ■ formulating and revising explanations and models, ■ analyzing alternative explanations and models, ■ accurately and effectively communicating results and responding appropriately to critical comments, and ■ generating additional testable questions.	The materials provide *frequent* opportunities to develop the abilities of scientific inquiry.	The materials provide a *limited number of* opportunities to develop the abilities of scientific inquiry.	The materials provide *none or very few* opportunities to develop the abilities of scientific inquiry.

FIGURE 4–2 AIM Scoring Rubric

(continued)

(*Source: Information in this table is synthesized from the following sources:* Bransford, J.D., Brown, A.L. and Cocking, R.R. (Eds.). (1999). *How people learn: Brain, mind, experience, and school.* Washington, DC: National Academy Press; and National Research Council. (1996). *National science education standards.* Washington, DC: National Academy Press.)

Criteria for examining the work students do	5	3	1
■ **1 hour lunch**	The materials provide students with *many* opportunities to understand the work scientists do and to make connections to student learning.	The materials provide students with *some* opportunities to understand the work scientists do and to make connections to student learning.	The materials provide students with *few* opportunities to understand the work scientists do and to make connections to student learning.
Accessibility When addressing the diversity of learners, consider the following: ■ Varied learning abilities and disabilities ■ Special needs (e.g., auditory, visual, physical, speech, emotional) ■ English language proficiency ■ Cultural differences ■ Different learning styles ■ Gender	The work students do is *consistently accessible* to diverse learners, providing opportunities for all students to achieve.	The work students do is *often accessible* to diverse learners, providing some opportunities for all students to achieve.	The work students do is rarely *accessible* to diverse learners, providing limited opportunities for all students to achieve.

FIGURE 4–2 *Continued*

SUMMARY

Most evidence indicates that science teaching is not now, and never has been in any significant way, centered in inquiry whether as content or as technique. Probably the closest the science education community came to teaching science as inquiry was during the 1960s and 1970s as we implemented the curriculum programs spurred by *Sputnik* and provided massive professional development experiences for teachers. The evidence does indicate that these programs were effective for the objectives related to inquiry that were emphasized in that era. Although science educators continue to chant the inquiry mantra, our science classrooms have not been transformed by the incantations.

The *Standards* have restated and provided details of what we mean by teaching science as inquiry. Appropriately viewed, inquiry as science content and inquiry as teaching strategies are two sides of a single coin. Teaching science as inquiry means providing students with diverse opportunities to develop the abilities and understandings of scientific inquiry while also learning the fundamental subjects of science. The teaching strategies that provide students those opportunities are found in varied activities, laboratory investigations, and inquiries initiated by students. Science teachers know this simple educational insight. It is now time to use the *Standards* and begin a new chapter where we act on what we know and teach science as inquiry.

—————————————   INVESTIGATING INQUIRY IN THE CLASSROOM   —————————————

ACTIVITY 4–1
WHAT IS TEACHING SCIENCE AS INQUIRY?

A beginning science teacher wanted to see inquiry in action so she visited three classrooms. Her considerations included content of lessons, teaching strategies, student activities, and student learning. During five days in each classroom, she made these observations.

Classroom 1

The students engaged in an investigation initiated by significant student interest. A student asked what happened to the water in a watering can. The can was almost full on Friday and almost empty on Monday. One student proposed that Willie the pet hamster had left his cage at night and drunk the water. Encouraged by the teacher to find a way to test this idea, the students covered the water so Willie could not drink it. Over several days they observed that the water level did not drop. The teacher then challenged the students to think about other explanations. The students' questions resulted in a series of full investigations about the disappearance of water from the container. The teacher employed strategies such as asking students to consider alternative explanations, using evidence to form their explanations, and designing simple investigations to test an explanation. The science teacher never did explain evaporation and related concepts.

Classroom 2

In a class studying evolution, the teacher distributed two similar but slightly different molds with dozens of fossil brachiopods. The students measured the lengths and widths of the two populations of brachiopods. The teacher asked whether the differences in length and width might represent evolutionary change. As the students responded, the teacher asked: "How do you know? How could you support your answer? What evidence would you need? What if the fossils were in the same rock formation? Are the variations in length and width just normal variations in the species? How would difference in length or width help a brachiopod adapt better?" The fossil activity provided the context for students to learn about the relationships between the potential for a species to increase its numbers, the genetic variability of offspring due to mutation and recombination of genes, the finite supply of resources required for life, and the ensuing selection by the environment for those offspring better able to survive and leave offspring. In the end, students learned about changes in the variations of characteristics in a population—biological evolution.

Classroom 3

In this science classroom, students selected from among several books that provided extended discussions of scientific work. Readings included *The Double Helix, The Beak of the Finch, An Imagined World,* and *A Feeling for the Organism.* Over a three-week period, each student read one of the books as homework. Then, in groups of four, all students discussed and answered the same questions: What led the scientist to the investigation? What conceptual ideas and knowledge guided the inquiry? What reasons did the scientist cite for conducting the investigation? How did technology enhance the gathering and manipulation of data? What role did mathematics have in the inquiry? Was the scientific explanation logically consistent? Was it based in evidence, open to skeptical review, and built on knowledge from other experiments? After reading the books and completing the discussion questions, the groups prepared oral reports on the topic, "The Role of Inquiry in Science."

   After completing the classroom visits, the science teacher summarized her observations (see Table 4–6).

   This introduction should have engaged your thinking about teaching science as inquiry. To further clarify your thinking, take a few minutes and respond to the questions here. Refer to the passages or summary table as often as necessary. Select the best answers and provide brief explanations for your choices.

   1. Which classroom would you cite as furnishing the best example of teaching science as inquiry?
      a. 1
      b. 2
      c. 3
      d. None of the classrooms
      e. All of the classrooms

TABLE 4–6 Summary of Observations

	Classroom 1	Classroom 2	Classroom 3
Content of Lesson	Changing water level in an open container	Investigation of variations in fossils	Stories of scientists and their work
Teaching Strategies	Challenge students to think about proposed explanations and use evidence to support conclusions	Provide molds of fossils and ask questions about student measurements and observations	Provide questions to focus discussions of readings
Student Activities	Design simple, but full investigations	Measure fossils and use data to answer questions	Read and discuss a book about scientific investigations
Student Outcomes	Develop the ability to reason using logic and evidence to form an explanation	Understand some of the basic concepts of biological evolution	Understand scientific inquiry as it is demonstrated in the work of scientists

Explanation

2. If teaching science as inquiry is primarily interpreted to mean using laboratory experiences to learn science concepts, which classroom was the best example?
   a. 1
   b. 2
   c. 3
   d. None of the classrooms
   e. All of the classrooms

Explanation

3. If students had numerous experiences with the same teaching strategies and the same activities devised by the students as in classroom 1, but pursued different questions, what would you predict as the results for students?
   a. Their thinking abilities, understanding of the subject, and understanding of inquiry will be higher than students who were in the other two classes.
   b. Their thinking abilities, understanding of the subject, and understanding of inquiry will be lower.
   c. Their thinking abilities would be higher and their understanding of the subject and of inquiry will be lower.
   d. Their understanding of the subject matter will be higher and their thinking abilities along with their understanding of inquiry lower.
   e. All learning outcomes would be the same as for students in the other two classes.

Explanation

4. Which of these generalizations about teaching science as inquiry would the observations of the three classrooms suggest to you?
   a. Overuse of one teaching strategy may constrain opportunities to learn the subject.
   b. Differing teaching strategies and student activities may bring differing benefits and trade-offs.
   c. The potential learning outcomes for any one sequence of lessons may be greater than for the sum of the individual lessons.
   d. Teaching strategies may need to differ in accordance with the result sought.
   e. All of the above

Explanation

5. If the teacher continues observing the three classrooms for another week, what would you recommend she look for in order to formulate an answer to the question, What is teaching science as inquiry?
   a. What the students learned about scientific inquiry
   b. What teaching strategies the teacher used

c. What science information, concepts, and principles the students learned

d. What inquiry abilities the students developed

e. What teachers should know and do to achieve the different learning goals of scientific inquiry

Explanation

6. Drawing on these observations, the science teacher proposes that teaching science as inquiry may have multiple meanings. Which of these would you recommend as a next step in her investigation?

   a. Explore how others have answered the question: What is teaching science as inquiry?

   b. See how the *National Science Education Standards* explain science as inquiry.

   c. Elaborate the implications of teaching science as inquiry.

   d. Try teaching science as inquiry in order to evaluate the approach in school science programs.

   e. All of the above

Explanation

As you engaged in this investigation, what were your ideas about teaching science as inquiry? If you have the opportunity, discuss your responses to these questions with classmates.

UNIT 2

HISTORICAL AND CONTEMPORARY PERSPECTIVES

Contemporary science education is in the process of reform. The federal government established priorities for education with legislation entitled, "No Child Left Behind" (Department of Education, 2004). This legislation has established goals for all of education; and national, state, and local school districts are implementing standards to help guide the reform and assessments, to help determine how well we have met our goals. Who determines why, when, and if science education should change? Are these decisions determined at the national level, or are they decided by the local school personnel? Teaching science in your classroom represents one small component of a larger system of science education. That system has a history of changes due to new scientific discoveries, new insights about student development and learning, and new issues in society.

Although your primary responsibility as a science teacher rests in the daily organization and introduction of productive learning experiences in your classroom, you also have a professional responsibility to understand the larger domain of science education. In order to appreciate contemporary reform, it is best to develop a historical perspective of the discipline. In this unit, we present such information and offer perspectives that you will find helpful as you design lessons and find strategies for teaching science and developing higher levels of scientific literacy among your students.

Developing students' scientific literacy means, in part, helping them to realize that throughout history philosophers and scientists have tried to clarify the process by which scientists generate scientific knowledge. In the seventeenth century, for example, individuals argued that the fundamental source of scientific knowledge was pure observations of nature. Scientists had the obligation to cleanse their minds of any ideas that might interfere with their observations. Thus, if scientists gathered facts and information without bias, they would eventually develop a correct theory. This may sound good until one asks if it is at all possible to observe nature with absolutely no preconceptions, no ideas, and no possible explanation for what is observed. The answer is no.

Over the years, philosophers, scientists, and science educators have proposed other formulations of the *scientific method*. For instance, the method often outlined in science textbooks usually includes (1) stating the problem, (2) forming a hypothesis, (3) designing an experiment, (4) collecting data, and (5) forming a conclusion. Scientists generally view such a formula with suspicion. Perhaps this method helps organize the results of scientific investigation, but it does not express the actual process of doing science, which is not neat and orderly.

You can see that science teaching is more than the process of designing learning experiences about life, earth, and physical science. It requires perspectives on science education, on science and technology, and on science and technology in society. Chapter 5 reviews the history of science education. For purposes of this discussion we have defined "history" as the late 1700s to the year 2000. Chapter 6 presents an introduction to the national standards for science education and perspectives on other contemporary trends and issues. Dates for contemporary trends and issues include the early twenty-first century.

HISTORICAL PERSPECTIVES ON SCIENCE EDUCATION

As society continues to change, so too must science education. The need for change is underscored by the widespread concern about social policies—debates over national security, economic stability, health and welfare; environment and cities; affluence and poverty. Weaving through these issues one identifies the recurrent themes of science and technology, ethics and values, education and learning. Present social conditions mandate a rethinking and reformulation of science education policies, programs, and practices. The changes that must occur in the early decades of the twenty-first century will be made by those who are entering the teaching profession as well as those already teaching science. Decisions you will make as a science teacher should be grounded in an understanding of the various forms and functions of science education in society. You should be aware of the history of science education and the present situation in science, society, and science education. Realize also that the decisions you make about your science curricula, instruction, classroom, and students help define the future.

This chapter has three parts. The first part has sections on science teaching in our first and second centuries. In the second section, we review the golden age of science curriculum. In the third, the view is toward the future and the role of science education in our changing national and global society.

THE FIRST TWO CENTURIES OF SCIENCE TEACHING

The First Century: 1776–1875, An Age of National Development

Even before the Declaration of Independence, the social institutions directed major efforts toward developing a nation. Ours was an agricultural society that later was to experience the tremors of industrial and civil revolutions.

In the decades after independence was declared, public education slowly was recognized as a necessary force for socialization. Education at this time was primarily religious and private. In 1779, Thomas Jefferson introduced a bill for educational reform in Virginia. The bill called for free public education for those of "worth and genius." At its base, however, in the Jeffersonian conception, education was designed to maintain social distinctions and a natural aristocracy between "the labour and the learned." In the late eighteenth and early nineteenth centuries, the government began granting land to each new state for public schools and to encourage universal free education. Although each state, county, and township had land, it generally lacked the necessary economic support and public enthusiasm to develop an adequate educational system.

Between 1820 and 1850, in the spirit of Jacksonian democracy, public schools received new support. By 1850, most elementary school children were receiving publicly supported education. The development of public high schools soon followed, so that, with the Jacksonian era, the social institution of public education was established. Later, the 1874 *Kalamazoo* decision set the precedent for tax-supported public high schools.

During the late eighteenth and early nineteenth centuries, religious indoctrination decreased and utilitarian objectives increased in schools. With this change, science education slowly gained a prominent place in American education.

The earliest forms of science instruction for children have been traced to the stories and didactic literature designed for home tutoring. These materials were based on the theories of John Locke and Jean Jacques Rousseau, and emphasized the firsthand study of "things and phenomena" as well as Christian doctrine. Originating about 1750, these materials reached their peak from 1800 to 1825. With the rise of group instruction, books for home use evolved into textbooks designed for school use. Science was included in many of the lessons, all of which stressed the memorization of factual knowledge, usually supporting theological concepts (Underhill, 1941).

Object teaching, from approximately 1860 to 1880, was a prominent movement in elementary science education. The primary aim of object lessons was personal development; science subject matter was of secondary importance. A method of teaching based primarily on the ideas of Johann Pestalozzi, this movement has had some impact on American education, but from its inception, it was strongly criticized for not emphasizing subject matter and was seldom fully implemented.

The mid-eighteenth to early nineteenth century marked the period of the academy in secondary level education. As religion ceased to dominate the instructional program, it was replaced with a more practical curriculum, which included science, such as agriculture and navigation.

Next came the early high schools (circa 1820 to 1870). The principal objectives of science education included learning practical arts and duties of citizenship. Sciences were firmly established in the curriculum during this period, although they were listed as natural philosophy (such as physics and chemistry) and natural history (such as biology and earth science).

After the depression of 1873, American schools were severely criticized by citizens asking a question common to such periods: "What are we getting for our money?" As social and economic patterns changed, educators followed with clear demands for more science in the classroom. The aim of science education was to give the public greater understanding of science and technology, the foundation of the emerging Industrial Revolution.

The Second Century: 1876–1976, An Age of Industrial Progress

The first 100 years of our nation held immense changes in the rate and direction of growth in American society. With the transition from an agricultural to an industrial economy, America became an industrial society. The end of World War II brought further technological and industrial development of an atomic age. As social development continued, however, negative trade-offs of technological development emerged. Suburban development influenced urban decay; corporate conglomerates increased while small businesses decreased; and society became affluent with new minorities of organizational men, lonely crowds, and other Americans. By the 1960s, almost every aspect of public policy—both domestic and foreign—was being severely criticized while basic institutions, including education, were being called to reform.

Periodically, throughout the century 1876 to 1976, schools were asked to make changes that more accurately reflected the realities of our developing society. Committee reports often reveal the nature of these reformations; several from this period will serve as examples of the suggested changes in education.

In 1893, the "Committee of Ten" (Committee on Secondary School Studies, 1893) stated that all students should be taught the same curriculum regardless if they planned to attend college. The committee detailed such matters as the subjects to be taught and the hours per week and weeks per year to be devoted to each subject. This report helped reduce the domination of colleges over high school programs and formed a stronger connection between high school and elementary school programs. It also stressed academic or intellectual goals.

The slow but steady recognition of the role of science and technology in developing an industrial society inevitably resulted in a popular interest in science and subsequently in science education. Laboratory instruction was popular because it contributed to a primary objective of the period: development of reasoning, observation, and concentration.

By 1915, the emphasis in science education shifted to goals broader than those for college entrance. A report of the Central Association of Science and Mathematics Teachers, Committee on Unified High School Science Courses (1915), suggested that science should (1) give pupils such a knowledge of nature as will help them get along better in everyday life, (2) stimulate people to more direct purposeful activity, (3) help them choose intelligently for future occupations, (4) give students methods of obtaining accurate knowledge, and (5) enable students to achieve a greater, clearer, and more intelligent enjoyment of life.

In 1918, the Commission on the Reorganization of Secondary Education completed its work by publishing, "The Cardinal Principles of Secondary Education." This report called for a shift in the goal of education from the narrower intellectual indoctrination to a broadened socialization of the student. The seven cardinal principles were health, command of fundamental processes, worthy home membership, vocation, civic education, worthy use of leisure, and ethics. School subjects were to be reorganized so that students would more effectively attain these objectives.

College domination of the high school science program was further eroded by the 1918 publication of the cardinal principles by the Commission on the Reorganization of Secondary Education. A report on the reorganization of science in the secondary schools was also published by a subcommittee of the original commission. This report discussed the contributions that science teaching could make to the cardinal principles of secondary education. In general, it stressed the importance of organization and sequencing of secondary science, but it also pointed out social goals beyond the traditional knowledge goals usually stressed in secondary school science.

By 1924, science teachers used the scientific process as a means to help students learn scientific knowledge. The Committee on the Place of Science in Education of the American Association for the Advancement of Science reported a study on the problems of science teaching. The report underscored the importance of scientific thinking as an objective of teaching. Science instruction, according to the committee, should be founded on scientific observation and experimentation for "a factual basis worthy of the spirit of science" (Caldwell, 1924).

In 1932, a national survey of secondary education reported on science teaching guides, courses of study, and syllabi. In general, the report stated that the knowledge taught lacked a coherent theoretical structure, grade-level placement of courses was confusing, and teaching methods were inconsistent. The report also indicated a variety of innovative practices to be considered when constructing new programs. Such considerations included problem methods of teaching, interpretation of the environment, use of illustrative materials, use of demonstrations, coordination of laboratory and textbook work, and greater use of visual aids.

These reports represent the change in values, as seen in science education, from the high ideals and social unity following World War I to the disillusionment of the economic depression of the late 1920s and 1930s.

The Great Depression raised doubts and questions concerning science education. Two publications during this period were of great importance. The National Society for the Study of Education book, *A Program for Science Teaching* (1932), emphasized the importance of broad scientific principles that aid students in a fundamental understanding of nature. The Progressive Education Association publication, *Science in General Education* (1938), stressed progressive goals such as personal–social relationships, personal living, economic relations, and reflective thinking. The general orientation of science programs was toward the more immediate needs of students; the content was of personal and social significance; and recommendations included programs in health, vocation, and consumerism. The greatest changes were in biology and general science courses, but physics and chemistry courses changed very little.

The period after the depression was a relatively calm one for science education. The National Society for the Study of Education published *Science Education in American Schools* (1947) with general objectives for science teaching, such as functional information, concepts and principles, skills and attitudes aligned with the scientific method, and the recreational and social values of science. With World War II, America recovered a sense of national purpose, which was reflected in the literature of science education.

After World War II, reports on the American school system stressed life-adjustment education. Examples included the Educational Policies Commission's *Education for All American Youth* (1952), *Planning for American Youth* from the Department of Secondary School Principals (1946), and *Life Adjustment Education for Every Youth*, published by the U.S. Department of Education (1951).

In the 1950s, during another economic recession, schools were again criticized for lacking adequate academic goals (Bestor, 1953; Rickover, 1970). The demand was for a return to the basics, emphasis on traditional subjects, and special attention to the gifted. This tide of criticism was aided by the October 1957 launching of *Sputnik I*, which became the symbol for a major reform in science education. The movement led to the most extensive period of curriculum revision and teacher education in American history. Reform of science curricula strongly influenced a model described by Jerome Bruner in *The Process of Education* (1960). Scientific knowledge was the dominant aim, and students used inquiry as a process to acquire knowledge. In Bruner's model, knowledge involved the concepts that formed the structure of a science discipline.

By the mid-1960s, however, a new group of social critics appealed for a greater understanding of student alienation, identity, and self-concept. The focus in education shifted from the space race to urban disgrace, and by 1976 the science education community felt tremors of a new reform.

THE GOLDEN AGE: SCIENCE CURRICULUM: 1958–1988

In the late 1950s, society focused attention on the cold war. One aspect included direct competition with the Soviet Union, especially in areas strongly associated with science and technology, for example, nuclear weapons and space exploration.

Although reform of the science curriculum began in the late 1950s, the movement was supported as a result of the Soviet Union's launch of *Sputnik I* in October 1957. Several years later, in 1961, President John F. Kennedy articulated a national goal when, in a special message to a joint session of Congress, he stated, "I believe that this nation should commit itself to achieving the goal, before this decade is out, of landing a man on the moon and returning him safely to the earth." From the president, the symbol and purpose of this goal was translated into support for science programs that encouraged students to enter careers in science and engineering. The curriculum materials developed and implemented in this period have had tremendous influences on education in general and science education in particular. In the next sections we examine many of the programs developed for junior and senior high schools.

Science Curriculum for the Junior High School

EARTH SCIENCE

Early in 1963, the American Geological Institute received a grant to implement the Earth Science Curriculum Project (ESCP) in the ninth grade. This course was interdisciplinary, involving geology, meteorology, astronomy, and oceanography. Its emphasis was on laboratory and field study.

ESCP materials included a textbook, *Investigating the Earth*; the laboratory was augmented by the text, teacher guide, films, laboratory equipment, maps, and a pamphlet series. After three years of testing and preparation of materials, the course was published commercially.

The table of contents from the first edition (1967) included the following chapters.

1. The Changing Earth
2. Earth Materials
3. Earth Measurement
4. Earth Motions
5. Fields and Forces
6. Energy Flow
7. Energy and Air Motions
8. Water in the Air
9. Waters of the Land
10. Water in the Sea
11. Energy, Moisture, and Climate
12. The Land Wears Away
13. Sediments in the Sea
14. Mountains from the Sea
15. Rocks within Mountains
16. Interior of the Earth
17. Time and Its Measurement
18. The Record in Rocks
19. Life—Present and Past
20. Development of a Continent
21. Evolution of Landscapes
22. The Moon: A Natural Satellite
23. The Solar System
24. Stars as Other Suns
25. Stellar Evolution and Galaxies
26. The Universe and Its Origin

The project continued its programs until 1969, when two offshoots, Environmental Studies (ES) and Earth Science Teacher Preparation Project (ESTPP), were initiated to deal specifically with the environmental problems and issues of teacher preparation in the earth sciences.

A serious problem that first faced ESCP was the preparation of persons qualified to teach the course, but continued efforts in teacher preparation have narrowed the gap between supply and demand. The advances made in the design and implementation of *Investigating the Earth* were commendable. The text design, integration of concepts from life and physical sciences, and the careful presentation of knowledge, process, and skills were unprecedented. Subsequent revisions of the text have replaced many innovative topics and realigned the book with older, traditional earth science texts.

PHYSICAL SCIENCE

Another program developed for the junior high school was the Introductory Physical Science (IPS) program of Educational Services, Incorporated. This project, supported by the NSF, was to develop a one-year course in physical science. Laboratory work and equipment were designed in such a way that students performed the experiments in ordinary classrooms. The table of contents of the IPS course included the following:

1. Introduction
2. Quantity of Matter: Mass
3. Characteristic Properties
4. Solubility and Solvents
5. The Separation of Substances
6. Compounds and Elements
7. Radioactivity
8. The Atomic Model of Matter
9. Sizes and Masses of Atoms and Molecules
10. Molecular Motion
11. Heat

The IPS course was tested in several centers throughout the United States, and the materials, which included textbooks, teacher guides, laboratory notebooks, and comprehensive apparatus kits, were eventually published commercially.

The attractiveness of the IPS course to better-than-average junior high school students was made clear in the results of a test survey of representative IPS students in the 1965–1966 school year. "In that year, 1,005 ninth-grade IPS students and 400 eighth-grade IPS students took the School and College Abilities Test (SCAT) Survey Form, a test of verbal and mathematical ability. The results made it clear that the IPS students were more scholastically able on the average than typical junior high school students in the nation (Education Development Center, 1968).

As the success of a new course depends on well-qualified teachers, the National Science Foundation supported a program to locate qualified science teachers and to prepare them to instruct other teachers in the use of IPS. The program was quite successful; in IPS workshops, teachers were trained by their peers in the local environment.

INTEGRATED SCIENCE

Among junior high school courses was the Intermediate Science Curriculum Study (ISCS) financed by the U.S. Department of Education and The National Science Foundation. "The fundamental assumption underlying the ISCS plan is that science at the junior high school level serves essentially a general education function" (Redfield & Darrow, 1970). Three levels were prepared, corresponding to the junior high school grades 7, 8, and 9. Level I for seventh grade was tightly structured. Its title, *Energy, Its Forms and Characteristics*, permitted students to delve into physical science principles by dealing with science in their environment. Level II put the students more on their own in designing experiments and recording and interpreting data. This level was titled, *Matter and Its Composition and Model Building*. Level III, *Probing the Natural World*, for the ninth grade dealt with biological concepts and was designed to use laboratory blocks six to eight weeks long as its basic plan of operation. The ninth grade student was expected to use the concepts and investigative skills acquired in the seventh and eighth grades. All of the class activity in the ISCS course was planned for individualized work, and the teacher's task was assisting students. No formal lectures or information-dispensing sessions were planned for the course, unless needed on a short-term basis by a small group of students.

An innovative feature of the ISCS course was the production of a complete course on computer-assisted instruction (CAI). Using behavioral objectives and a system of computer feedback, it was possible to obtain detailed information on the progress and problems encountered by each student. This information was used to modify and revise the trial versions of the course.

There were other smaller scale projects for revising junior high school science. Among them were the Interaction Science Curriculum Project (ISCP), Ideas and Investigations in Science (IIS), and a BSCS program, *Human Sciences Program*. Each was extensively field tested and met with some success.

Science Curriculum for the High School

At the high school level, advances in science and technology have traditionally exerted the greatest influence on programs. In this section, we review traditional disciplines for school science—physics, chemistry, and biology.

PHYSICS

Physics was first known as *natural philosophy* and appeared in the academies of the early 1700s. Content was organized into topics similar to those of many courses today. Mechanics, fluids, heat, light, sound, magnetism, and electricity were taught, mainly by recitation. The Civil War and the advent of land-grant colleges in the 1860s placed emphasis on military and vocational aspects of science, and the course became known as physics. Laboratory instruction was emphasized. A list of standard experiments, called *The Descriptive List*, was circulated by Harvard in 1886 for use by the high schools. Candidates for admission to Harvard who had taken physics as a prerequisite were then tested by use of these experiments.

Physical Science Study Committee: In 1956, a group of university physicists at Cambridge, Massachusetts, looked at the secondary school physics curriculum and found that it did not present the content or spirit of modern physics. From this group, the Physical Science Study Committee (PSSC) was formed, with the objective of producing a new physics course for the high school level.

In four years this group developed a textbook, laboratory guide, teacher guide, and set of apparatus, monographs, and films. These aids were correlated closely with one another to produce an effective curriculum package. In addition, they held summer institutes for upgrading teachers in physics and in the philosophy of the new course.

Important differences between the PSSC physics course and other high school physics became apparent.

- Fewer topics covered at greater depth
- Greater emphasis on laboratory work

- More emphasis on basic physics
- Less attention to technological applications
- Development approach showing origins of basic ideas of physics
- Increased difficulty and rigor of the course

Teachers and administrators had conflicting opinions about the merits of the PSSC course. There was general agreement that it was a definite improvement over traditional courses, especially for better-than-average college-bound students. For average or below-average students, its merit was questionable.

In a 1971 study by John Wasik, PSSC students showed significantly higher performance than non-PSSC students in the process skills of application and analysis (Wasik, 1971); however, non-PSSC students performed at a higher level on the taxonomic process measure of knowledge. Wasik concluded that the results supported the position of new curriculum writers that the PSSC instructional materials were most effective in developing higher cognitive-process skills.

A 1983 analysis of the effects of new science curricula on student performance revealed that the physics curricula was second only to the biology curricula in terms of overall advances in student performances. Studies of achievement and analytic skills showed that students participating in the new physics courses gained at least a half-year more than students in traditional courses (Shymansky, Kyle, & Alport, 1983). This result indicates that the new physics curricula was partially successful in achieving its stated goals. The goal generally not assessed was student perceptions of physics. This omission is unfortunate, because it could have given some insights to help slow the long and steady decline in physics enrollments.

Project Physics: Project Physics, a course designed for the average student and produced at Harvard University, attempted to treat physics as a lively and fundamental science, closely related to achievements both in and outside the discipline itself (Harvard Project Physics, 1967).

Financial support for the project was provided by the Carnegie Corporation of New York, the Ford Foundation, the National Science Foundation, the Alfred P. Sloan Foundation, the U.S. Office of Education, and Harvard University. Hundreds of participating schools throughout the United States tested the course as it went through several revisions.

The philosophy of this course is emphasized in eight points.

1. Physics is for everyone.
2. A coherent selection within physics is possible.
3. Doing physics goes beyond physics.
4. Individuals require a flexible course.
5. A multimedia system stimulates better learning.
6. The time has come to teach science as one of the humanities.
7. A physics course should be rewarding to take.
8. A physics course should be rewarding to teach.

Materials of Project Physics included a textbook, teacher guide, student guide, experiments, films, transparencies, tests, film loops, readers, and other items. Chapter headings for the Project Physics course were as follows:

Unit 1: Concepts of Motion
Unit 2: Motion in the Heavens
Unit 3: The Triumph of Mechanics
Unit 4: Light and Electromagnetism
Unit 5: Models of the Atom
Unit 6: The Nucleus

Several studies attempted to find reasons for the decreasing enrollments in high school physics. In a questionnaire sent by Raymond Thompson to 1,382 high school physics teachers, 79 percent believed that students stayed away because the course was too difficult (Thompson, 1970). Of these students, 40 percent ascribed their reluctance to fear of jeopardizing their grade average, and 16 percent attributed it to fear of mathematics.

In a study of 450 physics students enrolled in Project Physics in 1966–1967, Wayne Welch concluded that students received lower grades in physics than in their other courses (Welch, 1969). In the sample studied, the median IQ was at the 82nd percentile, but the average grade received by these bright students was in the C + to B − range. Thus, the students were dissatisfied with their experience.

The course was extensively evaluated during its development. Results were encouraging, both with respect to the performance of Project Physics students on standard tests such as the College Board Examinations and to attracting increasing numbers of high school students to elect physics in their junior or senior years. The percentage of girls taking the course also appeared to have increased over PSSC or traditional physics courses.

CHEMISTRY

The teaching of high school chemistry began in the early 1800s in girls' academies, while the Civil War years provided a stimulus to the course because of military and industrial applications. Laboratory work increased during the late 1800s, and efforts were made to reproduce many of the classical experiments of early chemists such as Joseph Priestly and Antoine-Laurent Lavoisier. As with physics, Harvard in 1886 placed chemistry on the optional list for college entrance and controlled the quality of entering students by publishing *The Pamphlet,* containing 60 experiments, on which the prospective enrollee was tested in the laboratory. Influence of *The Pamphlet* was profound, and the high school chemistry course became highly standardized. Laboratory workbooks were developed, containing experiments that were mainly exercises in observation and manipulation of chemical reactions.

Chemical Bond Approach: In 1957, a summer conference of chemistry teachers at Reed College in Portland, Oregon, produced a plan for a new type of chemistry course and initiated the Chemical Bond Approach (CBA) Project. There followed a series of writing conferences, use of the new materials by trial schools, and the production of a commercial textbook in 1963. The major theme of this course was the chemical bond, and particular attention was given to *mental models* (conceptual schemes) of structure, kinetic theory, and energy.

The laboratory program and textbook paralleled and reinforced each other. No unusual chemicals or equipment were required, and the cost of conducting the CBA chemistry course was not significantly different from that of conducting conventional courses.

Chemical Education Materials Study: A second course-improvement project in chemistry was initiated at Harvey Mudd College in Claremont, California, in 1959. Called the Chemical Education Materials Study (CHEM), the project developed a course that was strongly based on experiment and included a text and laboratory manual, teacher guide, a score of excellent films, and a series of wall charts.

Both the CBA and CHEM chemistry programs received grants from the National Science Foundation, which supported numerous inservice and summer institutes for teachers.

Enrollment in CBA and CHEM classes increased initially. In 1968, approximately 40 percent of high school chemistry taught in the United States was the CHEM course (Lockard, 1970). Approximately 10 percent of the schools were using CBA (Cawelti, 1968). At this time, the CHEM project terminated its work, and commercial publishers were invited to prepare courses based on the philosophy and materials of the CHEM course. Several publishers produced high school chemistry textbooks influenced by the philosophies and pedagogies of the CHEM and CBA programs.

In a survey by Frank Fornoff in 1970, in which 2,395 students were queried, the most widely used high school chemistry textbook was *Modern Chemistry;* *Chemistry—An Experimental Science* was second; and *Chemical Systems* was third (Fornoff, 1970). The latter two texts represented the commercial editions of CHEM study and CBA chemistry, respectively. Other information obtained in the study showed that most chemistry classes met five times per week for 40 to 59 minutes,

and 13 percent of students reported taking a college-level chemistry course in high school.

In a 1978 report it was estimated that fewer than 25 percent of chemistry teachers were using either CHEM study, a CBA approach, or a combination of the two (Weiss, 1978). The same study found that CHEM study was used in 15 percent of school districts; yet, neither textbook appeared on the list of most commonly used textbooks. A 1983 report on the effects of new curricula found that the new chemistry curricula, both CBA and CHEM study, produced the least impact in terms of student cognitive achievement and process skills (Shymansky et al., 1983).

Interdisciplinary Approaches to Chemistry: In March 1972, a new chemistry course was developed by the University of Maryland: the Interdisciplinary Approaches to Chemistry (IAC). The IAC course approached the teaching of chemistry somewhat differently by using a group of modules dealing with special topics of an interdisciplinary nature. Titles of the modules were as follows:

- Reactions and Reason (Introductory)
- Diversity and Periodicity (Inorganic)
- Form and Function (Organic)
- Molecules in Living Systems (Biochemistry)
- The Heart of the Matter (Nuclear)
- Earth and Its Neighbors (Geochemistry)
- The Delicate Balance (Environmental)
- Communities of Molecules (Physical)

Among the goals of IAC was the

realization that a student's attitudes or feelings about chemistry are just as important in the long run as his acquisition of special chemical concepts.

Thus, in molding the IAC program, equal emphasis has been placed on providing the student with a sound background in those basic skills and concepts normally found in an introductory high school chemistry course as well as on developing the attitude that chemistry is not a dry, unrealistic science, but an exciting, relevant, human activity that can be enjoyable to study (IAC, 1973).

Several characteristics made the IAC chemistry different from traditional chemistry courses or previous curriculum projects, with an emphasis on making chemistry more relevant and successful for the student. The program was modular, instead of being a single, structured text. Each module was devoted to a different aspect of chemistry and its relationship to the other sciences and society. This format allows for many degrees of flexibility within the program.

A module consisted of chemistry content and laboratory experiments integrated into a unified whole. The program included suggested readings for students, problems and activities, safety precautions, and relevant chemical data, such as periodic tables and charts. Each module dealt with a specific area of chemistry as indicated in the titles, relating chemistry to other sciences and phenomena encountered in the natural world.

IAC was revised in 1979 to update its content and its teaching techniques in concepts and in laboratory experiments. It was well received by chemistry teachers who enjoyed the freedom to experiment with different modules in their classes and to rearrange content in accordance with student and teacher interests.

Research by Robert Stephenson in 1977–1978 on the use of IAC chemistry in high school indicated that age, sex, and attitude had no effect on the achievement level of students; that cognitive-reasoning ability and grade-point averages were highly correlated with achievement success; and that achievement success on the introductory module tests could be used to predict success on subsequent modules (Stephenson, 1978).

BIOLOGY

In school science programs, biology began in botany, physiology, and zoology courses and in the nineteenth century was patterned after college courses in these subjects. A course of study in biology appeared in New York in 1905, and the College Entrance Examination Board prepared an examination for the course in 1913. Biology was placed either in the ninth or tenth grade.

Of all the high school sciences, biology had the largest enrollment due to a combination of factors to include placement in the ninth or tenth grade where the effect of school dropouts is less pronounced, the effect of compulsory education laws, the nonmathematical nature of the course, and the general requirement of a minimum of one science course for graduation from high school. These factors combined to increase enrollment in biology over the years. In 1958, approximately 68 percent of tenth-grade students were enrolled in a biology course (Brown & Obourn, 1961).

Biological Sciences Curriculum Study: The American Institute of Biological Science organized the Biological Sciences Curriculum Study (BSCS) at the University of Colorado in 1958, with Arnold B. Grobman as director. In discussing the design of a new biology course, he said:

> A realistic general biology program must take into account a wider range of student ability, interests, and potential than exists in other high school science courses. It must be a course that most tenth-grade students can handle and at the same time prove challenging to the above-average student. For these reasons, the committee thought it undesirable to limit the course to a single design (Grobman in AAAS, 1963).

Three courses were developed, based on a molecular approach (blue version), a cellular approach (yellow version), and an ecological approach (green version) to the study of biology. Although the courses differ in emphasis, nine common themes run throughout (AAAS, 1963).

1. Change of living things through time—evolution
2. Diversity of type and unity of pattern of living things
3. Genetic continuity of life
4. Biological roots of behavior
5. Complementarity of organisms and environment
6. Complementarity of structure and function
7. Regulation and homeostasis: the maintenance of life in the face of change
8. Science as inquiry
9. Intellectual history of biological concepts.

Among the course materials were textbooks, laboratory guides, supplementary readings, and tests. Innovations included laboratory blocks consisting of a series of interlocking and correlated experiments on a special topic of biology. Eleven laboratory blocks were developed, including Plant Growth and Development; Microbes: Their Growth and Development; and Interdependence of Structure and Function. A second-level course was prepared for advanced biology, and a course called *Patterns and Processes in Science* was designed for unsuccessful learners.

Other supplementary materials included excerpts from historical papers, BSCS Invitations to Inquiry, discussion outlines for the laboratory, films on laboratory techniques, *The Biology Teacher's Handbook,* and the BSCS Pamphlet Series.

The BSCS biology courses received a generally favorable response throughout the country. Two versions (green and blue) of the course are still available, and it has been found that different versions are chosen in different regions. Several foreign countries are also using the course.

Several researchers have studied the effects of BSCS biology in the schools. In one study, Kenneth George (1965) found that students taking the blue version scored significantly higher on critical thinking, as measured by the Watson Glaser Critical Thinking Appraisal Form ZM, than did students taking conventional biology. B. J. Adams (1968) found no difference in the retention of biological information between BSCS students and those taking traditional biology; however, he did find significant relationships between retention and intelligence, reading scores, and teacher grading, with the BSCS students generally scoring higher. Charles Granger and Robert Yager (1970) found no significant difference between students experiencing BSCS and non-BSCS backgrounds with respect to achievement in either high school or college-level biology. However, a significantly larger percentage of BSCS students felt their background was better in meeting individual needs, as well as preparing them for college-level biology (Shymansky, 1984). Jack Carter and Alan Nakosteen (1971), in a study with 8,500 college freshmen, found that BSCS students scored higher on inquiry and recall items on the BSCS Comprehensive Biology Tests than did students who enrolled in a non-BSCS course in high school.

In a 1983 report, BSCS fared very well in the major review of curricula developed in the 1960s and 1970s. Biology curricula showed the greatest effect on student performance, particularly in the area of developing analytic skills. In a 1984 report on the BSCS programs, James Shymansky had this to say:

> We found the new science programs to be consistently more effective than their traditional counterparts. Moreover, we found Biological Sciences Curriculum Study (BSCS) to be the most effective of all the new high school programs (Shymansky et al., 1983).

COMMON ELEMENTS OF GOLDEN AGE COURSES

A survey of various course materials developed in secondary school science during the 1960s and 1970s shows close similarity both in types of materials offered and in general objectives. The following common elements can be discerned.

- Less emphasis on social and personal applications of science and technology than in the traditional courses
- More emphasis on abstractions, theory, and basic science—the structure of scientific disciplines
- Increased emphasis on discovery—the modes of inquiry used by scientists
- Frequent use of quantitative techniques
- Newer concepts in subject matter
- An upgrading of teacher competency in both subject matter and pedagogical skills
- Well-integrated and designed teaching aids to supplement the courses
- Little emphasis on career awareness as a goal of science teaching
- Primarily an orientation toward college-bound students
- Similarities in emphasis and structure in the high school and junior high school programs

AN ERA OF EDUCATIONAL REFORM: SCIENCE EDUCATION IN SECONDARY SCHOOLS: 1980–FUTURE

Beginning in the early 1980s, science education entered a new era of reform. In 1981, Norris Harms and Robert Yager published the results of Project Synthesis, a major effort to evaluate the status of, and make recommendations for, science education. In a larger context, the publication *A Nation at Risk* in 1983 symbolized a wider and deeper national effort to reform education. Though varied in approach and recommendations, the national reports on education in the United States consistently identified science and technology as a vital area with a pressing need for reform. What brought about this national concern with science and technology education were a number of disturbing trends, including declines in the following:

- Science enrollments in secondary schools
- Science education in elementary schools
- Achievement test scores
- Students entering science and engineering careers
- Qualified science teachers
- Public attitudes toward science education
- Quality and quantity of American science education compared to that of other countries (Aldridge & Johnston, 1984, in Bybee, Carlson, & McCormack (Eds.), 1984; Hurd, 1983; Gardner & Yager, 1983)

The history of American education had never witnessed such widespread calls for educational reform. By the late 1980s, more than 300 reports admonished those within the educational system to improve. Depending on who published the report, recommendations emphasized such issues as updating scientific and technological knowledge, applying learning theory and new teaching strategies, improving approaches to achieve equity, and providing better preparation for the workplace. Various calls for reform continued into the 1990s and 2000. The need to improve continues in the twenty-first century.

For science education at the secondary school level, there are significant differences between the 1960s and 1990s reforms. The 1960s reform began at the secondary level and progressed to the elementary level. In the 1990s, reports have generally addressed all levels, K through 12, but the specific curriculum reform began at the elementary school level and progressed to secondary schools. The impetus for this sequential reform was initiated by funding from the NSF for new elementary and middle school programs. In the early twenty-first century, educators can anticipate curricular changes at the secondary school level. The important point is that school science programs structured from the top down, from twelfth grade physics to elementary programs, are quite different from school science programs that are structured from the bottom up, or when the science curriculum is viewed more holistically as a total K through 12 program.

A second difference between these two decades is that in the late 1990s and early twenty-first century there are fewer curriculum projects at the national level. Reform efforts are being initiated through national standards and benchmarks, as well as state-level frameworks and guidelines, but they are being completed through local development of materials. Such efforts have the advantage of higher levels of implementation and the disadvantage of lower levels of actual program reform. These lower levels of reform result from a lack of time and money to develop new materials, so, subsequently, school districts adopt textbooks. Additionally, staff development programs to update teachers in science and technology content and innovative teaching strategies are not implemented as a complement to the instructional materials. The result is a nationwide low level of reform in both quantity and quality.

REVIEWING THE GOALS OF SCIENCE EDUCATION

As soon as discussions of reform in science education began, so did talk of rethinking goals. Obviously the direction of reform had to be guided by new goals. Anna Harrison called attention to the inadequacy of science education goals in an editorial in *Science* (Harrison, 1982). Ronald Anderson asked the rhetorical question, "Are yesterday's goals adequate for tomorrow?" (Anderson, 1983) He, too, called attention to the inadequacy of contemporary goals. In the 1980s these were only two instances in which people began directing science educators toward the reform of goals for science teaching.

Others began addressing the need and substance for new goals in more detail. In a short monograph entitled, *Reforming Science Education: The Search for a New Vision*, Paul DeHart Hurd summarized the emerging vision of goals. "The rationale and goals are derived from a consideration of how science and technology influenced social well-being and human affairs. The goals for teaching science are based on scientific and technological systems in social, cultural, and individual contexts" (Hurd, 1984).

A major report issued by the National Science Board (NSB, 1983) was titled, *Educating Americans for the 21st Century*. This report was quite comprehensive, including a section on goals for science and technology education. The report clearly describes a vision that would eventually be set in place by the national standards. Following are the general outcomes recommended by this report:

- Ability to formulate questions about nature and seek answers from observation and interpretation of natural phenomena
- Development of students' capacities for problem solving and critical thinking in all areas of learning

- Development of particular talents for innovative and creative thinking
- Awareness of the nature and scope of a wide variety of science- and technology-related careers open to students of varying aptitudes and interests
- The basic academic knowledge necessary for advanced study by students who are likely to pursue science professionally
- Scientific and technical knowledge needed to fulfill civic responsibilities, improve the student's own health and life, and ability to cope with an increasingly technological world
- Means for judging the worth of articles presenting scientific conclusions

The NSB report continues by saying that materials to achieve these outcomes must be developed and tests devised to measure the degree to which these goals are met. The section then concludes with a summary statement of the goals.

In summary, students who have progressed through the Nation's school systems should be able to use both the knowledge and products of science, mathematics and technology in their thinking, their lives and their work. They should be able to make informed choices regarding their own health and lifestyles based on evidence and reasonable personal preferences, after taking into consideration short- and long-term risks and benefits of different decisions. They should also be prepared to make similarly informed choices in the social and political arenas (NSB, 1983, p. 45).

The goal statement is finally extended to the curriculum.

New science curricula that incorporate appropriate scientific and technological knowledge and are oriented toward practical issues are needed. They also will provide an excellent way of fostering traditional basic skills. The introduction of practical problems which require the collection of data, the communication of results and ideas and the formulation and testing of solutions or improvement would: (1) improve the use and understanding of calculation and mathematical analysis; (2) sharpen the student's ability to communicate verbally and to write precisely; (3) develop problem-solving skills; (4) impart scientific concepts and facts that can be related to practical applications; (5) develop a respect for science and technology and more generally for quantitative observation and thinking; and (6) stimulate an interest in many to enter scientific, engineering, and technical careers (NSB, 1983, p. 45).

The need to develop a new reform for goals is based on the national standards that education in science and technology should be grounded on recent advances in scientific and technologic disciplines, needs and aspirations of society, and the interrelationship of science, technology, and society.

First and foremost is the need to develop a contemporary perspective of goals for science and technology education. There have been tremendous advances in science, changes in social needs, and newly recognized interactions between science and society. These changes have been generally recognized in the goals expressed in the *National Science Education Standards* (NRC, 1996) and *Benchmarks for Science Literacy* (AAAS, 1993).

Science Education in Secondary Schools

The science curriculum in secondary schools is largely determined at the state and local levels by science teachers, science supervisors, administrators, and school boards (Council of Chief State School Officers [CCSSO], 2000). Research studies supported by the NSF have shown that even with significant autonomy there is considerable uniformity of science programs nationwide, and curriculum and methods of instruction have not changed significantly (Mullis & Jenkins, 1988; Weiss, 1978, 1987; Weiss, Banilower, McMahon, & Smith, 2001).

SCIENCE COURSES

Typically, the science curriculum presents general or earth science at the ninth grade, biology at the tenth grade, and chemistry and physics at the eleventh and twelfth grades, respectively. In 1978, the largest science enrollment in junior high schools was general science, with approximately 5 million students. Another 2 million students in schools with grades 7–12 or 9–12 were also enrolled in general science. Earth science enrollments were approximately 1.25 million. Enrollments did not change substantially in a decade, although they changed in the late 1980s due to the emergence of middle schools (Bybee et al., 1990). General biology is offered to all students and enrolls approximately 3 million students each year. About 80 percent of graduating seniors have taken high school biology. However, this statistic is misleading and has an important bearing on reform of science education at the secondary level. For 50 percent of high school students who graduate each year, biology is their last experience with any science course. High school chemistry and physics courses are generally perceived as college preparatory, as are the majority of other courses offered in the high school curriculum. As a result, many students lack an understanding of physical science. This observation is supported by results from the Trends in International Mathematics and Science Study (U.S. Department of Education, 1996).

TEXTBOOKS

The nature of the high school science curriculum can be determined by examining textbooks for the respective disciplines. The similarity among textbooks for a discipline—and even among textbooks for different disciplines—is remarkable. These characteristics include presenting a significant number of facts in simple and condensed form and an emphasis on extensive vocabulary and technical terms. In addition to being encyclopedic, science texts currently in use implicitly suggest a pedagogy of *inform, verify,* and *practice.* The NSF materials developed in the 1960s and 1970s espoused goals of understanding conceptual schemes (the structure of disciplines) and using scientific processes (the modes of inquiry); changes in textbooks and, subsequently, teaching evolved in different directions. For example, reviews of the inquiry goal in science teaching found that teachers give little attention to inquiry and associated skills (Costenson & Lawson, 1986).

STUDENT ACHIEVEMENT

The need for contemporary reform is supported by poor student achievement in science that was first recorded in the 1960s. In 1988, Ina Mullis and Lynn Jenkins summarized two decades of results from the National Assessment of Educational Progress (NAEP) in the *Science Report Card.* Following are summaries of achievement for 17-year-olds, that is, those students leaving high school.

1. At age 17, students' science achievement was well below those of students graduating in 1969. Steady declines occurred throughout the 1970s, followed by an upturn in performance between 1982 and 1986.
2. More than half of the nation's 17-year-olds were inadequately prepared for jobs that require technical skills or for specialized on-the-job training. The thinking skills and science knowledge possessed by high school students in the 1980s were inadequate for participation in the nation's civic affairs.
3. Only 7 percent of the nation's 17-year-olds had the prerequisite knowledge and skills to perform well in college-level science courses.

The NAEP completed assessments in 1996, 2000, and 2005. The national results present achievement levels for students in grades 4, 8, and 12. The National Assessment Governing Board (NAGB) set student performance standards (Bourque, Champagne, & Crissman, 1997; NCES, 2001). The levels of student performance are reported as *basic, proficient,* and *advanced.*

How did American students do? In 1996, 3 percent of the nation's students reached the *advanced* level at all three grades—4, 8, and 12. In the year 2000, 3 percent of the nation's fourth and eighth graders reached the *advanced* level. Only 2 percent of twelfth graders reached such levels.

Twenty-six percent of fourth- and eighth-grade students and 18 percent of twelfth-grade students performed within the *proficient* level. Again, in 2000, fourth graders remained the same—26 percent were *proficient*. Eighth graders had 28 percent proficiency in 2000 compared to 26 percent in 1996. The percent of twelfth graders who were *proficient* dropped from 19 percent in 1996 to 16 percent in 2000. Thirty-eight percent, 32 percent, and 36 percent performed within the *basic* level for grades 4, 8, and 12, respectively. In 2000, these percentages were 37 percent, 29 percent, and 34 percent, respectively. Concerning the results at the *basic* level, we can look at these results another way; namely, how many students were *below basic levels*. The answer is both disappointing and a challenge for science teachers. Respectively, 33 percent, 39 percent, and 43 percent of fourth-, eighth-, and twelfth-grade students were *below basic levels* of achievement in 1996. In the year 2000, these percentages were 34 percent, 39 percent, and 47 percent for grades 4, 8, and 12, respectively. These results are summarized in Figure 5–1.

Compared to middle and high school students, younger students are making the most progress in science. In 2005, a representative sample of more than 300,000 students in grades 4, 8, and 12 were assessed in science. This website presents national results for all three grades, and state results for grades 4 and 8. The 2005 results are compared to those from 1996 and 2000. Sample questions are presented to illustrate the types of skills and knowledge that were assessed at each grade. Aspects of schooling—such as teachers' time spent on instruction, teachers' preparation, and courses taken by students—are also reported.

At grade 4, the average science score was higher in 2005 than in earlier years. The percentage of students performing at or above the *basic* achievement level increased from 63 percent in 1996 to 68 percent in 2005. An example of the knowledge associated with the *basic* level is identifying two organs in the human body that work together to supply oxygen. Twenty-nine percent performed at or above the *proficient* level. Relating the amount of time a candle burns to the amount of air available is an example of the knowledge and skills at the *proficient* level. At grade 8, there was no overall improvement. In 2005, 59 percent of students scored at or above the *basic* level. An example of the knowledge and skills at the *basic* level is being able to compare changes in heart rate during and after exercise. Twenty-nine percent performed at or above the *proficient* level. Identifying the energy conversions that occur in an electric

fan is an example of the knowledge and skills at the *proficient* level.

At grade 12, the average score declined since 1996. In 2005, 54 percent of students scored at or above the *basic* level. Knowing the function of a neuron is an example of knowledge at the *basic* level. Eighteen percent performed at or above the *proficient* level. Identifying the source of heat energy released in a combustion reaction is an example of knowledge at the *proficient* level (NAEP, 2006).

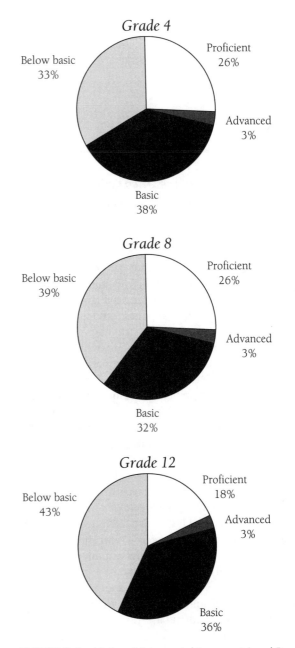

FIGURE 5–1   National Science Achievement-Level Results
(Source: The Nation's Report Card: Science Highlights 2000.)

FIGURE 5–2 Summary of NAEP Science Results at Grades 4, 8, 12

(*Source:* U.S. Department of Education, Institute of Education Sciences, National Center for Education Statistics, National Assessment of Educational Progress (NAEP), 1996, 2000, and 2005 Science Assessments.)

	4th Grade Across the board improvements		8th Grade Scores remain flat		12th Grade Scores steady from 2000, but lower than in 1996	
	Since 1996	Since 2000	Since 1996	Since 2000	Since 1996	Since 2000
Overall	↑	↑	↔	↔	↓	↔
White	↑	↑	↔	↔	↔	↔
Black	↑	↑	↑	↔	↔	↔
Hispanic	↑	↑	↔	↔	↔	↔
Gaps						
White – Black	↓	↓	↔	↔	↔	↑
White – Hispanic	↔	↓	↔	↔	↔	↔

↑   Indicates the score was higher or the gap increased in 2005

↓   Indicates the score was lower or the gap decreased in 2005

↔   Indicates there was no significant change in the score or the gap in 2005

ACHIEVEMENT OF UNDERREPRESENTED GROUPS

Social and economic realities have influences that far exceed the effect of school in general or a science program in particular. Still, the science program should contribute, in some small measure, to the future opportunities of all students. The NAEP data indicate continued and substantial disparities in science proficiency among groups of differing race, ethnicity, and gender. See Figure 5–2.

International comparisons of student achievement have also been made. In particular, the science education community has been, and will be, influenced by results from the Third International Mathematics and Science Study (TIMSS). This was the largest and most comprehensive comparative international study of education that has ever been undertaken. TIMSS reported results for eighth-grade students in November 1996, fourth-grade students in June 1997, and twelfth-grade students in February 1998. In all, the study assessed a half million students from 41 countries in 30 languages to compare their mathematics and science achievement. In addition to achievement results, TIMSS also included thorough reviews of curriculum materials and instructional methods in the countries. A brief summary of 1996 achievement levels for students in the United States: At fourth grade, our students are above the international average and among the best in the world. At eighth grade, our students are just above average in science and just below average in mathematics. At twelfth grade, U.S. students' performance was among the lowest of the participating countries in mathematics and science general knowledge, physics, and advanced mathematics. These results indicate a steady decline in U.S. students' achievement during their school years.

In 1999, TIMSS was replicated at the eighth grade. Involving 41 countries and testing at five grade levels, TIMSS was originally conducted in 1995 to provide a base from which policy makers, curriculum specialists, and researchers could better understand the performance of their educational systems. Conducted under the auspices of the International Association for the Evaluation of Educational Achievement (IEA), TIMSS was the first step in a long-term strategy, with further assessments in mathematics and science planned for 2003 and beyond.

TIMSS 1999, also known as TIMSS-Repeat or TIMSS-R, was designed to provide trends in eighth-grade mathematics and science achievement in an international context. Thirty-eight countries participated in TIMSS 1999. Of these, 26 countries also participated in TIMSS 1995 at the eighth grade and have trend data included in this report. Also, 1999 represents four years since the first TIMSS, and the population of students originally assessed as fourth graders had advanced to the eighth grade. Thus, for 17 of the 26 countries that participated in TIMSS 1995 at the fourth grade, TIMSS 1999 also provides information about whether the relative performance of these students has changed in the intervening years.

Six content areas were covered in the TIMSS 1999 science test: earth science, life science, physics, chemistry, environmental and resource issues, and scientific inquiry and the nature of science. About one-fourth of the questions were in the free-response format, requiring students to generate and write their answers. The achievement data are accompanied by extensive questionnaire data about the home, classroom, school, and national contexts within which science learning takes place (Martin, Mullis, et al., 2000).

U.S. students scored above the international average in both mathematics and science at the fourth-grade level. At the eighth-grade level, U.S. students performed above the international average in science and below the international average in mathematics. In the final year of secondary school (twelfth grade in the United States), U.S. performance was among the lowest in both science and mathematics, including among our most advanced students (Gonzales, Calsyn, et al., 2000).

It is also important to be aware of the Programme for International Student Assessment (PISA). Although not as popular as TIMSS in the United States, PISA is having an international impact.

The results of NAEP, TIMSS, and PISA provide substantial evidence that our educational system is not attaining the goal of scientific literacy. Indeed, it is failing to provide our students an adequate science education. The twelfth-grade students who did most poorly on TIMSS entered school in the late 1980s. Their science education consisted of traditional textbooks and instructional methods, and their achievement is dismal. Indeed, it was the worst in the world. The national and international results show that American science education needs improvement. Further, the TIMSS results also provide some indications of how we should reform curriculum, instruction, and assessments (Schmidt, McKnight, & Raizen, 1997; Schmidt et al., 1998; Valverde & Schmidt, 1997–98; Schmidt et al., 1996).

Trends in Secondary School Science

There is widespread support for continued improvement of the educational system. Scientific and technological literacy is the main purpose of science education in grades K through 12. This goal is for all students, not just for those individuals destined for careers in science and engineering.

In the early decades of the twenty-first century, the curriculum for science education at the secondary school level is not meeting the challenge of achieving scientific and technological literacy. Many scientists and science educators are urging a review of school science programs, a review that would affect millions of school personnel in thousands of autonomous school districts, but one that is necessary. Increasing the scientific and technological literacy of students also requires several fundamental changes in science curricula at the secondary school level. First, the information presented must be balanced with key conceptual themes that are learned in some depth. Second, the rigid disciplinary boundaries of earth science, biology, chemistry, and physics should be softened; greater emphasis should also be placed on connections among the sciences and among disciplines generally thought of as outside of school science, such as technology, mathematics, ethics, and social studies (Confrey, 1990; Newmann, 1988).

Achieving the goal of scientific and technological literacy requires more than understanding concepts and processes of science and technology. Indeed, the need exists for citizens to understand science and technology as an integral part of society. Science and technology are enterprises that shape, and are shaped by, human thought and social actions (Bybee, 1987; Yager, 1996). Our recommendation includes some understanding of the nature and history of science and technology. There is recent and substantial support for this recommendation, though few curriculum materials. Including the nature and history of science and technology provides opportunities to focus on topics that blur disciplinary boundaries and show connections between such fields as science and social studies.

The substantial body of research on learning should be the basis for making instruction more effective (Bransford et al., 2000; Tobin, Tippins, & Gallard, 1994). This research suggests that students learn by constructing their own meaning of the experiences they have. A constructivist approach requires varied methods of science instruction in the secondary school (Driver & Oldham, 1986; Sachse, 1989; Watson & Konicek, 1990; Bruer, 1994; McGilly, 1995; Bransford et al., 2000).

Related to the implications of research on learning theory is the recommendation that science teaching should consist of experiences exemplifying the spirit, character, and nature of science and technology. Students should begin with questions about the natural world (science) and problems about human beings adapting (technology). They should be actively involved in the processes of inquiry and design. They should have opportunities to present their explanations for phenomena and solutions to problems and to compare their explanations and solutions to those concepts of science and technology. They should have a chance to apply their understandings in new situations, as well. In short, the inquiry-oriented laboratory is an infrequent experience for secondary school students, but it should be a central part of their experience in science education. Extensive use of the inquiry-oriented laboratory is consistent with the other recommendations made in this section, and it has widespread support.

The issue of equity must be addressed in science programs and by school personnel. For the past several decades, science educators at all levels have discussed the importance of changing science programs to enhance opportunities for historically underrepresented groups. Calls for scientific and technological literacy assume the inclusion of *all* Americans. Other justifications—if any are needed for this position—include the supply of future scientists and engineers, changing demographics, and prerequisites for work. Research results, curricula recommendations, and practical suggestions are available to those developing science curricula for the secondary school (Gardner, Mason, & Matyas, 1989; Linn & Hyde, 1989; Malcom, 1990; Oakes, 1990).

Science education in middle schools is a special concern as educators look toward achieving higher levels of scientific literacy. Numerous reports and commissions have addressed the need for educational reform for high school science education, but few have specifically recognized the emergence of middle schools in the 1980s. The movement toward implementing middle schools, and phasing out junior high schools, was a significant trend in education. Yet, thus far, the middle school reform has not thoroughly addressed the particular issues of subject-matter disciplines—in this case, science and technology. Contemporary reform must not allow the science education of early adolescents to be overlooked or assumed to be part of either the elementary school or secondary school curriculum.

Improving curriculum and instruction will be a hollow gesture without concomitant changes in assessment at all levels, from the local classroom to the national and international levels. In general, the changes in assessment practices must reflect the changes described earlier for curriculum and instruction. Incongruities, such as teaching fewer concepts in greater depth but testing for numerous facts in fine detail, will undermine the reform of science education. New forms of assessment are available and being recommended by researchers, policy makers, and practitioners (Frederiksen & Collins, 1989; Murnane & Raizen, 1988; Shavelson, Carey, & Webb, 1990).

Reform of science education at the secondary school level must be viewed as part of the general reform of education. Approaching the improvement of science education by changing textbooks, buying new computers, or adding new courses simply will not work. Fortunately, widespread educational reform, which includes science education, is underway. The improvement of science education in the secondary school must be part of the reconstruction of science education for K–12 and must include all courses and students, a staff development program, reform of science teacher preparation, and support from school administrators. This comprehensive or systemic recommendation is based on the research on implementation (Fullan, 2001; Hall, 1989) and research literature on school change and restructuring.

Early in the twenty-first century we think the improvement of science education is a national mandate. You will be a part of that process. Although the challenge is large, we have clear guidance in national standards and benchmarks. These guidelines will be followed through changes in instructional materials and increased support of professional development to help science teachers improve. We have all the tools for the job; now we need commitment at the local, state, and national levels.

SUMMARY

The need for changes in secondary school science programs became increasingly evident midway through the twentieth century. A number of forces produced conditions that affected the curriculum. The rapid increase in scientific knowledge, the competitive nature of the race for space, technological advancements in teaching tools, a gradual dissatisfaction with the encyclopedic approach to the teaching of science, and new understandings of student learning and development combined to encourage changes.

In the 1950s and 1960s, the first secondary science curriculum course to react to these pressures was physics, followed by chemistry, biology, and junior high science, in that order. New courses for all these subjects appeared, stimulated by massive financial support from the National Science Foundation and other agencies.

Students of the investigative sciences were given opportunities for increased laboratory work and application of inquiry methods for learning. They were directed to better understandings of how scientists work and how knowledge is obtained.

The reform reached further than the materials developed under National Science Foundation grants. Authors of popular science textbooks incorporated many aspects of the new science materials.

In the late 1960s and early 1970s, problems in urban environments began to influence science programs. By the mid-1970s, a new set of social forces redirected the attention of science educators: population growth, pollution, economic problems, and energy and resource shortages.

The 1980s witnessed increasing support for educational reform, including science education. By the 1990s, general calls for reform had become more focused on national, state, and local standards. The *National Science Education Standards* and *Benchmarks for Science Literacy* established a solid foundation for achieving higher levels of science literacy.

This historical survey has shown the changes in science education resulting from the needs and demands of society. It seems that a clear relationship exists between social needs and the type of curricula and instruction that science educators are called on to provide in our schools. The major social pressures have been the early development of a nation, growth of an industrial-technological society, demands of a depressed economy, emergence of an atomic age, start of the space race, and the recent appearance of alienation and anxiety.

CHAPTER 6

CONTEMPORARY ISSUES IN SCIENCE EDUCATION

This chapter is divided into two major sections. In the first section we elaborate on the idea of scientific literacy. The second section of the chapter reviews several trends and issues that present a contemporary perspective on science teaching.

SCIENTIFIC LITERACY

Your goal as a science teacher is to help individuals achieve higher levels of scientific literacy. Most directly, this goal applies to your students, but it also applies to professional colleagues, parents, and community. In this section, we first elaborate the idea of scientific literacy and then establish the connection between the general idea of scientific literacy and your specific need to teach students science in a manner that helps them to become more scientifically literate. One author of this textbook, Rodger Bybee, has written *Achieving Scientific Literacy: From Purposes to Practices* (Bybee, 1997). You may wish to refer to this book for a more detailed discussion of scientific literacy.

The Purpose of Science Education: Scientific Literacy

In Chapter 1, we introduced *scientific literacy* as the term used to express the major purposes of science education. In fact, we went a step beyond this definition and suggested that you could define some aspects of scientific literacy by answering the question, "What should the scientifically and technologically literate person know, value, and do—as a citizen?" In answering

this question you should note several things. First, the question includes both science and technology. Second, the question includes knowledge, values, and skills. Third, and very important, the question asks to justify the answer in terms of citizenship.

In the history of science education, many individuals have addressed the goals of science teaching and the idea of scientific literacy (DeBoer, 1991; Bybee & DeBoer, 1993). In Tables 6–1, 6–2, and 6–3, we present discussions of scientific literacy so you can see what others have included in the translation of the idea to actual topics or themes for school science programs.

Scientific literacy expresses general education purposes of a science education. The goal represents an orientation of the science curriculum and instructional practices that includes experiences and outcomes for all students. You should contrast the general education orientation with a specific or vocational education that would orient school science programs toward the knowledge, values, and skills required in scientific and technological careers.

Note the domains of scientific literacy described in Table 6–3. These domains parallel content in the *National Science Education Standards* and the *Benchmarks for Science Literacy*. In Table 6–4, we summarize the content from these two documents. This summary of two reports provides a contemporary description of the domains of scientific literacy.

The Domains of Scientific Literacy

Clearly, scientific literacy includes *more* than the knowledge, values, and skills associated with a specific discipline

TABLE 6–1   Characteristics of Scientific Literacy: The 1960s

National Science Teachers Association Theory into Practice (1964) Conceptual Schemes	National Science Teachers Association Theory into Practice (1964) Processes of Science	Milton Pella (1967)
(1) All matter is composed of units called *fundamental particles;* under certain conditions these particles can be transformed into energy and vice versa. (2) Matter exists in the form of units that can be classified into hierarchies of organizational levels. (3) The behavior of matter in the universe can be described on a statistical basis. (4) Units of matter interact. The basis of all ordinary interactions are electro-magnetic, gravitational, and nuclear forces. (5) All interacting units of matter tend toward equilibrium states in which the energy content (enthalpy) is a minimum and the energy distribution (entropy) is most random. In the process of attaining equilibrium, energy transformations or matter transformations occur; nevertheless, the sum of energy and matter in the universe remains constant. (6) One of the forms of energy is the motion of units of matter. Such motion is responsible for heat and temperature and for the states of matter: solid, liquid, and gaseous. (7) All matter exists in time and space, and since interactions occur among its units, matter is subject in some degree to changes with time. Such changes may occur at various rates and in various patterns.	(1) Science proceeds on the assumption, based on centuries-old experience, that the universe is not capricious. (2) Scientific knowledge is based on observation of samples of matter that are accessible to public investigation in contrast to purely private inspection. (3) Science proceeds in a piecemeal manner, even though it also aims at achieving a systematic and comprehensive understanding of various sectors or aspects of nature. (4) Science is not, and will probably never be, a finished enterprise, and there remains much more to be discovered about how things in the universe behave and how they are interrelated. (5) Measurement is an important feature of most branches of modern science because the formulation, as well as the establishment, of laws are facilitated through the development of quantitative distinctions.	(1) Interrelationships between science and society (2) Ethics of science (3) Nature of science (4) Conceptual knowledge (5) Science and technology (6) Science in the humanities

TABLE 6–2   Characteristics of Scientific Literacy: The 1970s

Michael Agin (1974)	Victor Showalter (1974)	Benjamin Shen (1974)
(1) Science and Society (2) Ethics of Science (3) Nature of Science (4) Knowledge of the Concepts of Science (5) Science and Technology (6) Science and the Humanities	(1) Nature of Science (2) Concepts in Science (3) Processes of Science (4) Values of Science (5) Science and Society (6) Interest in Science (7) Skills Associated with Science	(1) Practical Science Literacy (2) Civic Science Literacy (3) Cultural Science Literacy

TABLE 6–3   Characteristics of Scientific Literacy: The 1980s

National Science Teachers Association, Science-Technology-Society: Science Education for the 1980s (NSTA, 1982)	National Commission on Excellence in Education, A Nation at Risk (NCEE, 1983)	Improving Indicators of the Quality of Science and Mathematics Education in Grades K–12, (Murnane & Raizen, 1988)	American Association for the Advancement of Science, Science for All Americans (AAAS, 1989)
(1) Scientific and technological process and inquiry skills	(1) Concepts, laws, and processes of physical and biological sciences	(1) The nature of the scientific worldview	(1) The nature of science
(2) Scientific and technological knowledge	(2) Methods of scientific inquiry and reasoning	(2) The nature of the scientific enterprise	(2) The nature of mathematics
(3) Skills and knowledge of science and technology in personal and social decisions	(3) Applications of knowledge to everyday life	(3) Scientific habits of mind	(3) The nature of technology
(4) Attitudes, values, and appreciation of science and technology	(4) Social and environmental implications of scientific and technological development	(4) Science and human affairs	(4) The physical setting
(5) Interactions among science-technology-society via context of science-related societal issues			(5) The living environment
			(6) The human organism
			(7) Human society
			(8) The designed world
			(9) The mathematical world
			(10) Historical perspectives
			(11) Common themes
			(12) Habits of mind

TABLE 6–4   Content Summary for the National Science Education Standards and Benchmarks for Science Literacy

National Science Education Standards	Benchmarks for Science Literacy
Unifying Concepts and Processes	The Nature of Science
Science as Inquiry	The Nature of Mathematics
Physical Science	The Nature of Technology
Life Science	The Physical Setting
Earth and Space Science	The Living Environment
Science and Technology	The Human Organism
Science in Personal and Social Perspectives	Human Society
History and Nature of Science	The Designed World
	The Mathematical World
	Historical Perspectives
	Common Themes
	Habits of Mind

such as biology or chemistry. Concepts associated with scientific disciplines must be included, but students also should develop understandings and abilities associated with scientific inquiry and technological design, as well as understandings associated with personal and social aspects of science, the history and nature of science, and major unifying ideas of the sciences. Table 6–5 should help clarify the different domains of content associated with scientific literacy. We adapted the model for this framework from original work of Mortimer Adler and the *Paideia Proposal* (Adler, 1982). Also note that the content parallels the *National Science Education Standards* and, with some modification of titles, *Benchmarks for Science Literacy.*

The framework for scientific literacy (see Table 6–5) depicts three columns, each with a distinctive orientation for content. As the elements of this framework might be translated to curriculum and instruction, you should recognize that all three columns are essential to the development of scientific literacy. You might also note the parallel between the earlier question— "What should the scientifically and technologically literate person know, value, and do—as a citizen?"—and the three different columns. We suggest that the development of scientific literacy includes the acquisition of organized knowledge, the development of intellectual abilities and manipulative skills, and the enlarged understanding of ideas and values.

TABLE 6–5   A Framework for the Content of Scientific Literacy

Goal	Acquisition of Organized Knowledge	Development of Intellectual Abilities and Manipulative Skills	Enlarged Understanding of Ideas and Values
Domains of Content	*In the Subject Matter of* Physical Science Life Science Earth Science Unifying Concepts Nature of Science and Technology	*In the Processes of* Scientific Inquiry and Technological Design	*In the Contexts of* Personal Matters Social Challenges Historical Perspectives Cultural Perspectives

Column one centers on the acquisition of knowledge in five domains—physical sciences, life sciences, earth sciences, unifying concepts in the sciences, and the nature of science and technology. It is important to note that these are domains of knowledge and not necessarily the curriculum or courses of study for middle and high school science. In fact, the science curriculum should include content from all three columns and may have an emphasis on social challenges, inquiry, or an integrated approach to science content (Roberts, 1982).

Why these five domains of science content? There are several reasons. First, these domains, especially the physical, life, and earth sciences, have a tradition as branches of the sciences. These are generic in that more specific branches, such as particle physics and molecular biology, could be included but are not emphasized for educational purposes. Unifying concepts include scientific ideas, such as Isaac Newton's laws of force and motion, the laws of thermodynamics governing energy and entropy, and the atomic structure of matter, that can provide connection among the traditional subject-matter domains. Science teachers can use the unifying concepts to show the interconnectedness and interdependence among the sciences and to develop understanding of the larger theories of science. Unifying concepts become especially useful in many research studies and in developing explanations for such things as social challenges and health issues. Science education programs traditionally have done little to help students understand the nature of science and technology, yet this understanding (or lack of it) relates to many discussions of the role, limits, and possibilities of science and technology in society.

Second, you will notice that these domains provide linkage between the national standards and benchmarks. Finally, it is important to see students acquiring scientific knowledge as a part of developing scientific literacy. Some educators have interpreted the constructivist approach as acceptance of students' explanations as scientific. This view fails to recognize the body of knowledge recognized as science and to view scientific literacy as the students' development of explanations more closely aligned with those we recognize as scientific.

Column two emphasizes the development of skills and abilities associated with scientific inquiry and technological design. If you examine the national standards for *Science as Inquiry* and *Science and Technology,* you will notice the specific cognitive abilities related to inquiry and design (see Figures 6–1 and 6–2).

Using science as the example, abilities include applying science processes (observing, inferring, experimenting, classifying, controlling variables), constructing scientific explanations (interpreting data, using critical thinking and logic to link evidence to explanation, formulating models, defining operationally), recognizing alternative explanations (maintaining an open mind, accepting the tentative nature of explanations, being skeptical), and communicating (reading, writing, speaking, listening).

If column one is know-about, column two is know-how. In column two, the learning outcomes indicate that students know how to do scientific investigations and technologic problem solving. The skills and abilities proposed in column two have very close connections with the domains of science outlined in column one. Developing scientific literacy includes developing the intellectual skills and abilities outlined in column two. If we wish students to acquire and use these skills, they must have experience doing investigations in science classrooms. That is to say, these skills must be a part of the students' science education. The method of teaching these skills cannot be lecture; rather, students must be engaged in investigations, and the science teacher should act as a coach, helping students to acquire the best techniques, pointing out strengths and weaknesses, giving directions, demonstrating the right moves, and sequencing actions to achieve a goal.

The innovative aspect of this domain consists of having students engage in inquiry and design. Most evidence indicates that students have few such experiences in their science education (Costenson & Lawson, 1986; Weiss et al., 2001; 2003). From your point of view as a science teacher, implementing the standards implies innovations through combinations of such teaching strategies and good coaching.

FIGURE 6–1 Abilities of Scientific Inquiry

By the end of eighth grade, all students should have developed the following abilities of scientific inquiry:

- Identify questions that can be answered through scientific investigations.
- Design and conduct a scientific investigation.
- Use appropriate tools and techniques to gather, analyze, and interpret data.
- Develop descriptions, explanations, predictions, and models using evidence.
- Think critically and logically to make the relationships between evidence and explanations.
- Recognize and analyze alternative explanations and predictions.
- Use mathematics in all aspects of scientific inquiry.

By the end of high school, all students should have developed the following abilities of scientific inquiry:

- Ask and identify questions and concepts to guide scientific investigations.
- Design and conduct scientific investigations.
- Use appropriate technology and mathematics to enhance investigations.
- Formulate and revise explanations and models.
- Analyze alternative explanations and models.
- Accurately and effectively communicate results and respond appropriately to critical comments.
- Generate additional testable questions.

- **Identify a problem or design an opportunity.** Students should be able to identify new problems or needs and have the ability to change and improve current technological designs.
- **Propose designs and choose between alternative solutions.** Students should demonstrate thoughtful planning for a piece of technology or technique.
- **Implement a proposed solution.** A variety of skills can be needed depending on the type of technology that is involved. The construction of artifacts can require the skills of cutting, shaping, or forming; treating; and joining common materials, such as wood, metal, plastics, and textiles.
- **Evaluate the solution and its consequences.** Students should test any solution against the needs or criteria it was designed to meet. At this stage students may review new criteria not originally considered.
- **Communicate the problem, process, and solution.** Students should present their results in a variety of ways, such as orally to other students, in writing, and in a variety of forms, including models, diagrams, and demonstrations.

FIGURE 6–2 Abilities of Technological Design

The content in column three provides important contexts for teaching and learning science. Whereas column one is know-about and column two is know-how, column three is know-why. Recall that scientific literacy places science in the context of history, society, and individual decisions. The content of column three engages students in content that provides meaning for science knowledge and intellectual skills. It is here, as students encounter the personal and social contexts of science, that they will recognize the ideas and values of science and further develop their own ideas and values. The development of understanding occurs because students have to use their knowledge and skills to respond to the proposed challenges of understanding science and technology in their own lives, in societal problems, in historical contexts, and in different cultures.

The content of column three serves the purpose of developing scientific literacy, because the topics require students to use their intellectual skills and scientific knowledge as they examine and analyze various positions. Sometimes those positions present a marked difference from their own. They become aware of their own ideas and values of science and technology. To help fulfill the requirements of citizenship, the content of column three requires students to correct misconceptions and improve their understanding of science and technology.

The Dimensions of Scientific Literacy

Developing scientific literacy is a lifelong goal for all individuals. Many discussions of scientific literacy use the terms and various domains we have described as a goal that one achieves or does not. It is the either/or, all-or-none position one often hears. It is much more helpful to recognize that all of your students occupy positions somewhere on a continuum of literacy for various scientific concepts. It also seems clear that one can associate different levels of understanding with scientific concepts. For example, students might correctly spell and use the word *cell* in a simple sentence; however, the same students might not recognize several other important concepts about cells, for example, that they convey information and reproduce. Further, what if you asked these students about the function of cells in cancer and they indicated that they had no idea about the relationship? Well, what would you say—are these students scientifically literate? If you look at the situation using a strict definition of literacy, one would have to say they are scientifically literate for this life science topic. What about the fact that the same students did not understand the structure and function of cells or the fact that cells have a role in cancer? It might be easier to use the either/or approach to scientific literacy, but it will probably not be helpful in deciding what to do to further these students' understanding of cells and other domains of science.

As a science teacher you should help students advance their scientific understandings and abilities. In order to help you, we provide a model of different dimensions of scientific literacy. In the following descriptions note that these dimensions are not developmental levels, nor do they represent a teaching sequence. These are different dimensions of scientific literacy that you should be aware of, as they relate to your decisions about how to structure lessons and units for your classes and how to respond to individual students who indicate a lack of understanding.

SCIENTIFIC ILLITERACY

In this model, some individuals may be scientifically illiterate because of age, stage of development, or impaired cognitive abilities. These students are small in number and for various reasons will probably not be in your science classroom. The indicator of scientific illiteracy is they cannot relate or respond to a reasonable question about science. They do not have the vocabulary, concepts, contexts, or cognitive capacity to identify the question as scientific.

NOMINAL SCIENTIFIC LITERACY

Suppose you begin a lesson on force and soon discover that students' statements about force indicate that they think force is a property of the moving object. They make statements such as, "A moving object has a force inside it; that is what makes it move." You try to introduce the idea that force is not a property of an object, but forces are characteristics of action between objects. Still, the students' ideas persist. These students exemplify nominal scientific literacy for the concept of force. The example comes from *Making Sense of Secondary Science* (Driver, Squires, Rushworth, & Wood-Robinson, 1994). The students understood the topic as scientific, but the level of understanding clearly indicates a misconception. You should recognize that such examples will be evident in your class and that they will usually express the students' current understanding.

FUNCTIONAL SCIENTIFIC LITERACY

Students may know scientific terms through other science classes, television, or reading. Students can memorize appropriate definitions of terms, and in this sense have some scientific knowledge, but they have limited knowledge and lack a full scientific understanding. Science textbooks and programs that exclusively emphasize rote memorization lead to functional levels of scientific literacy. Unfortunately, this has been the emphasis of many science textbooks and classrooms, and the result is emphasis on only one dimension of scientific literacy. Teaching that emphasizes functional scientific literacy leaves students with little or no understanding of the discipline, no experience with the excitement of inquiry, and probably little interest in science.

CONCEPTUAL AND PROCEDURAL SCIENTIFIC LITERACY

In this dimension, students develop some understanding of the conceptual schemes of a discipline related to the whole discipline. They begin to understand central ideas such as matter, energy, and motion in physical sciences and evolution in biological sciences.

Procedural abilities and understandings include the processes of scientific inquiry and technological design. Students actually have ability and understand that scientific inquiry includes asking questions, designing scientific investigations, using appropriate tools and techniques, developing explanations and models using evidence, thinking critically and logically about the relationship between evidence and explanation, recognizing alternative explanations, and communicating scientific procedures and explanations.

MULTIDIMENSIONAL SCIENTIFIC LITERACY

This perspective of scientific literacy incorporates an understanding of science that extends beyond the concepts of scientific disciplines and procedures of scientific investigation. It includes philosophical,

FIGURE 6–3 Dimensions of Scientific Literacy

Nominal Scientific Literacy

- Identifies terms, questions, as scientific but demonstrates incorrect topics, issues, information, knowledge, or understanding.
- Has misconceptions of scientific concepts and processes.
- Gives inadequate and inappropriate explanations of scientific phenomena.
- Expresses scientific principles in a naive manner.

Functional Scientific Literacy

- Uses scientific vocabulary.
- Defines scientific terms correctly.
- Memorizes technical words.

Conceptual and Procedural Scientific Literacy

- Understands conceptual schemes of science.
- Understands procedural knowledge and skills of science.
- Understands relationships among the parts of a science discipline and the conceptual structure of the discipline.
- Understands organizing principles and processes of science.

Multidimensional Scientific Literacy

- Understands the unique qualities of science.
- Differentiates science from other disciplines.
- Knows the history and nature of science disciplines.
- Understands science in a social context.

historical, and social dimensions of science and technology. Here students develop some understanding and appreciation of science and technology as they have been and are a part of the culture. Students begin to make connections within scientific disciplines, between science and technology, and between science and technology and the larger issues of social challenges.

Although a number of individuals have presented frameworks for scientific literacy that incorporate the dimensions just described (Pella, O'Hearn, & Gale, 1966; Agin, 1974; Showalter, 1974; Murnane & Raizen, 1988), two examples dominate the contemporary scene in science education, the *National Science Education Standards* and the *Benchmarks for Science Literacy*. Figure 6–3 summarizes the dimensions of scientific literacy.

CONTEMPORARY ISSUES IN SCIENCE EDUCATION

In this section we introduce the *National Science Education Standards* (NRC, 1996). We begin with background on the project and then review the project's major goals through a discussion of scientific literacy and the social orientation of national standards. We

then summarize the components of the *National Science Education Standards*. Next, we review Project 2061 and reports on *Science for All Americans* and *Benchmarks for Science Literacy*. Both the *Standards* and *Benchmarks* have had, and will continue to have, a major influence on science education at national, state, and local levels.

BACKGROUND ON NATIONAL STANDARDS

The National Council of Teachers of Mathematics (NCTM) introduced the word *standards* into the public dialogue on education when they published *Curriculum and Evaluation Standards for School Mathematics* in 1989. This statement of a profession's vision for what students should know and be able to do as a result of their mathematics education identified educational goals and provided a means of helping teachers of mathematics achieve them.

In the late 1980s and 1990s, politicians in the United States expressed their intense interest in improving education. This was symbolized by the *National Education Goals* created by President George Bush and the nation's governors, with leadership from then-governor Bill

GUEST EDITORIAL ◆ JEFF MOW

Science Education Student
Environmental Education
Carleton College, Northfield, Minnesota

ENVIRONMENTAL EDUCATION AND SCIENCE TEACHING

As a junior at Carleton College, I am just beginning my career in science education. Originally a Geology major, later I changed to Environmental Education. As I completed a science methods course, I realized that the informal teaching and educational opportunities found outdoors have the most meaning for me. I would like to be an outdoor educator or perhaps a visiting teacher and curriculum developer. One reason for this choice is that I have a strong interest in geology and would like to explore the career opportunities in this field. Another reason is that I have been teaching and developing curriculum materials for the U.S. Geological Survey. Because of this opportunity, I have already been exposed to some novel approaches to environmental education. This experience, in conjunction with my own personal education and teacher training, has made me think about issues in environmental education.

The first question I have is, "What is environmental education?" A common conception of environmental education is that it is recreationally oriented. Also, environmental programs often offer such a different subject-matter focus that students are unable to relate the environmental activity to an everyday experience such as going to school. This lack of integration often results in an ineffective environmental program. Is environmental education going hiking in the woods, viewing a film on pollution, or hugging a tree? Or is environmental education calculating the rate of erosion on a poorly managed farm field or making physical measurements of the forest regeneration process? I think that environmental education should take the latter form, as it allows students to integrate concepts learned in the classroom with an actual life experience. I also think that it is important that the outdoor experience can and should be used as a laboratory; that is, "a classroom without walls." I have developed and taught a map unit of the U.S. Geological Survey in which I have secondary students make detailed maps of their local environment. When I first taught this course, many of the students took the opportunity to run off. Since then, I have learned that for the exercise to be successful, I have to lay down some initial ground rules. The result of outlining my expectations of them is that I am able to focus the students' activity despite the loss of the classroom's physical constraints. I have found that the environmental activities I have taught have been successful, and I would hope that you might also try this approach.

A much larger issue is the role of science education in our society. My own education and what I have seen in the schools indicate a distinct gap or void between the science taught in the classroom and that encountered in life. As a future science educator, how can I help bridge this gap? For example, in your high school physics course, how much exposure did you have to daily scientific issues such as nuclear technology and electronic technology? A poll of my peers has revealed that these issues were not dealt with and I realized that, in hindsight, they should have been. I believe it is important that, as a future science teacher, I try to relate classroom material to everyday science applications. I think that it is clear that science and technology will be an important factor in solving many of our world's problems and that, as a science teacher, I have the responsibility of creating an increased awareness of the importance of science in our society.

Clinton, in their unprecedented summit in 1989. The *National Education Goals Panel* established the idea of subject-matter standards and performance-based assessments. These bipartisan *National Education Goals* were the basis for the Goals 2000: Educate America Act signed by President Clinton in 1994 (see Figure 6–4 for a summary of these goals).

National standards define expectations and minimal competencies; they set focus and direction. From the beginning of this discussion it is important to understand that *Standards* for science education are policies, not a curriculum; they are national, not federal; they are voluntary, not mandatory; and they are dynamic, not static.

FIGURE 6–4 The National Education Goals. In stressing quality education from early childhood through lifelong learning, the president and the governors adopted the National Education Goals, which became law in 1994 when Congress passed the Goals 2000: Educate America Act

The Goals state that by the year 2000:

1. All children in America will start school ready to learn.
2. The school graduation rate will increase to at least 90 percent.
3. All students will leave grades 4, 8, and 12 having demonstrated competency over challenging subject matter, including English, mathematics, science, foreign languages, civics and government, economics, arts, history, and geography; and every school in America will ensure that all students learn to use their minds well, so they may be prepared for responsible citizenship, further learning, and productive employment in our nation's modern economy.
4. The nation's teaching force will have access to programs for the continued improvement of their professional skills and the opportunity to acquire the knowledge and skills needed to instruct and prepare all American students for the next century.
5. United States students will be the first in the world in mathematics and science achievement.
6. Every adult American will be literate and will possess the knowledge and skills necessary to compete in a global economy and exercise the rights and responsibilities of citizenship.
7. Every school in the United States will be free of drugs, violence, and the unauthorized presence of firearms and alcohol and will offer a disciplined environment conducive to learning.
8. Every school will promote partnerships that will increase parental involvement and participation in promoting the social, emotional, and academic growth of children.

The National Science Education Standards Project

In the spring of 1991, Dr. Bonnie Brunkhorst, the president of the National Science Teachers Association (NSTA), acting on the basis of a unanimous vote of the NSTA board, wrote to the chairman of the National Research Council (NRC) requesting the NRC to convene and coordinate a process leading to national science education standards, grades K through 12. This was seconded by the presidents of several leading science and science education associations, as well as the U. S. secretary of education, the assistant director of education and human resources at the NSF, and the co-chairs of the National Education Goals Panel. The NRC agreed to take the lead, and the U.S. Department of Education provided initial funding. Throughout that autumn the NRC developed a general design and time line for the project, and Dr. James Ebert, vice president of the National Academy of Sciences, was designated chair of a National Committee on Science Education Standards and Assessment (NCSESA). His job was to oversee both development of science education standards and a nationwide critique and consensus process. In early 1994, Dr. Richard Klausner of the National Institutes of Health assumed Dr. Ebert's responsibilities.

As 1992 began, a chair's advisory committee was formed. Consisting of representatives of several national science education organizations, it worked to assist in planning and directing the project. This group participated directly in the process of identifying and recruiting staff.

Early in the project, staff and committee members decided to develop an integrated volume containing content, teaching, and assessment standards, all displayed in mutually reinforcing ways. Another decision involved a serious and extensive critique and consensus process, which would issue frequent updates on the project and materials suitable for intense critique by teachers, educators in colleges and universities, scientists, engineers, policy makers, and others interested in science education. The project released discussion and working papers in October and December of 1992, February 1993, and June 1993. In spring 1994, the NRC prepared a draft copy of standards for internal review. The first integrated draft of content, teaching, assessment, program, and system standards appeared for extensive national review in late 1994, and the *National Science Education Standards* were released in December 1995 with a 1996 copyright (Collins, 1995).

CONTEMPORARY SCIENCE EDUCATION

As you become a professional science teacher you will hear about national standards, federal legislation, national and international assessments, and other policies and programs that influence classroom practices. This section introduces several important policies and programs in contemporary science education. We begin with the *National Science Education Standards* (NRC, 1996).

NATIONAL SCIENCE EDUCATION STANDARDS: AN OVERVIEW

National standards in science education have several functions, depending on who is using them and the purpose for which they are being used. For example, standards can serve as vision, aspiration, and attainment; they also can be used as measures to judge the quality of current science education and criteria to design school science programs.

The *National Science Education Standards* offer a coherent vision of what it means to be scientifically literate. The standards describe what *all* students must understand and be able to do as a result of their cumulative learning experiences. The standards also provide criteria for judgments regarding programs, teaching, assessment, policies, and initiatives that can provide opportunities for all students to learn in ways that are aligned with the standards. Use of the adjective *national* means a nationwide agreement, not a federal mandate, on what defines successful science learning and the school practices that support the learning. National standards neither define a national curriculum nor are they a form of national standardization.

The eight categories of content standards are displayed in Figure 6–5. The first seven categories have standards for grade levels K through 4, 5 through 8, and 9 through 12. The final category (Unifying Concepts and Processes) crosses all grade levels. Within each of the areas represented in Figure 6–5 are fundamental understandings. The content described in the standards *does not* represent a science curriculum. Curriculum includes not only the content but also the structure, organization, balance, and presentation of the content. The selection of the fundamental concepts in these standards was based on the following criteria: It represents scientific ideas; it has rich explanatory power; it guides fruitful investigations; it applies to situations and contexts common to everyday experiences; it can be linked to meaningful learning experiences; and it is developmentally appropriate for students at the grade level specified.

Science as Inquiry
Physical Science
Life Science
Earth and Space Science
Science and Technology
Science in Personal and Social Perspectives
History and Nature of Science
Unifying Concepts and Processes

FIGURE 6–5 *National Science Education Standards:* Science Content

Science as Inquiry should be recognized as a basic in curriculum organization and in students' science education experiences. This standard highlights the ability to *do* inquiry and the fundamental concepts *about* scientific inquiry that students should develop. The emphasis on inquiry moves beyond the processes of science and emphasizes the students' cognitive development based on critical thinking and scientific reasoning required in the use of evidence and information to construct scientific explanations.

Physical, Life, and *Earth and Space Science* standards express the traditional subject matter of science. This subject matter focuses on those science concepts, principles, and theories that are fundamental for all students.

The *Science and Technology* standard establishes useful connections between the natural world and the designed world and offers essential decision-making abilities. This standard has two components. One emphasizes the development of abilities associated with technological design and problem solving. The second centers on developing understanding about the similarities and differences between science and technology, and their respective influences within society.

The standard on *Science in Personal and Social Perspectives* connects the students with their social and personal world. It helps students understand health, populations, resources, environments, and natural hazards that will enable them to fulfill their obligations as citizens.

The standard on the *History and Nature of Science* includes an understanding of the nature of science and uses history in school science programs to clarify different aspects of science in society, the human aspects of science, and how scientific advances occur.

The *Unifying Concepts and Processes* standard provides students with powerful ideas that help them understand the natural world. These conceptual and procedural schemes are integral to any school science program and students' learning experiences in science. The understanding and abilities associated with this standard should be developed over the entire K through 12 continuum.

Science Teaching Standards identify the characteristics of and provide a vision for good science teaching. Those standards center on the practice of teaching and are criteria for judging the quality of teaching in the science classroom. They describe roles and responsibilities in the areas listed in Figure 6–6.

The *Professional Development Standards* underscore the idea that becoming an effective science teacher is a continuous process, beginning with your current experiences and stretching throughout your career (see Figure 6–7).

Teachers of science plan an inquiry-based science program for their students. In doing this, they:
- develop a framework of year-long and short-term goals for students;
- select science content and adapt and design curricula to meet the interests, knowledge, understanding, ability, and experiences of students;
- select teaching and assessment strategies that support the development of student understanding and nurture a community of science learners; and
- work together as colleagues within and across disciplines and grade levels.

Teachers of science guide and facilitate science learning. In doing this, they:
- focus and support inquiries as they interact with their students;
- orchestrate discourse among students about scientific ideas;
- challenge students to accept and share responsibility for their own learning;
- recognize and respond to student diversity and encourage all students to participate fully in science learning; and
- encourage and model the skills of scientific inquiry as well as the curiosity, openness to new ideas and data, and skepticism that characterize science.

Teachers of science should engage in ongoing assessment of their teaching and of student learning. In doing this, they:
- use multiple methods to systematically gather data about student understanding and ability;
- analyze assessment data to guide teaching;
- guide students in self-assessment;
- use student data, observations of teaching, and interactions with colleagues to reflect on and improve teaching practice; and
- use student data, observations of teaching, and interactions with colleagues to report student achievement and opportunities to learn to students, teachers, parents, policymakers, and the general public.

Teachers of science should design and manage learning environments that provide students with the time, space, and resources needed for learning science. In doing this, they:
- structure the time available so that students are able to engage in extended investigations;
- create a setting for student work that is flexible and supportive of science inquiry;
- ensure a safe working environment;
- make the available science tools, materials, print, media, and technological resources accessible to students;
- identify and use resources outside the school; and
- engage students in designing the learning environment.

Teachers of science develop communities of science learners that reflect the intellectual rigor of scientific inquiry and the attitudes and social values conducive to science learning. In doing this, they:
- display and demand respect for the diverse ideas, skills, and experiences of all students;
- enable students to have a significant voice in decisions about the content and context of their work, and require students to take responsibility for the learning of all members of the community;
- nurture a collaboration among students;
- structure and facilitate ongoing formal and informal discussion based on a shared understanding of rules of scientific discourse; and
- model and emphasize the skills, attitudes, and values of scientific inquiry.

Teachers of science actively participate in the ongoing planning and development of the school science program. In doing this, they:
- plan and develop the school science program;
- participate in decisions concerning the allocation of time and other resources to the science program; and
- plan and implement professional growth and development strategies for themselves and their colleagues.

FIGURE 6–6 Standards for Science Teachers

Science Assessment Standards identify essential characteristics of fair and accurate student assessments and provide criteria for judging the quality of assessment at the classroom, district, state, and national levels. The definition of assessment includes not only familiar tests but also a range of strategies for collecting and interpreting information about student attainment, teacher performance, and the work of educational institutions. Very important, the *Science*

Assessment Standards include an evaluation of the opportunities that all students have to learn science. Assessment standards are not tests, and they do not describe strategies to judge student learning or a school science program. Figure 6–8 displays standards for assessment in science.

Program Standards describe how content, teaching, and assessment are coordinated in school practice over a range of school experience to provide all students the

Professional development for teachers of science requires learning essential science content through the perspectives and methods of inquiry. Science learning experiences for teachers must:

- involve teachers in actively investigating phenomena that can be studied scientifically, interpreting results, and making sense of findings consistent with currently accepted scientific understanding;
- address issues, events, problems, or topics significant in science and of interest to participants;
- introduce teachers to scientific literature, media, and technological resources that expand their ability to access further knowledge;
- build on the teacher's current science understanding, ability, and attitudes;
- incorporate ongoing reflection on the process and outcomes of understanding science through inquiry; and
- encourage and support teachers in efforts to collaborate.

Professional development for teachers of science requires integrating knowledge of science, learning, pedagogy, and students; it also requires applying that knowledge to science teaching. Learning experiences for teachers of science must:

- connect and integrate all pertinent aspects of science and science education;
- occur in a variety of places where effective science teaching can be illustrated and modeled, permitting teachers to struggle with real situations and expand their knowledge and skills in appropriate contexts;
- address teacher needs as learners and build on their current knowledge of science content, teaching, and learning; and
- use inquiry, reflection, interpretation of research, modeling, and guided practice to build understanding and skill in science teaching.

Professional development for teachers of science requires building understanding and abilities for lifelong learning. Professional development activities must:

- provide regular, frequent opportunities for individual and collegial examination and reflection on classroom and instructional practice;
- provide opportunities for teachers to receive feedback about their teaching and to understand, analyze, and apply that feedback to improve their practice;
- provide opportunities for teachers to learn and use various tools and techniques for self-reflection and collegial reflection, such as peer coaching, portfolios, and journals;
- support the sharing of teacher expertise by preparing and using mentors, teacher advisors, coaches, lead teachers, and resource teachers to provide professional development opportunities;
- provide opportunities to know and have access to existing research and experiential knowledge; and
- provide opportunities to learn and use the skills of research to generate new knowledge about science and the teaching and learning of science.

FIGURE 6–7 Standards for Professional Development for Teachers of Science

Assessments should:

- Be deliberately designed for the decisions they are intended to inform
- Measure both achievement and opportunity to learn
- Clearly relate decisions to data
- Demonstrate fairness in design and use
- Support their inferences with data

FIGURE 6–8 Standards for Assessment in Science

opportunity to learn science. They describe criteria for judging the quality of a K through 12 science program.

System Standards for science education guide the policies that must be implemented and the alignments that must be pursued by policy makers and others in order to support science learning described in the standards. System standards also address the essential functions that serve to build and sustain the capacities demanded by the standards of teachers and school communities.

NATIONAL STANDARDS, SOCIAL COMMITMENTS, AND SCIENTIFIC LITERACY

The *National Science Education Standards* define the level of understanding of science that all students should develop, regardless of background, future aspirations, or interest in science. The standards embody the belief that all students can learn science. These standards encourage all students—including members of populations defined by race, ethnicity, economic status, gender, and physical and intellectual capacity—to study science throughout their school years and to pursue careers in science. By adopting the goal of science for all, the standards will promote the participation of all students in challenging opportunities to learn science.

The *Standards* forcefully advocate the inclusion of those who traditionally have not received encouragement and opportunities to learn science—women and girls, all racial and ethnic groups, the physically and educationally challenged, and those with limited proficiency in English—as well as those who have traditionally made achievements in science: the gifted and talented students.

Various methods of learning and different sources of motivation are accommodated because the curriculum, teaching, and assessment standards take into account the diversity of the student population, disparate interests, motivation, experience, and ways of understanding science. The standards define criteria for high-quality instructional experiences that engage all students in the full range of science content. These experiences teach the nature and processes of science. In addition to the subject matter, they will reinforce the belief that people of diverse backgrounds can engage and participate in science. They will uphold the premise that all students have a claim on understanding science as a common human heritage.

The *National Science Education Standards* present an explicit definition of scientific literacy. School science education contributes to the broader goals of education by providing students with a scientific understanding of the natural world through knowledge of the basic concepts of science, scientific modes of inquiry, the nature of the scientific endeavor, and the historical, social, and intellectual contexts within which science is practiced. The ability to apply such scientific knowledge to aspects of one's personal and civic life is referred to as *scientific literacy*.

Goals of school science education include the preparation of students who understand the following:

- A limited number of the basic concepts of science and the fundamental principles, laws, and theories that organize the body of scientific knowledge and can apply them
- The modes of reasoning embodied in scientific inquiry and can use them
- The nature of the scientific endeavor and its ways of knowing, laws, and theories
- The history of scientific development, the relationship between science and technology, and the historical, cultural, and social contexts in which this relationship is embedded

To support and develop the broad social goals of education, school science must attend to students' understanding of scientific knowledge and provide opportunities for them to practice using that knowledge. Therefore, school science programs must provide experiences that:

- Are personally and socially relevant
- Call for a wide range of knowledge, methods, and approaches to analyze personal and societal issues critically
- Encourage students to act in ways that reflect their understanding of the impact of scientific knowledge on their lives, society, and the world
- Encourage students' appreciation of the scientific endeavor and their excitement and pleasure in its pursuit
- Develop in students an appreciation of the beauty and order of the natural world

Notice that these statements both identify goals and provide recommendations for achieving those goals, while allowing for a diversity in approaches and teaching styles. Eventually, science teachers will transform these general policies into actual curriculum materials and teaching practices.

NO CHILD LEFT BEHIND: FEDERAL LEGISLATION INFLUENCING SCIENCE EDUCATION

On January 8, 2002, President George W. Bush signed into law the "No Child Left Behind Act" (NCLB), the new federal education reform law that now affects virtually every aspect of K through 12 education.

The law affects science educators in several important ways. First, in the 2007–2008 school year, all states must administer an annual science assessment to students in grades 3 through 5, 6 through 9, and 10 through 12. Testing of science must be in one grade level of these grade-level sets. (Annual testing for students in grades 3 through 8 in math and reading began in 2005.)

Second, several new provisions under NCLB influence the professional development provided to all teachers. NCLB requires that **all states must ensure that every core subject classroom teacher is "highly qualified."** This includes science teachers. To meet this definition, a teacher must be certified or licensed, hold a bachelor's degree, and have demonstrated competencies in his or her teaching area (as determined by the state).

The federal government distributed grants to the states and districts for professional development (and other teacher quality programs) to help states, and teachers, reach the goal of highly qualified teachers.

District administrators can use Title II grant funds for a variety of purposes, including professional development, recruitment, and hiring, as long as the activities meet the law's requirements, increase the number of "highly qualified" teachers in the district, and lead to increased student achievement.

Develop a Professional Development Plan

You can work with schools and districts to decide how federal education funds can be used. To be eligible for NCLB Title II funds, a district must first conduct a needs assessment to determine the professional development needs of the district's science teachers. *Teachers must be involved in the needs assessment process.*

With the results of the needs assessment, the district is then required by law to develop a local improvement plan, which will address the determined needs and ensure all the district teachers are highly qualified. *Teachers must also be actively involved in the planning and implementation of the district's local improvement plan.* The local improvement plan is submitted to the state education agency.

With federally mandated science assessments and the requirement that all teachers, including science teachers, be "highly qualified," it is important that schools and districts have a plan that ensures that continuing professional development programs are available to science educators.

Create Your Professional Development Plan

You can take an active role in professional development by working with your school and district to create a needs assessment, then charting your own professional growth with an individual professional development plan that can be a part of the district's local improvement plan.

A successful professional development plan should reflect multiple opportunities and activities for science teachers to learn, practice, and enforce new behaviors. It should include a variety of professional development experiences, including workshops and seminars, immersion into inquiry science, study groups, research experiences, mentoring and coaching, and partnerships with scientists (Loucks-Horsley, Hewson, Love, & Stiles, 2003).

NATIONAL ASSESSMENT OF EDUCATIONAL PROGRESS: SCIENCE 2009

The National Assessment of Educational Progress (NAEP) is a measure of how well the goal of scientific literacy for all students is being met. The *Science Framework*

for the 2009 National Assessment of Educational Progress (NAGB, 2006) sets forth recommendations for a science assessment that will begin new NAEP measures of student progress in science beginning in 2009.

In 1988, Congress created the National Assessment Governing Board (NAGB) to set policy for NAEP. The National Center for Education Statistics (NCES, a division of the U.S. Department of Education) carries out NAEP. As the ongoing national indicator of the academic achievement of U.S. students, NAEP regularly collects information on representative samples of students in grades 4, 8, and 12 and periodically reports on student achievement in reading, mathematics, writing, science, and other subject areas. NAEP scores are always reported at the aggregate level, not for individual students or schools. For science, NAEP results are reported at the national, state, and select district levels.

NAEP produces comparative student achievement results according to demographic factors such as gender, race/ethnicity, and geographic region. Results are also provided in terms of student, teacher, and school background variables related to science achievement. Taken together, this information from NAEP helps the general public, educators, and policy makers make informed decisions about education. You can access performance results and released questions through NAEP reports and websites.

A new framework to guide the science assessment in 2009 was necessary for several reasons described in this chapter and book. Examples influencing the development of a new framework include publication of national standards for science literacy, advances in both science and cognitive research, growth in national and international science assessments, and increases in innovative assessment approaches. This 2009 *Framework* presents the content to be assessed, as well as the conceptual base for the assessment.

Key Features of the NAEP Science Framework

The Science *Framework* for NAEP 2009 (the *Framework*) was developed by hundreds of individuals across the country, including some of the nation's leading scientists, science educators, policy makers, and assessment experts. Under contract to the National Assessment Governing Board, WestEd and the Council of Chief State School Officers conducted an 18-month process to develop the *Framework* involving committees, regional hearings, and other public forums. The NAGB also engaged an external review panel to evaluate an early draft of the *Framework* and convened a public hearing to gather additional input during the development process.

The new *Framework* incorporates the following key features:

- Widely accepted national science education standards and assessments, in addition to state curriculum standards; however, the *Framework* does advocate for a particular approach to instruction or represent the entire range of science content and skills
- Special consideration to international assessment frameworks, such as those for *Trends in International Mathematics and Science Study* (TIMSS) and *Programme for International Student Assessment* (PISA)
- Focus on foundational and pervasive knowledge within each discipline and reducing the science content to be assessed
- Scientific knowledge and processes derived from tested explanations and supported by accumulated empirical evidence (Explanations of natural phenomena that rely on nonscientific views are not reflected in the *Framework*.)
- Detailed, grade-specific charts that also allow the reader to see the progression in complexity of ideas across grades
- Error-free and nontechnical description of the science content (The language used is intended to be accurate and accessible to a wide audience.)
- Focus on students' conceptual understanding, that is, their knowledge and use of science facts, concepts, principles, theories, and laws (Students' abilities to engage in some components of scientific inquiry and technological design also are reflected in the *Framework*.)
- New types of items, including the use of interactive computer tasks

Content of the NAEP Science Framework

The *Framework* describes the science content and the science practices that form the basis for the 2009 NAEP Science Assessment. It also presents item distribution, types of items, and proposed achievement levels.

SCIENCE CONTENT

The science content for the 2009 NAEP describes key facts, concepts, principles, theories, and laws in three broad areas.

- Physical Science
- Life Science
- Earth and Space Science

Physical Science deals with matter, energy, and motion; Life Science with structures and functions of living systems and changes in living systems; and Earth and Space Science with earth in space and time, earth structures, and earth systems.

SCIENCE PRACTICES

The *Framework* presents four science practices.

- Identifying Science Principles
- Using Science Principles
- Using Scientific Inquiry
- Using Technological Design

These practices can be combined with any science content statement to generate student performance expectations, and assessment items can then be developed based on these performance expectations. The cognitive demands placed on students as they engage in assessment tasks are also described.

DISTRIBUTION OF ITEMS

As measured by student response time, the distribution of items by content area should be as follows: approximately equal across Physical Science, Life Science, and Earth and Space Science at grade 4; more emphasis on Earth and Space Science at grade 8; and a shift to more emphasis on Physical Science and Life Science at grade 12. With respect to science practices, at all grades, the greatest emphasis should be on Identifying and Using Science Principles; and slightly less than a third of the time should be spent on items related to Using Scientific Inquiry.

TYPES OF ITEMS

Item types for the 2009 NAEP Science Assessment fall into two broad categories: selected-response items such as multiple-choice items and constructed-response items such as short answer items. As measured by student response time, 50 percent of the assessment items at each grade level will be selected-response items and 50 percent will be constructed-response items. In order to further probe students' abilities to combine their understandings with the investigative skills reflective of practices, a subsample of students at each grade level will receive an additional 30 minutes to complete hands-on performance or interactive computer tasks.

Hands-on Performance Tasks: In hands-on performance tasks, students manipulate selected physical objects and try to answer a scientific question involving the objects. NAEP hands-on performance tasks provide students with a concrete task along with equipment and materials. Students will be given the opportunity to determine scientifically justifiable procedures for arriving at an answer. Students' scores should be based on both the answer and the procedures created for carrying out the investigation.

Interactive Computer Tasks: Interactive computer taks will be of four types: (1) information search and analysis, (2) empirical investigation, (3) simulation, and (4) concept maps. Information search and analysis items pose a scientific question and ask students to query an information database and analyze relevant data to address the question. Empirical investigation items put hands-on performance tasks on the computer and invite students to design and conduct a study to draw conclusions about a problem. Simulation items model systems (e.g., food webs), manipulate variables, and predict and explain resulting changes in the system. Concept map items probe aspects of the structure or organization of students' scientific knowledge by providing concept terms and having students create a logical graphic organizer.

Achievement Levels

Results of the NAEP Science Assessment are reported as average scores for groups of students and as percentages of students who attain the basic, proficient, or advanced achievement levels.

INTERNATIONAL ASSESSMENTS

In the early 1960s, the science education community knew little about educational systems in other countries. Some academics maintained an interest, but for the most part, educators centered their interest on issues within the U.S. borders. The 1960s launched initial efforts in what has become a tradition of international comparative studies of science and mathematics education. These early efforts have grown into major international assessments that the educational community now knows as TIMSS (Trends in International Mathematics and Science Study), and in the year 2000, the newest addition PISA (Programme for International Student Assessment). TIMSS and PISA have contributed to a clear understanding that we are all part of an international educational community.

TIMSS 2003: AN INTRODUCTION AND OVERVIEW

The 2001 Trends in International Mathematics and Science Study (TIMSS) is the third comparison of mathematics and science achievement completed since 1995. TIMSS combines science and mathematics in one assessment and assesses student learning at different grades; in 2003, those grades were fourth and eighth.

Since 1995, TIMSS has been coordinated by the International Association for the Evaluation of Educational Achievement (IEA), an international organization of national research institutions and governmental research agencies. TIMSS is funded by the U.S. Department of Education, the National Science Foundation, the World Bank, the United Nations Development Project, and participating countries. IEA is located in Boston, Massachusetts. In 2003, a total of 49 countries participated in TIMSS at the fourth-grade level, the eighth-grade level, or both.

TIMSS provides a curriculum perspective by linking assessments to the science content of curricula in cooperating countries. Thus, TIMSS provides an indication of the degree to which students have learned concepts in the mathematics and science they have had the opportunity to learn in school programs. TIMSS's goal is to answer the question: Based on school curricula, what knowledge and skills have students learned by grade four? Grade eight? The achievement scores from TIMSS represent the "attained" or "learned" curriculum at different grade levels, specifically fourth and eighth.

How Did U.S. Fourth Graders Do?

In 2003, U.S. fourth graders exceeded the international average (495) in mathematics achievement. Between 1995 and 2003, fourth graders did not show any change in average mathematics achievement. The United States scored 518 in both assessments.

In 2003, U.S. fourth graders exceeded the international average in the TIMSS science assessment. However, U.S. fourth graders' average score decreased between 1995 and 2003, but this decrease did not represent a statistically significant difference.

Table 6–6 shows the science content domains and the average score for U.S. fourth graders compared with the TIMSS average.

In all science content areas, U.S. fourth graders' average scores were above the international average. In life science and earth science, U.S. students were outperformed by only three and four countries, respectively. In physical science, six countries outperformed the United States.

TABLE 6–6 U.S. 4th Graders' Achievement in Science Content Areas

Science Content Area	Number of Items	U.S. Average	TIMSS Average
Life science	65	537	489
Physical science	53	531	489
Earth science	34	535	489
Total	152	536	489

How Did U.S. Eighth Graders Do?

In 2003, U.S. eighth graders exceeded the international average in mathematics achievement. Nine countries of the 48 participating countries outperformed the United States. In the eight-year period between 1995 and 2003, U.S. eighth graders showed significant improvement in average performance.

U.S. eighth graders achieved above the TIMSS averages for all science content areas assessed in 2003. Compared with other countries, U.S. eighth graders were outperformed by the fewest countries (four) in environmental science and by the most countries (11) in chemistry.

How Did Different Groups of U.S. Fourth Graders Perform?

Because U.S. education is guided by the belief that all students, regardless of gender, race, ethnicity, or family background, should have equal educational opportunities, it is useful to look at the comparative performance of different student groups. In its contemporary form, this goal is expressed in the "No Child Left Behind" legislation.

In 2003, U.S. fourth-grade boys scored higher than girls in both mathematics and science. For race and ethnicity, the average mathematics and science scores for white fourth graders was higher than the average of either black or Hispanic fourth graders. Hispanic students outperformed black students in both mathematics and science.

In mathematics and science, the average score of fourth-grade students whose parents were both born in the United States was higher than when either parent was foreign born, or when both parents were foreign born.

One measure of poverty in U.S. public schools is the percentage of students eligible for the free or reduced-price lunch program. To determine the relationship between poverty and fourth graders' average achievement in mathematics and science, schools in the U.S. TIMSS sample were classified by the percentage of students eligible for the federal free or reduced lunch. Because this is a federal program, only public school data are reported. In mathematics and science, the higher the poverty level of the participating school, the lower the average achievement score of U.S. fourth graders in 2003.

How Did Different Groups of U.S. Eighth Graders Perform?

A look at the same five categories of U.S. population groups for eighth graders reveals similar trends. In both mathematics and science, U.S. eighth-grade boys outperformed girls. However, both U.S. boys and girls have improved their mathematics and science performance since 1995.

In 2003, the average mathematics and science scores for U.S. white students were higher than for either black or Hispanic students. In both cases, Hispanics outperformed black students. However, the overall scores of black and Hispanic eighth graders have improved significantly in both mathematics and science since 1995. This result indicates some narrowing of the achievement gap.

In both mathematics and science, the average scores of students whose parents were both foreign born were lower than the scores of students whose parents were both born in the United States. In science, students with one U.S.-born and one foreign-born parent also had a higher average score than students with two foreign-born parents.

In 2003, parents' level of education was another characteristic that correlated with a difference in the average performance in mathematics and science of U.S. students. Students who reported that their mother (or female guardian) completed college or completed some college had higher average scores than students who reported their mother did not complete college or had no more than a high school education. The same relationships were found when considering the fathers' education.

As with fourth graders, the measure of poverty used in TIMSS was the percentage of students eligible for the federal free or reduced lunch program in the sample schools. In mathematics and science, eighth graders in U.S. public schools with the highest poverty levels had lower average scores, compared with their counterparts in public schools with a lower percentage of students participating in the federal lunch program.

PISA 2003: An Introduction and Overview

The Programme for International Student Assessment (PISA) measures 15-year-olds' capabilities in reading literacy, mathematics literacy, and science literacy every three years. PISA was first implemented in 2000, and the most recent results are for the 2003 assessment. Each three-year cycle assesses one subject in depth. The other two subjects also are assessed, but not in the same depth as the primary domain. In 2003, mathematics was the primary subject assessed, and in 2006 it was science. PISA also measures cross-curricular competencies. In 2003, for example, PISA assessed problem solving.

PISA is sponsored by the Organisation for Economic Co-operation and Development (OECD), an intergovernmental organization of 30 industrialized nations based in Paris, France. In 2003, 41 countries participated in PISA, including 30 OECD countries and 11 non-OECD countries.

PISA uses the term *literacy* within each subject area to indicate a focus on the application of knowledge and abilities. Literacy refers to a continuum of knowledge and abilities; it is not a typological classification of a condition that one has or does not have. PISA assessments do not provide data to determine who is literate or illiterate.

For the 2003 assessment, mathematical literacy was defined as an individual's capacity to identify and understand the role that mathematics plays in the world, to make well-founded judgments, and to use and engage with mathematics in ways that meet the needs of that individual's life as a constructive, concerned, and reflective citizen (OECD, 2003, p. 24).

Problem solving is defined as an individual's capacity to use cognitive processes to confront and resolve real, cross-disciplinary situations where the solution is not immediately obvious and where the literacy domains or curricular areas that might be applicable are not isolated within the single domain of mathematics, science, or reading (OECD, 2003, p. 156).

Scientific literacy is defined as having the "capacity to use scientific knowledge, to identify questions and to draw evidence-based conclusions in order to understand and help make decisions about the natural world and the changes made to it through human activity" (OECD, 2003).

Compared to the curricular orientation of the Trends in International Mathematics and Science Study (TIMSS), PISA provides a unique and complementary perspective by focusing on the application of knowledge in reading, mathematics, and science in problems and issues in real-life contexts. PISA's goal is to answer the question: Considering schooling and other factors, what knowledge and skills do students have at age 15? The achievement scores from PISA represent a "yield" of learning at age 15, rather than a measure of the attained curriculum at grades 4 or 8, as is the case with TIMSS. The framework for assessment is based on content, processes, and situations. For example, in 2003, the content for mathematical literacy consisted of major mathematical ideas such as space and shape, change and relationships, quantity, and uncertainty. The processes describe what strategies students use to solve problems, and the situations consist of personal

contexts in which students might encounter mathematical problems.

In PISA, a situation may be presented and several questions asked about it. Although some items are answered by selected response, the majority of items require a constructed response, for which partial credit may be given. The typical PISA item makes more complex cognitive demands on the student than the typical item from TIMSS or the National Assessment of Educational Progress (NAEP) (Neidorf, Binkley, Gattis, & Nohara, 2004).

How Did U.S. 15-Year-Olds Do?

In 2003, U.S. performance in mathematics literacy and problem solving was lower than the average performance for the OECD countries.

In both mathematics literacy and problem solving, the United States had fewer students at the highest proficiency levels than the other OECD countries. That result was in stark contrast with the 2000 reading literacy results, in which the United States had a greater percentage of students at the highest proficiency level than other OECD countries (Lemke et al., 2001).

Table 6–7 shows the number of items on the problem-solving assessment and the average score for U.S. 15-year-olds compared with the average across all 29 OECD countries.

The U.S. average performance in problem solving is slightly lower than in mathematical literacy.

Although it was a minor domain in 2003, PISA did include assessment items on science literacy. There was no measurable difference between the U.S. average score of 499 in 2000 and 491 in 2003; however, the relative position of the United States compared with the OECD average did change. Specifically, the U.S. average score in 2000 was not statistically different from the OECD average, and in 2003, the U.S. average was measurably below the OECD average.

Are There Differences in How U.S. 15-Year-Olds Do?

VARIABILITY

The variation in mathematics literacy (measured by the standard deviation of students' scores) was slightly greater in the United States than in the average OECD country. Ten OECD countries had less variation in

TABLE 6–7 U.S. Average Scores in Problem Solving

Cross-curricular Competency	Number of Items	U.S. Average Score	OECD Average Score
Problem solving	10	478	500

mathematics literacy performance than the United States, and only two countries (Belgium and Germany) had more. The variation in problem solving was not measurably different in the United States from the average OECD variation. Sixteen OECD countries had less variation in problem-solving performance, and only two countries (Belgium and Japan) had more. In general, the variation within countries, including the United States, was much greater than the variation in average scores across countries.

SOCIOECONOMIC DIFFERENCES

PISA 2003 used an index of student socioeconomic status (the International Socioeconomic Index or ISEI) that was based on the occupational status of the student's father or mother (whichever was higher) as reported by the student. The average ISEI score in the United States was higher than that of all but two OECD countries (Norway and Iceland). Also, low ISEI students in the United States had a relatively higher socioeconomic status than their peers in most OECD countries. The United States is one of the OECD countries in which high student socioeconomic status is strongly associated with high performance on PISA 2003. In only three countries (Belgium, Germany, and Hungary) was there a stronger relationship between mathematical literacy and ISEI than in the United States, and in six OECD countries the relationship was weaker. For problem solving, there was a stronger relationship with ISEI in five countries (Belgium, Germany, Hungary, Czech Republic, and Poland), and there was a weaker one in six countries.

GENDER DIFFERENCES

In 20 of the 29 OECD countries, including the United States, male students outperformed female students. In the United States, this difference was due in part to more male students among the high performers and not to more female students among the low performers. In only five of the OECD countries, not including the United States, were there any differences between male and female students in performance on the problem-solving assessment. In all five countries where there were differences, the female students did better.

RACIAL AND ETHNIC DIFFERENCES

As in NAEP and in PISA 2000, blacks and Hispanics in the United States scored lower, on average, than whites, Asians, and students of more than one race in both mathematics literacy and problem solving.

SUMMARY

National Science Education Standards provide the qualitative criteria and framework for judging science programs (content, teaching, and assessment) and the policies necessary to support them. Among other objectives, the *Standards* and *Benchmarks* (1) define the understanding of science that all students—without regard to background, future aspirations, or prior interest in science—should develop; (2) present criteria for judging science education content and programs at the K through 4, 5 through 8, and 9 through 12 levels, including learning goals, design features, instructional approaches, and assessment characteristics; (3) include all natural sciences and their interrelationships, as well as the connections with technology, social science, and history; (4) provide criteria for judging models, benchmarks, curricula, and learning experiences developed under the guidelines of ongoing national projects, under state frameworks, or under local district, school, or teacher-designed initiatives; and (5) provide criteria for judging teaching, the provision of opportunities to learn (including such resources as instructional materials and assessment methods), and science education programs at all levels.

The national standards provide a broad view of scientific literacy, one that includes all students. Although the effort encompasses the entire nation, the *National Science Education Standards* honor the diversity of school districts, schools, and science teachers. Science teachers such as you can use many means to achieve the standards and the primary goals of developing higher levels of scientific literacy for all citizens.

UNIT 3

GOALS, OBJECTIVES, AND ASSESSMENTS

A 30-year veteran science teacher, Jim Jefferson continually demonstrated the characteristics of effective teaching. He knew the content of science, he used different instructional strategies, he efficiently managed the classroom, he was enthusiastic, and he had a good rapport with students. Jim's activity as a science teacher impressed everyone. He used discussions with students and gently challenged their ideas, he directed them to science knowledge, he helped them formulate new ideas, and he always asked them to justify their ideas. Jim's teaching revealed a consistency that enhanced student learning. Recognizing Jim's effectiveness required extended observations in a variety of classrooms for even the careful observer to see the patterns.

We asked Jim about his approach to science teaching.

I think of science education as consisting of knowledge and abilities related to science and the application of science to personal and social issues. These might be the big goals. I also think of scientific literacy as having several different dimensions. These goals provide frameworks that help me make decisions about the structure and content of my interaction with students. In teaching biology I keep major conceptual schemes from the *National Science Education Standards* (NRC, 1996) and *Benchmarks for Science Literacy* (AAAS, 1993) in mind; for example, I try to keep ideas like evolution of living systems, genetic continuity, energetics, biosphere, and interdependence in mind. I also know that students have to develop more specific terms and ideas, such as carrying capacity and limiting factors, gene regulation, DNA, and metabolism. Students need to know the terms *and* they need to see how the terms relate to big ideas in biology. Not only that, they need to see how the whole discipline of biology connects to other sciences and the student's life and social issues. I realize this is a lot, but you don't have to teach all of this at once, you teach a little at a time by making sure the students have meaningful experiences.

Let me say that the same ideas apply when I emphasize scientific inquiry. I try to get students to clarify their questions, obtain data using the best methods they can, and then develop their answer to the question. I know this emphasis is different from just teaching biological knowledge. I cannot emphasize the importance of inquiry enough. Students should be able to formulate a testable hypothesis and demonstrate the connections between the science concepts that guide the investigation. At some time in a student's experience in secondary school science, students should design and conduct a full scientific investigation. Every lesson does not have to be a full investigation, but I really think this is the best way to develop both the abilities of scientific inquiry and the understandings about scientific inquiry. In other lessons I try to incorporate different aspects of the inquiry goal. Sometimes it is as simple as asking a question about another student's explanation, sometimes it involves asking students to explain the connection between evidence and explorations, sometimes I ask students to explain what scientists have said about the topic. I think all of this contributes to students' understanding, and, for me, this emphasis on inquiry is one of the most exciting goals of science teaching.

Jim used this framework to help organize his science program and to guide his daily interactions with students. He also let the students know when he was emphasizing concepts or inquiry and when he was trying to get them to understand the nature of science or interaction between science and society. Whatever the goals, Jim seemed to know how to organize, emphasize, and present science. Even when students would take him off track, he returned to his goals and objectives.

Jim's teaching demonstrated not only constant variation, but also consistent structure. He knew his goals and what he was trying to accomplish with any individual student. Jim responded to the difficulty of concepts and the current conception of students with his repertoire of teaching strategies. We would say that, among other things, Jim Jefferson had a clear view of the goals of science education and the objectives of particular science lessons.

THE GOALS OF SCIENCE TEACHING

Begin this chapter by completing an activity concerning the goals of science teaching. Do Activity 7–1: Goals of Science Teaching, at the end of this chapter.

Science teachers continuously reexamine the goals and objectives of their programs. "Which units will I teach this year?" "What new topics shall I introduce?" Questions such as these, and the answers, are the bases of revised goals and changes in science programs. Only the individual science teacher knows the variables that must be evaluated in the decision-making process. "What is my budget?" "What are the abilities and attitudes of my students?" "What are my interests?" "What was the students' response to last year's units?" "What new ideas did I get from the NSTA convention I attended?" There are, of course, other questions, but these examples illustrate how goals are revised by individual science teachers.

We are not using the terms *goals* and *objectives* synonymously. There is a clear distinction. Goals are broad statements that give a general direction to a science curriculum and classroom instruction. Broad goals have the advantage of relating to many aspects of science, society, and education, and, simultaneously, of giving some direction to classroom planning and instruction. The disadvantage of goals is precisely that they are too broad for specific direction concerning grade levels, science subjects, and personal aims and preferences of science teachers. It is necessary to reformulate goals into objectives that are appropriate for each science teacher. Although goals and objectives differ, they are logically related because objectives are derived from goals.

BASIC GOALS OF SCIENCE EDUCATION

As you found in the introductory activity, there are many goals of science teaching. By using the following simple criteria, most goals can be summarized into a few categories.

- Goals should be comprehensive enough to include the generally accepted aims and objectives of science teaching.
- Goals should be understandable for other teachers, administrators, and parents.
- Goals should be neutral, that is, free of bias and not oriented toward any particular view of science teaching.
- Goals should be few in number.
- Goals should differentiate concepts and abilities.
- Goals should be easily applicable to instructional and learning objectives.

Science teachers use a small number of goals when they construct lessons or design curricula. If you are interested in the role of goals in the history of science education, you may wish to read George DeBoer's *A History of Ideas in Science Education* (1991), and "Research on Goals for the Science Curriculum" by Rodger Bybee and George DeBoer (1994), in *Handbook of Research on Science Teaching and Learning*.

Using the aforementioned criteria, we can identify the following categories of goals for science education: scientific knowledge, scientific methods, social issues, personal needs, and career awareness. You probably recognize many of the goals in the introductory activity

GUEST EDITORIAL ◆ MICHAEL URBAN

Earth Sciences Graduate Student
University of Northern Colorado

TEACHING: IDEOLOGY VERSUS REALITY

In the fall of 1999, I began what amounted to a three-year adventure as an eighth-grade earth science teacher in the small town of Detroit Lakes, Minnesota. I look back on my first year of teaching through rose-colored glasses at a blur of memories, and wonder how I ever managed to survive. There was so much to do that first year: prepare lessons; research topics; write worksheets, laboratory exercises, and tests; meet and work with new colleagues; learn how to deal with and develop rapport with students; creatively and resourcefully utilize the lab equipment I had; and muster every bit of restraint I could to refrain from stooping to the level of misbehaving students. Overall, though, the experience I gained from my first year made it well worth enduring.

We all know the adage that you learn more in your first year of teaching than in all of your previous years of schooling combined. This is true because you need to thoroughly understand a concept before you can effectively teach it, and also because you are constantly quizzed by your students when they ask questions (in many cases, the likes of which you have never heard before). We all leave college with at least some understanding of our subject area, but it is never enough. I spent a lot of time researching "simple" concepts; college was great at providing an advanced education, but I needed to bring it down to the *eighth-grade* level. Two sources of information I found invaluable were older textbooks (geared for the level I was teaching) and the "ask the expert" e-mail links found on many websites. You may think it strange to refer to out-of-date textbooks from the 60s, 70s, and 80s, but they can be a wealth of information because they tend, generally speaking, to go into more detail on explanations of *why* than do most of their modern counterparts (and in most cases, in the field of earth science, the information they provide has changed little).

I consider myself fortunate to have worked in a very progressive school where there existed an ample supply of both technology and expertise in effectively utilizing it. All schools possess some state-of-the-art equipment, but many have such limited quantities that teachers must share it heavily and so can use it only sporadically. Familiarity with overheads, filmstrips, and slide projectors is helpful as they still make up the bulk of most school AV departments. While it would be more efficient (and colorful) to project a computer-generated slide show onto the screen, an overhead projector can be just as effective. Teachers become experts at making the most of what they have.

Field trips, Internet research projects, phenology journals, creative writing assignments, brief excursions outdoors to make observations, and science fairs are good ways to break up any monotony that may be taking place in the classroom. They can be undertaken with teachers of other subject areas both inside and out of the science disciplines. One of the most appealing aspects of a science class is its ability to be so diverse; math, reading, writing, and art can all be easily combined with studies of nature, making science the epitome of the interdisciplinary model. As long as teachers are well rounded, there seems to be no limit to the extent of their ability to flex some creative muscles.

Science affords the perfect opportunity to unite learning with imagination and discovery. Like the early explorers of centuries ago, our students have a chance to voyage into a land filled with mystery and splendor. The teacher is charged with the responsibility of bringing this journey to life by providing students with a launching platform (concepts), a means to carry out exploration (scientific method, critical thinking skills), and a challenging voyage (hands-on activities). Students can become frustrated by problem-solving exercises, especially if they are not well grounded in the related fundamental concepts. Therefore, it is vital to realize that our students need constant encouragement and facilitation. As science teachers, we need to introduce our students to nature by actively engaging them in the *process* of science, while at the same time stimulating creativity, promoting critical thinking, and providing a physically and emotionally safe environment in which to have fun while learning.

If we are brave enough to expose our inner selves and let our passion and love for our subject shine through, we can truly captivate students. A student who sees the relevance, importance, and excitement of science will have meaningful learning experiences and might one day devote his or her life to science or teaching. Perhaps one day a student will look at you the way you once looked at an inspirational teacher. Can you imagine what it must feel like to ignite the spark of passion for science in someone else?

as relating to these categories. Many objectives can be deduced from these goals, but keep in mind that at any time all of the goals are not equally important. Still, they have been the goals underlying science curriculum and instruction.

1. *Scientific knowledge.* There is a body of knowledge concerning biological, physical, and earth systems. For over 200 years, our science education programs have aimed toward informing students of these natural systems. This goal has been, and will continue to be, of significant importance for science teachers. Stated formally, this goal is: *Science education should develop fundamental understandings of natural systems.*

2. *Scientific methods.* A second goal has centered on the abilities and understandings of the methods of scientific investigation. Descriptions of the goal have changed; for example, the terms *inquiry* and *discovery* have been used to describe the scientific methods goal. The goal can be stated as: *Science education should develop a fundamental understanding of, and ability to use, the methods of scientific inquiry.*

3. *Societal issues.* Science education exists in society and should contribute to the maintenance and aspirations of the culture. This goal is especially important when there are social challenges directly related to science. This goal is: *Science education should prepare citizens to make responsible decisions concerning science-related social issues.*

4. *Personal needs.* All individuals have needs related to their own biological/psychological systems. Briefly stated, this goal is: *Science education should contribute to an understanding and fulfillment of personal needs, thus contributing to personal development.*

5. *Career awareness.* Scientific research, development, and application continue through the work of individuals within science and technology and through the support of those not directly involved in scientific work. Therefore, one important goal has been: *Science education should inform students about careers in the sciences.*

SCIENCE EDUCATION GOALS AND PROGRAMS: PRELUDE TO REFORM

In the late 1970s, three national surveys assessed the status of science education: *The Status of Pre-College Science, Mathematics, and Social Science Education* (Helgeson, Blosser, & Howe, 1977); *Report of the 1977 National Survey of Science, Mathematics, and Social Studies Education* (Weiss, 1978); and *Case Studies in Science Education* (Stake & Easley, 1978). The following discussion is based on an extensive review of these

studies.[6] In addition, we used Hurd's (1978) review, "The Golden Age of Biological Education: 1960–1975," in *Biology Teachers Handbook* and the *1976–1977 National Assessment of Education Progress—Science* (NAEP, 1978a; 1978b).

This review of goals is especially important because it is a landmark in the history of science education. These studies present the first major national assessment of science education. We shall first give a general review of science education and then discuss the specific goals outlined earlier.

AN OVERVIEW OF GOALS FOR SCIENCE EDUCATION

You can gain a better understanding of science education by examining the long-standing goals described earlier: scientific knowledge, scientific methods, societal issues, personal needs, and career awareness. In the period 1955 to 1975, these goals were in transition. Between 1975 and approximately 1995, the science education community reformed the goals. The publication of *Science for All Americans* (AAAS, 1989), *Benchmarks for Science Literacy* (AAAS, 1993), and the *National Science Education Standards* (NRC, 1996) clearly set new goals for science education. The following discussion describes the status of goals in 1975 to 2009 and suggests the direction of change.

Scientific Knowledge

Science programs are primarily oriented toward knowledge of the academic disciplines. In the classroom, knowledge goals become the scientific facts, concepts, and principles that reflect the structure of science. Science teachers report that they want their students to understand the subject matter of science. For example, they want the students to know scientific concepts and definitions of scientific words, and to develop inquiry abilities and critical thinking skills. Understanding science is generally interpreted as passing a test.

Scientific Method

There is little effort by science teachers to realize the goal of understanding and using the methods of science. For example, teachers do not use questioning techniques or instructional procedures that facilitate the cognitive abilities of scientific inquiry.

However, evidence indicates that students can attain an understanding of scientific inquiry as a process, develop essential inquiry skills, and use these skills to improve their ability to think critically about science-related problems (NRC, 2000).

Several factors hinder the implementation of the scientific methods goal. First, science teachers are neither *model inquirers* for their students nor have they been educated in methodologies of scientific research. Second, most science teachers lecture for more than 75 percent of the class time, leaving students few opportunities to ask questions. Third, inquiry as a goal of science teaching is generally not seen as productive and is not accepted by most science teachers. Fourth, teachers who are aware of scientific methods as a goal of teaching feel that only bright, highly motivated students can profit from inquiry teaching. Fifth, inquiry teaching is seen by teachers as time consuming, thus reducing the time available for basics, that is, learning facts and getting so-called right answers. The current improvement of science education and national support for the goal of scientific inquiry should change the lack of emphasis on this goal.

Societal Issues

Increasing interest in science literacy and societal goals is evident in science programs. Science teachers are including these goals to make science relevant to the concerns of all students.

The goals for teaching science indicate more emphasis on environmental concepts, world problems, decision making, and interdisciplinary studies—all areas related to the goal of teaching students how to deal with societal issues. *National Science Education Standards* are having a direct impact on state and local frameworks for science education. State departments of education are influencing changes in goals through their legislative and regulatory powers, such as specific requirements to include energy conservation, environmental problems, and health, alcohol, and drugs in educational programs.

Personal Needs

School personnel and parents express their concerns about meeting the personal needs of students through science education. This rhetoric takes the form of life-and-work and school-to-work skills related to science, the preparation ethic, and vocational or career education. In response, science courses often emphasize content that is seen as useful in everyday living.

Attempts to meet personal needs are made primarily through health or advanced placement courses. Some of the other goals, such as career awareness, overlap with these courses. Sometimes personal needs are met as a secondary effect of another goal. A socially relevant course on environmental science may provide fundamental knowledge that stimulates students to examine the life worth living.

The goal of meeting personal needs has always been subordinate in science education programs, especially when compared to goals such as knowledge. In the past three decades, the goal of fulfilling students' personal needs has become increasingly important. This goal is closely related to both career and societal goals.

Career Awareness

One of the currently important goals of science education is to provide information and training that will be useful in future employment. You might hear this expressed as the need for science education that supports a twenty-first-century workforce. Recent increased emphasis on this goal is due in part to public opinion and concerns by business and industry. The career awareness goal was found consistently across science programs, although it was not the primary goal of science education. What mattered most was the scientific and technological knowledge needed for the next course and whether all the courses were eventually related to one's future job.

There is some resistance to implementing the career goal in science education. Several issues emerge: Teachers and communities have questioned whether the school should serve labor needs, that is, whether the school should help prepare for work. They have questioned the apparent conflict between work of the school and the world of work. Science teachers are reluctant to sacrifice the scholastic program to help youth prepare for jobs. When teachers, parents, and science coordinators were asked about vocational goals of science courses, they all agreed that these goals should be included—however, the majority selected general education goals over vocational goals.

In recent decades, the inclusion of career goals in science programs has been increasingly important. Although the career goal has been emphasized and is important, it probably will become an increasingly important goal of science education in the twenty-first century. This is an excellent place to stop and complete Activity 7–2: The Status of Goals and Programs, at the end of this chapter.

SCIENCE EDUCATION GOALS FOR THE TWENTY-FIRST CENTURY: NATIONAL STANDARDS AND BENCHMARKS

In contemporary reform, the configuration of goals for science education should relate to the overall purpose of achieving scientific literacy. Thus, any review of national standards should assess the degree to which the standards incorporate the acquisition of scientific knowledge, development of inquiry abilities and understandings, and

Science as Inquiry
Physical Science
Life Science
Earth and Space Science
Science and Technology
Science in Personal and Social Perspectives
History and Nature of Science
Unifying Concepts and Processes

FIGURE 7–1 National Science Education Standards: Science Content

understanding of the applications of science (especially personal and social aspects of science, and the history and nature of science and technology). Further, those implementing the *Standards, Benchmarks,* and state and local frameworks should review the priorities and emphases suggested for the different goals. To what degree and in what form are the goals expressed? Do the standards suggest one orientation for the structuring of the goals, or do they suggest variations? Do the standards allow for a variety of curriculum materials and instructional approaches to achieve the goals? These questions should help focus your review of the national standards and the following discussion of science content in the standards.

The science content presented in the *National Science Education Standards* (NRC, 1996) describes major concepts as well as fundamental concepts and abilities for all students. Content only represents one component of a comprehensive view of science education expressed by the national standards. This comprehensive view includes teaching *and* assessment. As we mentioned in Chapter 6, the *National Science Education Standards* organize science content into eight categories, displayed in Figure 7–1.

Scientific Methods

The standard *Science as Inquiry* represents the goal we have discussed under scientific methods. The standard on inquiry has two features, the ability to *do* inquiry and the development of understandings *about* scientific inquiry. The inquiry standard emphasizes the students' ability to ask scientific questions; plan and conduct investigations; use appropriate tools, techniques, and educational technologies; think critically and logically about the relationship between evidences and explanations; construct and analyze alternative explanations; and communicate scientific investigations and explanations.

Understandings about scientific inquiry generally parallel abilities. For example, the national standards encourage the students' development of knowledge about the types of questions scientists ask, the various reasons for conducting investigations, technology's role

in inquiry, criteria for acceptable scientific explanations, and the results and use of scientific inquiry.

The inquiry standard emphasizes the students' ability to think critically and to use observations and knowledge to construct scientific explanations. The *Standards* have moved science education a step beyond the traditional *processes of science*, which centered on students engaging in activities emphasizing skills such as observing, inferring, hypothesizing, experimenting, and controlling variables. These processes of science are obviously included in *Science as Inquiry*, but the *Standards* require students to use the processes, combined with existing knowledge, as a means to gather evidence used in their analysis, reasoning, and construction of other scientific understanding.

The *Standards* include *Science and Technology*, in which students would develop abilities of technological design as well as greater understanding of science and technology. The standard intentionally parallels the *abilities* outlined in *Science as Inquiry*. The difference between the standards is based on the difference between scientific inquiry and technological design. The latter includes identifying a problem, proposing designs and selecting from alternative solutions, implementing a solution, evaluating the solution, and communicating the problem, process, and solution.

In the *National Science Education Standards,* inquiry and design serve to (1) assist students in the development of their understanding of scientific concepts, (2) help students answer the question, "How do we know what we know in science?" (3) introduce one aspect of the nature of science, (4) develop abilities of critical thinking, scientific reasoning, and critical analysis, and (5) acquire the habits of mind associated with science and technology.

Scientific Knowledge

The *Standards* and *Benchmarks* have defined a wide range of scientific knowledge and emphasize that the content of secondary school science programs is not strictly confined to the *physical, life,* and *earth sciences.* However, three standards outline major concepts and fundamental understandings of physical, life, and earth sciences, three major divisions of the scientific disciplines. Figures 7–2, 7–3, and 7–4 present the conceptual organizers for these major divisions of science. Although the focus of this book is on secondary schools, we thought it important to present the conceptual organizers for grades K through 4 so that you can review the overall development of concepts.

In the section on scientific methods, we discussed the standards on *Science as Inquiry* and portions of the standard on *Science and Technology.* Both of these standards also elaborate fundamental understandings for their respective areas. These understandings extend the goal of scientific knowledge from a narrow focus on the disciplines to a broader view that includes understanding

Physical Science K–4	Physical Science 5–8	Physical Science 9–12

Properties of Objectives
Position and Motion of Objects
Light, Heat, Electricity, and
  Magnetism
	Properties and Changes in Properties
	  of Matter
	Motions and Forces
	Transfer of Energy
		Structure of Atoms and Materials
		Structure and Properties of Matter
		Chemical Reactions
		Motion and Force
		Conservation of Energy and
		  the Increase in Disorder
		Interactions of Energy and Matter

FIGURE 7–2 Conceptual Organizers for Physical Science Standards

Life Science K–4	Life Science 5–8	Life Science 9–12

Characteristics of Organisms
Life Cycles of Organisms
Organisms and Environments
	Structure and Function in Living
	  Systems
	Reproduction and Heredity
	Regulation and Behavior
	Populations and Ecosystems
	Diversity and Adaptations of
	  Organisms
		Cell
		Molecular Basis of Heredity
		Biological Evolution
		Interdependence of Organisms
		Matter, Energy, and Organization in
		  Living Systems
		Behavior of Organisms

FIGURE 7–3 Conceptual Organizers for Life Science Standards

Earth and Space Science K–4	Earth and Space Science 5–8	Earth and Space Science 9–12

Properties of Earth Materials
Objects in the Sky
Changes in Earth and Sky
	Structure of the Earth System
	Earth's History
	Earth in the Solar System
		Energy in the Earth System
		Geochemical Cycles
		Origin and Evolution of the
		  Earth System
		Origin and Evolution of the
		  Universe

FIGURE 7–4 Conceptual Organizers for Earth and Space Science Standards

scientific inquiry, science and technology, and the history and nature of science. We discussed some examples from understanding scientific inquiry in an earlier section. Generally, these understandings elaborate various aspects of scientific investigations. For example, scientific concepts guide investigations; technology enhances accuracy of data; scientific explanations use evidence, logically consistent arguments, and propose, modify, or elaborate principles, models, and theories in science; and science advances through legitimate skepticism.

In the standards on *Science and Technology,* understandings highlight the connections between science and technology and maintain a view of the scientific and technologic enterprise (for example, a larger and external view of science and technology in society). Examples of understandings include the similarities and differences between science and technology; the contributions of science to technology and technology to science; and the understanding that different people in different cultures have made, and continue to make, contributions to science and technology.

The scientific knowledge outlined in the *Standards* also includes the *History and Nature of Science* (see Figure 7–5). This standard does not imply that students develop understandings of a complete history of science. Rather, science teachers can present history to clarify various aspects of scientific inquiry, the human dimensions of science, and the various roles science has played in Western and non-Western cultures. Science teachers might use case studies from history, classical experiments, and perspectives of normal and revolutionary science in order to provide students with opportunities to develop the understandings described in this standard.

The *National Science Education Standards* also include *Unifying Concepts and Processes* within the goal of scientific knowledge. These standards present major conceptual and procedural schemes that unify science disciplines and, when understood, provide

History and Nature of Science K–4	History and Nature of Science 5–8	History and Nature of Science 9–12
Science As a Human Endeavor	Science As a Human Endeavor Nature of Science History of Science	Science As a Human Endeavor Nature of Scientific Knowledge Historical Perspectives

FIGURE 7–5   Overview of the History and Nature of Science Standards

Unifying Concepts and Processes K–12
Systems, Order, and Organization Evidence, Models, and Explanation Constancy, Change, and Measurement Evolution and Equilibrium Form and Function

FIGURE 7–6   Overview of Unifying Concepts and Processes

students with powerful ways of understanding the natural and designed world (see Figure 7–6). *Unifying Concepts and Processes* do not have specific grade-level designations; rather, science teachers should continually bring these ideas to awareness in appropriate contexts, based on students' experiences. Specific understandings included in this standard are as follows:

- *Systems, order, and organization.* Levels of organization, systems, prediction, and a statistical view of nature
- *Evidence, models, and explanation.* Observations, data, models, hypothesis, law, and theory
- *Constancy, change, and measurement.* Interactions, rate, scale, patterns, quantitative aspects of change, conservation of energy and matter
- *Evolution and equilibrium.* Gradual changes, present as connected to the past, descent from common ancestors, homeostasis, and energy content and distribution
- *Form and function.* Complimentarity, natural and designed world, and systems and subsystems

Personal Needs and Societal Issues

As mentioned in the first section describing goals, one fundamental purpose of science teaching is to help students understand and act on various issues and challenges they will confront as individuals and as citizens. The *Standards* recognize this goal through inclusion of *Science in Personal and Social Perspectives* (see Figure 7–7).

These standards provide a context and topics for science curriculum and instructions. You should notice that the national standards include different aspects of health at each grade level, and an implied development of understanding about population, resources, and environments at all grade levels. The standards at grades 5 through 8 and 9 through 12 include natural hazards such as earthquakes, volcanoes, floods, and hurricanes. Finally, this standard recommends that students come to understand and act on science and technology challenges at local (grades K through 4), social (grades 5 through 8), and global (grades 9 through 12) levels.

Career Awareness

The *Standards* have an explicit goal supporting career awareness; however, they do not have a standard emphasizing careers. It should be clear that the experience implied by the understandings and abilities outlined in the *Standards* would have a positive benefit on students' attitudes and inclinations toward careers in, for example, science, engineering, and the health professions.

The *National Science Education Standards* present a fairly balanced approach to the goals of science education, with career awareness as the exception. Further, the *Standards* align quite well with the dimensions of scientific literacy described in Chapter 6. The content standards form a complete set of outcomes for students. Development of students' understandings, attitudes, and abilities are grounded in scientific investigations, and they form a solid foundation in life, earth, and physical sciences and apply fundamental understanding and ability within various personal, social, and historical perspectives. Although balanced, thorough, and clearly aligned with long-standing goals of science education, the *National Science Education Standards* must be transformed in curriculum materials, instructional practices, and assessment strategies, all topics discussed in later chapters. Complete Activity 7–3: Goals of Science Textbooks, and Activity 7–4: Reforming Goals to Align with National Standards and Benchmarks.

Science in Personal and Social Perspectives K–4	Science in Personal and Social Perspectives 5–8	Science in Personal and Social Perspectives 9–12
Personal Health	Personal Health	Personal and Community Health
Characteristics and Changes in Populations	Populations, Resources, and Environment	Population Growth
Types of Resources	Natural Hazards	Natural Resources
Changes in Environments	Risks and Benefits	Environmental Quality
Science and Technology in Local Challenges	Science and Technology in Society	Natural and Human-Induced Hazards
		Science and Technology in Local, National, and Global Challenges

FIGURE 7–7 Conceptual Organizers for Science in Personal and Social Perspectives

SUMMARY

This chapter provided an overview of five enduring goals of science education: scientific knowledge, scientific methods, societal issues, personal needs, and career awareness. We reviewed the status and changes of these goals in light of reports assessing science education for the period 1955 to 1975 and reform efforts of the 1980s.

Entering the twenty-first century, national standards have had, and will continue to have, a profound influence on the goals of science education. *National Science Education Standards* incorporate the enduring goals. Scientific knowledge includes the major divisions of *Physical, Life, and Earth Science* and other areas such as *Science and Technology,* the *History and Nature of Science,* and *Unifying Concepts and Processes.* The goal of scientific methods is expressed as the standard on scientific inquiry, which includes both abilities and understandings associated with inquiry. Personal needs and societal issues are consolidated in the standard on *Science in Personal and Social Perspectives.*

The national standards provide a balanced and fairly thorough expression of traditional goals. It is clear that some areas, such as technology, personal and societal perspectives, the history and nature of science, and the unifying concepts and processes, will require science teachers to broaden their understanding on content. It is significant that the aforementioned areas have the status of national standards.

———————————— **Investigating Science Teaching** ————————————

Activity 7–1
Goals of Science Teaching

Directions

1. In the blank in front of the goal statements, indicate whether you agree (A) or disagree (D) with the goal or have no opinion (NO).

2. Review and discuss your individual responses in a group of three or four persons. At this point you can add new goals, combine, modify, or omit goals. As a group you should agree on the goal statements.

3. Compile the goals from the small groups into a class set of goals for science teaching.

Goals. Science Teaching Should:

_____ 1. Make students aware of good health practices.

_____ 2. Include contemporary social problems and solutions for those problems.

_____ 3. Emphasize analytic skills more than the skills of synthesis.

_____ 4. Prepare students for careers in science-related fields.

_____ 5. Help individuals cope with their environment.

_____ 6. Provide students with an understanding of the crucial role of science and technology in our society.

_____ 7. Provide students with the ability to form a hypothesis and plan an experiment to test the hypothesis.

_____ 8. Be more concerned with scientific facts than with broad generalizations since students cannot comprehend the generalizations.

_____ 9. Develop skills basic to technical occupations and professions.

_____ 10. Be related to and clarify individual beliefs, attitudes, and values.

_____ 11. Make students aware of the fact that science is the only answer to our many social problems.

_____ 12. Help students organize concepts into broad conceptual schemes.

_____ 13. Make students aware of science-related careers.

_____ 14. Enable students to use the scientific method to solve daily problems.

_____ 15. Present fundamental knowledge and not contemporary, relevant information. If students understand the fundamentals, they can deal responsibly with personal and social issues.

_____ 16. Be future oriented; the past and present should receive marginal emphasis.

_____ 17. Place more emphasis on the methods and processes of scientific investigation.

_____ 18. Train the intuitive, inventive, creative talents more than the rational, logical, and methodological; the former more than the latter talents are responsible for new knowledge.

_____ 19. Actually involve students in science activities.

_____ 20. Develop the following abilities: creative thinking, effective communication, and decision making.

_____ 21. Demonstrate the aesthetic and ethical values of science.

_____ 22. Place great emphasis on recognizing the moral obligation of science and technology to the individual and to society.

_____ 23. Deal with broad, encompassing knowledge, since it is impossible to determine the best specific knowledge that most students will need.

_____ 24. Focus on the nature of scientific inquiry since this is the one aspect of the scientific enterprise that does not change.

_____ 25. Help students differentiate between facts and opinion and determine which is the best information available concerning problems.

Activity 7–2
The Status of Goals and Programs

As you enter this profession, it is important to reflect on your goals of science teaching in comparison with our best estimate of what is actually happening in the field. To assist you in this process, answer the following questions.

1. Why did the goals of science remain unchanged for approximately 20 years (1955–1975), then go into a period of transition?
2. What is your position on teaching science by inquiry?
3. What do you think are the important goals of science teaching?
4. What is the best way of achieving those goals?
5. What is your reaction to the teaching of science as "a body of information to be learned as dogma and accepted on faith"?

ACTIVITY 7–3
GOALS OF SCIENCE TEXTBOOKS

You have seen that the goals of textbooks are, essentially, the goals for science programs. In this activity you will first compare the goals of three textbooks or curriculum programs in your discipline. In the second part of the activity you will observe a science class for several days to see if goals are recognizable aspects of daily science teaching.

First, select three textbooks in your discipline (e.g., physics, chemistry, biology, or earth science) at the level at which you plan to teach (e.g., junior high, middle, or high school). Next, examine the textbooks and teacher guides carefully and identify the goals of the program. Are they stated clearly? Did you have to derive the goals from the text materials? Complete the following information about goals.

	Text 1	Text 2	Text 3
1. Which goals were present and recognizable? (Y = yes, N = no, or M = marginal)			
Scientific knowledge	_____	_____	_____
Scientific methods	_____	_____	_____
Societal issues	_____	_____	_____
Personal needs	_____	_____	_____
Career awareness	_____	_____	_____
2. Rank the importance of goals presented in the text. (1 = very important, 2 = important, 3 = somewhat important, 4 = marginally important, 5 = not important)			
Scientific knowledge	_____	_____	_____
Scientific methods	_____	_____	_____
Societal issues	_____	_____	_____
Personal needs	_____	_____	_____
Career awareness	_____	_____	_____
3. Were the goals: (Y = yes, N = no, M = marginal)			
Comprehensive enough to include the generally accepted objectives of science teaching?	_____	_____	_____
Understandable to other teachers, administrators, and parents?	_____	_____	_____
Free of bias toward a particular philosophy of science teaching?	_____	_____	_____
Few in number?	_____	_____	_____
Conceptually different?	_____	_____	_____
Applicable to teaching and learning objectives?	_____	_____	_____

Now that you have reviewed the goals of three texts:
1. Which text do you prefer?
2. How does the text reflect your own goals for science teaching?
3. What did you learn about the transfer of goals to the science classroom?

ACTIVITY 7–4
REFORMING GOALS TO ALIGN WITH NATIONAL STANDARDS AND BENCHMARKS

The initial task of redesigning science programs is to identify what it is about science and technology that has significance for students. This statement applies to national curriculum reform or the local development of a science program. Take a few minutes to answer the following questions.

1. What knowledge, values, skills, and sensibilities relative to science and technology are important for citizens in the twenty-first century?
2. What scientific and technological knowledge do you think is important? Why?
3. What values of science and technology would you emphasize? Why?
4. What skills and abilities are important? Why?
5. What are the sensibilities required of citizens?

CHAPTER 8

The Objectives of Science Teaching

Teachers often talk about "teaching objectives." What is meant by this term? Are they really necessary in one's day-to-day teaching? How can they help you? Might they stifle your creative impulses? Most science teachers would agree that some form and recognition of teaching objectives are necessary to become an effective teacher.

As Robert Mager (1997) in "Preparing Instructional Objectives" once said, "If you don't know where you are going, you might end up someplace else." Do objectives help you determine where you are going? This chapter may help you get a clearer picture of "where you are going" with your class. Meeting objectives involves at least two different aspects. You have certain objectives you wish to accomplish with respect to your *own* teaching progress. Then you set certain objectives you wish to have your *students* achieve. We shall concentrate on the latter group in this chapter.

As a teacher your purpose is to make it possible for students to develop an understanding of what their objectives should be. Is it factual knowledge? Is it changes in attitude? Is it recognition of their own potential as lifelong learners? Most teachers would subscribe to all of these, plus many more. This chapter will help you think about all of these possibilities.

One of the best ways to learn is to be actively involved in and with the material to be studied. To apply this principle, start by completing Activity 8–1: Objectives of Science Teaching, at the end of this chapter. In the previous chapter, we described larger purposes and directions of science education; now we will discuss specific objectives for science teaching. General goals are related to specific objectives, and both types of goals should be related to your purposes as a science teacher.

Be sure you have the most appropriate objectives for your purposes.

New Thrust in Teaching Objectives

Today, emphasis is put on the development of scientific literacy, for scientifically literate citizenry is essential in a highly technological society such as ours. Students in secondary schools form a preferred group for developing this objective.

To realize success in their efforts to develop scientifically literate students, science teachers must have a clear idea of what comprises scientific literacy and proceed to formulate classroom objectives that emphasize appropriate activities and foster the desired learning and skill development. *Achieving Scientific Literacy* (Bybee, 1997) has detailed various levels of scientific literacy as they apply to the goals and objectives of science teaching. These levels have relevance to other areas of science teaching and are discussed below.

The lowest level of literacy is the *nominal level*. Students may enter a class with minimal recognition of science terms but may not be able to give adequate or correct explanations of the scientific phenomena under discussion and may have misconceptions about them. A common problem in middle school classes is that students, when presented with a new topic to study, may believe they have already covered the material, thus diminishing their enthusiasm for the task ahead. In fact, they may have only name recognition of the topic and little or no conceptual understanding of the depth of the subject being proposed. A teacher's objective in this

GUEST EDITORIAL ◆ CARYL E. BUCHWALD

Professor of Geology and Director of the Arboretum
Carleton College, Northfield, Minnesota

TEACHING SCIENCE

Science is important to all of us. The world is in desperate need of more and better science precisely because it has been one of the dominant forces in our lives and the life of the world for several hundred years. Science and its derivative, technology, have increased the life expectancy and material well-being of Western people but at the same time have led us to the brink of disaster through ecological catastrophe or nuclear war. Science raises the hope that we can truly progress to a higher understanding of ourselves and our interrelationships with nature.

There can scarcely be a higher calling or more honorable occupation than teaching science to young people. It is important because, when well taught, science leads us to discover two characteristics that are important not only to our own lives but to the future of humanity. Science should help us to discover humility on the one hand and the ability to affect our own futures on the other.

Humility comes from studying science, for the obvious reason that we learn about our own place in nature. That we are minuscule in the universe, but domineering in the biosphere, is a position not always easy to grasp. That we are a part of the very biosphere that we dominate should lead us to realize that we cannot deny the integration of our own lives with nature.

Science is often portrayed as possessing facts and laws. Yet, when we attempt explanation in our own research, most of the time we discover that facts are contextual in time and place. Because science is really explanation and not discovery, the explanations change as we learn more or see causal relations that were previously unsuspected. When reflecting on my own career as a teacher, I am constantly amazed by how the so-called facts have changed. What has not changed is the search for data and their meaning, the use of logic, the need for verification, and the consequences of knowledge.

The consequences of knowing are important. They lead us to moral dilemmas time and time again. Atomic research has given us improved medical treatment but also nuclear bombs. Better medical treatment has eased human suffering, extended our lifetimes, and contributed to the population explosion. It is hard to do one thing at a time. The reality remains: Knowledge requires action.

What can we do with and for our students to improve their understanding of science? It seems to me that the best teachers possess two essential attributes: enthusiasm and patience. Enthusiasm stems from a love of what is being done, a belief that science is important and worth doing. Patience is needed because science is a process that must be internalized. Science is not a set of operating procedures that goes one, two, three . . . conclusions. Often it is difficult to figure out the steps that were actually taken in framing a question and seeking an explanation. To require a lock-step progression from data gathering through hypothesis to conclusion not only denies the reality of scientific activity but is likely to make students seek preconceived answers rather than to invent their own explanations.

Patience means letting students seek the relationships and explanations that fit their experience. If we insist that they hunt for the right answers, we end up teaching them the wrong thing; that is, that science is discovering the hidden. We want to teach them that science is a way to perceive nature. Seeking right answers also leads to the conclusion that science has answers entrusted to an elite and that is counter to the democratic idea.

So, we must be enthusiastic. This enthusiasm will flow from belief in what we are doing and confidence with our subject. We must be patient because science is a complex way of thinking, and it takes time for it to develop and mature.

Science teachers should consider their perceptions of themselves, students, the teaching task, and the subject before starting an instructional theory. Once this is done, they can begin to formulate such a theory by clarifying goals and preferences, understanding the theories and methods of science teaching, analyzing similarities and differences of theories and methods, and synthesizing their goals and preferences with appropriate theories and methods. Above all, science teachers should realize that they are the most important aspect of the instructional theory.

situation might be to develop a realization of the breadth and depth of the topic under consideration.

At a higher *functional level,* students may be able to define science terms correctly from memory but have little understanding of purpose, interrelationships between parts, or organizational hierarchy of terms. Teachers may want to consider objectives that emphasize the role scientific terms play in classification, in organization, and in delineating scientific usage from everyday usage of some words.

Students may achieve *conceptual and procedural literacy* if they can construct appropriate explanations based on their experiences in class or out of school, and can explain concepts in their own terms. Objectives and activities at this level should emphasize development of interrelationships between parts, applications of scientific phenomena to everyday experiences, and personal relevance of the newly learned material.

In addition, this level includes the understanding and abilities of scientific inquiry. This is what is meant by the term *procedural.*

At the *multidimensional level,* students can apply the knowledge they have gained and the skills they have developed to solve authentic problems that may require integration from other related disciplines, such as social studies, reading, and language arts. Objectives and activities at this level should provide many opportunities to work on real problems with alternate solutions that bring out the trade-offs that frequently are needed to make progress in the solutions of real-life problems.

Objectives for Constructivist Teaching

What is the main purpose of teaching? What is the science teacher attempting to do? What is the teacher's role when facing a roomful of eager (or perhaps apathetic) students? Unfortunately, there exists a residual belief that teaching is like filling a bucket—pouring knowledge in like water or sand until the student's mind (the bucket) is overflowing. A study by Aguirre, Haggerty, and Linder (in Hewson, 1995) used an open-ended questionnaire to elicit preservice science teachers' conceptions of teaching science. They found students entering preservice education programs "possessed a variety of views about science teaching and learning. For example, almost half of 74 prospective science teachers believed that teaching is a matter of knowledge transfer from teachers to the 'empty' minds of students, in contrast to about one third who believed that for learning to occur, new information should be related to existing understanding." Perhaps the encouraging feature is that as many as one third of the preservice teachers viewed teaching in a quasi-constructivist manner.

Appleton (1997) has described a constructivist-based model used during science classes. He points out, "Constructivist ideas have had a major influence on science educators over the last decade. . . . This study has resulted in a model for science lessons which allows the identification and description of students' cognitive progress through the lessons." Appleton also asserts, "The main tenet of constructivist theories is that existing ideas which learners may hold are used to make sense of new experiences and new information. Learning therefore occurs when there is a change in the learner's existing ideas, either by adding some new information or by reorganizing what is already known."

Methods for conducting science classes frequently focus on use of discrepant events. These seem to generate "cognitive conflict" or "disequilibrium." Examples of three useful approaches are: (1) teacher demonstrations to present the discrepant event, (2) teacher discussion including questioning and identifying examples drawn from students' experiences, and (3) students' conduct of the discrepant event followed by small group discussion of possible explanations. Such discrepant events as the Cartesian diver and the double pendulum were cited as examples.

The recent emphasis on inquiry-oriented science has put constructivism in the middle of learning theories relevant for teaching and learning science. The basic premise of constructivism is that learners receive sensory input, compare it to existing ideas of what appears to be similar events, modify if necessary, and construct explanations that seem to make sense (Appleton & Asoko, 1996). What learners actually construct from a given learning experience varies from student to student and often deviates from what the teacher had intended. According to George Bodner of Purdue University, "There is no conduit from one brain to another. All teachers can do is disturb the environment. Effective instruction depends on our ability to understand how students make sense of our disturbances (stimuli) rather than how we make sense of those stimuli ourselves. Knowledge is constructed by the learner" (Hackett, 1992).

Appleton and Asoko have outlined the characteristics of constructivist teaching as follows: (a) a prior awareness of the ideas which children bring to the learning situation, and/or attempts to elicit such ideas; (b) clearly defined conceptual goals for the learners and an understanding of how learners might progress toward the (ideas); (c) use of teaching strategies which involve challenge to or development of the initial ideas of the learners and ways of making new ideas accessible to them; (d) provision of opportunities for the learners to utilize new ideas in a range of contexts; and (e) provision of a classroom atmosphere which encourages children to put forward and discuss ideas (Appleton & Asoko, 1996).

Considering these factors, it becomes necessary to develop and refine classroom objectives in science. Highly effective instructional models based on constructivism include the Learning Cycle and the BSCS 5E Instructional Model (BSCS, 2006) (see Chapter 13). These employ five phases: engagement, exploration, explanation, elaboration, and evaluation. Working objectives for each of these phases are as follows:

- *Engagement.* Mentally engage students in the big ideas or concepts of the lesson. Access prior knowledge and understandings. Whet interest and curiosity.
- *Exploration.* Investigate and explore ideas together to establish a common experience base and share prior understandings.
- *Explanation.* Put forth explanations based upon prior knowledge. Develop vocabulary. Provide experiences to reinforce and strengthen understandings.
- *Elaboration.* Challenge and extend students' conceptual understanding and skills. Transfer and apply understandings of concepts to different situations. Make connections to other curriculum areas.
- *Evaluation.* Encourage students to assess their understandings and abilities and provide opportunities for teachers to evaluate progress toward achieving the educational objectives.

SELECTING OBJECTIVES FOR SCIENCE TEACHING

As you probably discovered during the introductory activity, there are many objectives for science teaching. Rather than giving our answers to your questions about objectives, we will clarify different types of science objectives and then discuss the preparation of objectives for science teaching. First, we examine six criteria that will help differentiate objectives from goals and give you a guide to selecting objectives for science teaching.

Science objectives:
1. should be general enough to be identifiably related to science goals and specific enough to give clear direction for planning and evaluating science instruction.
2. should be understandable for students, teachers, administrators, and parents.
3. should be few in number but comprehensive for any lesson, unit, or program.
4. should be challenging yet attainable for your students.
5. should differ conceptually from each other.
6. should be appropriate for the subject you are teaching.

TYPES OF OBJECTIVES FOR SCIENCE TEACHING

Objectives can be stated in terms of instructional or learning results. In the first example, the emphasis is on what the teacher does; in the second example, it is on what the student does.

- "To demonstrate to students how to use a barometer"
- "Students should be able to describe correct procedures in the use of a barometer"

The advantage of stating objectives as instructional results is that it gives you direction. The disadvantage is that you may not be clear as to whether the students learned anything. In general, we suggest that you concentrate on learning results when forming objectives. Doing so will help define the instruction sequence, set the stage for evaluation, and define acceptable criteria for assessment.

Objectives can be classified as either behavioral or nonbehavioral. Behavioral objectives state an observable indication that learning has occurred. Examples of behavioral objectives are as follows:

The student should be able to:

- identify symbols on a weather map,
- describe predator and prey relationships, and
- define the term energy.

For contrast, examples of nonbehavioral objectives are as follows:

The student should be able to:

- learn scientific names for common animals,
- comprehend the concept of work,
- know how to use the scientific method, and
- note the action verb in each stated objective.

All seven of these examples could be objectives for science lessons, and they are all stated in terms of learning results for students. In the first set, the specific behaviors have been stated: if students can identify . . ., describe . . ., and define . . ., then they have learned. The second set is a little less clear as to how you will know whether students have learned . . ., do comprehend . . ., or do know. Are behavioral objectives better than nonbehavioral? Here are some advantages and disadvantages of behavioral objectives.

Advantages of behavioral objectives include the following:

- They help the science teacher become more precise in teaching.
- They clarify exactly what is expected.
- They provide performance criteria for student achievement and accountability for the teacher.

- The teacher plans more carefully because she or he knows what performance the students should display after finishing a science lesson, unit, or course of study.
- The teacher knows what materials are needed and is able to give more specific help to students in directing them to outside sources of information.
- The teacher who prepares behavioral objectives finds them very helpful in evaluation. When preparing paper and pencil tests, the questions can be matched to the objectives and, by deciding on certain criteria of performance, questions can be phrased in such a way that the teacher has precise knowledge of the ability of the student to perform certain tasks.

Disadvantages of behavioral objectives include the following:

- They may tend toward an emphasis on trivial behaviors and ignore important objectives that are too difficult to define behaviorally.
- They may inhibit the teacher's spontaneity and flexibility.
- They may provide a precise measurement of less important behaviors, leaving more important outcomes unevaluated.
- They may be used against teachers who are held accountable for the performance of students who do not learn.
- They tend to focus the teacher's attention on the small, less-significant aspects of teaching, leaving the larger picture unattended.
- They represent only one particular psychology and philosophy of education (namely behaviorism).

DOMAINS OF OBJECTIVES FOR SCIENCE TEACHING

It is customary to think of objectives in three aspects: *cognitive, affective,* and *psychomotor.* These terms come from the work of Benjamin Bloom and others who developed taxonomies of educational objectives (Bloom et al., 1950; Krathwohl et al., 1965; Kibler et al., 1970). Cognitive objectives deal with intellectual results, knowledge, concepts, and understanding. Affective objectives include the feelings, interests, attitudes, and appreciations that may result from science instruction. The psychomotor domain includes objectives that stress motor development, muscular coordination, and physical skills.

Traditionally, cognitive objectives have received far more attention over the years than affective or psychomotor objectives. With increased attention to behavioral objectives and performance competencies,

the cognitive area becomes fertile ground for writing objectives that stress performance in science knowledge and conceptual understanding. Still, science teachers should not omit important learning results in the affective and psychomotor domains.

Your understanding of the three domains will be one of the most helpful aids in formulating objectives for science teaching. We have used categories from the cognitive, affective, and psychomotor domains as the basis for tables summarizing instructional objectives in science (see Tables 8–1 through 8–6). The tables are based on the original work of Bloom et al. (1950), Krathwohl et al. (1965), and Norman Gronlund (1970). The domains are arranged in Table 8–1, in a hierarchical order, from simple to complex learning results.

The Cognitive Domain

The cognitive domain starts with acquiring simple knowledge about science and proceeds through increasingly difficult levels: comprehension, application, analysis, synthesis, and evaluation. The categories are inclusive because higher level results incorporate the lower levels. For example, students must know a science concept before they can apply it. Science teachers usually have concentrated on the cognitive domain and the lower levels of learning within the domain. Understanding the hierarchical nature of this and other domains increases your awareness of higher levels of science objectives and, subsequently, higher levels of student achievement. (See Tables 8–1 and 8–2 for a

A science teacher and her supervisor review objectives for science lessons.

TABLE 8–1   Cognitive Domain for Science Teaching

Knowing

Knowledge represents the lowest level of science objectives. The definition of knowledge for this level is remembering previously learned scientific material. The requirement is to simply recall, that is, bring to mind appropriate information. The range of information may vary from simple facts to complex theories, but all that is required is to remember the information.

Comprehending

Comprehension is the first step beyond simple recall. It is the first level, demonstrating and understanding of scientific information. It is the ability to apprehend, grasp, and understand the meaning of scientific material. Comprehension is shown in three ways: (1) translation of scientific knowledge into forms, (2) interpretation of science knowledge by reordering and showing interrelationships and summarizing material, and (3) extrapolation and interpolation of science knowledge. Here the students can estimate or predict future trends or infer consequences between two points or items of data.

Applying

Application is the ability to show the pertinence of scientific principles to different situations. At this level students may

apply scientific concepts, methods, laws, or theories to actual concrete problems.

Analyzing

Analysis requires more than knowledge, comprehension, and application. It also requires an understanding of the underlying structure of the material. Analysis is the ability to break down material to its fundamental elements for better understanding of the organization. Analysis may include identifying parts, clarifying relationships among parts, and recognizing organizational principles of scientific systems.

Synthesizing

Synthesis requires the formulation of new understandings of scientific systems. If analysis stresses the parts, synthesis stresses the whole. Components of scientific systems may be reorganized into new patterns and new wholes. A bringing together of scientific ideas to form a unique idea, place, or pattern could be a learning result at this level.

Evaluating

Evaluation is the highest level of learning results in the hierarchy. It includes all the other levels plus the ability to make value judgments based on internal evidence and consistency and/or clearly defined external criteria.

---

summary of the cognitive domain and examples of general and specific instructional objectives in science.)

WRITING COGNITIVE OBJECTIVES

Much of science learning in the past has been concerned with gaining knowledge of factual or conceptual nature on science topics. This is still true, but it now comes with some recent recognition that the volume of such knowledge has become overwhelming with the rapid advancements in science. The information overload for science students has become intolerable. What is a realistic solution to this problem?

One solution is to make appropriate selections within the topical field and reduce the number of topics taught. Judicious use of well-defined cognitive objectives can help in this process. To do this, prepare a short list of cognitive objectives that progress from simple to more complex levels. For example, suppose the topic you plan to teach is "weather" with a subtopic of "severe storms."

You do not have to spell out in detail every cognitive objective that might seem necessary to learn about severe storms. Instead, use Bloom's taxonomy of educational objectives as a guide and prepare one

objective for each level (knowledge, comprehension, application, analysis, synthesis, and evaluation). As illustration, under knowledge, you might have, "Student should be able to describe two differences between tornadoes and hurricanes." Or, under evaluation, you might have, "Student should be able to assess the probable damage to beach-side residences as a result of a close passage of a moderate hurricane on the East Coast of the United States."

Keep in mind that every objective should contain an action verb that describes what the student should be able to do as a result of studying the particular topic under concern. In the two previous examples the words *describe* and *assess* are the action verbs.

The Affective Domain

Affective objectives deal with feelings, interests, and attitudes. Science teachers are becoming increasingly concerned with this area in our schools today. Neglect or lack of attention to attitudes has produced some unexpected results. Often students are losing interest in science at a time when scientific advances are unparalleled in the history of humanity. Greater numbers of students and adults

TABLE 8–2 Examples of General Objectives, Behavioral Objectives, and Terms for Specifying Objectives for Science Instruction in the Cognitive Domain

	General Objectives	Behavioral Objectives	Terms for Objectives
Knowing	Knows scientific facts Knows scientific methods Knows basic principles of earth science, biology, chemistry, physics Knows the conceptual schemes of science	To label the parts of a frog To list the steps in the scientific method To state the second law of thermodynamics	Define, describe, identify, label, list, name, select, state
Comprehending	Understands scientific facts Interprets scientific principles Translates formulas to verbal statements Estimates the consequences of data Justifies procedures of scientific investigation	To distinguish between scientific facts and theories To explain Newton's laws To give examples of density To infer the results of continued population growth To defend procedures in problem solving	Convert, defend, interpolate, estimate, explain, extrapolate, generalize, infer, predict, summarize
Applying	Applies scientific concepts to new situations Applies theories to practical events Constructs graphs from data Uses scientific procedures correctly	To apply the theory of natural selection to new data To predict the results of fossil fuel depletion To prepare a graph of temperature changes of ascending and descending air masses	Apply, compute, discover, modify, operate, predict, prepare, relate, show, use
Analyzing	Identifies stated and unstated assumptions of a scientific theory Recognizes logical fallacies in arguments Differentiates between facts and inferences Evaluates the appropriateness of data Analyzes the structure of a scientific inquiry	To identify the assumptions of Newtonian physics To point out logical connections in the reasoning of scientific principles applied to practice To distinguish fact from assertion To select relevant data for the solution of a problem	Analyze, diagram, differentiate, discriminate, divide, identify, illustrate, infer, relate, select
Synthesizing	Gives an organized account of two theories applied to a problem Proposes procedures for solving a problem Integrates principles from meteorology, biology, and chemistry in a discussion of pollution Formulates a scheme for resolving an interdisciplinary problem	To combine the second law of thermodynamics and principles of supply and demand in discussing energy To solve an original scientific problem To relate different scientific principles To design procedures for classifying unrelated objects	Arrange, combine, compile, compose, construct, devise, design, generate, organize, plan, relate, reorganize, summarize, synthesize
Evaluating	Judges the adequacy of a theory to explain actual phenomena Judges the value of a solution by use of internal and external criteria	To criticize the theory of continental drift To evaluate the Green Revolution as a solution to world food problems	Appraise, compare, conclude, contrast, discriminate, explain, evaluate, interpret, relate, summarize

are questioning science, perhaps because of a poor understanding of its role in society or because of confusion over the relationships between science and technology.

Writing affective objectives usually is more difficult than writing those in the cognitive area. It requires more care to formulate criteria for feelings, interests, and attitudes. It is impossible to peer inside the student's head and determine what attitudes are there. However, certain behaviors are indicative of students' attitudes or interests. Students have attitudes and values toward the scientific enterprise, an enterprise that is, of course, valuable in itself.

As science teachers we are as much obligated to present scientific attitudes and values as we are to present scientific facts and concepts. What are some of these attitudes and values? In Chapter 3 we described scientific values. Others are curiosity, openness to different ideas, objectivity, precision, accuracy in reporting, perseverance in work, and questioning of ideas. Tables 8–3 and 8–4 should further clarify science objectives for the affective domain.

WRITING AFFECTIVE OBJECTIVES

Turning the student objectives in the affective domain into behavioral objectives requires attention to the use of action verbs that describe behavioral changes in such things as interest development, changes in attitudes, appreciations, and development of values. These are all legitimate objectives and important in the growth of

understanding the essence of science and technology in society today.

Because the observation and evaluation of behavioral changes among students in the affective areas is somewhat more difficult than in cognitive and psychomotor domains, it is important to design objectives that are carefully thought out and stated with precision. The teacher can observe many affective changes in behavior during the course of instruction. These might be called overt behavioral changes. Others, more subtle, may not be directly observable and, therefore, can be called covert.

Here are some examples of overt and covert behavioral objectives in the affective domain.

> Overt: Students should be able to give evidence of behavioral change in the development of interest in the study of crystals by voluntarily selecting three or more books from the library and reading them for their own understanding of crystals.

Note that in the statement of this behavioral objective, the word *voluntarily* is included. This is important because evidence of behavioral change in interest development can only be credible if the student shows a voluntary response. If it is in the form of a teacher assignment, extra credit, or other structured request, there is doubt about whether the response represents a true behavioral change.

> Covert: Students will give evidence of behavioral change in development of a set of values in classroom demeanor

TABLE 8–3 Affective Domain for Science Teaching

Receiving

Receiving or attending to stimuli related to science is the lowest level of learning result in the affective domain. Receiving means that students are aware of the existence of and are willing to attend to scientific phenomena. When students are paying attention in science class, they are probably behaving at this level. The three levels of receiving are: (1) awareness that science-related topics and issues exist, (2) willingness to receive information about science, and (3) selective attention to science topics.

Responding

Responding means that the learner does something with or about scientific phenomena. The student not only attends to but also reacts to science-related materials. Learning results can have three levels of responses: (1) acquiescence—meaning that the student does what is assigned or required, (2) willingness—meaning that the student does science study above and beyond requirements, and (3) satisfaction—meaning that the student studies science for pleasure and enjoyment.

Valuing

Valuing refers to consistent behavior that indicates the student's preference for science. The valuing level is based

on internalized values related to science. Again, valuing includes three levels: (1) acceptance of scientific values, (2) preference for scientific values, and (3) commitment to scientific values. Instructional objectives related to attitudes and appreciation would be included at this level of the affective hierarchy.

Organizing

Organizing means that the student brings together different scientific values and builds a consistent value system. Learning results include the conceptualization of scientific values and the organization of a personal value system based on science. The student is organizing a philosophy of life based on scientific values.

Characterizing

Characterizing means that, in effect, the individual has developed a lifestyle based on the preferred value system— in this case science. The individual's behavior is consistently and predictably related to scientific values. Learning results related to general patterns of behavior would be aligned with this level.

TABLE 8–4 Examples of General Objectives, Behavioral Objectives, and Terms for Specifying Objectives for Science Instruction in the Affective Domain

	General Objectives	Behavioral Objectives	Terms for Objectives
Receiving	Attention to activities in science Awareness of the importance of science Sensitivity toward science-related social issues	To listen during chemistry class To ask questions about physics To select a book on geology to read	Ask, attend, choose, follow, identify, listen, locate, look, select, tell
Responding	Completes assignments in science Participates in science class Discusses science Shows an interest in science Helps other students with science	To respond to questions related to photosynthesis To complete a report on glaciers To discuss the limitations and potential of science in social issues	Answer, assist, complete, discuss, do, help, perform, practice, read, recite, report, select, tell, watch, write
Valuing	Demonstrates confidence in science and technology Appreciates the role of science and technology Demonstrates the values of scientific problem solving Prefers science over other subjects	To initiate further study in ecology To work on community projects relating to recycling To complete a science project To accept leadership in the science club	Accept, argue, complete, commit, describe, do, explain, follow, initiate, invite, join, prefer, propose, read, report, study, work
Organizing	Recognizes the responsibility of science and technology to society Develops a rationale for the place of science in society Bases judgments on evidence Accepts scientific values as personal values	To present scientific values as one's own To defend the right of scientists to do research To argue using fact, evidence, and data	Adhere, alter, argue, combine, defend, explain, integrate, modify, organize, synthesize
Characterizing	Uses problem solving for daily problems in work Displays scientific values Shows a consistent philosophy of life based on scientific values	To solve problems objectively To verify knowledge To display scientific attitudes	Act, confirm, display, influence, perform, practice, propose, question, refute, serve, solve, use, verify

by voluntarily self-reporting that they plan to assist other students to improve their skills of sharing with other classmates.

In this statement, note the addition of the word *self-reporting*. In a covert objective there can be no outward sign of the behavioral change, although such change may have taken place in the student. Therefore, the teacher must rely on the student's own statement of intent. Although this may not ensure complete validity, it is an improvement over complete lack of observable evidence. Many covert objectives involving feelings, likes and dislikes, and valuing fall into this category.

The Psychomotor Domain

In science, psychomotor objectives concern learning results which involve physical manipulation of apparatus, proficiency in using tools—such as scientific instruments and devices, and developing abilities associated with inquiry. Many of these desired behaviors are not ends in themselves but are means for cognitive and affective learning. This observation points out the interrelation of the three domains and stresses the importance of total learning by the individual. Since one of the goals of education is to produce fully competent individuals who are self-reliant and capable of pursuing learning on their own throughout their lives, the psychomotor objectives occupy an important place in the overall educational endeavor. Although psychomotor objectives play a major role in physical activities, their importance in science classes should not be overlooked, especially since much of science instruction involves laboratory work requiring the physical handling and manipulation of materials. In Tables 8–5 and 8–7,

TABLE 8–5 Alternative View of Psychomotor Domain for Science Teaching

Simple

This initial state of psychomotor behavior is one which confirms positive readiness and mental set for the learner's further development in this skill area. It is not to be viewed as an objective in "performance" terms. Learner objectives need not be written at this level. However, if the teacher is keenly observing the learner's imitative activity, and reads the learner's need accurately, the teacher can, at this point, identify appropriate objectives(s) to move the learner through the succeeding stages (manipulation, etc.).

Imitation

Imitation refers to perceptual readiness (eyes, touch, muscle sense, etc.). When learners are exposed to an observable action they begin to make covert imitation of that action. Such covert behavior appears to be the starting point in the growth of psychomotor skill. This is then followed by overt performance of an act and capacity to repeat it. The performance, however, lacks neuromuscular coordination or control and hence is generally in a crude and imperfect form. This level is characterized by impulse, crude reproduction, and repetition, as well as a low degree of learner control, accuracy, and confidence.

Manipulation

This domain emphasizes the development of skill in following directions, performing selected actions, and fixation of performance through necessary practice. At this level learners are capable of performing an act according to instruction rather than just on the basis of observation as is the case at the level of imitation. They are able to follow directions, give attention to form, and begin to integrate their motor responses.

Precision

The proficiency of performance reaches a higher level of refinement in reproducing a given act. Here, accuracy, proportion, and exactness in performance become significant. The actions are characterized by minimal errors, higher degree of control, and increased self-confidence.

Articulation

Articulation involves the coordination of a series of acts by establishing appropriate sequence and accomplishing harmony or internal consistency among different acts. Accurate, controlled performance incorporates elements of speed and time. Learners' responses become habitual, yet are capable of being modified.

Naturalization

A high level of proficiency in the skill or performance of a single act is required. The behavior is performed with the least expenditure of psychic energy. At this level, the performance is smooth and natural. It is routinized, automatic, and spontaneous, and performed with a high degree of learner confidence.

---

we have relied on our own experience and understanding of psychomotor skills required for learning science. Table 8–5 represents a view used in music education and may be applicable in science education as well.

WRITING PSYCHOMOTOR OBJECTIVES

In science teaching, one is particularly concerned that objectives include developing the types of behaviors involving physical movement relating to the use of equipment in laboratories, field observations, and investigative activities that require careful and precise measurements. The skills that are to be developed are those that will be used repeatedly in all science classes and will form the basis for good scientific study as students progress to higher class levels in high school and college.

As with cognitive and affective objectives, keep in mind the use of action verbs that designate clearly what the student should do or perform to satisfy the objective. Repeated attention to this will develop habits that automatically ensure the performance outcomes to be desired. The cognitive, affective, and psychomotor domains have been outlined for your use in preparing instructional objectives for science teaching

(Table 8–6). Each domain has a hierarchical order that goes from simple to complex learning results. As you prepare objectives for science teaching, we suggest that you use Tables 8–1 to 8–6 as guides to the levels of learning and the formulation of general and specific objectives.

- ◆ Clarify objectives for an instructional unit.
- ◆ Identify appropriate levels for instructional objectives.
- ◆ Define objectives in meaningful terms.
- ◆ Prepare comprehensive lists of objectives for instruction.
- ◆ Integrate the cognitive, affective, and psychomotor domains in your teaching.
- ◆ Communicate intentions, levels, and nature of learning, relative to your instructional unit.

Don't be a slave to the classification systems. You may have some objectives that do not fit in any domains and others that fit all three. Be less concerned about classifying your objectives and more concerned about how they will contribute to making you more effective as a science teacher so that your students will become better learners.

TABLE 8–6 Examples of General Objectives, Behavioral Objectives, and Terms for Specifying Objectives for Science Instruction in the Psychomotor Domain

	General Objectives	Behavioral Objectives	Terms for Objectives
Moving	Walking smoothly in science class Moving around the science class without problems Keeping up with the class on science field trips	To clean and replace science materials To carry a microscope properly To obtain and carry materials for laboratory activities	Adjust, carry, clean, follow, locate, move, obtain, store, walk
Manipulating	Manipulating science materials without damaging them Coordinating several activities during laboratory periods Performing skillfully in the science laboratory Operating science equipment safely	To set up science laboratory equipment quickly To adjust a microscope so that the image is clear To dissect with precision To operate scientific instruments correctly To assemble science apparatus To pour chemicals safely	Adjust, assemble, build, calibrate, change, clean, connect, construct, dismantle, fasten, handle, heat, make, mix, repair, set, stir, weigh
Communicating	Informing the teacher of problems Communicating results of science activities Drawing accurate reproductions of microscopic images Talking and writing clearly and logically Explaining science information clearly	To communicate problems in handling equipment To ask questions about problems To listen to other students To write legibly To report data accurately To graph data accurately	Ask, analyze, describe, discuss, compose, draw, explain, graph, label, listen, record, sketch, write
Creating	Creating new scientific apparatus for solving problems Designing new scientific devices Inventing different techniques	To create different ways of solving problems To combine different pieces of equipment to form a new science instrument or device To plan ways to solve problems	Analyze, construct, create, design, invent, plan, synthesize

PREPARING OBJECTIVES FOR SCIENCE TEACHING

The task of writing objectives can be simplified by following these steps:

1. *Have your overall instructional objectives in mind.* What are your general objectives for the lesson or unit you are going to teach? Is it improvement of a skill? Developing the understanding of a concept? Stimulating interest in a new area of science? A combination of these objectives? Are your objectives cognitive? Affective? Psychomotor? Is there congruence between the levels of objectives and your instructional aims?

2. *Select the content desired to achieve the objectives of the unit.* In many teaching situations, unit goals may depend on the sequence of topics found in a science textbook or curriculum guide. However, the presence of a topical outline should not influence your teaching objectives. After all, you are trying to achieve certain objectives for a unique group of students. The topics chosen should be vehicles to achieve these objectives. Usually, several subject-matter topics can be used to accomplish the task. Select those that are appropriate in terms of student interests and needs, your interest, suitability to the background of the students, and other factors. If you live in a mountainous area, use mountain terrain and topography to teach about variations of

Students and teachers work together to establish appropriate teaching and learning objectives.

weather in different locations. Adapt your teaching to local situations. If brachiopods and trilobites can be found in a local limestone quarry, use that resource to teach about fossils rather than discussing forms that can be found only as pictures in books or in exotic collections from laboratory supply houses. Selection of content is very important. Try to find content that is both appropriate to your objectives and personally meaningful to your students.

3. *Write general statements describing how the student should perform.* Begin these statements with a verb (*knows, defines, responds, calibrates,* etc.), and then state what it is you intend to accomplish. It is helpful to write these statements in terms of learning results for the students. Be sure you have stated only one learning result per objective. Three or four general objectives should be sufficient for any lesson and six to eight for sets of lessons or units. When the general objectives are completed, you should be able to relate them to the general goals of science education and to identify an instructional plan or sequence for your lesson. (See the first column of Tables 8–2, 8–4, and 8–6.)

4. *Write specific objectives under the general statements.* Again, the objective should start with a verb and state a learning result that is related to the general objective. Usually two or three specific objectives will be sufficient to describe the specific learning results. You may wish to change general and/or specific objectives after the closer analysis provided by this step. (See the second and third columns of Tables 8–2, 8–4, and 8–6.) Following is an example using the general objective stated in step 3, "Interprets scientific principles:"

a. Defends inquiry-oriented procedures in problem solving
b. Distinguishes between scientific facts and theories
c. Identifies correct and incorrect inquiry procedures in the work of others

Note that the conditions for good objectives are clear in the example; that is, both the general and specific objectives are clear, since they use a verb and they define observable learning results. Satisfactory performance of the task can be shown by the student's ability to apply the inquiry process to his or her own problem, to summarize the process, and to identify correct and incorrect procedures in the work of other students. Certainly there could be other learning results for this problem, but this one should serve as an example.

5. *Review and evaluate objectives in terms of their comprehensiveness, coherence, and contribution to the science lesson unit or program.* The evaluation should identify any imbalance between levels of objectives or domains. Are all your objectives at the lower levels of the cognitive domain? We hope not. (Use Tables 8–2, 8–4, and 8–6 to help in the review.)

SUMMARY

You should have good, clear objectives for science teaching. Without objectives, teaching may become a confused and directionless experience, frustrating to the teacher, and ineffective for the students. Good objectives include a statement that uses action verbs, signifies learning results in observable or measurable terms, describes the conditions under which the performance can be expected, and indicates the level of attainment needed to satisfy the objective. Objectives often are divided into cognitive, affective, and psychomotor types. The first pertains to conceptual understandings or knowledge objectives. The second refers to attitudes, feelings, interests, and appreciations. Psychomotor objectives refer to skills and competencies that involve manipulation, coordination, or sensory achievements.

The steps in preparing objectives are as follows: (1) Review your general intentions; (2) select the content; (3) write general objectives; (4) write specific objectives; and (5) review your objectives for comprehensiveness, coherence, and contribution to the lesson.

The use of clearly stated objectives in science teaching is significant. Although critics have cited certain pitfalls to be avoided, the overall effect of good objectives appears to be beneficial. Science teachers are more conscious of the performance they expect from their students. Evaluation becomes more precise and progress toward the attainment of goals is more easily measurable.

— **INVESTIGATING SCIENCE TEACHING** —

ACTIVITY 8–1
OBJECTIVES OF SCIENCE TEACHING

Directions

1. In the blank provided before each statement of objectives, indicate your evaluation of each. Is it excellent (E), good (G), fair (F), poor (P), or not an objective (NO)? Complete this portion individually.

2. Review your individual responses in a small group of three or four persons. At this point you should discuss why you evaluated the objectives the way you did.

3. As a class, review the strengths and weaknesses of the objectives as you presently understand them.

Objectives

_____ 1. Describe the relationship between pressure and volume of an enclosed gas and predict either variable when the other is changed independently.

_____ 2. Demonstrate skill in setting up science laboratory materials.

_____ 3. Know science.

_____ 4. Appreciate the nature of scientific inquiry.

_____ 5. Teach students the concept of density.

_____ 6. Enjoy interacting with friends in science class.

_____ 7. Given a scientific problem, define variables, formulate hypotheses, and test the hypotheses.

_____ 8. Handle a microscope properly.

_____ 9. Record data appropriately.

_____ 10. At the completion of the lesson, prepare a growth curve showing the relationship of the age of a bacterial culture to the density of organisms and predict the results of continued growth.

_____ 11. Really show curiosity.

_____ 12. Show scientific attitudes (e.g., openness, reality testing, risk-taking, objectivity, precision, perseverance).

_____ 13. Perform skillfully while working in the laboratory.

_____ 14. Judge the logical consistency of a scientific theory.

_____ 15. Display habits of safety.

_____ 16. Know common scientific terms.

_____ 17. Demonstrate to the students different geologic processes.

_____ 18. Having fun in science.

_____ 19. Identify energy chains in a community.

_____ 20. Is able, upon completion of the lesson, to draw, label, and explain it.

_____ 21. Science teaching should make students aware of the relationship between the scientific enterprise and society.

_____ 22. At the completion of this lesson the student should understand the meaning of science as it relates to the good life.

_____ 23. Operational definition of scientific truth.

_____ 24. The student shows the scientific attitude of perseverance by pursuing a problem to its solution.

_____ 25. Understands the basic principle of density.

    a. States the principle in his or her own words.

    b. Give an example of the principle from life, physical, and earth science.

    c. Distinguish between correct and incorrect applications of the principle.

CHAPTER
9

ASSESSMENT OF STUDENT LEARNING

As a teacher of science, you have incredible power—the power to help others learn, the power to improve your teaching. Where do you get this power? From assessment! Do you know that you can influence the motivation of students to learn science, and can modify the study habits of students in your classes? Do you know that you have the power to change attitudes and develop new interests and directions for learning?

Most science teachers look at assessment as an unpleasant task—one that unfortunately has to be done, and the quicker the better! Because of this, assessment is frequently left until the end of a unit or lesson and used in less than constructive ways. Then tests are often hastily developed and given to the student—sometimes the test aligns with what was taught, sometimes it does not. However absurd this sounds, the scenario is more true than false. These test results are then often put into the form of grades and given to the students, mainly for ranking students and providing reports to parents. The teacher relaxes in the knowledge that the students have been tested, at least for the time being.

Happily, assessment involves much more than this. With careful planning and sufficient time to prepare the form of assessment, evaluation can be an integral part of the teaching and learning process, which is what it should be. Diagnostic evaluation helps you understand your students' background, knowledge, and abilities as you begin teaching. Formative evaluation in the assessment helps you learn about student difficulties as you go through class instruction. The kind of assessment you do at the end of your instruction is called *summative evaluation* and is generally used for giving grades, ranking students, or placing them in groups.

Throughout this book we have been talking about innovative and effective teaching and learning strategies, such as inquiry-oriented learning. These methods require different kinds of assessment than are found in traditional, expository teaching. Especially with the greater emphasis on developing lifelong learning skills, new assessments, including tests, have to be devised that assess those skills.

A common perception among teachers is that assessment is limited to giving tests. The broader aspects of assessment—including self-evaluation by students; evaluation of laboratory work; diagnostic, formative, and summative evaluation; and other aspects of the total assessment process—are sometimes misunderstood by teachers. Most teachers have received little formal training in evaluation, and so their evaluation methods have traditionally tended to be formal, concentrating on quizzes and end of chapter or unit tests.

As a result, instruction and evaluation are thought of as separate entities. In addition, an adversarial relationship seems to exist between the evaluator and those being evaluated, thus minimizing the evaluation's effectiveness and destroying one of the very reasons for doing it—the valid assessment of achievement, attitudes, skill development, and progress. Assessment should be considered a vital part of instruction and inseparable from it. In this chapter, many illustrations will show the connections between instruction and assessment.

ASSESSMENT STANDARDS

The *National Science Education* Standards (NRC, 1996) contain assessment standards. We also note an addendum on assessment that was developed to elaborate assessment principles and practices described in the standards. That addendum is *Classroom Assessment and the National Science Education Standards* (NRC, 2001).

In Assessment Standard A—Coordination with Intended Purposes—assessments are deliberately designed, and have explicitly stated purposes.

Under Assessment Standard B—Measuring Student Achievement and Opportunity to Learn—the data collected should focus on science content that is most important for students, and equal attention should be given both to opportunities to learn and to assessment of student achievement.

Under Assessment Standard C—Matching Technical Quality of Data with Consequences—it should be clear that features that are claimed to be measured are actually measured and that assessment tasks are authentic, that is, that they represent similar tasks or performance that is being assessed. Students should have adequate opportunities to demonstrate their achievements.

In Assessment Standard D—Avoiding Bias— assessment practices must be fair. Avoid the use of stereotypes or language that may be offensive to a particular group. Do not assume that experiences or perspectives of a particular group will apply equally to other groups with different backgrounds.

An important goal of assessment is to develop self-directed learners. Thus, the students must understand the purpose of the assessment and have opportunities for conversations and input into the assessment practices.

In summary, the standards include focusing on what is most important for students to learn in science and providing data that may lead to valid inferences about students' science attainment. The data collected should be consistent with the particular aspect of science attainment being assessed and should be equally fair for all students. Science teachers should be involved in the design and implementation of the assessment materials and procedures and should consider the intended use of the resulting information. Finally, equal attention should be given to the assessment of the opportunities to learn as well as to student attainment.

THE CASE FOR STRENGTHENING ASSESSMENT IN THE SCIENCE CLASSROOM

Evaluation involves the total assessment of student learning. It includes evaluating their understanding of the process of science, subject-matter competence and achievement, multiple talents, scientific attitudes, laboratory skills, and willingness to work. The progress of the students toward the goals of your course, in particular,

and of the school, in general, need to be considered. Good evaluation indicates the strengths and weaknesses of instruction. Once a teacher has made a thorough assessment, she has an indication of how to improve her teaching. Evaluation acts as feedback in the experimental process of teaching. Teachers must experiment in order to progress and become more skilled. They must be willing to try new methods and new techniques and, by so doing, evolve toward teaching mastery.

Multiple Purposes of Assessment

Science teaching is a scientific inquiry where teachers gather data in the laboratory, in daily classroom activities, and in the many and varied encounters they have with students. An inquiry approach assumes collection of data to verify the success of the methods used and the areas that require improvement. Assessment techniques are a great source of data. The better the evaluation instruments, the greater the information available to the teacher for improving teaching. Classroom assessment usually falls into one of three categories: diagnostic, formative, or summative.

Diagnostic evaluation normally precedes instruction but may be used during instruction to uncover student learning problems. Diagnostic evaluation can provide information to teachers about the knowledge, attitudes, and skills of the students entering a course and can be used as a basis for individual remediation or special instruction.

Formative evaluation is carried on during the instructional period to provide feedback to students and teachers on how well the material is being taught and learned. Because teaching is a dynamic process, formative evaluation can provide useful information that teachers can use to modify instruction and can improve teaching effectiveness so that greater learning and understanding occur. Black and Wiliam (1998a) define formative assessment as "all those activities undertaken by teachers and by their students [that] provide information to be used as feedback to modify the teaching and learning activities in which they are engaged."

The third kind of evaluation, *summative*, is the kind that is used most often by teachers and is primarily aimed toward providing student grades and reports of achievement. It is most frequently based upon cognitive gains and rarely takes into consideration other areas of learning and growth. Summative assessment is generally used at the end of an instructional unit to assess the final outcome of that unit in terms of student learning.

The authors of *Classroom Assessment and the National Science Education Standards* (NRC, 2001) recommend that you consider three questions when designing and integrating assessment into your classroom practice:

- Where are you now?
- Where are you trying to go?
- How can you get there?

By keeping these questions in mind when planning your assessments, you will be able to keep a focus, communicate expectations clearly to your students, and achieve more in your classroom.

The Case for Formative Assessment

Certain research supports the importance of formative assessment in ensuring student understanding of science. For example, in Black and Wiliam's (1998a) review of more than 250 articles and books, they were able to conclude that formative assessment is an essential component of classroom instruction and, in fact, a necessary component when attempting to raise standards. The significance of formative assessment can only be realized, however, when teachers and students *use* the information gained from the assessment to inform teaching and influence learning. The learning gains possible from systematic attention to the data from formative assessment has been documented to be larger than for any other type of educational intervention (Black & Wiliam, 1998b). To make sure that formative assessment is an effective tool for increased learning, teachers must focus on the *quality* of their feedback. Research indicates that the use of descriptive, criterion-based feedback is much more useful and effective for the student than numerical scoring or letter grades that do not relate back to clear criteria (Bangert-Downs, Kulik, Kulik, & Morgan, 1991; Sadler, 1989; Butler & Neuman, 1995; Cameron & Pierce, 1994; Kluger & deNisi, 1996).

The Case for Summative Assessment

Effective summative assessment has a clear and valued target; attends to many facets of learning, including content understanding, application, processes, and reasoning; and includes a role for student reflection (NRC, 2001; Stiggins, 2001; McTighe & Ferrara, 1998). You can accomplish all this in your summative assessment if you plan ahead, use assessment resources, and vary the types of assessments you use. Table 9–1 offers a way to think about approaches for classroom assessment.

The Impact of High-Stakes Assessment

The United States is in an era of high-stakes, large-scale testing that has not been seen since standardized tests were introduced in the early 1900s. At that time, standards tests were used by the Army to determine which specialty to assign to each recruit in preparation for World War I. In the 1920s, IQ tests were used by schools to sort students into different programs, such as college preparation, general education, or vocational program. Then in the 1930s and 1940s, colleges began using national examination as part of the admission process. These uses of national testing pale in comparison to the use of state and national level assessments today (NRC, 2001; Shepard, 2003).

These assessments are now administered to every student in districts at multiple grade levels. Public officials then use the scores to rank schools, make financial decisions, determine continued certification, and set teachers' salaries. When you are visiting schools during your teacher education, ask about the role and

TABLE 9–1 Assessment Approaches in the Classroom

Selected Response Format	Constructed Response Format			
Multiple choice True-false	Brief Constructed Response	Performance Assessment		
Matching	Fill in the blank	Product	Performance	Process-Focused
Enhanced multiple choice	Words	Research paper	Oral presentation	Debate
	Phrases	Poem	Lab demonstration	Teach-a-lesson
	Short answer	Portfolio	Enactment	Oral question
	Sentences	Project		Observation
	Paragraphs	Model		Interview
	Label a diagram	Video/audio tape		Conference
	Visual representation	Spreadsheet		Think aloud
	Essay	Lab report		Journal

Source: Adapted from McTighe & Ferrara, 1998.

influence of national, state, and local standardized tests in each school. Use what you learn to formulate questions to ask when you are interviewing for teaching positions.

EVERYONE HAS A ROLE IN ASSESSMENT

The Teacher's Role

Because good assessment is varied, the role of the teacher is varied, also. Above all, the teacher must be prepared. Know what you want your students to learn and what sort of information will count as evidence that the learning has occurred. You will need to have clear criteria that you communicate to students and you will have to allow time to teach your expectations and criteria to the students. Good assessment is not an afterthought; it takes instructional time and should be part of your planning. If you plan for multiple and varied assessments, you will find that you play many roles—coach, facilitator, negotiator, responder, provider of feedback. At the end of this chapter you will see a variety of assessment examples. Review these examples and consider what role you would have for each type of assessment.

The Student's Role

One of the key activities that students must engage in is self-assessment. Most middle and high school students are not inclined to be reflective about their school work. In your role as coach, you will want to encourage self-reflection and assessment. The goal of this is to help students bridge the gap between what they know and understand and what they *can* know and understand. Brown (1994) points out that learning is most effective when the learner has insights into inner strengths and weaknesses as a learner. To encourage this type of reflection you can provide students with journaling tasks, conduct class discussions about learning, or use a peer assessment strategy, help students set goals and develop plans, or teach time management skills.

The School's Role

To be able to use a variety of assessment tools comfortably and effectively, it is critical that the school and the district support the use of varied assessments. If teachers do not have this type of support, it will limit their effectiveness in the classroom. As indicated in the assessment standards listed earlier in the chapter, as well as by the data supporting the roles of formative and summative assessment, learning is more effective if instruction and assessment are seamless. To learn more about support for varied assessment, find out the district and school's policies on these issues. Also invite an administrator to talk with you about the role of the school in supporting varied assessment in addition to high-stakes assessments.

AN OVERVIEW OF ASSESSMENT TECHNIQUES

Forms of Assessment That Are Not Tests

With the realization that teaching methods in science are expanding to include more inquiry and investigative techniques, comes an equally important realization that assessment methods must be adjusted to match the newer teaching methods. No longer can teachers rely on traditional paper-and-pencil tests as the sole means of assessing student progress and achievement. Students are aware that for fairness in evaluation of their work in science classes, efforts must be made to develop authentic assessment techniques that get to the heart of the tasks they are expected to perform. Teachers sensitive to this need are developing a host of alternative assessment techniques to deal with the enlarged variety of activities students engage in during their studies in science. Among these techniques are concept mapping, creative assessments, journals, oral interviews, essay, portfolios, observations, projects, extended tasks, open-ended labs, and others. These techniques should be planned to fit the type of activity or instruction in which students are engaged.

Concept Mapping

Concept mapping is a means of organizing ideas. It is used in instruction and can be used in assessment as well. Students begin by identifying the major and minor concepts of a topic under study, then organizing these concepts in hierarchical relationships. When used as assessment tools, concept maps provide the teacher with information on how students relate the concepts they have learned. In this way, a better picture of the students' understanding of the topic can be ascertained.

When analyzing the concept maps produced by students, the teacher should look for concepts that are definitely related to the topic at hand, show a hierarchical relationship from simple to more complex, are informative as to scientific accuracy, and are replete with examples showing how the concepts are or can be applied in real situations. Assessments of this type are, of necessity, quite subjective and should be used

Some assessment tasks will require making arrangements for your student to go to the library.

to glean clues as to the students' misunderstandings or misconceptions.

Creative Assessment

In creative assessment, students are given the opportunity to show what they have learned in a nontraditional manner. Some students might use scrap books, home videos, or cartoons to show information and relationships that illustrate what they have learned in the unit. Instead of simply recalling facts, they can use higher level thinking skills, such as application, analysis, synthesis, or evaluation. To implement creative assessment in the classroom, the teacher might spend a short time suggesting the kinds of things students could do to show their knowledge. This should not in any way limit their creativity, but many students need guidance to avoid frustration, especially if this is the first time they have been exposed to nontraditional ways of assessing their progress. By its very nature, this form of assessment is quite subjective and should be used as motivation or formative evaluation during instruction in a unit.

Journals and Oral Interviews

Journals provide a teacher with information of a sequential nature showing how students have progressed in their study of the science material. Some teacher guidance is needed to help students focus on the topics at hand and avoid irrelevancies. Questions such as, "How might this information help you plan a traveling vacation?" or "What new facts did you learn that could make your life more interesting?" might help guide the students' responses. Journal entries should be regular and need not be voluminous. They should promote reflective thinking and may generate further questions for study. There is also an increasing body of research that indicates the power of teacher feedback in the context of student journals. In other words, when teachers comment selectively in student journals, students learn more and push their thinking more (e.g., Ruiz-Primo, Li, Ayala, & Shavelson, 2004).

Some students are more adept at speaking than writing. Oral interviews in a relaxed atmosphere may supply information to the teacher and student alike that will benefit future work. They give the teacher an opportunity to provide verbal support to students as well as to obtain clues about their study habits, difficulties of understanding certain topics, misconceptions, and gaps in knowledge. Students, at the same time, may gain a better understanding of what is expected, the location of resources, and a realistic measure of their own strengths and weaknesses. This type of assessment is most useful when coordinated with instruction in the formative stages of development of the unit or chapter.

Portfolios

A portfolio is put together by a teacher for individual students, using materials produced by the student. These materials can include a large variety of products, such as worksheets, pictures, assignments completed, data sheets, written conclusions, experiment reports, maps, stories, plans, and any other written materials related to the work completed for a unit or course. It is usually long range—perhaps up to a year or longer—and can form the basis for other types of assessments, such as interviews and conferences. An advantage of a portfolio is that it is highly individualized and avoids to some extent a tendency all teachers have—that of comparing students with other students in a competitive atmosphere. Another advantage is that the students can use the enclosed materials to evaluate themselves and gain a more realistic picture of their own accomplishments.

Practical Assessment

Practical assessment provides information on students' skill and problem-solving abilities through the use of apparatus setups, experiments, and open-ended situations that can reveal certain thinking processes. Students who have become familiar with investigative learning will be able to display their abilities to their best advantage. Students who have been taught in highly traditional, expository classes will find this method of assessment distasteful and possibly unfair. One should not expect students to perform satisfactorily in an assessment procedure that is strange or different from the instructional methods they have experienced.

GENERAL GUIDELINES FOR USING TESTS

When you are confronted with the prospect of preparing a test, several methods will contribute to appropriate, effective evaluation. Guidelines for testing are as follows:

♦ Use tests as learning and diagnostic devices. Give students opportunities to demonstrate that they have learned what they missed on a test; adjust the grade.

♦ Use different forms of items to obtain different types of data that will help make decisions about student achievement and instructional practices.

♦ Use tests or self-evaluation inventories to evaluate all of your objectives, including inquiry abilities and attitudes.

♦ Spend time with students going over missed questions. This simple activity will help many students fill in gaps in their understanding. Some students may need individual tutoring if their gaps are more substantial.

♦ Remember that tests are only a sample of what has been learned, and probably not a very good one. Therefore, they should not be used as the only means of evaluation.

♦ Ask questions to determine students' attitudes toward topics and methods.

♦ Place the easier questions at the beginning of the test so students gain confidence and minimize their frustration and fatigue.

♦ Consider the time factor. How long will it take students to complete the test? Some students will finish much sooner than others. Plan for students who finish before others, so they do not present discipline problems.

♦ Rather than having the students write on the test, have them place their responses on an answer sheet. This procedure ensures ease of recording and saves paper since the test may be used for more than one class.

♦ Encourage honesty. For example, you can remove the temptation to copy by spreading students out or by making two versions of the same test and alternating them when you pass out the tests.

Accounting for Student Individuality When Using Science Tests

Problems in interpreting and using tests may occur for students who are not native English speakers, have a learning disability, read below grade level, have low motivation, or have test anxiety. Every student should be given the best opportunity to demonstrate knowledge. Accommodating differences in test taking is one strategy for mediating the range of experiences students bring to school, which may not provide opportunities to learn the types of tasks included on the tests. Techniques a science teacher can use to minimize the differences in test results include the following:

♦ Nonverbal tests can be prepared, using diagrams and pictures familiar to the various culture groups being tested. In the case of language difficulties, use of translations might be considered.

♦ Attempts can be made to use items that are intrinsically interesting to the students to encourage motivation. Selection of items that have relevance to the experiences of the test takers will increase their likelihood of success.

♦ Make time less of a factor—write tests so they are not dependent on speed as an important condition for success on the test.

♦ Keep the test procedures simple and the instructions clear.

♦ Base the content of the test on intellectual skills and knowledge that are familiar to the group being tested.

Problem Tests

This kind of test presents a problem that students work on individually. The test usually contains a series of questions that the students must answer to solve the problem. A problem test can be constructed with relative ease if it is based on a problem that has actually confronted a scientist—problems that can be easily obtained from a scientific journal. The teacher provides the students with information about the problem and has them devise their own hypotheses, research designs, or methods of collecting and recording data. A problem test can best be used to acquaint students with scientific processes. The test may have an answer sheet similar to that for a self-test, or it may be used to stimulate discussion.

Open-ended scientific problems are preferable for this kind of test. Some examples of problems that might be used in constructing a test of this nature are:

♦ How would you reduce the amount of pollution from a smoke stack?

♦ A citizen thought the local river was polluted. How could he find out? What experiments could he do?

♦ A scientist thought fungus might produce a chemical that inhibits the growth of bacteria. What kind of experiments must she conduct to verify her hypothesis?

True-False Tests

What are some general considerations to be kept in mind when making a true-false, a multiple-choice, and a completion test? If the examination is limited to true or false questions, statistics show that 75 or more items are necessary to overcome the guessing factor. On a 100-question true-false test, many students are able to answer about 50 questions correctly merely by guessing. According to some, this problem can be eliminated by subtracting the number of wrong answers from the number of right ones to determine the score; they penalize for guessing. This procedure is not recommended, however, because students usually think the instructor is using the technique maliciously. It is also undesirable because the student is penalized for guessing; in science, we wish to have students make hypotheses, that is, good guesses.

Avoid overbalancing the test with too many true or too many false questions. Try to make them fairly even in number so that a student who knows a little about the material cannot get a high score simply by assuming that more questions are true (or false). Here are some other suggestions:

- Avoid using statements that might trick students.
- Do not use the same language as in the text, or students will tend to memorize.
- Do not use double negatives in a statement.
- Avoid ambiguous statements. For example, do not write, "Erosion is prevented by seeding."
- Avoid using complex sentences in your statements.
- Do not use qualitative language if possible. Do not write, for example, "Good corn grows at a slower rate than hybrid corn," or "The better metals conduct electricity faster."
- Arrange your statements in groups of 10 to 20. This procedure relieves excessive tension for students.
- Put answer blocks on one margin so that they can be easily checked using a key.

Selected-Response Tests

A selected-response (multiple-choice) test is composed of items having more than three responses. If there are not at least four possible responses to each question, a correction formula should be used. A selected-response test differs from a multiple-response test in that only one answer is correct for each question in the first type of test. We suggest the following approaches:

- In a selected-response test, make all responses plausible.
- All answers should be grammatically consistent.

- Try to keep all responses about the same length.
- Randomize the correct answers to avoid creating patterns in the examination. Students may look for the pattern.

Remember that the correct response often can be determined by a process of elimination as well as by knowing the correct answer. Try to prevent this in phrasing all of the responses in a plausible manner.

- Present first the term or concept you wish to test for.
- Test for the higher levels of understanding as much as possible.
- Require a simple method for the response. Provide short lines for the answers along one margin of a page so they can be easily keyed.
- Use scenarios or graphical representations of data as the source for a cluster of several questions. This technique allows you to gradually increase the complexity of the questions.
- Group your items in sections. This system makes it easy to refer to various sections of the test and helps break the monotony in taking the test.
- Group together all questions with the same number of choices.

Completion and Matching Tests

Because completion and matching tests usually emphasize recall and are often verbally tricky, they should be minimized. If matching questions are used, they should be grouped. When there are more than 15 matching items in a group, the test becomes cumbersome. Number your questions and use letters for your answers, or the reverse, but be consistent. Provide more matching choices than questions to minimize obtaining answers by elimination. Although matching tests have traditionally stressed recall, they can be used to test for recognition or application principles. Three sample matching questions follow:

1. A machine that would require the least amount of friction to move it 20 feet.
2. A machine that could best be used to pry open a box.
3. Which of the listed devices is made up of the greatest number of simple machines?
   a. Pliers
   b. Wheelbarrow
   c. Ice tongs
   d. Seesaw
   e. Doorknob
   f. Pencil sharpener
   g. Saw

SUMMARY

Classroom assessment can be characterized as diagnostic, formative, or summative. In addition, students and teachers may have to participate in district or state-mandated assessments. In designing classroom assessments it is important to remember the significance of high-quality formative assessments as a powerful, positive effect on student learning and achievement. Teachers should think of assessment as a means for improving their own classroom practice, planning curricula, developing self-reflecting learners, and reporting student progress. Student participation in the assessment process is essential. You will need to vary your assessment tools and techniques to provide ample opportunities for students to demonstrate their growing competencies and understandings. By making assessment seamless with instruction, you will not lose instructional time when you stop to assess—you will gain it!

UNIT 4

UNDERSTANDING THE SCIENCE CURRICULUM

When you think of the science curriculum, what comes to mind? Is it expressions of what students *should learn*, that is, the content of district guidelines, course syllabi, and science textbooks? Is this curriculum made up of the *experiences* students have with laboratory investigations, computer programs, readings, and discussions that science teachers present to students? Or is the science curriculum the knowledge, values, and skills that students actually *learn* as a result of all the varied experiences in a school science program? The science curriculum may consist of all of these perspectives. Certainly, you can find examples of them in any school system or science classroom. The three perspectives just mentioned—the *intended* science curriculum, the *taught* science curriculum, and the *learned* science curriculum—all contribute to an understanding of what we mean by the science curriculum.

Think of other questions. What should be emphasized in the students' experiences with science? Should the emphasis be on science principles and concepts? Should the curriculum emphasize scientific inquiry? Should science teachers orient the curriculum toward science- and technology-related social issues? How would you justify answers to these questions?

Should you consider different orientations for science curricula at middle schools and high schools? You can see that an answer to the lead question of this section—When you think of the science curriculum, what comes to mind?—involves much more than the science textbook. The science curriculum consists of the science content, your expected actions and teaching behaviors, students' experiences, educational technologies, laboratories, and the textbook. As a science teacher you have the responsibility of organizing and orchestrating the curriculum for students.

Your career as a science teacher will include improving the science curriculum in your school. The chapters in this section on understanding the science curriculum provide you with information and understanding about the science curriculum and help you answer some of the questions we posed in this introduction.

By now you probably recognize that curriculum is really more than content. Your curriculum includes science content, manipulative skills, attitudes you wish students to develop, the context or environment of the classroom, various teaching strategies, and the means you use to assess student progress. There will be a difference between the science curriculum represented in your school district syllabus, the national standards, state and local frameworks, science textbooks, and what your students learn. Discussing the curriculum is more complex than it may see. Rather than resolve all the issues surrounding curriculum, in these chapters we direct attention to the national standards and benchmarks, instructional materials representing different courses of study you may encounter, and a general process for the design and development of curriculum.

CHAPTER

10

HOW SCIENCE CURRICULA ARE DEVELOPED

Among the twenty-first-century issues and trends in science education, teachers must acknowledge the fundamental importance of the science curriculum. The science curriculum is the one component that brings together social aspirations, content standards, research on learning, appropriate assessments, and meaningful professional development. The curriculum has a long-standing place of fundamental importance (Kliebard, 1992), and certain contemporary trends relate directly to the curriculum (Ravitch, 1995) and the theme of national standards in general (Cobb, 1994) and science in particular (NRC, 2002).

As we begin the twenty-first century, we have the NCLB era in which assessments—international, national, state, and local—represent dominant forces for educational reform. We have perspectives from reforms past and present; but one lesson stands out—the reforms that had the most impact changed the curriculum, improved teaching, and provided professional development for teachers.

In this chapter we begin with a discussion of standards and develop the connections between standards, the science curriculum, and teaching. The next section addresses the design and development of science curricula.

STANDARDS, THE SCIENCE CURRICULUM, AND TEACHING

The Power of Standards

The power of standards lies in their capacity to change the fundamental components of the educational system.

Standards, as a set of national or state policies, provide a comprehensive approach to changing science education policies, programs, and practices. By their design, standards direct attention to these domains and inform decisions about various components of the educational system, including the science curriculum. To the degree various agencies, organizations, institutions, and districts embrace the standards, they have the potential to bring greater coherence and unity to diverse components such as state frameworks and assessments, teacher education, continuing professional development of science teachers, textbook adoptions and implementations, and resources and support for science education K through 12.

A Standards-Based Approach

A standards-based approach to educational improvement emphasizes what all students should know and be able to do. Using standards shifts our educational perspective from "inputs," that is, changes that may enhance achievement such as time in school, homework, and use of instructional technologies, to "outputs," such as defining the goals for middle and high school science education. Standards define the goals of science education and then leave to the educational community how to change various components, such as the curriculum, to achieving those aims.

Taking a school district as an example, the district uses standards as the basis for identifying goals for the science education program—what all students should know and be able to do. The district could then either select or design assessments aligned with those outcomes and do the same for curriculum materials and instructional strategies. Such an approach would result in greater coherence for the school science program.

The Content of Standards

The content of national and many state standards emphasizes fundamental concepts of life, earth, and physical science and expands these traditional content domains to include the contexts of inquiry, technology, personal and social perspectives, and the history and nature of science. Although it may seem that this discussion places standards at the center of science education, it is the science curriculum and teaching that matter most. In the end, students learn the content they are taught. Indeed, the standards help define that content. This said, school districts make decisions about the textbooks and materials used in the science program, and science teachers decide the particular emphasis and activities that students will experience. It is worth noting that the national standards recommend the development of fundamental scientific concepts and intellectual abilities of scientific inquiry.

One insight from TIMSS and comparisons of U.S. curricula with high achieving countries is the need to reduce the number of science topics students encounter in a school year and to focus efforts on fundamental concepts and abilities. The national standards do this. Those with responsibility for the science program can reduce topics and reform programs so the science curriculum presents students with opportunities to learn fundamental science concepts.

The national standards present a new view of inquiry. Based on the historical importance of scientific inquiry, the standards extend and elaborate views based on process skills such as observing, inferring, hypothesizing, and the like, to include the development of cognitive abilities such as reasoning, critical thinking, and using evidence and logic to form explanations. In addition, the standards recommend that students develop some understanding of scientific inquiry. Teaching science as inquiry should become a part of *content* for the science curriculum

Finally, the standards provide a context within which such fundamental concepts can be presented. Technology, personal and social perspectives, and history and nature of science all provide appropriate contexts for use in curriculum reform.

Standards Are the Foundation

The standards provide the basis for a science curriculum that is educationally coherent, developmentally appropriate, and scientifically accurate. If a school district uses standards as the basis for deciding the content of a school program, then it is important to make further decisions about how the content should be organized. That is, topics should represent an organized and coordinated K through 12 structure for content. The parts should make a whole. Most programs present a grade-level course orientation, especially at the secondary level. Curricular coherence requires a strong vertical perspective that is then complemented by the traditional course or horizontal view.

By developmentally appropriate, we refer to a curricular perspective that includes the number, duration, repetition, sequencing, specificity, and difficulty of science concepts in the curriculum. Decisions relative to these issues should be based on students' developmental and learning capacities (NRC, 1999) and the fundamental concepts and intellectual abilities as presented in the standards.

The term "scientifically accurate" expresses the idea that science concepts must be correct, given the age and developmental level of students. In general, the national standards have recognized this criterion in the K through 4, 5 through 8, and 9 through 12 grade-level orientations for content. Another essential feature of "scientifically accurate" is expressed by the requirement of fundamental topics at the heart of the sciences. Biological evolution is an example of this point. Omitting fundamental concepts that are central to science disciplines for a curriculum is scientifically *inaccurate*. Holding the line on socially controversial concepts is a part of our educational responsibility to the disciplines of science and the learning of our students. In a very real sense, representatives of states, school districts, and professional science teachers are the first line of defense in battles over the integrity of science.

Science Teaching in an Age of Diversity

Science teaching should consist of coordinated and systematic strategies that provide opportunities to learn for a diversity of students. In the earlier section on curriculum, we stated, "In the end, students learn the content they are taught." Here we propose that how much students learn is directly influenced by how they are taught. The key idea, of course, is *how* they are taught. To be more specific, we recommended coordinated and systematic strategies for teaching. In Chapter 13 we present several models for effective science teaching. The models complement the overall structure of the science curriculum.

At this point we recommend that you complete Activity 10–1: Evaluating A Science Curriculum, at the end of this chapter.

DESIGNING STANDARDS-BASED SCIENCE CURRICULA

Design refers to a process of identifying a goal and selecting the means to achieve that goal. Our use of the term *design* is intentionally associated with the disciplines of engineering and technology and applied to the science curriculum. For many teachers, the dominant model of curriculum includes thinking of a topic, clarifying science content, developing one or several activities associated with the topic, and finally figuring out some form of assessment. Fundamentally, this approach centers on activities and gives reduced emphasis to considerations of student learning as an important constraint in curriculum development. Viewing curriculum as a design problem holds the promise of improving the quality of instructional materials and subsequently student achievement.

Recently, several books have used the term *design* in reference to curriculum in general and science curriculum in particular. Examples include the helpful and pragmatic book by Grant Wiggins and Jay McTighe, *Understanding by Design* (2005), the National Research Council publication, *Designing Mathematics or Science Curriculum Programs* (NRC, 1999), and *Designs for Science Literacy* (AAAS, 2001) developed by the AAAS Project 2061. *Designs for Science Literacy* addresses the attributes of design (e.g., designs are purposeful, deliberate, require compromise, can fail, and have stages), essential elements of design (e.g., designs have goals, such as achieving scientific understanding; and constraints, such as developmental abilities students), and decisions in design (e.g., benefits and costs, risks, and trade-offs). Fundamental issues of curricular design include curriculum specifications, student learning, and national standards.

Design Specifications: Student Learning

Design is a deliberate effort to attain a specific goal. Achieving scientific literacy states a major goal for science education. Here, the specifications for student learning should focus on science concepts and understanding as well as the abilities and processes of scientific inquiry. The national standards define, at a fairly specific level, what students should know and be able to do. These standards are the learning outcomes for the science curriculum.

While identifying and clarifying goals, one has to consider the limits and possibilities of what can be learned. In curriculum development, time and budget are clear examples. Other examples include scientific discipline and grade level. In this discussion, we emphasize one particular class of constraints; namely, how students learn. By analogy, if you are building a bridge,

the laws of nature impose constraints on the design. If you are developing a curriculum, what we know about student learning imposes constraints on the design. Enhancing student achievement will rely on implementing research that has advanced our understanding of how students learn science. The National Research Council reports, *How People Learn: Brain, Mind, Experience, and School* (Bransford et al., 2000), *How People Learn: Bridging Research and Practice* (Bransford, Pellegrino, & Donovan, 1999), and the more recent *How Students Learn: Science in the Classroom* (NRC, 2005) present a major synthesis of research on human learning. Three findings from these NRC reports have both a solid research base and clear implications for curricular design. The following findings are from *How People Learn: Bridging Research and Practice* (Bransford et al., 1999).

> Students come to the classroom with preconceptions about how the world works. If their initial understanding is not engaged, they may fail to grasp the new concepts and information that are taught, or they may learn them for purposes of a test but revert to their preconceptions outside the classroom (p. 10).

This finding directly relates to science teaching, specifically, how we structure experiences to draw out students' current understandings, bring about some sense of the inadequacy of the ideas, and provide opportunities and time to reconstruct ideas so they are consistent with basic scientific concepts.

A second finding refers to the conceptual foundation of a curriculum.

> To develop competence in an area of inquiry, students must: (a) have a deep foundation of factual knowledge, (b) understand facts and ideas in the context of a conceptual framework, and (c) organize knowledge in ways that facilitate retrieval and application (Bransford et al., 1999, p. 12).

The science curriculum should incorporate fundamental knowledge and be based on, and contribute to, the students' development of a strong conceptual framework. The research findings that compare the performance of novices and experts (e.g., Crismond, 2001), as well as research findings on learning and transfer (e.g., Robertson, 2000), show that experts draw upon a richly structured information base. Although factual information is necessary, it is not sufficient. Essential to expertise is the mastery of concepts that allow for deep understanding.

The last finding relates to students' ability to think about their thinking.

> Students can be taught strategies that help them monitor their progress in problem solving (Bransford et al., 1999, p. 13).

Research on the performance of experts suggests that they monitor their understanding of a scientific investigation.

They note the requirement of additional information, the alignment of new information with what is known, and use analogies that may provide insights and advance their understanding. For experts, there are often internal conversations grounded in the processes of scientific inquiry. The latter can be learned if taught in the context of science subject matter and investigations. This finding has clear implications for the theme of teaching science as inquiry.

In summary, the school science curriculum should acknowledge the fact that students already have ideas about objects, organisms, and phenomena; and, many of these ideas do not align with contemporary science. The challenge for curriculum developers and teachers is not so much the fact that students have these misconceptions, but how to change the current concepts. In contrast to many contemporary programs, research on learning indicates that curriculum and instruction should include a clear conceptual framework as well as facts and information. Finally, students can enhance their own learning through self-reflection and monitoring, as taught in the context of school science programs.

Design Specifications: Science Content and Processes

Whether carefully designed by professional curriculum developers or quickly compiled by teachers, any science curriculum answers the question—What should students know and be able to do? The general answer to the question seems clear. Students should learn both facts and concepts. The curriculum should be structured using a conceptual framework. The goal of learning with understanding includes factual knowledge placed on a conceptual framework. You should recognize the complementary nature of these two ideas, because many contemporary programs and assessments give much greater emphasis to facts without attention to the underlying concepts. Should the science curriculum emphasize "big ideas" or "many facts"? The answer to this question is both.

Although the research synthesis is recent, the idea of basing the science curriculum on a major conceptual framework is not new. In *The Process of Education* (1960), Jerome Bruner addressed the organization of knowledge.

> The curriculum of a subject should be determined by the most fundamental understanding that can be achieved of the underlying principles that give structure to a subject. Teaching specific topics or skills without making clear their context in the broader fundamental structure of a field of knowledge is uneconomical (p. 6).

The school science curriculum should be structured using a framework that includes ideas central to the disciplines of science, for example, the structure and properties of matter, biological evolution, and geochemical cycles. In addition, students should learn about science; that is, ideas fundamental to the process of science should be part of the curriculum. The content of school science should include scientific inquiry and the nature of science and fundamental ideas such as the empirical nature of science and the role of evidence in scientific explanations.

You likely have noted that this discussion has only answered part of the question—What should students know and be able to do? Still to be addressed is the issue of the abilities that should be developed in a school science curriculum based on the *National Science Education Standards* (NRC, 1996). These five ideas from the standards are a good starting place:

- Identify questions and concepts that guide scientific investigations.
- Think critically and logically to make the relationships between evidence and explanations.
- Formulate and revise scientific explanations and models using logic and evidence.
- Recognize and analyze alternative explanations and predictions.
- Communicate and defend a scientific argument.

Of course, these abilities will have to be developed in the context of investigations and experiments.

Design Specifications: Rigor, Focus, and Coherence of Science Content and Processes

Criticisms about the lack of rigor in the curriculum center on its content, particularly the conceptual orientation of programs. For example, one can ask whether a curriculum is oriented toward scientific concepts fundamental to a discipline, or timely topics that may be interesting but do not emphasize scientifically fundamental concepts or processes. Focus refers to the depth of treatment of content. For example, content may only receive brief and superficial time in the curriculum. Finally, concerns about coherence refer to the connections among science concept and inquiry abilities in both horizontal and vertical dimensions of the curriculum. The cumulative effect of the lack of these qualities is a lack of student achievement. Because the qualities of rigor, focus, and coherence can be addressed as issues of curricular design, it is important to introduce them, along with science content and processes and understanding of student learning, as issues in curricular design.

To the questions of rigor, school science programs should be based on fundamental or essential scientific concepts and inquiry abilities. Documents such as the *National Science Education Standards* (NRC, 1996),

Benchmarks for Science Literacy (AAAS, 1993), and *NAEP Science 2009* (NAGB, 2006) have answered questions about what students should know and be able to do (see Table 10–1 for an example from the national standards).

However, identifying the content for school science is not enough. One must attend to other curricular and instructional issues.

Design of science curricula must address the focus and coherence for the organization of content. Focus is the depth of treatment for fundamental concepts and procedures. It is a measure of the time and opportunities given within classes, courses, and across the extended curriculum; for example, units, courses of study, and the K through 12 science programs. Table 10–2 presents an example of depth from the national standards.

Coherence is the number of concepts and procedures developed in a period of study (e.g., lesson, unit, course) and within a school science curriculum

(e.g., elementary, middle, high school, college). It is a measure of the connectedness among science concepts and procedures that students experience during their study of science. Note these are both horizontal (that is, courses) and vertical (that is, school science programs) dimensions to curricula coherence. Table 10–3 presents a contemporary example of a framework for a high school science curriculum. The framework is from the program, *BSCS Science: An Inquiry Approach* (2005).

THE PROCESS OF CURRICULUM DEVELOPMENT

This discussion begins with an example. *BSCS Science: An Inquiry Approach* is currently under development (funded by the National Science Foundation in 2000) and is conceptualized as a standards-based science program for grades 9 through 11. The program explicitly

---

TABLE 10–1 Example from the *National Science Education Standards*

Design Specification: Rigor

Rigor centers on the content of the curriculum, particularly the conceptual orientation of science disciplines.

Example from the *National Science Education Standards*:

• STRUCTURE AND PROPERTIES OF MATTER (Grades 9–12)

Source: National Research Council. (1996). *National Science Education Standards*, p. 129. Washington, DC: National Academy Press.

TABLE 10–2 Example from the *National Science Education Standards*

Design Specification: Focus

Focus refers to the depth of treatment of content.

Example from the *National Science Education Standards*:

STRUCTURE AND PROPERTIES OF MATTER (Grades 9–12)

• Atoms interact with one another by transferring or sharing electrons that are furthest from the nucleus. These outer electrons govern the chemical properties of the element.
• An element is composed of a single type of atom. When elements are listed in order according to the number of protons (called the atomic number), repeating patterns of physical and chemical properties identify families of elements with similar properties. This "Periodic Table" is a consequence of the repeating pattern of outermost electrons and their permitted energies.
• Bonds between atoms are created when electrons are paired up by being transferred or shared. A substance composed of a single kind of atom is called an element. The atoms may be bonded together into molecules or crystalline solids. A compound is formed when two or more kinds of atoms bind together chemically.
• The physical properties of compounds reflect the nature of the interactions among its molecules. These interactions are determined by the structure of the molecule, including the constituent atoms and the distances and angles between them.
• Solids, liquids, and gases differ in the distances and angles between molecules or atoms and therefore the energy that binds them together. In solids the structure is nearly rigid; in liquids molecules or atoms move around each other but do not move apart; and in gases molecules or atoms move almost independently of each other and are mostly far apart.
• Carbon atoms can bond to one another in chains, rings, and branching networks to form a variety of structures, including synthetic polymers, oils, and the large molecules essential to life.

Source: National Research Council. (1996). *National Science Education Standards*, pp. 178–179. Washington, DC: National Academy Press.

TABLE 10–3 A Contemporary Framework for a High School Science Curriculum

Units	Major Concepts Addressed at Each Grade Level		
	Grade 9	Grade 10	Grade 11
Science as Inquiry	• Questions and concepts that guide scientific investigations	• Design of scientific investigations • Communicating scientific results	• Evidence as the basis for explanations and models • Alternative explanations and models
Physical Science	• Structure and properties of matter • Structure of atoms • Integrating chapter	• Motions and forces • Chemical reactions • Integrating chapter	• Interactions of energy and matter • Conservation of energy and increase in disorder • Integrating chapter
Life Science	• Cell structure and function • Behavior of organisms • Integrating chapter	• Biological evolution • Molecular basis of heredity • Integrating chapter	• Matter, energy, and organization in living systems • Interdependence of organisms • Integrating chapter
Earth-Space Science	• Origin and evolution of the universe • Origin and evolution of the Earth system • Integrating chapter	• Geochemical cycles • Integrating chapter	• Energy in the Earth • Integrating chapter
Science in a Personal and Social Perspective; Science & Technology	• Personal and community health • Natural and human-induced hazards • Abilities of technological design	• Population growth • Natural resources • Environmental quality	• Science and technology in local, national, and global challenges • Understanding about science and technology

Source: Based on the program: *BSCS Science: An Inquiry Approach* (BSCS, 2005).

uses the *National Science Education Standards* (NRC, 1996) as the conceptual basis for designing and developing this program (see Table 10–3). Each year of the program begins with a two-week Science As Inquiry unit and is followed by three core units (eight weeks each): Life Science, Earth-Space Science, and Physical Science. In each of these core units, the first several chapters are devoted to helping students build conceptual understanding of the core concepts. The latter chapters help the students understand how these core concepts play a part in problems and events in the integrated setting of the natural world. The final unit uses problems and projects that are relevant to the lives of high school students to develop an integration of ideas across the sciences.

Design Studies

The process of curriculum development by professional organizations begins with a design study. These studies involve a current review of science education at the level or levels under study, national and state priorities, careful consideration of curricular elements such as content, instructional strategies, use of laboratory investigations, tests and assessment exercises, and issues of implementation and professional development.

Design studies help identify what to include in the program, for example, student materials, teacher editions, and implementation guides. Further, the design studies clarify the goals and constraints prior to initial development. Since the mid-1990s, professional development groups have used the *National Science Education Standards* (NRC, 1996) and *Benchmarks for Science Literacy* (AAAS, 1993) as the basis for several aspects of curricular design (e.g., content and professional development).

Backward Design

Beginning in the late 1990s, the backward design process was described by Grant Wiggins and Jay McTighe in *Understanding by Design* (2005). In this process, development begins with a content standard and determining the acceptable evidence of student attainment for that content, then deciding what learning experience(s) would develop students' knowledge and understanding of the content.

After identifying the standard and stating the content outcomes, an assessment activity and design activity assess students' knowledge and understanding of the content.

Forward Development

After clarifying the desired outcomes and means to assess for those outcomes, we design and develop the experience that will provide students with the opportunities to learn the content. This process may result in further clarification and modifications of the assessment activities (see Figure 10–1).

Teaching and the Science Curriculum

In this section, science connects the science curriculum and teaching. Table 10–4 summarizes many of the points and extends them to practical issues for teaching and learning. The latter are addressed as what teachers need to know and do. This table is an adaptation of an earlier work (Powell, Short, & Landes, 2002).

By this point in the discussion it should be clear that designing and developing a new science curriculum is a complex process. This discussion only scratches the surface of the complex and interrelated issues that must be addressed. A coherent, focused, and rigorous science curriculum consists of a conceptual framework based on major scientific ideas that have been sequenced with a learning trajectory for the concepts, the integration of scientific inquiry as content, and a consistent instructional model.

Summary

Achieving scientific literacy will require a curriculum that is rigorous, focused, and coherent. Briefly, rigor was discussed as content that is conceptually fundamental; focus is a measure of attention given scientific concepts and procedures; and, coherence is a measure of connectedness among the concepts and procedures students experience during their study of science. Based on design principles of rigor, coherence, and focus, this discussion addressed student learning and curricular design including the scope of content and instructional sequences that will enhance student learning. The discussion included examples of curricular materials and the process of designing and developing contemporary instructional materials.

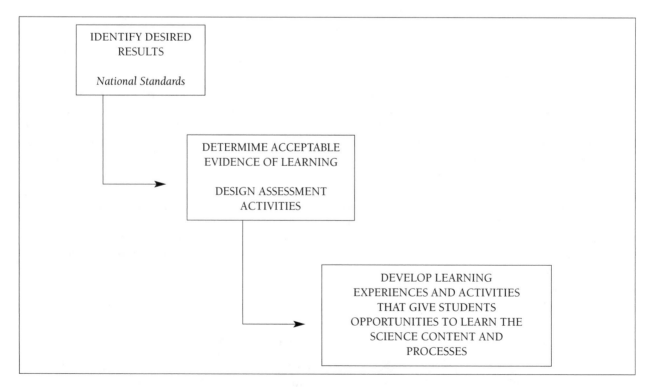

FIGURE 10–1   The Backward Design Process and the BSCS 5E Model

TABLE 10–4 Science Teaching and the Curriculum

What We Know about Student Learning	What to Consider in Designing a Science Curriculum	What Science Teachers Need to Know	What Science Teachers Need to Do
Students have current concepts about objects, organisms, and phenomena	• Sequence that elicits current concepts • Provide opportunities and time for conceptual change	• Students' misconception • Processes of conceptual change	• Challenge current misconceptions • Provide time and opportunities for conceptual change
Learning requires both a conceptual framework and facts	• Base curriculum and teaching on concepts fundamental to science • Connect facts to concepts	• Conceptual understanding of fundamental science • Abilities of scientific inquiry	• Make continual reference to concepts • Connect facts to concepts
Learning is facilitated by self-reflection and monitoring	• Make learning outcomes explicit • Incorporate metacognitive skills in curriculum experiences	• Strategies to enhance metacognition • Processes of metacognition	• Include goal setting in class time • Teach metacognitive skills

―――――――――――――――― **INVESTIGATING SCIENCE TEACHING** ――――――――――――――――

ACTIVITY 10–1
EVALUATING A SCIENCE CURRICULUM

Project 2061 is the ongoing work of AAAS that included the development of *Benchmarks for Science Literacy*. With funding from the National Science Foundation and in collaboration with hundreds of K through 12 teachers, curriculum specialists, teacher educators, scientists, and materials developers, Project 2061 has been developing a process for analyzing curriculum materials. Field tests suggest that Project 2061's curriculum-analysis procedure will not only serve the materials' adoption needs of the schools but also help teachers revise existing materials to increase their effectiveness, guide developers in the creation of new materials, and contribute to the professional development of those who use it. The Project 2061 curriculum-analysis procedure involves the following five steps:

1. *Identify specific learning goals to serve as the intellectual basis for the analysis.* This is done before beginning to examine any curriculum materials. The source for appropriate goals can be national standards or benchmark documents such as those mentioned above, state or local standards and curriculum frameworks, or sources like them. To be useful, the goals must be precise in describing the knowledge or skills they intend students to have. If the set of goals is large, a representative sample of them should be selected for purposes of analysis.

2. *Make a preliminary inspection of the curriculum materials to see whether they are likely to address the targeted learning goals.* If there appears to be little or no correspondence, the materials can be rejected without further analysis. If the outlook is more positive, go on to a content analysis.

3. *Analyze the curriculum materials for alignment between content and the selected learning goals.* The purpose here is to determine, citing evidence from the materials, whether the content in the material matches specific learning goals—not just whether the topic headings are similar. At the topic level, alignment is never difficult, since most topics—heredity, weather, magnetism, and so forth—lack specificity, making them easy to match. If the results of this analysis are positive, then reviewers can take the next step.

4. *Analyze the curriculum materials for alignment between instruction and the selected learning goals.* This involves estimating the degree to which the materials (including their accompanying teacher's guides) reflect what is known generally about student learning and effective teaching and, more important, the degree to which they support student learning of the specific knowledge and skills for which a content match has been found. Again, evidence from the materials must be shown.

5. *Summarize the relationship between the curriculum materials being evaluated and the selected learning goals.* The summary can take the form of a profile of the selected goals in terms of the content and instruction criteria, or a profile of the criteria in terms of the selected goals. In either case, a statement of strengths and weaknesses should be included. With this information in hand, reviewers can make more knowledgeable adoption decisions and suggest ways for improving the examined materials.

In addition to its careful focus on matching content and instruction to specific learning goals, the Project 2061 procedure has other features that set it apart. For example, its emphasis on collecting explicit evidence (citing page numbers and other references) of a material's alignment with learning goals adds rigor and reliability to decisions about curriculum materials. Similarly, the Project 2061 procedure calls for a team approach to the analytical task, providing opportunities for reviewers to defend their own judgments about materials and to question those of other reviewers. These and other characteristics help make participation in the analytical process itself a powerful professional development experience.

Choose one middle school curriculum that interests you and try this adaptation of the Project 2061 procedure:

1. Identify specific learning goals to serve as the intellectual basis for the analysis.

2. Make a preliminary inspection of the curriculum materials to see whether they are likely to address the targeted learning goals.

3. Analyze the curriculum materials for alignment between content and the selected learning goals. Base this alignment on the degree of match between the relevant NSES or Benchmarks and the information in the curriculum you are examining. Use questions such as the following:

   ◆ Does the content called for in the material address the substance of a specific benchmark/standard or only the benchmark/standard's general "topic"?
   ◆ Does the content reflect the level of sophistication of the specific standard/benchmark, or are the activities more appropriate for targeting standards/benchmarks at an earlier or later grade level?
   ◆ Does the content address all parts of a specific benchmark/standard or only some?

4. Analyze the curriculum materials for alignment between instruction and the selected learning goals. Seven criteria clusters have been identified to serve as a basis for the instructional analysis:

   Cluster I. Providing a sense of purpose: Part of planning a coherent curriculum involves deciding on its purposes and on which learning experiences will likely contribute to those purposes. Although coherence from the curriculum designers' point of view is important, it may not give students an adequate sense of what they are doing and why. This cluster includes criteria to determine whether the material attempts to make its purposes explicit and meaningful to students, either by itself or by instructions to the teacher.

   Cluster II. Taking account of student ideas: Fostering better understanding in students requires taking time to attend to the ideas they already have, both ideas that are incorrect and ideas that can serve as a foundation for subsequent learning. Such attention requires that teachers be informed about prerequisite ideas/skills needed for understanding a benchmark or standard and what their students' initial ideas are—in particular, the ideas that may interfere with learning the scientific information. Moreover, teachers can help address students' ideas if they know what is likely to work. This cluster examines whether the material contains specific suggestions for identifying and relating to student ideas.

   Cluster III. Engaging students with phenomena: Much of the point of science is explaining phenomena in terms of a small number of principles or ideas. For students to appreciate this explanatory power, they need to have a sense of the range of phenomena that science can explain.

   Cluster IV. Developing and using scientific ideas: Science literacy requires that students see the link between phenomena and ideas and see the ideas themselves as useful. This cluster includes criteria to determine whether the material attempts to provide links between phenomena and ideas and to demonstrate the usefulness of the ideas in varied contexts.

   Cluster V. Promoting student reflection: No matter how clearly materials may present ideas, students (like all people) will assign their own meanings to them. Constructing meaning well is aided by having students: (1) make their ideas and reasoning explicit, (2) hold their ideas and reasoning up to scrutiny, and (3) recast their ideas as needed.

   Cluster VI. Assessing progress: There are several important reasons for monitoring student progress toward specific learning goals. Having a collection of alternatives can ease the creative burden on teachers and increase the time available to analyze student responses and make adjustments in instruction based on those responses.

   Cluster VII. Enhancing the learning environment: Many other important considerations are involved in the selection of curriculum materials: for example, the help they provide to teachers in encouraging student curiosity and creating a classroom community where all can succeed, or the material's scientific accuracy or attractiveness.

5. Summarize your assessment of what is being taught by the curriculum you selected and what instructional approach is being promoted. Are these materials you would use in the classroom? Why or why not?

CHAPTER 11

INTEGRATED APPROACHES TO THE SCIENCE CURRICULUM

WHY AN INTEGRATED APPROACH?

As the world changes, more and more recognition is being given to the broad nature of education in science. No longer is it sufficient to think narrowly of physics, chemistry, geology, or biology, although these are the traditional core science subjects in our high schools. The advent of earth sciences in the mid-twentieth century was a major step in recognizing the commonality of earth problems that demanded broad approaches to their solution. It has become more apparent that solutions to problems, as for example, environmental concerns, demand integrated viewpoints with their varied techniques and expertise. Similarly, integration of science with other disciplines such as mathematics, reading, social studies, history, technology, and other school subjects is an important step in bringing about a better understanding of world problems. At the same time, science teachers must realize the role science plays in one's overall education. At present there seems to be a lack of understanding of science principles among citizens. Their "scientific literacy" appears to be low. This makes your task even more important. Perhaps the solution is to develop greater recognition of the integrated nature of science in their education. This chapter will enhance your understanding of integrated approaches to the science curriculum.

Many science teachers, school districts, and state frameworks are integrating science with other disciplines (BSCS, 2000). Justification for such approaches includes the fact that knowledge growth requires individuals to understand broader concepts that link science disciplines; the observation that schools impose artificial boundaries and constraints on students; the commonsense notion that world problems do not present themselves in discipline-bound packages; and the understanding that fragmentation of the curriculum reduces relevance and meaning for students. What do educators mean when they talk about integrated approaches to curriculum? We can begin with ideas of disciplines and curriculum. Disciplines such as physics, chemistry, and biology represent specific bodies of knowledge with their own history, procedures, and methods. From these disciplines educators, curriculum developers, and science teachers select specific knowledge, methods, historical people, and advances to include in school science programs. As Bruner (1960; 1968) points out, students must know the structure of science disciplines to further their development and acquire understandings of how things are related. From a teaching point of view, disciplinary approaches to the curriculum make sense because students can direct attention to specific content and closely related concepts and methods. Focusing on a subject for a period of time, for instance earth science for a year, allows students time and opportunity to progressively develop the fundamental concepts, methods, and history associated with the Earth sciences. In science, the integrated approach may begin with a theme, local issue, global problem, school event, or science topic and applies the concepts and methods from more than one discipline to the realm of study or investigation. Whereas the disciplinary approach stresses thorough understanding of the conceptual schemes of a discipline such as biology or physics, integrated approaches emphasize connections and linkages among disciplines in the pursuit of understanding objects, organisms, and events in the natural and designed world.

Defining Integrated Science

In seeking a definition of integrated science, you will discover a range of ideas about exactly what it is and what such a curriculum should look like. Within the mix of integrated science, you will find the terms of coordinated science, unified science, alternated science, and interdisciplinary studies as well. For some, the term "integrated science" encompasses all of the terms; for others, each term means something specific and excludes each of the others.

Most often you will hear a distinction between integrated science and coordinated science. In integrated science, students explore cross-disciplinary concepts in each lesson. For example, in a lesson about weather patterns, students might uncover concepts in earth science (rotation of the earth and orientation of the earth in space), concepts in physical science (convection and flow of energy), and concepts in life science (the effect of weather on living organisms). To contrast, in true coordinated science, students explore discipline-specific concepts in a layered fashion where the students' experience is coordinated in a logical way, but there are not explicit connections between the disciplines. For example, students might explore a concept in physical science for several weeks before moving on to a lesson in the life sciences. Next, they would complete a lesson in earth science before returning to explore another set of concepts in the physical sciences.

Many science teachers think that it is not realistic to expect that each lesson in an integrated science program would integrate all of the sciences. They correctly argue that often in a lesson only two of the sciences are integrated and sometimes only one predominates. This feature is important, because in some cases students must have a clear understanding of a basic concept in one of the disciplines before they can explore the concept further in an integrated context. Take the example of weather patterns again. It is likely that students would need to complete an activity that focuses only on the physics of energy before they explore how energy contributes to various weather patterns.

Some educators use the term *interdisciplinary* as a synonym for integrated. It seems more common, however, to use the term *interdisciplinary* for course work that brings together content from more widely separated disciplinary areas such as science and social studies, science and language arts, or social studies and language arts.

Discussions about defining integrated science can begin with the issue of content. What content is it that should be integrated? What content should we teach to students who do not pursue the traditional earth science–biology–chemistry–physics sequence? It is clear that the answer to that question is not qualitatively different from the answer to the related question, What content should we teach to students to pursue the traditional sequence? In fact, if you understand that *Standards* and *Benchmarks* really do define scientific literacy, then the answer to both questions is the same. *Standards* and *Benchmarks* should define the content of any science program, regardless of whether it is traditional or integrated in structure.

In the case of integrated science, then, we agree that *Standards* and *Benchmarks* for grades 9 through 12 represent the core scientific content that *all* students should learn. Of course, that content includes not only understandings and abilities related to the various science disciplines and inquiry, but also related concepts in the history and nature of science, the personal and social perspectives of science, and science and technology.

From both conceptual and political standpoints, defining content in this way offers an obvious advantage: It does not assume or require that ability be considered when determining whether integrated science is appropriate for a particular audience. The content itself can be presented in more or less challenging ways regardless of whether it is organized in the familiar sequence or as an integrated course of study. The concept of energy flow through systems, for example, is independent of the structure of the curriculum and of the students in the course. Curricula can present energy flow to students in concrete ways—by following what happens to packaging materials as they move from the manufacturing plant to the consumer to the landfill or recycling center—or in more abstract ways—by tracing how energy is captured from the sun and stored in the structure of organic molecules. Thus, we can develop an integrated science program for honors students and another for average students, just as we have done for decades in biology, chemistry, and physics.

To successfully address the needs of a diversity of students with respect to interest level, motivation, and ability, there must be flexibility and excellence throughout the overlapping layers of the broader system, which includes policies and philosophies at the district level, the structure and scope of the science program, and the fine art of teaching and assessing student learning. Each of these areas has its own set of standards, and each represents often-overlooked, yet critical, elements of a sound school science program.

Our analysis of *Standards* suggests that a minimum of two years is necessary to provide learning experiences that introduce the *core* science content. That estimate assumes a focus on inquiry, life, earth and space, and physical sciences and minimizes substantive exposure to science and technology, science in personal and social perspectives, and history and nature of science standards.

Given all that we have said up to this point, why do we think that integrated science represents a viable alternative to the traditional sequence and addresses many of the converging needs in school districts across the country? A survey of teachers and administrators in 46 states indicates that integrated science is a valuable and viable alternative, because it engages a greater diversity of students, it reflects the unifying concepts and principles of science, it reflects the reality of the natural world, and it may better prepare students to think comprehensively about an increasingly complex world (BSCS, 2000).

Because integrated science reflects the unifying concepts and principles of science as well as the reality of the natural world, teachers indicate that, in their experience, this makes science seem relevant and connected to the lives of a diversity of students. Problem- and project-based approaches, for example, that blur the boundaries of the sciences and allow students to investigate a range of concepts across the disciplines present students with a "need to know." This need to know engages the students when it is connected to a problem that the students find meaningful. Broad themes and unifying principles also provide a rich context and a creative learning environment. Integrated science programs tend to engage the students and keep them motivated to learn.

Because all students are not equally engaged by science for science' sake, integrated science, which seems relevant and connected to real experiences in their lives, may be a more effective way to teach a diversity of students. Regardless of whether students are in a traditional sequence or an integrated sequence, as they are presented with in-depth opportunities to explore cross-discipline concepts and solve cross-discipline problems, it is likely that they will be better prepared as science-literate citizens to interact and participate more fully in a complex world.

States and districts are developing their own set of standards and curriculum frameworks, many of which are modeled after *Standards* and *Benchmarks*.

Completing the Definition: Models, Vehicles, and Grain Size of Integration

Experiences in integrated science can take on many shapes by making use of a range of different vehicles of integration and by being developed for a range of grain sizes. As a result of this mix, BSCS (2000) has developed six major models of instruction (see Figure 11–1). It is possible to view these models along a continuum, and each model may have several variations. For example, in one model, students might experience a single activity that integrates two or three of the science disciplines and takes up only one or two class periods. In another model, students might experience a multiyear program that integrates all of the major disciplines of science in an ongoing experience.

Each of the six models represents a different pathway through science teaching and learning. A school district would need to discuss all aspects of each model

FIGURE 11–1 Six Models of Integrated Science

I. The first model is a traditional sequence of earth science, biology, chemistry, and physics, with no conceptual connections among the sciences. This model includes no integrated content.

II. One variation of the second model is the traditional, discipline-based sequence with some conceptual connections *within* each discipline. This model includes no integrated content. A second variation of the second model is the traditional, discipline-based sequence with some conceptual connections *between* the disciplines.

III. The third model is a coordinated program with each discipline being taught each year (perhaps grades 9 through 11). Several variations are possible here, some with equal emphasis given to each science and some with certain sciences predominating at specific points.

IV The fourth model is a disciplined-based or coordinated program for most of each year of a three- or four-year program, with one integrated science unit at some point during the year, perhaps an initial or a final unit.

V. The fifth is a model that includes a full year of integrated science at ninth grade followed by the traditional, discipline-based sequence for grades 10 through 12. Another version of this model might be the traditional sequence for grades 9 through 11 and a capstone course at twelfth grade.

VI. The sixth model includes two, three, or four years of a full integrated science program.

thoroughly and then determine which best matches its goals for students with respect to what it wants its students to know and be able to do in science. For example, a school district might ask the following questions: What represents excellence for us? What will offer us the most coherence in our science program? What are the advantages and disadvantages of each model with respect to the students and learning, the teachers and teaching, the science disciplines, and assessment? What are the implications of our decision?

Vehicles for Integration

Curriculum developers use a variety of approaches, perspectives, or themes to increase students' interest in science, to carry a message that has social or historical importance, or to provide an intellectual and scholarly coherence to a body of work. Developers refer to these approaches, perspectives, or themes collectively as *vehicles. Active Physics*, for example, uses as a vehicle a series of relevant challenges that require students to draw conclusions from experiments in sports, medicine, transportation, or other integrating topics. BSCS has used integrating themes as a vehicle for more than 40 years in its high school biology texts, *An Ecological Approach* (Green Version), *A Molecular Approach* (Blue Version), and more recently, *A Human Approach* (Human Version).

Broadly speaking, vehicles for integration may include a variety of themes—content themes such as energy or systems, process themes such as inquiry or the nature of science, and issues such as science-technology-society (STS) topics. Vehicles also include project- and problem-based approaches and research initiatives at the local, national, or global level, as shown in Figure 11–2.

The Grain Size of Integrated Science

When considering the possible ways in which to construct an integrated science curriculum, one can imagine a range of time frames. Edmund Burke's *Connections* series on television thoroughly presents integrated science and technology in self-contained, one-hour segments, which might be the equivalent of a single classroom lesson. This is one example of a small grain size. At the other end of the continuum, one can imagine integrating a student's entire high school science experience during a three-year sequence using a spiraling thematic approach to science content and process. This would be an example of a large grain size. In between, teachers can integrate science content across a week, a multiweek unit, or a full semester, with the remaining time devoted to more traditionally organized content.

In general, when planning for an integrated science experience of a particular grain size, either small or large, you might want to consider a range of vehicles. To demonstrate the flexibility of a particular vehicle of integration with respect to grain size, it might be useful to consider one vehicle, such as issues in science-technology-society and examine the possibilities in a range of grain sizes (see Figure 11–3).

For an example of model II, a teacher in an earth science class might end a unit on the behavior of matter within the earth with a lesson on recycling. In this lesson, the teacher might use this STS issue to bring together concepts from earth science (cycles of matter) and life science (the effects of certain materials on living organisms) and then examine how we can recycle materials safely. In model IV, another earth science teacher might design an entire unit on recycling that gives the students the opportunity to explore related concepts in the earth and life sciences as well as to investigate concepts from the physical sciences such as tracing the flow of energy and the chemical breakdown of matter.

In another school, a teacher teaching a yearlong integrated science course (model VI) might design a series of units using several different STS issues such as global warming, natural disasters, sustainability, and world population. In another district, teachers might use similar STS issues to develop a two- or three-year program in integrated science.

A fundamental consideration when developing any integrated science curriculum is whether the content is conceptually coherent. If big ideas do not connect logically and obviously, then student learning is uncertain and tentative. Lacking power, scientific ideas presented without conceptual coherence have little chance of enduring in the minds of many students.

Vehicle	Example
Broad-based themes	patterns, systems, evolution
Science-technology-society issues	pollution, transportation, energy use
Process themes	inquiry, nature of science
Topics	wildfires, earthquakes, properties of materials
Projects	building an effective greenhouse
Research initiatives	local issues such as "Why are the fish dying in our lake?"

FIGURE 11–2 Possible Vehicles for Integrating the Sciences

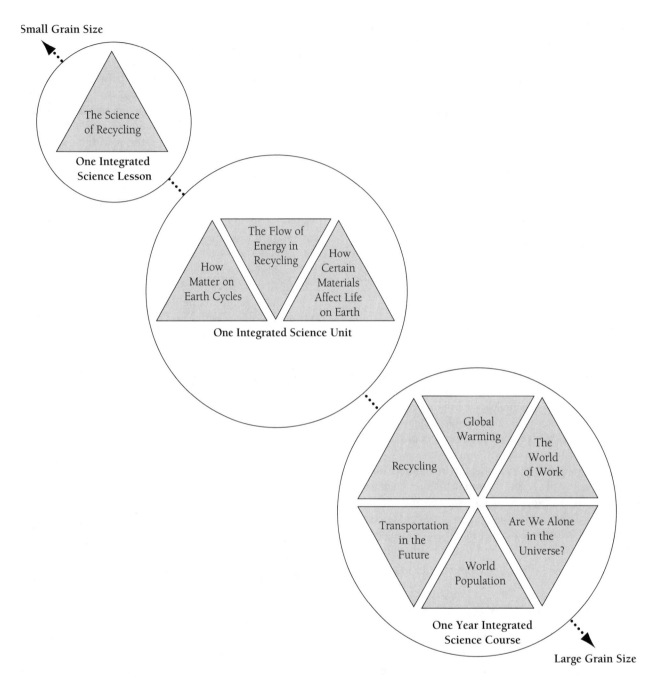

FIGURE 11–3 Grain Sizes

Issues Associated with Integrated and Interdisciplinary Science

Heidi Hayes-Jacobs (1989) has pointed out problems associated with content selection for interdisciplinary courses. One problem is what she terms the "potpourri" problem. That is, units are a sampling of knowledge from different disciplines without any central focus, scope, or sequence in the curriculum. A second issue emerges as a polarity problem where the differences between disciplinary and interdisciplinary approaches become polarized and result in conflicts with departments, schools, or states. To avoid these problems, Dr. Jacobs recommends two criteria for interdisciplinary programs. First, such programs must have carefully articulated designs that include a scope and sequence, a framework for thinking skills, indicators for attitudinal change, and thorough and consistent assessment. Second, the curriculum must include both disciplinary and interdisciplinary approaches. There are many good reasons to involve students in interdisciplinary studies as part of their science education. One way to encourage the development of understandings and abilities associated with science is to focus on epistemological issues through questions such as, "What do we know?" and "Why do we believe what we know?" Frequently, focusing on these questions brings forth interrelationships between disciplines not usually considered. For example, what benefits accrued to industrial processes in the nineteenth century from the research of chemists and physicists of that era in relation to thermodynamic processes, research on the nature of electricity, and clarifications of the periodic table in chemistry? Students can gain a better understanding of the interdisciplinary nature of science by actively involving themselves in proposing new relationships. A technique sometimes used for this purpose is "morphological analysis," in which a two-axis chart is constructed with the horizontal axes listing forms of energy, such as light, heat, electrical, or nuclear, for example, and the vertical axes depicting various types of transportation systems such as automobiles, airplanes, submarines, rockets, human-powered vehicles, animal-powered vehicles, moving sidewalks, and so forth. By imagining new vehicles that make use of some or all of the forms of energy available, creative designs can be invented that may have practical uses.

Although many advocate interdisciplinary studies, others urge caution. Kathleen Roth, who taught science at a middle school, has expressed some second thoughts about interdisciplinary studies. Her concerns grew out of work on a unit that combined science and history. After designing and teaching an interdisciplinary unit on "Seeds of Change," she realized the theme and teaching approach did not help students connect with the important concepts, especially science, that she had first thought they would. She also found that the interdisciplinary approach did not allow for adequate development of ideas and concepts related to science. It also seemed that the social studies connection constrained some science activities. In conclusion, Dr. Roth suggests, "Before we jump on the interdisciplinary bandwagon, let us engage in debate and study of the kinds of integration that are compelling, meaningful, and powerful for children" (Roth, 1994). Discussions about interdisciplinary curriculum often point to the use of themes as a central focus. Both the *National Science Education Standards* (NRC, 1996) and *Benchmarks for Science Literacy* (AAAS, 1993) identified themes that you might use in the design of science curriculum. (See Figures 11–4 and 11–5 for those concepts and processes.) The national standards and benchmarks include conceptual and procedural schemes that cross traditional disciplinary boundaries and provide students with powerful ideas to help them understand the natural and designed world. The content of these unifying and common themes can be introduced at any level in the K through 12 science program. In the following sections we provide examples and approaches to interdisciplinary approaches to science curricula.

Order and Organization
Evidence, Models, and Explanation
Change and Measurement
Evolution and Equilibrium
Form and Function

FIGURE 11–4 *National Science Education Standards* Unifying Concepts and Processes

Systems
Models
Constancy and Change
Scale

FIGURE 11–5 AAAS *Benchmarks for Science Literacy* Common Themes

HISTORY OF SCIENCE AND TECHNOLOGY IN SCIENCE CLASSES

There are several well-grounded reasons for integrating the teaching of the history and nature of science and technology in science classes (Bybee et al., 1991; BSCS, 2000), as well as a thrust for developing improved scientific literacy among students and the lay public. Many also have renewed interest in instruction in history of science and technology as perceived by policy documents such as the NRC's *National Science Education Standards* (1996) and *Benchmarks for Science Literacy* (1993) and an additional trend toward inclusion of science-technology-society themes in science classes in contemporary school programs.

SCIENCE AND MATHEMATICS

The alliance between science and mathematics has a long history, dating back many centuries. Science provides mathematics with interesting problems to investigate, and mathematics provides science with powerful tools to use in analyzing data. . . . Science and mathematics are both trying to discover general patterns and relationships, and in this sense, they are part of the same endeavor (AAAS, 1989).

No scientific discipline has become truly respectable until bolstered by data compiled and analyzed by mathematical methods. The evidence provided by natural phenomena, experimentally tested in the laboratory or in the field, and subjected to intensive scrutiny by mathematics forms the foundation on which science rests. For example, data collected by Tycho Brahe did not contribute substantially to the understanding of astronomy until the mathematical genius of Johannes Kepler put it into order and formulated several laws of planetary motion. A second example is more recent. The hypothesis, developed by Jonas Salk, of polio inoculation by weakened virus did not gain public acceptance until it was supported by statistical methods on a large scale.

Science teachers in middle and senior high school have an obligation to convey to students an understanding of the role of mathematics in science. Every opportunity should be used to show the integral nature of mathematics courses in grades 7 through 12, although little crossover between these disciplines is currently afforded. Students are led to believe that science and mathematics are unrelated entities. This attitude is often perpetuated by the teachers of both subjects, perhaps because they are unfamiliar with possible common objectives and applications. In practice, the difficulty of incorporating mathematics into science classes is compounded by extreme variations in mathematical ability among students. At any grade level, students in the science classes have mathematics competencies that range several grade levels above and below the average for the particular grade. Some students may have difficulties with simple addition and subtraction operations, while at the same time other students may have an understanding of ratio and proportion, percentage, and use of science notation. Science teachers confront this great variation and should plan science activities accordingly. The mathematical requirements for any given activity or experiment are also extremely varied. By suitably individualizing the instruction, students can be challenged at their level and in the process gain competence in the particular mathematical skill. Science and mathematics do have some common features including a belief in understandable order, an interplay of imagination and rigorous logic, ideals of honesty and openness, the critical importance of peer criticism, the value placed on being the first to make a key discovery, the international scope, and even, with the development of electronic computers, the ability to use technology to open up new fields of investigation.

The National Council of Teachers of Mathematics (NCTM) standards (NCTM, 2000) emphasize problem solving, communication, reasoning, connections, estimation, measurement, patterns and relationships, and other areas that are equally important in science and mathematics education.

Occasional joint planning between the mathematics and science teachers can bring about improved conditions, in both areas, for relating mathematics and science. If mathematics teachers are aware of the uses of mathematics in the science classes at particular grade levels, they may point out the possible applications to their students. In assigning homework problems they may use currently significant examples from science. Mathematics textbooks can be improved significantly on this point. The scientist is concerned with proper use of units and measurement. Attaching appropriate units to the figures given in word problems in mathematics can develop skills in usage, recognition, and manipulation of units by the students. The problems will take on increased meaning and show the applications of mathematics to science. Coordinated teaching between science and mathematics teachers can afford many opportunities for connecting the two disciplines. Many teachers are trained equally well in both areas and have teaching responsibilities in both. In this case, maximum effectiveness should be achieved.

MATHEMATICS AND ITS CONNECTIONS WITH SCIENCE DISCIPLINES

Too often the mathematics learned by secondary school science students seems to have little relevance to the mathematics used in their science courses. There needs to be increased cooperation and planning between mathematics and science teachers to bridge the gap that now exists to make the mathematics relevant to the science being studied. For example, developments in the teaching of biology at all levels reveal the need for students to have a mathematical background and an ability to bring mathematical experience and skills to bear on practical problems of measurement, classification, observation, and recording. It is equally clear that in studying biology meaningful, relevant situations can provide a springboard and motivation for learning and applying mathematics. The authors of biology textbooks assume that students understand the mathematics of measurement. The student may be asked to use a hand lens and to place the object being examined at the focal length of the lens, which is perhaps 6 centimeters (cm). Understanding of the metric system is required here. Reference may be made to the size of a human cell, which may be measured in micrometers and is frequently expressed using exponential notation. This also requires the student to be familiar with the metric system as well as the use of powers-of-ten notation. All sciences now work in the world of the very small. "Nanoscience" in biology, elementary particle physics, computer chip design, extremely short time intervals discussed in cosmology, and many other areas routinely use the prefix "nano" to refer to "billionths of" a meter, a second, or other measurement unit.

Ratio and proportion are other important mathematical concepts frequently used in biology. The ratio of length to width of plant leaves and the proportion of biomass to nutrition provided for plant growth are two concepts that require these mathematical understandings.

Statistical understanding is needed because frequently such things as the mean, median, and mode are expressed when talking about population and growth. When frequency tables are used, students must have the knowledge of collecting a sample in order to make a statistical count. It also is important for students to understand the idea of using discrete and continuous data in graphing notations.

Calculating relationships between two sets of unit measurements such as Fahrenheit and Celsius temperature scales requires mathematical understanding. To be able to make conversions from one temperature scale to another is a skill required not only in biology but in many other sciences.

The concept of very small and very large numbers is another mathematical tool frequently used in biology. For example, giving students a problem involving bacteria growth where the number of bacteria doubles every 25 minutes provides a beautiful opportunity for them to calculate exponentially.

Another important concept is the idea of scaling and scaling factors. One exercise is to have students determine the food requirements of a small mammal, such as a mole, and of a very large animal, such as an elephant. Does the food requirement alter with respect to size, volume, mass, or other factors? This concept also can be applied to heat loss and the necessary rate of metabolism to maintain life. All of these are mathematical concepts that are needed in biology and whose application will help students to better understand the use of mathematics in science.

Mathematics concepts used in chemistry at a more sophisticated level are those of ratio and proportion. Concepts of pressure, volume, and temperature change and the use of the general gas laws provide opportunities for students to apply these mathematical operations. Manipulations of equations and formulas also require mathematics. Calculations need to be made in balancing equations. A chemical equation is similar to a mathematical formula in its application. It is evident that mathematics has much to offer chemistry, biology, and other science subjects. Conversely, mathematics also can gain greatly from these subjects if the teachers of mathematics and the sciences make an effort to plan and to standardize the notation systems they use. If the mathematics teachers in their applications will use science examples and if the science teachers will apply the mathematics at every opportunity in working science problems, students will understand that mathematics and science are inseparable entities and highly important to scientific endeavor.

Simple Statistics

An aspect of mathematics in science that needs greater attention is the use of simple statistical techniques.

Mathematics, science, and environmental sciences find common ground in technological advances.

Students should have opportunities to assemble data, construct frequency distributions, and calculate certain measures of central tendency (such as the mode, median, and mean) and certain measures of dispersion (such as the range, average deviation, and standard deviation). Exercises requiring these operations will emphasize the intimate relationships between science and mathematics. Certain experiments lend themselves well to statistical computations, particularly those dealing with biological populations or probability problems.

SCIENCE AND READING

A frequently neglected connection is that of reading and science. Because students obtain information from science textbooks, their reading skills play an important role, yet too often the level of the reading matter is inappropriate for their grade level. Often students are unaware that reading and understanding science material is quite different from reading novels or short stories. As a result, they lose effectiveness in their reading.

Research by Larry Yore (1991) notes several points bearing on the beliefs and attitudes school teachers have regarding reading in science. He found that science teachers place high value on reading as an important strategy to promote learning in science and generally accept responsibility for teaching content reading skills to science students. Many teachers accept the importance of science reading as a component of scientific

Mathematics and science teachers must work together and with students to make better connections between mathematics and science curricula.

literacy and as a means of improving science achievement. Jeffrey Mallow's (1991) research concluded that students have a great range of misconceptions regarding science reading. Among these misconceptions, students believe: (1) science vocabulary is the same as ordinary vocabulary, (2) science textbook materials are to be memorized, (3) one can read science as rapidly as literature, and (4) all science reading is of the same sort and at the same level. Students commonly think, "If I can't understand a popular account of science, then I must be incapable of grasping science altogether." Some suggestions Mallow makes regarding improving students' ability to read science materials are: (1) use objectives and reviews for orientation toward the material, (2) read slowly and reread, going back and forth between sections, and read any margin notes provided, (3) use questions and exercises interactively with specific chapter sections, and (4) use problems interactively with the whole chapter.

GUEST EDITORIAL ◆ F. JAMES RUTHERFORD

American Association for the Advancement of Science

COHERENCE AND INTEGRATED SCIENCE CURRICULA

Coherence, it appears, is held in high esteem. Its presence in most objects, activities, processes, organizations, and systems is applauded, its absence deplored. In general, the notion of coherence itself is simple enough. It has to do with relationships. Things are coherent if their constituent parts connect to one another logically, historically, geographically, physically, mathematically, or in some other way to form a unified whole. Coherence calls for the whole of something to make good sense in the light of its parts, and the parts in the light of the whole.

Fair enough. But difficulties show up when one tries to apply the general idea of coherence to particular entities or domains. Picasso's *Guernica,* Shakespeare's *Hamlet,* the U.S. Congress, highway systems, newspapers, farms, clocks, space missions, department stores—in each, purposes, constraints, understandings, traditions, and values shape how the idea of coherence is put to work. In a word, coherence is extremely contextual. Here, the context is high school science, more specifically the conceptual coherence of high school science courses that feature integrated content.

Integrated courses are not automatically interesting, relevant, or understandable, and certainly not intrinsically coherent. They have to be made so, just as do discipline-centered courses. In fact, when it comes to coherence, the latter have a leg up. As put in *Designs for Science Literacy* (AAAS, 2001):

> Although many kinds of coherence are possible, traditionally coherence is assumed to reside naturally in the college disciplines. Since each of the disciplines at any time more or less defines a body of knowledge and its organization, language, and practices, the disciplines themselves seem to provide a

ready-made framework for creating a coherent curriculum. The prominence of biology, chemistry, and physics in the science curriculum reflects this premise, as do arithmetic, algebra, and geometry in the mathematics curriculum.

In principle, if not always in fact, a discipline-based high school science course gives primacy to the knowledge, methods, structure, language, and applications of a discipline, or significant parts of a discipline, and reflects the coherence of that discipline. By the way of contrast, the content of integrated courses is selected and limited and perhaps justified by themes, social or environmental issues, phenomena, problem solving, or other nondisciplinary organizers, or by some combination of disciplines, and can be quite idiosyncratic. In essence, integrated courses have no ready-made framework for creating coherence, and so it must deliberately be built into them.

Discipline-based high school science courses may have a conceptual head start with regard to coherence, but an examination of textbooks quickly makes it clear that few of them are in fact impressively coherent. They contain the words but not the music. Perhaps designers of discipline-based courses assume—quite mistakenly—that the intrinsic coherence of the discipline will automatically appear along with the borrowed content, and consequently invest little thought in creating the interconnections, themes, and story lines that are essential for coherence. As just noted, however, designers of integrated courses can be under no such illusion—and that is good news. It alerts developers of integrated courses that if they want coherence, they will have to create it. Simply characterizing the disciplines as being too compartmentalized, abstract, and remote from the interests and concerns of most people to serve as a framework for organizing content, and claiming the greater relevance of integrated courses for most students, will not get the coherence job done. The challenge depends to some extent on what approach is being taken to content integration.

If what is intended is the creation of a course that connects two or more sciences, as in interdisciplinary courses, the challenge is not to mistake patchwork for coherence. A little physics followed by a little chemistry followed by a little biology, for example, does not necessarily tell a story, or even three little stories. For coherence to prevail, the physics, chemistry, and biology must be woven into a discernable whole that draws on but transcends the coherence that characterizes each of the individual disciplines.

If the intention is to create a course in which something other than science itself is in the foreground—say problem solving or environmental issues—then the challenge is to make sure that the science itself does not get lost in the shuffle. A *science* course can be coherent only if the science is there, and not merely in some offhand or emaciated way. Moreover, coherence will not be served by inserting little nuggets of science content here and there, for the science must be integral with and woven into the story being told.

A new generation of high school science courses is needed that feature both integrated content and conceptual coherence. Once some exist and gain adoptions, careful assessments can determine if in fact better learning occurs—better than in discipline-based courses or than in integrated courses lacking coherence. But of course, the proper measure of "better" is what students learn. Thus, to emphasize a point made earlier, the first and most fundamental step in creating new high school science courses, whether discipline-based or integrated, is to identify a coherent set of explicit learning goals to be targeted. After that, the challenge is for developers to create integrated courses that result in the attainment of those learning goals. The courses themselves should be no less coherent than the goals they claim to serve.

INTEGRATED APPROACHES TO HIGH SCHOOL SCIENCE AND TECHNOLOGY

Global Science: Energy, Resources, Environment is an environmental science program designed for high school students. This program integrates chemistry, biology, physics, and earth science into a laboratory-oriented curriculum. Labs or classes allow students to analyze social problems and understand how science is relevant to their personal lives. By viewing the world as a dynamic, self-supporting ecosystem, students gain a new appreciation of our planet and the knowledge to manage its resources intelligently. Figure 11–6 provides an annotated table of contents for Global Science, which gives an indication of the program's integrated approach. We also include the science disciplines in Global Science (see Figure 11–7). This is an example of the second criteria outlined by Hayes-Jacobs (1889); namely, curriculum must include both disciplinary and interdisciplinary approaches.

BSCS Science: An Inquiry Approach is a thee-year science program for grades 9, 10, and 11. This program presents the core concepts in physical science, life science, earth-space science, and inquiry as articulated in the *National Science Education Standards* (NRC, 1996).

1. *The Grand Oasis in Space*
   Students build an understanding of ecosystems.

2. *Basic Energy/Resource Concepts*
   Students develop an understanding of the laws governing energy and mineral resource use.

3. *Mineral Resources*
   Students learn how mineral deposits are formed, where they are located, and how they are mined.

4. *Growth and Population*
   Students learn about exponential growth and population issues.

5. *Food, Agriculture, and Population Interactions*
   Students examine nutrition and the fundamentals of food production, modern agricultural practices, and the world food situation.

6. *Energy Today*
   Students build understandings of the energy sources for modern societies.

7. *Nonrenewable Resource Depletion*
   Students examine the depletion pattern for nonrenewable resources and examine resource lifetimes.

8. *Nuclear Energy*
   Students understand the basic principles of nuclear energy and consider its potential as an energy option.

9. *Energy Alternatives*
   This chapter focuses on the energy source alternatives to oil, gas, coal, and nuclear power.

10. *Strategies for Using Energy*
    Students examine energy options and consider options for future planning.

11. *Water: Quantity and Quality*
    This chapter builds an understanding of the importance of having adequate quantities of high-quality water for modern societies.

12. *Resource Management: Air and Land*
    Students examine ways of improving our ability to use air and land.

13. *The Economics of Resources and Environment*
    Students combine scientific information and economic principles related to resource and environmental challenges.

14. *Options for the Future*
    Students develop models of the future.

FIGURE 11–6 *Global Science: Energy-Resources-Environment* Annotated Table of Contents

Chapter	Life Science	Earth Science	Chemistry	Physical Science	Physics
1. The Grand Oasis in Space	●	●	●	●	
2. Basic Energy/Resource Concepts	●		●	●	●
3. Mineral Resources		●	●	●	●
4. Growth and Population	●				●
5. Food, Agriculture, and Population Interactions	●	●	●		
6. Energy Today		●	●	●	●
7. Nonrenewable Resource Depletion		●		●	●
8. Nuclear Energy	●	●	●	●	●
9. Energy Alternatives	●	●	●	●	●
10. Strategies for Using Energy		●	●	●	●
11. Water: Quantity and Quality	●	●	●	●	
12. Resource Management: Air and Land	●	●	●	●	●
13. The Economics of Resources and Environment					●
14. Options for the Future	●	●	●	●	●

FIGURE 11–7 Disciplinary Representation in Global Science

In addition, the program engages students in integration across the disciplines in relevant, social contexts to address other standards. This program provides high school students and teachers nationwide with a coherent alternative to the traditional sequence of biology, chemistry, and physics.

Across the country, school districts and teachers are interested in an inquiry-based science program that spans the disciplines.

◆ Teachers seek a coherent alternative to the discipline-based sequence.
◆ States are establishing standards across the disciplines and implementing tests in science that span the disciplines. Teachers see a multidisciplinary science program as a way to help students meet those standards and help students prepare for tests related to those standards.
◆ Science that integrates across the disciplines engages a greater diversity of learners.
◆ Science that integrates across the disciplines reflects the unity of the natural world.

The key features of *BSCS Science: An Inquiry Approach* include:

◆ Rigorous, standards-based content
◆ Activity-centered lessons
◆ Opportunities for structured and open inquiry in relevant contexts
◆ A constructivist, student-centered approach
◆ The BSCS 5E instructional model
◆ A collaborative learning environment
◆ Assessment that aligns with instruction
◆ The use of student science notebooks

The program consists of six modules at each grade level, as follows:

1. Two-week science as inquiry unit
2. Eight-week physical science core
3. Eight-week life science core
4. Eight-week earth-space science core
5. Eight-week integrated unit
6. Full-inquiry that begins mid-year

Each core unit includes three chapters that expose the students to fundamental concepts in each discipline. The fourth chapter in each unit allows students to apply what they have learned in an integrated context. This approach builds a foundation of knowledge across time and provides a compelling context for learning— an approach supported by recent research in learning (Bransford et al., 2000; Pellegrino, Chudowsky, & Glaser, 2001).

SUMMARY

Justification for interdisciplinary approaches to curriculum varies. Some authors think that fewer students are interested in science courses because of economic reasons; they do not see job possibilities in science, so they pursue other studies. Another proposed explanation for a lack of interest in science is that students often think science is dull, particularly when the only science they encounter is presented in a form that lacks connections to personal and social contexts. Many individuals and reports have proposed that the scientific and technologic understanding and skills that students need should be developed in personally meaningful and socially relevant contexts. These recommendations support an interdisciplinary approach to the science curriculum; that is, curriculum connections should exist not only between science disciplines but also among other areas of educational and intellectual growth. Increasingly, science teachers recognize the need to integrate science with other disciplines. The ability to synthesize information, to view world problems holistically, and to look at the interrelated dimensions of problems that affect human life are becoming more important.

Interdisciplinary programs and unified approaches to studying science appear to be growing. There is a need for greater emphasis on relating mathematics and secondary school sciences. Students of mathematics should have opportunities to apply their mathematical skills to the solution of scientific problems; applications should be called to their attention. The use of inquiry methods in science teaching provides many opportunities for incorporating mathematics. In this way mathematics is seen as a tool of science for quantifying and testing hypotheses. Students practice, on a realistic and meaningful level, the skills learned in their mathematics classes. In addition to practice in the usual skills of addition, subtraction, scientific notation, logarithms, use of calculators, and so forth, students in modern science learn to evaluate measurements, express precision of data and results, work with significant figures, and apply statistical tests to their data. These skills are practiced at all levels of junior and senior high school. The *National Science Education Standards* and *Benchmarks for Science Literacy* encourage the inclusion of other areas such as technology, history and nature of science, and personal and social issues in the curriculum. There are examples of interdisciplinary approaches to curriculum that emphasize science concepts and skills as well as other disciplines.

THE SCIENCE CURRICULUM AND CONTROVERSIAL ISSUES

Every science teacher encounters controversial issues in discussions in the science classroom. These may emerge unexpectedly, or they may be an integral part of lessons. If they are anticipated, you will have the advantage of preplanning, thinking through strategies, and arranging for necessary materials and information. If they occur unexpectedly, our advice is to use an understanding of the science, the ethics, and a general plan of action that you considered and prepared in advance. It is wise to remember and respect the facts that students have beliefs, opinions, and biases, that they have a right to their opinions, and that the teacher's role is not one of promoting a particular point of view, but one of fostering orderly discussion of the issues. As appropriate, the discussions should clarify the science concepts, appeal to evidence, and present scientific and technological alternatives.

Controversial issues may include a range of topics and will often reflect national, state, or local conflicts of ideas or values. For example, issues that have gained notoriety include: stem cell research, environmental degradation, conservation of resources, protection of endangered species, genetic engineering, use of animals in medical research, biological evolution, controlling population growth, limiting growth of cities, and restrictions on smoking in public places. There is no foreseeable end to these issues, nor to the inevitable controversies that develop among the public.

Part of science education for students in our schools is learning how to deal with opinions of persons whose views differ from their own. Avoiding discussion of the issues will not benefit a democratic society in the same ways that using controversial issues to provoke

learning, encourage changes in attitudes, increase understanding of others' opinions, and improving interaction skills will do. Incorporating activities that address controversial issues will enhance student learning and present opportunities to develop abilities to think critically and resolve conflicts. As a result, students will build a foundation of civic responsibility.

Controversy in the classroom confronts the teacher with issues of ethics and conflict resolution. In this chapter we present a brief introduction to these areas.

ETHICS IN THE SCIENCE CLASSROOM

Ethics is the study of the general nature of morals and of the moral choices made by individuals and groups. In everyday terms, ethics is concerned with right or wrong actions and judgments about whether individuals are good or bad. For most of the controversial issues in science classrooms, ethics relates to the moral quality of a course of action. For example, decisions about the use or nonuse of medicines, cutting or not cutting forests, or using or not using human growth hormones.

As a science teacher you will encounter ethical positions that range along a continuum and it is best to understand the many origins of these positions. The various sources for ethical positions include the law, family traditions, cultural practices, community expectations, religious traditions, and the influence of friends. Because of this variety, addressing ethical issues in the science classroom can be frustrating and confusing. With care and attention you can use controversy to help students develop their ability to think critically and formulate evidence-based arguments. However, you will have to focus on *ethics as a process of critical thinking and argument as a reasoned expression of a particular point of view* and not on picking a solution or deciding on an answer.

It is safe to assume that the future will require citizens to make personal and social decisions that involve aspects of science and technology. For the most part, such decisions will center on issues such as population growth, resource use, environmental quality, and health issues. This is where ethics enters, and where these citizens will be presented with competing points of view. How can you best help students decide between (or among) competing points of view? You can help them develop the language and skills to do the following:

- Clearly communicate their moral concerns
- Understand others' points of view
- Clarify the scientific concepts and processes involved
- Rigorously analyze our own points of view and those of others
- Respectfully argue about and criticize differing points of view

In short, approach ethics in the science classroom as a process of thinking critically about morally complex matters. This process of critical thinking should be approached in a way that promotes respect for and serious consideration of the views of others. When implemented in careful, consistent, and patient ways, ethics in the science classroom contributes directly to one of the primary aims of education—citizenship.

ETHICAL ANALYSIS IN THE SCIENCE CLASSROOM

Ethical analysis and scientific inquiry share a commitment to rational discourse. Scientific inquiry is a form of rational analysis of facts and empirical matters. Scientists ask, "What is the evidence, and how can we best explain it?" Ethics is a form of rational analysis into right and wrong action and good and bad character. Ethicists ask, "What ought we to do or be, and what justifies our answers to such questions?" Scientific inquiry insists on rigor and on following rules of rational analysis for developing an explanation for natural phenomena. Similarly the study of ethics includes a set of rules for rational analysis and discourse.

- Assumptions about rules and character must be examined and supported. Opinions have no weight. This requirement is similar to the requirement in science that proposed explanations be supported by empirical data. Unsupported explanations command no respect. In the absence of justification, the process of ethics breaks down.
- Arguments justifying a point of view must appeal to reasons that any reasonable person can accept, regardless of personal beliefs. Justifications must be as universal and objective as possible. Here, "objective" means they should be as free of idiosyncrasy as possible. "Universal" means that they should be widely shareable.
- Arguments justifying a point of view must always be open to criticism, including and especially self-criticism. "How could I be incorrect, confused, or inconsistent?" is a question that is essential for ethical analysis.
- The results of ethical analysis are arguments that establish a point of view as reasonable, a point of view that reasonable people should be willing to accept. The persuasive power of ethics, like that of science, relies on the mutual commitment to rational, disciplined inquiry.
- Results of ethical analysis are, therefore, tentative; they are never final or certain, any more than the results of a scientific inquiry. One must, as a result, always be open to the possibility of ending with poor results, or "getting it wrong," thus, the possibility of beginning another round of ethical analysis.

Following are four elements to the process of ethical analysis that you can develop in the classroom:

1. *Interpretation*. This task involves helping students communicate clearly and carefully what each has to say. The task of interpretation requires students to define and clarify terms. Thus, the first element of ethical analysis is to establish clearly the meaning of key terms and to use those terms with *consistent meaning* throughout the process of justification.

2. *Analysis*. The task here is to identify the nature of the reasons that someone is proposing as the justification for a point of view. The conceptual tools of ethics are brought to bear at this stage of ethical analysis in an attempt to answer the question, "What is the focus of a justification?" The nature of the reasons that students use includes negative consequences, for example, results are detrimental to health or safety; or positive consequences, for example, eliminating hunger or disease. Other reasons include respect for individual rights and beliefs. Finally, fairness or justice is often one of the reasons students argue in analysis.

3. *Argument*. This task involves giving and testing reasons that together support or justify a point of view. The task here has several steps. First, we need to identify the premises that are asserted in support of a conclusion. Arguments, to be complete, must

have both premises and conclusions. Second, we need to examine the warrants for premises—why their proponent thinks them to be true. Third, we need to determine whether the conclusion does indeed follow the premises.

4. *Critique of the justification.* Critique proceeds by asking these questions about each of the first three elements of doing ethics:

   ◆ Has the proponent been clear and consistent in the use of key terms?

   ◆ Has the proponent focused on all of the relevant moral considerations? Has the proponent identified the full range of ethical implications of the science or technology issue being considered?

   ◆ How well has the proponent structured her or his argument?

      ◆ Is it complete? Are there missing premises?

      ◆ Are the warrants for its premises established on rational grounds? How could one disagree with the warrants that are offered?

      ◆ Does the conclusion follow from the premises? Do other conclusions follow from the premises?

This is an excellent place to stop and turn to Activity 12–1: An Exploration of Ethical Analysis in the Science Classroom, at the conclusion of the chapter. This activity centers on the distribution of resources and provides an introduction to the process of ethical analysis.

ETHICAL DEVELOPMENT OF STUDENTS

Many of the issues that pose controversial problems for discussion in science classrooms are of an ethical nature. This situation creates the need to consider the development and maturity of students with respect to their innate abilities to deal with complex ethical problems. In the 1970s, Lawrence Kohlberg (1977) studied matters of moral development of children. Kohlberg used Piaget's research on moral development as the foundation for his studies. He carried out numerous studies in the United States and in other countries striving to better define moral development.

One of his main works, started in 1958, involved a longitudinal study of boys at ages 10 and 16, and followed their development past the ages of 24 and 30. Kohlberg also made several cross-cultural investigations. His research generally substantiated the proposition that moral development is hierarchical in character. Kohlberg proposed that moral development consists of three levels, each containing stages identified as *preconventional*, *conventional*, and *postconventional*. The following paragraphs describe these levels.

At the preconventional level, children are responsive to such rules and labels as good and bad, right and wrong.

They interpret these labels in purely physical or hedonistic terms—if they are bad, they are punished; if they are good, they are rewarded. They also interpret labels in terms of the physical power of those who enumerate them. Two stages in this level consist of punishment avoidance and reward seeking.

At the conventional level, expectations of the individual's family, group, or nation are perceived as valuable in their own right, regardless of immediate and obvious consequences. The attitude is one not only of conformity to the social order but also of loyalty to it—of actively maintaining, supporting, and justifying the order, and of identifying with the persons or group involved in it. Two stages are recognized in this level: socially approved orientation and law-and-order orientation.

At the postconventional level, there is a clear effort to teach to others a personal definition of moral values—to define principles that have validity and application apart from the authority of groups or persons and apart from the individual's own identification with these groups. Two stages in this level consist of a social-contract legalistic orientation and an orientation toward universal ethical principles. In the first of these stages, there is a clear awareness of the importance of personal values and opinions, and a corresponding emphasis on procedural rules for resolving conflicts. In the latter stage, rights are defined by the conscience in accordance with self-chosen principles, which are based on logical comprehensiveness, universality, and consistency. These principles are abstract and ethical, such as the golden rule.

Because Kohlberg's study population was all male, other recent studies have been conducted to find out whether his ideas could be universally applied to all students (Gilligan, 1985; Belenky, Clinchy, Goldberger, & Tarule, 1986; Noddings, 1992). This scholarship shows that females are relational, connected learners. In other words, girls and women tend to view the world holistically and see how things are connected. This means that females are more likely to follow an ethic of care and responsibility whereas males are more likely to view things separate and independent of each other. You may see this difference in approaches when you ask students to support a specific side of an issue. Students who view things as connected will have difficulty choosing one idea over another because they may see the strengths and weakness in both choices.

CONFLICT RESOLUTION IN THE SCIENCE CLASSROOM

By their very nature, incorporation of science-related social issues within science classes brings forth many situations subject to differing interpretations, differing values, and differing points of view. Frequently, environmental concerns come to the foreground. Matters of resource allocation and conservation can generate intense interest and strong opinions among students. Pitting the economic benefits of cutting forests against the endangerment of flora and fauna living in these areas is often personalized by students, who take strong positions. Such situations present opportunities for students to learn how to resolve science and technology-related social conflicts. The Key Issues Program of Keystone Science School has developed a mediation process for resolving conflicts. It is especially important to understand that individuals have preferred ways of resolving conflicts and that any one way of resolving a conflict is appropriate in some cases and inappropriate in others. Table 12–1 displays five different ways of resolving controversial issues.

In addition to the problems of providing opportunities for fair and objective discussions of the conflicting points of view found in one's classes, the teacher must also be concerned about student achievement and anxiety while sensitive topics are being discussed. Such concerns take one beyond the realms of simple evaluation and grading into areas of concern for feelings, attitude development, and values formation.

Jon Pedersen (1992) studied the effects of controversy relating to a science-technology-society issue on achievement and anxiety among secondary school science students. He found, "A controversy can exist when one student's ideas, information, conclusions, theories, or opinions are incompatible with those of another student or when incompatible activities occur and the students involved try to reach an agreement."

A group of students using the CHEM-COM chemistry program was divided into two subgroups. One group used a method called cooperative controversy, and the other group used individualistic study. In the cooperative controversy model, student groups of four each were formed and divided into pairs—one pair to present a pro position, and the other pair to present a con position of the issue being studied. Each pair, after sufficient preparation, presented its position, and the positions were debated by the group which then reached a consensus and wrote a collaborative report.

In the individualistic model, students worked on their own and were told to read, study, and research the assigned issue using any resources available.

TABLE 12–1 Mediation in the Science Classroom

Methods	What Happens When Used	Appropriate to Use When. . .	Inappropriate to Use When. . .
Denial or Withdrawal	Person withdraws to solve the problem.	The issue is relatively unimportant, timing is wrong, cooling off period is needed, withdrawal offers a short-term solution.	The issue is important, will not disappear, and builds.
Suppression or Smoothing Over	Differences are played down; *surface* harmony exists. May result in resentment, defensiveness, and possible sabotage if primary issues remain unresolved.	Preservation of the relationship between parties is more important than resolving the controversy.	Reluctance to deal with the conflict leads to evasion of an important issue or when players are ready and willing to deal with the issue.
Power or Dominance	One's authority, position, majority rule, or a persuasive minority settles the conflict.	Power comes with the position of authority and when this method has been agreed upon.	Losers have no way to express their needs. Could result in future disruptions.
Compromise or Negotiation	Each party gives up something in order to meet halfway.	Both parties have enough leeway to give, resources are limited, or when win/lose stance is undesirable.	The original position is inflated and unrealistic, the solution is too diluted to be effective, and the commitment is doubted by the parties involved.
Collaboration or Mediation	Each player's position is clear and the abilities, values, interests, and expertise of all are recognized.	Time is available to complete the process, parties are committed and trained in use of the process.	The conditions of time, abilities, and commitment are not present.

Source: Adapted from Key Issues Mediation Techniques, a program of the Keystone Science School, Keystone, Colorado. Used with permission.

Student interaction is an important aspect of understanding and responding to controversial issues.

The period of time involved was 20 days. At the end of the period, two measures were used for evaluation. Anxiety levels were measured using a State-Trait Anxiety Inventory. Class achievement was measured by a teacher-made achievement test.

The researchers concluded that the cooperative controversy treatment had a positive effect on the dependent variable—anxiety, but had no effect on the dependent variable—achievement. Anxiety was reduced, possibly because of the opportunities for sharing information and tasks, which may have minimized difficulties of understanding among individuals. Working independently on an issue did not provide this kind of help and reinforcement.

DESIGNING CONTROVERSIES FOR THE SCIENCE CLASSROOM

Before continuing, you may wish to complete Activity 12–2: Which Issues to Introduce in School Programs.

For the teacher, consideration of the moral development and maturity of students provides clues for structuring discussions of controversial issues. Damon (1999) argues that it is not enough for children to distinguish right from wrong, they must develop a commitment to acting on their ideals. Here is a suggested flow of steps to guide your students through in their study of science-based social issues:

1. Identify the conflict and theme for the controversy (e.g., life, liberty, justice, truth).
2. Introduce the scientific or technological problem.
3. Clarify the conflict.
4. Be sure there is a controversy (i.e., a choice between two or more alternatives).
5. Describe the situation and controversy to the student in understandable terms.
6. Delineate the possible decision in the dilemma.
7. Review the ethical positions and describe what you perceive to be the pro/con positions for each stage.
8. Ask for a definitive decision with reference to the controversy.
9. Remember that a good controversy is simple, straightforward, and relevant to students.
10. Ask for a justification for the response.

After introducing the controversy, the science teacher should guide the discussion, making sure the students stay on the topic. The teacher can point out inconsistencies in reasoning and more adequate resolutions to the controversy. Be sure to let the students answer and justify their positions.

OTHER STRATEGIES FOR TEACHING ABOUT CONTROVERSIAL ISSUES

For teachers faced with the perplexing problem of how to approach discussion of controversial issues in class, the debate format just described offers a positive strategy. The benefit of using this approach is the opportunity for creative modifications and diversions of the method.

Biology teaching provides many examples of issues that are controversial in today's world. One is the issue of genetic engineering. This is a topic that deals with genetic screening/eugenics, cloning, gene therapy (modification of human genes that cause disease), and gene alteration (of plants and animals including humans). A teaching strategy for dealing with this and similar issues in the classroom is debate. An experimental procedure carried out by two teachers in Minnesota has taught us much about what makes debate an effective strategy for teaching (Armstrong & Weber, 1991).

Outcomes for the unit included understanding of topics of genetic engineering and biotechnology; identification of different issues within the field, such as cloning; gene therapy and gene alteration; and production of a final essay summarizing the students' learning in genetic engineering.

After thorough planning and adherence to the rules of debate, the *debate format* worked well. A selected judge monitored the debate procedures, and a jury of peers rendered a decision at the end of the debate. The total time required to carry out the sequence of preparation, debate time, and final discussions was seven days of class time, which was considered reasonable considering the benefits achieved.

Some of the obvious benefits were that many students indicated they had formed their own opinions on the issues, rather than just following the crowd. Pre- and post-test results showed a decrease in the number of unsure responses concerning resolution of the issues. Each student was accountable for some part of the exercise, and students maintained a high interest level throughout the period.

Other effective methods to use in science classrooms when exploring and discussing current issues of concern are role-playing, morphological analysis, creativity-synectics, and others. *Role-playing* is a particularly useful technique because it allows students to place themselves in someone else's shoes. One example deals with the problem of the proposed construction of a superhighway through valuable agricultural land. The issue centers on the selection of an appropriate route that would minimize the agricultural damage. Obviously, there are more than two positions or views to such an issue.

To set up the situation, the instructor described the following: There is the head of the federal transportation department, a cabinet-level appointee who has jurisdiction over interstate highways. There is the truckers' union, which is concerned with economy of delivering goods. The agricultural community, represented by several state and federal agencies, is intimately concerned and affected by any decisions. In addition, a number of organizations are concerned with environmental issues; business groups from small cities and towns that might be bypassed by such a superhighway express their concerns; and other groups interested

in aesthetics and general quality of life are also vocal in their expressions of concern.

To get the teaching activities started, the instructor suggested a number of roles that might properly be included in the exercise. Such roles might include the representative of the highway department, chair of one or more agricultural agencies, president of a local environmental club, a number of farmers along the proposed route who would be directly affected by the construction, a lawyer for the highway department, as well as a lawyer for the agricultural agencies, and others. Students were encouraged to suggest other roles that might enhance the discussion of the issues.

A short prospectus was written by the instructor for each of the proposed roles. The prospectus in each case was general and suggested points of view that the player might take. Ample opportunity was provided for role-players to create, amplify, or embellish their points of view. This generated superb interest on the part of class members and led to much humor and good feeling. Roles were chosen or assigned, and the portion of the class not involved in the role-playing function was assigned the task of evaluating the effectiveness of each presentation and deciding on the outcome.

After one or two days of preparation to gather facts and figures, prepare statements, discuss pros and cons, and research data, a day was chosen for the meeting of the various representatives. This hearing was open to the public, that is, other members of the class. The meeting was chaired by an impartial moderator and was carried on during a normal 50-minute class period.

An obvious benefit of this teaching strategy was the high interest generated by the discussion. No students were apathetic or bored, even those with a peripheral role to play. Preparation for the event was excellent as students sought out supporting data for their arguments. An extension of the role-playing strategy could be made by inviting other classes to sit in as observers. The author's experience led him to believe the method could be used frequently, with variations on other issues and topics covered in the science class.

Morphological analysis has potential as a method for exploring and explicating solutions for problems arising in controversial situations. This is a creative problem-solving strategy that helps to identify and relate various independent variables or factors. The approach involves several steps:

◆ A problem is stated in terms as general as possible.
◆ Students are invited to identify as many independent variables as possible.
◆ Students state these variables or factors in as many ways as possible.
◆ Each of the factors becomes an axis on a grid of a two-dimensional or three-dimensional model.

TABLE 12–2   Model Grid

		Type of Energy				
		Fossil	Solar	Nuclear	Water Power	Wind Power
Efficacy	Cost	____ / ____	/ ____	/ ____	/ ____	/ ____
of	Speed	____ / ____	/ ____	/ ____	/ ____	/ ____
Use	Upkeep	____ / ____	/ ____	/ ____	/ ____	/ ____
	Convenience	____ / ____	/ ____	/ ____	/ ____	/ ____
	Conversion	____ / ____	/ ____	/ ____	/ ____	/ ____
	Other	____ / ____	/ ____	/ ____	/ ____	/ ____

◆ Students then combine the axes or locate intersections within the grid that provide multiple ways of viewing and resolving the problem.

To illustrate this analysis: Suppose the issue was how to rationalize the problem of replacing all of the vehicles dependent on burning fossil fuels in the United States with vehicles that use some other nonpolluting source of energy, such as electricity, solar power, or wind power.

The first step would be to have the class identify independent variables associated with each form of energy (presently in use or proposed). Two axes of a grid might be type of energy versus efficacy of use in a national transportation system. In the first category might be listed fossil fuels, solar energy, nuclear energy, wind energy, water power, or others. The second axis might contain cost per mile, average highway speed, maintenance of vehicles, convenience of use, conversion costs, and other factors.

A grid might be set up as shown in Table 12–2.

Studying the grid by placing intersecting points at desired places and by inserting estimated but realistic values for each factor would enable students to decide what traits of the new transportation system to consider as viable alternatives to the present system. The exercise could be done in a group or individual format as desired. A general discussion could be held after the exercise to consider the advantages or flaws of each system suggested. The level of interest in this exercise would likely be higher than traditional methods of lecture, recitation, or discussion.

Another technique, *creativity-synectics* developed by William J. J. Gordon and colleagues in the 1960s, offers a teaching strategy for stimulating creative talents.

Synectics requires students to form three types of metaphors to gain different perceptions of a problem. These are used to break mental *structures* or *psychological set* in looking at a problem, thereby contributing to the stimulation of creative thought. The three metaphors are *direct analogy, personal analogy,* and *compressed conflict.*

In *direct analogy,* students compare and contrast two objects or concepts and state how they are similar or different. For example, in a controversy about cutting down the rain forest, they might be asked to compare and contrast birds with airplanes, or tropical woods with corn, or pharmacists with medicine men.

In *personal analogies,* students state how they would feel if they were an endangered species of animal. They might be encouraged to identify with an object or concept such as a river or an evaporating water molecule. They might express their feelings about their potential future or fate in the rain forest.

The two steps above may then lead to a situation of *compressed conflict.* Students are asked to identify contradictions in the analogies and work to resolve them by making certain concessions or accommodations.

The above strategy helps students perceive problems in a more diverse and creative manner. They will have motivation to explore something unfamiliar and create something new or different. One desirable outcome also may be the ability to see a problem from another person's point of view and to avoid responding to problems in stereotypical ways.

Small-group discussions on an identified topic, followed by an all-class discussion, with small-group leaders presenting the consensus of their groups, will become an effective method of dealing with controversial issues in the classroom. The creativity-synectics strategy will set the stage for more fruitful class discussion.

SUMMARY

Facing the prospect of dealing with controversial issues in science classes is almost a certainty for science teachers. Well-prepared teachers will not wait until a serious issue suddenly makes its appearance in the classroom. Instead, the teacher will think through many possibilities and potential strategies for dealing with the issues and plan to teach their students the basics of ethical analysis.

Current issues may develop out of various referendums that appear on the ballot during elections or that have a global nature, frequently have an environmental context, and are invariably extremely complex, affecting many segments of society in diverse ways. In addition, highly vocal groups often express their points of view through the media, committees, and political agendas. Rather than to be feared, these should be looked upon as opportunities for students to think critically and develop ethically.

Teachers should understand some of the basic ideas of ethics and ethical analysis, as these are the bases for a rational inquiry into controversial topics. Strategies for teaching about controversies suggested in this chapter include class debates, role-playing, morphological analysis, creativity-synectics, small-group discussions, and other techniques.

An important principle when dealing with controversial issues is that the teacher's job is to provide suitable opportunities for discussion and explication of the issues and maintain a culture of respect in the classroom for all views, while at the same time avoiding injecting personal views (Veugelers, 2000). To do otherwise is to invite repercussions from parents, school authorities, and community groups.

EXPERIENCING ETHICAL ANALYSIS

ACTIVITY 12–1
AN EXPLORATION OF ETHICAL ANALYSIS IN THE SCIENCE CLASSROOM

Distributing Resources

This activity is designed as an introduction to ethical analysis. The openness and ambiguity of the task is intentional. It provides ample opportunity for discussion about an issue that is not laden with prior information or understanding. Thus, you can concentrate on the elements of ethical analysis, which are as follows:

1. *Interpretation.* Clarify and define terms, and use them consistently.

2. *Analysis.* Identify the reasons that various individuals propose as justification for their point of view. Do they want to:

   ♦ Avoid negative consequences?
   ♦ Nurture positive consequences?
   ♦ Honor individual values and beliefs?
   ♦ Pursue fair and equitable solutions?

3. *Argument.* Develop a rationale for the position. Do the individuals provide:

   ♦ Premises and conclusions?
   ♦ Support for premises?
   ♦ Premises and conclusions that are consistent?

4. *Critique.* Analyze the arguments and information presented. Pursue answers to the interpretation, analysis, and argument as part of the ethical analysis.

Your problem is to decide how to distribute resources among three groups who have requested your help. For this activity we are using the term *resources* to include many different things, such as food, minerals, fuels, and other items needed by people. Here is the only information you have to make your decisions:

You have 300 units of resources.

You presently use 200 units of resources.

You can survive on 100 units of resources.

Three groups want some of your resources. Here are their situations:

Group 1—needs 250 units of resources to survive; wants 250 units of resources

Group 2—needs 100 units of resources to survive; wants 200 units for survival *and* improvement

Group 3—needs 50 units for survival; wants 100 units for improvement

Group 4—needs no units for survival; wants 200 units for improvement

First, decide how you would distribute the resources. Complete the chart below.

Individual Decisions

Distribution of Resources	Group 1	Group 2	Group 3	Group 4
Reasons for Decision				

Now join a group of three or four individuals and use the process of ethical analysis on the discussion of a group decision about the allocation of resources.

Distribution of Resources	Group 1	Group 2	Group 3	Group 4
Reasons for Decision				

Activity 12–2
Which Issues Would You Introduce in School Programs?

Take a few minutes and complete the following survey. Your responses will be the basis for discussing the inclusion of controversial issues in science programs. There are many public policy problems confronting citizens. The policy concerns below are related to one another. This makes selection of one problem over another somewhat difficult. With this understanding, we ask that you do your best to rank the most significant policy issues with a number 1, the second with a number 2, and so on to number 12.

   The easiest way to rank the 12 issues is to first rank those items you think are most important (i.e., 1, 2, 3, 4). Then rank the least important items (i.e., 12, 11, 10, 9). Finally, rank the middle options from most to least important (i.e., 5, 6, 7, 8).

_____ Air Quality and Atmosphere (acid rain, CO_2, depletion of ozone, global warming)

_____ Energy Shortages (synthetic fuels, solar power, fossil fuels, conservation, oil production)

_____ Extinction of Plants and Animals (reducing genetic diversity)

_____ Hazardous Substances (waste dumps, toxic chemicals, lead paints)

_____ Human Health and Disease (infectious and noninfectious disease, stress, diet and nutrition, exercise, mental health)

_____ Land Use (soil erosion, reclamation, urban development, wildlife habitat loss, deforestation, desertification)

_____ Health Issues (stem cell research, stem cell therapies, gene therapy)

_____ Mineral Resources (nonfuel minerals, metallic and nonmetallic minerals, mining, technology, low-grade deposits, recycling, reuse)

_____ Nuclear Reactors (nuclear waste management, breeder reactors, cost of construction, safety)

_____ Population Growth (world population, immigration, carrying capacity, foresight capability)

_____ War Technology (bioterrorism, nerve gas, nuclear development, nuclear arms threat)

_____ Water Resources (waste disposal, estuaries, supply, distribution, groundwater contamination, fertilizer contamination)

_____ World Hunger and Food Resources (genetically modified organisms, food production and distribution, agriculture, cropland conservation)

_____ Other (please specify)

UNIT 5

PLANNING EFFECTIVE SCIENCE TEACHING AND PROGRAMS

The fun of teaching science involves figuring out the most interesting strategies and techniques to enhance learning. The most dismal thing that can happen is to get in a rut and keep teaching in the same ways day after day.

The solution to this is to create new, effective, and innovative ways to present material, use games to stimulate interest, and get students personally involved in their learning. For too long science teachers have looked at students as receptacles for knowledge—the fount for which is the teachers themselves, or the science textbook. But things are changing as we employ new ways of teaching and learning. If we look at science classes as a place where students can use their fertile minds to solve problems, gather data, explore new avenues, or create different solutions, then we will find that they respond favorably and learn science. There will be excitement in every class as students look for changes in things they are growing, see the results of an experiment, or learn of exciting information that relates to the natural or designed world. Students are curious and responsive to new challenges. The job of science teaching is to direct these traits so that learning occurs.

In the process of becoming involved in their own learning, students develop certain desirable knowledge, skills, and attitudes that stay with them throughout their lives. Whether they go into science as a career or not, certain understandings, habits of careful observation, deliberation before drawing conclusions, and healthy skepticism all will be useful characteristics in any field of endeavor. The development of scientific literacy is not merely being able to read science materials with understanding, but also to develop a full appreciation of where scientific information originates, the differences between science and technology, and how each of these impinges on society.

Our goal as science teachers should be to produce scientifically literate citizens who can make valid and considered judgments about decisions relating to science and technology. It certainly is true that we live in an increasingly scientific and technologic world that is likely to become even more complex in the future. What a responsibility we have as science teachers to ensure that these children will be well equipped to cope with the challenges ahead! You have chosen an exciting career. With thoughtful preparation, you are destined for success.

CHAPTER 13

MODELS FOR EFFECTIVE SCIENCE TEACHING

Publication of the *National Science Education Standards* places *Science as Inquiry* very high on science teachers' instructional agenda. The standards on inquiry focus science teachers' attention on developing students' abilities to use observations and knowledge as they construct scientific explanations. The *Standards* incorporate the traditional processes of science with instructional strategies that require students to use scientific knowledge and evidence from their investigations to formulate scientific explanations. The *Standards* shift instructional emphasis toward empirical criteria, critical thinking about evidence, and scientific reasoning in the construction of explanations.

Figures 13–1 and 13–2 summarize the inquiry abilities in the national standards. These standards do **not** represent an instructional model. They present learning outcomes that should be based on student investigations. Because inquiry is a central theme in the *Standards*, we emphasize that "Science as Inquiry" as represented in Figures 13–1 and 13–2 presents learning outcomes for students. *An assumption underlying these outcomes is that students will engage in laboratory-oriented investigations.*

The chapter outlines instructional models that will help you organize for effective instruction. These constitute the planned sequence of instruction. The flexible component is something you will develop with experience in science teaching. The chapter concludes with a general instructional model that incorporates many elements of other models. This model is presented in detail and is recommended as a model that is both usable and effective for science teaching.

DESIGNING YOUR INSTRUCTIONAL SEQUENCE

A National Research Council report entitled, *America's Lab Report: Investigations in High School Science* (2006), presents important ideas in your considerations of

---

Identify questions that can be answered through scientific investigations.

Design and conduct a scientific investigation.

Use appropriate tools and technologies to gather, analyze, and interpret data.

Develop descriptions, explanations, predictions, and models using evidence.

Think critically and logically to make the relationships between evidence and explanation.

Recognize and analyze alternative explanations and predictions.

Communicate scientific procedures and explanations.

Use mathematics in all aspects of scientific inquiry.

FIGURE 13–1   Science as Inquiry: Grades 5–8

Identify questions and concepts that guide scientific investigations.

Design and conduct scientific investigations.

Use technology and mathematics to improve investigations and communications.

Formulate and revise scientific explanations and models using logic and evidence.

Recognize and analyze alternative explanations and models.

Communicate and defend a scientific argument.

FIGURE 13–2   Science as Inquiry: Grades 9–12

designing lessons for effective teaching. Based on contemporary principles of learning, authors of this report reviewed research on the outcomes of laboratory experiences. One very important finding centered on how to sequence science instruction, including laboratory experiences, in order to support student learning. Authors of the National Research Council report (2006) proposed the phrase "integrated instructional units" to describe the sequence of instruction they identified as effective. Integrated instructional sequences link laboratory experiences with other instructional strategies such as reading, demonstrations, computer simulations, direct instruction, and discussion. When compared to traditional laboratory experiences, studies conducted using integrated instructional sequences show greater effectiveness for improving the mastery of subject matter, developing scientific reasoning, and cultivating interest in science. In addition, integrated instructional units also appear to be effective in helping diverse groups of students progress toward these goals.

In the following descriptions of the learning cycles, cooperative learning, the Hunter approach, and the 5E instructional model, you will be reading about various ways individuals have designed integrated instructional sequences.

THE LEARNING CYCLE

The learning cycle originated in the 1960s with the work of Robert Karplus and his colleagues during the development of the Science Curriculum Improvement Study (SCIS). Originally, the learning cycle was based on the theoretical insights of Piaget, but it is also consistent with other theories of learning, such as those developed by Ausubel (Karplus, 1980).

Originally there were three phases to the learning cycle: *Exploration, Invention,* and *Discovery.* Later, these terms were modified to *Exploration, Concept Introduction,* and *Concept Application.* Although other terms have been used for the three original phases, the goals and pedagogy of the phases have remained similar.

During the first, or *Exploration,* phase of the learning cycle, students learn through their involvement and actions. New materials, ideas, and relationships are introduced with minimal teacher guidance. The goal is to allow students to apply previous knowledge, develop interests, and initiate and maintain a curiosity toward the materials. The materials should be carefully structured so involvement with them cannot help but engage concepts and ideas fundamental to the lesson's objectives. During the exploration, teachers can also assess students' understanding and background relative to the lesson's objectives.

Concept Introduction is the next phase. Various teaching strategies can be used to introduce the concept. For example, a demonstration, DVD, CD-ROM, textbook, or lecture can be used. This phase should relate directly to the initial exploration and clarify concepts central to the lesson. Although the exploration was minimally teacher directed, this phase tends to be more teacher guided.

In the exploration stage of the instructional model, students are actively involved in investigating new materials and ideas.

STEPS FOR DESIGNING LESSONS

Applying the Learning Cycle

Concept Exploration

1. Identify interesting objects, events, or situations that students can observe. Student experiences can occur in the classroom, laboratory, or field. Many instructional methods can be used to explore a concept.

2. Allow students time to explore the objects, events, or situations. During this experience, students may establish relationships, observe patterns, identify variables, and question events. In this phase, the unexpected can be used to your advantage. Students may have questions or experiences that motivate them to study what they have observed.

3. The primary aim of the exploration is to have students think about concepts associated with the lesson.

Concept Introduction

4. The teacher directs student attention to specific aspects of the exploration experience. Initially, the lesson should be clearly based on student explorations. In this phase, the key is to present the concepts in a simple, clear, and direct manner.

Concept Application

5. Identify different activities in which students extend the concepts in new and different situations. Several different activities will facilitate generalization of the concept by the students. Encourage students to identify patterns, discover relationships among variables, and reason through new problems.

In the Exploration phase of the learning cycle, students are actively involved in exploring new materials and ideas.

In the next phase, *Concept Application,* students apply the newly learned concepts to other examples. The teaching goal is to have students generalize or transfer ideas to other examples used as illustrations of the central concept. For some students, self-regulation, equilibration, and mental reorganization of concepts may take time. Having several activities where a concept is applied can provide the valuable time needed for learning. An excellent introduction to and science teaching examples of the learning cycle have been developed by Howard Birnie (1982) and Karplus and colleagues (1977).

John Renner and his colleagues examined the effectiveness of altering the sequence of the learning cycle. They found that the normal sequence (described above) is the optimum sequence for achievement of content knowledge (Renner, Abraham, & Birnie, 1985).

Anton Lawson (1988) has made important connections between research on student misconceptions and use of the learning cycle. Lawson suggests that use of the learning cycle provides opportunities for students to reveal prior knowledge (particularly, their misconceptions) and opportunities to argue and debate their ideas. This process can result in cognitive disequilibrium and the possibility of developing higher levels of reasoning.

Lawson proposes three types of learning cycles: *descriptive, empirical-inductive,* and *hypothetical-deductive.* Although the sequence is similar to that described above, the difference among the types of learning cycles is the degree to which students gather data in a descriptive manner, or in a manner that empirically tests alternative explanations. In descriptive learning cycles, students observe natural phenomena, identify patterns, and seek similar patterns elsewhere. According to Lawson, little or no disequilibrium occurs in descriptive learning cycles.

Empirical-inductive learning cycles require students to explain phenomena, thus expressing any misconceptions and providing opportunities for dialogue and debate. Hypothetical-deductive learning cycles require students to make explicit statements of alternative explanations of phenomena. Higher order reasoning patterns are required to test alternative explanations.

COOPERATIVE LEARNING

As a science teacher, you will be in a position to structure lessons in several different ways. Most commonly, lessons are structured so students compete with one another for recognition and grades. You also might design your lessons so students can follow an individual approach, or learn on their own. There is a third option that lends itself to science teaching, especially when the laboratory is a central part of instruction. This is a cooperative approach where students are arranged in pairs or small groups to help each other learn the assigned material. David Johnson, Roger Johnson, and their colleagues have developed a substantial research base for the use of a cooperative learning model (Johnson et al., 1981). Over the years, the Johnsons also have developed the practical instructional approach based on their model. We base this discussion on their book, *Circles of Learning: Cooperation in the Classroom* (Johnson, Johnson, Johnson, Holubec, & Roy, 1986). (We recommend that you read the guest editorial by David

Cooperative learning provides an opportunity for full engagement by all students.

and Roger Johnson, "A Message to Teachers on Structuring Student Interactions in the Classroom" later in this chapter.)

There are four basic elements in cooperative learning models. To be truly cooperative, small group work must be structured for *positive interdependence, face-to-face interactions, individual accountability,* and *use of interpersonal and small group skills.*

Positive interdependence is established when students perceive that they are in affirming and cooperative relationships with other members of their group. There are several ways of achieving positive interdependence. You can establish mutual goals for the group; establish a division of labor for a mutual task; divide materials, resources, or information to ensure cooperation among group members; assign students different roles, such as recorder, researcher, organizer; or create joint rewards for the group.

Face-to-face interactions among students is a central aspect of cooperative learning. Cooperative work and verbal exchanges among students form the learning experience. Though they work in groups, students must still be individually accountable for learning the assigned materials. Cooperative learning is not having one person do a report for two or three others. The aim is for all students to learn the material. To accomplish this, it is necessary to determine the level of mastery among students and then assign groups to maximize achievement.

Finally, students have to learn to use interpersonal and small group skills. Most students are not naturally skilled at cooperative learning. They must learn the social skills of collaboration, they must be given time and experience in collaboration, and they must be taught to analyze the group process to see if effective working relationships have been maintained.

As a science teacher you will have to teach your students the skills of cooperation. This statement leads to the obvious questions, What skills need to be taught? and How does one teach these skills? In answer to the first question, there are four levels of cooperative skills. The first are *forming skills,* that is, the basic skills needed to organize a group and establish norms of behavior for cooperative interaction. Here are some suggestions to help the initial formation of cooperative groups:

- Students should move into groups without undue noise and unnecessary interaction with other students.
- Students should stay in their group.
- Students should speak softly.
- Students should encourage each other to participate.
- Students should use names and look at each other during discussions.
- Students should avoid sarcastic remarks toward other people.

Group functioning is the second skill level that you will need to develop. Here the lessons involve those skills that will maintain the group and facilitate effective working relationships. Important skills of group maintenance include:

- Students should understand the purpose, time allotment, and most effective procedures to complete their work.
- Students should support each other's ideas and work.
- Students should feel free to ask for help, information, or clarification from other group members or the science teacher.
- Students might learn how to paraphrase and summarize another student's ideas.
- As appropriate, students should learn how to express their feelings about the assignment and group process.

The next phase is *formulating understanding* of the concepts, processes, and skills of the assigned lesson. The skills are designed to maximize each student's learning. Here are some suggestions:

- Each student should summarize aloud important ideas contained in the material.
- Other students should correct and clarify summaries.
- Students should elaborate on each other's summary.
- Students can give hints about ways to remember ideas.
- All group members should participate in the discussion.

The last stage is *fermenting ideas and understandings.* Students should develop skills that will help reconceptualize and extend ideas. At this level, there is

GUEST EDITORIAL ◆
ROGER JOHNSON

Professor of Science Education
University of Minnesota, Minneapolis

DAVID JOHNSON

Professor of Social Psychology
University of Minnesota, Minneapolis

A MESSAGE TO TEACHERS ON STRUCTURING STUDENT INTERACTIONS IN THE CLASSROOM

There are instances where traditional practice in schools has gone one way, while empirical research indicated that another course was more productive and desirable. Such is the case with the use of cooperative, competitive, and individualistic student–student interaction patterns for instruction. In the past 40 years, competition among students has been emphasized in most American schools. In the past 15 years, individualistic efforts toward achieving learning goals have been increasingly emphasized. The research indicates, however, that cooperative interaction among students would be more productive on a wide range of cognitive and affective instructional outcomes than either competitive or individualistic interaction patterns.

Perhaps the major reason for this discrepancy between educational practice and research is the fact that how students interact with one another has not been emphasized in the development of curriculum and in teacher preparation. The spotlight has been on the ways that students interact with materials and the role of the teacher; however, how students interact with each other during instruction has powerful and important effects on their learning and socialization.

The three basic choices for student–student interaction patterns are competitive, individualistic, or cooperative. A competitive interaction pattern exists when students see that they can obtain their goals if and only if the other students with whom they are linked fail to obtain their goals. An example would be a spelling bee where students spell against each other to find the best speller in the class. Norm-referenced evaluation systems, such as rank-ordering students from best to worst or grading on a curve, set up competitive interaction between students. An individualistic interaction pattern exists when the achievement of students' learning goals are unrelated to the goal achievement of other students. An example of this we're-all-in-this-alone situation would be a spelling class where each student has his or her own set of words to learn and a criterion for measuring individual success, so that the achievement of one student has no effect on the achievement of another.

A cooperative interaction pattern exists when the students perceive that they can obtain their goal if and only if the other students with whom they are linked obtain their goals. An example of this sink-or-swim-together situation is a group of students working together as a spelling group, preparing each other to take the spelling test individually on Friday. Each student's score is the number of words his or her group spells correctly. Competition involves a negative interdependence in terms of goal attainment, the individualistic situation involves independence between goal attainment, and cooperation involves a positive interdependence in terms of goal attainment.

Many research studies have compared cognitive and affective results for students working cooperatively, competitively, and individualistically. The results indicate that, in comparison to competition and working individually, cooperation produces the following:

1. Higher achievement and longer retention of the material learned
2. More positive attitudes about the subject matter and the teacher
3. Higher self-esteem
4. More effective use of social skills
5. More positive feelings about each other (This *positive cathexis* works regardless of differences between students and has implications for the integration of different ethnic groups, mainstreaming of handicapped students into regular classroom settings, and managing the heterogeneity present in every classroom.)

These results represent only a few of the many which have been researched, but they emphasize the powerful nature of cooperative learning. Furthermore, the importance of cooperative learning experiences goes beyond improving instruction and making teaching more satisfying and productive for teachers, although these are worthwhile goals. The ability of all students to cooperate with others is the keystone to building and maintaining friendships, stable families, career success, neighborhood and community membership, and contributions to a society. Knowledge and skills are of no use if the students cannot apply them in cooperative interaction with other people.

With strong empirical support for cooperative learning and the fact that it makes sense for students growing up in society, we must be careful not to overgeneralize. The research into cooperative learning does not say that having students work together cooperatively is a magic wand that will solve all classroom problems. It does say that those problems probably have a better chance of being solved in a cooperative than in a competitive or an individualistic setting, but it is not reasonable to expect hyperactive students to suddenly become calm or low mathematics students to suddenly master all the material. It does give the teacher a powerful edge to go to work on the problems of orchestrating effective instruction for students.

We recommend that all three interaction patterns be used in a classroom setting. Students must learn how to compete appropriately and enjoy the competition, win or lose; they must learn how to work independently and take responsibility for following through on a task; and they must learn how to work with one another effectively in cooperative relationships. Each of these interaction patterns must be used appropriately and integrated effectively within instruction, realizing that cooperation is the most powerful of the three.

There is little doubt that teachers who master the strategies needed to set up appropriate interaction patterns, maximizing the use of cooperation, will have a powerful and positive effect on their classroom learning environment. This addition to the teacher's repertoire does not mean a new curriculum. It takes only a few minutes to make clear to students the kind of student–student interaction that is expected, with some additional time needed at first to teach the appropriate interaction skills to the students.

The initial effort on the teacher's part and the time needed to carefully structure student–student interaction are effort and time well spent. It would be exciting to see the gap between the research findings and traditional classroom practice disappear so the students would say, "School is a place where we work together to learn and share our ideas, argue our point of view, and help each other find the most appropriate answers and understand the materials. Sometimes we have a fun competition and sometimes we work individually, but most of the time we learn together."

already a firmly developed group structure, so it is possible to introduce challenges, conflicts, and controversies. Because of already developed skills, challenging situations can bring about deeper thinking, further synthesis of ideas, gathering of more information, and constructive arguments about conclusions, decisions, and solutions. In this case, the science teacher may be the person who encourages the extension of ideas. It is possible, even desirable, for students to function at this level. The teacher will have to decide about the degree of group development and level of interaction as this level is reached. Skills that facilitate this stage include:

- Criticize ideas, not other students.
- Clarify disagreements within the group.
- Synthesize different ideas into a single statement.
- Ask other students to justify their conclusions.
- Ask probing, clarifying questions.
- Generate several answers or conclusions, and select the best for the given situation.

We now turn to the second question, How does one teach these skills? As a science teacher interested in cooperative learning, it will be critical to identify students who have not developed the group skills discussed earlier. Following are ways that you can teach the skills required for cooperative learning:

- Be sure that students understand the need for group skills.
- Be sure that students understand the skill and when to use it.
- Be sure that students have time and situations where they can practice the skills.
- Be sure that students have the opportunity and procedures for discussing their use of group skills.
- Be sure that students continue using the skills until they are a natural part of group work.

Since work in science classes, and later life, is dependent on group work, we think your time and effort required to implement cooperative skills will be well spent. There is still a time and place for individual and competitive learning. The cooperative learning model provides an excellent complement to other models used in science teaching.

STEPS FOR DESIGNING LESSONS

Applying the Cooperative Learning Model

Objectives

1. *Clearly specify the objectives for the lesson.* You should make clear the two types of objectives: academic and collaborative skills. The former objective is used in most science lessons. The latter provides students with the specific skills used for cooperative learning.

Decisions

2. *Decide on group size.* This decision may be influenced by time, materials, equipment, and facilities. A general recommendation is to use pairs or groups of three.

3. *Decide on who is in the group.* Generally, it is best to have heterogeneous groups randomly assigned. Other alternatives include homogeneous grouping and having students select their own group.

4. *Decide on the room arrangement.* Again, this decision may be influenced by facilities and equipment. For optimum cooperative learning, group members should sit in a circle and be close enough for effective communication.

5. *Decide on the instructional materials to promote interdependence.* In early stages of developing cooperative learning groups, pay attention to the ways materials are used to facilitate interdependence. Three ways are suggested: materials interdependence (e.g., one set of materials for the group); information interdependence (e.g., each group member has a resource needed by the group); and interdependence with other groups (e.g., intergroup competition).

6. *Decide on roles to ensure interdependence.* You can assign roles—such as summarizer, researcher, recorder, and observer—that will encourage cooperation among group members.

Explanations

7. *Explain the assignment.* Be sure students are clear about the academic task. Make connections to past experience, concepts, and lessons. Define any relevant concepts, and explain procedures and safety precautions. Check on students' understanding of the assignment.

8. *Explain the collaborative goal.* Students must understand that they are responsible for doing the assignment and learning the material, and that all group members are to learn the material and successfully complete the assignment.

9. *Explain individual accountability.* All individuals should understand that they are responsible for learning, and that you will assess learning at the individual level.

10. *Explain intergroup cooperation.* Sometimes you may want to extend the cooperative group idea to include the entire class. If so, the method and criteria of success should be clear.

11. *Explain the criteria for success.* In the cooperative learning model, evaluation is based on successful completion of the assignment. It is therefore important to explain the criteria by which work will be evaluated.

12. *Explain the specific cooperative behaviors.* Since students may not understand what is meant by cooperative work, you should give specific examples of your expectations of their behaviors. For instance: "stay as a group," "talk quietly," "each person should explain how he got the answer," "listen to other group members," and "criticize ideas, not people."

Monitoring and Intervention

13. *Monitor student work.* Once the students begin work, your task is to observe the various groups and help solve any problems that emerge.

14. *Provide task assistance.* As needed, you may wish to clarify the assignment, introduce concepts, review material, model a skill, answer questions, and redirect discussions.

15. *Teach collaborative skills.* Because collaboration is new, it may be important to intervene in groups and help them learn the skills of collaboration.

16. *Provide closure for the lesson.* At the end of the lesson, it may be important for you to intervene and bring closure. Summarize what has been presented, review concepts and skills, and reinforce their work.

Evaluation

17. *Evaluate the quality and quantity of student learning.* Evaluate the previously decided upon product (e.g., a report).

Processing

18. *Assess how well the groups functioned.* If group collaboration is truly a goal, then some time should be spent on assessment. Point out how the groups could improve next time.

THE 5E INSTRUCTIONAL MODEL

In the early 1960s, J. Myron Atkin and Robert Karplus first proposed a learning cycle (Atkin & Karplus, 1962). Karplus, Herb Thier, and their colleagues based the original learning cycle on the psychological theories of Piaget and used the cycle as the basis for organizing lessons in Science Curriculum Improvement Study (SCIS) materials. A variation on this teaching model was also proposed by David Hawkins (1965) and used in the Elementary Science Study. We have extended and elaborated the original design for a learning cycle by Atkin and Karplus and have based the 5E model proposed in this chapter on that work.

Over the years, many curriculum designers have elaborated, modified, and applied teaching models in different educational programs (Renner & Abraham, 1986). The approach in this chapter is the first to describe the form and function of a teaching model, then to discuss the psychological basis for the proposed model, and finally to describe the model.

Form and Function

The 5E instructional model has five phases: engagement, exploration, explanation, elaboration, and evaluation. Each phase has a specific function and is intended to contribute to the learning process. We have described the phases in terms of: (1) assumptions about the mental activity of students, (2) activities that students would be involved in, and (3) strategies used by the teacher. Later in this section we shall discuss the five phases in detail.

An instructional model has two functions. A model provides guidance for curriculum developers as they design a program. Depending on the instructional model, curriculum developers can use the model at different levels of organization. One level is equivalent to a yearlong sequence; another is equivalent to a unit; and another is equivalent to a series of daily lessons. The second function of an instructional model is to help the classroom teacher improve instructional effectiveness through a systematic approach to and use of strategies closely aligned with models of learning and educational outcomes.

A Constructivist Orientation

Historically, educators have explained learning by classifying it into one of three broad categories. In simple terms, these are transmission, maturation, and construction (see Figure 13–3). In recent years, cognitive scientists and science educators have focused on a constructivist model in their work on the misconceptions of students, that is, differences between novice and expert explanations of phenomena, and naive versus canonical theories individuals hold (Anderson, 1987; Champagne, 1987; NRC, 2000).

In the constructivist model of learning, students reconstruct core concepts, or intellectual structures, through continuous interactions between themselves and their environment (which includes other people). Applying the constructivist approach to teaching requires the teacher to understand that students have some conceptions or prior knowledge of the world. Such conceptions may be inadequate (i.e., misconceptions) and need further development (i.e., conceptual change) (Wandersee, Mintzes, & Novak, 1994). In teaching for conceptual change, teachers should be sure that students are focusing on objects or events that engage concepts of interest to the science teacher, that is, objects or events that are related to science or technology. Then, students can encounter problematic situations that are slightly beyond the current level of understanding. In so doing, the student will experience a form of cognitive disequilibrium. Teachers then structure learning experiences that assist the reconstruction of core concepts. New constructions can then be applied to different situations and tested against other conceptions of the world.

Science teachers are implementing the constructivist view (Kyle & Shymansky, 1989; Anderson, 1987). Doing so requires: (1) teaching in a manner that recognizes the students' level of conceptual understanding, and (2) an understanding that the students' construction of knowledge occurs through the confrontation and resolution of problem situations. The key here is that confrontation should be intellectually challenging but within students' parameters of intellectual accommodation. Intellectual challenges that are actually included as instructional strategies are described by terms such as moderate

Perspective	View of Students	View of Knowledge	Approach to Teaching
Transmission	They must be filled with information and concepts.	Core concepts are a copy of reality.	External to Internal
Maturation	They must be allowed to mature and develop.	Emergence of core concepts.	Internal to External
Construction	They are actively involved in learning.	Construction of core concepts.	Interaction between Internal and External

FIGURE 13–3 Perspectives on Education

novelty, appropriate dissonance, optimal discord, tolerable mismatch, and reasonable disequilibrium.

Research by Peter Hewson and his colleagues suggests that conceptual change may occur in several different ways (Hewson, 1981; Hewson & Thorley, 1989; Hewson & Hewson, 1988; Posner, Strike, Hewson, & Gerzog, 1982). There may be the addition of new conceptions, a reorganization of current conceptions, and a rejection of conceptions. An important instructional aspect of the model proposed by Hewson and others is that students must be *dissatisfied* with the current conception, and the new conception must be *intelligible*, *plausible*, and *fruitful*. You can imagine this from a teacher–students interaction point of view. A science teacher introduces a new concept, and students are unable to reconcile the new concept with current knowledge and experience. The teacher then provides experiences and information that helps students make sense of the new conception. As students consider and try to incorporate the new conception, they must see that a world in which the conception is true is generally reconcilable with their worldview. Finally, students must see that there are instances where there is good reason to supply the new conception—namely, it works and it helps explain things. Regardless of the specific instructional model, helping students to develop more adequate scientific concepts is an important goal of science teaching. It is also a difficult task.

An assumption of the 5E model is that using sequences of lessons designed to facilitate the process described above will assist in students' construction of knowledge. Another is that concrete experiences and computer-assisted activities will assist in the process of constructing knowledge. The following are general strategies based on the constructivist view of learning:

* Recognize students' current conceptions of objects, events, or phenomena.
* Present situations slightly beyond the students' current conceptual understanding. One could also present the student with problems, situation conflicts, paradoxes, and puzzles.
* Choose problems and situations that are challenging but achievable.
* Have students present their explanations (concepts) to other students.
* When students are struggling with inadequate explanations (misconceptions), first help them by accepting their explanations; second, by suggesting other explanations of the same phenomena or activities designed to provide insights; and third, by allowing them time to reconstruct their explanations.

The 5E instructional model is based on a constructivist view. Because this model of learning is important, we summarize it before introducing the different phases of the 5E model. Constructivism is a dynamic and interactive conception of human learning. Students redefine, reorganize, elaborate, and change their initial concepts through interactions among the environment, classroom activities and experiences, and other individuals. Individual learners interpret objects and phenomena and internalize the interpretation in terms of their current concepts similar to the experiences being presented or encountered. In other words, changing and improving conceptions often require challenging the current conceptions and showing them to be inadequate. From a science teacher's point of view, the instructional and psychological problem is to avoid leaving students with an overall sense of inadequacy. If a current conception is challenged, there must be opportunity, in the form of time and experiences, to reconstruct a more adequate conception than the original. In short, the students' construction of knowledge can be assisted by using sequences of lessons designed to challenge current concepts and provide opportunities for reconstruction to occur.

The 5E Instructional Model: The Phases

Again, the model's five phases are engagement, exploration, explanation, elaboration, and evaluation.

ENGAGEMENT

In the first phase, you engage the student in the learning task. The student mentally focuses on a problem, situation, or event. The activities of this phase make connections to past and future activities. The connections depend on the learning task and the different dimensions of scientific literacy (see Chapter 6); they may be conceptual or procedural.

Asking a question, defining a problem, and showing a discrepant event are all ways to engage students and focus them on the instructional task. The teacher's role is to present the situation and identify the instructional task. The teacher also sets the rules and procedures for establishing the task.

Successful engagement results in students being puzzled and actively motivated in the learning activity. Here we are using *activity* in both the constructivist and behavioral sense—that is, students are mentally and physically active; in other words, they have a "minds-on, hands-on" experience. If we combine the external events with the basic needs and interests of the students, instruction contributes to successful learning. Figure 13–4 summarizes the engagement phase.

EXPLORATION

Once you have engaged the students' interest in ideas, they need time to explore these ideas. You can specifically design exploration activities so that students in the class have common, concrete experiences that

Orientation

This phase of the teaching model initiates the instructional task. The activity should: (1) make connections between past and present learning experiences, and (2) anticipate activities and organize students' thinking toward the learning outcomes of current activities.

Students

Establish an interest in, and develop an approach to, the instructional task.

Teachers

Identify the instructional task.

Activities

May vary, but should be interesting, motivational, and meaningful to students.

Learning

Initiated by, exposure to, and experience with concepts, processes, and skills.

FIGURE 13–4   Engagement

begin building concepts, processes, and skills. Engagement brings about disequilibrium, whereas exploration initiates the process of equilibration. Key words used to describe the type of activities used in this phase are *concrete* and *hands-on*. Courseware can be used in the phase, but it should be carefully designed to assist the initial process of conceptual reconstruction.

The aim of exploration activities is to establish experiences that the teacher or small groups of students can use later to formally develop a concept, process, or skill. During the activity, students have time in which they explore objects, phenomenon, events, or situations.

As a result of their mental and physical involvement in the exploration activity, students establish relationships, observe patterns, identify variables, and question events.

The teacher's role in the exploration phase is that of facilitator or coach. The teacher initiates the activity and allows students the time and opportunity to investigate objects, materials, and situations based on each student's own concepts about phenomena. If called upon, the teacher may coach or guide students through questions, suggesting avenues of activity or thought, and hints that may avoid frustration and begin the process of mental reconstruction. Use of concrete materials and experiences is essential. However, it is important to remember that the teacher's role is subordinate to the students' activity. The exploration phase is an excellent time to use cooperative learning. Figure 13–5 summarizes the exploration phase.

EXPLANATION

The word *explanation* means the act or process in which concepts, processes, or skills are made plain,

Orientation

This phase of the teaching model provides the students with a common base of experiences within which current concepts, processes, and skills may be identified and developed.

Students

Complete activities directed toward learning outcomes.

Teachers

Facilitate and monitor interaction between students and instructional situations, materials, and/or courseware.

Activities

Provide mental and physical experiences relative to the learning outcomes. These activities provide an initial context for students' explanations as they have unanswered questions based on the exploration.

Learning

Directed by objects, events, or situations.

FIGURE 13–5   Exploration

comprehensible, and clear. The process of explanation provides the students and teacher with a common use of terms relative to the learning task. In this phase, the teacher directs student attention to specific aspects of the engagement and exploration experiences. First, students are asked to give their explanations. Second, the teacher, text, or other students introduce scientific or technological explanations in a direct and formal manner. Explanations are ways of ordering the exploratory experiences. The teacher should base the initial part of this phase on students' explanations and clearly connect the explanations to experiences in the engagement and exploration phases of the instructional model. The key to this phase is to present scientific concepts, processes, or skills in a simple, clear, and direct manner, and move on to the next phase. The explanation phase can be relatively short because the next phase allows time for restructuring and extends this formal introduction to concepts, processes, and skills.

The explanation phase can be teacher, student, textbook, or technology directed. Teachers have a variety of techniques and strategies at their disposal. Educators commonly use oral explanations, but there are other strategies such as reading, DVD, film, and educational courseware. This phase continues the process of cognitive construction and provides scientific words for explanations. In the end, students should be able to explain exploratory experiences using appropriate scientific concepts and terms. Students will not immediately express and apply the explanations—learning takes time. Students need time and experience to establish and expand concepts, processes, and skills. For a summary of the explanation phase, see Figure 13–6.

Orientation

This phase of the teaching model focuses students' attention on a particular aspect of their engagement and exploration experiences and provides opportunities to demonstrate their conceptual understanding, process skills, or behaviors. This phase also provides specific opportunities for teachers to introduce concepts or skills.

Students

Describe their understanding, use their skills, and express their attitudes.

Teachers

Direct student learning by clarifying misconceptions, providing vocabulary for concepts, giving examples of skills, modifying behaviors, and suggesting further learning experiences.

Activities

Provide opportunities to identify student knowledge, skills, and values; and introduce language and/or behaviors related to learning outcomes.

Learning

Directed by teacher and instructional courseware.

FIGURE 13–6 Explanation

ELABORATION

Once students begin developing an explanation of their learning tasks, it is important to involve them in further experiences that extend or clarify the concepts, processes, or skills. In some cases, students may still have misconceptions, or they may only understand a concept in terms of the exploratory experience.

Elaboration activities provide further time and experiences that contribute to learning. According to Audrey Champagne (1987):

> During the elaboration phase, students engage in discussions and information-seeking activities. The group's goal is to identify and execute a small number of promising approaches to the task. During the group discussion, students present and defend their approaches to the instructional task. This discussion results in better definition and gathering of information that is necessary for successful completion of the task. The teaching cycle is not closed to information from the outside. Students get information from each other, the teacher, printed materials, experts, electronic databases, and experiments they conduct. This is called the information base. As a result of participation in the group's discussion, individual students are able to elaborate upon the conception of the tasks, information bases, and possible strategies for its completion.

Interactions within student groups is an application of Vygotsky's psychology to the teaching model. Group discussions and cooperative learning situations provide opportunities for students to express their understanding of the subject and receive feedback from others who are close to their own level of understanding.

Orientation

This phase of the teaching model challenges and extends students' conceptual understanding and skills. Through new experiences students develop deeper and broader understanding, more information, and adequate skills.

Students

Present and defend their explanations and identify and complete several experiences related to the learning task.

Teachers

Provide an occasion for students to cooperate on activities, discuss their current understanding, and demonstrate their skills.

Activities

Provide experiences through challenges, repetition, new activities, practice, and time.

Learning

Encouraged through challenges, repetition, new experiences, practices, and time.

FIGURE 13–7 Elaboration

The phase is also an opportunity to involve students in new situations and problems that require the application of identical or similar explanations. Figure 13–7 is a summary of the elaboration phase of the teaching model.

EVALUATION

At some point, students should receive feedback on their achievements. Informal assessment can occur from the beginning of the teaching sequence. The teacher can complete a formal assessment after the elaboration phase. As a practical educational matter, teachers must assess student learning. This is the phase in which teachers administer tests or performance activities to determine each student's understanding. This is also the important opportunity for students to use the skills they have acquired and evaluate their own understanding. In addition, one justification for such a model lies in providing adequate opportunities for all students to learn science.

The 5E instructional model is aligned with many processes involved in scientific inquiry. In science, the methods of scientific inquiry are an excellent means for students to evaluate their explanations. These methods are, after all, congruent with science. How well do student explanations stand up to review by peers and teachers? Is there a need to reform ideas based on experience? Figure 13–8 summarizes the evaluation phase.

Figure 13–9 provides additional details about what the teacher does and what the student does at different stages in the instructional model. We have provided descriptions of methods and activities that are both consistent and inconsistent with this model.

In addition, one author has provided a detailed discussion of the 5E model in *Achieving Scientific*

Literacy: From Purposes to Practices (Bybee, 1997), and the BSCS (2006) has conducted a thorough review of research supporting the model.

Summary

This chapter describes several instructional models. *America's Lab Report: Investigations in High School Science*

Orientation

This phase of the teaching model encourages students to assess their understandings and abilities and provides opportunities for teachers to evaluate student progress toward achieving the educational objectives.

Students

Examine the adequacy of their explanations, behaviors, and attitudes in new situations.

Teachers

Use a variety of formal and informal procedures for assessing student understanding.

Activities

Evaluate concepts, attitudes, and skills of the students.

Learning

Repeat different phases of the teaching model to improve conceptual understanding and/or skills.

FIGURE 13–8   Evaluation

(NRC, 2006) proposed the idea of integrated instructional units as a way of thinking about and designing sequence of lesson that enhances student learning. The idea of integrated instructional sequence connects to discussion of learning cycles, cooperative learning, and the 5E model.

One instructional model is the learning cycle. This cycle is a three-step instructional sequence that includes the following:

- Concept exploration
- Concept introduction
- Concept application

Cooperative learning is an effective strategy in the science classroom. Students learn a number of strategies that help them develop and function as a group. Formation of a group, group functioning, formulating understanding of the task, and time to discuss and reform concepts are all important aspects of cooperative groups.

The 5E instructional model includes the phases of engagement, exploration, explanation, elaboration, and evaluation. The basis of the 5E instructional model is the original learning cycle used in the SCIS program. We have modified and extended this learning cycle and drawn on research in the cognitive sciences—research that deals primarily with student misconception and conceptual change. Three factors support the use of this instructional model: (1) research from the cognitive sciences, (2) concordance of the model with the scientific process, and (3) utility to curriculum developers and classroom teachers.

Stage of the Instructional Model	What the Teacher Does	
	That Is Consistent with This Model	*That Is Inconsistent with This Model*
Engage	Creates interest Generates curiosity Raises questions Identifies what the students know about the topic	Explains concepts Provides definitions and answers States conclusions Provides closure Lectures
Explore	Encourages students to work together without direct instruction from the teacher Observes and listens to students as they interact Asks probing questions to redirect students' investigations when necessary Provides time for students to puzzle through problems Acts as a consultant for students	Provides answers Explains how to solve the problem Provides closure Tells students that they are wrong Gives information that answers the question Leads students step-by-step to a solution
Explain	Encourages students to explain concepts and definitions in their own words Asks for justification (evidence) and clarification from students Formally provides definitions, explanations, and new labels Uses students' previous experiences as the basis for explaining concepts	Accepts explanations that have no justification Neglects to solicit students' explanations Introduces unrelated concepts or skills

FIGURE 13–9   Applying the 5E Instructional Model

(continued)

Elaborate	Expects students to use formal definitions and explanations	Provides definite answers
	Encourages students to apply the concepts and skills in new situations	Tells students that they are wrong
		Lectures
	Reminds students of alternative explanations	Leads students step-by-step to an answer
	Refers students to data and evidence and asks: What do you already know? Why do you think . . . ?	Explains how to work through the problem
Evaluate	Observes students as they apply new concepts and skills	Tests vocabulary words, terms, and isolated facts
	Assesses students' knowledge and/or skills	Introduces new ideas or concepts
	Looks for evidence that students have changed their thinking or behaviors	Creates ambiguity
	Allows students to assess their own learning and group-process skills	Promotes open-minded discussion unrelated to the concept or skill
	Asks open-ended questions, such as: Why do you think . . . ? What evidence do you have? What do you know about? How would you explain . . . ?	

Stage of the Instructional Model	What the Student Does	
	That Is Consistent with This Model	*That Is Inconsistent with This Model*
Engage	Asks questions, such as: Why did this happen? What do I already know about this? What can I find out about his?	Asks for the "right" answer
		Offers the "right" answer
		Insists on answers or explanations
	Shows interest in the topic	Seeks one solution
Explore	Thinks freely, but within the limits of the activity	Lets others do the thinking and exploring (passive involvement)
	Tests predictions and hypotheses	Works quietly with little or no interaction with others (only appropriate when exploring ideas or feelings)
	Forms new predictions and hypotheses	
	Tries alternatives and discusses them with others	
	Records observations and ideas	Plays around indiscriminately with no goal in mind
	Suspends judgment	Stops with one solution
Explain	Explains possible solutions or answers to others	Proposes explanations from thin air with no relationship to previous experiences
	Listens critically to another student's explanations	
	Questions other explanations	Brings up irrelevant experiences and examples
	Listens to and tries to comprehend explanations offered by the teacher	Accepts explanations without justification
	Refers to previous activities	
	Uses recorded observations in scientific explanations	Does not attend to other plausible explanations
Elaborate	Applies new labels, definitions, explanations, and skills in new, but similar, situations	Plays around with no goal in mind
		Ignores previous information or evidence
	Uses previous information to ask questions, propose answers, make decisions, design experiments	Draws conclusions from thin air
		Uses in discussions only those labels that the teacher provided
	Draws reasonable conclusions from evidence	
	Records observations and explanations	
	Checks for understanding among peers	
Evaluate	Answers open-ended questions by using observations, evidence, and previously accepted explanations	Draws conclusions, not using evidence or previously accepted explanations
	Demonstrates an understanding or knowledge of the concept or skill	Offers only yes-or-no answers, memorized definitions, or explanations as answers
	Evaluates his or her own progress and knowledge	
	Asks related questions that would encourage future investigations	Fails to express satisfactory explanations in his or her own words
		Introduces new, irrelevant topics

FIGURE 13–9   *Continued*

―――――――――――――――― **INVESTIGATING SCIENCE TEACHING** ――――――――――――――――

ACTIVITY 13–1
WHAT DOES IT MEAN TO CONSTRUCT AN UNDERSTANDING OF A SCIENTIFIC CONCEPT?

In this chapter we have discussed various models for organizing your approach to how you present ideas and opportunities in the classroom to maximize learning. A constructivist approach is one of the key ideas emerging in many areas of educational reform, including science education. Despite the support in the research for the value of this approach, it is probably the least common approach of instruction. Use this activity to think about what the value of a constructivist approach might be and why it is seldom used.

1. Draw a concept map that demonstrates your understanding of *photosynthesis*. Your map should answer this question: What are the key ideas related to the concept and how are they related?

2. Circle the areas on the map that you think should be taught in middle school in one color and the areas that should be taught in high school in another color.

3. Watch the video *Lessons from Thin Air*, and then prepare to discuss these questions:

   ◆ What does the teacher do to help students build an understanding of photosynthesis?
   ◆ What else could the teacher do?
   ◆ What do you think of the student's reaction to his own videotape?
   ◆ Do you think photosynthesis is a valuable concept to teach? Why?
   ◆ What is your explanation about why so few people could accurately explain how an acorn grows into a large oak tree?

4. Look at your concept map in light of what you learned watching the video. How does your map represent both accuracies and inaccuracies in understanding the big ideas behind the concept of photosynthesis?

5. Review the areas on your map that you indicated as being appropriate to teach in middle and high school. What changes would you make based on the video and the discussion?

6. What do you see as the role of an instructional model in helping students develop accurate understandings of key scientific concepts?

   If you would like to learn more about videos like *Lessons from Thin Air*, check the Annenberg website at www.learner.org.

CHAPTER 14

PLANNING FOR EFFECTIVE SCIENCE TEACHING

Science teachers are especially fortunate because of the many interesting and motivational things connected with science that they can use in their teaching. Examples of natural and scientific phenomena abound. The daily cycle of news events, the endless variety of clouds and weather, the growth of plants and animals, and the passage of the seasons all contribute to an endless store of materials for scientific and technologic discussions.

Alert and enthusiastic science teachers do not miss the opportunity to incorporate these in their teaching plans. Clever use of appropriate items and examples will inject a degree of interest and spontaneity into science classes that is unmatched in other disciplines. How does the science teacher put the things of science to use? Are there meaningful ways to plan for effective teaching? Can the teacher maintain sequence and organization and at the same time stimulate interest? Can the objectives of science teaching be realized while permitting the objects of science to dominate the scene? These are questions teachers must face when planning their yearly and daily work.

At this point, we recommend that you complete at least one of the following: Activity 14–1: Planning a Simple Lesson, or Activity 14–2: Evaluating a Lesson, at the end of this chapter.

The next sections introduce elements and strategies of effective teaching. These are the "pieces" that science teachers use in designing individual lessons or teaching units. The chapter is structured so that you develop an idea of different types of planning for effective science teaching. This chapter presents the practical how-to of science teaching—the actual planning of a science program, a teaching unit, and daily lesson plans.

PLANNING A UNIT OR COURSE OF STUDY

The prospects of designing a course, unit, or even a daily lesson plan may be quite daunting for a new teacher. Fortunately, the instructional materials you use will have done much of the preplanning of the organization and content of your prospective unit. Your particular goals and objectives, however, will certainly dictate the specific manner in which the accomplishment of these goals and objectives will be met. At this point you should complete Activity 14–3: Planning a Limit—Preliminary Questions. The activity is at the end of this chapter.

In your planning there are several components to consider. First, you should have a clear idea of the rationale for the course or unit. Why is this material being included? How does the new information fit into the overall course or unit? You will need to think about the intended learning outcomes. What specific student objectives are to be accomplished? Which of these are conceptual, which are skill objectives, and which are expected values outcomes?

It is helpful to construct a conceptual framework showing the relationships among the ideas of the unit or course. Which are major ideas? Which are minor or subordinate ideas? In what order should they be presented?

The instructional plan is an important component which will consume much of your planning time. How can you best accomplish your objectives? What materials lend themselves best to the task? How can you make it interesting? How will students become actively involved? How can you avoid a traditional didactic approach and employ inquiry methods? These are all important questions you will need to answer.

Good advance planning for a lesson or unit is effective teaching. Sharing of ideas with other teachers is important.

Finally, you need to think about your evaluation plan. There are many forms of evaluation, each of which can serve a specific purpose in your teaching. Think about evaluation as you plan your unit or course, not as you approach the end of it. One helpful approach is called "backward design." In this process you begin by identifying the desired results and next determine acceptable evidence, via an assessment, that would indicate the students attained your goals. Then, and only then, you plan the learning experiences for your program. This process is based on the work of Grant Wiggins and Jay McTighe and elaborated in their book, *Understanding by Design* (2005).

ELEMENTS AND STRATEGIES OF EFFECTIVE SCIENCE TEACHING

Effective teaching requires a great deal of thought, preparation, and design. In the following sections we introduce ideas that you might keep in mind while designing a lesson.

Before a Lesson

Several times in this book we have indicated the importance of goals and learning outcomes. They emerge here as the fundamental consideration of the planning process.

Goals and learning outcomes are like maps. They indicate the journey and the destination, respectively. They also indicate where you are going and tell you when you have arrived. In teaching, it is often important

to remember that, like travel, the destination defines the trip, and the means of travel accommodates other aspects of the trip (e.g., budget, time, and access). We recommend careful thought and identification of the desired results and especially the evidence that you have attained those results. Once you actually have designed the lesson and begun teaching, it is important to continually direct and redirect teaching to your goals and learning outcomes. To use the trip analogy again, one can have educational side trips, but it is essential to continue in the general direction of your learning outcomes.

Beginning a Lesson

How you begin sets the stage for the entire lesson. The beginning of a lesson should achieve several things. First, it should connect what has been learned in the past with what is going to be learned in the present lesson. While the connections may seem obvious to you as the teacher, it is not always as clear to the students. Second, a good beginning should provide a focus or context for the present lesson. Effective beginnings answer the why and what questions that students may have. Third, the beginning should be exciting and engaging. Students should be enthusiastic about what they are going to study.

There are many effective ways to begin a lesson. Current events, confrontation with problems, pictorial riddles, discrepant events, counterintuitive demonstrations, and challenging questions are all ways to begin a teaching sequence.

Middle of a Lesson

Once the lesson is under way, you can incorporate more elements and strategies into science teaching. Here are a few initial ideas to consider as you design lessons. Active participation with materials, equipment, and electronic media are good ways to engage the learner's attention and develop the concepts, skills, and values of your learning outcomes.

You want to optimize the amount of time students are engaged in learning tasks. There are different means of capturing, maintaining, and enhancing students' attention. These motivational strategies include showing students the personal meaning of the lesson through a rationale, or by connecting an idea or concept to the students' lives or answering a personal question.

Once you are into the lesson, remember to apply the principles of learning and development. At a minimum, use reinforcement to discourage nonproductive behaviors. When introducing skills it is often essential to model what you want the students to do. For example, demonstrate how you want them to set up and dismantle laboratory equipment or use the probes of a computer-based laboratory.

Practice is another element of learning. Some ideas, skills, and values are learned because they have great personal meaning. In others, proficiency is achieved through repetition of a task. Don't hesitate to schedule time to practice the skills that you perceive to be important. Sometimes practice can be done with the entire class, usually at the initial stages of learning; other times practice can be individualized and either distributed throughout or clustered at the end of the learning sequence.

As you teach the lesson, it is valuable to monitor student progress. How are they doing? Do they understand what has been taught? If students are not progressing as you had anticipated, it is well worth adapting the sequence or method to better enhance student learning. The assessment can be as simple as spot-checking papers, asking questions, or giving a quiz. The crucial point is to change instruction based on feedback from the assessment.

Another sometimes elusive set of factors is important for planning and teaching. These factors can be thought of as the classroom climate. What plans should be made to establish a classroom environment that enhances student learning? Planning your lesson or unit should include communicating expectations of achievement—your goals, procedures for a safe and orderly work environment, anticipation and sensible management of disruptive behavior, and establishment of cooperative learning (Berliner, 1984).

There is a lot that goes into teaching. Some of the factors described above can actually be a part of your planning, while others are part of your instructional theory.

Ending a Lesson or Unit

Too often lessons just stop. Plan an ending to your lesson. There should be closure, an opportunity for you or your students to summarize what has been taught. At the lesson's end, you should be able to indicate how well the learning outcomes were met. Students ought to leave the room with a feeling of accomplishment and closure for the day's lesson or the unit.

After a Lesson or Unit

When a lesson is over, you should have some measure of the lesson and student achievement. The measure can be an informal assessment of how things went and what they learned, or a formal evaluation of the lesson through an assessment of student achievement. These procedures are feedback for you and the students. They indicate what might be changed in the instructional sequence and the problems students may be having with the material. The next section is a more complete description of planning for effective science teaching.

DESIGNING PROGRAMS, UNITS, AND LESSONS

This section is designed to have you take steps toward the practical, everyday matter of science teaching. You have just read about general strategies of effective lessons. Here many of the elements and methods are combined into a sequence of instruction. Although there are many models and methods for teaching science, the purpose of this section is for you to begin thinking generally about your science program and specifically about planning science lessons. We take the approach of beginning with the science program, the yearlong plan. Although this is probably not your most immediate concern, having the big picture of your science program provides the framework for consistent and coherent units and lessons. The sequence of this discussion is the science program, unit plans, and lesson plans.

THE LONG-RANGE PLAN: A SCIENCE PROGRAM

Our goal for this section is to have you begin thinking about a full year's science program. To accomplish our goal of conceptualizing a total science program—seeing the forest before looking at trees—complete Activity 14–4: Designing a Full-Year Program, at the end of this chapter. Designing your science program will be a major challenge. You will have to synthesize many diverse ideas and recommendations into your program. Remember to begin with the learning outcomes and acceptable evidence that you have achieved those outcomes. Topics and activities come from a variety of sources. These sources may include the following:

- ◆ Science department requirements
- ◆ District syllabi
- ◆ State standards and assessments
- ◆ Textbook organizations
- ◆ National organizations

Sorting all of these recommendations is not easy. Fortunately, many of the recommendations are consistent. In the end, you will decide on your science program. That is why we encourage you to begin thinking about how to organize your program. There are several ways to organize programs. We briefly describe some of those ways in the next sections.

Conceptual Structure of the Discipline

Science disciplines are organized by major conceptual ideas. Themes such as thermodynamics in physics, bonding in chemistry, and diversity in biology are examples of conceptual schemes that organize disciplines. Many contemporary curriculum projects are organized by the structure of disciplines.

Nature of Scientific Inquiry

Inquiry refers to the ways scientists within disciplines determine the truth or falsehood, validity or invalidity, of knowledge claims. Inquiry includes the processes scientists use—observation, classification, controlling variables, forming hypotheses, and designing experiments. Organizing on the basis of inquiry also includes the study of how and why scientific propositions are accepted or rejected. If scientists have competing theories, how does one know which is acceptable?

Science Topics

Topics can be used to organize science courses. Electricity, magnets, rocks and minerals, cell division, and photosynthesis are examples of topics.

Science-Related Social Issues

In recent years, the trend has been toward using issues to organize courses. If carefully and properly done, organizing a program by issues can be exciting for students and will include many important science concepts and processes. Examples of issues include air quality and atmosphere, water resources, land use, population growth, food resources, mineral resources, and environmental quality.

Organizing a science program can take the form of a yearly calendar. The calendar indicates the order of units and time allotted to them. Table 14–1 is a calendar for a course organized by both integrating concepts and social issues. Examination of textbooks and state syllabi will provide other examples of yearly calendars.

In preparing this calendar, the order of issues and concepts generally moves from simple to complex. The more complex problems come later in the year, and more time is allotted for study of these issues. The calendar includes 180 days, the average number of classes a science teacher has in a school year.

THE MIDDLE-RANGE PLAN: A SCIENCE UNIT

A beginning teacher is assisted by a teaching-unit plan designed in moderate detail for a period of a month or six weeks. The unit topic is usually a cohesive area of study that fits into long-range plans and objectives. The teaching unit frequently contains the following sections and characteristics:

1. Title
2. Purpose statement
3. Learning outcomes
4. Content
5. Methods
6. Materials
7. Assessments
8. Teaching sequence

TABLE 14–1   Yearly Calendar for a Course Organized by Concepts and Issues

Unit	Issue	Concepts	Days Allotted
I	Science and technology in society	The nature of science and technology	10
II	Air quality	Cycles	20
III	Land use	Scale	20
IV	Water quality	Equilibrium	20
V	Hazardous substances	Gradient	25
VI	Space exploration	Systems	40
VII	Population, resources, environment	Interactions	45
			(Total 180 days)

The *title* is simply an identifying name for the unit. It need not be anything complicated, for example, "An Introduction to Physics," "Human Ecology," or "Earth Processes: Folds and Faults."

A *purpose statement* is a synopsis of why this unit is important and generally what will be accomplished by the teaching unit.

The *learning outcomes* should be specific, brief statements of objectives for the unit. They should serve as constant reminders to the teacher of the things to be accomplished in the time allotted. They should be practical, timely, and carefully suited to the capabilities of the class. Learning outcomes should be clearly written and testable.

Content refers to the actual material to be taught in the unit. Because this material may be extensive, the teaching-unit plan cannot list all of it in detail; however, the plan may list major principles, pertinent facts of major importance, examples and illustrations, and references to specific knowledge in text material deemed important for the unit. An outline form may be used in this part of the unit plan. Because of the chronological nature of the teaching unit, specific content and references to subject matter can be distributed sequentially throughout the unit.

Methods to be used in teaching should be planned as carefully as possible. This is where the use of one instructional model is highly recommended. Plan through the sequence of lessons using a model. Based on the model and your outcomes, certain parts of the teaching sequence may be taught more suitably by one method than by another. For example, a DVD may be the most effective teaching agent for an introduction (e.g., engagement), and a simulation game may be most appropriate as an elaboration of the lesson's concepts. At another time you may deem a discussion or individual project to be the best teaching method.

Materials must be planned with care to ensure their availability when needed. In some cases, ordering a few weeks in advance is necessary. Apparatus should be checked to see whether it is in working order. Development of the teaching unit will undoubtedly involve hours of library work, searching the web for ideas, and reading materials and activities. Consideration should be given to the needs of slow and gifted learners, and suitable materials should be arranged for them.

Assessment should be thought of as a continuing process throughout the unit. One of the major functions of assessment is to keep students informed of their progress and to give them realistic feedback about their abilities. Assigned work, short quizzes, conferences, and unit tests must be planned in the teaching unit. Not all of the assessment strategies and techniques can be planned in advance, but provision for them can be made. Assessment should be based on the learning outcomes of the unit and be developed *before* you identify other plans; that is, apply the backward design strategy discussed earlier.

The *teaching sequence* may be outlined for the period of time involved, but flexibility for change must be provided. This can be done by arranging for alternative procedures, omitting or adding certain subject matter, and providing for unplanned periods that can occasionally be interspersed to take up slack or give needed time for completing a topic. The teaching unit should be thought of as a guide for action rather than a calendar of events. Reasonable attention to the sequence, outcomes, and procedures of the teaching unit can promote better learning, satisfaction, and accomplishment. A general outline for a unit is presented here.

Outline for a Science Teaching Unit
- Title
- Purpose Statement
- Outline for a Year Program (Use Activity 14–4: Designing a Full-Year Program, and indicate where your unit is located in the total program.)
- Learning Outcomes for the Unit
- Weekly Schedule for the Unit (See Table 14–2 for an example.)
- Pretest
- Daily Lesson Plans (Use a specific model or combination of models.)
- Unit Assessment

CHECKLIST OF REQUIREMENTS FOR THE SCIENCE UNIT

Your instructor may indicate requirements for a science unit. You can use this checklist to organize your science unit:

1. *Title page.* Give the title of the unit, grade level, and whether it is based on a new curriculum. If it uses a modern curriculum, state its name. List your name, the title and number of the course, and leave a space for the unit evaluation.
2. *Purpose statement.* Give the reason for the scope and sequence of the unit. Indicate the broad goals to be achieved through the unit.
3. *Learning outcomes.* These should be clearly stated.
4. *Weekly schedule of the unit.* A brief, one-page survey of what will take place each day as shown in Table 14–2.
   a. Include assignments.
   b. Include homework activities.
   c. Include web searches.

TABLE 14–2 Example of a Weekly Schedule for a Middle School Science Class Studying Environmental Change

Content Outline	Class Period	Phase of Teaching Model	Class Activity
Environmental problems in paper	Homework	Engagement	Students collect examples of newspaper articles dealing with environmental problems, e.g., hazardous substances or pollution.
Evidence of environmental change • Change is common • There are good, bad, and neutral changes	1	Exploration	Class goes outside and gathers evidence of changes in local environment. They should find good, bad, and neutral changes.
Factors related to environmental change • Immediate • Delayed • Cycles • Growth	2	Explanation	Show DVD, *The Saga of DDT*. Use DVD to focus discussion on key concepts. End class with short lecture, defining and giving examples of immediate change, delayed change, cyclical change, and change through growth.
Changing environmental systems	3	Elaboration	Do silent demonstrations of changes in aquatic and terrestrial ecosystems. Have students identify potential immediate, delayed, cyclical, and growth changes.
Limits to change in environmental systems	4	Elaboration	Do invitation to inquiry on "Tragedy of the Commons." Use cooperative groups.
End of section	5	Evaluation	Quiz on concepts. Students will define concept and give one local and one global example.

5. *Laboratory exercises.* These should be laboratory activities, including the following:
   a. The subject outcomes (concepts and abilities) the laboratory will teach
   b. Critical-thinking and problem-solving processes the lesson will develop
   c. A discussion section preceding the lesson and open-ended possibilities following the lesson
   d. Other (assigned by your instructor)
6. *Invitations to inquiry.* You are to prepare these invitations.
7. *Discussion questions during or at the end of the unit*
   a. List the questions you will ask to determine whether the students understood the material studied and whether they can apply what they have learned.
   b. When possible, the questions should develop critical-thinking and problem-solving processes. The type of mental process the student must use—for example, predicting or inferring—should be placed in the margin to indicate what is required.
8. *Demonstrations.* Include only if they are required because of a shortage of equipment or for safety reasons.
9. *Bulletin board display.* Prepare a diagram for at least one bulletin board display, indicating how it will appear and contribute to the learning outcomes.

10. *Supplemental materials*
    a. Laboratories or investigations
    b. Web searches
11. *Multimedia materials*
    a. CD-ROMs
    b. Use of the Internet
    c. Videos
    d. PowerPoint presentations
    e. Models, charts
12. *Consideration of safety precautions.* What special considerations should be made about safety?
13. *Consideration of special students.* You might wish to include the variations on the lesson you would implement if you have special students.
14. *Resource materials.* Include magazine materials, books, and web resources you might want to use to improve your knowledge about the topic.
15. *Assessments.* Assessments should evaluate your learning outcomes.
    a. Quizzes
    b. Performance activities
    c. Assessments
16. *Self-evaluation of the unit*
    a. After compiling this unit outline, go back over it and write what problems you think you might have in teaching.
    b. After teaching this unit, evaluate how you think it could be improved.

THE RESOURCE UNIT

Many science teachers prepare a resource unit for the different topics they teach. A resource unit is, as the title indicates, a collection of resource materials that can be used for a specified topic (e.g., acids and bases, the laws of thermodynamics, the rock cycle, or photosynthesis) or various issues (e.g., population growth, air quality, world hunger, or health and disease). Rather than assemble the resources in a teaching sequence such as we have discussed previously, a resource unit is usually arranged by teaching strategies or methods. If you begin organizing resource units now, in only a few years you will have an extensive collection of ideas and methods. Although you will have to determine the topics or issues for your science program, we can provide some general organizational categories for resource units. You would probably want to develop resource units for each of the major topics in your curriculum.

Possible Organizational Categories for Resource Units
- Goals
- Learning Outcomes
- Bulletin Boards
- Computer Software
- Demonstrations
- Discussion Topics
- Field Trips
- Homework
- Invitations to Inquiry
- Lecture Notes

- Multimedia
- Projects
- Supplementary Readings
- Assessments
- Videos
- Websites
- Miscellaneous

You will probably not use all of these categories, and will perhaps add some of your own, but this list should help you begin organizing your resource units. Use of a personal computer and a database will greatly enhance your organization, filing, and search capacity. Table 14–3 is a more complete description of the categories and examples of materials for a resource unit.

THE SHORT-RANGE PLAN: THE SCIENCE LESSON

The sequence of topics in this chapter may have seemed unusual to the science teacher facing a first lesson. We think there is an added advantage for all teachers who have thought through the year's program and a unit before organizing a daily lesson plan. At this point complete Activity 14–5. Planning gives direction. A yearly plan guards against disconnected units, and unit plans protect against disconnected lessons. For all teachers, planning is an essential component of effective instruction. Approaching a science class with a well-organized plan gives the teacher personal assurance and leaves the students with confidence in the teacher's abilities.

Stimulating interest in science and technology is an important goal in resource or teaching units.

TABLE 14–3   Resource Unit: Examples of Categories and Contents

Categories	Contents
Aims and Goals	Lists of aims and goals from your local district, state education agency, national organizations, and textbooks
Learning Outcomes	Lists of objectives from your local district, state education agency, national organizations, and textbooks
Bulletin Boards	Sketches and designs, newspaper and magazine articles, pictures, and maps
Computer Software	CAI programs, microcomputer-based laboratory, tutorial, simulation, HyperCard, models
Demonstrations	Collections of good demonstrations from journals such as *Science Scope,* the *Science Teacher,* the *American Biology Teacher,* the *Physics Teacher;* ideas from workshops and college courses
Discussion Topics	Questions and issues that are successful with students
Field Trips	Description of where to go, what to do, and who to contact
Games	List of games in science department, local media center
Homework	Unique and interesting homework assignments for the topic
Invitations to Inquiry	Lists of appropriate invitations from *Biology Teachers Handbook,* invitations you have developed, ideas for invitations.
PowerPoint Presentations	List (by title or content) of PowerPoint slides on file
Lecture Notes	Revised notes from past courses
Projects	Problems and ideas for projects
Supplementary Readings	List of books and articles in media center, your file, or public library
Assessments	Quizzes, tests, and questions for the unit
Videos	List of videos from *NOVA, DISCOVERY,* etc., for VCR replay
Websites	List of sites that relate to the concepts and topics of the unit

Thorough planning should precede any written plans. Ask yourself the following questions:

- What are my goals?
- How can I best achieve my goals?
- How will I know that students have achieved the goals?
- How can the concepts, processes, or skills be presented most effectively?
- How can I evaluate the lesson's effectiveness?

Because students vary in abilities and interests, plans must provide for these variations. Only by knowing something of the background of each student can the teacher be effective. This fact argues strongly for taking a personal interest in the students in one's classes. The small human contacts in a friendly classroom, an interested question here and there, can motivate students better than any other method.

Planning for effective science teaching is more than just making sure that there is something to do for the entire class period. For example, unless it is the very first lesson of the year, it is probable that assignments have been made and that the nature of the subject matter is understood. Thus, the basis for planning has already been established.

To conduct an interesting class period, the teacher must vary the methods from day to day and even within the class period itself. It is eventually ineffective to use the same pattern of teaching every day. Even an excellent method can suffer from overuse. With the great variety of methods from which to choose and with the potential excitement of inventing a new technique or of modifying an existing one, the science teacher is in an excellent position to plan a highly effective lesson.

The lesson plan should be concise and functional. The format may vary with the situation and individual teacher, but most important, it should be a practical, usable plan. In general, provision should be made for listing outcomes and the related concepts. The learning activities and required procedures should be listed. For example, the procedures ought to be given in adequate detail; written questions and directions ensure a smooth class. All materials needed for the class period should be listed and checked. Two last essentials are assignments and evaluation. A skeletal form for a daily lesson would include the topics listed below:

1. Learning Outcomes
2. Concepts
3. Activities/Procedures
4. Materials
5. Assignments
6. Assessments

During the class period, a teaching plan should be as unobtrusive as possible, yet referred to when needed. Main ideas, questions, and procedures may be memorized. Be sure the plan is handy if you need it for reference. As we mentioned above, a plan gives direction. You should also plan for flexibility—realize that you will have to make some decisions about the direction of a particular lesson based on circumstances that arise in class.

TABLE 14–4 An Instructional Sequence for Planning Lessons

Engagement

This phase of the instructional sequence initiates the learning task. The activity should: (1) make connections between past and present learning experiences, and (2) anticipate activities and focus students' thinking on the learning outcomes of current activities. The student should become mentally engaged in the concept, process, or skill to be explored.

Exploration

This phase of the teaching sequence provides students with a common base of experiences within which they identify and develop current concepts, processes, and skills. During this phase, students actively explore their environment or manipulate materials.

Explanation

This phase of the instructional sequence focuses students' attention on a particular aspect of their engagement and exploration experiences and provides opportunities for them to verbalize their conceptual understanding, or demonstrate their skills or behaviors. This phase also provides opportunities for teachers to introduce a formal label or definition for a concept, process, skill, or behavior.

Elaboration

This phase of the teaching sequence challenges and extends students' conceptual understanding and allows further opportunity for students to practice desired skills and behaviors. Through new experiences, the students develop deeper and broader understanding, more information, and adequate skills.

Evaluation

This phase of the teaching sequence encourages students to assess their understanding and abilities and provides opportunities for teachers to evaluate student progress toward achieving the educational objectives.

After each lesson, we recommend evaluating the lesson plan. The experience gained in teaching a lesson should be recorded with brief notations on the written plan, either during the class period or immediately after class. Suggestions for timing, organization, student involvement, or modification of a technique can be noted for future use. (See Activity 14–6: Evaluation of Instructional Skills, at the end of this chapter.)

To help organize your planning in advance, the following are some features of lessons for inquiry-oriented science teaching:

- Students are involved in broad, open-ended questions related to science, technology, and/or social issues related to science and technology. Generally, students do not know the answer to the question.

- Students are required to understand the question before designing an investigation.
- Students design investigations and make observations and conclusions.
- Students write their results using the standard protocol of science papers.
- Planning for such experiences should be done with the following points in mind:
  - Students probably have not had many previous opportunities of this type. Some may feel the need for explicit directions. The initial progress made by these students may be disappointing and frustrating, both to student and teacher.
  - Accepting responsibility for one's own learning is a challenge that some students may tend to resist. Passive learning in which the teacher has been the key person for initiating a course of action has probably been the students' experience.
  - First attempts should be on a small scale, with opportunities for greater choice and greater responsibility increasing as the student gains experience.
  - The teacher should provide situations in which questions are asked. Students should be encouraged to formulate and ask questions that can be answered through inquiry.
  - Means must be provided for students to gain experience in analyzing the results of an inquiry. The ability to see relationships, to organize data so that meaningful patterns emerge, to draw inferences, and to visualize ways of improving the investigation is a necessary skill that must be developed for effective learning.

As you conclude this section pause and complete Activities 14–7 and 14–8.

◆

Sample Inquiry Lesson Plan—Grades 8–10

Overall Plan of the Lesson

The Problem

Learning Outcomes

Materials

Class Groupings

Background and Discussion (entire class)

Pupil Investigation (in groups)

Post-experiment Discussion (entire class)
    a. Hypotheses
    b. Concepts
    c. Comparison of group results
    d. Conclusions

Teacher's Notes

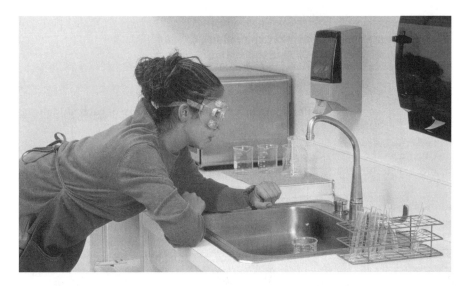

Adequate materials and facilities for inquiry teaching are essential components for success.

Problem: How can we measure the speed of sound by resonance?

Learning Outcomes: Students should be able to:
a. Explain what causes resonance
b. Perform the experiment to measure the speed of sound by resonance
c. Hypothesize what effect temperature may have on the speed of sound

Materials:

Tuning fork—Middle C (256 vps or G-384 vps)
Rubber mallet for striking the tuning fork
Glass tube at least 1 inch in diameter and 16 inches long
Deep container for water, such as a tall cylinder

Class groupings: Suggest five to seven persons per group

Background and Discussion: This can be established by discussion and questioning of the students, with some information provided by the teacher.

1. Have you ever pushed a friend on a swing? How did you decide when to push? Was it decided for you by when the swing came back to you?
2. If you pushed each time the swing came back to you, what happened to the height of the swing? If you stopped pushing, what happened to the height of the swing?
3. This was an example of resonance because you added energy periodically to make the swing go higher. Can you think of any other examples of resonance?
4. What is a tuning fork used for?
5. In music, what might be the vibration rate (frequency) of a common tuning fork used for getting the proper pitch?

6. How fast does sound travel through air? Does this change sometimes? What might cause it to change?
7. How might we find the speed of sound in air? (The method we will use will involve a tuning fork and resonance.)

Pupil Investigation

1. Obtain a tuning fork with the number of vibrations per second marked on it.
2. Obtain a glass tube about 16 inches long and 1 inch in diameter, open at both ends. Hold the tube upright with the lower end in a tall container of water (see Figure 14A).

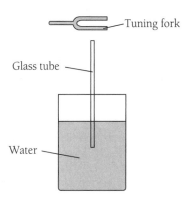

3. Strike the tuning fork a sharp blow with a rubber mallet and hold it above the open end of the glass tube.
4. Slowly move the glass tube up and down, keeping the vibrating tuning fork close to the open end of the tube, until a place is found where the sound of the tuning fork is greatly magnified.
5. When you have found the best resonance, measure the length of the tube from the top to the surface of the water in the bottom of the tube.

6. Multiply the length you have measured (in feet) by 4 and then by the number of vibrations per second marked on the tuning fork. This gives you the speed of sound in feet per second.

Postinvestigation Discussion

1. Why do you multiply the length of the tube by 4? Why do you multiply by the frequency of the tuning fork? Why do you use water in the large container? Could you use another liquid? Try it.

2. The glass tube closed at the bottom by water is called a "closed tube." Could you obtain resonance with an "open tube"? How could you perform this experiment with an open tube?

Conclusion: What do you conclude from this investigation? Briefly state your conclusion.

Teachers' Notes: The relationship among wavelength, frequency, and speed of sound is wavelength times frequency equals speed of sound. To get the wavelength in this investigation, the length of the glass tube is multiplied by 4 because the sound wave travels the length of the tube four times for each wave before resonance is produced (see Figure 14B).

Explanation of Resonance in a Closed Tube
While tuning fork goes from:

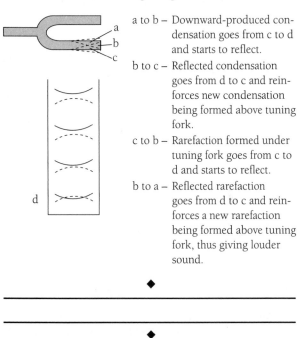

a to b – Downward-produced condensation goes from c to d and starts to reflect.

b to c – Reflected condensation goes from d to c and reinforces new condensation being formed above tuning fork.

c to b – Rarefaction formed under tuning fork goes from c to d and starts to reflect.

b to a – Reflected rarefaction goes from d to c and reinforces a new rarefaction being formed above tuning fork, thus giving louder sound.

◆

◆

5E Model Lesson Plan—Lung Capacity

A useful strategy for teaching science to middle school pupils is that of the BSCS 5E Model. The five phases to this format are as follows:

- ◆ Engagement
- ◆ Exploration
- ◆ Explanation
- ◆ Elaboration
- ◆ Evaluation

Problem: To find the lung capacity of each student

Materials:

Large glass container of at least 2 liters capacity. A cider jug may serve the purpose for this large open plastic or metal container for water. The container should hold at least 5 liters of water.

Rubber tubing, about 5 millimeters inside diameter, and about 30 centimeters in length (see Figure 14C for the proper setup of the apparatus).

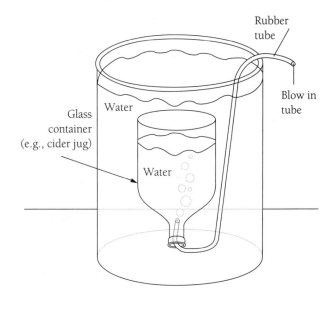

Small container of water in which a few milliliters of chlorine bleach has been mixed for disinfectant.

Engagement: What is lung capacity? Why is a large lung capacity desirable for humans? Who would be best served by a larger lung capacity on average—people who live at sea level or those who live at high altitudes? Suggest why this might be true. How might we determine a person's lung capacity?

Exploration:

a. Have students, in sequence, exhaust the air completely from their lungs and then take a very deep breath from the rubber tube. Note the height the water reaches in the cider jug.

b. Carefully measure the difference in height between the initial height and the final height with a metric ruler. Record this measurement for each person. (Note: Be sure to dip the end of the rubber tube into the bleach water after each use.)

c. After students have measured their "intake lung capacity," have them perform the experiment again— this time by filling their lungs to capacity and then expelling the air into the cider jug that has been filled with water. Measure the difference in height of the water in the jug after all lung air has been expelled. Record this measurement next to the measurement of "intake lung capacity."

d. To obtain the lung capacity of each pupil in liters, multiply the height difference you measured by *p* times *r* squared. The formula for volume of a cylinder is height times *p* times *r* squared. For example, if the height measurement was 10 centimeters and the radius of the cider jug was 8 centimeters, the volume would be 10 centimeters times 64 square centimeters times *p*, which equals 2011.6 cubic centimeters, or 2.012 liters.

Explanation:

What caused the water to go into the cider jug on the intake phase of the experiment? (Remember a vacuum cannot "pull" on anything. There must have been "pushing" to get the water to go into the jug. What might it have been?)

What caused the water to leave the jug on the "expelling" phase of the experiment?

Generally, how did the two measurements obtained in the two phases compare for each student? What might account for any differences noticed?

Elaboration:

In some countries, divers take a deep breath and dive for oysters or other shellfish. They can stay under water for several minutes. What kind of lung capacity must they have? How could you increase your lung capacity?

Whales are mammals that breathe air. They dive and remain below the surface for many minutes. What might happen to your lung capacity if you breathed pure oxygen instead of ordinary air? (Be careful how you answer this.)

Evaluation:

What factors should be evaluated in this experiment?

Was the apparatus functional? How could you improve it?

How many trials should one take to obtain a representative lung capacity measurement for each pupil?

What conclusions might you draw after completing this experiment?

◆

SUMMARY

Planning is a critical aspect of effective science teaching. When designing a lesson, teaching unit, or total course, keep in mind ideas that are fundamental to effective instruction: Use learning outcomes; focus teaching on the objective; be sure students actively participate; apply principles of learning and motivation; and develop lessons with a beginning, middle, and end that are educationally productive.

A variety of methods are used in contemporary science teaching. Some of the key methods are questioning, discussing, demonstrating, reading, role-playing, presenting reports, doing projects, working in the laboratory, solving problems, taking field trips, preparing multimedia presentations, conducting simulations, and debating.

Science teachers can use models of teaching that combine strategies and methods into an effective instructional sequence. Using teaching models contributes to more efficient design of science lessons, and the synthesis of many elements of instruction into a workable and effective form.

The long-range plan of science teaching is the full-year program. The process for this plan was introduced. There are at least two kinds of middle-range unit lesson plans. A resource unit can be planned with a time sequence in mind and usually provides for statements of learning outcomes, outlines of content, methods, materials, and assessment techniques. A resource unit is not usually concerned with chronology but a reservoir of activities, websites, and PowerPoint slides that the teacher uses for daily lesson planning. It also may contain lists of aims, important knowledge outcomes, lists of activities and projects, computer software, suitable demonstrations and experiments, references, bibliographies, sample tests, assignments, and other teaching aids.

The lesson plan is a guide for action, not a rigid blueprint to be followed unswervingly. It should be flexible and modified when necessary. Much thought should precede the writing of a lesson plan. Consider these questions before planning the teaching sequence: What is the purpose of the lesson? What major generalizations are to be taught? How is the material best presented? What kinds of individuals are in the class?

The format of the lesson plan should be functional and comfortable to the teacher. Individual teachers select the format most useful to them. Lesson plans should be as concise as possible within the limitations of effective teaching. While teaching, the lesson plan should be unobtrusive but available for reference.

Planning for contemporary science teaching usually requires a somewhat different approach than more traditional methods. The role of the teacher becomes one of guidance and direction, with students accepting greater responsibility for learning. Plans must provide more time, more questioning, greater variety of materials, and willingness on the part of the teacher to allow individual variations in progress by students.

Thorough lesson planning is a necessary facet of effective science teaching. Good teaching does not happen by accident. A prospective teacher of science recognizes the value and benefit to be derived from careful, inspired planning in the art of science teaching.

———————————— **INVESTIGATING SCIENCE TEACHING** ————————————

ACTIVITY 14–1
PLANNING A SIMPLE LESSON

1. Select a simple and specific learning outcome for a science class, such as "to develop skill in correct use of the microscope," "to learn how to use a balance," or "to operate a microcomputer." Plan a lesson to achieve this outcome, incorporating the features of a good lesson plan.

2. Using the lesson plan prepared above, or a similar one, teach your classmates the lesson. Invite them to play the role of a secondary science class, with appropriate questions and activities. Solicit their constructive criticisms and comments on your lesson and the effectiveness of your teaching.

ACTIVITY 14–2
EVALUATING A LESSON

A lesson plan for an eighth-grade science class is described below. Read through the description of the teacher's preparation and topic, and study the teacher's written lesson plan. Then respond to the questions at the end of the section.

Mr. Foster looked forward to planning the eighth-grade science class on Monday morning. The topic for consideration was the simple Mendelian ratio of 1:2:1 for the offspring in the first generation produced by crossing of two pure strains. As he thought of the students in his class, it seemed that he might involve them in class participation and generate enthusiasm by doing a demonstration experiment. He would use the crossing of pure white and pure black guinea pigs as a simple case to illustrate this phenomenon.

In pure strains the genes for coat color in the parents could be represented by BB and ww. The only possible combinations in the first generation offspring would be Bw. These animals would be black, but each would carry the gene for white. If animals of this genetic makeup were crossed, the possible combinations in their offspring (second generation) would be BB, Bw, wB, and ww.

To demonstrate the purely statistical nature of the results obtained in this cross and of the effect of dominant over recessive genes, Mr. Foster decided to make a simple arrow spinner that would be attached to the blackboard with a suction cup. Then a circle could be drawn on the blackboard, around the spinner, and labeled as shown in the figure. With this device, he could engage the class in a "game of chance," give them practice in keeping a record of the data shown as follows, and put across the point of the lesson in an interesting manner.

After constructing the spinner, Mr. Foster decided to give it a trial run to see whether it would perform satisfactorily and whether the demonstration could be accommodated in the 50-minute class period. Out of 40 trials, the results he obtained in his trial run were

	BB	Bw	wB	ww
Trials:	11	8	11	10

The activity took 10 minutes and the results appeared to be close enough to the expected values to illustrate the point. He decided to plan his class period around this demonstration experiment.

On paper, Mr. Foster's lesson plan looked like this:

Topic: Simple Mendelian ratio
Learning Outcome: To show the statistical nature of the Mendelian ratio
Objective: At the completion of this lesson the student should be able to predict the approximate proportions of each gene combination obtained with 100 trials of the spinner.

Introductory questions (10 min.):

1. What is meant by dominant gene? By recessive gene?
2. Suppose a purebred black and a purebred white guinea pig (BB, ww) were mated. What genes have they for color? What would be the color of their offspring?
3. What are the possible combinations of dominant and recessive genes for color of coat? (BB, Bw, wB, ww)
4. What might be the proportions of each of these combinations in the offspring? (1:1:1:1—since Bw and wB are the same, the ratios appear as 1:2:1)
5. How would we show that this is the result of statistical probability?

Activity: Set up the blackboard spinner. Select a volunteer to spin it. Select another volunteer to keep a record on the blackboard under the headings BB, Bw, wB, and ww. Continue for 10–15 minutes.

Discussion (20 min.):

1. What are the actual colors of offspring that have each of the possible gene combinations? (three black and one white)
2. Why aren't the results in an exact ratio of 1:2:1? (change variations when few trials are used)
3. Could we improve the results? (more trials)
4. Student questions (anticipated)

Assignment (a volunteer assignment): Two boys or girls might run this experiment for more trials to see what the results would be.

Evaluation:

　　Time OK? _____ Interest? _____ Understanding? _____ Student Learning? _____

1. How would you improve Mr. Foster's lesson?
2. What pitfalls and precautions would you advise Mr. Foster about?
3. What features would you identify as a well-planned lesson?

ACTIVITY 14–3
PLANNING A UNIT—PRELIMINARY QUESTIONS

Suppose you are faced with the task of planning and carrying out a unit of work (e.g., four to five weeks) in your teaching area. What questions might you ask yourself? How will you organize your thoughts and plans? Consider each of the following questions:

1. What will be some important factors to take into consideration?
2. How might you involve students in the planning? How much student involvement is desirable?
3. What different levels of planning will probably be necessary?
4. What parts of your plans will you, of necessity, put down in written form?
5. What parts of your plans might you prefer to note mentally but not necessarily write down?
6. How much importance will you grant to a time budget?
7. How will you provide for the anticipated procedure questions and activities of the class? For the unanticipated questions and activities?
8. How will you provide for flexibility so that unexpected events can be handled adequately?
9. What purpose will evaluation serve in subsequent planning?
   a. From the standpoint of knowledge acquired by the students?
   b. From the standpoint of modification of the plans for the next teaching session?

ACTIVITY 14–4
DESIGNING A FULL-YEAR PROGRAM

As best you can, design a year's science program. We have found it best to complete the preliminary items as a way of thinking through your ideas. Then, complete the weekly schedule. You may wish to indicate major units within the weekly outline. Finally, complete the question at the end of the investigation.

Title of Program: Preliminary Textbook:

Discipline: Supplemental Textbook(s):

Grade Level:

Purpose Statement:

Weekly Schedule for an Academic Year: *Unit Topics for an Academic Year:*

1.

2.

3.

Question:

What was your rationale for the sequence, or order, of topics outlined?

ACTIVITY 14–5
A COMPLETE LESSON PLAN

Think through all aspects of a lesson plan. The experience will contribute to your doing this on a less formal basis for future lessons.

Topic

Goals

Learning Outcomes

Materials

Instructional Plan

Assessment

ACTIVITY 14–6
EVALUATION OF INSTRUCTIONAL SKILLS

This form is provided for a self-evaluation of a lesson you teach. The evaluation is directed toward the use of strategies, methods, and models discussed in this chapter.

Selects appropriate objectives

Makes learning outcomes and purposes of lesson clear to students

Teaches to the objective

1. Asks questions relevant to outcome
2. Provides information relative to outcome
3. Responds to learned questions/problems related to outcomes

Demonstrates continuity in lesson

◆ Beginning
◆ Middle
◆ End

Uses different methods

Applies strategies and a model of teaching

◆ Concept Mapping
◆ The Learning Cycle
◆ Cooperative Learning
◆ Textbook
◆ 4MAT

Shows continuity of plans

◆ Long Range (year)
◆ Middle Range (unit)
◆ Short Range (daily)

Activity 14–7
Student Attention

The following technique can be used to analyze student attention in class. Enlist the aid of another teacher or friend to observe your teaching for a full class period. Provide her with a form similar to the following:

OBSERVATION SHEET

Name _____ Class _____

Date _____ Time _____

Instructions: (a) At intervals of three minutes, count the class members and determine the number of students who are actively paying attention to the lesson or activity. Use your best judgment as to whether a student is paying attention. (b) Keep a record of the types of activities engaged in by the teacher and/or class (e.g., lecture, discussion, demonstration, experiment, film, student report). Note the time of transition from one type of activity to another. Note any major occurrences, such as disciplinary action, public address system coming on, entrance of a visitor, or any unusually distracting event. Plot a graph of percent attention versus time for each class observed.

Total attendance _____

Time	Class Count	Percent	Comments
0	_____	_____	_____
3	_____	_____	_____
6	_____	_____	_____
•			
•			
•			
•			
•			

ACTIVITY 14–8
EFFECTIVENESS OF METHODS

The effectiveness of different teaching methods can often be judged by student attention. In this investigation you are provided with a class attention record for a middle school physical science class. The record is for a week, and the different activities are noted. You are to review the high and low points of the week and draw conclusions about the different methods used and pupil attentiveness.

- ◆ How many methods did the teacher use?
- ◆ Which methods seemed most effective?
- ◆ What can you tell about transitions between activities?
- ◆ If you were to redesign the lessons for this, what would you change?

Good advance planning for a lesson or unit is essential for effective teaching. Sharing of ideas with other teachers is important.

CHAPTER 15

DESIGNING AN EFFECTIVE SCHOOL SCIENCE PROGRAM

In this chapter we first provide background on middle and high school curriculum reform. Then we present standards for a science program and review national standards for the content of school science programs. In the latter part of the chapter, we discuss processes for designing a school science program.

A BACKGROUND ON CURRICULUM REFORM

Adolescence is a period of significant physical, intellectual, social, and emotional development. The fact that adolescence generally spans the years of secondary education makes understanding this period generally important, but of particular importance is the period of middle school. Education during the middle school years, generally from ages 10 to 14, must extend the experiences of elementary school. The goals, curriculum, and instruction for science should be conceptualized and implemented as unique and congruent with the particular needs of the developing adolescent.

History of the Junior High

In the latter part of the nineteenth century, most elementary schools included grades 1 through 8 and high schools included grades 9 through 12. By 1920, about 80 percent of students graduating from high school had experienced eight years of elementary school and four years of high school. Although the schools were actually structured in this eight-four plan, leading educators

continually debated school organization for three decades beginning in the 1890s. Junior high schools, or school systems with six years of elementary school, three years of junior high school, and three years of high school, emerged in the early 1900s. Not until the 1918 Commission on the Reorganization of Secondary Education (CRSE) did the junior high become firmly established in the American educational system. The 1918 CRSE report, *Cardinal Principles of Secondary Education*, stated:

> We, therefore, recommend a reorganization of the school system whereby the first six years shall be devoted to elementary education designed to meet the needs of pupils approximately 6 to 12 years of age, and the second six years to secondary education designed to meet the needs of pupils approximately 12 to 18 years of age. The six years to be devoted to secondary education may well be divided into two periods which may be designated as the junior and senior periods (CRSE, 1918).

With the CRSE report, the concept of junior high schools was established. Their numbers grew, from an estimated 800 junior high schools in the United States in 1920 to 1,787 by 1930. The reasons for the rapid increase of junior high schools included shortages of facilities and economic restraints placed on schools between World War I and World War II. Justifications for junior high programs cited the needs of adolescents, the transition to high school, the elimination of dropouts, and vocational preparation. By 1940, prominent educators had developed a rationale for the junior high school. W. T. Gruhn and N. R. Douglas (1977) summarize the essential functions of junior high schools as follows:

- *Integration.* Basic skills, attitudes, and understanding learned previously should be coordinated into effective behaviors.
- *Exploration.* Individuals should explore special interests, aptitudes, and abilities for educational opportunities, vocational decisions, and recreational choices.
- *Guidance.* Assistance should be provided for students making decisions regarding education, careers, and social adjustment.
- *Differentiation.* Educational opportunities and facilities should provide for varying backgrounds, interests, and needs of the students.
- *Socialization.* Education should prepare early adolescents for participation in a complex democratic society.
- *Articulation.* Orientation of the program should provide a gradual transition from preadolescent (elementary) education to a program suited to the needs of adolescents.

In reality, most science teachers were trained for the high school and had little desire to teach in junior high schools. A junior high school teaching job was perceived as a stepping stone to a high school position. Most educators forgot or ignored the important goals of education for early adolescents, and education in grades 7, 8, and 9 became scaled-down versions of grades 10, 11, and 12.

Science Programs in Junior High Schools

General science was the course offered in the ninth grade of 84 schools when the first junior high schools came into existence. Begun in the decade 1910–1920, the course was designed to satisfy the needs and interests of students in early adolescence. The first course was established through research and was designed to fill a perceived need.

Junior high school science encountered several difficulties. For one, there was a shortage of well-trained general science teachers. Many teachers at this level were physics, chemistry, and biology teachers whose primary interest was not the problems of junior high school science. Second, teachers in other disciplines, such as English, mathematics, and physical education, were recruited to teach science. For these reasons, the general science texts for these grades were written in an effort to relieve these problems, but the variations in school and grade-level organization, such as six-three-three, eight-two-two, and eight-four, necessitated much repetition of science topics to produce universally saleable textbooks.

Deficiencies also existed in equipment and facilities for teaching science. Many science classes were taught in ordinary classrooms without water or gas outlets and without adequate facilities for demonstrations and experiments. Further, no one had clear knowledge of what junior high school science should actually accomplish. Objectives ranged from "preparation for the rigorous science courses in the senior high school" to "general education for good citizenship." Science educators and teachers gave considerable thought to development of attitudes and interests. Some believed general science should be exploratory in nature. Courses designed on this premise became rapid surveys of chemistry, physics, astronomy, meteorology, biology, and geology. Others believed that students should study the applications of science in the world around them. Courses of this kind centered on home appliances, transportation, communication, health problems, and natural resources.

Enrollments in general science grew to about 65 percent of the ninth-grade classes by 1956, then declined as new courses began to permeate the ninth grade and as the seventh and eighth grades took over more of the general science offerings (Brown & Obourn, 1961).

Usually the junior high school science program is organized in one of three patterns: (1) a one-, two-, or three-year program called general science; (2) a three-year program in which life, physical, and earth sciences are taught individually for a year each; or (3) a one-, two-, or three-year program of integrated or thematically organized science. One of the first two patterns is found in the majority of schools (Hurd, Robinson, McConnell, & Ross, 1981). Revision of junior high school science programs through national curriculum studies of the 1960s did not occur until late in the reform movement. Attention centered on the senior high school courses. The reform movement of the 1960s and 1970s made no effort to improve general science. In fact, many educators hoped that by implementing new life, earth, and physical science programs, the traditional general science program would eventually be replaced. This did not occur.

Emergence of Middle Schools

During the 1960s, several factors contributed to the emergence of middle schools as an alternative to junior high schools. Those factors included general criticisms of the schools and a need to increase the quality of education; an emphasis on curriculum improvement in science, mathematics, and foreign language; renewed interest in preparation for college; recognition of Piaget's work in developmental psychology; the need to eliminate de facto racial segregation; the need to restructure schools due to overcrowding; and a general desire to improve education. These and other factors contributed to an increase from 100 middle schools in 1960 to over 5,000 in 1980. In 1988, there were 12,000 separate middle schools with an estimated enrollment of 8 million students.

The middle school represents an important conceptual and physical change in the American educational system. Vital characteristics of the middle school were described in *The Status of Middle School and Junior High School Science* (Hurd et al., 1981).

- Program specifically designed for pre- and early adolescents
- Program that encourages exploration and personal development
- Positive and active learning environment
- Schedule that is flexible with respect to time and grouping
- Staff that recognizes students' needs, motivations, fears, and goals
- Instructional approach that is varied
- Emphasis on acquiring essential knowledge, skills, and attitudes in a sequential and individual manner
- Emphasis on developing decision-making and problem-solving skills
- Interdisciplinary learning and team teaching

Middle schools, in structure and function, have the following advantages:

- The middle school has a unique status; the school and program are not junior to another program.
- Specific subjects, such as science and mathematics, can be introduced at lower grades by specialists.
- Developing new middle schools provides the impetus for redesigning goals, curriculum, and instruction for the early adolescent learner.
- Developing middle schools can facilitate changes in teacher certification standards, and subsequently teacher education programs.
- Some discipline problems can be eliminated through different groupings of students, primarily the inclusion of some younger students.
- Middle schools can be designed to provide greater guidance and counseling at the time it is needed.

High School Science Programs in Transition

In an earlier chapter we reviewed the history and major programs developed during the golden age of science education. We now turn attention to the present era of reform.

We should first note that in about half of the states in the United States, the high school science instructional materials are selected at the local level by science teachers, administrators, and school boards. In making their decisions, they use suggestions and guidelines from national frameworks and policies (such as the national standards) and state departments of education. Even with significant autonomy, recent NSF studies have shown two things: There is considerable uniformity of programs, and the curriculum has not changed significantly in recent history (Weiss et al., 2001).

Typically, the senior high school science curriculum is biology at the tenth grade and chemistry and physics at the eleventh and twelfth grade, respectively. In 2000, Horizon Research conducted a study funded by NSF that indicated that approximately 30 percent of the science courses offered in grades 9 through 12 are first-year biology courses. Nineteen percent of the courses are first-year chemistry, 10 percent are first-year physics, and physical science and earth science account for 7 percent each. The remaining courses fall out with 9 percent of high school offerings covering general, integrated, or coordinated science and 11 percent including advanced courses in biology, chemistry, or physics (Weiss et al., 2001).

By nature of the traditional emphasis on science facts and vocabulary, little attention is paid to the goals of scientific inquiry, investigation, or analytical thinking. A review of the inquiry goal in science teaching found that teachers gave little attention to the aim of inquiry and associated skills (Anderson, 2002). Despite the research (Shymansky et al., 1983) supporting the effectiveness of the NSF-funded programs from the golden age, school programs are dominated by basic science concepts with less emphasis on the nature of science and the conducting of scientific inquiries (Weiss et al., 2001). Subsequently, in the early 1990s, the NSF began funding proposals to develop a new generation of programs for high school science.

STANDARDS AND FRAMEWORKS FOR SCIENCE PROGRAMS

The *National Science Education Standards* (NRC, 1996) included the chapter, "Science Education Program Standards." The aim is to provide criteria that science teachers can use to make judgments about current programs and to improve programs. The standards most appropriate for your understanding are summarized here.

Program Standard A

All elements of the K–12 science program must be consistent with the other *National Science Education Standards* and with one another and developed within and across grade levels to meet a clearly stated set of goals.

- In an effective science program, a set of clear goals and expectations for students must be used to guide the design, implementation, and assessment of all elements of the science program.
- Curriculum frameworks should be used to guide the selection and development of units and courses of study.
- Teaching practices need to be consistent with the goals and curriculum frameworks.
- Assessment policies and practices should be aligned with the goals, student expectations, and curriculum frameworks.
- Support systems and formal and informal expectations of teachers must be aligned with the goals, student expectations, and curriculum frameworks.
- Responsibility needs to be clearly defined for determining, supporting, maintaining, and upgrading all elements of the science program.

Program Standard B

The program of study in science for all students should be developmentally appropriate, interesting, and relevant to students' lives; emphasize student understanding through inquiry; and be connected with other school subjects.

- The program of study should include all of the content standards.
- Science content must be embedded in a variety of curriculum patterns that are developmentally appropriate, interesting, and relevant to students' lives.
- The program of study must emphasize student understanding through inquiry.
- The program of study in science should connect to other school subjects.

Program Standard C

The science program should be coordinated with the mathematics program to enhance student use and understanding of mathematics in the study of science and to improve student understanding of mathematics.

This brief introduction should give you an orientation for the discussions that follow. You will have to make decisions about various aspects of the science program in your classroom, school, and perhaps district. It will be well to remember that the course(s) you teach will be part of a school science program.

Several frameworks for curriculum have significantly influenced state and local reform of middle school and high school science programs. Those frameworks include the AAAS reports *Science for All Americans* (AAAS, 1989) and *Benchmarks for Science Literacy* (AAAS, 1993) and the *National Science Education Standards* (1996). In addition, the 2009 framework for the National Assessment of Educational Progress (NAEP) may well be an influential framework for school science programs.

Science for All Americans

Late in the 1980s, F. James Rutherford established Project 2061 at AAAS. He designed Project 2061 to take a long-term, large-scale view of education reform in the sciences. This reform is based on the goal of scientific literacy. The core of *Science for All Americans* and in 1993 the subsequent publication *Benchmarks for Science Literacy* consist of recommendations by a distinguished group of scientists and educators about what understandings and habits of mind are essential for all citizens in a scientifically literate society.

Project 2061 staff used the reports of five independent scientific panels. In addition, Project 2061 staff sought the advice of a large and diverse array of consultants and reviewers—scientists, engineers, mathematicians, historians, and educators. The process took more than three years, involved hundreds of individuals, and culminated in the publication of *Science for All Americans* and the characterization of scientific literacy. Thus, the project's recommendations are presented in the form of basic learning goals for American students. A premise of Project 2061 is that science teachers do not need to teach more; they should teach less so that content can be taught better.

Science for All Americans covers an array of topics. Many already are common in school curricula (e.g., the structure of matter, the basic functions of cells, prevention of disease, communications technology, and different uses of numbers). The treatment of such topics, however, differs from traditional approaches in two ways. One difference is that boundaries between traditional subject-matter categories are softened and connections are emphasized through the use of important conceptual themes, such as systems, evolution, cycles, and energy. Transformations of energy, for example, occur in physical, biological, and technological systems; and evolutionary change appears in stars, organisms, and societies. A second difference is that the amount of detail students are expected to learn is less than in traditional science, mathematics, and technology courses. Key concepts and thinking skills are emphasized instead of specialized vocabulary and memorized procedures. The ideas not only make sense at a simple level but also provide a lasting foundation for learning more science. Details are treated as a means of enhancing, not guaranteeing, students' understanding of a general idea.

Recommendations in *Science for All Americans* include topics that are not common in school curricula. Among those topics are the nature of the scientific enterprise and how science, mathematics, and technology relate to one another and to the social system in general. The report also calls for understanding something of the history of science and technology.

Identify questions that can be answered through scientific investigations.

Design and conduct a scientific investigation.

Use appropriate tools and technologies to gather, analyze, and interpret data.

Develop descriptions, explanations, predictions, and models using evidence.

Think critically and logically to make the relationships between evidence and explanation.

Recognize and analyze alternative explanations and predictions.

Communicate scientific procedures and explanations.

Use mathematics in all aspects of scientific inquiry.

FIGURE 15–1 Conceptual Organizers from *National Science Education Standards* for Grades 5–8

NATIONAL SCIENCE EDUCATION STANDARDS AND BENCHMARKS FOR SCIENCE LITERACY

In previous chapters we introduced the *National Science Education Standards (NSES)*. In this section we direct attention to the content standards, in particular those for grades 5 through 8 and 9 through 12 (see Figures 15–1 and 15–2). These standards describe the knowledge, understandings, and abilities that students should develop as a result of their educational experiences. They also represent one aspect of a comprehensive vision of science education, which also includes science teaching and assessment. We state this to make the point that as you consider the science curriculum, it is imperative to consider more than content. You also should review teaching and assessment in the consideration of any commercial program or the design of your local science curriculum.

Figures 15–1, 15–2, and 15–3 present the conceptual organizers for the content standards. As you consider curriculum for middle school science, try to incorporate opportunities for students to develop the fundamental understandings and abilities associated with these conceptual organizers.

CONSIDERATIONS IN THE DESIGN OF SCHOOL SCIENCE PROGRAMS

The content standards presented in both the *National Standards* and *Benchmarks* elaborate what students should understand and be able to do in natural science, and the personal and social context that should be considered in the design of science curriculum. These standards emphasize inquiry-oriented activities, connections between science and technology, and the history and nature of science as students develop an understanding of

Identify questions and concepts that guide scientific investigations.

Design and conduct scientific investigations.

Use technology and mathematics to improve investigations and communications.

Formulate and revise scientific explanations and models using logic and evidence.

Recognize and analyze alternative explanations and models.

Communicate and defend a scientific argument.

FIGURE 15–2 Conceptual Organizers from *National Science Education Standards* for Grades 9–12

fundamental ideas and abilities in science. The content standards of NSES represent one component of a comprehensive vision of the science curriculum, a vision that also includes science teaching, assessment, professional development, school programs, and the educational system. If you only review and use the content standards and ignore other standards, for example, on teaching and assessment, or only use a subset of content—such as subject matter for physical, life, and earth science—then the use of the *National Science Education Standards* in the science program is incomplete.

Many different individuals and groups use the content standards for a variety of purposes. However, there are some groups who use them immediately and concretely—for example, curriculum developers, science supervisors at state and local levels, and classroom teachers of science. The concepts and understandings described in the content standards do not represent a science curriculum. Content is what students should learn. Curriculum includes the way content is organized, what is emphasized, how it is taught, and how it is assessed. The science curriculum includes a structure, organization, balance, and presentation of the content in the classroom, and the curriculum can be organized in many different ways. The national standards indicate what should be learned, not how content should be organized in school science programs.

As you think about your science curricula, teaching, and assessment and begin incorporating the *National Science Education Standards,* consider the following criteria:

♦ Content standards must be used in coordination with the standards on teaching and assessment. Using the content standards with traditional teaching and assessment strategies misrepresents the intentions of the *National Science Education Standards.*

♦ Science content, at the level of standards, cannot be eliminated. For instance, students should have opportunities to learn "Science in Personal and Social Perspectives" and "History and Nature of Science" in the school science program.

The Nature of Science	The Nature of Mathematics	The Nature of Technology	The Physical Setting
The Scientific Worldview Scientific Inquiry The Scientific Enterprise	Patterns and Relationships Mathematics, Science, and Technology Mathematical Inquiry	Technology and Science Design and Systems Issues in Technology	The Universe The Earth Processes That Shape the Earth Energy Transformations Motion Forces of Nature

The Living Environment	The Human Organism	Human Society	The Designed World
Diversity of Life Heredity Cells Interdependence of Life Flow of Matter and Energy Evolution of Life	Human Identity Human Development Basic Functions Learning Physical Health Mental Health Group Interdependence	Cultural Effects on Behavior Group Behavior Social Change Political and Economic Systems Social Conflict	Agriculture Materials and Manufacturing Energy Sources and Use Communication Information Processing Health Technology

The Mathematical World	Historical Perspectives	Common Themes	Habits of Mind
Numbers Symbolic Relationships Shapes Uncertainty Reasoning	Displacing Earth from the Center of the Universe Uniting the Heavens and Earth Relating Matter and Energy and Time and Space Extending Time Moving the Continents Understanding Fire Splitting the Atom Explaining the Diversity of Life Discovering Germs Harnessing Power	Systems Models Constancy and Change Scale	Values and Attitudes Computation and Estimation Manipulation and Observation Communication Skills Critical-Response Skills

FIGURE 15–3   Conceptual Organizers from *Benchmarks for Science Literacy*

♦ Science content, at the level of conceptual organizers, cannot be eliminated. For instance, "Biological Evolution" cannot be eliminated from the life science standards.

♦ Science content can be added to elaborate conceptual organizers. In the translation of content to curriculum, the connections, depth, detail, and selection of topics can be varied as appropriate for students and school science programs.

The content standards, like the discipline of science itself, will continue to change. The national standards identify important and enduring ideas rather than current topics and contemporary research. The conceptual organizers, fundamental understandings, and abilities outlined in the national standards will provide students with basic concepts, a knowledge base, and skills that will continually improve their scientific literacy.

The *National Science Education Standards* and other reports on science education have identified important outcomes for all students. Although the reports are different they represent considerable agreement on the essential outcomes within the domains of science education. The *National Science Education Standards* incorporate many outcomes of the AAAS report. If you are actively involved in the science program, do not view these as mutually exclusive reports. Having said this, it is also important to understand that the *National Science Education Standards* and the AAAS reports were developed over an extended time; had input from thousands of scientists, engineers, science educators, and science teachers; and used an overall conceptual framework for scientific literacy.

This is an excellent point to complete Activity 15–1: Gathering Information About Curriculum Materials, at the end of the chapter.

FIGURE 15–4   Ralph Tyler's Approach to Curriculum and Instruction

I.   Examination of Traditional Factors Influencing the Curriculum to Determine an Initial Set of Instructional Goals
   • Examine student interests and characteristics
   • Analyze social trends and issues
   • Synthesize information from disciplines
II.   Development of Preliminary Curriculum Program
   • Synthesize objectives from step I into a cohesive program
III.   Reconsideration of Objectives in Terms of Philosophy and Psychology
   • Review program objectives for congruence with curriculum designer's philosophy
   • Review program objectives for congruence with current learning theories
IV.   Development of Curriculum Program
   • Arrange curriculum objectives into an organized program
V.   Evaluation of Learning Experiences

DESIGNING YOUR SCIENCE PROGRAM

Discussion in this chapter has been directed toward national policies and the implications for development of science programs. In some cases, national groups will develop new programs. In these cases, large-scale projects will require a team of scientists, science educators, and classroom teachers of science. Often with the help of major funding, primarily from government agencies such as the NSF, materials are developed, field tested, revised, field tested again, revised, and then published. This is one approach to curriculum development. This model of curricular reform can be characterized as: (1) occurring at a national or state level, (2) being heavily funded, and (3) approached from the top down—that is, developed and published first and then implemented by classroom teachers.

Though there is a need for improvement, curriculum development in the near future will also be: (1) at the local or district level; (2) funded within the usual budgets of schools and school districts, perhaps with some assistance from state, federal, or private agencies; and (3) approached from the bottom up—that is, initiated and developed by classroom teachers and then implemented within the school district.

The second approach to curriculum development is a smaller scale approach to change. Here an individual science teacher or team of science teachers is appointed to initiate, develop, and implement a science curriculum. This could encompass anything from a minor revision of an extant course to development of a new K–12 science program for the entire school district.

The new demands for educational improvement, combined with the level of funding at the national level for the "No Child Left Behind" legislation and the implementation of state standards and assessments, suggest that the burden for change will increasingly fall to the local school district and science-teaching personnel.

Consider a third approach to curriculum development. The adoption of new science textbooks, software, and kit materials represents the selection and implementation of a science curriculum. The curriculum then can be *adapted* to align with the needs and requirements of local school districts and science teachers. In this approach, the emphasis is on adaptation through professional development.

With the preceding paragraphs as background and rationale, we direct your attention to a discussion that will be useful to science teachers confronting the task of designing a science program. We begin by noting several resources that form the basis of our discussion, starting with Ralph Tyler's 1949 classic, *Basic Principles of Curriculum and Instruction*. More than 50 years of age, Tyler's model (see Figure 15–4) has not lost its vitality as an important process for identifying curricular objectives and learning experiences. This model is applicable today because it outlines procedures for developing a program. The utility and simplicity of Tyler's model is found in four basic questions.

   ◆ What educational purposes should the school seek to attain?
   ◆ How can learning experiences likely to attain these objectives be selected?
   ◆ How can learning experiences be effectively organized?
   ◆ How can we determine whether these purposes are being attained? (Tyler, 1949)

Several helpful books also address various aspects of curriculum development: *Developing a Quality Curriculum* (Glatthorn, 1994), *Analyzing the Curriculum* (Posner, 1994), and *Understanding by Design* (Wiggins & McTighe, 2005).

Although this discussion is about local science programs, the national projects have some important processes and advice. Joseph McInerney, past director of

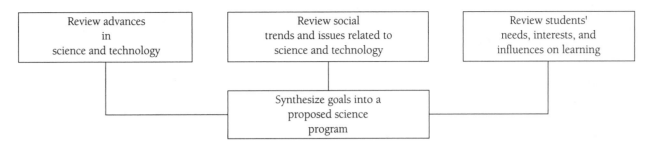

FIGURE 15–5 Program Review and Synthesis Flowchart

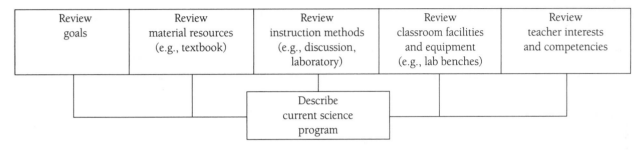

FIGURE 15–6 Program Description Flowchart

the Biological Sciences Curriculum Study (BSCS), outlined several criteria for the selection of content for science programs. These criteria are (paraphrased) as follows:

- How well does the information being considered illustrate the basic, enduring principles of the scientific discipline?
- Do other teachers, administrators, and parents perceive the proposed materials as useful and important?
- What is the relationship between the proposed curriculum materials and the prevailing context of general education? (McInerney, 1987)

Asking and answering questions such as these will help with the difficult issue of deciding what content should be included and ensure that the program is understandable and acceptable to the scientific and educational communities.

The following discussion is our synthesis of approaches and recommended steps for redesigning and implementing a science program.

Step 1—Review Influences on the Science Program

In the first phase of improving a school science program, you should spend time reading, thinking, and discussing three traditional influences on the program: advances in science, changes in society, and understanding the influences on student learning. What are the recent advances in science and technology that are

important for students to use in their personal lives and as citizens? Obviously, all scientific knowledge and technology advances cannot be incorporated into school science programs. Science teachers must decide what knowledge is of most worth.

What are the trends, issues, and problems in society that are related to science and technology? Reviewing these issues provides another goal component of the science program. An examination of student needs, interests, characteristics, and processes of learning is also essential. Here you can include the unique needs of students in your school or district. After reviewing current priorities regarding science, society, and students, state a first set of general objectives. This first step is presented graphically in Figure 15–5, a flowchart for reviewing major influences on the science program. Figure 15–6 provides a flowchart of areas to review when considering the school science program.

Step 2—Synthesize Goals into a Proposed Science Curriculum

Phase two consists of bringing the objectives identified in the first phase into a proposed framework. At this point, do not make an effort to evaluate or filter the learning outcomes based on various constraints such as time, personnel, or budget. Synthesize your learning outcomes into a program that has a scope and sequence, as well as classroom facilities, materials, equipment, instructional approach, and evaluation components. This can be an exciting exercise, so use your creativity.

	Proposed	Present
Goals (e.g., learn science knowledge and processes)		
Grade Levels (e.g., 5–8, 9–12)		
Time Requirements (e.g., 55 min./day at 9–12)		
Student Population (e.g., all students, at-risk)		
Type of Schools (e.g., urban, rural)		
Academic Subjects (e.g., life science, integrated)		
Description of Program (e.g., STS, standards-based)		
Relationship to Other Subjects (e.g., complements health, supports reading)		
Curriculum Materials (e.g., textbook, student modules)		
Instructional Emphasis (e.g., reading, active learning)		
Instructional Strategies (e.g., reading, active learning)		
Instructional Model (e.g., 5E model)		
Education Materials (e.g., kits, local equipment)		
Educational Courseware (e.g., MBI use of Internet)		
Evaluation (e.g., built into instruction, end-of-unit tests)		
Implementation (e.g., concerns-based adoption model, professional development)		
STS—Science–Technology–Society		
MBL—Microcomputer-Based Laboratory		

FIGURE 15–7 Characteristics of the Proposed and Present School Science Program

Step 3—Describe the Present Science Program

One mistake often made in local development is the omission of consideration of the present program. What are the present goals? What is the current textbook? What about the scope and sequence of the present program? What about the role and use of computers in the science program?

Reviewing the present program also includes reviewing any special topics, units, or lessons that you develop. This phase of improvement is a matter-of-fact approach, outlining what exists in terms of materials, equipment, time, space, budget, and your competencies. Use categories such as goals, instructional materials, teacher interests and competencies, classroom facilities and equipment, instructional methods, and assessment. This phase is represented in Figure 15–7, which is a chart for recording the proposed and present program characteristics.

Step 4—Analyze the Discrepancies Between the Proposed and Present Science Program

Using the same categories—that is, material resources, instructional methods, classroom facilities, and teacher interests and competencies—provides a convenient way to identify the differences between where your science program is and where you want it to be. As a result of this stage, you should have a good idea of what is needed in order to improve your science program.

Analysis of the Proposed and Current Programs						
	What Is the proposed change?	*Who has the responsibility to change?*	*Where will change occur?*	*What is the actual form of change?*	*How will the change be implemented?*	*What support is required?*
Goals						
Grade levels						
Time requirements						
Student population						
Type of schools						
Academic subjects						
Description of program						
Relationship to other subjects						
Curriculum materials						
Instructional emphasis						
Instructional strategies						
Instructional model						
Educational courseware						
Evaluation						
Implementation						

FIGURE 15–8   Changes in the School Programs

Step 5—Evaluate the Proposed Science Program

The fifth step is critical, because this is the point at which you reevaluate what you propose doing in terms of what is possible. The phase is infused with reality. Things such as educational philosophy, learning theory, time, budget, and any other real-world items should be factored into the possible science program. Screening everything at this point sets the stage for the review, purchase, development, or synthesis of materials; changes in goals; and suggestions for professional development appropriate to your proposed program. At the end of this phase you should have a realistic picture of what can be done, who is required to do what, and how long it will take. Figure 15–8 provides one way to organize this information.

Step 6—Select and Implement the Science Program

Remember two things at this point. First, you do not have to develop the program de novo. You can select new materials and adapt materials in the current program. Second, the new science program does not have to be developed in a week, month, or even year. As a result of your analysis and synthesis to this point, you should have a long-range plan for your professional development;

material acquisition; development of lessons, units, or modules; adoption of new textbooks; and so on. Implementation can occur over an extended time.

Step 7—Evaluate the Science Program

From time to time it will be necessary to reevaluate the science program. Ideally, you will monitor and improve the science program continuously. Doing this will allow you to maintain those curricular components that are appropriate to the present state of science, society, and students, while changing those aspects of the program that have become outdated and outmoded. The seven steps we have outlined are summarized in Figure 15–9.

Up to this point, the process of improving the science program has primarily focused on materials. The success of your program also depends on the awareness, interactions, and work of the people directly and indirectly involved in the process. The materials of the science program are relatively easy to change, and although changing materials is necessary, it is not sufficient. Efforts to improve a science program also must take into account the beliefs, attitudes, and perceptions that teachers, administrators, and the public have about science and technology education and the particular need to design a new program.

FIGURE 15–9 Proposed Process for Designing a Science Program

I.   Review Influences on the Science Curriculum
- Look at advances in science and technology that have personal and social utility for students.
- Evaluate social trends and issues related to science and technology.
- Consider student needs, interests, and characteristics, including national concerns and local issues.
- Outline goals relative to the three areas reviewed

II. Synthesize Goals into a Proposed Science Curriculum
- Curriculum materials
- Instructional strategies
- Facilities, materials, equipment
- Teacher competencies
- Evaluation

III. Describe the Present Science Curriculum
- Goals
- Curriculum materials
- Instructional strategies
- Facilities, materials, equipment
- Teacher interests and competencies
- Evaluation

IV. Analyze Discrepancies between Proposed and Present Program
- Contrast differences and identify priorities in terms of categories listed above

V.   Reevaluate the Proposed Science Curriculum
- Reevaluate proposed program in terms of priorities and possibilities (e.g., budget).
- Review proposed program in terms of educational philosophy and policies of district, school, and/or science department.
- Revise proposed program incorporating contemporary educational psychology, e.g., development and learning theory.

VI. Development and Implementation of the Science Curriculum
- Review curriculum materials appropriate for the proposed program (e.g., textbooks, teaching modules).
- Consider adaptation of extant materials for proposed program.
- Develop curriculum materials (e.g., lessons, units, modules as necessary).
- Implement new materials in an organized fashion.

VII. Evaluation of the Science Curriculum
- Monitor and adjust curriculum periodically.
- Repeat process of redesign of science curriculum.

In regard to this assertion, we suggest the addition of other components for the successful selection and implementation of a science program.

- Establish the need to change the science education curriculum among the science faculty and with other teachers and administrators.
- Describe the nature, direction, and realities of change to those interested and concerned—especially administrators and the public.
- Obtain endorsement and support from the principal, school board, and community.
- Select materials within the budget.
- Establish a realistic timeline for selection and implementation.
- Provide for released time, inservice programs, and summertime pay for personnel directly involved in the project.
- Monitor and adjust the process of development and implementation.

As a final activity in this chapter, we recommend completion of Activity 15–2, Evaluating Middle/Junior High School Science Programs.

SUMMARY

Adolescence is a unique period in life. Throughout our educational history we have seen changes in the science curriculum for this age group. The junior high school was created in the late 1800s, and in the late 1900s, the middle school emerged. Junior high schools were junior versions of high school programs, but the middle school curriculum is uniquely designed for the early adolescent.

Although textbooks were significantly changed during the 1960s and 1970s, the 1980s and 1990s witnessed a return to models similar to those prior to the 1960s.

In the 1980s, a new wave of educational reform was initiated. Numerous national reports on education in general and on science education in particular have stimulated new interest in the science curriculum. Of particular importance are the *National Science Education Standards* and *Benchmarks for Science Literacy*. Aspects of the new emphasis can be summarized as follows:

- Standards (national, state, local) will be the basis for school science programs.
- Inquiry will be expanded to include cognitive abilities, knowledge about scientific inquiry, and teaching strategies.

- Laboratory activities will include both holistic and reductive analysis approaches.
- Decisions about science curricula will be largely determined by science teachers in local school districts.
- Interrelationships and interdependence of science, technology, and society will be contexts for study.
- Science and technology literacy for personal, social, and civic understanding will be the primary emphasis of the secondary science curriculum.

In the 1990s, the initial wave of reforms was sustained by development and implementation of national standards and benchmarks for science education. In the early 2000s, "No Child Left Behind" legislation (nochildleftbehind.gov), the emphasis on accountability, and the critical role of standards provide support and direction for the improvement of science education in general and the science curriculum in particular.

To design, develop, and implement your own science curriculum, we outlined the following seven steps:

1. Review influences on the science program.
2. Synthesize goals into a proposed science program.
3. Describe the present science program.
4. Analyze the discrepancies between proposed and present programs.
5. Evaluate the proposed science program.
6. Select and implement the science program.
7. Evaluate the science program.

--- **Investigating Science Teaching** ---

Activity 15–1
Gathering Information About Curriculum Materials

The publishing industry has entered an electronic age, which allows for fairly rapid revisions of textbooks and curriculum materials. One of the greater challenges you will have as a teacher is trying to stay abreast of advances in science education outside of your own classroom, school, and district. The Internet is one place where you can quickly gather a lot of information without traveling, writing letters, or making phone calls. Use the information below to identify the usefulness in each website. (Please note that the addresses listed were accurate late in 2006; if they do not work when you try them, do a search for the particular organization listed instead.)

Your Task

Visit each website below and respond to the following questions:

a. What are the strengths of this site?

b. What are the limitations or weaknesses of this site?

c. When would it be useful to access the information available at this website?

d. Based on when you think it would be useful to visit this site, what would be your next step after visiting this website?

Visit These Websites

The Textbook Letter
http://www.textbookleague.org/
   This website publishes independent appraisals of textbooks that publishers are selling. Their emphasis is on textbooks. The Textbook League was established in 1989 to support the creation and acceptance of sound schoolbooks. They publish The Textbook Letter (or TTL), which is mailed to subscribers throughout the United States. The subscribers include classroom teachers, officers of local school districts, officers of state or county education agencies, and private citizens who take a serious interest in the quality of the instruction offered in the public schools.
   Each issue of TTL is built around reviews of schoolbooks, with emphasis on middle school and high school books in history, geography, social studies, health, and the various branches of natural science. These book reviews are augmented by evaluations of classroom videos and by articles about topics that are important to people who must choose instructional materials.

NSTA Science Suppliers list
http://www.suppliers.nsta.org/
   The National Science Teachers Association has published a supplement to its journals each year called the Science Education Suppliers Guide. This useful tool includes the names and addresses of nonprofit organizations that work in science education as well as all the contact information for publishers, suppliers of materials and lab equipment, and companies that produce software. This supplement is now available on the Internet at the address listed here.

ACTIVITY 15–2
EVALUATING MIDDLE/JUNIOR HIGH SCHOOL SCIENCE PROGRAMS

At some time in your career, you will select a new science program. This activity introduces you to that process. The form you will complete is adapted from the American Association for the Advancement of Science publication Science Books & Films.

Select three programs from the discipline and grade level you intend to teach. Review the textbooks and complete the following chart. List the textbooks you compare by author(s), title, publisher, and copyright date.

Science Program

1.

2.

3.

1. Were the programs for middle school, junior high school, or high school?
2. How were the programs similar? Different?
3. Describe an outstanding feature of each program.
4. Describe the weakest feature of each program.
5. Which program would you select to use? Why?

UNIT 6

STRATEGIES FOR SCIENCE TEACHING

It has often been said that science is not really science unless it is accompanied by experimentation and laboratory work. In the secondary schools, there continues to be interest in the laboratory as the focal point for the study of science. It is worth noting that this is not the first time in the history of science education in the United States that the laboratory has come into prominence. The late 1800s saw the construction of laboratories in secondary schools and colleges with a corresponding change in emphasis in the methods of science instruction. The recitation method and the catechetical approach for learning science principles were gradually replaced by experiments in laboratories with the expressed purpose of verifying the laws of physics and chemistry. It was believed that students would learn science best by repeating, in an abbreviated fashion, the classical experiments of Newton, Galileo, Hooke, Priestley, Boyle, and many others. Students would see principles of natural science at work, enabling them to understand the underlying science concepts. Laboratories and apparatus were designed to duplicate as nearly as possible the materials and equipment used in the original experiments, with modern refinements to ensure reasonable accuracy in the hands of science students.

The two aspects of science teaching that have long characterized the nature of this endeavor are demonstrations and laboratory experiences such as those first described. Some would say that science teaching without these two components is really not science. Regardless of one's position on this topic, the two strategies remain at a high level in most science classrooms. With contemporary emphasis on inquiry teaching, it is likely that demonstrations and experiments will remain important.

Other strategies at the center of effective science teaching are asking questions, guiding discussion, and using the textbook. These strategies along with the role of educational technologies form the core of this unit.

THE LABORATORY AND DEMONSTRATIONS

Although the rhetoric about the role of laboratories continues to be loud, the reality is that many science teachers continue to lecture more than engage students in laboratory work, and when they do use laboratories, the procedures are often "cookbook" approaches. First, we discuss means to improve traditional approaches and follow this with information from a National Research Council study on laboratories. Finally, we present information that will help you safely incorporate laboratories in your classroom.

THE LABORATORY AND SCIENCE TEACHING

Traditional Laboratory Investigations

Unfortunately, traditional laboratory investigations do not provide enough opportunities for students to use their minds to solve problems posed in the laboratory. Frequently, all that is required is to make sure the detailed instructions found in the laboratory manual are carried out, and that all the blanks are filled in after the investigation is completed. Laboratory manuals have often been compared to a cookbook, which fails to excite students and often leaves them unsure about what they were studying, or what they found out in the activity. Paul German and others (1996) analyzed several biology textbooks and found little evidence of scientific inquiry. They reported, "Results indicated that while some manuals have made efforts to include a few science process skills, they seldom call upon students to use their knowledge and experience to pose questions,

solve problems, investigate natural phenomena, or construct answers or generalizations."

Suggestions for improving traditional laboratory experiments have been offered by William Leonard (1991). These suggestions are included here for consideration by science teachers in secondary schools because of their relevance to investigative methods of teaching.

- Give the student a simple task or goal to accomplish. This task can be explained verbally by the teacher or by brief explanations in written form. The purpose is to engage students' attention on a question and to encourage creative thinking.
- Give the student only essential procedures. Get the student started with general suggestions. Let students struggle for awhile. If frustration becomes apparent, give some help in the form of possible exploration.
- Have students work in small, cooperative groups. Ideas for possible procedures can be shared and discussed.
- Provide students with ideas and lists of potential resources to use in the investigation.
- Resist telling students how to carry out the investigation. Although this will undoubtedly require more time, it will provide opportunities for reflection and deliberation by the students themselves and help to develop necessary investigative skills.
- Add meaningful questions at the end of the investigation. Emphasize analyzing why certain procedures were used, why certain hypotheses were tested, and why certain conclusions were drawn.

The purpose of these questions is to cause students to think about their work, the decisions they made, and even the possible faulty pathways they took in arriving at a result.

Research on the Laboratory's Role in Science Teaching

Over the years, science educators have examined the influence of the laboratory on achievement and other variables such as reasoning, critical thinking, understanding science, process skills, manipulative skills, interests, retention, and ability to do independent work. Much of this research gave inconclusive results, but science teachers in general believe the laboratory is a vital part of science teaching.

Joseph Novak (1988) described the problems graphically.

> The science laboratory has always been regarded as the place where students should learn the process of doing science. But summaries of research on the value of laboratory for learning science did not favor laboratory over lecture—demonstrations . . . and more recent studies also show an appalling lack of effectiveness of laboratory instruction . . . . Our studies showed that most students in laboratories gained little insight regarding the key science concepts involved or toward the process of knowledge construction.

Some positive findings can be cited. Three studies done between 1969 and 1979 found that laboratory instruction increased student problem-solving abilities. Other researchers reported positive results encouraging cognitive development, introducing scientific ideas, giving concrete examples, and learning how to manipulate materials when working with disadvantaged students in the laboratory (Blosser, 1983).

INTEGRATING LABORATORIES AND INSTRUCTIONAL MODELS

In 2006, the National Research Council published *America's Lab Report: Investigations in High School Science*. This report examined the status of science laboratories and developed a vision for their future role in high school science education. The NRC committee (NRC, 2006) used the following definition for laboratory experiences.

> Laboratory experiences provide opportunities for students to interact directly with the material world (or with data drawn from the material world), using tools, data collection techniques, models, and theories of science (p. 31).

This definition includes physical manipulation of substances, organisms, and systems; interactions with simulations; interactions with actual (not artificially created) data; analysis of large databases; and remote access to instruments and observations, for example, via World Wide Web links.

The committee was clear that science education includes both learning about the methods and processes of scientific research and the knowledge derived from those processes. The learning goals that should be attained as a result of laboratory experiences include the following:

- Enhancing mastery of subject matter
- Developing scientific reasoning
- Understanding the complexity and ambiguity of empirical work
- Developing practical skills
- Understanding the nature of science
- Cultivating interest in science and interest in learning science
- Developing teamwork abilities (NRC, 2006, pp. 76–77)

In the analysis of laboratory experiences, the committee applied results from the large and growing body of cognitive research (Bransford et al., 2000; Donovan & Bransford, 2005; Duschl et al., 2007). Some researchers have investigated the sequence of science instruction, including the role of laboratory experiences, as these sequences enhance student achievement of the aforementioned learning goals. The NRC committee proposed the phrase "integrated instructional units":

> Integrated instructional units interweave laboratory experiences with other types of science learning activities including lectures, reading, and discussion. Students are engaged in forming research questions, designing and executing experiments, gathering and analyzing data, and constructing arguments and conclusions as they carry out investigations. Diagnostic, formative assessments are embedded into the instructional sequence and can be used to gauge the students' developing understanding and to promote their self-reflection on their thinking (NRC, 2006, p. 82).

Integrated instructional units have two key features. First, laboratory and other experiences are carefully designed or selected on the basis of what students should learn from them. Second, the experience is explicitly linked to and integrated with other learning activities in the unit.

The features of integrated instructional units map directly to the BSCS 5E instructional model described in Chapter 13. Stated another way, the BSCS model is a specific example of integrated instructional units. According to the NRC committee's report, integrated instructional units connect laboratory experience with other types of science learning activities including reading, discussions, and lectures.

TABLE 16–1 Attainment of Goals: Typical Laboratory Experience versus Integrated

| | Instructional Units | |
Goal	Typical Laboratory Experience	Integrated Instructional Unit
Mastery of subject matter	Is no better or worse than Other modes of instruction	Increases mastery compared with other modes of instruction
Scientific reasoning	Aids the development of some aspects	Aids the development of more sophisticated aspects
Understanding of the nature of science	Shows little improvement	Shows some improvement when explicitly targeted as the goal
Interest in science	Shows some evidence of increased interest	Shows greater evidence of increased interest
Understanding of the complexity and ambiguity of empirical work	Has inadequate evidence	Has inadequate evidence
Development of practical skills	Has inadequate evidence	Has inadequate evidence
Development of teamwork skills	Has inadequate evidence	Has inadequate evidence

Source: NRC. (2006). *America's lab report: Investigations in high school science.* Washington, DC: The National Academies Press.

Typical (or traditional) laboratory experiences differ from the integrated instructional units in their effectiveness in attaining the goals of science education. Research shows that typical laboratories suffer from fragmentation of goals and approaches. Although the studies are still preliminary, research indicates that integrated instructional units are more effective than typical laboratory research for improving mastery of subject matter, developing scientific reasoning, and cultivating interest in science. In addition, integrated instructional units appear to be effective for helping diverse groups of students progress toward these three goals. Table 16–1 compares typical laboratory experiences and integrated instructional units.

Many teachers say students are apathetic about laboratory work and that labs are difficult to stock, maintain, and control. However, it is not likely students will experience much of the nature, methods, and spirit of science without this important component of science teaching.

Thus, while much lip service is commonly given to the value of laboratory work in science classes, many science teachers appear to discount its value when faced with the realities of organization, materials procurement, time constraints, and lack of familiarity with investigative approaches to laboratory instruction.

Development of Skills and Abilities in the Laboratory

The complaint has frequently been lodged against science teaching that students and teachers alike have difficulty in expressing exactly what the goals of science teaching should be. In taking up this challenge, we will identify the types of skills that science students ought to

be able to do better after having taken middle and senior high school science. We have listed five categories of skills: acquisitive, organizational, creative, manipulative, and communicative. No attempt is made to rank these categories in order of importance, or even to imply that any one category may be more important than any other. Within each of the categories, however, specific skills are listed in order of increasing difficulty. In general, those skills that require only the use of one's own unaided senses are simpler than those that require use of instruments or higher orders of manual and mental dexterity.

In laboratory work students can develop the skills and abilities of scientific inquiry.

Categories of Skills and Abilities

A. *Acquisitive:* skills and abilities of gathering information
   - Listening—being attentive, alert, questioning
   - Observing—being accurate, alert, systematic
   - Searching—locating sources, using several sources, being self-reliant, acquiring library skills and the ability to use computer search programs
   - Inquiring—asking, interviewing, corresponding
   - Investigating—formulating questions
   - Gathering data—tabulating, organizing, classifying, recording
   - Researching—locating a problem, learning background, setting up investigations, analyzing data, drawing conclusions

B. *Organizational:* skills and abilities of putting information in systematic order
   - Recording—tabulating, charting, working systematically, recording completely
   - Comparing—noticing how things are alike, looking for similarities, noticing identical features
   - Contrasting—noticing how things differ, looking for dissimilarities, noticing unlike features
   - Classifying—identifying groups and categories, deciding between alternatives
   - Organizing—putting items in order, establishing a system, filing, labeling, arranging
   - Outlining—employing major headings and subheadings, using sequential, logical organization
   - Reviewing—identifying important items
   - Evaluating—recognizing good and poor features, knowing how to improve grades
   - Analyzing—seeing implications and relationships, picking out causes and effects, locating new problems

C. *Creative:* skills and abilities of developing new approaches and new ways of thinking
   - Planning ahead—seeing possible results and probable modes of attack, setting up hypotheses
   - Designing—identifying new problems
   - Inventing—creating a method, device, or technique
   - Synthesizing—putting familiar things together in a new arrangement, hybridizing, drawing together

D. *Manipulative:* skills and abilities of handling materials and instruments
   - Using an instrument—knowing the instrument's parts, how it works, how to adjust it, its proper use for a given task, its limitations
   - Caring for an instrument—knowing how to store it, using proper settings, keeping it clean, handling it properly, knowing its rate capacity, transporting it safely
   - Demonstrating—setting up apparatus, describing parts and functions, illustrating scientific principles
   - Experimenting—recognizing a question, planning a procedure, collecting data, recording data, analyzing data, drawing conclusions
   - Constructing—making simple equipment for demonstrations and investigations
   - Calibrating—learning the basic information about calibration, calibrating a thermometer, balance, timer, or other instrument

E. *Communicative:* skills and abilities of transferring information correctly from one experimenter to another
   - Asking questions—learning to formulate good questions, to be selective in asking
   - Discussing—learning to contribute ideas, listening to ideas of others, keeping on the topic, arriving at conclusions
   - Explaining—describing to someone else clearly, clarifying major points, exhibiting patience, being willing to repeat
   - Reporting—orally reporting to a class or teacher in capsule form the significant material on a science topic
   - Writing—writing a report of an experiment or demonstration; describing the problem, method of attack, data collected, methods of analysis, conclusions drawn, and implications for further work
   - Criticizing—constructively criticizing or evaluating a piece of work, a scientific procedure, or conclusion
   - Graphing—putting in graphical form the results of a study or experiment, being able to interpret the graph for someone else

Is There a Need for Science Development of Skills and Abilities?

Courses in elementary and secondary schools should emphasize skills and abilities of science inquiry as much as the concepts and generalizations. Understanding a process improves skill competencies, while learning how to learn requires adequate learning tools. In addition, students need confidence in their ability to perform the tasks needed in self-learning.

Development of Skills and Abilities Can Be Guided Through a Sequence of Activities

This progression is possible because of certain characteristics of skills themselves, such as level of difficulty and complexity. For example, skills requiring the use of unaided senses are usually simpler than those requiring the use of instruments. It is easier for students to use their unaided eyes to compare the colors of minerals than to operate a petrographic microscope to do the same thing at a higher level of sophistication. Also, groups of simple skills may be included in more difficult complex skills. Graphing, for example, requires competency in the simpler skills of counting, measuring, and using a ruler (instrument). In the same way, higher levels of learning—such as analysis, synthesis, and evaluation—require higher levels of skill proficiency.

Development of Skills and Abilities Enhances Concept Development

Growth in conceptual understanding is enhanced by expertise in the use of skills and abilities. In teaching skills, concepts form the vehicle by which the skills are learned. One cannot learn a skill in a void—there must be substantive information on which to operate. The skill of comparing, for example, is useless unless there are things to compare. In the same context, a hierarchy of skills forms a framework to which concepts can be attached. As one learns increasingly sophisticated skills, the subject matter (concepts) can be adapted and changed as required.

Achievement of Skills and Abilities Can Be Tested

There is ample evidence that skill achievements can be structured in behavioral terms. Performance can be observed and evaluated. Various performance levels of individual skills can be graded on a continuum from minimum to maximum success. Not only is it possible for teachers to create testing situations using performance objectives, but also it is possible to provide self-evaluation opportunities for students to gain knowledge of their own progress and levels of performance.

Implications for the Development of Skills and Abilities in the Science Classroom

Conditions necessary for success when emphasizing the skill or process goals are as follows:

- Time must be provided for practice and experience in the skills being developed. One does not become proficient without practice.
- Teachers must clearly understand the skill objectives. Planning must center on these objectives rather than traditional content goals.

- Ample materials must be available. There must be a responsive environment permitting students to operate with the materials of science.
- A variety of conceptual materials may be selected to facilitate skill development. In planning for teaching, however, it is important to concentrate on a few skills in any particular lesson.
- Assessments must emphasize performance. Performance and depth of understanding and development of skills and abilities should be brought to the foreground.

To aid in skill development and ultimate mastery of the desired skills, the teacher must devise suitable teaching plans and student activities. In this type of learning, learning by doing is an important maxim. Students must be involved in inquiry-oriented activities that give repeated practice in the desired skills and abilities. The laboratory becomes an important facility at this point because most of the skills and abilities involve procedures that, to a greater or lesser extent, require materials and apparatus.

Organizing Laboratory Work

Effectiveness of the laboratory experience is directly related to the amount of students' individual participation. Such participation means active involvement in the experiment with definite responsibilities for its progress and success. The ideal arrangement would be to have each student wholly responsible for conducting the experiment from start to finish. In this way, the preliminary planning, gathering materials, preparation of apparatus, designing the method, collecting data, analyzing results, and drawing conclusions are unmistakably the work of the individual student, with a maximum level of learning.

In reality, for certain students, maximum learning may be achieved by working in pairs or very small groups. With good cooperation and shared duties, the stimulation of pair or small group activity may be beneficial. In group work, some students may be stimulated into action and thought processes not possible when working alone. Other students may assume directive and leadership qualities not developed in individual work. The science teacher must be aware of these possibilities and plan the methodology of laboratory work accordingly.

Experiments will vary in complexity. Even in a typical laboratory science, such as chemistry, experiments may be no more than carrying out a preplanned exercise of observation and data gathering, or they may be as extensive and demanding as research on a problem whose solution is totally unknown. Arrangements for laboratory work must accommodate these extremes. Students of general science in the middle school may need more of the exercise type of experiment to gain the skills needed for complex experiments. However, they should also be given opportunities to work on true experiments so that they might sense the joy of discovery in the same way as a practicing scientist.

Orienting Students for Laboratory Work

In general, students of the sciences look forward to a laboratory class with pleasant anticipation. Being pragmatic by nature, they sense that this is truly science and that an exciting experience awaits them. This attitude, most prevalent in the middle school, must be carefully nurtured and guided as the student progresses to more rigorous disciplines. If laboratory work becomes a bore because of excessively rigid formality, unexciting exercises, cookbook techniques, or for other reasons, the student will probably be lost as a potential science participant. An atmosphere of excitement, curiosity, interest, and enthusiasm for science should be encouraged in the laboratory, tempered by care and restraint in use of apparatus and diligence in the tasks assigned. Obviously, a hands-off policy regarding equipment cannot be adopted, nor can a complete laissez-faire attitude be condoned. Respect for the problem, the materials, and the probable results of experimentation must be developed.

Orientation for laboratory work may involve creating a suitable frame of mind for investigating a problem. The problem must appear real to students and worthy of study. Students must have some knowledge of possible methods of attack, and they should know what equipment or apparatus is needed and be familiar with its use.

Students also must have time to work on the problem. In a given situation, the science teacher may need to give attention to one or more of these factors to begin students on their laboratory investigations.

Laboratory Work as Part of Integrated Instructional Units

We recommend thinking of the laboratory as part of an integrated instructional sequence that may include other class activities such as discussion. Laboratory work often is followed by class discussion or question periods. During these activities, student questions are answered, observed phenomena are clarified, and certain misconceptions may be discussed. Other activities—such as problem assignments, projects, extra reading, reports, tests, and demonstrations—may be integrated as part of the teaching and learning process.

In this method it is likely that more than half of the total class time may be spent in laboratory activities.

Follow-up sessions become extremely important. The teacher usually must ascertain the accuracy of the learned concepts, correct misconceptions, and promote maximum learning more than in a conventional course. At the same time, students are more directly involved in the task and may be more highly motivated than they would be otherwise.

Laboratory Work in the Middle School

Extension of laboratory practices to middle school is occurring with greater frequency. Facilities for effective laboratory work are being built into modern middle schools and students of this age are beginning to experience laboratory work on a regular, planned basis.

Middle school students are enthusiastic participants in the laboratory method of teaching. Curiosity and a buoyant approach to learning make this group responsive to the laboratory method, and proper teacher guidance can make this method a fruitful one. Because middle school science leads to more rigorous and laboratory-oriented sciences in the senior high school, it is worthwhile to consider its contributions to more effective learning when the student reaches earth science, biology, chemistry, or physics. It is reasonable to assume that certain attitudes, knowledge, and skills learned in the middle school contribute to better and perhaps more rapid learning in the senior high school.

Following is a suggested list of basic knowledge and skills that might be developed in fifth- through ninth-grade science and that are considered desirable prerequisites for senior high science.

- Understanding the purposes of the laboratory in the study of science
- Understanding and being familiar with the simple tools of the laboratory
- Understanding and using the metric system in simple measurement and computations
- Understanding the need to properly report observations
- Keeping accurate records of laboratory investigations
- Understanding simple ratios and proportions
- Understanding the construction and reading of simple graphs
- Understanding simple forms of exponential notation
- Using the calculator for simple operations
- Putting together simple equipment in performing laboratory experiments
- Measuring accurately in linear, cubic, and weight units
- Using the computer for data gathering, record keeping, word processing, and data storage

A difficult problem in any effort to emphasize inquiry strategies in laboratory experiences is to get students to create or design investigations that will hold promise of producing answers or solutions to problems selected for study. Care must be taken to design investigations that are neither too simple nor too ambitious, that have controls, that can be replicated, and that make clear to the students the need to have a structured and organized approach. Paul German and others (1996) have researched the problems of experiment design among seventh-grade students. They have concluded that "development of the science process skills of formulating hypotheses and identifying variables, together with model examples, may be a means to facilitate student success in designing science experiments."

Laboratory work in the middle school can be broadened to include such features as out-of-doors observations, excursions, and certain types of project activities, as well as conventional experimentation in laboratory surroundings. Systematic nighttime observations of planets, constellations, meteors, the moon, and other astronomical objects may properly be considered laboratory work. Similarly, meteorological observations and experiments involving record keeping and correlations of data are included under this heading. Excursions for collecting purposes, observations of topographical features, studies of pond life, and ecological investigations are true laboratory work. The narrow connotation of laboratory work as something that takes place only in a specially designed room called a laboratory must be avoided in the middle school sciences.

The range and variety of activities performed by students in laboratory work make it necessary to use a variety of assessment methods. A teacher of science must be aware of these prerequisites and alert to new possibilities as well. Increasing emphasis on laboratory methods is almost certain to broaden, rather than narrow, the range of individual differences among students. Suitable means must be devised for assessing the progress and achievement of these students in their laboratory experiences.

SAFETY PRECAUTIONS IN THE LABORATORY

An inevitable result of greater student participation in laboratory work is increased exposure to potentially dangerous apparatus and materials. Instead of viewing this fact as a deterrent to the laboratory method of teaching, the alert and dedicated science teacher will approach the problem realistically and will take the proper precautions to avoid accidents among students in the laboratory.

Accidents and injuries often occur because students lack knowledge of the proper techniques and

Students learn about behavior of liquids and solids by personal involvement under safe conditions.

procedures. If the teacher plans properly, these techniques can be taught in advance. Certain minimum standards of acceptable procedures may be demanded of students before they are allowed to work in the laboratory. The motivation to engage in laboratory work is usually strong enough to overcome students' reluctance to develop the requisite skills, particularly if they are convinced of the inherent dangers and the need for proper safety precautions.

According to the National Safety Council, about 32,000 school-related accidents occur each school year, about 5,000 of which are science related. Middle school grades 7–9 experience the highest frequency of accidents.

The prevention of accidents can be accomplished through a positive science safety educational program that emphasizes teacher and student awareness of the potential dangers in science-related activities. "Safety First" should be the basic motto for the school science program. Safety considerations may rule out a science lesson. Effective planning sometimes can be used to capitalize on safety problems. Developing and maintaining positive attitudes toward safety require continual efforts in safety education. Safety training in the science program will instill in the student the importance of safety in all areas of work and play.

General laboratory skills that will prepare the student to work safely are the following:

- Handling glass tubing—cutting, bending, fire-polishing, drawing tubing into capillaries, inserting tubing into rubber stoppers, and removing tubing from rubber stoppers
- Heating test tubes of chemicals—knowledge of proper rate of heating, direction, use of test tube racks

- Handling acids—pouring, proper use of stoppers to avoid contamination, dilution in water, return of acid bottles to designated shelves
- Testing for presence of noxious gases safely
- Treating acid spillage or burns from caustic solutions
- Operating fire extinguishers
- Setting up gas generators properly
- Using standard carpenter's tools
- Using dissecting equipment, scalpels

The following safety precautions to be observed in the chemistry laboratory may be put into effect in a school by discussing them with the students, supplying copies for students' notebooks, and posting them in a prominent place in the laboratory.

List of Safety Precautions in the Chemistry Laboratory

The work you do in the chemistry laboratory is an important part of your chemistry course. Here you will learn to observe experiments and draw your own conclusions about your observations. Following is a list of safety rules to follow in making your laboratory work as safe and efficient as possible.

- Observe all instructions given by the teacher. Ask for help when you need it.
- In case of an accident, report to your teacher immediately.
- Be careful in using flames. Keep clothing away from the flame, and do not use flames near inflammable liquids.
- Follow the directions carefully when handling all chemicals.
- If acids or bases are spilled, wash immediately with plenty of water. Be sure you know where the neutralizing solution is located in the laboratory. Ask your teacher how to use it.
- Read the labels on all reagents carefully. Make a habit of reading each label twice on any reagent used in an experiment.
- Dispose of waste materials in the proper receptacles. Solid materials should be placed in special crocks provided for the purpose.
- Be sure you know the location and proper usage of the fire extinguishers and fire blankets provided in the laboratory.
- Consider the laboratory a place for serious work. There is no excuse for horseplay or practical jokes in a science laboratory.

SAFETY AND THE LAW

The principal is responsible for the overall supervision of the entire school's safety program. The science teacher is similarly responsible for the supervision of safety in the science class.

Individual teachers can be held liable for negligent acts resulting in personal injury to students. Some school boards have liability coverage that might support teachers if legal action is brought against them. Teachers should inquire about the nature of local board coverage and/or their own personal liability coverage. The extent of a teacher's liability is discussed in the NSTA publication, *Investigating Safely: A Guide for High School Teachers.*

DEMONSTRATIONS AND SCIENCE TEACHING

A demonstration has been defined as the process of showing something to another person or group. Clearly, there are several ways in which things can be shown. You can hold up an object such as a piece of sulfur and say, "This is sulfur," or you can state, "Sulfur burns, light some sulfur, and show that it burns." Showing things in this way mainly involves observation or verification.

A demonstration also can be given inductively by the instructor asking several questions but seldom giving answers. An inductive demonstration has the advantage of stressing inquiry, which encourages students to analyze and form explanations based on their knowledge. Their motivation is high because they like riddles, and in an inductive demonstration they are constantly confronted with riddles. The strength of this motivation becomes apparent if you consider the popularity of puzzles. Inviting students to inquire why something occurs taxes their minds and requires them to think. Thinking is an active mental process. The only way in which students learn to think is by having opportunities to do so. An inductive demonstration provides this opportunity because students' answers to the instructor's questions act as feedback. The teacher has a better understanding of students' comprehension of the demonstration. The feedback acts as a guide for further questioning until the students discover the concepts and principles involved in the demonstration, and the teacher is sure that they know its meaning and purpose.

Demonstrations, in addition to serving as simple observations of material and verification of a process, may also be experimental in nature. A demonstration can become an experiment if it involves a question for which the answer is not immediately apparent to the class. Students particularly like experimental demonstrations because they usually have more action. Students enjoy action more than words! They love to watch something happening before their eyes.

Students learn about acceleration by gravity in a hands-on experiment.

Demonstration Versus Individual Experimentation

Laboratory work, because it involves the individual directly in the learning process, as well as imparting working skills, is thought to be superior to teaching by demonstration. Students working on a laboratory problem should have learned far more than just the answer to the problem. They may learn to be efficient, self-reliant, and analytical; to observe, manipulate, measure, and reason; to use apparatus; and, most importantly, to learn on their own. Individual laboratory work helps to attain these goals better than demonstrations. For this reason, demonstrations should play a lesser role in science instruction, with individual student investigation receiving top priority.

Demonstrations, however, add value to a student's science education. Demonstrations can be justified for the following reasons:

◆ *Lower cost.* Less equipment and fewer materials are needed by an instructor doing a demonstration. It is, therefore, cheaper than having an entire class conduct experiments. Note, however, that cheaper education is not necessarily better education.

◆ *Availability of equipment.* Certain demonstrations require equipment not available in sufficient numbers for all students. For example, not every student in a physics class needs to have an oscilloscope.

◆ *Economy of time.* Often the time required to set up equipment for a laboratory exercise cannot be justified for the educational value received.

◆ *Less hazard from dangerous materials.* A teacher can safely handle dangerous chemicals or apparatus requiring sophisticated skills.

◆ *Direction of the thinking process.* In a demonstration, a teacher has a better indication of the students' thinking processes and can do much to stimulate the students to be more analytical and synthetic in their reasoning.

◆ *Show the use of equipment.* An instructor may want to show the students how to use and prevent damage to a microscope, balance, oscilloscope, and so forth.

Planning a Demonstration

To plan an efficient and effective demonstration requires extensive organization and consideration of the following points:

1. Identify the concept and principles you wish to teach. Direct the design of the entire demonstration and assessment to their attainment.
2. If the principle you wish to teach is complex, break it down into concepts and give several examples for each concept. For example, photosynthesis involves understanding concepts of radiant energy, chlorophyll, carbon dioxide, glucose, water, temperature, a chemical change, and gases.
3. Choose an activity that will show the concepts you wish to teach.
4. Design the activity so that each student becomes as involved as possible.
5. Gather and assemble the necessary equipment.
6. Practice the demonstration at least once before class.
7. Outline the questions you will ask during the demonstration. This procedure is especially important in doing an inquiry-oriented demonstration.
8. Consider how you may use visual aids in the demonstration.
9. Decide on the assessment.
   Written Techniques
   a. *Essay:* Have students take notes and record data during the demonstration, and then have them write a summary of the demonstration.
   b. *Quiz:* Have students write answers to questions or prepare diagrams to see if they really understand the demonstration. Stress application of scientific principles.

Verbal Techniques

   a. Ask students to summarize the purpose of the demonstration.

   b. Give them problems in which they must apply the principles they have learned.

10. Consider the time a demonstration will take. Try to move it rapidly enough to keep students attentive. Prolonged or complicated demonstrations are generally undesirable because they fail to hold students' attention.

11. When you plan a demonstration, do it well, with the intention that you will probably use it for several years. Evaluate a demonstration immediately after giving it to determine its weaknesses and strengths.

Giving a Demonstration

When giving a demonstration, keep the following guidelines in mind:

1. Make it easily visible. If you are working with small things, make sure all students can see the demonstration.

2. Speak loudly, and modulate the tone and volume of your voice to avoid monotonous delivery.

3. Display excitement in giving the demonstration. Make it "come alive."

4. Stage the demonstration. Involve everyone immediately. One suggestion is to place unique objects on a demonstration desk. For example, a transfusion container or a van de Graff generator placed on a desk immediately motivates students' inquisitive minds. Before you begin, have the students with you, wondering what will happen.

5. Teach inductively. Start your demonstration with a question. If you have interesting equipment, ask your students what they think you are going to do with it. Spend some time asking questions about the apparatus.

6. Ask questions. Constantly ask what's happening, why they think it is happening, and what the demonstration is proving or illustrating.

7. Know the purpose of the demonstration. Be ready to pick up suggestions from the questions students ask while they are observing the demonstration.

8. Give positive reinforcement. Always recognize all students' answers.

9. Allow at least three seconds for students to reply to your questions. This wait time is important so that the students may think about and reason out the demonstration.

10. Evaluate your lesson, orally or in a written summary.

Ways to Present a Demonstration

Of the several ways in which a demonstration can be given, a teacher-centered demonstration is seldom the best method, because it does not provide enough student involvement. When students participate actively in giving a demonstration, they are more interested and, consequently, learn more. Here are five ways in which a demonstration can be presented:

1. *Teacher demonstration.* The teacher prepares and gives the demonstration to the class. This approach has the advantage usually of better organization and more sophisticated presentation.

2. *Teacher–student demonstration.* In this team approach, the student assists the teacher. This type of demonstration recognizes the student. The class may be more attentive because they like to watch one of their peers perform.

3. *Student–group demonstration.* This method can be used on occasion; it has the advantage of more actively involving students. The group approach can be used to advantage if students are allowed to select their group members. The teacher should evaluate the group as a whole and assign the same grade to each group. The groups will form at first among friends; however, if some of the members are not productive, they will be rejected the next time groups are selected. The peer pressure to produce and become actively involved replaces the necessity for a teacher to encourage students to work. This group arrangement may also be effective in organizing laboratory work.

4. *Individual student demonstration.* This method can produce effective demonstrations. One successful way to conduct individual student demonstrations is to have eleventh or twelfth graders, from advanced science classes, demonstrate to the nineth graders. A freshman general-science class may become enthralled when a physics or chemistry senior comes into the class to give a demonstration. The older student, excited about giving a demonstration, helps to convey that excitement to the younger students.

5. *Guest demonstration.* Guest demonstrators can do much to relieve a boring pattern of routine class activities. Other science teachers in the school may be called in to present a demonstration or activity in which they have special competence. Professional scientists are also often willing to give special demonstrations.

Silent Demonstration

Some authors have stressed the importance and desirability of the silent demonstration. The following passage compares a verbal demonstration with a silent one.

The usual kind of demonstration by which science teachers give their students visual or auditory experiences is the teacher-talking demonstration. In this performance the teacher is actor and commentator. The pupils, who are supposed to be learning from the new experience how to attack a difficulty or develop a concept, are spectators. But they do not necessarily learn scientific facts or principles from a demonstration in which everything is done for them. Pupils really learn when they observe and react to what is presented.

There is a kind of demonstration that is likely to ensure, on the part of the student, careful observation, accurate recording of data, and practical application, later, of the ideas gained from the experience. This procedure is the silent demonstration (Obourn, 1961).

The silent demonstration, since it cannot be supplemented or strengthened by explanation, requires more careful planning than other demonstrations (see Table 16–2). In preparing the silent demonstration, the teacher may find this general procedure a good one. First, fix clearly in mind the learning outcome of the demonstration and select the apparatus and materials best suited for the demonstration. Then determine the beginning point of the demonstration. The beginning is based on what the teacher assumes that pupils know.

Consider difficulties as learning steps. Perform the techniques so that they can be observed from all areas of the room. The steps should follow order in relation to the learning steps. Give pupils an outline of the steps to be used. Outlines may be photocopied, mimeographed, or put on the chalkboard.

Silent demonstrations should not be used frequently because there is no way for the teacher to determine if the students are achieving the objectives while the demonstration is being given. Silent demonstrations can, however, provide a welcome change in the routine activity of the class. They can be used effectively if an instructor's movements are accentuated so that the students can see and have some hints about what is relevant. In a silent demonstration, visibility is extremely important and must be ensured; otherwise, the students will quickly become frustrated and discipline problems will ensue.

Storage of Demonstration Equipment

Store equipment after use so that it may be found easily in the future and set up again with little effort. One way to do so is to establish a list of headings under which to store materials. For example, in physics, storage areas might be labeled "electricity," "magnetism," "heat," "light," "sound," or "atomic structure." In biology, storage categories might be "glassware", "chemicals," "slides," or "preserved plant and animal specimens." The next time you wish to find the equipment, it is readily available under the proper storage title. Such a system also makes it easy for students to assist you in storing or obtaining equipment for use in demonstrations.

An efficient way to store small demonstration materials is to use several boxes or containers. Place all the materials you need for a demonstration in the box and label the end. For example, a box might be labeled "electrostatic demonstration materials." You might also include in the box a sheet of paper describing the demonstration. This helps lessen future preparation time for the same demonstration. This storage procedure works particularly well with general science and simple physical materials. A drawback is that when many materials and articles of equipment are stored in the boxes, they are not then easily available for other demonstration work during the year.

Stressing the Higher Levels of Learning

A demonstration should contribute to the objectives of the course and school. It should be used to stimulate

TABLE 16–2 Comparison of Teacher-Talking and Silent Demonstration

Teacher-Talking Demonstration	Silent Demonstration
Teacher states purposes of the demonstration.	Pupils must discover purpose as the demonstration progresses.
Teacher names pieces of apparatus and describes arrangement.	Teacher uses apparatus. Pupils observe equipment and arrangement.
Teacher is manipulator and technician, tells what is being done, points out and usually explains results.	Teacher performs experiment. Pupils observe what is being done and then describe results.
Teacher often points out the things that should have happened and accounts for unexpected results.	Pupils record results as observed. Teacher checks for accuracy and honesty in reporting. Teacher repeats the experiment if necessary.
Teacher summarizes the results and states the conclusion to be drawn. Pupils usually copy the conclusions as stated.	Pupils summarize data and draw their own conclusions based on what they observed. Teacher checks conclusions and repeats experiment if necessary.
Teacher explains the importance of the experiment and tells how it is applied in everyday life.	Pupils attempt to answer application questions related to the demonstration.

critical thinking and offer opportunities for creativity. A demonstration may further be used to develop understanding of the philosophical basis of science. For example, the instructor may ask questions that elicit responses relating to the degrees of certainty or uncertainty in the data, the social implications of new findings in science, and the responsibilities of scientists in the release of new findings to the public. What questions need to be asked and what decisions need to be made?

Questions of this type can be used discriminately throughout a series of demonstrations to build a philosophical awareness of the foundations of modern science. The responsibility to impart knowledge of this sort offers great challenge to the teacher in formulating lessons.

SUMMARY

Laboratory work in the middle and senior high school is constantly changing. From the emphasis on verification experiments in the traditional mode, the student is now invited to inquire into or investigate a problem. Laboratory experience becomes the initial introduction to a new topic of subject matter, followed by discussion, reading, and further experimentation. The experiment may lead to new problems that warrant investigation.

The middle school is becoming increasingly oriented toward a laboratory approach. Not only does this approach give students an early start in learning science methods, but also it introduces and allows practice of certain skills that will have value in senior high school sciences.

With more of the responsibility for learning in the laboratory being allocated to the student, the matter of safety becomes even more important. The science teacher must carefully train students in the use of laboratory apparatus and materials. This training may precede actual work in the laboratory or be an intrinsic part of the laboratory work early in the students'

experience. The promise of science for the future continues. A breakthrough has been achieved in which students at last have become participants in the search for knowledge, not mere recipients of facts and generalizations dispensed by authoritative teachers and textbooks. The laboratory is the key instrument in science teaching.

A demonstration has been defined as showing something to a person or group. The techniques of planning a demonstration involve determining the concepts and principles to be taught, deciding on activities, gathering the materials, practicing the demonstration, outlining the questions to be asked, and deciding on the evaluation methods to be used.

Plan a demonstration with the intention of using it again. A teacher, in giving a demonstration, should be aware of visibility, audibility, and all of the aspects that go with good staging. The teacher should have zest, present the demonstration inductively, ask inquiry-oriented questions, give positive techniques, and summarize and evaluate the demonstration. A demonstration may be conducted by the teacher, by the teacher and students together, by a group of students, by an individual student, or by a guest. More attention should be given to demonstrations other than those presented by the teacher, with accompanying comments. Silent demonstrations offer a different approach and emphasize observational techniques.

Equipment should be stored so that it is easily located for future demonstrations. Special equipment can often be secured from local industries without cost. The overhead projector, LCD projector, and TV screen are excellent teaching aids for demonstrations.

Individual experimentation is usually a more desirable teaching technique than are demonstrations; but demonstrations have the advantage of economy of time and money, allow for greater direction by the teacher, and provide certain safety precautions. Demonstrations should contribute to the higher levels of learning—those requiring critical thinking and creativity.

CHAPTER 17

QUESTIONING AND DISCUSSION

This chapter presents three general categories for teaching science that constitute the foundation of interactions between teachers and students. We recommend that you begin by completing the Activity 17–1: Recognizing Good Questions, at the end of this chapter. Complete only Part 1. After you complete that brief activity, return to the following section on questioning.

QUESTIONING AND SCIENCE TEACHING

Throughout this book we have underscored the importance of inquiry-based teaching. One central feature of inquiry-based teaching is questioning. Sometimes the question may center on a laboratory investigation, and at other times it may be the basis for group discussion. Regardless, the aim of questioning is to engage students: critical thinking, reasoning, and analysis of phenomena. The implied result of a question should be thought and a reasoned answer, often based on evidence. Let's begin by reviewing types of questions and then proceed to useful strategies for questioning in the science classroom.

TYPES OF QUESTIONS

Questions may be planned before class or may arise spontaneously because of student interaction. It is always wise to prepare a series of questions before entering an inquiry-oriented class. Having thought about the questions gives you direction and a sense of security, thus enhancing your ability to carry on a discussion.

Inquiry-oriented teachers must remain constantly flexible. Even though they have planned a series of questions, they must be willing to deviate from them and formulate new ones as they interact with students. These unplanned, spontaneous questions may be difficult to create at first, but through developing good questioning techniques, instructors become more sophisticated and more likely to interact appropriately with students.

Before you formulate your own questions, answer the following questions:

- What critical thinking processes will you try to nurture?
- What learning outcomes do you want to achieve?
- What types of answers will you accept?
- What skills do you wish to develop?
- What attitudes and values do you wish to emphasize?

Questions and Learning Outcomes

Just as learning outcomes can be classified by Bloom's taxonomy, so can questions. Bloom's abbreviated taxonomy is repeated to help you.

BLOOM'S TAXONOMY

Cognitive Domain	Affective Domain
Evaluation	Receiving
Synthesis	Responding
Analysis	Valuing
Application	Organizing
Comprehension	Characterizing
Knowledge	

Group discussions of laboratory experiences can enhance learning.

In general, questions requiring responses from the higher levels of the hierarchy are more desirable because answering them involves more critical and creative thinking and indicates a better understanding of concepts.

USING BLOOM'S AND KRATHWOHL'S TAXONOMIES TO CLASSIFY QUESTIONS

Classification	*Sample Question*
Knowledge	◆ How many legs has an insect?
Synthesis	◆ What explanation would you make using the data?
Application	◆ Knowing what you do about heat, how would you get a tightly fitted lid off a jar?
Analysis	◆ What things do birds and lizards have in common?
Comprehension	◆ Operationally define a magnet.
Evaluation	◆ If you were going to repeat the experiment, how would you improve it?
Receiving	◆ Do you watch science shows on television?
Responding	◆ Do you talk to your friends about science?
Valuing	◆ What is your interest in earth science now compared to when you began the course?
Organizing	◆ Can you argue using scientific facts, evidence, and data?
Characterizing	◆ Do you use problem-solving techniques for solving problems at school or at work?

QUESTIONS AND SCIENTIFIC INQUIRY

Another way to classify questions is to use the process integral to scientific inquiry. This approach ensures that the basic structure of science and critical thinking is taught. Following is a guide of how you might classify questions using inquiry processes such as hypothesizing, designing, observing, graphing, and others.

CLASSIFYING USING THE PROCESSES OF SCIENTIFIC INQUIRY

Classification	*Sample Question*
Observing	◆ What do you observe about the landscape?
Hypothesizing	◆ What do you think will happen to the solution when I heat it?
Designing an Experiment	◆ How would you determine the absorption of the different wavelengths of light in water?
Graphing	◆ How would you graph these data?
Setting up Equipment	◆ Obtain the following equipment and set it up as directed.

Reducing Experimental Error	◆ How many measurements should be made to report accurate data?
Inferring	◆ What inferences can you make from the data?

Convergent and Divergent Questions

Another way to classify questions is to determine whether they encourage many answers or just a few. Questions allowing for a limited number of responses and moving toward a conclusion are called *convergent*. Questions allowing for a number of answers are called *divergent*; they provide for wider responses plus more creative, critically considered answers. In an inquiry discussion it is generally desirable to start with divergent questions and move toward more convergent ones if students appear to be having difficulties.

Generally speaking, convergent questions, particularly those requiring only a yes or no answer, should be minimized because they allow for fewer responses, thereby giving students little opportunity to think critically. The fundamental purpose in using the inquiry approach is to stimulate and develop critical thinking, creative behavior, and multiple talents. Convergent questions generally contribute less to achieve this end. Remember that, in an inquiry investigation, it is important that students have a chance to think. Unfortunately, some teachers are so concerned with getting the right answer that they prevent students from going through a thought process. We as teachers would, of course, like for students to think and obtain the correct answer. However, recall for a moment a mathematics teacher who only accepts the correct answer to a problem, ignoring the procedures used in obtaining it. Students may have used very good thinking processes to obtain the answer yet misplaced the decimal point. Is the teacher justified in saying that students have not learned because they don't have the right answer? Students probably will never have that problem again but they undoubtedly will have many situations requiring them to use similar logical strategies. It is the thinking that is most important! Complete Activities 17–2 through 17–4: Classifying Questions—Divergent or Convergent?, at the end of the chapter to test your understanding of the different types of questions.

Teleological and Anthropomorphic Questions

Teleological (the Greek word *teleos* means "an end") questions are those that imply that natural phenomena have an end or purpose. The word *anthropomorphic* comes from two Greek words: *anthropos,* meaning "man," and *morphos,* meaning "form." An anthropomorphic question implies that some natural phenomenon has the characteristics of humanity. For example, such a question might state that some natural phenomenon has a want or wish: Rocks fall because they want to.

Why do you think teleological questions should be avoided? What do they do as far as developing critical thinking and leading to further investigation? How do they contribute to misconceptions? Complete Activity 17–5: Classifying Questions—Teleological or Anthropomorphic?, at the end of the chapter.

QUESTIONING PROCEDURES

Wait Time Affects Quality of Responses

Mary Budd Rowe (1970) and her coworkers have done an extensive study of the questioning behavior of teachers. In their analysis of taped classroom discussions, they discovered that teachers, on an average, wait less than a second for students to reply to their questions. Further investigations revealed that some instructors waited an average of three seconds for students to answer questions. An analysis of student responses revealed that teachers with longer wait times (three seconds or more) obtained greater speculation, conversation, and argument than those with shorter wait times.

Rowe also found that when teachers were trained to wait five seconds, on the average, before responding, the following occurred:

◆ Students gave longer and more complete answers.
◆ Speculative and creative thinking increased.
◆ Suggested questions and experiments increased.
◆ Slower students increased their participation.
◆ Teachers became more flexible in their responses.
◆ Teachers asked fewer questions, but the ones they asked required more reflection.
◆ Students gave a greater number of qualified inferences.
◆ Teacher expectations for student performance changed; teachers were less likely to expect only the brighter students to reply.

Rowe believed that the expectancy levels of students are more likely to change positively if students are given a longer time to respond. She also found that the typical pattern of discussion, teacher–student–teacher, can be altered by training instructors to get student–student–teacher responses. This pattern will occur when students are involved in controversy, for example, determining the best design for an experiment or deciding what conclusions can be drawn from data.

For inquiry-based teaching to occur, most instructors should increase their wait-time tolerance so that students have more opportunities to think and create.

In addition, sociocultural factors may play a part in the effectiveness of the questioning and wait-time procedures. In school systems where high authoritarian classroom environments prevail, low levels of student questioning may exist, which would tend to negate teachers' efforts to apply suitable wait-time and inquiry techniques, especially in discussion situations in the science classroom (Olugbemiro & Olajide, 1995).

PRECAUTIONS IN QUESTIONING

It has long been thought that the practice of questioning promotes student thinking and participation, and in most cases it does. However, sometimes certain questioning techniques have the reverse effect and actually reduce student thinking. Frequently what the teacher actually does is initiate a question-and-answer practice that does not develop into true classroom discussion and does not promote expressiveness, active participation, or independent thinking. Instead, the process may encourage student passivity and dependency. A few precautions are outlined in the following paragraphs to alert teachers to practices that may hinder discussion.

First, sometimes using questions simply results in a back-and-forth interchange between teacher and students in which the teacher is the questioner and the student is the respondent. (See Figure 17–1 for an example.) Instead, try holding back from asking questions at the start, thus encouraging students to take

some responsibility for carrying on the discussion, rather than simply being targets of teacher questions.

Second, questions are sometimes used to make a point in which a particular piece of information or idea is underscored. This practice can be counterproductive, because the same information would be more effective as a declarative statement.

Third, questions are often asked to help students who pause or falter in their responses. Teachers sometimes condition students to speak in short bursts in answer to our direct questions, and students don't expect to have to do anything beyond this. True discussion, however, requires thoughtful, sustained reasoning on the part of the students. It requires more time to express complex thoughts or interpretations.

Fourth, questions are sometimes used to elicit predetermined answers. In this case, the teacher has a particular answer in mind and phrases questions so that the student produces the expected answer. This again reduces speculative responses from students.

Fifth, teachers occasionally ask questions in reply to a student's question. While sometimes recommended as a way of promoting inquiry, the danger is that it may convey the idea that only the teacher gets to ask the questions and that whenever students ask questions, all they get is a redirected question.

Sixth, questions are sometimes used to draw out the nonparticipating students. This assumes that every student is in the frame of mind to respond equally when compared to every other student. The practice may instead intimidate some students and cause others to become wary of future questions. Students may thus prepare answers in advance and fail to listen to the argument or the discussion. Such practices may cause students to withdraw even more rather than to draw them out.

Seventh, using questions to probe the students' personal feelings and experiences in the classroom is risky. This may make the student feel fear and resentment.

Alternative practices can help you avoid these pitfalls. For example, instead of asking a question, make a declarative statement. This can still present the problem or issue to the students and open up avenues for further discussion.

Another alternative to questioning would be to restate the speaker's words. Try to make a statement that interprets what the student has said, thus giving the class an opportunity to reconsider the information. Declare your perplexity when you do not understand something a student has said. Simply state, "I am confused about what you are saying." Invite elaboration. Use a statement such as, "I'd like to hear more of your views on that." Encourage class questions. In a discussion it should be possible for students to ask other students questions or to direct their

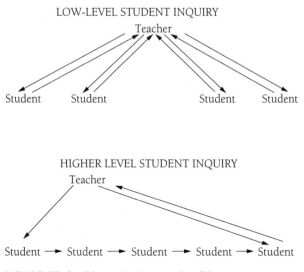

FIGURE 17–1 Discussion Interaction Diagrams

questions to the person who is speaking, whether the speaker is a teacher or a student. Let the speaker pause and ask a question. This promotes discussion, indicates the speculative nature of the statements that are being made, and gives the student an opportunity to obtain feedback.

Finally, simply maintain silence. Use a longer wait time to indicate to the student that you are conducting a leisurely practice and you want to provide opportunities for reflection, introspection, and thoughtful answers (Diller, 1982).

RESEARCH ON QUESTIONING IN THE CLASSROOM

Because of its potential in stimulating thinking and learning, questioning remains one of the most influential teaching behaviors in the classroom. The first major systematic research on questioning was conducted by Stevens at Columbia University in 1912. Almost all the research conducted from that time until the 1950s focused primarily on describing teacher questioning behavior. Results uniformly supported the finding that questions stimulating memory and recall were the type being emphasized in classrooms.

Around 1970, a new increase of activity on teacher questioning began. The emphasis in this research was on identifying specific questioning levels and skills that had an impact on pupil growth.

Full-functioning teachers almost certainly have educational outcomes not only at the fact level, but also at the concept level, and even at the personal meaning and values levels. This necessitates asking high-order questions of students. Teachers then need not determine whether to ask high-level questions but rather need to determine how to find an appropriate balance of lower- and higher-order questions to achieve instructional goals.

Research exists on the use of questions as a learning strategy. Questions in textual material have been defended on the basis that they provide "advance organizers" for the material to be learned. The use of questions at the higher levels of cognition (such as application, analysis, synthesis, and evaluation) has been shown to have a significant positive effect on student learning. Questions placed within the text material appear to produce better understanding and retention than text material without questions. In a study on presentation style, groups of students reading material with questions at the beginnings of paragraphs scored higher on an immediate posttest than groups reading without questions.

As a result of the research over the past 75 years, we can draw several tentative conclusions concerning questioning in the classroom. Teachers appear to persist in asking questions that require students primarily to recall knowledge and information. It is important to consider stressing high-level questions and devising a variety of instructional objectives that balance low-level memory questions with preplanned high-convergent and divergent questions. Teachers can be effectively trained to raise the cognitive emphasis of their questions. There is a tendency for the cognitive levels of questions asked by teachers and responses from pupils to be positively related.

The extent of wait time teachers use after asking questions dramatically influences the quantity and quality of pupil responses. Teacher educators need to provide training opportunities for teachers to practice increasing their wait time to a minimum of three seconds.

At the primary level, the tendency is to use lower cognitive level questions related to pupil achievement. Teachers need to stress the importance of balancing low and high cognitive level questions to stimulate productive thinking at all grade levels (Wilen, 1984).

Questioning in the Content Areas

Students in science classes experience general questioning techniques and encounter questioning in the content of their science classes. The skills of formulating good questions in science and of seeking solutions to questions posed by their teachers, their textbooks, and their laboratory experiments are practiced and developed in the context of the science discipline being studied.

Research on reading and questioning in content areas is reported by Bonnie Armbruster and others (1991). Results showed that most questions were directly related to textbook material that was to have been read by the students in their assignments and were largely questions on factual information. Only about 15 percent of the questions required students to analyze, predict, or apply information from the text. These questions came from only a small number of the teachers involved in the study, indicating that the use of high-level questions was somehow related to individual teaching styles. There was also a high percentage of rhetorical questions whose purpose was not clear other than perhaps to form a bridge to foster continuity in class discussions.

Gender Differences

Science educators are becoming increasingly concerned about gender differences with respect to expectations, types of experiences, and participation in science classrooms. Roberta Barba and Loretta Cardinale (1991) have investigated student questioning interactions in secondary school science classrooms. Results of the study suggest that female students have fewer interactions with science teachers and receive less attention than males.

Questions asked of female students were predominantly low-level questions. Males received more teacher interaction, including more questions of higher levels. This trend in questioning female students seems to give females a signal that they have low ability in the sciences. It is also apparent that such behavior occurs before the secondary school level is reached, causing many females to believe that they are incapable of success in science.

Levels of Questions

Studies of teachers' classroom interactions indicate that 60 to 80 percent of teachers' questions require the lowest level of thinking for satisfactory answers (Otto, 1991).

A practical questioning technique divides teacher questions into soliciting moves and reacting moves. Soliciting moves are categorized as follows:

- Recall questions that draw upon past experience or knowledge
- Data-collecting questions where students react to direct observations
- Data-processing questions where students hypothesize, analyze, compare, or suggest solutions
- Verification questions where students evaluate or judge responses

Reacting moves by the teacher involve the following:

- Accepting or informing the student that the response is correct
- Rejecting or informing the student of the incorrectness of the response
- Requesting clarification or further evidence
- Asking another person

Employment of the above strategies can raise the level of questions, provide opportunities to practice thinking skills beyond mere factual recall, and foster skills that support inquiry and investigative methods.

Development of effective questioning skills among students is as important as developing better questioning techniques among teachers. As science classes adopt more investigative learning and teaching methods, the ability to ask higher-order questions becomes imperative. As with all learning, frequent opportunities to practice the desired skills results in greater improvement.

Now, return to Activity 17–1: Recognizing Good Questions, and complete Part 2.

FACILITATING DISCUSSIONS AND SCIENCE TEACHING

In the last section on questioning, we alluded to classroom discussions. Here we provide a more detailed introduction and suggest strategies that will help you in your science classroom.

Advantages of Discussion

Students become more interested when they are involved, thus discussion is a desirable approach for class procedures. Since an aim of modern science instruction is to teach science as inquiry, with an emphasis on the individual's cognitive development, students must have time and opportunities to think. A student can't think unless given opportunities to do so. The presentation of questions in a discussion requires students to think before they can formulate answers. A teacher who tells students all about a subject offers only an opportunity to soak up information and memorize it.

A discussion leader interested in developing inquiring strategies seldom gives answers but asks questions instead. In answering, students learn to evaluate, analyze, and synthesize knowledge. They are often thrilled to discover fundamental ideas for themselves. Another benefit of discussion is that the teacher receives feedback. An astute discussion leader learns quickly from student comments about how much students understand. The leader then guides the discussion, moving it rapidly when students understand the information and slowing it down when they have difficulty. A lecture-oriented teacher seldom knows what students are comprehending. This teacher may concentrate on a point that the class understands or may speed through information that confuses students. One of the greatest mistakes a beginning teacher can make is to assume that the lecture method will be effective in a secondary school.

How to Lead a Discussion

Leading a discussion is an art that is not easily learned. There is nothing more exciting than to see a master teacher conducting an interesting and exciting discussion. How can you bring students to this point? Excellent class discussions do not just happen. Inexperienced instructors may think they will walk into a class and talk about a subject off the top of their head. After all, don't they know more about the subject than the students? While it's true they may know about the material, they are faced with the problem of helping students discover information and develop their abilities. This process requires as much preparation as any other class procedure. The first step in preparing for a discussion is to determine what it is you wish to accomplish. Ask yourself, "What are my learning outcomes?" Next, outline questions you think may help students reach these outcomes. Good discussion leaders use the "What do you think?" approach to learning. They ask questions such as were suggested in the section on questioning. For example:

- Why did you do this experiment?
- What did the data show?

- Why did you use this approach?
- How would you go about finding answers to this question?
- How else could you find the answer?
- How does this answer relate to your daily life?
- What steps did you take in solving the problem?
- How many variables were involved in the experiment?

Spend Time Analyzing Thought Processes

Every discussion should stimulate critical and creative thinking. You should spend time analyzing the types of questions you will ask in a discussion to ensure that they require the exercise of these abilities. You will contribute positively to their expectancy level of their critical thinking. Showing students that they are performing relatively sophisticated inquiry abilities—inferring, hypothesizing, evaluating data, and so forth—will encourage them to accept that they can use their minds to derive answers to relatively complex questions. We come to believe that we are good thinkers only by being successful in thinking and by receiving feedback about our thinking abilities. Furthermore, teachers build positive student self-concepts when they involve students in tasks requiring thinking and show them how they are developing their minds. An actual inquiry discussion might follow these steps.

Present a problem such as, "What is the lifetime of a burning candle?" Encourage students to formulate hypotheses and give evidence. For example, say an apparatus is set up as follows: A burning candle is placed upright in a pan in which there is some water, and the candle is then covered with a glass container. Show how the experiment is set up by projecting a transparency of it on a screen. Some types of questions to ask are: "What will happen to the candle when it is covered?" "What else will happen to the apparatus as this is done?" "What would happen if the candle were lengthened, the size of the jar above it were increased, or the amount of water in the container holding the candle were decreased?" "How would you find out?"

After the students have progressed this far, have some students reflect back on what has been said and summarize the high points of the discussion. As a discussion leader, at times you might have to assist a student in doing this by repeating, "What was the problem?" Review the cognitive processes students used in solving the problem. Ask: "What hypotheses were made?" "What was the best hypothesis and why?" "How were the conclusions reached?" "On what are they based?" "What is required to make better conclusions?"

Questions Must Be Directed at the Students' Level

A less-experienced discussion leader may begin a discussion with a question that is too difficult. If there is no response to a question, the teacher should rephrase it to make it simpler. This procedure may have to be followed several times before there is a response. A question implies an answer. Similarly, if the question is too vague, the students may not respond, and rephrasing it may give them some insight. Leading a discussion by questioning without giving answers is a skill that brings great satisfaction, but to be an astute questioner requires practice and a keen awareness of students' comprehension. By questioning correctly, the experienced discussion leader can guide students toward understanding the concepts and principles involved in the lesson or experiment. The questions must be deep enough to require critical thinking rather than a simple yes or no answer.

Eye contact is also an important aspect in leading a discussion. A teacher's eyes should sweep a class, constantly looking for boredom, a student with an answer or a question, or one with a puzzled look. Eye contact gives the instructor feedback and motivates students to think and participate in the discussion. It also shows that you are more interested in the students than in the information being covered.

A Discussion Started in a Novel Way Gains Attention

A motivational technique useful in beginning a discussion is to start it with an interesting demonstration. Burning a candle can lead to a discussion of several scientific concepts and principles. A good rule to follow is to start a discussion with a precept or observation when possible. Not all discussions will lend themselves to this procedure, but those that involve the discovery of a concept almost always do.

GENERAL RULES FOR LEADING A LARGE GROUP DISCUSSION

General rules to follow in using discussions are presented here.

- Create an atmosphere in the class in which questions not only welcomed but expected.
- Include students' interests.
- When you give reinforcement, do it positively and as often as you can. Use very little negative feedback. Say, "That's a good answer." "That's right, you have the idea." No response should be a form of

negative feedback. If students have the wrong answer, do not say, "That's wrong" or "No, that answer is no good." Rather, challenge the response by saying, "Well, that is not quite right." "You may have something there, but I am not sure I understand the point," or "Good, you are thinking; but that is not quite what I was leading up to."

♦ When you encourage a student to think, evaluate the result on the basis of the student's level of comprehension. Even when you are aware that the student's idea is a misconception, indicate that the student has made effective use of the information, but should evaluate the adequacy of the response.

♦ Praise a student for being a good listener when the student calls attention to a mistake you have made.

♦ When leading a discussion, try to remember previous comments and integrate them. If at all possible, give recognition by referring to the name of the student who made the comment. For example, a teacher in responding to the idea of a student might say, "Joan believes that there are other factors besides temperature determining the rate of expansion of a metal. George has just suggested that possibly humidity and air pressure may have a minor effect."

♦ Maintain a positive and accepting attitude. Your attitude in leading a discussion does much to determine the quality of that discussion. If you walk into a class feeling and looking very glum and with the weight of the discussion on your shoulders, the students' response will be lukewarm. However, if you start a discussion with the attitude that you and the students are going to have fun wrestling with ideas, their response is more likely to be impressive. In leading a discussion with adolescents, you must be able to laugh at yourself; discreet use of humor captures interest and gains participation.

♦ When questions arise for which science does not yet provide an adequate explanation, state that, as yet, there is no answer. This gives students insight into avenues of research which we still need to explore.

♦ Call on students who are willing to answer as well as those who are reluctant.

♦ Do not rush discussions. Remember that the major reason for having discussions is to give students time to think. When there is silence during a discussion, this may be the period where most of the thinking is going on. Remember that a desirable wait time averages five seconds.

Special Precautions in Leading a Discussion

At times, the following suggestions are proper, but you should give serious consideration to their potential disadvantages as well.

♦ Repeat a question when it is asked of you; or have another student repeat the question in its entirety.

♦ Encourage the class to take notes.

♦ Avoid the appearance of carrying on a private conversation with the person who asked the question.

♦ Deliberately let your eyes roam over the entire class while giving the answer.

♦ Use questions requiring the abilities of scientific inquiry.

♦ Avoid sarcasm.

♦ Encourage students to seek recognition before answering or have them be courteous of another and wait until that person finishes before they respond.

♦ Do not let students make derogatory remarks about another student's question or answer.

SPECIAL DISCUSSION TECHNIQUES

Invitations to Inquiry

In its Biology Teacher's Handbook, the BSCS gives 44 class-discussion outlines under the title, "Invitations to Inquiry." The main purpose of these outlines is to involve students in the strategies of solving scientific problems—not to teach science subject matter. The invitations engage students in the process of solving problems in the way that scientists are engaged. A typical outline for an invitation is provided here.

FORMAT FOR AN INVITATION

Present a problem to the students and ask how they would go about solving it. Describe the actual experimental design used by the scientist. Ask the students what they would hypothesize about the experimental results.

Then give the students the data the scientists collected and ask: "What conclusions can you make about these data?" Finally, ask: "If you were the scientist, what would be your next problem and why?" BSCS authors state that the primary aim [of invitations] is an understanding of scientific inquiry and the development of inquiry abilities. It is mainly for the sake of these aims that the active participation of students is invoked. Both practical experience and experimental study indicate that concepts are understood best and retained longest when students contribute to their own understanding. You can easily make your own invitations. The steps are as follows:

1. Determine your science processes and subject-matter objectives.
2. State a problem related to your objectives. The idea for problems can come from actual scientific research reported in journals.
3. Devise questions that give students opportunities to set up experiments, make hypotheses, analyze and synthesize, and record data. Stress the understanding

Dividing the class into small groups permits more individual attention and opportunities to answer in laboratory activities.

of science as a process and the cognitive skills involved.

4. Write the invitation as a series of steps. In different sections insert additional information to help students progress in depth in the topic or methods of research.
5. Evaluate the effectiveness of your invitation.

Invitations to inquiry can be written for various levels of learning. As much as possible, they should stress the development of students' cognitive abilities. In addition to the science processes, students should also learn the necessity for having a control, understand cause-and-effect relationships, learn when to use quantitative data and how to interpret it, learn the role of argument and inference in the design of experiments, and so forth.

Write an invitation! Your first invitation may lack sophistication, but in the process of writing it you will gain insight into how to construct invitations and gain a better understanding of how to involve students in understanding science as a process.

Pictorial Riddles

Another technique for developing motivation and interest in a discussion is to use pictorial riddles, that is, pictures or drawings made by the teacher to elicit student response. A riddle is drawn on the chalkboard or on poster board or is projected by PowerPoint, and the teacher asks a question about the picture.

Pictorial riddles are relatively easy to devise. They can be as simple or as complex as a teacher desires. In devising a riddle, follow these steps.

1. Select a concept or principle you wish to teach or emphasize.
2. Draw a picture or show an illustration that demonstrates the concept.

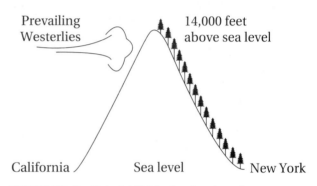

FIGURE 17–2   Pictorial Riddle (earth science)

3. An alternate procedure is to change something in a picture and ask students to find out what is wrong in the picture. An example might be a picture of a large child being held up on a seesaw by a small child. Ask, "How is this possible?" Or show a farming community in which all of the ecological principles are misapplied and ask what is wrong with what has been done in the community.
4. Finally, devise a series of questions related to the picture which will help students gain insights into the principles involved.

Figures 17–2, 17–3, and 17–4 provide three examples of pictorial riddles.

The format for a riddle which lends itself particularly well to PowerPoint is the before-and-after type of riddle. Students are shown a diagram or picture, some factor is then altered, and the students are shown another picture of the same situation after modification. Students are to hypothesize what happened in the before situation to reach the modification shown in the after diagram.

talents and self-concepts. For dedicated teachers, there is probably no greater satisfaction than to walk out of class knowing that they have developed the students' mental abilities to the point where their presence is practically unneeded except as an organizer. To acquire this facility requires preparation and constant self-analysis, but it is one of the intellectual satisfactions that comes only with good teaching. Activity 17–6: Leading a Discussion, provides the opportunity to practice your skills in this area. Activity 17–7: Self-Evaluation Instrument for Rating your Questioning Ability, can be used anytime you lead a discussion that is audio or video recorded.

USING TEXTBOOKS AND SCIENCE TEACHING

Science textbooks continue to be a basic source of information in the classroom. When they are used judiciously

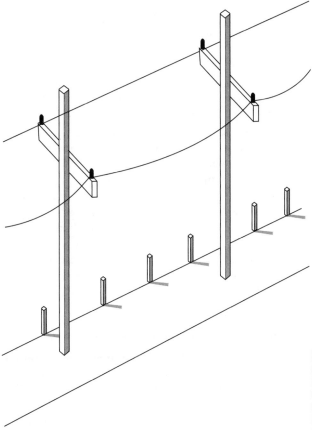

FIGURE 17–3 Pictorial Riddle (physical science)

DISCUSSION AS A TECHNIQUE OF REVIEW

All of the preceding discussion techniques can be used to good advantage for class review. Discussion also may be used as an excellent review for laboratory work. After you have had a class conduct several experiments in a unit, take time to discuss the conclusions that can be drawn from the laboratory work. Also consider how the information was obtained, what types of problem-solving and cognitive behaviors were involved in determining the answers, and what assurance the students have that their information is correct. A discussion of this type can do much to reinforce learning and divide the trivia from the important aspects of learning.

Learning to Lead a Good Discussion Never Ends

Teachers never quite perfect their ability as discussion leaders, but they should never stop trying to improve. Excellence in discussion comes only with wisdom, not only in subject matter but also in learning how to develop

BEFORE		AFTER
Cell ⊙ Cell ⊙	?	Cell ⊙ Cell ⊙
	?	
Animal Tracks	?	No More Tracks
NaOH	?	Precipitate Formed
Nail 1 Nail 2	?	Nail 1 Nail 2

FIGURE 17–4 Sequential Pictorial Riddles. Can you Supply the Missing Form?

and with recognition of their limitations, textbooks contribute substantially to student learning. We recommend that you complete Activity 17–8: Readability Analysis, at the end of this chapter.

USING TEXTBOOKS EFFECTIVELY

In spite of common myth, textbooks in and of themselves are not bad; most good teachers use textbooks, and textbooks can enhance student learning. The majority of teachers use textbooks. In a 1985 survey, Iris Weiss (1987) found that 93 percent of science teachers in grades 7 through 12 used a published textbook. Interestingly, the majority of science teachers did not consider textbook quality to be a significant problem in their schools. The most high-rated aspects of science textbooks were their organization, clarity, and reading level. Others however, see problems with the quality and usability of textbooks (Osbourn et al., 1987; Gould, 1988; McInerney, 1986; Champagne et al., 1987).

Since the 1960s, the prevailing view in science education has been that programs should be activity based and not textbook dominated. Research reported in 2001 shows that the opposite is the case—teachers are using fewer activities and relying more on the textbook (Weiss et al., 2001). Use of textbooks is prevalent in science teaching due to the need for science teachers to plan for several subjects, the reduction of budgets, and the scheduling of science classes in nonlaboratory rooms.

In this section we assist you in becoming an intelligent user of the textbook, that is, to help you recognize the potentials and limitations of textbooks, and to use them to enhance learning. The section relies on the research of Kathleen Roth and Charles Anderson (1988).

Science teachers use textbooks in several ways. Textbooks help teachers make decisions about the curriculum. Questions about topics, activities of coverage, depth, sequence, and emphasis are answered by reference to the textbook. Keep in mind that although the textbook helps teachers make efficient decisions, they do not necessarily help them make the best decisions for student experiences and learnings.

Textbooks help teachers select teaching strategies. Again, this use of textbooks has both advantages and disadvantages. The clear advantage is efficiency. It takes considerable effort to manage an activity-based program. It is much easier to have students read the textbook. The disadvantage is that reading the textbook may not facilitate student learning. We discuss this in detail later.

Textbooks provide scientific explanations. Descriptions of key concepts and information are usually straightforward and succinct in textbooks. Providing students with good descriptions of scientific ideas is difficult; it is especially difficult when teachers are teaching out of their discipline. So textbooks can be a useful resource for scientific explanations.

Given the function of textbooks, it is easy to see why the majority of teachers rely on them. What do science teachers need to understand in order to use textbooks more effectively? First in importance is to understand how students use textbooks.

We have pointed out that students have prior knowledge about science. Often this knowledge is inadequate or incomplete when compared to accepted scientific knowledge. Students' prior knowledge is important to understand when considering students' reading strategies. What happens when students are asked to read a text that has explanations about phenomena that are incompatible with their current explanations? Students seem to use several strategies to accommodate the difference between their conceptions and those presented in textbooks (Roth, 1985). Here are the different strategies students use.

Reading for Conceptual Change

A few students use the text to change current conceptions to more appropriately scientific conceptions. As students confront concepts that conflict with their own ideas, they give up their concepts and assimilate those presented as formal scientific explanations in the textbook.

Over-Relying on Prior Knowledge and Distorting Text

Here students use elaborate strategies to link prior knowledge with text knowledge. These students genuinely try to make sense of the text and integrate text ideas with their own knowledge. Still, they just cannot give up their own strongly held ideas. Theirs is the strategy of linking scientific knowledge with their own ideas.

Over-Relying on Facts in the Text

These students focus on the memorization of vocabulary and facts and they rely on separating their prior knowledge from the text knowledge. They do not relate the facts and vocabulary to each other or to their prior knowledge. Reading for conceptual change is not possible.

Over-Relying on Details in the Text—Separating Prior Knowledge and Text Knowledge

These students pay great attention to the text. They attend to the details, as opposed to concepts, and fail to

STEPS FOR DESIGNING LESSONS

Using Textbooks Effectively

1. Direct students' attention to important concepts.
2. Challenge students' thinking and misconceptions.
3. Ask students to construct explanations of everyday phenomena.
4. Probe student responses.
5. Provide accurate feedback to students.
6. Construct alternative representations of textbook explanations.
7. Make explicit the connections between textbook explanations and student misconceptions.
8. Select activities that create conceptual conflict and encourage conceptual understanding.

attach any meaning to details. The details, most often specialized vocabulary of science, are isolated words that have no relationship to anything. These students think they understand science if they are able to decode the words and identify details in the textbook.

Over-Relying on Prior Knowledge and Ignoring Text Knowledge

Some students rely on their own experiential knowledge to interpret the textbook. If asked about text knowledge, they equate textbook explanations with their own explanations, ones that have nothing to do with scientific explanations. To them the text makes sense in terms of their prior knowledge.

What can teachers do? There are a few recommendations for effective use of science textbooks. The principles are based on studies of text-based science teaching (Anderson & Smith, 1983) and understandings gained from studies of students' reading strategies (Roth, 1985).

Directing Students' Attention to Important Concepts

Textbooks typically contain numerous ideas and vocabulary words. This situation causes students to memorize facts and lists of words rather than focus on strategies that will result in conceptual change. Focusing students on central issues that are problematic, keeping lessons related to the concepts, and keeping vocabulary to a minimum will contribute to conceptual change.

Challenging Students' Thinking and Misconceptions

Most textbooks are written from a scientist's perspective. Seldom do textbook authors consider students' perspectives as they organize textbooks. Still, students will interpret text material in terms of their prior knowledge. Effective teachers identify the differences between students' concepts and those in the textbook. By asking questions and challenging students' thinking, teachers can initiate the process of conceptual change. The questions should be stated in relation to ideas in the textbooks, or students may not make the connections.

Asking Students to Construct Explanations of Everyday Phenomena

Questions in textbooks seldom have students apply knowledge to everyday experiences. Encouraging students to compare, challenge, and debate each other's explanations are all methods that result in conceptual change.

Probing Student Responses

Listen for students' thinking rather than for right answers. Ask questions that will have students justify and clarify their responses.

Providing Accurate Feedback to Students

Teachers typically respond to student answers by praising correct answers and ignoring incorrect answers. The greatest concern is the latter. Although teachers think this approach helps students, in actuality it does not. Giving positive feedback for any answer encourages students to maintain their current conceptions and to use ineffective strategies to find correct answers. Give clear and accurate feedback about the strengths and limitations of student responses.

Constructing Alternative Representations of Textbook Explanations

Give the students time to struggle with explanations in the textbook. Most textbooks are packed with explanations that are presented in one way only, and then the text moves to the next explanation. There is little time and variation to help students consider alternative explanations and construct new concepts. After students have time to grapple with concepts, provide different representations of the ideas. The representations will be most effective if they clearly contrast the students' and the text's explanations. The goal of this struggle is to help students make explicit the relationships between scientific explanations and their own understanding.

Selecting Activities That Create Conceptual Conflict and Encourage Conceptual Understanding

Selection of activities is based on criteria such as student interest, a sense of important science concepts, and the need to do inquiry-oriented activities. Discrepant events are good examples of the types of activities that create conceptual change. In the end, doing activities is not as important as helping students make sense of their experiences.

SUMMARY

The ability of the teacher to ask questions to stimulate creative and critical thinking is basic to inquiry teaching. Inquiry types of questions may be involved in all areas of science teaching, such as discussion, laboratory demonstrations, student worksheets, visual aids, and evaluations. Instructors should plan their questions before class but remain flexible and adapt their instruction as dictated by student interaction. Before outlining the question, teachers should decide what critical thinking abilities and subject-matter outcomes they hope to develop and the answers they will accept.

Questions may be classified as convergent or divergent according to Bloom's taxonomy or by the inquiry processes they are trying to develop. Divergent types of questions and those requiring more cognitive sophistication should be stressed. Teleological questions, anthropomorphic questions, and those that could be answered by yes or no responses should be avoided.

The time a teacher waits for a response, called wait time, is important. Most teachers wait, on an average, less than one second. A five-second average wait time results in more responses by slow learners, more creative answers, more complete-sentence answers, more questions, and more suggestions for experiments.

This chapter suggests questioning techniques to involve students in investigations and to stimulate creativity. Research indicates that teachers trained in questioning techniques do change their questioning behavior in the classroom, asking questions requiring

greater cognitive ability. Teachers who emphasize higher-level types of questions are more likely to see their students do better on national tests, which tend to test for all cognitive levels.

Inquiry-based discussions motivate students and involve them more in cognitive processes than do lectures. There are definite techniques to be used in leading inquiry-oriented discussions. Primarily, the instructor should question and give minimal information; the type of question asked by the teacher helps students discover concepts and principles.

To lead a good discussion requires extensive preparation. Discussion leaders should know their objectives, outline a series of relevant questions, and spend time at the end of the discussion analyzing how conclusions were reached. Part of the discussion should be devoted to reflecting on the thought processes used in arriving at these conclusions.

Discussion leaders should give as much positive reinforcement as possible. They should compliment students on good ideas and suggestions and never deride or make sarcastic remarks about poor suggestions. When misconceptions emerge in discussions, careful and sensitive challenging becomes necessary. The teacher should structure a question that engages the students in conceptual conflict and then continue the discussion in a manner that helps students construct a more accurate scientific conception. A good method for starting a discussion is to use a demonstration or PowerPoint projection pertaining to a subject or topic of interest to students. In leading the discussion, attempt to recall previous comments and interrelate the suggestions with the names of the individuals who made them.

Although textbooks are used by the majority of science teachers, there has been little effort to use them effectively. Science teachers should recognize that students' use of textbooks is influenced by their prior knowledge (i.e., misconceptions) and that this prior knowledge can dominate or distort text material. Some recommendations for using a textbook include the following:

- ◆ Direct students' attention to important concepts.
- ◆ Challenge students' misconceptions.
- ◆ Ask students to construct explanations of everyday phenomena.
- ◆ Probe student responses.
- ◆ Provide accurate feedback to students.
- ◆ Construct alternative representations of textbook explanations.
- ◆ Select activities that create conceptual conflict.

———————————————— **INVESTIGATING SCIENCE TEACHING** ————————————————

ACTIVITY 17–1
RECOGNIZING GOOD QUESTIONS, PART 1

Read the following questions and mark them according to whether they are poor (P), fair (F), good (G), or excellent (E).

_____   1. Why do roots thirst for water?

_____   2. Why does water seek its own level?

_____   3. Are all big trees the same size, shape, and age?

_____   4. How does a siphon work?

_____   5. How do seeds sprout?

_____   6. How does soap clean?

_____   7. What will happen if clothes are soaked with a bleach before instead of after washing?

_____   8. How can the bleaching action be accelerated?

_____   9. If ethylene glycol prevents avalanches, what other chemicals do you suspect might also prevent them?

_____ 10. If you were going to repeat the experiment with yeast, how would you improve it?

_____ 11. How would you design an experiment to _____?

_____ 12. If you have a straight-line graph indicating a relationship between population growth and time but the period ends at two days, what could you say about the population at four days?

_____ 13. How would you define a magnet operationally?

_____ 14. How could you be more certain about the conclusions you made from the data?

_____ 15. What do you think will happen to a potted geranium plant if it is placed near a window?

_____ 16. What evidence does the process of diffusion contribute to the molecular theory?

_____ 17. Look at the culture plates and describe what you see.

_____ 18. Place the organisms into any two groups you wish.

_____ 19. If the distance is doubled between two masses in Newton's gravitational formula, what will happen to the force?

Now provide an explanation for your responses. Why do you think some questions are poor, fair, good, or excellent?

RECOGNIZING GOOD QUESTIONS, PART 2

Below are several questions related to the first part of this activity. Read each question and attempt to answer it. Record your answers in the space provided and refer to them again after completing this chapter to see how well you did.

_____   1. Of the preceding questions, which three are the best?

_____   2. Which are teleological or anthropomorphic questions?

_____   3. Which questions require the student to analyze?

_____   4. Which questions require the student to synthesize?

_____   5. Which questions require the student to evaluate?

_____   6. Which questions are convergent?

_____   7. Which questions are divergent?

_____   8. Which questions require students to demonstrate in their responses the processes of science?

_____   9. Which questions require students to reason quantitatively and what are they required to do?

_____ 10. Which questions require creative responses?

_____ 11. Which questions require students to formulate an operational definition?

_____ 12. Which questions require students mainly to observe?

_____ 13. Which questions require students mainly to classify?

_____ 14. Which questions require students to demonstrate experimental procedure?

_____ 15. Which questions require students to formulate a model?

_____ 16. Which questions require students to hypothesize?

_____ 17. Which question would an authoritarian personality most likely guess at if he or she didn't know the answer?

_____ 18. Which of the following two types of questions suggest a test?

    a. How do seeds sprout?

    b. What is needed for seeds to sprout?

_____ 19. It has been said that "how" questions do not lead to experimentation. Comment on this statement.

After you have answered these questions, compare and discuss your answers with other students in the class.

Activity 17–2
Classifying Questions in Normal Conversation

Observe normal conversation and classify the questions asked according to one of the classification systems suggested in this chapter.

ACTIVITY 17–3
CLASSIFYING QUESTIONS USING BLOOM'S TAXONOMY

Write discussion questions to be used in a class discussion and classify them according to Bloom's taxonomy and science processes.

ACTIVITY 17–4
CLASSIFYING QUESTIONS—DIVERGENT OR CONVERGENT?

In the blank before each question, place a "D" if you think the question is divergent, a "C" if you think it is convergent.

_____   1. What do you think I am going to do with this apparatus?

_____   2. What conclusions can you make from the data?

_____   3. Can anything else be done to improve the growth of the plants?

_____   4. Is heat an important factor in the experiment?

_____   5. Do you think the salt precipitated because the solution was cooled?

_____   6. Which of these three rocks is hardest?

_____   7. What can you tell me about the geology of this area from the picture?

_____   8. Would you say you have sufficient data?

_____   9. In what ways can you make the lights burn with the wire, switch, and power supply?

_____ 10. What things can you tell me about the biological make-up of this earthworm from your observations?

Which questions are the most convergent? What answers are possible for these questions? What words start these sentences? How would you change the sentences to make them more divergent?

ACTIVITY 17–5
CLASSIFYING QUESTIONS—TELEOLOGICAL OR ANTHROPOMORPHIC?

In the blank before each question, indicate whether the question is teleological (T) or anthropomorphic (A).

_____ 1. How do you think bacteria feel when ultraviolet light is shined on them?

_____ 2. Why does water seek its own level?

_____ 3. Why do plants seek the light?

_____ 4. Why will a body in motion want to stay in motion?

_____ 5. Why is the end of evolution to become increasingly more complex?

ACTIVITY 17–6
LEADING A DISCUSSION

Lead a small discussion and have someone check your wait time and how well you get students to talk to students instead of students to teacher to student.

ACTIVITY 17–7
SELF-EVALUATION INSTRUMENT FOR RATING YOUR QUESTIONING ABILITY

Lead a discussion and use a cassette tape recorder to record it. Read through the following questions. Then listen to the tape. Put a check mark in the blank before the statement for each time the action described in the statement occurred.

_____ 1. You asked what students knew about the topic before starting the discussion.

_____ 2. You asked a convergent question.

_____ 3. You developed student–student rather than teacher–student interaction.

_____ 4. You asked an effective question.

_____ 5. You reinforced an answer without saying that the response was correct.

_____ 6. You did not stop discussing a point when the right answer was given but asked students if there were other answers or further discussion.

_____ 7. You asked a question requiring science-process thinking (e.g., hypothesizing, designing an experiment, inferring).

_____ 8. You interrupted a student without giving the student proper time to complete the thought.

_____ 9. You paraphrased a student's statement to clarify or focus for others on the topics.

Conclude this activity by noting the following information for future reference.

_____ 1. Measure how many seconds on the average you waited for a response.

_____ 2. Measure how much class time (in seconds) you devoted to routine (e.g., roll taking, announcements), student activity, and teacher talk.

_____ Routine

_____ Student activity

_____ Teacher talk

_____ 3. Rate yourself as a listener:

1   2   3   4   5   6   7   8   9   10

Poor listener   Average   Good listener

_____ 4. Rate yourself as a questioner:

1   2   3   4   5   6   7   8   9   10

Poor questioner   Average   Good questioner

Evaluate your responses and list those things you most want to change in your teaching. Record and rate yourself again at a later date or have a student or aide do it and note your improvement.

ACTIVITY 17–8
READABILITY ANALYSIS

For the busy teacher or review committee selecting textbooks, a primary consideration is ease of use. Fortunately, one of the readability formulas, the Fry readability graph, is a simple tool which can be used by the average classroom teacher in selecting textbooks. It is a good exercise to try your hand at determining the readability of a textbook that you might use for your particular subject, to familiarize yourself with the difficulty and usefulness of such a formula. Remember, however, that the results are only approximate and largely dependent on the technical nature of the material being analyzed. Many of the readability formulas do not take into adequate consideration the technical nature of science subjects.

Fry's Readability Graph

The Fry graph is used for narrative and expository writing only; do not use it for poetry, dialogue, drama, or unusual styles of writing. The Fry graph assesses technical difficulty, not interest, style, or content.

Directions for using the readability graph

1. Select three 100-word passages from near the beginning, middle, and end of the book. For anthologies, average nine samples (three samples from each of three stories or essays).

2. Avoid samples from the beginnings and ends of chapters.

3. Include proper nouns (except for common names such as Dick or Sue) in your word count.

4. Count the total number of sentences in each 100-word passage (estimating to the nearest tenth of a sentence). Average these three numbers.

5. Count the total number of syllables in each 100-word sample. There is a syllable for each vowel sound; for example: *cat* (1), *blackbird* (2), *continental* (4). Don't be fooled by word size; for example: *polio* (3), *through* (1). Endings such as -y, -ed, -el, or -le usually make a syllable; for example: *ready* (2), *bottle* (2). Average the total number of syllables for the three samples.

6. Count numbers in figures (1973) as one syllable. If the number is written out, count it in full syllables.

7. Plot on the graph the average number of sentences per 100 words and the average number of syllables per 100 words. The point where these plots coincide designates the grade level. If your computation places the estimated reading level in the shaded area on the graph, start over again with different samples. (Plot these two points on the Fry graph shown as follows. What is the approximate grade difficulty level of this material?) Most plot points fall near the heavy curved line. Perpendicular lines mark off approximate grade-level areas.

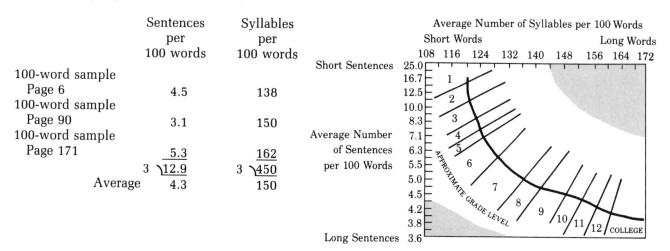

8. If the material has been translated from another language, add one year to the estimated reading level.

9. If the material was written before 1900, add one year to the estimated reading level.

10. If great variability is encountered either in sentence length or in the syllable count for the three selections, randomly select several more passages and compute their average before plotting.

EDUCATIONAL TECHNOLOGY IN THE SCIENCE CLASSROOM

The U.S. Department of Education (2004) reports "explosive growth in the availability of online instruction and virtual schools, complementing instruction with high quality courses tailored to the needs of individual students. Tests now can be taken online, giving students, teachers, and parents almost instant feedback . . . New student data management systems will greatly facilitate the collection and use of test, demographic and other data for more effectively designing and managing instructional programs" (p. 7).

"Yet, we have not realized the promise of technology in education. Essentially, providing the hardware without adequate training in its use—and in its endless possibilities for enriching the learning experience—meant that the great promise of Internet technology was frequently unrealized. Computers, instead of transforming education, were often shunted to a 'computer room,' where they were little used and poorly maintained. Students mastered the wonders of the Internet at home, not in school. *Today's students, of almost any age, are far ahead of their teachers in computer literacy*" [emphasis added] (p. 10).

In this chapter we do not attempt to provide a comprehensive review of all the options for incorporating educational technology into the science classroom. Instead we will provide an overview of the status of educational technology use in the United States and a brief review of the potential of technological tools in the science classroom. Although many forms of educational technology exist, we are emphasizing the role of computers because they are the most prevalent tool available in schools today.

The information presented in this chapter is shared with you, a beginning teacher, with the approach that you are more advanced in your use of technology than the more senior teachers with whom you will soon be working. As indicated in the quotation above, the Department of Education recognizes that students may be ahead of their teachers in their use of computers. We added italics to this statement because we heartily concur with this idea and believe it extends into the teaching profession—newer teachers are more likely to be far more proficient in their use of computers than more experienced teachers. A wise department chair or principal will take advantage of your expertise. If you are in a school that does not do this, we encourage you to be a leader in the use of educational technology.

The authors of *Benchmarks for Science Literacy* present science teachers with the dual challenge "to build technology education into the curriculum, as well as to use technology to promote learning, so that all students become well informed about the nature, power, and limitations of technology" (AAAS, 1993). Although many different tools, instruments, and machines should be encountered in science classes, nowhere is there a better opportunity to "build technology into the curriculum" and "use technology to promote learning" than through the use of computers.

This chapter on computers in science teaching has five main purposes. The first is to consider the status of computer and Internet use in schools.

The second purpose is to portray educational technology as an example of technology in general. Many educators have equated computers with technology.

In science education, however, it is important to consider the term *technology* much more broadly. Learning *about, with,* and *through* computers can help students to better understand how science, technology, and society interact.

The third purpose is to examine the multiple roles of educational technology in the science classroom. These roles include being a tool for collecting, analyzing, or presenting data; being a machine that provides learning experiences via software, simulations, CD-ROM, and videodiscs; and providing access to reference material and people beyond the school building by using the telecommunications applications available to science teachers and students today. The foundations in educational theory of each of these technologies and how and where they might be used in the science classroom will also be explored.

The fourth purpose is to review equity issues related to the use of computers in the science classroom. The fifth purpose is to consider the future of computers and Internet-based information in the science classroom.

STATUS OF COMPUTER AND INTERNET USE IN SCHOOLS

In 2006, the National Center for Educational Statistics released a report titled, *Internet Access in U.S. Public Schools and Classrooms: 1994–2005* (Wells & Lewis, 2006). This review of 10 years of changes in schools listed a number of key observations. In this chapter we share the findings. The main point of this information is to provide some context for the world in which you will enter when you take your first teaching position.

Key Points (Based on Data Collected in 2005 from Public Schools)

- Nearly 100 percent of public schools in the United States have access to the Internet. In 1994, this was true of only 35 percent of schools. Ninety-seven percent of the access is broadband and 45 percent of schools also have wireless access.
- Researchers found no differences in school Internet access by any school characteristics.
- The ratio of students to instructional computers with Internet access in public schools is 3.8 to 1. The ratio of students to instructional computers varied by all school characteristics. For example, small schools had better student-to-computer ratios than medium-size and large schools (2.4 to 1 compared with 3.9 to 1 and 4.0 to 1, respectively). In addition, schools with the lowest level of minority enrollment had better student-to-computer ratios than schools with higher minority enrollments.

- Nineteen percent of public schools provide hand-held computers (PDAs) to either students or teachers for instructional purposes. The overwhelming majority of school-provided PDAs are provided to teachers, not students.
- Ten percent of public schools lend laptop computers to students. In these schools, 47 percent report that students can borrow them for less than 1 week, 17 percent report that students can borrow them for a period of 1 week to less than 1 month, 16 percent report lending laptops for the entire school year, and 5 percent report lending laptops for some other maximum length of time.
- Of the 90 percent of schools without laptop computers available for loan to students, 3 percent are planning to make laptops available for students to borrow during the next school year.
- Eighty-three percent of public schools with Internet access indicate that their school or school district has offered professional development to teachers in their school on how to integrate the use of the Internet into the curriculum in the year prior to completing the survey.
- Eighty-nine percent of schools indicate they use the Internet to provide data to inform instructional planning at the school level.
- Eighty-seven percent of schools report using the Internet to provide assessment results and data for teachers to use to individualize instruction.
- Eighty-seven percent of schools report using high-quality digital content for teaching (i.e., learning materials brought in from the Web, such as digital libraries and museums, or any text, images, sounds, and video that have been digitized).
- Fifty-one percent report providing online professional development courses to teachers.
- Thirty-two percent provide access for students to online distance learning for courses that are otherwise unavailable at the school.

LEARNING *ABOUT, WITH,* AND *THROUGH* COMPUTERS

Modern science and modern technology are highly interactive, with science influencing technological developments, and technology, in turn, contributing to advances in science (Bybee et al., 1990). The impetus for technology is the problem of human adaptation to natural, constructed, and social environments. Through technological advances people are provided with new ways of adapting to and even shaping their surroundings. New technologies can make even more powerful technological innovations possible. Further, new instruments and techniques enable new observations of and scientific explanations about the world.

Science teachers still can facilitate student learning—about, through and with—computers.

The story of the development of computers provides many excellent examples of the interactions among technology, science, and society. The world's first electronic, digital computer was dedicated in 1946 (Boraiko, 1982). By the 1980s, computer technology had advanced from the 30-ton ENIAC computer to the microprocessor, a computer on a silicon chip made possible through progress in solid-state physics. Chips were thousands of times cheaper than the ENIAC, operated on the power of a night-light rather than that of 100 lighthouses, and could perform a million calculations a second, more than 200 times as many as ENIAC.

Although the data listed in the previous section indicates that we have met our goals as a country to have every classroom in America wired for Internet access by the year 2000, the more important question is whether these technological tools are being used effectively and how their educational potential can be maximized in the classroom (Songer, 1996).

Technology can greatly affect the job market, as well as the type of education that workers need. The multiple uses of computers in business and industry—such as in data processing, communications, robotics, and inventory and quality control—have resulted in the reduction or elimination of many jobs, particularly at the lower level. At the same time, a broad array of new occupations, demanding higher levels of cognitive functioning, have opened up. Because of the rapid pace of technological developments, workers need continual updating, as well as retraining every few years. It is more important than ever that education, particularly in science, mathematics, and technology, focus on real understanding of conceptual and principled knowledge and on the development of higher-order thinking, decision-making and problem-solving processes and strategies, and learning skills and attitudes that support lifelong learning.

Computers and Learning

Alan McKay, a researcher with Apple Corporation who has extensively explored the use of computers by children, has identified a number of potential benefits of using computers in education (1995). First, computers have the potential of providing instant access to any and all existing media. Texts, images, sounds, and movies can be readily accessed, manipulated, and placed in appropriate form to support learning through the use of word processors, desktop publishing, and multimedia systems. Second, and more important, computers can provide for great interactivity. For example, students can mold presentations to fit their own tastes, and ideas can be explored from many different perspectives. Third, computers can go beyond static representations to present dynamic simulations of attributes, processes, and relationships that can be used to test conflicting theories. Fourth, pervasively networked computers are fast becoming a universal library, offering resources once beyond the capacity of an individual computer (e.g., supercomputers for complex simulations, information being gleaned by satellites, and large compilations of data). In science classes the use of computers can demonstrate the course of technological progress, enrich instructional presentations, encourage students to become more active explorers of their environment, and significantly enhance curiosity and motivation—all of which lead to deeper understandings and improved thinking and problem-solving capabilities.

The uses of computers and associated technologies in science education might be placed into three categories:

1. Learning about computers
2. Learning through computers
3. Learning with computers

In learning about computers, students develop technological literacy. In the process of learning through computers, computers either take over or assist the teacher with various functions of instruction. In learning with computers, students use computers as a tool in data acquisition, analysis, and display; communication with other people; information retrieval; and the myriad other ways computers are used by research scientists, medical professionals, technicians, managers, and others in the workplace.

Learning About Computers

Activities in this category have generally been treated in relation to computer literacy—that is, to acquiring computer-related terminology, learning about the history and development of computers, understanding uses of the computer as a tool, learning to communicate instructions to the computer through simple programming, and learning about problems and issues related to the use of computers in society. In science classes, computer literacy should be considered to be merely one aspect of the more comprehensive goal of understanding technology and its relationships to science and society.

Learning With and Through Computers

One of the most difficult tasks in science teaching is to help students develop real conceptual understanding. In 1995, Joseph Snir, Carol Smith, and Lorraine Grosslight, researchers with Harvard University's Educational Technology Center, proposed the use of "conceptually enhanced computer simulations" to address the problem of teaching for conceptual understanding. Though their ideas are more than 10 years old, they are still consistent with learning theory today and highly relevant to thinking about the best use of technology in the classroom. The Educational Technology Center group has identified three levels of students' understanding of natural phenomena:

Level 1: Knowledge of facts and simple generalizations

Level 2: Conceptual and theoretical understanding

Level 3: Metaconceptual understanding

At the first level are directly observable facts and simple generalizations based on these facts. At the second level, students learn theories that enable the facts and simple generalizations learned at this level to be conceptualized and explained. These first two levels of understanding in Snir et al's model are similar to the levels of understanding addressed by the exploring and inventing phases in Karplus's learning cycle and the exploring and explaining phases in the 5E instructional model. The third level of understanding is a metacognitive, or metaconceptual, level in which students reflect about the basis of the level 2 conceptual relationships. At the third level of understanding, students must learn what a model is and how scientists develop and test models to help them understand phenomena.

In terms of the Harvard model, the problem in teaching for understanding is to help students make the transition from the concrete facts and empirical generalizations of level 1 to the conceptual and theoretical understandings of level 2. This transition is difficult for three main reasons. First, concepts and theories are abstract; they cannot be directly observed by the learner. Second, conceptual and theoretical understandings are complex, consisting of many aspects that must be held in mind simultaneously. Third, students already have their own misconceptions about the phenomenon, which can be almost impervious to change. In teaching for understanding, each of these three factors—the abstractness and complexity of concepts and theories and the misconceptions of students—must be addressed.

At the core of Snir et al's conceptually enhanced simulations are computer-generated visual representations of the abstract, unobservable concepts and complex relationships used in explaining a specific phenomenon. Students manipulate the visual analogue in the computer simulation in learning to think about the phenomenon conceptually. Thus, the visual representation serves as a bridge from the concrete to the conceptual level. Further, the visual representation is a kind of model, which helps students to think about the general problem of models in a more concrete way.

Examples of various applications of educational technology in science teaching are described and discussed in terms of learning and instruction models in the following sections.

ROLES OF EDUCATIONAL TECHNOLOGY IN THE CLASSROOM

In this brief overview of ways that educational technology is used in the classroom, we start with those options that are least complex and move to considerably more complex options. The complexity comes from both the role of the software and hardware interface and the role of the teacher and the learners.

Computer-Assisted Instruction

Computer-assisted instruction (CAI) is the use of a computer to provide course content and interactive instruction in a variety of forms. Main methods of CAI include drill and practice, simulations, and tutorials.

Drill and Practice

Drill and practice, a repetitive approach emphasizing rote memory, was an early form of CAI. An example of a drill and practice program in mathematics is *Space Mouse*, which is aimed at middle school and high school students. In the program the computer randomly generates problems related to the multiplication and division of fractions. If the student solves the problems correctly, he is rewarded by being allowed to fly a rare space mouse through a maze in a video game–type setting. Through enhanced motivation and ample practice afforded by the CAI program, learners improve their abilities to solve the type of problems presented. Software design has now gone well beyond the drill and practice stage; this form of CAI is rarely utilized today (Chambers & Sprecher, 1983).

Simulations and Tutorials

Many CAI programs combine tutorials and simulations. Tutorials use the computer in a traditional question-and-answer, dialogue-type format. Industry has long been using computers to simulate and explore complex phenomena and processes. Simulations provide a computer model of the attributes, concepts, and relationships in the real world.

In CAI simulations, the student plays an active role in manipulating various factors in the computer simulation to better understand real-world phenomena. Through the variation of various factors, the computer generates creative, perhaps even impossible, environments. The computer may, for example, permit time compression by condensing a great amount of data into a very short time frame, or it may expand the time base to allow longer looks at changes that take place within a short time span. It can produce graphic displays of processes at work and the effects of different variable factors on the processes. Simulations allow the effects of changes to be seen in a model before irrevocable changes are made in the real system. In this sense, minor or hypothetical risks can be taken without the cost or danger of carrying out the experiment in real life. Students using simulations are often forced to make decisions on the basis of incomplete data, and the results of these decisions can be seen quickly. This is excellent practice for the real world, in which important decisions frequently need to be made on the basis of meager information.

Computer sky simulations can be used in many ways in understanding sky relationships. For example, the rise and set times and azimuths (i.e., angular displacements toward the east from true north) of stars over the course of a year might be studied. Although the rise positions of stars are fixed over the short term of a few years, explorations with the planetarium simulator reveal that they vary systematically over the centuries, a consequence of the phenomenon known as precession, the slow wobbling of the earth's polar axis.

Microcomputer-Based Laboratories

A microcomputer-based laboratory (MBL) is a microcomputer equipped with a sensing probe for collecting data on physical phenomena in real time, and special software for recording and displaying the results (Ruopp & Pfister, 1993). For instance, temperature data might be collected with a temperature-sensing probe over a fixed time sequence, such as every five minutes, and the data converted into line graphs and data tables.

The powerful MBL tools for investigation have been available to students at the secondary level only since the mid-1980s. The Technical Education Research Center (TERC) in Cambridge, Massachusetts, has played a pivotal role in their development. Probes are available for measuring a wide variety of phenomena including the following: temperature, sound, light intensity, motion, atmospheric pressure, pH, EKG, EMG, heart rate, brain waves, humidity, wind speed, and wind direction. Commercial packages for computer-based laboratories are marketed by a variety of companies.

A goal of MBL instruction should be to increase students' intuitive feel for events and to build causal links between external events and the graphs (Kimball, 1993). Time for exploring the probes and finding out what they can tell us about the world is necessary in developing a general sense about what to expect for certain natural phenomena such as temperature changes over time. Writing about all aspects of an experiment and telling the story of the graph is a good way to help students build correlations between the world and the graph and to reveal what students are seeing and thinking. Used in this way, computer-based laboratories represent another way to help bridge between the concrete physical world and abstract conceptualizations.

Microcomputer-based laboratories provide for an almost unlimited range of traditional and new investigations by students. TERC researchers have emphasized the importance of using the probes in student science projects (Ruopp & Haavind, 1993). For example, a student might use a temperature probe to investigate the effects of adding ice cubes to drinks (Dublin, Pressman, Vaughn, 1994). In the investigation, an ice cube of a given mass might be added to a given volume of water at room temperature and the temperature of the water measured over an extended time. Using the graphing option of the MBL software, a line graph of the temperature versus time might be drawn and printed out. The investigation might focus on questions with consequences in daily life, such as:

- How quickly does the water temperature begin to change after an ice cube is added?
- How low can the temperature of water be brought with ice cubes?
- How many ice cubes (or what mass of ice) are needed to lower the water to 0°C? How does this depend on the volume of the water?
- What factors affect the rate at which the water is cooled by the ice? Do more ice cubes increase the rate? Does stirring the water help?
- What kind of container can keep water (without ice) at cold temperatures longer?

A project in environmental science might use a pH probe to explore the effect of acid rain on seed germination and plant growth. Water at different levels of acidity might be prepared and the pH measured with the sensor probe. The effect of water at different pH levels on the rate of germination of seeds and the growth rate and health of plants could then be explored. Additionally, the pH of soil that has been soaked with water at different pH levels might also be investigated.

Multimedia Presentations

Interactive multimedia is a collection of computer-centered technologies that give a user the capability to access and manipulate text, sounds, and images. Multimedia authoring software enables the user to control computer text, graphics, and sound, as well as external multimedia devices, including videodisc, audiodisc, and CD-ROM players.

Student-Developed Multimedia Presentations

In Frank Hinerman's high school biology class in Pennsylvania, as part of a course assignment students develop multimedia lessons on the DNA and RNA molecules using a special authoring system (1994). Working in cooperative groups of four, students develop a concept map on the topic, then break into groups of two to construct a flowchart. When the flowchart is completed, students go to the computer lab to complete their final project. Each of the student programs contains drawings, questions, and videodisc references. The DNA and RNA video images are taken from commercially available videodiscs in biology. According to Hinerman, the use of a multimedia application in instruction creates an active atmosphere in the classroom and fosters student enthusiasm and communication, as well as creativity and learning. Student presentations enable the elaborate linking of ideas that otherwise might remain isolated and separate.

Commercial Interactive Media Presentations

Interactive media presentations, combining the interactivity of the computer with images, sound, and music presented on videodisc, are available from various commercial sources. An example is the National Geographic Society's *Planetary Manager,* available from Glencoe Publishing. This production provides for an examination of the state of the earth, with students cast in the roles of planetary managers. Overviews of major environmental issues are featured on one side of the disc. Nine shows illustrate broad concepts such as the complexity of environmental issues and human impact on the environment. Eight shows on the other side of the disc focus on specific environmental topics, such as the complexity of environmental issues and human impact on the environment. The presentations feature the stunning photography and folksy communication style that characterize *National Geographic.*

As an example, a show on water pollution, "Shall We Gather at the River?" shifts the normal water pollution discussion away from faceless factories and industry out of control to the pollution that arises out of our own personal worlds. The narrator, in oratorical tones, framed by the faint background strains of the religious song from which the title is taken, emphasizes that all of the world's rivers come together (a watershed), and he traces the ills of the oceans, rivers, and aquifers to bad practices that arise out of everyday actions (water pollution). In dramatic fashion, still and moving pictures play out the story line simultaneously with the narration.

Along with the narration, captions and additional information about who, what, when, where, and why of each scene are available on the computer screen. Also, the interactivity of the computer allows the teacher or students to write their own captions or provide their own relevant information. Search features in the computer software enable the user to locate images on a variety of environmental topics, for example, fossil fuels. Still and moving pictures on the topic can be selected in any combination to create custom presentations to fit individual curriculums.

Network Projects

KIDS AS GLOBAL SCIENTISTS

The atmospheric science network project called *Kids As Global Scientists* (KGS) was developed originally by a team at the University of Colorado in collaboration with Weather Underground at the University of Michigan and now operates out of the University of Michigan. Middle school students study general weather topics such as wind, precipitation, temperature/pressure, and clouds/humidity collaboratively with students and professional meteorologists around the world. Students collect local weather data with weather instruments that are shared with students from various sites via email and, currently, a message board. A message board is a page online where students can post messages and others can respond to these messages. Students use real-time satellite imagery and investigate current weather phenomena locally and at distant locations by sharing and critiquing ideas and data. This model led to the development and pilot testing of a new series of projects called *One Sky, Many Voices*—projects centered around the investigation of severe weather topics such as hurricanes, blizzards, and tornadoes.

CoVis (www.covis.northwestern.edu/)

CoVis, the *Learning through Collaborative Visualization* project is based at Northwestern University. This project is designed to enable high school students to connect with practicing scientists and their scientific tools. The *CoVis* project team has developed software programs for students that facilitate the understanding and use of satellite weather imagery and communication tools. These software programs give students access to real-time satellite imagery, weather maps, and scientific data as well as provide tools for students to make their own weather forecasts with high-quality weather maps. Students use a collaboratory notebook to record project information as well as other communication tools such as a desktop video telephone system and a commercial screen sharing tool.

NGS Kids Network (www.terc.edu)

NGS Kids Network was launched in 1989 as a collaboration between TERC and the National Geographic Society, and funded in part by the National Science Foundation. This innovative telecommunications-based science program (grades 3 through 9) provides teachers with software, curriculum units, classroom materials, and equipment kits, and links classrooms across the nation in collaborative, hands-on, project-based investigations.

Hands-On Universe™ (www.terc.edu)

Hands-On Universe™ (HOU) is an educational program that enables high school students to do investigations in astronomy while applying tools and concepts from science, math, and technology. Using the Internet, program participants around the world request observations from a network of automated telescopes at astronomical observatories, download images, and use image processing software to visualize and analyze the data. Through the investigation of the solar system, galaxies, variable stars, and supernovae, students develop problem-solving techniques and critical-thinking skills. HOU is developing activities and tools for middle school students as well as continuing to implement HOU in high schools. TERC is working with the developers at the Lawrence Berkeley Lab to create curriculum, teacher enhancement materials, and activities for informal science education centers.

Globe (www.globe.gov)

The Global Learning and Observations to Benefit the Environment (GLOBE) project, initiated by Al Gore when he was vice president, elicits participation by students, teachers, and scientists around the world to monitor the global environment. Students take scientific measurements relevant to environmental issues near their schools such as temperature, precipitation, water temperature, and water pH. Students send their data to the GLOBE Student Data Archive via the Internet. The data are then tabulated and posted graphically on the World Wide Web. Practicing scientists and other students use the data to conduct research on environmental conditions.

GLOBE is an interagency program funded by the National Aeronautics and Space Administration (NASA) and the National Science Foundation (NSF), supported by the U.S. Department of State, and implemented through a cooperative agreement between NASA, the University Corporation for Atmospheric Research (UCAR) in Boulder, Colorado, and Colorado State University in Fort Collins, Colorado. GLOBE is a cooperative effort of schools in partnership with colleges and universities, state and local school systems, and nongovernment organizations. Internationally, GLOBE is a partnership between the United States and over 100 countries that manage and support their unique national and regional program infrastructure and activities.

Continuing Technological Education for Science Teachers

It is important for teachers to feel at ease with technological equipment, software, and information resources and be able to effectively integrate technology in instruction to improve student motivation and learning. One way of learning about available new technologies is to attend the annual national and area conventions of the NSTA and spend considerable time in the exhibit area. Virtually every supplier of educational technology for science will have a booth and a helpful staff to demonstrate products and to help you feel comfortable in working with them. Workshops, summer institutes, and college courses are also often available to help you learn to use new technologies. Nothing, however, can substitute for extended hands-on, trial-and-error exploration of computer-based materials individually or in a small group.

A set of technology-related objectives for teachers has been developed by the BSCS technology education project, ENLIST-MICROS. These objectives provide new and experienced science teachers with an excellent framework for establishing personal and professional development goals related to educational technology. The ENLIST-MICROS objectives are divided into three categories—general technological literacy, technology in education, and integrating technology in instruction, as follows:

General Technological Literacy
- Demonstrate an awareness of the major types and applications of technology, such as information storage and retrieval, simulation and modeling, and process control and decision making.
- Communicate effectively about technological equipment.
- Recognize that one aspect of problem solving involves a series of logical steps and that programming is translating those steps into instructions.

- Understand thoroughly that computers only do what they are instructed to do.
- Respond appropriately to common error messages when using software.
- Load and run a variety of software packages.

Technology in Education
- Demonstrate an awareness of technology usage and assistance in the field of education.
- Describe the ways technology can be used to learn *about* computers, to learn *through* computers, and to learn *with* computers.
- Describe appropriate uses for technology in education, including:
  - Computer-assisted instruction (simulation, tutorial, drill and practice)
  - Computer-managed instruction
  - Microcomputer-based laboratory
  - Problem solving
  - Word processing
  - Equipment management
  - Record keeping
- Value the benefits of technology in education.

Integrating Technology in Instruction
- Use technology to individualize instruction and increase student learning.
- Demonstrate appropriate uses of technology for basic skills instruction.
- Demonstrate ways to integrate the use of technology-related materials with other educational materials, including textbooks.
- Respond appropriately to changes in curriculum and teaching methodology caused by new technological developments.
- Plan for effective technology interaction activities for students (e.g., debriefing after a simulation).
- Locate commercial and public domain software for a specific topic and application.
- Use an evaluative process to appraise and determine the instructional worth of a variety of computer software.
- Voluntarily choose to integrate technology in instructional plans and activities.

SCIENCE, COMPUTING, AND EQUITY

The computing culture shares many similarities with the culture of science. Research indicates that computer technology is also viewed as a heavily masculine domain and that girls experience biased treatment by teachers, peers, parents, and course materials, which contributes to their lack of interest in the field when compared with boys (Mistler-Jackson & Songer, 2000; Schofield, 1995). When computer technology is used in the science classroom, as is becoming more commonplace, the combination of the science and computing cultures may compound these notions of masculinity and further alienate girls and others already disengaged from science. Much research has been conducted on students' responses to the use of computer technology in the classroom and evidence suggests that most students, both boys and girls, have positive attitudes toward computers.

In particular, research has shown that students enjoy the change from typical classroom instruction which using computers brings, and that so far there has not been a novelty effect in which interest has dissipated over time. Computer lab environments are typically more social and offer students more opportunities for personal control than the regular classroom environment, contributing to increased motivation. Collaborative Internet projects, in particular, offer unique opportunities that have been shown to positively affect student interest.

Gender differences in computer use at school are remarkably similar to gender differences noted in science classes. Boys tend to do the work while girls watch when in mixed-gender groups, or girls perform the secretarial tasks while the boys make project decisions. Girls in advanced high school computer science classes are few and far between and are often subject to more sexual harassment and isolation in these classes than in others. The higher ratio of boys to girls in these courses has been offered as an explanation for this occurrence. In one case study, the only girl who managed to interact respectfully with the boys in an advanced computer science class publicly denigrated her own abilities and fit accepted feminine images, such as saying "she was attractive, nice, and a cheerleader" (Hrabowski, 2002; Schofield, 1995).

The gender equity literatures in science and computer technology share common goals. The works examine how the cultures of scientific and computer technology communities create climates that are open and closed to different groups of people. They contend that cultural barriers, not innate or biological differences, are responsible for disparities in achievement and participation. Today, both pieces of literature suggest that it is not the girls who need to catch up with science or computers, but that science and computers need to catch up with them. In other words, girls' legitimate concerns should focus attention on changing the software and curricula, pedagogy, and goals for science and computer technology education. A successful transformation would enable more women and other reticent groups to be able to visualize themselves as legitimate participants and those fields as interesting and meaningful. The pieces of literature share the belief that increasing the participation of women in scientific and computer professions will benefit the fields by bringing in more diverse perspectives. Both argue that changing educational practices, curricula, and culture will ultimately benefit both the "haves" and "have-nots" by creating more opportunities for engagement, and will not eliminate what has worked for those already engaged (American Association of University Women [AAUW], 2004).

THE FUTURE OF COMPUTER AND INTERNET USE IN SCHOOLS

The report from the Office of Educational Technology (U.S. Department of Education, 2004) makes seven recommendations for continuing to improve the use of educational technology in schools. The majority of the recommendations are targeted at parts of the public school system that do not directly involve teachers such as states, districts, and school personnel responsible for technology infrastructure. One of the seven recommendations could profoundly impact teachers because it is focused on the nature of curriculum and instruction, a move toward digital content.

Move Toward Digital Content

A perennial problem for schools, teachers and students is that textbooks are increasingly expensive, quickly outdated and physically cumbersome. A move away from reliance on textbooks to the use of multimedia or online information (digital content) offers many advantages, including cost savings, increased efficiency, improved accessibility, and enhancing learning opportunities in a format that engages today's web-savvy students.

Recommendations to states and districts include:

◆ Ensure that teachers and students are adequately trained in the use of online content.
◆ Encourage ubiquitous access to computers and connectivity for each student.
◆ Consider the costs and benefits of online content, aligned with rigorous state academic standards, as part of a systemic approach to creating resources for students to customize learning to their individual needs (p.43).

It is highly probably that during your teaching career you will participate in a shift away from the curriculum being defined by textbooks. Today's learners are ready for more interactive, highly visual, nonlinear forms of instruction. The integration of online content, computer-based imagery, and multimedia tools with more traditional forms of instruction is the beginning of this shift. As a new teacher and someone who probably uses technology regularly, you are poised to lead this transition. As you do so, be sure that your decisions about when and how to incorporate technology-based options are informed by what the students need to learn and which strategies and tools make that learning most effective for the majority of students.

In 2001, those attending the National Conference on the Revolution in Earth and Space Science Education developed a report emphasizing the role of technology in science education, with a strong emphasis on earth and space science. The authors of this report emphasized that students have access to many of the same tools that scientists use and this access can improve the authenticity of the students' experience in the science classroom. Examples of the tools available to students include the following: visualization software, geographic information systems (GIS), and the digital camera onboard the International Space Station. In addition, Internet access makes it possible to bring scientific images and data from sources such as earth-orbit satellites, Martian probes, deepwater marine expeditions, and other schools around the world into classrooms.

The authors note, (DOE, 2004) "Education technologies are strategic resources that enhance students' ability to sense, measure, question, understand, communicate, and learn. They empower students to learn as active scientists rather than as passive consumers of textbook-based curricula. They enable students to learn core concepts more clearly by offering visual representations of ideas that otherwise might seem confusing or unclear. They transform science from canned labs and the passive memorization of content to a dynamic, hands-on, authentic process of investigation and discovery. By using the same technologies as scientists, students acquire vital process skills and deepen their understanding of science. Additionally, they familiarize themselves with many of the same tools and processes that they will encounter as adults, particularly in the workplace."

It is this vision of legitimate science occurring in the secondary science classroom that makes the investment in educational technology worthwhile. If we are going to use computers as glorified worksheets that provide novel mechanisms to review terms and definitions, then we should save our money for something else. But if science teachers bring the universe—literally and through data—to their students, then we have made a worthwhile investment in educational technology. Use Activity 18–1: Reviewing Educational Technology Materials and Systems, to further your understanding.

SUMMARY

This chapter, at best, is introductory. You will need to expend considerable effort throughout your career in learning about and keeping up with the latest advances in educational technology. How successfully the new educational technologies will be integrated into the science classroom to develop technological understanding and to promote science learning among future generations of students will depend on you, the science teacher.

Computers in the classroom do not represent a cure-all for science education problems but should be seen as complementary to other approaches to teaching science. Computers are tools that you can use to vary your instruction. The ubiquitous access to the World Wide Web in schools and homes is a trend that science teachers can capitalize on when considering how to individualize instruction. The role of computers as an instructional aid has changed dramatically in the last 20 years, and the true power of the computer lies in two areas: providing nonlinear, highly visual options to help students develop conceptual understandings, and providing authentic scientific information and experiences.

INVESTIGATING SCIENCE TEACHING

ACTIVITY 18–1
REVIEWING EDUCATIONAL TECHNOLOGY MATERIALS AND SYSTEMS

Examine and evaluate several CAI programs, multimedia presentation systems, or online projects available to you. Using a computer, perhaps with a partner, study the teacher guide accompanying the materials, load the software, and work your way through the instructional phases of the materials. Evaluate the programs or systems in terms of the following questions.

1. What are the instructional goals of the program or package?
2. What is the quality of the graphics and text in the program or package?
3. How easy is the program or package to use?
4. Which phases of BSCS's 5E constructivist model of instruction are provided for or utilized in the program or package?
5. How would you integrate the program or system into your science classes?

UNIT 7

UNDERSTANDING STUDENTS

For several decades, the issue of equity in science classes has received attention but little action. Beginning in the 1990s, science educators rallied to the slogan, "Science for All Students," as this was a prominent theme in *Science for All Americans* (AAAS, 1989), *Benchmarks for Science Literacy* (AAAS, 1993), and the *National Science Education Standards* (NRC, 1996). Embracing science for all students means that science teachers will have to translate general ideas such as "all students can learn" and "all students can participate in science activities" into actual classroom practices.

Whether the discussion centers on helping girls succeed in science (Milne & Ransome, 1993), multicultural education (Atwater, 1994; Banks, 1993; Madrazo & Hounshell, 1993), disabilities (Roberts & Bazler, 1993), or differing levels of literacy, the unifying value that science teachers should recognize is equity. Equity in this case means that all students, regardless of gender, race, ethnicity, or disability, will have access to high-quality science education programs and fair opportunities and treatment in science classrooms. Equity in science classrooms also means that students develop an understanding of views and perspectives of groups and cultures other than their own. It is certainly the case that science teachers must maintain a balance among the unique perspectives of individuals, common values and ideals of society, and the defining characteristics of science. Science, mathematics, and engineering have been spheres predominately dominated by white males from middle- or upper-level economic settings. The issue now is not recitation of past sins but a remedy that informs and improves future practices. As a beginning teacher, what do you need to know and do to implement the goal of science for all students in your classroom? Chapter 19 focuses on issues related to various special needs that individual learners may have. Chapter 20 looks at a bigger picture by examining the research about female students and nonwhite learners and the challenges brought on by the variable literacy levels of students in your classroom. The implications of this research are easiest to apply when you think of your class as a multicultural environment. Chapter 21 turns to the practical matters of attending to classroom management and conflict resolution. To work with *all* the students in your classroom, you will need to synthesize the information in all three chapters, consider each child as an individual, and then try different combinations of ideas and strategies with each learner to help bring out his or her best every day.

Banks (1994) says that multicultural education "tries to create equal educational opportunities for all students by ensuring that the total school environment reflects the diversity of groups in classrooms, schools, and the society as a whole." He goes on to point out that in this environment students learn to form knowledge for themselves. Another way to think about a multicultural environment is to consider what type of environment facilitates the internalization of a value system that helps those who feel disempowered to do or learn science become aware, knowledgeable, and empowered for change.

Therefore, a multicultural environment is one in which the diversity of the people in the environment is celebrated and used to improve the quality and quantity of learning that takes place. This environment can be an informal setting such as a neighborhood, community center, or a local park, or it can be a more formal setting such as a church, school, or city government. In this unit, we will limit the discussion to multicultural environments in the school setting. We will discuss general strategies for developing multicultural environments and look at some of the learning characteristics of different cultures.

INDIVIDUAL DIFFERENCES IN SCIENCE CLASSROOMS

A great diversity of students come to science classes. They come from urban, suburban, and rural environments; they come from poor, middle-class, and affluent homes. Some can read, others cannot; some are interested in science, others are not. Some are gifted, some are slow, and most are average. The list could go on and on. In fact, if we started a classification system, it could continue until we described each individual in each school. Saying that each student is a unique individual is to state the obvious. Few teachers disagree, in principle, with the logical educational implication of such a statement—namely, all students require individual attention and opportunities to learn.

EXCEPTIONAL STUDENTS IN EDUCATION: A RATIONALE

Of the many issues that educators face in the future, perhaps one of the most encompassing is that of a right to education for *all* students. In the late 1970s, attention was focused on the educational rights of students who were traditionally placed in restricted, special-education programs. One result of this movement is the recognition of individual differences and the conclusion that has been clear to many teachers for a long time—all students are exceptional.

All educators stand to gain from having exceptional students in science classrooms. Although it is only natural to expect some initial hesitation, frustration, or fear on the part of students and teachers alike, once these feelings pass, the gains are clear: Exceptional students encounter a whole new range of educational opportunities; all students learn that in terms of basic human needs and wants, exceptional students are not very different from themselves; and teachers become more sensitive to the realities of different learning styles, subtleties of instruction, and modifying curricula to meet students' personal needs. In the end, we all learn more about what it means to be human.

Aside from the points made in the preceding paragraph, there is another reason for having exceptional students in science classrooms: It is the just thing for science teachers to do. We have a responsibility to provide the best science program for all of our students. Science teachers know that students have unique needs that are not fulfilled by curriculum materials alone. An essential task for science teachers is accommodating our programs and teaching to the needs of students, not to making students adapt to our science programs and teaching strategies.

EXCEPTIONAL STUDENTS IN SCIENCE PROGRAMS: THE LAW

Appeals to personal and professional benefit and to justice do not completely convince teachers of the need to include exceptional students in the science classroom. The most immediate and forceful argument seems to be the law. We have a legal responsibility to include exceptional students in the mainstream of school programs.

One of the first laws that included protection of the rights of exceptional students was the Rehabilitation Act of 1973, Public Law 93-112, Section 504, which states:

> No otherwise qualified handicapped individual in the United States . . . shall, solely by reason of his handicap, be excluded from participation in, be denied the benefits

of, or be subjected to discrimination under any program or activity receiving federal financial assistance.

Since most, if not all, school systems receive federal financial assistance under this law, exceptional students must be allowed to participate in, receive the benefits of, and have open access to educational programs.

Other federal legislation that included safeguards concerning the rights of exceptional students was Public Law 93-380, the Education Amendments of 1974. This law mandated due process procedures at the state and local levels for the placement of exceptional students, ensured placement of exceptional students in the least restrictive environment, and set a goal of providing full educational opportunities for all handicapped students within each state. Public Law 94-142, the Education for All Handicapped Children Act of 1975—the regulation with which most U.S. school personnel are probably familiar—requires that exceptional students be integrated into regular classrooms when possible.

It is the purpose of this Act to assure that all handicapped children have available to them . . . a free appropriate public education which emphasizes special attention and related services designed to meet their unique needs, to assure that the rights of handicapped children and their parents or guardians are protected, to assist states and localities to provide for the education of all handicapped children, and to assess and assure the effectiveness of efforts to educate handicapped children.

Specifically, Public Law 94-142 requires the following of school personnel:

1. *Zero rejection.* No student may be rejected from a free public education and related services. Court cases, such as *Pennsylvania Association for Retarded Children v. Commonwealth of Pennsylvania*, 334 F. Supp. 1257 (E. D. PA, 1971), and *Mills v. Board of Education of the District of Columbia*, 348 F. Supp. 886 (D. D. C., 1972), have resulted in a legal commitment to the public schools for the education of all school-age students. That all students have a "right to education, regardless of their present level of functioning" results in a principle of zero rejection. You also should note that education is defined as the development of students from their present level to the next appropriate level. In brief, the assumption is that all students are educable.

2. *Classification and placement.* Evaluation of students shall be nondiscriminatory. Diagnostic and assessment procedures are to be established by each state to ensure that cultural and racial bias are not evident in the system used for identifying exceptional students. Tests shall be a fair evaluation of the student's strengths and weaknesses.

3. *Appropriate education.* This stipulation is a requirement for an Individualized Education Program (IEP). An IEP should have statements concerning the student's present level of performance, how the student will participate in the regular educational program, the type of special services needed, the date special services were initiated, and the expected length of services. In addition, the IEP should set short- and long-term minimum standards, measures of achievement, and an evaluation of educational progress that includes a conference among school personnel, parents, and the exceptional student.

4. *Least restrictive placement.* To the maximum extent possible, exceptional students will be educated with all other students. "Least restrictive placement" means that exceptional students should be educated in the "mainstream," the regular educational environment. They can be educated in special programs when the nature or severity of their handicap requires such treatment.

5. *Due process.* The exceptional student (usually through parents or a guardian) has a right to question testing and placement; that is, exceptional students are guaranteed procedural safeguards in the placement and provision of special services.

6. *Parental participation.* Parents of the exceptional student have the right to be present for their child's evaluation, placement, and development of the IEP.

Public Law 101-476 was passed in 1990 to reauthorize P.L. 94-142. This reauthorization accomplished several things, including changing the name of the law to the Individuals with Disabilities Education Act (IDEA), with the purpose of reflecting a more contemporary philosophy. Rather than focusing on handicapped people, the language was changed to emphasize the *individuals* with disabilities and send a "person-first" message. The reauthorization upheld the major provisions of the original law, but added provisions for very young children with disabilities, added students with traumatic brain injuries and those with autism, and for students preparing to leave secondary school. The transition services are designed to make sure disabled students who are leaving high school receive assistance when finding a job or attending vocational school or a university or college. P.L. 101-476 emphasized inclusion of *all* students, even those with severe disabilities (Friend & Bursuck, 1996).

Public Laws 93-112, 93-380, 94-142, and 101-476 stand on fundamental principles guaranteed in the Constitution. Exceptional students have been systematically excluded from many educational programs, which, in essence, has been a violation of the constitutional rights of approximately 35 million Americans. The Fourteenth

Amendment guarantees equal protection under the law for all Americans. Recall that the *Brown v. Board of Education of Topeka*, 347 U. S. 483 (1954) overturned the earlier "separate but equal" ruling of *Plessy v. Ferguson*, 163, U. S. 537 (1896). It is instructive to read the *Brown v. Board* decision and make appropriate changes in the wording, such as *disabled* or *challenged* for *Negro* or *race*, and *classroom* for *school*. Separate educational facilities for some students are, by definition, unequal; thus, exceptional students have been deprived of the equal protection of the laws guaranteed by the Fourteenth Amendment of our Constitution.

Of these laws, Public Law 94-142 was probably the most significant piece of educational legislation of the 1970s, and its effect will continue to be felt into the twenty-first century. There are several reasons for this fact. First, Public Law 94-142 incorporates parts of the other laws and clarifies the fundamental right of all students to an education. Second, because it is a federal law, it establishes the right to education as a national priority. Third, Public Law 94-142 commits us to recognize individual differences and to appropriate educational programs for all students because it is permanent legislation with no expiration date. This fact demonstrates the importance Congress placed on this legislation.

RACIAL INEQUITIES IN SPECIAL EDUCATION

Minority students are overrepresented in public school special-education programs and underrepresented in gifted education programs. African American students are one and one half to four times more likely to be identified as mentally retarded or emotionally disturbed. Native American students tend to be overrepresented in categories related to cognitive disabilities. Asian American students are typically underrepresented in special education and well represented in gifted education. Even more disturbing is that students of color are more often placed in a restrictive, substantially separate setting. As elaborated in Chapter 20, the low expectations that teachers have for students of color is part of the problem in special-education placements as well as in regular classroom settings (Losen & Orfield, 2002).

GUIDELINES FOR EXCEPTIONAL STUDENTS IN SCIENCE CLASS

Teachers' concerns are not in understanding why exceptional students should be in science classrooms, but in dealing with the fact that they are in our classrooms. Therefore, the problems may be stated: What can be done to provide the best science education program

possible? What are the first steps? What should I do now? The following sections address these questions. The ideas about teaching exceptional students have been synthesized from many sources and should give you some information, confidence, and direction in working with exceptional students. We write with the assumption that all teachers will do their best to be responsive to the pedagogical needs of all students. Students with disabilities may have unique educational needs and you may receive direction regarding academic adjustments and accommodations through IEPs and Section 504 plans for specific students. In the long run, you can benefit all of your students best by thinking about the broad range of abilities, disabilities, and other characteristics of potential students as you design your curriculum. This approach is called universal design of instruction. See http://www.washington.edu/doit/Brochures/Academics/instruction.html for details about universal design.

In addition, you can do simple, straightforward things to help most students. Certainly, there are unique problems in integrating any exceptional student into the science classroom. You can anticipate personal tension and educational problems during the period of adjustment. Understandably, we cannot provide suggestions that will cover all situations. Nevertheless, some approaches have proved helpful with most exceptional students.

General Guidelines for Helping Exceptional Students

- Obtain and read all the background information available on the student.
- Spend time educating yourself on the physical and/or psychological nature of the student's exceptionality and how it affects the student's potential for learning.
- Determine whether special help is available to you through the resources of experts within and outside the school system.
- Determine any special equipment needed by the student.
- Talk with the student about limitations and particular needs in the science class.
- Use resource teachers and aides to assist you.
- Establish a team of fellow teachers (including resource teachers and aides) to share information and ideas about the school's exceptional students. A team approach is helpful in overcoming initial fears and the sense of isolation in dealing with the student. You may need to take responsibility for contacting appropriate school personnel and establishing the team; if so, have courage and do it.

Effective teachers work to individualize their instruction to meet the needs of each learner.

♦ Other students are often willing to help exceptional students. Encourage them to do so.

♦ Be aware of barriers, both physical and psychological, to the fullest possible functioning of each student.

♦ Consider how to modify or adapt curriculum materials and teaching strategies for exceptional students without sacrificing content, processes, or activities.

♦ Do not underestimate the capabilities of exceptional students. Teachers' perceptions of students' abilities have a way of becoming self-fulfilling prophecies. If these perceptions are negative, they may detrimentally affect students and your ability to create new options for them.

♦ Use the same standards of grading and discipline for exceptional students as you do for the rest of the class.

♦ Develop a trusting relationship with all students.

♦ Educate the other students about exceptionality in general, as well as about specific handicaps of students in their class.

Auditorially Challenged Students

From an early age, most children learn through listening—and there is every indication that most teaching is through telling. So, it becomes quite difficult for students with hearing problems; science teachers have to adjust. Hearing impairment is defined as an auditory problem that may adversely affect the student's educational performance. Students with hearing impairments often have developmental delays in speech and language. These delays have obvious effects on the ability to communicate. Students with hearing impairments will not necessarily have problems acquiring science concepts, although they may have difficulty learning the written or oral language to communicate their understanding.

Helping Auditorially Challenged Students Learn Science

1. Individuals with hearing impairments depend heavily on visual perception. Therefore, seat the student for optimal viewing.

2. Determine whether an interpreter will be needed and the nature of the student's speech/language problems.

3. Learn the student's most effective way of communicating.

4. Find the student a listening helper.

Visually Challenged Students

Like students with hearing impairments, students with visual impairments are those whose vision is limited enough to require adaptations in materials and strategies. Students who can read material with the use of magnifying devices and/or enlarged print are classified as partially seeing. Students who require Braille or taped materials are classified as educationally blind.

Helping Visually Challenged Students Learn Science

- Students with visual impairments learn through sensory channels other than vision, primarily hearing. Therefore, seat students for optimal listening.
- Determine from the student what constitutes the best lighting.
- Change the room arrangement when necessary, but always make a special effort to reorient the student.
- Allow the student to manipulate tangible materials, models, and, when possible, real objects. Do not unduly protect students from materials.
- Speak aloud what you have written on the board and charts.
- Use the student's name; otherwise, the student may not know when he or she is being addressed.
- Since smiles and facial gestures might not be seen, touching is the most effective means of reinforcing the student's work.
- Be aware of eye fatigue. This fatigue can be overcome by varying activities, using good lighting, and providing close visual work.
- Have the student use visual capacity when possible (unless otherwise directed).

Physically Challenged Students

Students with physical and health impairments represent a diverse group of special needs, for this category includes students with allergies, asthma, arthritis, amputations, diabetes, epilepsy, cerebral palsy, spina bifida, and muscular dystrophy. Some are mobile and others are confined to wheelchairs; some have good use of their limbs and others do not. Some have a single condition and some have multiple disabilities. The range of needs is such that some can work in the regular science classroom with little or no problem, whereas others require full-time care.

Helping Physically Challenged Students Learn Science

- Eliminate architectural barriers.
- Become familiar with the basic mechanics and maintenance of braces, prostheses, and wheelchairs.
- Understand the effects of medication on students and know the prescribed dosage.
- Obtain special devices, such as pencil holders or reading aids, for students who need them.
- Learn about the symptoms of special health problems and appropriate responses.

Speech and Language Challenged Students

Until recently, classroom teachers had more contact with students with speech and language impairments than with any others with disabling conditions. This situation may still be true in most schools, but learning disabilities programs are growing rapidly. Speech and language disabilities that you might encounter are articulation (the most common problem), dyslexia, delayed speech, voice problems, and stuttering. In addition, students with other disabilities, such as cleft palate, cerebral palsy, and hearing loss, may have speech and language problems.

Helping Speech and Language Challenged Students Learn Science

- Help the student become aware of the problem; students must be able to hear their own errors.
- Incorporate and draw attention to newly learned sounds in familiar words.
- Know what to listen for and match appropriate remedial exercises with the student's problem.
- Be sure your speech is articulated; students often develop speech and language patterns through modeling.

Students with Learning Disabilities and Mild Mental Disabilities

Because the difference is too technical to summarize here, suffice to say there is a distinction between learning disabilities and mild mental disabilities. Students with mild mental disabilities should be identified only through the use of multiple criteria. Classroom teachers may observe indications of mental disabilities in a student's social interaction, general intelligence, emotional maturity, and academic achievement. In contrast, students with learning disabilities show a significant discrepancy between their achievements and the apparent ability to achieve. The problem is manifest as a disorder of learning and not mental ability. Science teachers may observe learning disabilities in the areas of arithmetic, listening, reading, spelling, logical thinking, speaking, and writing.

Helping Learning Disabled and Mentally Challenged Students Learn Science

- Listen closely so you can understand the student's perception and understanding of concepts and procedures.
- Use an individualized approach based on the student's learning style, level of understanding, and readiness.
- Use multisensory approaches to learning: visual, auditory, kinesthetic, and tactile.
- Find and use the student's most refined sensory mode to aid in development of mental capacities.
- Make use of the students' strengths and work on diminishing their deficiencies.
- Since many exceptional students have short attention spans, reduce or control interruptions.

- Stay within the students' limits of frustration. Rely on your judgment, not the level of curriculum materials.
- Begin conceptual development at a sensory-motor or concrete level, and work toward more abstract levels.
- Work on speech and language development.
- Help students to develop self-esteem; a good, firmly grounded self-concept is essential to their continued development.

Emotionally Challenged Students

Students who are emotionally challenged probably cause the greatest concern and frustration for science teachers. As it turns out, they also are the ones who have been in science classrooms all along. Emotionally challenged and disruptive students show behavior that ranges from mild, attention-getting pranks to violent assault. They also may demonstrate withdrawn behavior ranging from mildly withdrawn to clinically depressed and suicidal. Other examples of behavior that teachers might identify as disturbed or disruptive include regression, fears and phobias, chronic complaints of pains and illness, aggressiveness, overdependence, social isolation, perfectionism, excessive dieting, obesity, chemical dependency, defiance, and vandalism.

The student's behavior may be a result of forces within or from the environment. The first may be either physiological or psychological in origin. Environmental factors might include violence in the home, school pressures, and/or social problems. In some cases, schools and teachers may contribute to the development of disruptive behaviors, in the form of extreme emphasis on grades, teacher comments, harsh and punitive treatment, unwarranted social comparison, unrealistic physical and academic requirements, and teacher conversations about student behavior that in turn become fulfilled prophecies when other teachers have the same student.

Helping Emotionally Challenged Students Learn Science
- Spend time with students when they are not being disruptive.
- Make rules reasonable and clear.
- Provide realistic, reasonable, and appropriate consequences if rules are broken.
- Disruptive behavior ranges from low levels at which a student may merely be looking for attention or recognition through a spectrum that ends in rages, tantrums, or complete withdrawal. Always try to be alert to behaviors that, though minimally disruptive, could become more serious problems.
- Avoid personal confrontations or situations that provoke troubled students.

- Make directions for assignments, class work, and laboratory procedures direct, clear, and complete.
- Be aware of and prepare for transitional times in the classroom.
- Provide troubled students with success experiences.
- Resolve conflicts by talking about specific behaviors, reasoning, and involving the student in the problem-solving process. Once a course toward aggressive or uncontrolled behavior begins, it is hard to stop.
- Convey your intention to help resolve the problem mutually: "We have a problem here, and we are going to resolve it."
- If behavior problems escalate, try to talk about the process while providing solutions to the problem. For example, "We are both getting angry; can't we settle this calmly?" or "I see you are upset; let's try to solve the problem."
- Avoid using comparison, embarrassment, ridicule, and unwarranted threats to change behavior.

Academically Unsuccessful Students

Students who are academically unsuccessful have normal abilities and do not have significant physical or psychological disabilities, yet they are below their expected level of achievement. Their challenges may be caused by such things as extreme poverty, a home environment that does not encourage learning, poor reading abilities, diminished self-concept, negative attitudes toward school, and language problems due to a first language other than English. In the past, these students were labeled culturally deprived, slow learners, economically disadvantaged, and underachievers. We have used the words "academically unsuccessful" to suggest that the science teacher's attention should be directed toward the educational problems and their remediation or resolution, not to the student's culture, home, or economic condition. The role of the science teacher is to help these students overcome their educational problems and continue their development. It is neither to identify a cause for the problem nor to excuse one's self from important educational goals, such as developing scientific literacy.

Helping Academically Unsuccessful Students Learn Science
- Identify the educational problem (e.g., reading) and concentrate on resolving this problem.
- Convey your expectations for achievement within a realm of reasonable possibilities for the student.
- See that physiological, physical, and psychological needs are fulfilled.
- Use concrete learning experiences, such as the laboratory.
- Provide experiences where the student will succeed.

GUEST EDITORIAL ◆ ELIZABETH KARPLUS

Special Education Campolindo High School,
Moraga, California

SCIENCE FOR EXCEPTIONAL STUDENTS

Every science teacher is familiar with the case of Albert Einstein who failed mathematics as a young student because he could not memorize and had a nonverbal style of thinking. Or, they have heard of Thomas Edison, who was declared mentally retarded and whose mother taught him at home because she did not believe he was stupid.

Einstein and Edison are not just special isolated cases. I remember Alan, a very tall, skinny, slightly stooped, dark-haired student. In high school, he carried all of his books and papers in total disarray in a large backpack. As a child, he had been diagnosed as dyslexic, dysgraphia, and dyscalculic at the California State Diagnostic School for the Neurologically Handicapped. This diagnosis was based on his profound problems with orientation in time and space, mild cerebral palsy evidenced in shaking hands, poor coordination, and poor throat-muscle control (and, therefore, poor speech). He was very distracted by the sensory stimuli around him and unable to attend selectively because he could not decide which signal of many was the important one for the current task.

After diagnosis, he was placed in a self-contained class for the learning disabled, where remedial mathematics and reading were begun by a loving woman. He ran away from school. The drill on symbols and phonics frustrated him because he was unable to get meaning from them in isolation. What he needed was an awareness that the events in the world, including symbols, were consistent and made sense and that the symbols were only useful in helping to describe that sense. He needed hands-on experiences where he could observe what happened. He needed contact with ideas and with other bright students who could discuss those ideas, since reading about them was so difficult. Alan needed to learn to sequence his symbols (writing 73, not 37, when he meant seven tens and three units) and sequence directions according to the meaning or the expected result rather than trying to remember them in step-by-step detail since his memory was so poor. He needed taped textbooks so that he could listen to them to get information. He needed to ask "why" and "what." He needed the

encouragement of accepting teachers who weren't dismayed by his poor writing or his unusual approaches to problems. Those teachers, in turn, often needed to reword their explanations as class work became increasingly abstract, because words never carried quite the same meaning for him that they did for most of the class.

It was in the science classes that he had the greatest triumphs, and it was the activities in these classes that provided the best environment for him to learn from his mistakes and to monitor his own learning, developing a style of learning he could apply to other subject areas. He went on to major in physics at a California State University—a modern success story.

Learning-disabled students, such as Alan, need science or other activity courses (shop, home economics, arts, crafts) as much or more than nondisabled students. In science classes, the students themselves can control variables, change conditions, observe results, and learn to discriminate between variables that affect the outcome of the experiment and those that do not.

The science classes can provide exposure to new equipment and ideas in a hands-on setting. New learning can be firmly embedded in a situational context so that it is easier to remember and reapply. Old learning can be applied in new situations so that concepts are refined. Language usage itself can be refined and vocabulary increased. Science activities are filled with opportunities to measure along, around, through, diagonally, up, and down. The student can easily distinguish among thin, narrow, short, light, and weak, and learn when each is an appropriate replacement for "little." Position and direction are encoded in the prepositions *in, out, among, under, over, between, by,* and *up,* as well as in adjectives such as *contiguous* or nouns such as *circuit, test tube,* or *beaker.*

In science classes, instructions make sense and are usually monitored by the progress of the experiment, not by remembering an a priori order. You cannot filter a precipitate before the two interacting solutions have been mixed. If you haven't connected the battery, the bulb will not light. Most importantly, the student learns that failures do not represent disaster but are useful as sources of new information. The creative teacher can use each failure of an experiment, each mismeasurement, to help the student to a new understanding of the phenomenon.

As the science teacher of the learning-disabled student, you must observe two cautions. Take special pains to recognize the learning-disabled student's preferred sensory channels (visual-reading; auditory-listening; kinesthetic-demonstration) for information input and preferred channels for output or reporting understandings to you (visual-writing or diagrams; auditory-oral speech; kinesthetic-demonstration). You also may need to change your preferred methods of presentation to match the student's methods; otherwise, the student may not be able to understand the lesson or you may not be able to discover how much the student has actually learned. In my classes, we often read test questions or put laboratory instructions and text on cassette tapes so that the student may listen and understand rather than read and misunderstand.

Sometimes, it is necessary to change laboratory setups to make them more usable for students, particularly the physically handicapped, whose movements may be jerky or ill defined. Equipment can be clamped tightly to the desk or otherwise anchored. Special laboratory measuring devices are available for the blind or deaf, and they are often useful to the learning-disabled student, who can then use more than one sense and thus monitor his or her own collecting of accurate information.

Science classes are for everyone, including the learning-handicapped student. Learning science involves attention, reasoning, and questioning skills that are of constant value throughout life. Learning science can bring great satisfaction to the learning-disabled high school student, because it is an important academic discipline and because he or she can develop skills so necessary for self-esteem in these classes. We owe these students their chance to learn how to learn—a skill most easily taught through well-designed science experiments.

♦ Eliminate educational approaches that have not worked and try something new.
♦ Give recognition to talents the student does have.
♦ Approach the educational impairment with an attitude of, "When you are in science, we are going to work on this."
♦ Provide time, materials, and experiences within the learning capabilities of the student.
♦ Adapt instruction and the curriculum to the student, not the reverse.

GIFTED AND TALENTED STUDENTS IN SCIENCE CLASS: PERSPECTIVE AND RESOURCES

If you had a serious illness, you would want the best physician. If you had economic problems, you would want the best financial adviser. Everybody recognizes the need for unusual gifts and talents, yet this is a much-neglected area in education.

Definitions of giftedness vary. Most, however, are paraphrased from the congressional report submitted by past Commissioner of Education Sidney Marland in *Education of the Gifted and Talented* (1972). Gifted and talented students are those identified by professionals who, by virtue of their abilities, are capable of high achievement. These students require educational programs beyond those normally provided to fulfill their personal potentials and to encourage their contribution to society. In a less-cumbersome definition: Gifted students have superior academic abilities. Talented students have special aptitudes in specific areas. The difference between giftedness and talent is not distinct, since most gifted students have talents and most talented students are gifted in some areas. Gifted and talented students may have demonstrated abilities in any of the following areas: academics (general or specific), leadership, visual and performing arts, music, creativity, mechanics, and athletics.

Characteristics of the Gifted and Talented Student in Science Class

♦ Enjoys asking scientific questions
♦ Solves problems easily and logically
♦ Demonstrates advanced ethical, cognitive, and aesthetic development
♦ Learns science faster than other students
♦ Understands scientific concepts quickly
♦ Asks many questions about science
♦ Shows an awareness of science far beyond that of other students
♦ Is motivated to read and study science independently
♦ Demonstrates unique abilities in designing laboratory equipment to solve problems
♦ Is highly creative

You may also observe a few negative behaviors such as boredom, frustration, acting out, and complaints.

This list gives a subjective and preliminary means of identifying gifted and talented students. If you think you have such a student, it is best to consult the school counselor so that appropriate tests can be administered to confirm your initial impressions.

Adapting school programs for gifted and talented students can be achieved in many ways. Businesses, industries, colleges, and universities often have programs for students showing special abilities. There are special honors classes, programs, and schools. Gifted students can work on advanced placement courses and accelerated schedules, take extra classes, enter college early, and work part time and/or summers in projects where they can develop their talents. You can easily find options for the gifted students in your school.

Although resources are available, probably the crucial question is, "What can I do to help the gifted and talented student in science class?"

Helping Gifted and Talented Students Learn Science

- Use questions, problems, and projects that will facilitate higher levels of cognitive, affective, and psychomotor development.
- Develop independent study programs.
- Have special honors seminars.
- Initiate extracurricular science activities, such as having science fairs or having gifted students help teach an elementary science club.
- Assign special projects in lieu of routine work that is boring the students.
- Emphasize scientific inquiry and problem solving in your teaching.
- Individualize a program based on the student's interests.

TEACHING SCIENCE FOR INDIVIDUAL DIFFERENCES

After reading the previous sections, it should be clear that, as a science teacher, you will encounter a broad range of students. All students have individual differences that should be recognized in the science classroom. With increased recognition of the science-for-all orientation and because of the laws cited earlier, more and more school systems are modifying their instructional programs to give greater attention to individual differences. Psychological research indicates that there are human differences that have implications for teaching. This research indicates the following:

- Individuals come to the classroom with different conceptions of natural phenomena.
- Individuals vary in the rate at which they learn concepts.

- Individuals have different levels of motivation toward learning.
- Individuals have different levels of psychomotor skills.
- Individuals have different attitudes, values, and concepts in regard to science.

Many more such statements could be made concerning individual differences among students in the science classroom. Commonsense and observation confirm the statements as much as research evidence. Yet, teachers have been reluctant to modify instruction. In this section, we describe several ways you can individualize instruction in your science classroom.

Individualized instruction is a process of adapting curriculum materials and instructional procedures to the student's needs. The aim of individualization is to maximize student learning. Many schools have used grouping as a way of reducing instructional differences in a classroom or grade level. However, grouping alone cannot meet the needs of all students. Other approaches are important.

There are some variations on individualized instruction in science. The entire science program may be individualized for all students, or only for students with exceptional needs. Individualized instruction may be based on any or all of the following: rate of learning (e.g., accelerated, extra time), direction of learning (e.g., independent study, student-selected projects), different methods (e.g., alone, small group, teacher directed), different materials (e.g., reading, laboratory activities), and levels of achievement (e.g., assessments, projects completed). Clearly there are many variations available to science teachers. These approaches only describe things you can do in the classroom and do not include approaches requiring administrative or schoolwide reorganization. The following sections are brief descriptions of different approaches to teaching science for individual differences.

Grouping

In one plan, students are grouped according to ability. They are assigned units of work to complete, and when they finish these units, they may be moved at the end of the semester to another group of higher ability and achievement. Sometimes teachers group within a classroom so that there might be high, middle, and low groups in a class of 30. This system allows the teacher to adjust instruction to the different levels. It is usually not a good idea to maintain these groups on a permanent basis, because such grouping defines a class structure, the disadvantages of which outweigh the advantages.

Continuous Progress

A second approach is the continuous-progress plan. It allows students to progress from subject to subject with no time restriction. A student who finishes biology in six weeks and passes an examination is then eligible to move into chemistry. This approach is linear; that is, it progresses through the regular sequence of science courses.

Enrichment Programs

Enrichment programs provide extra opportunities for students who complete the regular program and the extra time needed for others to complete the chapter or unit. Here, the faster students have the opportunity to work in depth and breadth within the science course. Using an enrichment program may require extra materials and a resource center.

Team Teaching

Another attempt to give greater attention to individual differences is to use some large group instruction in a team-teaching situation on certain days, with small group and individualized instruction on other days. This method is a compromise between having traditional group instruction and completely individualized instruction. This approach has the advantage of releasing teachers during the large group instruction so that they may prepare and organize materials. When this method is used, there is no reason why the students cannot be taught on an individualized basis when the group is divided into smaller sections.

TEACHING SCIENCE FOR INDIVIDUAL DIFFERENCES: ADVANTAGES AND DISADVANTAGES

Now that you have information about what is possible, it is appropriate to review the advantages and disadvantages in teaching science for individual differences. The aforementioned approaches endeavor to respond to the overwhelming evidence on individual variation. They are efforts to respect the person. Science teachers who have gone from group-centered to more individualized instruction often state that they didn't realize how futile it was in the traditional approach to try to have all students learn particularly difficult material at the same rate. The fact that the slower academic students are not demeaned and frustrated because they don't learn rapidly or gifted students are not held back until their classmates catch up is perhaps the major advantage of recognizing individual differences.

Furthermore, there is a shift in emphasis from extrinsic to intrinsic rewards. Students doing an assignment at their own rate gain self-confidence and a sense of competence that may not manifest so easily in group instruction. The real joy of learning in this manner comes in students completing the task on their own initiative, not simply because of grades given by the teacher.

Although an individualized approach ideally has many practical advantages, there also are several disadvantages. A science teacher considering taking a position in a school or seriously thinking about the implementation of such a system should be aware of these disadvantages before making the pertinent decisions.

Staff

Individualizing a science program means that the faculty must operate as teams. Instructors must be well prepared in several subjects, because they may be supervising a large laboratory containing students working on units spread over several areas in different subjects. Because students are often working on different units within each of these subjects, a teacher cannot read a chapter ahead of the students the night before and be prepared. Teachers of individualized instruction must know the subjects and curriculum well to interact appropriately with each student's needs.

Acting as a member of a fully functioning team is often difficult because of the differences in how members view their functions as teachers and because of what they think are appropriate requirements for the learners. For example, if some teachers believe that students should be directed to cover a lot of material, and other teachers think students should be given considerable freedom to become autonomous investigators, then conflicts are bound to occur among the faculty team members.

Materials

Individualized science instruction demands more reading matter and audiovisual aids than conventional teaching, because multilevel learning aids must be available to adjust materials to students' academic abilities. For example, some students may read college-level books or use computers and videodiscs while others work on laboratory investigations.

SUMMARY

Because of the call to educate *all* students in science and because of clear legal mandates, science teaching requires that teachers recognize the unique disabilities, gifts, and talents of their students. Exceptional students will be mainstreamed in regular classrooms, and the gifted also will receive special attention. Although each exceptional student, whether disabled or gifted, presents a distinctive case, certain guides and suggestions can help the science teacher meet the specific needs of students.

Science teachers have recognized the needs of students at either end of a continuum, from disabled to gifted. The process has clarified individual differences in general, and it emphasizes the theme of this chapter—*all students can learn science.*

Students vary in their perceptions of school and science and in their cognitive, affective, and psychomotor development. Schools ordinarily have not taught for individual differences because of traditional philosophy and practices, problems of scheduling, poor teacher preparation, instructional costs, poor facilities, and poor equipment. In spite of these problems, many schools are now endeavoring to change the traditional pattern of instruction. This change also has been encouraged by laws requiring individualized programs for exceptional students who are being taught in the regular classroom. Individualized grouping, continuous progress, enrichment programs, team teaching, honors classes, seminars, second-level science courses, and special science classes have been successful.

Although there are advantages and disadvantages to teaching science for individual differences, on balance, the advantages outweigh the disadvantages. To achieve the goals of teaching science for individual differences, all students must develop their understanding of science and abilities of inquiry. You can embody these aspirations in a vision that includes expectations that all students will achieve national standards in science, provision for rich and varied experiences with science content, instruction that accommodates different needs and learning styles, direct action on equity issues, and appropriate assessment strategies.

◆
─────────

RESOURCES

DO-IT (Disabilities, Opportunities, Internetworking, and Technology) serves to increase the successful participation of individuals with disabilities in challenging academic programs and careers such as those in science, engineering, mathematics, and technology. DO-IT is a collaboration of Computing & Communications and the Colleges of Engineering and Education at the University of Washington.

DO-IT
University of Washington
Box 355670
Seattle, WA 98195-5670
doit@u.washington.edu
http://www.washington.edu/.

National Center for Learning Disabilities: www.ld.org
Council for Exceptional Children: www.cec.sped.org
LD Resources: www.ldresources.com
Gifted Students: www.kidsource.com

TEACHING SCIENCE FOR DIFFERENCES: GENDER AND CULTURAL

Research on classroom interactions among teachers and students and between students sheds light on the ways boys, girls, and students of color can have quite different experiences in school. Most of the differences are subtle, some are blatant, yet both can be powerful in molding students' identities (Mistler-Jackson, 2003). In this chapter, we present an overview of gender issues, which have been studied extensively, and issues related to cultural differences especially, which have not been studied as extensively, and then conclude with ideas that you can implement in your classroom to make sure that *all* students learn science.

Myra and David Sadker have spent several decades studying gender differences in schools. Their 1994 book, *Failing at Fairness: How Our Schools Cheat Girls*, documents the variable treatment that boys and girls receive in the classroom. They note that the differences are often so subtle and engrained in our culture that when others watch a classroom video full of gender bias, they don't see any of it until it is pointed out. Then participants in their workshops have an "aha!" experience about what subtle gender bias is all about. The Sadkers also illustrate the gender bias pervasive in course materials and how significantly the images presented in these materials can influence students' perceptions of male and female ability. Klein and Sherwood (2005) conducted research that shows that young women learn science better when certain characteristics of the classroom and curriculum are met. Their work indicates that girls learn science better when the curriculum makes specific links from mathematics, science, and technology to the real world. They found that girls also learn well in collaborative settings that require the use of verbal skills. Klein and Sherwood emphasized

that educators should encourage girls to concentrate on how the right answer is determined and not just what the right answer is. Others have shown that girls learn science well in classrooms that use hands-on investigations while encouraging girls to be experts and technology controllers. Emphasizing characteristics such as these helps girls develop a level of self-efficacy that combats negative attitudes and personal disbeliefs.

Additionally, parents play an important role in classroom culture through the expectations they maintain for their children and the ways they reinforce or challenge the gendered expectations students encounter at school. In sum, these various forces help create the particular culture of a classroom that, when biased against girls' full participation, can be detrimental to girls' academic and social development.

TEACHER BIAS

In my A.P. physics class in high school there were only three girls and 27 boys. The three girls, myself included, consistently scored at the top end of the scale. On one test I earned a 98. The next closest boy earned an 88. The teacher handed the tests back saying, "Boys, you are failing. These three pretty cookies are outscoring you guys on every test." He told the boys it was embarrassing for them to be beaten by a girl (Sadker & Sadker, 1994).

Teachers play a central role in determining the climate of their classrooms. Although most teachers are unaware that they treat boys and girls differently and some make a conscious effort to avoid gender bias, an examination of many classrooms reveals a subtle and pervasive gender bias that undermines girls' confidence. For example, Sadker and Sadker report that boys call out responses more than girls and demand more of the teacher's attention. While teachers get frustrated with the calling out and set rules that students must raise their hands and wait to be called on, the girls are more often reprimanded for breaking the rule. They write that this "system of silencing operates covertly and repeatedly" (1994, p. 43) throughout years of schooling and socializes girls not to be disruptive, aggressive, or demanding.

Boys' disruptive behavior is reprimanded, but expected, so it gets framed and tolerated differently by teachers than girls' disruptive behavior. Peggy Orenstein's (1994) qualitative study of adolescent girls provides many rich examples of phenomena discussed more broadly in Sadker and Sadker's book.

> In mid-November, Mrs. Richter is giving out grades . . . the teacher sits at her desk in the back corner of the room, and the students come up one by one . . . When Dawn's turn comes, Mrs. Richter speaks sharply to her. "You're getting a B," the teacher says, "but for citizenship, you're getting 'disruptive.' You've been talking a lot and there have been some outbursts." Dawn scrunches her mouth over to one side of her face, lowers her eyes, and returns to her seat.
>
> "Disruptive?" yells Nate from across the room where the teacher's voice has carried. "*She's* not disruptive, *I'm* disruptive." Mrs. Richter laughs. "You've got that right," she says. When his turn comes, Nate gets a B plus. "It would've been an A minus if you turned in your last homework assignment," Mrs. Richter says. As predicted, his citizenship comment is also 'disruptive,' but the bad news isn't delivered with the same sting as it was to Dawn—it's conferred with an indulgent smile. There is a tacit acceptance of a disruptive boy, because boys *are* disruptive. Girls are too, sometimes, as Dawn illustrates, but with different consequences.
>
> Over the course of the semester, Dawn slowly stops disrupting; she stops participating too. At the semester break, when I check with Mrs. Richter on the classes' progress, she tells me, "Dawn hardly talks at all now because she's overpowered by the boys. She can't get the attention in class, so she's calmed down."
>
> Nate, however, hasn't changed a bit, but whereas Dawn's behavior is viewed as containable, the teacher sees Nate's as inevitable. "I'll go through two weeks of torture before I'll give him detention," Mrs. Richter says. "But you have to tolerate that behavior to a certain extent or he won't want to be there at all, he'll get himself kicked out" (1994, pp. 16–17).

As a result of different expectations, girls and boys learn what they can and cannot get away with in class. Many girls learn too well the lesson that they are to be cooperative, and their education suffers because of it. Girls are often model students. They get better grades and receive fewer punishments than boys. Their good behavior allows the teacher more time to work with the more-difficult-to-manage boys. As a result, girls receive "less time, less help and fewer challenges. Reinforced for passivity, their independence and self-esteem suffer. As victims of benign neglect, girls are penalized for doing what they should and lose ground as they go through school" (Sadker & Sadker, 1994, p. 44).

Girls are cognizant of these behavior differences and often consider themselves superior to boys, especially at the elementary level. They complain that boys are more off task, raise their hands even when they don't know an answer, and dominate the class in inappropriate ways. This early confidence fades as girls progress through school. By middle school, many girls place so much importance on being correct and not looking foolish in class that they are afraid to be wrong. A female student in the gifted program at her suburban middle school explained, "Boys never care if they're wrong. They can say totally off-the-wall things, things that have nothing to do with class sometimes. They're not afraid to get in trouble or anything. I'm not shy. But it's like, when I get into class, I just . . . " She shrugs her shoulders helplessly. "I just can't talk. I don't know why" (Orenstein, 1994).

More than 10 years later, researchers from the University of Texas conduct research that helps explain this student's comments (Muller & Riegle-Crumb, 2006). Catherine Riegle-Crumb notes that "having friends that are high performers is associated with advanced course-taking in all three subjects [English, math, science]." Yet, what is unique to math and science is the positive association that comes from a friendship group that is predominantly female. Thus, the estimated effects of friends do vary based on the gender composition of the group, but only in math and science, areas where women have been historically underrepresented. "This suggests that the dominant presence of friends who are doing well is a visible reminder that females can do well in subjects stereotyped as male."

Chandra Muller notes that "since there are no social stereotypes or norms to discourage girls from taking advanced courses in English, having high-performing friends may help, but generally the girls may feel free to embark on this traditionally gendered path without the additional support of an academically successful female friendship group". (Muller & Riegle-Crumb, 2006)

> Because girls are often afraid of being wrong, they may take longer to respond to a question posed in class. This also works to their detriment, as wait-time analyses have shown that teachers usually give students less than a second to begin to respond to a question. As a result, girls are often bypassed as boys are more willing to offer an answer. Studies have also shown that boys are given slightly longer wait times but the reasons for this preference are unclear. However, the message sent to students who are

given more time to respond is that the teacher has confidence that they will get the answer right (AAUW, 1998; Sadker & Sadker, 1994).

Girls are also sometimes the victims of blatant teacher bias. Blatant bias against girls is often most pronounced in science, math, and technology classrooms in which some teachers believe that boys are more suited to excel in these fields than girls. One student teacher told Sadker and Sadker, "A lot of my female students complained about a science teacher who persisted in referring to them as 'dizzy' or 'ditzy' or 'airhead.' He often told the class, 'You can't expect *these girls* to know anything.'" A teacher from Louisiana told them about a science teacher who called the boys "Mr." or "Professor," but called the girls by their first names, if they were lucky, or "Blondie." In one extreme case, there is a story of a girl in a high school chemistry class whose repeated question to the male teacher was ignored until he threw a beaker at her and yelled, "What do you want?" Afterward, he told the researcher that girls aren't suited to do science.

The AAUW Educational Foundation has spearheaded several landmark publications synthesizing the literature regarding girls' experiences in schools. Their 1998 publication, *Gender Gaps: Where Schools Still Fail Our Children,* sought to examine the progress that had been made in the 1990s to reduce gender differences in educational outcomes. Even with some signs of improvement, they noted that studies of teacher–student interactions continued to document male domination in the classroom in both large and small groups. The most notable inequities occurred in math, science, and technology classrooms.

What Is the Root of Teacher Bias?

These inequities are not surprising when one considers the cultural bias at work in which girls are expected to excel in the humanities and boys in the sciences (Kahle, 1998; Orenstein, 1994; Sadker & Sadker, 1994).

Many teachers and students believe these generalities exist, and middle and high school level standardized test scores support it. But the root of how these generalizations come about is a topic of intense debate. Are girls biologically predisposed to excel at language and relationships and boys to excel at math and spatial relations? Most educational researchers and scientists maintain that it is impossible to separate "nature" from "nurture" in determining the relative impact of the many forces that shape people's lives (Brazelton & Greenspan, 2000; Bryant & Clark, 2000).

Cultural expectations and constructions of gender are extremely powerful in shaping individuals' behavior and are so engrained that it is difficult to examine one's own culture. In the equity literature, it is assumed that differences in educational outcomes among large groups of people are primarily the result of cultural expectations and classroom experiences, not biology.

STUDENT BIAS

Beliefs about what boys and girls are supposed to do are also transmitted through peer relationships. The messages boys send to girls are both subtle and blatant, and, as with teachers, powerful in defining girls' "place" in areas such as science and math. As stated in the teacher bias section, student bias against girls is most pronounced in areas such as science, math, and technology because of a cultural belief that boys should outperform girls in these areas. The following examples also illustrate this point. McLaren and Gaskell (1995) interviewed high school girls in physics class about their experiences and found that girls identified more biased treatment by boys than by teachers.

> In our class there is one guy and he is really, really smart; he has a 90% average and over and he kind of looks at me as if I'm not supposed to be in that class. And he kind of thinks that he's smarter than me and that I'm wasting my time in that class. And then when I get a good mark on my test, I feel really good because I proved to him that I'm not stupid, that I can do it too (p. 22).

McLaren and Gaskell suggest that boys may feel freer to harass girls in science than in other classes because of larger cultural messages that science is a male domain. They argue that gender should be an official part of the science curriculum to affect change in these attitudes, instead of leaving students to deal with it informally.

Girls may also act as if they do not want to or cannot do science because "acting girly" brings attention from boys. For example, Orenstein (1994) observed middle school girls shrieking when a boy dangled a spider in front of them that he had captured for extra credit in science class. They made a big deal about it, and the boys did, too. After the hoopla, a girl told Orenstein, "I'm not *really* afraid of that stuff, except snakes and blood. But guys like it if you act all helpless and girly, so you do (p. 22)." Orenstein reflected on these scenes she witnessed again and again and wrote,

> With each flight toward traditional femininity, I thought about who has permission, who has the right in our culture, to explore the natural world, to get dirty and muddy, to think spiders and worms and frogs are neat, to bring them in for extra credit in science. In fact, to be engaged in science at all (p. 26).

A loss in academic confidence is one piece of a larger picture of diminishing confidence experienced by adolescent girls in our society. Research on developmental issues unique to the adolescent years has shed light on how challenging these years are for all children (AAUW, 1998). It is generally the middle school years, ages 11 to 14, in which students must grapple with changes in their bodies, increased social pressure to conform to peer culture, hormonal ups and downs, increased awareness of sexuality and desire, and greater awareness of gender roles that apply to themselves. Both boys and girls struggle with these issues, but in general, girls emerge from the storm with their self-esteem less intact than boys. This plunge in self-confidence unique to adolescence is one of the major forces that has implications for middle school girls' participation, interest, and learning in school, especially in science.

COURSE MATERIAL BIAS

Students continue to encounter a male-dominated world in their textbooks, classroom posters, and course presentations. The historical contributions of men make up the majority of history (in all subject areas) that students learn in school. They study male inventors, writers, poets, artists, leaders, and warriors much more than they study women who also filled these roles and other roles that are not as valued in our culture. Not only do textbooks and other materials ignore all but the most "notable" women (e.g., Joan of Arc, Marie Curie, Amelia Earhart, Harriet Tubman), but also they do not discuss *why* women are omitted. Just as there is evidence of white men taking credit for the accomplishments of black men in U.S. history, the same is true for women. Historical education ideally would examine how having the legal power to vote, own property, publish, attend college, and so forth have framed the contributions of men and women to society, but they often do not (Sadker & Sadker, 1994).

Course material bias in male-dominated areas such as science is especially problematic for students' developing identities because it reinforces larger cultural stereotypes and girls' self-doubt that they can excel in "male" domains. The same girl in McLaren and Gaskell's study who admitted self-doubt because of putdowns by boys in science class also attributed her lack of confidence to curricular materials. She continued:

> You start thinking, in all the textbooks and stuff all you see is guys. . . . In the textbook you see, this guy invented this sort of thing, a lot in the math and sciences. That's all you really see. You start thinking, "Oh, maybe it's because females can't really do that," and I think, that sort of affects [girls], maybe not because they really particularly think about it, but I think that it may have something to do with it unconsciously or whatever. I just sort of get that impression (p. 148).

Boys continue to outperform girls on standard measures of achievement in secondary science (except biology), and girls opt out of advanced science coursework in greater numbers than boys. Science, like math, is often presented as factual, linear, numeric, and objective. "Cookbook" science "experiments" are designed to lead students to one right answer and have dominated the curriculum. Scientists would point out that these exercises, commonly referred to as "experiments," are not experiments at all, but only demonstrations or exercises in following a particular procedure. True experiments are far more creative, engaging, and open ended. Additionally, units or courses in science can vary so much that previous work may not seem relevant to new material (e.g., chemistry versus physics). Thus, like in math, the probability for difficulty in understanding new concepts and doubting one's ability is greater than in language courses where concepts have more of a spiraling nature.

PARENTAL BIAS

Parents' attitudes about their children's abilities also can have a powerful impact on the development of self-concept. Whereas some parents actively resist gender-stereotyped expectations for their children, less-critical parents may inadvertently contribute to larger cultural stereotypes. For example, many parents foster their sons' interest in traditionally masculine fields such as math, science, and computers by buying mechanical toys for them and putting a computer in their room while assuming these items wouldn't interest their daughters. Early exposure to science-related toys and hobbies has been shown to positively correlate with later science achievement (Orenstein, 1994, p. 49). Some parents maintain different expectations for the types of courses their sons and daughters should pursue and achievement in those courses based on gender stereotypes.

Orenstein recounts a story about Lindsay, a girl in the advanced math track at a suburban middle school. Lindsay was experiencing anxiety attacks at school and home, and doctors could find nothing wrong with her. It turned out that she was failing math and she was terrified of her parents' reaction. Interestingly, her parents were so relieved to find out what was wrong with her that they weren't angry at all. In a discussion with Lindsay's mother, Orenstein asked if the panic attacks could be seen as a warning that Lindsay was placing too much pressure on herself. Her mother instead thought that they were a result of her being placed in a class beyond her capabilities.

> We were surprised that Lindsay was placed in algebra at all. She has always gotten B's in math, so that's not her strong subject. . . . I think the panic was just from not

knowing what was going to happen if she brought home an F. We didn't kill her, and I think she was surprised. But I said, "Now if there's any other class where you *should* be doing well and you get and F—*then* you'll be killed for sure" (p. 49).

Perhaps Lindsay's mother really was basing this attitude on her daughter's academic record and not gender stereotypes, but given a larger culture in which women are viewed as less capable in math (and science) than men, her parents did nothing to counteract gender stereotypes and gave Lindsay permission to opt out of advanced math coursework. It is in this way that parents may reinforce the culture of the classroom and contribute to girls' lack of confidence in areas considered male domains.

ADDING ETHNICITY AND CULTURE TO THE MIX

Much research has been done on girls' passage through adolescence in the 1990s that offers meaningful perspectives on ways in which our cultural expectations demean girls. Individual girls and those from different ethnic groups have many varied experiences and responses to the challenges of these years. For example, far more African American girls retain their overall self-esteem during adolescence than white or Latina girls. They are almost twice as likely to say they are "happy with the way I am" (despite the messages from school) than girls from other groups and say "they are pretty good at a lot of things" at nearly the rate of white boys (AAUW, 1991). Latina girls, on the other hand, suffer the worst self-esteem drop. The number of Latina girls who are "happy with the way I am" plunges between the ages of 9 and 15 by 38 percentage points, compared to a 33 percent drop for white girls and a 7 percent drop for black girls (Orenstein, 1994). Numerous studies illuminate the complexities in girls' lives and indicate that some girls maintain a sense of self and direction better than others. These authors share the conclusion that many girls experience a loss of confidence through their interactions with others and in response to American culture; a loss that takes years to recover from, and, in some cases, only if one is aware of what has happened (Pipher, 1994; Brown & Gilligan, 1992).

Despite the number of studies about girls' passages, there has been little research on boys or the cognitive, metacognitive, and motivational characteristics of students in relationship to their ethnic or cultural background (Taylor & Lorimer, 2002; Guild, 1994). This dearth of work also means that the few studies that exist may not be parallel, so it is difficult to compare studies or begin to make generalizations for the multicultural populations found in many school settings.

In this section, we will describe the characteristics that influence learning of a variety of ethnic groups.

There is not clear agreement that various cultural and ethnic groups learn differently from each other. Wang's (1993) work suggests that the differences among ethnic groups are not significant enough to be considered when thinking about how students learn. Rather he suggests that socioeconomic status is a more significant factor than either race or culture. This study suggests that theories emphasizing racial differences in cognitive and metacognitive skills should be rethought in terms of the influences of a combination of cultural-familial factors.

When considering the characteristics of any large group, consider this caution: "One reason that the linkage between culture and learning styles is controversial is that generalizations about a group of people have often led to naive inferences about individuals within that group" (Guild, 1994, p. 17). The following characteristics help describe the strengths different groups of learners bring to the classroom based on the funds of knowledge taught within their culture. The purpose of these lists is to provide a sense of the range of strengths for each population in general. In reality, the lists oversimplify the whole issue. The hope is that this information will help you as a teacher recognize the great chasm between traditional Anglo ways and the strengths that non-Anglo children may bring to the classroom that are now being ignored or "assimilated." The learning characteristics emphasized by Anglo culture are listed first for comparison purposes. These are the characteristics that most curricula and instruction are focused on enhancing (Taylor & Lorimer, 2002; Bert & Bert, 1992; Howard, 1989). Keeping this perspective in mind makes the differences on other lists even more noticeable. The learning characteristics of Anglo culture include the following characteristics:

- Value individuality highly
- Believe that reality is material
- Encourage positive self-talk
- Relate to adults in a formal and task-oriented manner
- Reward males for achievement in academics and athletics, females for friendliness and physical appearance
- Value objectivity, analytical thinking, and accuracy

The learning characteristics of Mexican American culture include the following characteristics (Darder, 1995; Donato & Hernández, 1994).

- Seek friendly, personal, adult relationships
- Do not sanction physical contact among adolescent boys and girls
- Become bicultural or bicognitive to succeed
- Are more highly motivated in a cooperative learning environment than in a competitive environment

(friends and family form a safety net and support system in daily life)

- Have greater verbal productivity than whites
- Tend to need affiliation
- Family rituals form the basis of social networks and solidarity (families are large and extended)
- Social interactions developed from infancy and maintained through adult life
- Wide latitude given for error; lots of encouragement to try again
- Children learn by modeling adults at home
- Develop a "zone of comfort" at home due to the previous three characteristics; not reinforced at school

The learning characteristics of the African American culture include the following (Taylor & Lorimer, 2002; Murtadha, 1995; Guild, 1994; Howard, 1989):

- Value oral experience; use expressive language
- Emphasize social well-being, solidarity, interdependence, and cooperation to benefit society
- Stress loyalty in interpersonal relationships
- Believe that human beings are spiritual
- Treat human behavior as subjective
- Use an effective approach to knowledge
- Believe that the sense of self is collective
- Have a sense of mutual responsibility for other African people
- Get involved physically, cognitively, and emotionally in learning

The learning characteristics of the Native American culture include the following (Bert & Bert, 1992; Howard, 1989):

- Need to understand the whole picture (global learners)
- Make many observations before performing a task
- Find true-false and multiple-choice tests more difficult than essay tests
- Are stronger at synthesis and interrelating ideas
- Like to have "discussions with self"
- Come from a strong oral tradition
- Believe in balance in the universe
- Believe that humans are a part of nature, not superior to it
- Treat every individual with dignity
- Believe that reality is spiritual
- Value cooperation and harmony highly
- Believe that making eye contact with adults is disrespectful
- Include learning by doing, symbols, dreams, and humor in traditional education
- Show respect to adults by disagreeing with the elders
- Discourage the demonstration of achievement and individual competition unless it benefits the group in some way

Many of the dominant characteristics of nonwhite learners align well with ideas about how to improve students' success in learning science such as making observations, being able to consider the whole picture rather than the parts, and having strong social skills. What does not align well are the Western definitions of certain attributes. For example, consider the terms *academic time management, practice, goal-directedness,* and *sense of self-efficacy* in light of the characteristics of white learners and dominant white culture: We mean learners who can stick to a task, use their time efficiently, and believe in their ability to do the task. This perspective favors a learner who works quickly, quietly, and efficiently and is willing to tell the teacher what a good job she has done.

If we reframe those characteristics from a nonwhite perspective, we need to focus on such characteristics as putting the task into perspective, that is, fitting it into the big picture, doing the task cooperatively, creatively, and so that it honors the learner's culture. The more holistic approach of most nonwhite learners allows for greater reflection, if the instructor and the curriculum recognize this asset.

WHAT ARE THE IMPLICATIONS FOR CURRICULUM AND INSTRUCTION?

To help all learners have the opportunity to develop as successful science learners, change is necessary in three major areas of school: curriculum, instruction, and assessment. Banks (1994) and Ladson-Billings (1994) both endorse a transformation approach to curriculum. The essence of the transformation approach, according to Banks, is that it "changes the structure, assumptions, and perspectives of the curriculum so that subject matter is viewed from the perspectives and experiences of a range of groups."

An advantage of this approach is that it brings awareness of marginalized groups to all learners and therefore legitimates their experiences. In addition, it helps learners construct their own understanding of their culture and the cultures of others. Increased understanding decreases the stereotype images often reinforced by the "festival" approach to multicultural education.

In terms of instruction, the single biggest change that teachers in multicultural environments can make is to include cooperative learning strategies in their teaching. This does not necessarily mean doing more group work. These opportunities for cooperative learning must allow for students to construct their knowledge in a safe, social environment that allows all students to articulate their understanding.

In addition to this major change in instruction are a variety of strategies teachers can employ to help all students succeed in science (Bell, 2002; Hrabowski,

2002; Rolón, 2002; Taylor, 2002; Donato & Hernández, 1994; Howe, 1994; Ladson-Billings, 1994; Villegas, 1991; Pogrow, 1988). For example, try the following in your classroom:

◆ Set expectations as high for nonwhite students as for white students.
◆ Accept all students' experiences as legitimate.
◆ Use the language and understandings of the children.
◆ Provide access to higher-order thinking skills for all students, and use other students as language and cultural brokers.

Consider the following actions to help you develop a multicultural classroom.

Show Respect for Cultural Differences

Develop a perspective of cultural differences rather than cultural deficits. The former will help you see that cultural groups have different views and learning styles, the accommodation of which will greatly enhance learning science. The latter perspective perpetuates the myth that differences equal deficits and that girls, minorities, and exceptional students have problems learning science.

Respect for cultural differences means that you understand that there is not one best way to learn science and that every student has a unique perspective and approach to learning. Value what each student brings to the classroom, whether it is another language, travel to other countries, or just a different way of completing routine activities.

Consider the Cultural Resources of Your Students

Although diverse groups may be in your science class, it is difficult to know exactly which groups (and how many individuals) will predominate. The point here is your openness to understanding the groups represented in your classes. You might consider home visits, involvement in community activities, talking with parents, observing students in nonclassroom and nonschool settings, and reading about different cultures.

Use Understanding to Enhance Learning

In numerous sections of this book we have discussed the model of learning that begins with students' current conceptions of science and constructs more adequate conceptions aligned with science. So it is that some students will have prior knowledge influenced by their culture-bound experiences. You should not avoid using this as a foundation for teaching and learning.

Make Decisions That Enhance Learning

From the moment you begin teaching a lesson, you will receive feedback from students about their interest, attention, and understanding. You will have to decide what to do—how to adjust your plans—in order to enhance learning. In classrooms with culturally different groups, you will have to be more sensitive to student signals because some may vary from what you have previously experienced. Although the subtleties of culturally influenced responses may take time to understand, it is not too early to be aware of their influences and to carefully evaluate each lesson, asking where students had difficulty, if all students were involved, which students seemed interested, and what evidence you have that learning occurred.

Provide Time

Students need time to activate their prior knowledge. If activated, they will have more to share in class. Writing in journals, working in small groups on focus questions, or participating in paired brainstorming sessions are examples of strategies that will provide opportunities for you and the students to identify what is known and what is not.

Provide Positive Role Models

Students should learn from individuals who represent different cultural groups. Students have to recognize that women, minorities, and individuals with handicaps can all do science and make contributions to society.

As part of fulfilling the national standards on the History and Nature of Science, you should introduce students to the diversity of individuals who have contributed to advances in science, engineering, medicine, and other related professions.

Use Cooperative Groups

Research shows that cooperative groups, when adequately implemented, help all students become involved and learn science. Cooperative groups shift responsibilities among members and thus subtly confront stereotypes and prejudices while allowing for individual and cultural differences.

Use Hands-On Investigations

In general, all students are motivated through active involvement. The physical manipulation of materials, the intellectual encounter, and cooperation with peers that occurs while doing investigations contribute to all students learning more science.

Provide Equal Opportunities and Expectations

All students should have experiences with science equipment, computers, field trips, and materials. Again, we point out the advantage of cooperative group work in achieving the goal of equal opportunity for student involvement. You should also make it clear that you expect all students to become involved and develop the abilities associated with inquiry and the use of facilities, materials, and equipment.

Use Appropriate Language

When teaching science, you will often use analogies and metaphors. Try to balance male and female metaphors and use examples that incorporate other cultures or ask your students to generate metaphors as a means of building understanding.

Be Sensitive in Questioning

Science teachers ask a lot of questions. When you ask a question, wait, so all students have time to ponder and reflect on the answer. You should also be aware of who responds and who you ask to respond. Teachers often have different reactions to different students, and the differences too often reveal the teacher's perceptions of student abilities.

Communicate with Parents

Parents are your allies. Assume they care about what is happening in school as well as with their own children. Remember, though, that caring does not translate into specific knowledge about how to support their children in school. Let parents know about achievement gaps from national and international data that show the inequities by gender, race, culture, and geographic region. Often this awareness helps parents support higher standards at school and at home. Emphasize the importance of reading for improving all academic performance, and provide parents with lists of readings and websites that appeal to your students.

Keep parents informed by sending advance notice about major assignments and assessments. Prepare a copy of the syllabus to send home with students, in the mail, or by email. Send updates regularly. When talking to parents about their own children, point out what the student has done well and what is not going well and the reasons for each. Conduct workshops for parents

that model what you are doing in class or that help connect science to real life.

Maintain High Expectations

Regardless of the diversity in your science class, make it clear to students that you expect them to reach higher levels of achievement. Expect all students to participate, use complete sentences, and use correct grammar when speaking or writing, and make clear that you will do everything you can to help all students succeed in science class.

SUMMARY

Science teachers need to recognize the unique influences of culture on students' perceptions and learning styles. Two large ideas that are developed in other chapters in this book and in the *National Science Education Standards* will help you attend to each child in your classroom as a unique learner. The first is to use a constructivist approach to organize your teaching and the second is to use authentic assessment strategies.

Constructivism blends well with cooperative learning strategies and provides a methodology for accepting and legitimating all learners' explanations. Adherence to a constructivist philosophy also changes the pace in the classroom so that each learner has time to construct an understanding of a concept. Constructivist strategies in the classroom encourage learners to make use of what they already know and build new knowledge connections from there.

Authentic assessment tasks will build on the strengths many female and non-Anglo learners bring to the classroom, because they place the assessment in a context that is meaningful for the learner. Traditional forms of assessment remove this context, thereby handicapping most nonwhite learners. By authentic, we mean the use of assessment tasks that reflect the teaching and learning environment. For instance, in a science classroom that is rich in hands-on, inquiry-oriented laboratory activities, it is not authentic to use paper-and-pencil tests as the only form of assessment. Authentic assessment for this classroom would include hands-on, inquiry-oriented tasks.

Regardless of which specific changes you or your school choose to implement to improve the learning opportunities for all students, we all must move away from deficit models that emphasize what non-Anglo learners *cannot* do (or do not do) when compared to white learners. Schools should celebrate the diversity and range of approaches and experiences that each learner brings to the classroom. This celebration allows all learners to develop to the best of their ability and increases their chances of becoming lifelong, self-regulating learners.

CLASSROOM MANAGEMENT AND CONFLICT RESOLUTION

Two major concerns for beginning science teachers are student discipline and classroom management. You have probably asked yourself, "How will the students behave?" "Will they do what I tell them to do?" "What can I do if a student is disruptive in science class?" In this chapter we provide answers to such questions.

Many individuals share your concern about discipline. The American public consistently indicates that lack of discipline is one of the most important problems facing public schools. What about science teachers? Do they perceive discipline as an important problem? Actually, the majority of science teachers do not believe that discipline is a serious problem. A 2000 survey found that only six percent of teachers in grades 7 through 9 and five percent of teachers in grades 10 through 12 reported "maintaining discipline" as a serious problem in their school. If you include "lack of student interest in science," those percentages are increased by an additional four percent and eight percent, respectively (Weiss et al., 2001).

What do science teachers consider "lack of interest," and what is meant by "maintaining discipline"? There are many answers to these questions. Our discussion is primarily directed to conflicts between teachers and students and to the constructive resolution of conflicts.

Before proceeding, you should complete Activity 21–1: Conflicts—What Would You Have Done? and Activity 21–2: Resolving Conflicts, at the end of this chapter. Completing these will give you information about the ways you resolve conflicts and so will serve as a useful preparation for this chapter.

CLASSROOM CONFLICTS

Classroom conflicts occur when the activities of one or more individuals are incompatible; such conflicts can be interpersonal or intergroup. An action that is incompatible with another action interferes, obstructs, or reduces the effectiveness of the action (Deutsch, 1973). For the most part, we can discuss conflicts between teachers and students, because a teacher must often take action, even when two students are in conflict. In most classrooms, the difference between compatible and incompatible activities is defined by rules, policies, or expectations of behavior. A classroom conflict usually results in disruption of normal activities and educational objectives.

Note the neutrality of the preceding definition. We have not defined rules or passed judgment on whether certain rules or expectations of behavior are good or bad. Science teachers have a wide range of rules and expectations for students. Similarly, students have a remarkable ability to adapt to different teachers and classroom situations. Rather than trying to define rules, it is better to focus on classroom conflicts and suggest ways that science teachers can either prevent conflicts or resolve them constructively.

We begin by presenting two views of the same conflict. First is the report of a student teacher who had eight weeks of experience; the second is the report of the student teacher's supervisor, a science teacher with 10 years of experience.

The Student Teacher's Perceptions

A new seating chart was set up for the class. In the shuffle, a student (the most openly aggressive and hostile student I've seen) started to swing at a student sitting behind him. I'm not sure of the reason, but I suspect that the boy behind him had his feet sticking out under the desk and the student either kicked him or tripped over him or slid his chair into his feet, and words were exchanged. I was close enough to verbally stop him and then collar him and send him up to the front of the class. My words were something like, "All right, you're moved, right now, up to the front; turn forward and don't turn back around or away from the chalkboard or you'll be out of here immediately. If you can't get along with the people around you, then you can sit by yourself with no privileges until you're ready to be part of the class." I thought for a minute he was going to explode (both mentally and physically), but he moved, sat and did nothing, very belligerently withdrawn, incredibly strong, and negative.

The Teacher's Perceptions

A new seating chart was established in the class. As one student took his newly assigned seat he appeared to be belligerent but not verbally so. Another student immediately behind made a comment, and he responded by turning around and pushing the table, and made a comment which I did not hear. The action was bad enough to get the attention of the majority of the class.

The instructor (student teacher) responded by giving the student a seat at a lone table in the front corner of the room. He took the seat but refused to do any work in class for the next three days. Whenever he attempted to turn or communicate with others, he was told to turn around. The student remained belligerent during this entire three-day period. After the teacher made corrections or comments he, usually, unknown to the instructor, had some obscene comment or verbal reaction to the correction.

Teachers' perceptions of the same situation can vary, and their perceptions of students can also influence the way they interact with the student to resolve the conflict. This conflict was not unique as classroom conflicts go—it was short, resolved by the teacher, and ended with little difficulty.

We can continue by looking at another typical classroom conflict. What is unique about this conflict is that it has been described by *both* the student and the teacher.

The Student's View

I was sitting at a table in the science laboratory with a few friends. We had finished our work and were engaged in normal conversation. The teacher approached our table and told us to get some work out. "You can't just sit there and talk."

I ignored her, and after she left our presence, we resumed our conversation. She came back soon after that, a bit more perturbed, and repeated her previous order. This time I spoke and told her I must be responsible enough to know when and how to do my schoolwork since I had an A average in school. "So," I said, "I don't need you to supervise my study habits." I reminded her we weren't being noisy, just talking among ourselves; that we weren't bothering anyone.

She became angry. She told us we were bothering others and stated that there was a rule of no talking in the science laboratory. In general, she tried to control the situation with power and authority instead of tact and reason. I, in turn, got a little indignant, lost my temper, and smarted off. She then kicked me out of science for the remainder of that day.

The Teacher's View

It was about halfway through the period when I noticed three boys sitting at a table talking. I went over to the table and told them that this is a science class and they should finish their science laboratory. I said they should do something besides talk.

I went about my business until, a few minutes later, I noticed that the boys were still talking. So I went to the table again and explained that they should be working. I hadn't even finished what I was saying when one of the boys said he was "smart enough to take care of himself so you can just leave me alone."

At this, I told the boy that a few students do not have the right to talk and disturb other students who wanted to work. The boy got angry and said, "The hell with you and the other students." At this, I asked the boy to leave the room and he did.

This situation is a typical classroom conflict in several respects. The context was related to undefined time in class, apparently the conflict lasted only four to five minutes, and there apparently was a rule governing conduct.

The reports described above reveal several other factors common to school conflicts. The perceptions of the individuals in conflict were very different, as is clear in the descriptions of the confrontation. Communication was somewhat accurate at the beginning but deteriorated as the situation continued to the point of threats, name calling, and assertions of power. Characteristics of a trusting attitude were lacking. Finally, each party to the conflict thought he or she was correct; thus, the problem belonged to the other person. Note also that the conflict ended but was not resolved. Left the way it was, there is every reason to suspect that future problems would occur between the student and the teacher, and, in fact, they did.

All conflicts are different. Figure 21–1 outlines different levels of student behavior that may result in classroom conflicts. Understanding different student (and teacher) behaviors that lead to conflict situations can help prevent conflicts and give direction and guidelines on the intervention and resolution of others. Also, such understanding clarifies how conflicts escalate; that is,

FIGURE 21–1   Levels of School Conflicts

Level I: Normal conflicts for individuals of this age and stage. Although the behavior may have violated general rules or norms of peers or society, the conduct is not a typical pattern for the individual.

Active	Passive
Mischievous	Aloof
Temperamental	Sulky
Overeager	Slow to Warm Up

Level II: Occasional conflicts for the individual. The conflicts are violations of minor school policies, classroom rules, and age-appropriate societal norms. There may be an emerging pattern that is subtle but should not be overlooked.

Active	Passive
Clowning	Dawdler
Impulsive	Shy
Acting Out	Dreamer
Seeks Affirmation	Alienated

Level III: A pattern of behaviors that consistently conflict with minor school policies, classroom rules, and age-appropriate societal norms. The pattern is clear, but the major rules and basic rights of others are seldom violated.

Active	Passive
Disobedient	Avoidant
Oppositional	Shut Down
Negativistic	Withdrawn
Provocative	Alienated

Level IV: A pattern of behaviors that persistently violated major school policies, classroom rules, and the basic rights of others. The pattern is clear to school personnel and peers.

Active	Passive
Aggressive	Depressive
Destructive	Self-destructive
Angry	Substance Abuse

Level V: Episodes of behaviors directed toward the physical harm of self, others, or property.

Active	Passive
Violent	Substance Addiction
Vandalism	Suicidal

each party moves to a higher level, hoping the other party will withdraw. In some unfortunate cases, simple conflicts can escalate to violent and destructive episodes within the school.

Causes of Conflicts

Understanding the origins and causes of disruptive behavior can provide you with responses that prevent many conflicts. The causes discussed here are arranged from origins common to almost all adolescents to the beginnings of unique disorders of only a few adolescents.

The Middle School Student

The fifth- through ninth-grade student is going through the period of early adolescence. Students at this period are sometimes mature and reflective; they are also sometimes immature and impulsive. They sometimes want to separate themselves from adult authorities, such as science teachers, and they sometimes want to be directed by adults. They sometimes want to be treated as individuals who can make decisions and act responsibly, and they sometimes want to be told what to do and when to do it. You can probably see from this discussion that it is difficult to know the appropriate way to respond to early adolescents.

The classroom can be a place where there is a certain amount of testing of adult roles and learning to be responsible. The result can be real bursts of energy for learning science and, also, great energy lulls. Frustrating? Yes. What can you do? First and foremost, try to understand that these behaviors are part of the developmental process and more often than not you should not internalize them as something directed at you, your teaching, or science. Second, establish the limits of tolerable activity for your class. The limits vary from teacher to teacher, and so we cannot define your limits. But you must have limits, and it is in your interest to identify them early, be sure they are clear, and make them known to your students.

Classroom management for this age level is largely a matter of instilling controlled self-discipline. Thus, limited freedom must be permitted so that self-discipline can be exercised. Students will not develop self-discipline and reliability if they are never given the opportunity to practice them. Overly rigid, authoritarian control, in which the primary motivation for good behavior is fear of the teacher's reprisal, will not develop the kind of student who is capable of self-discipline. At the same time, you cannot permit chaos by allowing uncontrolled behavior. A productive environment allows students to show initiative and be responsible for their actions within a framework of supervisory control by the teacher.

Early adolescents are usually quite responsive and sensitive to their peers. You can provide a positive approach to discipline by showing them that their actions influence the actions of other class members. When students misbehave and take up valuable class time, they are infringing on the study time of classmates. As a result, they are likely to lose the favor of peers and be seen as troublemakers; their status will correspondingly change.

The middle school science teacher can use peer pressure to bring about improved classroom behavior. You should constantly refer to the need for cooperation, the value of class time, the real purposes of the study of science, and mutual obligations to one's classmates.

The Senior High School Student

Sharp character differences between middle school students and senior high students do not exist. You can easily find younger students who are as mature as those in the senior high school. The reverse also is true. In general, however, as students mature, one finds more inhibition and less boisterous behavior in the classroom. This change is a natural result of the student's nearing adulthood. More thought is given to future plans, career choices, or decisions about advanced education.

From the standpoint of discipline, this increased maturity is salutary. The frequency of classroom incidents requiring disciplinary measures usually decreases. The student is more likely to respond to treatment normally accorded adults. Because of the student's sensitivity in this regard, the most effective measures you can use in disciplinary matters are those that treat the student as an adult, with responsibilities for adult behavior.

Some students cause discipline problems because they are bored with the activities. Although you may think that science is interesting and exciting, many students do not. Many students may not understand the concept being discussed or demonstrated, but some may. These difficulties can cause boredom and subsequent behaviors that lead to conflicts. Gearing class activities to the needs and interests of a wide range of students is certainly desirable. We also recommend having interesting and relevant lessons.

For some students, negative attention is better than no attention at all. Often students who are not successful academically, athletically, musically, and so on, become the class clowns or enact other behaviors that result in minor conflicts with the science teacher's activities. Attention-seeking behavior is often hard for teachers to change because the responses that teachers think reduce or eliminate the disruptive behavior are the very responses that reinforce the students' behavior.

The best way to reduce this behavior is to give the student attention in educationally constructive ways. Give recognition for the types of behavior you desire and try to ignore the attention-seeking behaviors you do not wish to have reoccur.

Maslow's hierarchy of basic needs—food, water, sleep, safety and security, love and belongingness, and self-esteem—describes another source of discipline problems. Sometimes students' basic needs have not been fulfilled, and the result is inappropriate behavior as they attempt to fulfill their needs. The teacher's response is to try and fulfill those needs in the best way possible and in a way that is also educationally productive.

In other cases, students can be frustrated with the amount of effort required in science versus the amount of learning and the rewards they receive. Other problems can be students' resistance to required subjects; that is, they feel forced to do activities they are not interested in or do not like, and they occasionally must comply with rules that conflict with personal preferences (e.g., wearing safety goggles).

We are not suggesting that you can provide a frustration-free environment. If frustrations are mounting, you can change the pace, switch activities, take a break, let the students have a discussion day, and so on. Forcing a tense situation can result in a conflict that could have been avoided.

We turn to the origin of a persistent and difficult discipline problem, alienation. Simply defined, alienation is a feeling of being separated or removed from one's group or from society. There is also a weakening of the social bond between the individual and society or the school system as a subsystem of society. The latter situation results in the student's rejection of school and the appropriate behaviors for those in school. Melvin Seeman, a sociologist, suggests five components that influence alienation (1959). We present this discussion as background for many school-related problems, such as assaults, gangs, guns, and general alienation of youth in schools.

The first component is *powerlessness*. This is the individual's belief that he is unable to influence his life under the present rules. This feeling was described by Rowe (1979) as fate control. Control over one's life is directed by something besides the individual. Here, science teachers can show individuals that they can achieve and that there are positive results for appropriate behavior.

Second, *meaninglessness*, is the absence of a clear set of values and connections between the individual and society. We have heard this problem discussed as relevance of instruction and the curriculum. Trying to present the concepts and processes of science in a context that is meaningful to the student helps reduce this problem.

Third, *normlessness*, is a reduction in the regulatory power of social rules and laws over individual behavior. To overcome this problem, the science teacher should make classroom rules clear and enforce them consistently and fairly. Let the students know that there are rules, that you intend that rules be obeyed, and that all students are subject to the same rules and consequences for rule violation.

Fourth is the feeling of *isolation*. Here the individual feels left out of the group, class, or school. This problem occurs most frequently in large and impersonal schools and science classes. Be sure students know that you care for them and want them in your classroom, and that you show some personal attention to their work.

The last component is *self-estrangement*. The individual comes to rely on external rewards and is easily frustrated when they are not received. The individual lacks self-confidence. This problem suggests a need for experiences where the student's confidence in completing a task is supported, and he learns that there are some internal rewards for learning science.

Our discussion of the origin of students' discipline has been general. There are more specific descriptions and recommendations concerning behavior problems of adolescents. Too often science teachers construct their own explanations for adolescent behavior, and they do not consult individuals or resources who are knowledgeable. Science teachers provide explanations of adolescent behavior such as, "He only wanted attention," "She comes from a broken home," or "He associates with the wrong group." Although these are explanations, they are also incomplete and hold every possibility of having misconceptions about the causes of adolescent behavior. If you do not think you have an adequate understanding of a particular student, or if you think something is seriously wrong, consult a counselor, school psychologist, or a book on behavior problems of adolescents. If you are wondering about a student's behavior, ask yourself the following questions:

- Is there a *pattern* of behaviors? Does the student behave the same way in other classes?
- Does the student continually demonstrate inappropriate behaviors for his or her age?
- Are the basic rights of others (including you) consistently violated?
- Is there the possibility of personal harm, either to the student in question or to others?

If you find yourself answering yes to these and similar questions, you should consult other resources because the behaviors are probably not in the acceptable range for your classroom and school. Do not try and solve the problem yourself. Many of your colleagues in the school system (special educators and school psychologists) are immediate and valuable resources.

DISCIPLINE PROBLEMS AND THE SCIENCE CLASSROOM

Science has numerous applications to the daily lives of students. This relevance gives you many opportunities to engage students in the study of science and avoid discipline problems. Science classes also have the advantage of demonstration devices, laboratory equipment, and educational technologies that stimulate interest. Students may find themselves drawn away from unruly influences and toward scientific interests. Furthermore, for students whose poor behavior may stem from lack of recognition, science classes may offer opportunities to gain prestige in the eyes of their peers.

On the negative side, certain unique problems exist in science classes. The laboratory, by its very nature, offers freedom of movement that may lead to discipline problems. Students without self-discipline will find many opportunities to cause trouble. The teacher's control must be completely effective, although not rigid, or the learning opportunities of the laboratory will be sacrificed. Learning requires considerable self-direction and attention to the task; and the laboratory, under skillful guidance of the teacher, can be a place where students develop self-discipline. We recommend completing Activity 21–3: Classroom Discipline, at the end of this chapter.

CONFLICT RESOLUTION AND REGULATION

Social psychologists have studied the resolution and regulation of conflicts. *The Resolution of Conflict* by Morton Deutsch (1973) is probably the single most important synthesis of these research findings. For this reason, we rely on Deutsch's ideas in this discussion.

We assume that conflicts will occur in the science classroom. We also assume that you are interested in their *constructive resolution*. Further, we assume that in those rare situations of intense conflict, you are interested in regulating the conflict so that the results are not destructive to you or others.

David and Roger Johnson and their colleagues (1992) have used the *cooperative learning model* to help students learn how to mediate conflicts in the classroom. Science teachers also will find such strategies helpful.

GUEST EDITORIAL ◆ SUSAN STEWART
Physical Science Teacher
Kenny C. Guinn Junior High, Las Vegas, Nevada

PREPARING FOR THE FIRST YEAR

Are there really slot machines in the classrooms? Do cacti grow on the playground? Do most of the teachers lose their paychecks in the local casino once a week? These and similar questions were asked by the folks back home when I left my conservative midwestern hometown to start an adventure as an eighth-grade science teacher in Las Vegas. Regardless of the different images people have of this city, I am certain that my experiences as a first-year teacher here are very much like those of my fellow graduates in other parts of the country. Adolescents are adolescents no matter where they live. The first year of teaching junior high is frustrating and exhausting. But as my colleagues assure me, it gets easier with experience, and I believe them.

Las Vegas is growing by leaps and bounds and consequently is one of the few places in this country crying for teachers. Kenny C. Guinn Junior High just opened this fall with 1,150 students drawn mainly from a rapidly expanding part of town. Most of the parents in this area are employed by the hotels on the Strip. Because of the growth of this town and the fact that in most cases both parents work, Clark County is a fairly wealthy district. Comprehensive special education programs, vocational-technical education, and career exploration are emphasized at all levels. Strong emphasis is placed on basics, and comprehensive programs are offered in all schools for youngsters who need special help in reading and mathematics. The Clark County School District reflects all ethnic backgrounds in its student population, staff, and approach to learning. The ethnic distribution of students is 78 percent Caucasian, 15 percent Black, 5 percent Spanish-American, 0.4 percent American Indian, and 1.6 percent others.

With three new schools opening, the district had 110 schools. It is a privilege to be a member of the staff that opened one of these new schools. It is exciting and challenging to participate in setting precedents and in creating new curricula for over 1,100 students. Other "thrills of opening a new school" (as my principal loves to say) include dealing with unfinished rooms and laboratory facilities, as well as undelivered supplies and equipment; waiting for defective doors and pencil sharpeners to be repaired; and running a program that has never been tried

before. These are times that call for the highest virtues a teacher can possess: flexibility, creativity, and patience.

This first year as a junior high science teacher is an eye-opening experience. There are so many things I am facing now for which no college course or textbook ever prepared me. Who could have taught me how to handle the politics within an administration or of a district school board? What course trained me to deal with the parents of different students? Was there a textbook recipe on how to deal with the normal day-to-day stress that confronts anyone who works with teenagers up to eight hours a day?

I am very thankful for the preparation I did have in my undergraduate years. There I developed very important organization skills. I learned how to express my creativity and my love for science through writing curricula. I was challenged to develop an educational philosophy and to learn how to apply it to practical and realistic objectives for the classroom.

My strength as a teacher lies in my enthusiasm for my subject and in my wholehearted conviction that it is valuable for every youngster. I also have a certain empathy for junior high students and a genuine concern for guiding them through "those difficult years." Supposedly, those qualities are enough to start the young teacher off with a smooth-running classroom. Well, if you do not discover it in student teaching, you soon find out on your first job how fragile all those idealistic goals and perceptions of education are; they shatter before your eyes within the first three months. It takes persistence and faith to piece together again a modified educational philosophy consistent with the classroom realities.

One of the major areas for which college courses have failed to prepare teachers in the past is discipline. As a first-year teacher, I did not anticipate spending 70 percent of the class time in teaching students that there are logical consequences to their actions. Genuine concern, conscientious hard work, and creative lesson plans are not enough. The prospective teacher needs to be trained in effective classroom control. I, like many other teachers, have learned classroom management by trial-and-error and have ended up using methods that just seem to work. For certain periods of time, my actions became mechanical and inconsistent; they were designed to eliminate my stress and they did not always consider the best interests of the child. To create a workable and consistent philosophy of discipline, the young teacher needs more background in adolescent psychology and more practical experience in the classroom with time to apply, evaluate, and revise this philosophy.

Teaching is not an eight-hour-a-day job; you are a teacher around the clock. The demands by the public for what a good teacher should be are increasing. The trend to make teachers accountable for cranking out reading, writing, and calculating students is on the uprise. More and more guidelines and restrictions are being established as to what you can teach. College is the place to learn some self-preservation and sanity-saver techniques. Gather ideas for your future curricula. Learn how to express your creativity in concrete objectives. Spend as much time as you can in the classroom—observing, experimenting, and evaluating. Solidify what you believe about children, the role of the teacher, and the role of the school, and start to observe how it works in practice.

There are still several things for which no text or course can prepare you. At times, as a first-year teacher, there will appear to be few rewards, and even those few will not be immediately visible. You need to be aware of the potential morale problems you will face among your faculty. Although you confront disillusionment, you must resist being drawn into a negative attitude. Keep hold of those ideals; you may have to reconstruct them, but do not ever abandon them. Budget cuts, crowded classrooms, and apathetic parents are other challenges which await you. It is part of the occupation, however, and your decision to stick with it boils down to your own conviction that you possess a potential power to make a dent in it all.

My personal conviction is strong enough that I know I want to make teaching my career. I plan to finish coursework for a Master's degree in geology or biology. With that, I would like to try teaching overseas for a few years. Environmental education also appeals to me, and I may want to move into the position of consultant. This first year is just the beginning, of course, and there are many possibilities ahead.

Avoiding Destructive Conflicts

Destructive conflicts tend to escalate from minor encounters to major events in the classroom. Involved persons increasingly rely on power and authority to resolve, regulate, and finally control the situation. As the conflict takes a destructive course, threats, coercion, and demonstrations of power steadily displace open discussion and the processes of peaceful resolution. The destructive course is set once (1) the conflict becomes a win–lose situation, (2) communication decreases and, thus, misperceptions increase, and (3) commitments for personal and social consistency decrease. We can look to the opposite of these three ideas for means to avoid destructive classroom conflicts. We suggest that you consider the following to avoid destructive conflicts:

◆ Encourage cooperation.
◆ Communicate clearly.
◆ Commit yourself personally and socially to resolve the conflicts peacefully.

Encouraging Constructive Resolutions

Conflicts will take a constructive course when science teachers use a creative problem-solving model for intervention. This model includes: (1) motivation to resolve the problem, (2) finding conditions to redefine the problem, and (3) suggesting ideas that might solve the problem. Following are suggestions that contribute to constructive resolutions of conflicts:

◆ Define the conflict as small.
◆ Resolve the conflict as soon as possible.
◆ Focus on the problem, not the person.
◆ Reduce the conflict to several smaller problems and resolve them.
◆ Emphasize similarities and common goals.
◆ Be sure all parties agree on the problem.
◆ Acknowledge that a conflict exists.
◆ Use a third party to resolve the conflict.

On some occasions, problems persist and for many reasons cannot be easily resolved. What should one do when conflicts cannot be constructively resolved? When a situation such as this exists, try to *regulate* the conflict so it does not take a destructive course.

Regulating Classroom Conflicts

In regulating conflicts, you attempt to set limits or boundaries on the interaction between conflicting parties. Regulating conflicts is obviously harder than resolving them. Both parties are often on a thin edge leading to destructive conflict. In such situations, teachers fear both for their safety and of having intense emotional responses. Likewise, students who find themselves in these situations have similar reactions. Although we must accept the legitimacy of these human responses, we must also guard against the detrimental consequences of a destructive conflict. What can a science teacher do? The following recommendations will help you regulate conflicts:

◆ Wait until parties are calm, rational, and organized, and then begin talking about the conflict.
◆ Demonstrate the legitimacy of all parties in conflict.
◆ Reach agreement on the limits of interaction.
◆ Use new and different approaches when other ones have failed.
◆ Develop a sense of community for all parties.
◆ Make sure rules are known, clear, and unbiased.
◆ Remedy rule violations as soon as possible.
◆ Use counselors for third-party regulation when necessary.

This is an excellent time to complete Activity 21–4: Resolution and Regulation of Conflicts, at the end of this chapter.

RECOMMENDATIONS FOR SCIENCE TEACHERS

Developing Self-Discipline

The goal of all discipline training should be the development of responsible self-discipline. Students should reach a point of inner motivation to complete learning tasks. Discipline of this type is positive and self-rewarding.

To reach this goal, students should have numerous opportunities to practice self-discipline or peer-group discipline. As with the development of any skill, there must be time to practice.

Teaching science by inquiry provides a setting for developing self-discipline. Individual work in the laboratory or on projects carried out in the classroom or at home gives many opportunities to develop good work habits and qualities of self-reliance, persistence, and reliability.

The following suggestions may assist the science teacher in providing an environment in which student self-discipline can be developed.

◆ Capture interest through activities, experiments, projects, and other student-oriented learning methods.
◆ Allow a degree of unstructured work commensurate with the maturity and experience level of the students.
◆ Give suitable guidance to students who require direction and external control, until it is no longer needed.
◆ Treat students as adults from whom you expect mature behavior and evidence of self-discipline.

Developing Techniques to Influence Behavior

Science teachers have techniques they use to influence student behavior. In light of earlier discussions of conflicts, many of these techniques are early-warning signals for the student. In this respect, the actual conflict is prevented, usually because the student responds to the signal.

Following are suggestions to consider:

◆ Use nonverbal signals, such as staring, clearing your throat, shaking your head, or stopping discussion and waiting.
◆ Use physical closeness or proximity control. While continuing the discussion, move near the disruptive student.
◆ Use humor to let the student know that enough is enough. Humor should not be sarcastic or personally demeaning.
◆ Ask the disruptive student a simple, direct, and easy question that will bring him or her into the discussion.
◆ Provide individualized help for particularly difficult problems, laboratories, or assignments.
◆ Help the students through transitional periods in class, such as shifting from a laboratory to seat work. Provide the time and be sure not to expect immediate responses during transitional periods.
◆ Establish patterns for laboratory work, cleanup, and other routine or common activities in the classroom.
◆ Modify routines such as attendance and distributing papers.
◆ Remove particularly tempting laboratory equipment.
◆ Have well-prepared lessons, use a variety of instructional methods, and show a personal interest in students.

Developing Means to Resolve Classroom Conflicts

The following recommendations may help avoid serious conflicts and bring about constructive, as opposed to destructive, consequences.

◆ Try to recognize the consistent patterns of behavior that can result in conflicts (see Figure 21–1).
◆ Clarify classroom rules. This may require mentioning particular rules relating to daily activities.
◆ Clarify each person's perceptions of the conflict situation. "How does this situation seem to you?"
◆ Maintain communication between the parties in conflict. You should be able to keep the lines of communication open for several minutes by avoiding personal insults, threats, or the use of power.

◆ Define the conflict as a mutual problem. "Look, you would like to visit, and I would like it quiet so students can work. How can we resolve this?"

◆ Avoid using power to resolve the conflict. Use of power can escalate the conflict or end it without resolution.

Developing a Discipline Policy

One of the strongest recommendations we can make to science teachers is to develop a discipline policy. Having a policy will result in consistency and clear expectations for both you and your students. Once you have developed a set of rules (and we suggest you do this with the students), the following suggestions should be considered when there are rule violations or conflicts.

◆ Request that the student stop the behavior and remind the student of the rule being violated.

◆ If the behavior continues, inform the student that the behavior must stop and that "we will have to resolve the problem."

◆ Establish what the problem is and what can be done to resolve it.

◆ Help establish the new rules and procedures of the student's behavior, and make clear the consequences for any further rule violations.

◆ Avoid using personally or physically harsh or abusive measures.

◆ Be consistent with the rules and consequences you have both agreed to. Be kind and firm. Being kind shows respect for the student; being firm shows respect for yourself as a person and as a science teacher.

Meeting Parents to Solve a Discipline Problem

Occasionally, you will find it necessary to meet with parents concerning their child's behavior in school. As a first step, we recommend you do a thorough assessment of the student's discipline problems; the steps are outlined in Figure 21–2. Scheduling a meeting with parents indicates a high level of concern about the student, which suggests

FIGURE 21–2 Steps in Assessment of a Discipline Problem

Understand the Problem
• What happened in the last 48 hours of the student's life?
• What were the circumstances of the problem?
• What patterns of behavior are identifiable?

Clarification of Current Difficulties
• What is the nature of present school-related problems?
• What is the duration of all problems, i.e., academic, behavioral, with peers?
• Have there been any recent changes in behavior? Achievement? Friendships?

Review of Background
• What is the relevant family background?
• What is the student's relation to peers?
• How has the student related to other teachers? Administrators? Counselors?

Identification of Coping Style
• How does the student handle stress?
• What triggers a discipline event?
• How does the student think problems could be avoided?
• What resources are available to help the student avoid difficult situations?

Assessment of Psychological and Developmental Status
• What is the student's mood?
• What are the student's cognitive, moral, social, and emotional levels of development?

List All Current Problems
• What are the present problems as perceived by (1) the student, (2) school personnel, and, if appropriate, (3) parents?
• Which problems have highest/lowest priority?

Establish Help That Is Required
• What does the student want (or agree) to do?
• What do school personnel recommend?
• What will all parties agree to?
• Should anyone else be involved?

Develop a Contract
• What terms are acceptable to student, school personnel, and parents?
• Who is responsible for doing what? When? How?

the need for information, documentation, and understanding of the problems and their potential resolution.

As you approach the meeting, keep several things in mind. First, have with you the information (and examples) concerning the student's problems. Second, realize that you have two goals: to gain further understanding of the student's background and role in the family, and to join with the family in a cooperative approach to intervene and improve the student's behavior.

Outside of the natural nervousness about meeting with parents, you have other challenges to bear in mind. The family usually will be concerned and often quite defensive about being called to school. To work effectively, you must have the cooperation of other school personnel. Finally, to develop a plan of action to be implemented, you will have to identify and work with the central decision makers in the family. The following are suggestions for a meeting with parents to solve a discipline problem. Note that some of the ideas in this section are applicable to any meeting with parents concerning school-related problems, whether academic, social, or behavioral.

- Be sure the meeting is scheduled. Do not plan to just see the parents after school or stop by their home unannounced.
- Have data, documentation, and examples. The more specific you can be, the more the parents will realize the seriousness of the problem.
- Try to recognize and overcome the parents' anxiety and defensiveness. Simple statements such as, "I'm sure you are concerned about your child's problems" will help. Also acknowledge that the parents know about their child and can contribute to the problem's resolution.
- Define and clarify the current problem. Present the problem in a clear and concise manner. Direct the discussion toward actual behaviors, and avoid derogatory comments relative to the student.
- Allow the parents time to respond. If the parents do not respond, then review the problems to impress on them the serious nature of the issues. If the parents seem confrontational, then direct their attention to the problem and not other issues, such as the personalities of school personnel. If the parents are cooperative, then develop a list of means that might be used to help resolve the problems.
- Develop a plan of action. Use the following process to establish the plan:

  1. Identify the behaviors to be increased or decreased.
  2. Are there other educational problems that should be attended to—for example, reading difficulties or learning disabilities?
  3. Identify the consequences of inappropriate behaviors. A logical-consequence approach often works very well.
  4. Decide on who, what, when, where, and how the plan will be implemented.
  5. Clarify the responsibilities of school personnel, parents, and others.
  6. Determine what all parties would see as improvement.
  7. Schedule other meetings to review progress.

SUMMARY

The matter of class control and management is of primary concern to science teachers. The multiple problems of preparing for class, devising suitable teaching methods, and keeping the class orderly are frequently overwhelming.

The actual statistics indicate that most science teachers do not perceive maintaining discipline as a problem. Nor do they think that they need assistance with discipline and class management. Although statistics indicate that discipline problems are not a major concern, it is nonetheless true that inevitably there will be conflicts in the science classroom. Conflicts occur when the activities of one individual or group are incompatible with the activities of another individual or group.

The causes of conflicts vary, but some of the more prevalent origins of conflict are adolescent need for separation and individuation, the need for attention, boredom, frustration, tension, and alienation. It is also true that the very nature of the science classroom—laboratory work, small group discussions, transitions from one activity to another—can cause problems.

Conflicts can be resolved using a few simple procedures: Define the conflict when it is small, work to resolve the conflict immediately, focus on the problem, reduce the problem to smaller parts, be sure there is agreement on the problem, and use a third party if necessary. If conflicts are headed in a destructive direction, then wait until all parties are calm; recognize legitimacy; reach limits on interactions; use new approaches if old ones do not work; make rules clear, known, and unbiased; and, again, use a third party if necessary.

There are many possible ways to resolve conflicts in the classroom. For students, an important first step is to develop self-discipline. A second step is developing a set of techniques that can prevent or resolve a conflict before it develops. Next, it is recommended that the teacher use the various means of resolving conflicts. Finally, each teacher must develop a discipline policy. Such a policy will result in a fair and consistent pattern of conflict resolution in the science classroom. All of these methods converge in the recommendation to be firm, friendly, fair, and consistent in your interactions with disruptive students.

INVESTIGATING SCIENCE TEACHING

ACTIVITY 21–1
CONFLICTS—WHAT WOULD YOU HAVE DONE?

The following three incidents were recorded by student teachers. The incidents occurred in science classrooms and represent discipline situations you might encounter. Read each incident and decide what you would have done had you been in the situation. After this you might share your response with other students in class to see what they would have done.

Incident 1

I was tutoring seven students who had fallen behind in their ninth-grade general chemistry class. As I proceeded, two male students made sly remarks that related to my subject material. I laughed at first, but then said, "OK, fun is fun, but let's get down to business." Since they did not take this as a warning, I told them that if they did not keep quiet and listen, they would have to return to the classroom. At this point I realized that I had "threatened" them in the form of a warning—the old "do-or-die" situation.

The two students continued this behavior, so I asked them to leave and just stand and wait. It was tough for me since I really did not want them to leave. They needed the help I was there to provide, but they infringed on the learning opportunity of the five other students. Class went well after the two boys left.

What would you have done in this situation?

Incident 2

This was a conflict between two students during a laboratory period. I stepped in to try to resolve it before it grew out of control.

The laboratory required a perch made of books. One student borrowed a book from a laboratory partner that was large enough to meet his needs. However, the partner decided he wanted to have the book available for reading during the period and asked for his book back. The first student didn't want to move his setup since it was all prepared and checked, so he refused the other's demands. The partner was slowly losing patience when I stepped in. Since the problem wasn't very grave to me, I told the two that we could easily solve the conflict and asked for the student's help in exchanging the book and rechecking the setup while the partner cooled off. The tension subsided, and they were able to work together during the period.

What would you have done in this situation?

Incident 3

I passed out a test. An A⁺ student forgot to do one section of the test. I graded all the tests. This student received a B⁺. She is a talkative student, always making jokes or puns in class to gain attention. After I returned the test, she said nothing in class for two days.

On the second day, I approached the student to help her on some problems in balancing equations. She had some trouble, so I was able to help her. After class she came up to me and insisted that I change her grade. I listened to her explain her mistake. Then I asked her what she thought should be done. She said I should change her grade. She decided that it would be fair to give her a better grade.

What would you have done in this situation?

Activity 21–2
Resolving Conflicts

Many factors influence the direction and resolution of a conflict. In this activity you are to examine your preferred methods for resolving problems. In other words, how do you typically try to resolve conflicts with other people? The insights you gain from the exercise will be beneficial when you have to resolve conflicts with students in your science class.*

The following sayings can be thought of as descriptions of different ways individuals resolve conflicts. Read each of the statements carefully. Using a scale of 1 through 5, indicate how typical each saying is of your actions in a conflict situation.

5—Very typical of the way I act in a conflict

4—Frequently typical of the way I act in a conflict

3—Sometimes typical of the way I act in a conflict

2—Seldom typical of the way I act in a conflict

1—Never typical of the way I act in a conflict

_____ 1. Soft words win hard hearts.

_____ 2. Come now and let us reason together.

_____ 3. Arguments of the strongest have the most weight.

_____ 4. You scratch my back, I'll scratch yours.

_____ 5. The best way of handling conflicts is to avoid them.

_____ 6. If someone hits you with a stone, hit the person with a piece of cotton.

_____ 7. A question must be decided by knowledge and not by numbers if it is to have a right decision.

_____ 8. If you cannot make a person think as you do, make the person do as you think.

_____ 9. Better half a loaf than no bread at all.

_____ 10. If someone is ready to quarrel with you, the person isn't worth knowing.

_____ 11. Smooth words make smooth ways.

_____ 12. By digging and digging, the truth is discovered.

_____ 13. One who fights and runs away lives to fight another day.

_____ 14. A fair exchange brings no quarrel.

_____ 15. There is nothing so important that you have to fight for it.

_____ 16. Kill your enemies with kindness.

_____ 17. Seek till you find, and you'll not lose your labor.

_____ 18. Might overcomes right.

_____ 19. Tit for tat is fair play.

_____ 20. Avoid quarrelsome people—they will only make you unhappy.

Insights about your typical style of resolving conflicts can be gained by adding the responses to different sayings. Add your typical responses to the sayings as indicated.

Sayings	Total	Response Style
1, 6, 11, 16	_____	Smoothing
2, 7, 12, 17	_____	Negotiating
3, 8, 13, 18	_____	Forcing
4, 9, 14, 19	_____	Compromising
5, 10, 15, 20	_____	Withdrawing

*This activity is based on ideas from P. Lawrence and J. Torsch, *Organization and Environment: Managing Differentiation and Integration* (Cambridge, MA: Division of Research, Graduate School of Business Administration, Harvard University, 1967); and from David Johnson, *Human Relations and Your Career: A Guide to Interpersonal Skills* (Upper Saddle River, NJ: Prentice Hall, 1978).

Science teachers are concerned with two goals as they resolve conflicts. One goal is personal and involves achieving, gaining, or maintaining something; for example, achieving an educational goal, gaining personal recognition, or maintaining one's sense of security in the science classroom. The second goal has to do with preserving or changing the relationship with the conflicting party. In the science classroom, this usually means preserving the relationship with a student, while changing the patterns of behavior.

The five different response styles to conflicts have direct bearing on the personal and relational goals of science teachers. We describe briefly the results of typical conflict responses relative to personal and relational goals of teachers.

Withdrawing

Withdrawing from a conflict fulfills neither the personal nor the relational goals. Essentially it is a lose–lose approach to conflict resolution since the educator gives up whatever educational goals he or she had and does not try to maintain the relationship with the student. In brief it is:

PERSONAL—LOSE

RELATIONAL—LOSE

Smoothing

Smoothing over the conflict gives highest priority to maintaining the relationship, often at all costs, including giving up personal goals. This is a resolution that usually results in:

PERSONAL—LOSE

RELATIONAL—WIN

Forcing

Here, personal goals are achieved at any cost. The cost is often to give up a personal relationship with the students. We have a situation of:

PERSONAL—WIN

RELATIONAL—LOSE

Compromising

The educator gives up personal goals, and relational goals are modified to resolve the conflict. All parties to the conflict give up something and are often dissatisfied with the results. The grounds for resentment by both educator and students have been established. The amount of resentment will depend on the perceived amount of compromise by each party to the conflict. In essence, this is a resolution of:

PERSONAL—TIE

RELATIONAL—TIE

Negotiating

Educators and students resolve conflicts through cooperative problem solving. Though some changes occur, essentially the goals of both educators and students are achieved and relationships maintained. This approach is one of:

PERSONAL—WIN

RELATIONAL—WIN

At times each of the different means of resolving conflicts is an appropriate course of action. Science teachers should understand this and make judgments concerning the situation, the student, and their personal and relational goals.

Think of a classroom situation where each of the response styles would be appropriate.

Withdrawing:

Smoothing:

Forcing:

Compromising:

Negotiating:

ACTIVITY 21–3
CLASSROOM DISCIPLINE

One of the best ways for you to gain an understanding of conflicts in the science classroom is to analyze a situation that you perceive to be a serious discipline problem. You must spend time observing in a science classroom or recall a situation from earlier experience.

Incident

Describe the actual behaviors and statements between the science teacher and the student during a conflict incident. This should be an objective statement. What did the teacher say and do? What did the student say and do?

After describing the incident complete the following:

Grade Level _____   The conflict was between: Teacher   Student

School _____   Male _____   Male _____

Class _____   Female _____   Female _____

Other (specify) _____

How long did the conflict last?

_____ Less than 1 minute   _____7–10 minutes

_____ 1–3 minutes   _____Longer than 10 minutes

_____ 4–6 minutes   _____Indicate how long _____

Most classroom conflicts involving individuals can be categorized at one of the levels described in Table 14–1. Indicate the individual student's behaviors in terms of the categories outlined.

1. Affirmation _____   Alienation _____
2. Assertion _____   Withdrawal _____
3. Aggression _____   Depression _____
4. Violence toward others _____   Violence toward self _____

Was this incident part of a recurring or consistent pattern of behavior for the student?

Yes _____   No _____   Don't know _____

Context

Describe the classroom setting, circumstances, and origin of the conflict. What preceded the conflict? Complete the following questions concerning the context of the conflict.

1. Was the situation during: Comments

_____ Teacher presentation (e.g., lecturing)

_____ Class discussion (e.g., teacher leading)

_____ Class presentation (e.g., film)

_____ Group work (e.g., laboratory)

_____ Individual work (e.g., reading)

_____ Student presentation (e.g., discussion of project)

_____ "In-between time" (e.g., between a laboratory activity and class discussion)

_____ Free time in class (e.g., after a test before bell)

_____ Free time in school (e.g., hall, cafeteria)

_____ Free time outside of building (e.g., after school)

_____ Other (Specify)

2. Should any unusual circumstances be noted?

3. What was the rule, policy, or expectation of behavior?

4. Was the rule, policy, or expectation presented or enforced as:

_____ Prohibitive (e.g., You should not . . .)

_____ Prescriptive (e.g., You should . . .)

_____ Benefit to group (e.g., You must, so we can . . .)

_____ Benefit to individual (e.g., We must, so you can . . .)

_____ Other (specify)

5. To your knowledge was the rule, policy, or expectation:

Stated _____	Unstated _____	by either party to the conflict?
Written _____	Unwritten _____	prior to the conflict?
Known _____	Unknown _____	to the accused?

Comments:

Resolution

Describe how the conflict was ended or resolved. Would you say the resolution was:

_____ Mutual (e.g., agreed on by both parties)

_____ Coercive (e.g., one party got the other to stop through warnings)

_____ Assertive (e.g., one party threatened the other)

_____ Aggressive (e.g., one party physically did something to the other)

What happened in the brief period (3–5 minutes) after the conflict ended or was resolved?

Did the behaviors change for the persons directly involved in the conflict?

How did behaviors change for those indirectly involved (i.e., the other students)?

Were there any other consequences of the conflict/resolution?

Interpretation

How would you interpret the conflict you have described?
What general statements can be made concerning the conflict?

Recommendations

What could be done to avoid further conflicts such as the one you described?

What would you do if you had to resolve a similar conflict?

If the entire methods class completed this investigation, it may be interesting to compile the observations and discuss your findings.

ACTIVITY 21–4
RESOLUTION AND REGULATION OF CONFLICTS

In this exercise we present conflicts that may occur in science classrooms. Based on the earlier discussions of conflict resolution and regulation you are to suggest what should be done: First, list what you would do. Then join with other members of your class and share ideas about the resolution or regulation of the conflicts.

Incident 1

At the beginning of class, the last period of a Friday afternoon, the students came in talking and laughing. They didn't settle down when the bell rang. The teacher didn't say anything for a while, just watched the students with an amused half-smile on her face. After about a minute she said something like, "How much time are you going to waste? You've already wasted 45 seconds, and you're going to have to stay after class for 45 seconds to make up for it."

What would you do?

Incident 2

Mary Beth was extremely withdrawn in science class. When I talked to her she would say, "Leave me alone and go away." Yet she was failing class, mostly due to not completing her assignments.

What would you do?

Incident 3

Gil was always causing a disturbance. He would continually clown around in class. His antics would disrupt the other students and my teaching. I must admit that he was occasionally funny.

What would you do?

Incident 4

Glen had a "chip on his shoulder" from the first day he entered earth science. One day we were cleaning up and he dropped a beaker of sand. I told him to clean it up and he responded, "I don't feel like it." I then said he had spilled it and he had to clean it. He replied, "Make me."

What would you do?

Incident 5

This wasn't the first time Jane had been in trouble. She just could not follow the rules. It didn't ever seem serious, at least until this incident. She came into class and was chewing gum. I told her to get rid of the gum. Then she started talking to her neighbor. I told her to pay attention. Then she started making remarks about my discussion. I was at my wit's end.

What would you do?

UNIT 8

STUDENT TEACHING

You are rapidly reaching the culmination of many years of study in preparation for the career you have chosen. Soon you will be in charge of real live classes in science for which you have been prepared. This is an exciting prospect full of promise for your future.

Now you will face students and see their enthusiasm or disinterested natures, their understandings or perplexities. You will have a chance to interact with them, give help when they need it, praise them when warranted. At the same time, you will be gaining confidence as a teacher yourself.

Many new teachers become discouraged after a few months on the job. It may not be what they expected, or perhaps the particular teaching situation is too daunting. Try not to become disheartened. Make friends with dedicated, experienced teachers with whom you can converse. All have faced many of the same problems you are facing. Do not be influenced by certain cynical teachers who may try to dissuade you.

They may decry what they think is your idealism for the task. Schools need idealistic teachers who can think creatively and who are willing to try new methods. An understanding principal will look favorably upon people with ideas. Within the rules and norms of the school, use every opportunity to bring out the best in students. Above all, be enthusiastic yourself. Show that you know your subject and that you want to share your knowledge with others. Students will respond favorably.

The chapter which follows provides many ideas and suggestions for finding materials for teaching and for making a successful transition to practicing teacher of science. We are hopeful you will be happy in your new employment and will make it a lifelong career. Speaking from experience, your choice is an excellent one. Hopefully you will discover untold joys in being a participant and contributor to a most noble profession—the education of young people in science.

CHAPTER 22

STUDENT TEACHING AND BECOMING
A SCIENCE TEACHER

Preservice teachers nearing the end of their teacher education program grow increasingly anxious to get on the job. They may look forward with anticipation to trying their wings as full-fledged teachers in charge of a class. At the same time, they are apt to feel apprehensive at the prospect of facing a roomful of students. Will they be able to hide their nervousness? Will their knowledge of the subject be adequate for the task? Will they be able to handle discipline problems? These questions and many others may cause concern as they face the future—a future that will see them transformed from science students to teachers of science.

WHY STUDENT TEACH?

The student-teaching experience is designed to smooth the transition from the role of student to that of teacher. It is your opportunity to test your liking for the teaching task. You will discover whether you really enjoy teaching the subject for which you have prepared. You will learn through close contacts with students whether you are really interested in teaching students of the particular age level for which you are assigned. Most important of all, you will, it is hoped, find a genuine enthusiasm in the teaching task, and enthusiasm sufficient to convince you that this should be your chosen vocation. At the same time, the student-teaching assignment will give the training institution an opportunity to evaluate your teaching capabilities. Successful student-teaching experiences, under the supervision of qualified classroom teachers, will enable the training institution to place its "stamp

of approval" on your work, with reasonable assurance of your future success.

The prospective science teacher can confidently expect to gain the following values from the student-teaching experience. These values will not accrue automatically. Much of the responsibility rests with the student teachers as they attempt to profit from this culminating experience in their teacher training.

1. *Improvement in confidence.* Actual experience with a science class will take away the fear of the unknown that everyone experiences when faced with a new situation. Many of these fears may turn out to be groundless. The experience actually will prove to be fun and exhilarating once the initial uneasiness is overcome. Psychologists have learned that the way to overcome the butterflies of fear of the unexpected is to become deeply involved in the experience. The immediacy of the routine problems then supersedes the anticipated difficulties.

2. *Putting theories into practice.* Here new teachers will be able to test what they have learned in methods classes (and in other classes) about ways of handling various problems. Handling individual differences among students, discipline cases, techniques of presenting science material, laboratory methods, working with small groups, and so forth, will provide situations in which student teachers can apply educational theories to classroom reality.

3. *Learning about student behavior.* Firsthand, responsible relationships with students will give student teachers the chance to study them, observe their behavior under a variety of conditions, and

learn about motivation, competition, enthusiasm, boredom, and many other factors that make up the climate of a typical classroom.

4. *Testing knowledge of subject matter.* Regardless of your self-assurance and confidence in your own knowledge of the subject you are planning to teach, you are likely to have a certain amount of apprehension about your ability to transmit this knowledge to others. The responsibility of teaching enthusiastic and sometimes critical students can be unnerving and is certain to convince you of the necessity of knowing your subject thoroughly and of preparing for contacts with the class. One frequently hears the comment, even among experienced teachers, "I really learned my subject when I had to teach it."

5. *Receiving constructive criticism.* At no other time in your long-term teaching experiences will you have the benefit of prolonged, intensive observation of your teaching by an experienced teacher who can be constructive in criticism and advice. This valuable benefit is not to be taken lightly. If the criticism and suggestions are taken receptively, with the intention of putting them into practice, this experience can be the most valuable part of your assignment. It is important, therefore, to select one's supervising teacher wisely. The chance to observe and be observed by a master teacher in an atmosphere of mutual respect and helpfulness is immeasurably worthwhile.

6. *Discovering teaching strengths and weaknesses.* You will have the opportunity to discover your own strong and weak points in the handling of science classes. You may find that performing demonstrations results in the most successful teaching and gives you the most pleasure. It may be that organizing classes into effective discussion groups brings about maximum learning under your direction. The questioning technique and the Socratic method of conducting teacher–pupil discussions may be most successful under your guidance. Conversely, these same activities may be the least effective for you. Knowing these facts early in your career will enable you to improve your weaknesses and capitalize on your strengths. It is certainly to the advantage of a science teacher to be highly competent in many methods of teaching, but it is equally important to recognize that individual teachers have certain innate teaching strengths and should use techniques that capitalize on these strengths.

7. *Gaining poise and finesse.* Because teaching is as much an art as a technique, experience should improve ways of handling classes (such as anticipating student questions and problems, timing, exploiting enthusiastic and dramatic classroom events, sensing the proper time for introducing a new activity, and commending good work). These factors will contribute to smoother functioning of class activities and to generally more effective learning. It is important to recognize, of course, that this kind of improvement will continue as long as a teacher teaches and that rarely, if ever, does a teacher reach complete perfection in the art.

Selecting Your Supervising Teacher

Frequently, a certain amount of latitude is allowed prospective student teachers in their choice of school, subject, and teacher under whom they wish to work. The extent of this freedom will vary with the institution and circumstances in which the student-teaching program is operated, and it is entirely possible that assignments may be made quite arbitrarily. However, it is more likely that, within certain limitations, the wishes of the student will be taken into consideration.

Therefore, it is to your advantage to make a careful selection of school, subject, and supervising teacher. Often, new teachers feel that their student-teaching assignment was the most valuable experience in their training program. This can be true if the selection is well made and the experience fulfills its potential.

Prospective student teachers should obtain the maximum advantage by teaching in their major field. It is this area for which they are best prepared and in which they probably will feel the greatest confidence. If the situation permits, teaching in their minor field also, under a different supervising teacher, may be advantageous; they will benefit from constructive help from two experienced teachers. This experience may be analogous to an actual situation as a full-time teacher in a small or medium-size school system.

It would be wise to visit several classes in a number of schools in the quarter or semester before your student-teaching assignment. Arrangements can be made through the principal of the school, and advance notice can be given to the teachers involved. If the purpose of the visits is explained, you will probably be favorably received, particularly if it is a school in which student teachers customarily have been supervised.

The advantages of the visit can be manifold. You will be able to refresh your memory of the atmosphere and activities of a high school classroom. You will be able to observe an experienced teacher in action. You will mentally attempt to project yourself into an equivalent situation as a teacher in charge of a class, a desirable step in preparation for your actual student-teaching assignment. You may be able to talk briefly with the teacher at the close of class to gain further insights. After several such visits to a variety of classes (including several outside the field of science), you will be able to choose more intelligently the kind of teaching situation you wish to select for the student-teaching experience.

Keen interest and rapt attention are key hallmarks of science students in inquiry classes.

Suggestions of criteria to look for in the teaching situation are as follows:

1. Is the teacher well prepared, and teaching in a major field?
2. Does the teacher have good control of the class?
3. Do the students appear to be alert and interested in the activities?
4. Is there a genuine atmosphere of learning?
5. Do the facilities and materials appear to be adequate for the kind of science being taught?
6. Does it appear that the teacher is a person from whom one can learn valuable teaching techniques?
7. Is there opportunity for a certain degree of flexibility in carrying out one's teaching plans?
8. Does the teacher have a moderate workload, thus affording time for constructive help for a student teacher?
9. Does the teacher appear to be interested in serving as a supervisor for the student teacher?

Meeting Your Supervising Teacher

Once the assignment is made for a particular school, class, and teacher, it is imperative that the student teacher arranges a short interview before attendance at the first class. This interview can be brief but should be a day or two in advance and by appointment. You will then avoid incurring the displeasure of the supervising teacher by intruding on last-minute preparation for class and will provide for an interchange of questions and answers.

At the interview, be punctual, interested, enthusiastic, and suitably dressed. The purpose of the interview is to become acquainted and to exchange ideas and information.

The supervising teacher is interested in knowing your background and preparation, as well as in any special qualifications you may have, such as the ability to handle audiovisual equipment, take charge of a science club, or talk about travel experiences. You should learn what your role is to be in the classroom, what meetings to attend, what text materials are in use, and so forth.

The supervising teacher will probably suggest a period of class observation, perhaps a week or two at the outset. There may be certain room duties to perform, such as roll taking, reading announcements, and distributing materials. Each of these tasks will enable you to quickly learn the names of pupils, a necessary step in establishing rapport with members of the class. You probably will be encouraged to prepare a seating chart immediately. Text materials may be discussed and the teacher's long-range objectives clarified. You will probably be asked to read certain assignments so that you will be acquainted with the students' present studies. You will find it imperative to do this regularly in order to best assist students who need help.

Facilities and apparatus available for teaching the science class may be shown to you during the interview. Location of the library and special preparation rooms may be pointed out. The place in the classroom where you may observe the activities of the class may be designated. (In one school, it was customary for the student teacher to sit next to the demonstration desk, facing the class. In this way, she learned to recognize pupils more quickly; but, more important, this arrangement enabled the student teacher to see the expressions on the pupils' faces as they responded to questions or watched a demonstration, as they showed perplexity, or as they registered insight into problems under discussion.)

A new student teacher tries out her skills while the supervising teacher looks on.

Students who intend to teach in urban-area schools are advised to seek out student-teaching experiences that will give them the best possible preparation for such an assignment. Such an experience might involve student teaching in a school similar to the type in which they ultimately wish to be teaching.

BEING A STUDENT TEACHER

Your First Days in the Class

Observing pupils in the science class can be a profitable experience the first few days or weeks. You have an advantage in this situation because you are not preoccupied with teaching plans and conducting the class, as is the regular teacher. The alert observing student teacher can, in fact, be of assistance to the regular teacher in recognizing incipient discipline problems, lack of interest, or special conditions that might lead to better teaching if recognized early. You may wish to follow a systematic observation program to become familiar with all class members. For this purpose, a checklist of individual differences is suggested. Place a check mark in the column opposite the observed characteristic. The numbers represent individual pupils observed.

◆

Recognizing Individual Differences in a New Class During the First Few Weeks

Things to observe and consider:

Pupils 1 2 3 4

◆ Health
◆ Physical defects and differences
◆ Personality
◆ Basic skills
◆ Relationships with fellow pupils
◆ Relationship with teacher
◆ Class participation
◆ Class attitude and cooperation
◆ Dependability
◆ Probable ability combined with effort

◆

The first days in the student-teaching class should afford opportunities to give individual help to pupils who need it. Do not answer questions directly, but use inquiry methods, that is, ask guiding questions. It is wise to confer with the supervising teacher about the extent of such help. There may be some reason to withhold assistance on certain assignments. At the same time, contact with students on an individual basis is an excellent way to gain confidence in your ability to explain, teach, or convey information. You should capitalize on every possible opportunity to develop this skill.

If the science class is one in which laboratory work plays a large part (e.g., chemistry, physics, biology, or earth science), then you will have many opportunities to give individual help. The student teacher can also be of significant help to the regular teacher in preparing laboratory apparatus and supplies. In this situation, the student teacher will realize that teaching a laboratory science requires extensive planning and attention to detail.

Because the initial period of observation may be rather brief, perhaps only a few days or a week, student teachers will do well to begin thinking about the choice of a teaching area or unit. Such a choice may have already been made in conference with the supervising teacher. It will certainly depend on the subject-matter, goals of the course during the semester or quarter, or the assignment. In anticipation of student teaching, you will wish to gather appropriate materials and to prepare general plans. Certain details of the preliminary planning are considered in the next section.

Preparing to Teach a Lesson

A teacher facing a class for the first time may expect to accomplish far too much in a given amount of time. Although it is not necessarily wasteful to overplan a lesson, it is a mistake to try to teach everything on the lesson plan just because it is there. Sometimes the learning pace of the pupils does not allow the entire lesson plan to be completed. You must be in tune with your class constantly, sensing the proper pace and modifying your presentation as the situation demands.

A second common fault of the beginning teacher is the tendency to teach beyond the students' comprehension. This fault may be a result of recent contact with college courses, in which the level is very high, or the inability to place abstract ideas into concrete terms for comprehension by secondary school students. The problem is important enough that beginning teachers should make certain that presentations are at the appropriate level for the class involved. Perhaps they could try a few test trials with individual students to acquire a realistic sense of the proper difficulty level before teaching the entire class.

Construction of unit and daily lesson plans is an important task at this stage. It is important to have a clear idea of what you wish to accomplish in the allotted time and what specific objectives are to be met. Student teachers should attempt to place themselves in the position of a science pupil who is learning about the material for the first time. They should consider factors of interest, motivation, individual differences, time limitations, facilities, and equipment; they should try to anticipate the kinds of problems that may occur and prepare possible solutions. When student teachers have considered these elements, they will feel more secure and will have fewer discipline problems.

Beginning teachers should also anticipate questions from the class. First attempts at planning tend to neglect preparation for handling these questions and fail to provide enough time for dealing with them in the class period. Yet the frank interchange of ideas between teacher and students, which is provoked by questions, can be an effective teaching technique and should not be ignored. In planning, try to anticipate the kinds of questions students may ask. If you remember that the students may be encountering the subject matter for the first time, then it is not too difficult to foretell what questions may come to their minds. Jot down these probable questions on your lesson plan, along with suitable answers or with suggested procedures for finding the answers. Time spent in this manner is not wasted, even if the specific anticipated questions do not arise. You will gain confidence in your own understanding of the subject matter and in your ability to provide suitable answers.

A final point to consider is that of proper pacing and timing of the class period. The written lesson plans may have suggested time allotments for various activities, but the actual class is certain to deviate to some extent. The important idea to remember is to be flexible enough to accommodate minor variations within the class period. However, to avoid gross miscalculations of time requirements for certain activities, rehearse them in advance. A short lecture, for example, can be tried out on one's roommate, who will be able to give critical comments on clarity and organization, as well as timing. In the case of student activities or laboratory work, it is usually advisable to allot about 50 percent more time than appears adequate for the teacher to do the work. This leeway is also recommended in giving written tests.

At all stages of planning for the first day of teaching, it is imperative that student teachers keep the supervising teacher informed of their plans, solicit advice and assistance, and, in general, plan in such a way as to make the transition from regular teacher to student teacher as smooth as possible.

The First Day of Teaching

If you have had frequent opportunities to work with individuals and small groups before your first day of actual teaching, you will find the new experience a natural extension of these tasks and a challenging opportunity for growth in the art of teaching. A good introduction will get the class off to an interesting start. A brief explanation of the purpose of the lesson and the work at hand, followed immediately by plunging into the class activities, will convey to the students an appreciation of the tasks to be accomplished. A forthright and businesslike manner will elicit class cooperation and leave no doubt about who is in charge.

Attention should be given to proper speech and voice modulation. A good pace should be maintained, and, above all, genuine enthusiasm must be displayed. This enthusiasm will normally be infectious and will secure an enthusiastic response from the class. If possible, students should be encouraged to participate. Questions from students should be encouraged and a relaxed atmosphere maintained for free interchange of ideas.

It is usually advisable, especially with middle school classes, to vary the activity once or twice during the class period. Perhaps a short lecture can be followed by a brief video and the period concluded with a summarizing discussion. Or a demonstration might be followed by a period of individual experimentation. It is true that planning and execution of a varied class period requires more work on your part, but the dividends appear in the form of enthusiasm, alert attention, and better learning.

The last few minutes of a class period are often used to summarize the major points of the lesson and to make appropriate assignments. It is important to recognize that students need to have a feeling of accomplishment and progress to keep their motivation high. A final clarification of what is expected of them in preparation for succeeding lessons is worth a few minutes at the close of a class period.

Completion of your first day of teaching should be followed as soon as possible by reflection on the successes and failures of the class period and an effort to diagnose any problems that may have arisen. This evaluation can usually be done profitably in conference with the supervising teacher and can be a useful follow-up to the day. Any required adjustments in future plans can be made at this time, necessary additional materials can be gathered, and the stage can be set for a new day of teaching.

Your Responsibilities

The opportunity to student teach in a given school system under a competent supervising teacher should be considered a privilege. Contrary to an apprentice in a typical trade situation, the apprentice teacher is not working with inanimate materials, such as wood and metal, but with live human beings of infinite worth. You must never forget your responsibility to provide the best possible education for the students and to avoid possible harmful measures.

It is, therefore, extremely important to make lesson plans with care, to consider individual differences in interest and ability, and to conduct the class in an atmosphere of friendly helpfulness. Each student should be considered a potential "learning being" with capabilities for infinite growth. The teacher's responsibility is to develop this potential to the maximum extent.

The student teacher's responsibility to the supervising teacher rests in the area of recognition of authority and respect for experience. Certainly, there may be disagreements about teaching methods, but the final authority is the supervising teacher, who is officially responsible for the class. At the same time, an alert student teacher can be of great help by anticipating the needs of the class, suggesting materials, preparing materials, and in general earning the title of assistant teacher, which is used in some school systems. The varied backgrounds of student teachers and their willingness to share experiences and special talents can make the science classroom more interesting and educationally effective.

Also important is the responsibility of student teachers toward themselves and their potential as science teachers. It would be relatively easy to sit casually by, waiting for things to happen in the student-teaching assignment. The student teachers who gain the most, however, from the standpoint of personal growth, will be those who enter the experience with a dynamic approach, intent on learning everything they can in the time allotted. They will participate, when permitted, in meetings of the school faculty, in attendance and assistance at school athletic events, in dramatic and musical productions of the school, and in other functions relating to school life. In this way, they will see their pupils in many roles outside of the science classroom and will gain insight into the total school program. They will be able to achieve a balanced perspective of their own role as teachers of science among the other academic disciplines and curricular activities. Such experience will enable them to become mature teachers of science and will complete the metamorphosis from the role of college science student.

Concerns of the Student Teacher

A questionnaire listing nine areas of preparation was distributed to 40 student teachers of secondary science at the University of Northern Colorado. They were asked to indicate those areas in which they felt the need for greater preparation.

Four areas receiving the greatest number of responses were evaluating students and grading, handling discipline problems, answering students' questions, and stronger preparation in subject matter, in that order. Other areas of consideration were lesson planning, record keeping, extracurricular activities, demonstrations, and handling laboratory work.

In the same survey, when asked to suggest improvements in the methods courses in physical and biological sciences, students made the following suggestions.

1. Put more emphasis on discipline problems, and on answering students' questions.
2. Have more discussion on techniques for handling slow and fast learners.
3. Do more demonstrations and experiments.
4. Emphasize methods of evaluation.
5. Provide opportunities to hear the experiences of recent student teachers.
6. Evaluate the texts and materials of the new secondary curriculum projects.
7. Provide more opportunities to speak in front of a group and do demonstration teaching.
8. Cover a greater variety of topics, including test construction, extra-credit work, interest development, grouping of students, policies regarding student failures, and science fairs and exhibits.
9. Provide opportunities to observe several teachers in one's field.
10. Acquire more information on specific sourcebooks of activities, demonstrations, and experiments.

Matters of concern to the beginning teacher were investigated by Adams and Krockover in 1997. Foremost among these were concerns about potential job assignments, teaching responsibilities, and matters relating to curriculum development. Other more personal concerns were related to management of one's time, discipline control, and ways to present content information. In the same study, preservice teachers felt that content coursework for teachers was sometimes too specific and some of the pedagogical courses had limited usefulness. Also, the group surveyed believed that field experiences before graduation needed to be increased. To accomplish this, they felt that being an undergraduate teaching assistant helped to ease the transition to becoming a teacher.

PROFESSIONAL DEVELOPMENT STANDARDS

"Prospective teachers become active participants in schools through such activities as internships, clinical studies, and research" (NRC, 1996). This statement by the subcommittee on professional development standards of the *National Science Education Standards* (National Research Council) sets the tone for development of activities and experiences for prospective science teachers.

Professional Development Standard B—Learning to Teach Science—states that "professional development of teachers of science requires integrating knowledge of science, learning, pedagogy, and students, and applying that understanding to science teaching." A particularly appropriate suggestion in relation to student teaching is that "learning to teach science takes place in actual classrooms to illustrate and model effective science teaching and permit teachers to struggle with real situations, practice and expand knowledge and skills in an appropriate context."

The *National Science Education Standards* provide criteria for judging the opportunities and activities available for prospective and practicing teachers of science. Among these criteria is a recurring reference to the requirement of learning a breadth and depth of science content through the perspectives and methods of inquiry. Teachers must be actively involved in investigating scientific phenomena, interpreting results, and making sense of the findings. Problems should be organized around significant issues and events and should give opportunities to practice inquiry skills. There must also be opportunities to integrate science knowledge, pedagogy, and understanding of students.

A further interesting standard is that schools must become centers of inquiry that support the professional growth of science teachers. This includes involving teachers in leadership roles and providing an environment for support of new science teachers in their classroom responsibilities.

LICENSURE OPTIONS

Some states require prospective teachers to take certain mandated tests before securing approval to teach in the state's schools. One example is the state of Colorado, which requires, as a result of the recent passage of the Educator Licensing Act, four assessments in the field of preservice education. Licensure requires four tests. An entry test in basic skills is followed by three exit tests in (a) liberal arts and sciences (general education), (b) professional knowledge, and (c) content knowledge. The tests are called the Program of Licensing Assessments for Colorado Educators (PLACE) exams. The tests are designed by the National Evaluation Systems of Amherst, Massachusetts, in contract with the state of Colorado. Other states have implemented or are considering implementation of similar preservice licensing procedures.

Each state has its own requirements for licensure. A list of requirements can usually be obtained by writing directly to the state's Department of Education for which you wish information.

SECURING A TEACHING POSITION

Recent years have shown a fluctuating job market for teachers. Currently, there is a severe shortage of science teachers. Even so, prospective teachers must work diligently at finding a suitable position. Competition is high, and they must use all available avenues to secure a satisfactory teaching job. Frequently, schools or departments of education set aside certain days in the spring of the year as "job fairs" at which prospective teachers and school administrators can meet and exchange information about job possibilities. Be sure to take advantage of these to become acquainted with school needs and to display your own qualifications.

Preparing to Look for a Job

As preparation to enter the job market, there are several necessary steps. As prospective employees of a school system, you will wish to secure several recommendations from your college instructors in your major and minor fields, your methods instructors, and perhaps others of your own choosing. Be sure to obtain permission to use an instructor's name for a reference and request the recommendation personally, either by letter or by personal conversation. Remember that instructors

Personal Recommendation

FIGURE 22–1 Sample Recommendation Request Form

Name _____

Classes from me _____

_____

Grades _____

Because many of you will be applying for teaching jobs (or other jobs in the near future), you will be required to obtain letters of recommendation for your files at the Office of Appointments. If requested to write such a recommendation, I shall be happy to oblige but I should like to have some further information about you to include in the recommendation. It is my belief that the following types of information can be very meaningful to a prospective employer and may make the difference between being hired and not being hired.

Please give information on the following points:

1. Any experience you have had working with young people in any capacity other than practice teaching, such as scout leader, Sunday school teacher, swimming instructor, camp counselor, or other. Give specific information.

2. Any scientific hobbies or specialties you may have (past or present), such as specimen collecting, lapidary, ham radio, model airplane building, amateur telescope making, special reading in a topic, expertise with computers, etc.

3. Any travel you have done that may have been scientifically broadening or educational, such as to Carlsbad Caverns, the Grand Canyon, Yellowstone Park, or any others.

4. Any other experimental information that may be important for a prospective employer to know.

are asked to write many recommendations and that a thoughtful instructor will put in a reasonable amount of time toward writing a good one. To make the job as easy as possible, supply your instructor with specific information about yourself. For example, provide information on your hobbies and on your experiences in working with children, such as coaching, camp counseling, summer recreation programs, Sunday school teaching, and so forth. Relate any special competencies that you have, such as the ability to handle a photography club, or special knowledge of rocks and minerals, or model airplane building, or any other relevant experiences. Give specific evidence of the kinds of experiences that would qualify you to be a good science teacher. This kind of information will pay off and will secure for you the immediate attention of a thoughtful school administrator.

When requesting a recommendation, if the contact with the instructor is several months old, it is a good idea to supply a snapshot of yourself to refresh your instructor's memory. A sample recommendation request form is shown in Figure 22–1.

Using Placement Services

You will probably wish to use one or more teacher placement services to secure a satisfactory position. Most teacher-training institutions have placement offices. There may be an enrollment fee for this service. You would be well advised to get all your required materials submitted early, usually by January 1, because

the placement offices begin to make appointments with school administrators early in the new year to interview applicants for positions. If you are conscientious about submitting all of your requirements, you will be eligible to meet with prospective employers.

Many state departments of education have placement bureaus. It is wise to contact them and give them the necessary information so they can assist you in locating vacancies within the state where you plan to teach.

Letters of Application

Once you have been notified of a suitable vacancy for which you wish to apply, you must prepare a letter of application that will be considered favorably by the recipient. If you plan to type your own application letter, it is a good idea to check with someone to refresh your memory on style and form. In many cases, your letter of application will merely elicit a standard application form from the school to which you apply. In this case, give the complete information required by the school.

If possible, have your letter of application typed by a professional. A professional letter adds quality and dignity to the correspondence and will impress the recipient. A poorly constructed letter with typographical errors, erasures, and other evidence of carelessness certainly will get tossed into the reject file.

In your letter of application, be sure to include all of the necessary information to give a clear picture of your qualifications for the job for which you are applying. Include your major and minor teaching areas,

FIGURE 22–2 Sample
Letter of Application

January 12, 2007
123 Hope Avenue
Caton, Missouri

Dr. Harold Oglesby
Superintendent of Schools
Wichita Falls, Missouri

Dear Dr. Ogelsby:

I wish to apply for the position as teacher of middle school science announced as a vacancy in
your school system. The placement office at Webster State College, Webster, Kansas, will send
my complete credentials.

My major teaching area is junior high school science and my minor is mathematics. In addition,
I have secured a teacher's permit for driver education and am qualified to give the driver education course of the state of Missouri.

Photography has been a hobby and a vocation of mine for many years, and I would be interested
in supervising a junior high school photography club.

I shall be happy to come for a personal interview at your convenience.

Sincerely yours,

information on special competencies (such as ability to
handle specific types of clubs), and information on your
familiarity with new teaching trends (such as inquiry
teaching, team teaching, individualized instruction,
new curriculum projects, open-school concepts, and
other current trends).

You might conclude the letter by volunteering your
willingness to meet the superintendent for an interview
at a mutually convenient time. A sample letter of application you might use as a guide is shown in Figure 22–2.

The Job Interview

If you are interviewed by the principal or superintendent of schools, you will wish to present yourself in the
best possible manner. Be sure to arrive on time, dress
appropriately, and be well groomed. Allow the employer
to conduct the interview at her own pace and in her
own manner. Supply information about yourself as requested. If asked, discuss your philosophy of teaching
briefly, tell about your training and special competencies, and mention your professional memberships (such
as the NSTA, Academies of Science, National Association of Biology Teachers [NABT], and other organizations to which you belong).

You will have the opportunity to ask questions. You
will want to know some of the details of the position,
such as the level of the class, its probable size, the text
materials that are used, and the availability of supplies.
Perhaps you will want to ask questions about the community, such as the availability of housing, churches,
and recreation facilities. Let the interviewer supply you

with information on the prospective salary and other
fringe benefits associated with the job.

After Obtaining the Job

Securing a position as a new teacher is a major accomplishment and may give you the feeling that your teaching career is set for all time, but this would be a
shortsighted view. Of course, it should be your intention to remain on the job with the expectation of doing
excellent work, but you should also recognize that you
may want to move upward professionally. Therefore, it
is a good idea to keep your placement file up to date.
Keep in contact with the placement office by informing
them of any new coursework you have taken, such as
institutes or summer school attendance. Have updated
transcripts supplied to the placement office, which may
include the completion of a new degree or additional
coursework. When you are ready to apply for a new position, be sure to get recommendations from your principal and supervisor.

MAKING THE TRANSITION
TO A PROFESSIONAL TEACHER

Up to this point, you have been a student preparing to
meet the challenges of teaching science. You have studied your chosen subject(s) carefully, taking in volumes
of factual knowledge with the expectation of using it at
some time in the near future as a science teacher. You
have been regaled with information about teaching

methods and strategies and have observed other science teachers perform in the classroom. You have studied the psychology of adolescents and young adults to learn what makes them tick and what motivates them in and out of school. You have gotten your feet wet in the science classroom by doing your student teaching under the supervision of an experienced science teacher.

Now you are approaching the end of this long process and are looking forward to being a science teacher in a classroom of your own. Perhaps you are a bit apprehensive at this point. Perhaps you have seen enough of the reality of teaching to feel intimidated by the thought of taking full charge of a class. Or, alternatively, perhaps you have gained confidence, through your student-teaching experience and with the guidance of sensitive science teachers, so that you are enthusiastically anticipating the real world of science teaching. The authors hope this is the case. To put this situation in a more concrete setting, we shall present four examples of prospective teachers as they move toward this final stage of their preparation.

◆

Josh

Josh is a student teacher in Earth science at a medium-size high school. He teaches five classes of ninth-grade earth science under the tutelage of two different science teachers. His assignment of teaching was gradually increased from observing to teaching one class to ultimately taking over five classes. Although all classes were ninth-grade level, there were perceptible differences in the nature and character of the five classes. The vagaries of grouping children and the dynamics that prevailed in different classes promoted a distinctive character obvious even to an outside observer. Josh found it necessary to make adjustments in his planning, teaching style, and handling of each of the classes.

As is common with new teachers, who have most recently sat through dozens of college classes in which lectures were the prevalent form of presenting material, Josh tended to emphasize lectures in his classes, too. While the topics under study were potentially interesting, the lecture format didn't capture the interest of the ninth graders. They were restless, somewhat noisy, and they carried out Josh's assigned tasks rather perfunctorily. The main emphasis for them seemed to be to memorize the factual information Josh presented to be ready to give it back on a factual test. While some of the students were comfortable with this teaching method, the majority of the class looked upon it as a rather onerous way to learn science. In fact, they did not clearly understand what the purpose of learning the facts was and did not perceive how the information would benefit them.

The experienced teachers under whom Josh was working talked with Josh and suggested he try an activity approach to teaching the topics. They gave him some concrete suggestions of materials he could use and procedures to follow. Josh tried out some of the suggestions in his next class periods and found that the students enjoyed them. To his surprise, Josh found that he had fun using activity labs and was actually less exhausted at the end of the day. The students did as well on the tests as they had in the former lecture approach. In addition, they seemed to have a better attitude toward their learning. There were no discipline problems.

Barbara

Barbara is a student teacher in a junior high school in a midsize city. She teaches earth science to seventh graders three class periods a day and physical science to eighth graders two periods a day. She feels most comfortable with the seventh-grade classes, mainly because they are less disruptive and easier to manage.

Barbara's supervising teacher has not had a student teacher before. He feels a bit intimidated by the new responsibility and has turned over much of the class management to her. Although this is a challenge to Barbara, it is also a good experience because she is given considerable freedom to operate the classes as she wishes. Her teacher has operated his classes in a rather perfunctory manner and has not given much help to his student teacher other than to suggest that Barbara follow the standard format prevalent in the class.

Barbara has tried to provide a modicum of activity labs (at least once a week) in which the students participate in some type of investigation. These are followed by short postlab discussions. Students usually have some type of short write-up to turn in at the conclusion of the class period.

The discipline in the seventh-grade classes is average. Most students are serious learners, but one or two give way to their adolescent urges to show off or distract their classmates. Barbara has learned infinite patience in dealing with these children and has good results without having to resort to authoritarian measures of discipline control. This is perhaps the best indicator of Barbara's potential success as a teacher of junior high school children in the future.

Sam

Student teaching for Sam took place in a modern high school under the tutelage of an experienced science teacher with a reputation for good teaching and control of his classes. Sam has two tenth-grade physical science classes and one called global science, which is a class of students who have not taken a regular science sequence in high school but who need at least one science to graduate.

Although physical science was not Sam's major field in college, he had several courses in physics and chemistry that prepared him adequately for this assignment. He seemed to prefer teaching the physical science classes over the global science, mainly because of the quality and motivation of the physical science students. He has some very bright students in these classes, which lends challenge and satisfaction to his teaching. (It is not uncommon for beginning teachers to face two or three different subject assignments in their first year of teaching. A student-teaching assignment that gives varied experiences and responsibilities in different kinds of classes is an excellent preparation for this eventuality.)

Sam has a relaxed approach to his teaching and develops good rapport with the students. He is firm about tasks and requirements but is willing to listen to the students and is helpful in working with them. These traits, if carried over to his first job, will smooth the transition and raise considerably his chances of having a satisfying and productive teaching career in the sciences.

Erica

Erica teaches biology and chemistry as her student-teaching assignment. She has three biology classes and two of chemistry. She is fortunate to have two highly qualified, experienced teachers as her supervisors in the classroom. They feel that she is doing an excellent job and are lavish in their praise of her teaching.

Two of Erica's classes are college-prep classes, with more than 80 percent of the students planning to go on to college. Consequently, Erica instructs them largely in a typical college manner, with much lecture, note taking, and factual emphasis on terminology, taxonomy, and high-level concepts in biology. The students seem to eat it up. They realize, it seems, that Erica knows what she is talking about when she informs them that they are getting excellent preparation for their upcoming experience in college. The small fraction of students in the classes who are not college bound are not sure how the information they are getting will help them in their careers but are sure that somehow it represents science, which seems to be in the news quite often these days.

◆

The examples described here represent four different sets of experiences by prospective teachers of science. A common thread is that each experience is unique and is the result of many factors coming together—individual natures of the students, varying traits and expertise of the supervising teachers, class makeup and objectives, and the subject matter of the class, among others. So it will be in your first employment opportunity as well. Perhaps the lesson to be learned is to be prepared for anything. A teacher needs to be flexible and adaptable. Of course this is what makes teaching exciting and rewarding as well!

Throughout this book we have emphasized *Becoming a Science Teacher* to bring unity and clarity to the organization and presentation of chapters. Here, we are switching to the theme *Being a Science Teacher.* Why don't you pause here and complete two of the activities (22–1, 22–2, 22–3, or 22–4) at the end of this chapter.

Becoming is the process of developing suitable or appropriate qualities needed for science teaching. Becoming, then, represents a change from that which you were to that which you are now. It is your coming to be all that you potentially can be as a science teacher, given the time and constraints of this textbook, your life, the methods course, and so forth.

Being is the existence of a particular state or condition—in this case, that of a secondary school science teacher. The title of this chapter signifies that you are one step closer to actually being a science teacher. In many ways you have probably already developed many qualities and attitudes of science teachers. Paradoxically, you will always be at some degree of both becoming and being a science teacher. For example, during the science methods course you have been involved with a variety of experiences, all contributing toward your becoming a science teacher. Simultaneously, you have developed a set of interests and attitudes similar to those of science teachers. Perhaps you imagined yourself as a science teacher and, on occasion, actually experienced this position through teaching a class and working with students. We are referring to your own attitudes and values and your own interest and desire to be a science teacher. These are the most significant variables in the becoming-being equation.

If we had to identify one symbolic point at which the percentage of becoming and being shifted in favor of being, it would be the first day of your first job. Throughout the practice-teaching experience, becoming and being will probably be about equal. However, there has been some degree of being a science teacher from the moment of your career decision, and there will be some degree of continually becoming a better science teacher throughout your career.

These two situations, summarized in "Fulfillments and Frustrations" at the end of this chapter, are two ends of an emotional continuum for science teachers. There are indeed frustrations and fulfillment, and both are a part of becoming and being a science teacher. For some reason, more time is devoted to the frustrating aspects of science teaching than to the fulfillments; yet, without a doubt, the latter occur each day and in many ways. Science teaching is a source of personal fulfillment because it contributes to the development of students and ultimately to society. Occasionally, we lose sight of this simple fact because of the daily frustrations, dissatisfactions, and challenges.

SCIENCE-TEACHING STANDARDS

The current teaching standards of the *National Science Education Standards* provide criteria to be used in making judgments about the quality of teaching in science classrooms. They set forth a vision of good science teaching to be used as a model for prospective and practicing teachers of science. Several roles and responsibilities are outlined in the following areas.

1. Teachers of science should plan inquiry-based programs for their students. This means selecting science content and curriculum directions to meet student interests, knowledge, skills, and experiences. It also means using teaching strategies that develop understanding and skills for doing inquiry science.

2. Teachers should interact with students to focus and support their inquiries, recognize diversity and provide opportunities for all children to participate fully in science learning, and challenge students to take responsibility for individual as well as collaborative learning.

3. Teachers should engage in ongoing assessment of their teaching and of resulting student learning. There should be formal assessment activities, as well as guidance, for students to do meaningful self-assessment.

4. Conditions for learning should provide students with time, space, and resources needed for successful science learning. These conditions include adequate tools and materials, as well as a safe working environment.

5. Teachers should foster habits of mind, attitudes, and values of science by being good role models for these attributes.

6. It is important for teachers to become active participants in ongoing planning and development of the school science program. This includes taking leadership roles and developing their own professional growth potential.

CHARACTERISTICS OF A GOOD SCIENCE TEACHER

Administrators and supervisors constantly evaluate teachers for salary increments, promotions to department chair, differentiated staffing, and other reasons. Unfortunately, many evaluations are made on the basis of superficial characteristics or personal qualities that happen to please or displease the evaluator, rather than on more basic characteristics that exemplify good teaching. Following is a question checklist that can be used by an administrator or supervisor, or by the science teacher for self-evaluation (Adams & Krockover, 1997).

Question Checklist

1. Is the teacher enthusiastic about what he is doing and does he show it?
2. Is the teacher dynamic and does she use her voice and facial expression for emphasis and to hold attention?
3. Does the teacher use gadgets or other illustrative devices extensively to make each new learning experience as concrete as possible?
4. Does the teacher show originality in making teaching materials from simple or discarded objects?
5. Does the teacher have a functional knowledge of her subject so that she can apply what she knows to everyday living?
6. Does the teacher possess the ability to explain ideas in simple terms regardless of the extent of his knowledge?
7. Does the teacher stimulate actual thought on the part of his students, or does he make parrots out of them?
8. Is the teacher a have-to-finish-the-book type of teacher, or does she teach thoroughly?
9. Does the teacher maintain calm and poise in the most trying of classroom circumstances?
10. Does the teacher use a variety of teaching techniques, or is it the same thing day after day?
11. Does the teacher exhibit confidence, and are the students confident about his ability?
12. Does the teacher encourage class participation and questions, and does he conscientiously plan for them?
13. Does the teacher maintain a good instructional tempo so that the period does not drag?
14. Does the teacher use techniques to stimulate interest at the beginning of new material, or does he treat it merely as something new to be learned?
15. Does the teacher concentrate on key ideas and use facts as a means to an end?

Of a more formal nature is the *Stanford Teacher Competence Appraisal Guide* (1963). It may be used to assist the individual teacher in assessing her strengths and weaknesses, or it may be used for formal evaluation purposes. For rating, each item may be evaluated on the basis of eight points and totaled for a cumulative score. The ratings are

0 . . . . Unable to observe
1 . . . . Weak
2 . . . . Below average
3 . . . . Average
4 . . . . Strong
5 . . . . Superior
6 . . . . Outstanding
7 . . . . Truly exceptional

Stanford Teacher Competence Appraisal Guide

Aims

1. *Clarity of aims.*   The purposes of the lesson are clear.
2. *Appropriateness of aims.*   The aims are neither too easy nor too difficult for the pupils. They are appropriate and are accepted by the pupils.

Planning

3. *Organization of the lesson.*   The individual parts of the lesson are clearly related to each other in an appropriate way. The total organization facilitates what is to be learned.
4. *Selection of content.*   The content is appropriate for the aims of the lesson, the level of the class, and the teaching method.
5. *Selection of materials.*   The specific instructional materials and human resources used are clearly related to the content of the lesson and complement the selected method of instruction.

Performance

6. *Beginning the lesson.*   Students come quickly to attention. They direct themselves to the tasks to be accomplished.
7. *Clarity of presentation.*   The content of the lesson is presented so that it is understandable to the pupils. Different points of view and specific illustrations are used when appropriate.
8. *Pacing of the lesson.*   The movement from one part of the lesson to the next is governed by the students' achievement. In pacing, the teacher stays with the class and adjusts the tempo accordingly.
9. *Pupil participation and attention.*   The class is attentive. When appropriate, students actively participate in the lesson.
10. *Ending the lesson.*   The lesson is ended when the students have achieved the aims of instruction. The teacher ties together chance and planned events and relates them to long-range aims of instruction.
11. *Teacher–student rapport.*   The personal relationships between students and teacher are harmonious.

Evaluation

12. *Variety of evaluative procedures.*   The teacher devises and uses an adequate variety of procedures, both formal and informal, to evaluate progress in all of the aims of instruction.
13. *Use of evaluation to provide improvement of teaching and learning.*   The results of evaluation are carefully reviewed by teacher and students to improve teaching and learning.

Professional

14. *Concern for professional standards and growth.*   The teacher helps, particularly in her specialty, to define and enforce standards for (1) selecting, training, and licensing teachers; and (2) working conditions.
15. *Effectiveness in school staff relationships.*   The teacher is respectful and considerate of colleagues, and demonstrates awareness of their personal concerns and professional development.
16. *Concern for the total school program.*   The teacher's concern is not simply for her courses and her students. She works with other teachers, students, and administrators to bring about the program's success.
17. *Constructive participation in community affairs.*   The teacher understands the particular community context in which she works and helps to translate the purposes of the school's program to the community.

RESEARCH ON SCIENCE TEACHER CHARACTERISTICS

In 1980, using the principles of meta-analysis of research, Cynthia Druva and Ronald Anderson (1983) carried out a research project that focused on science teacher characteristics. The results were reported by displaying correlations between these identified teacher characteristics, teacher behavior, and student outcomes. The meta-analysis was conducted of research studies that used characteristics of gender, course work, IQ, and so forth, as independent variables; and as dependent variables, (1) teaching behavior in the classroom, such as questioning behavior and teaching orientation, and (2) student outcome characteristics, such as achievement and attitudes toward science. The subject population was chosen from teachers and students in science classes throughout the United States from kindergarten through twelfth grade.

With respect to the relationships between teacher characteristics and teacher behavior, the following outcomes were reported.

1. Teaching effectiveness is positively related to training and experience as evidenced by the number of education courses, student-teaching grade, and teaching experience.
2. Teachers with a more positive attitude toward the curriculum that they are teaching tend to be those with a higher grade-point average and more teaching experience.
3. Better classroom discipline is associated with the teacher characteristics of restraint and reflectivity.
4. Higher-level, more complex questions were employed more often by teachers with greater knowledge and less experience in teaching.

Science teaching is both personally and professionally fulfilling.

In making decisions, the effective teacher takes into account spontaneous happenings in the classroom as well as instructional theory.

With respect to the relationships between teacher characteristics and student outcomes, several relationships were discovered.

1. Student achievement is positively related to teacher characteristics of self-actualization, heterosexuality, and masculinity. It is also related positively to the number of science courses taken and attendance at academic institutes.

2. The process-skill outcomes of students are positively related to the number of science courses taken by teachers.

3. The outcome of a positive attitude toward science was positively associated with the number of science courses taken by teachers and the number of years of teaching experience.

One implication of the study is the relationship between teacher preparation programs and what their graduates do as teachers. Science courses, education courses, and overall academic performance are positively associated with successful teaching.

For student teachers, the research reported above is significant because it gives direction and guidance to their career and goal preparation. Although the results may seem to be natural, commonsense results, it is significant that data now shows that teachers with better preparation in science, as well as in the pedagogical areas, do a better job of teaching. Also significant is the finding that a positive attitude toward their task relates to better results for the students in their charge.

Hands-on workshops provide confidence and expertise in preparing for science instruction.

One of the difficulties brought about by the daily routine of hard, laborious work in teaching—the incessant planning, paper grading, and all such work—is that this often has a debilitating effect on young teachers. It may cause them to become cynical and skeptical of the results they are achieving. Many times they will tend to blame the students or the system, when in fact it may be the negative attitude they themselves bring to the teaching task that is at least partially responsible for their poor results.

It is important to maintain zest for teaching. In no other profession is it as important to exhibit a positive and enthusiastic relationship with individuals. Young minds in your charge are vulnerable to your attitudes and enthusiasm as well as to your obvious background of preparation and experience. A caring teacher is able to overcome many shortcomings in background and preparation, but an uncaring teacher cannot be successful, though he may have excellent preparation in terms of subject matter and teaching techniques.

OPPORTUNITIES FOR PROFESSIONAL GROWTH

Among the opportunities for professional growth while on the job are completing graduate work during the summer or at night, depending on the available opportunities; participating in inservice workshops and institutes; attending government- or industry-sponsored summer institutes; doing committee work on curriculum revision or evaluation; maintaining membership in professional organizations, with accompanying attendance at regular meetings and participation in committee work; reading professional journals, scientific publications, and current books in science and teaching; writing for professional publications; and keeping up to date on new materials, teaching resources, and education aids.

Graduate Work

There are many opportunities for graduate work. The usual requirement for completion of a master's degree in education is one year or four summers of coursework. Theses are generally not required, but comprehensive examinations in a major and minor field usually are. The monetary rewards for science teachers with master's degrees are well worth the time and expense involved in obtaining the degree. Most school systems have a salary differential of $1,000 or more for holders of master's degrees; furthermore, opportunities for higher-paying jobs are greater, and a better selection of teaching positions is available for the applicant who holds a master's degree.

Inservice Training and Institutes

Inservice workshops and institutes are usually sponsored by public school systems for improvement of the teachers within that system. Degree credit may or may not be offered, depending on the arrangements with the colleges or universities from which consultant services are obtained. Such workshops and institutes often have objectives designed to stimulate curriculum improvement or to improve teacher competencies in subject-matter understanding and teaching techniques. New teachers are encouraged to avail themselves of these opportunities to familiarize themselves with broad problems of curriculum improvements and to benefit from the experience of older teachers in the system.

Government- or industry-sponsored summer and inservice institutes provide excellent opportunities to grow professionally. Although fewer of these institutes are available now than before, the usual requirement is three years of teaching experience; however, this rule is frequently relaxed for one reason or another.

Improving Your Use of Educational Technology in the Classroom

It is important for teachers to feel at ease with equipment, software, and information resources and be able to effectively integrate technology in instruction to improve student motivation and learning. One way of learning about available new technologies is to attend the annual national and area conventions of the NSTA and to spend considerable time in the exhibit area. Virtually every supplier of educational technology for science will have a booth and a helpful staff to demonstrate products and to help you feel comfortable in working with them. Workshops, summer institutes, and college courses are also often available to help you learn to use new technologies. Another unique resource is the VideoPaper Builder developed by TERC. This tool allows teachers to create multimedia documents of best practices incorporating text, digital video, still photographs, and hyperlinks to web pages. [This tool can be downloaded free from the TERC website (www.TERC.org).] Nothing, however, can substitute for extended hands-on, trial-and-error exploration of computer-based materials individually or in a small group. You will find the Internet an excellent resource for learning more about what is available.

To check your own understanding of technology education as it relates to teaching science, consider the following list. Ask yourself how well you are able to use each skill—do you function at a beginning, proficient, or advanced level? You can base decisions about further professional growth on your assessment.

- Demonstrate an awareness of the major types and applications of technology, such as information storage and retrieval, simulation and modeling, and process control and decision making.
- Communicate effectively to students and other teachers about technological equipment.
- Respond appropriately to common error messages when using software.
- Load and run a variety of software packages.
- Demonstrate an awareness of technology usage and assistance in the field of education.
- Describe appropriate uses for technology in education, for example:
  - Computer-assisted instruction (simulation, tutorial, drill and practice)
  - Computer-managed instruction
  - Microcomputer-based laboratory
  - Problem solving
  - Word processing
  - Equipment management
  - Record keeping
- Use technology to individualize instruction and increase student learning.
- Demonstrate appropriate uses of technology for basic skills instruction.
- Demonstrate ways to integrate the use of technology-related materials with other educational materials, including textbooks.
- Respond appropriately to changes in curriculum and teaching methodology caused by new technological developments.
- Plan for effective technology interaction activities for students (e.g., debriefing after a simulation).
- Locate commercial and public domain software for a specific topic and application.
- Use an evaluative process to appraise and determine the instructional worth of a variety of computer software.
- Voluntarily choose to integrate technology in instructional plans and activities.

Committee Work

Committee activity is an excellent way to develop a professional attitude and become aware of the many problems facing the science teacher. Active school systems frequently have a curriculum committee, a professional committee, a salary and grievance committee, a textbook-selection committee, or other committees of temporary nature as needed. Participating on one or more of these committees can be enlightening and can contribute to the professional growth of the new teacher; however, committee responsibilities mean extra work, and the new science teacher should consider the total workload and weigh carefully the ultimate benefits of participation.

Professional Organizations

There are many professional organizations serving the science teacher. They are listed here along with their respective journals.

1. American Association of Physics Teachers, One Physics Ellipse, College Park, MD 20740-3845
   —*American Journal of Physics* and *Physics Teacher*
2. The American Chemical Society, 1155 16th St. NW, Washington, DC 20036
   —*Journal of Chemical Education*
3. The National Association of Biology Teachers, 12030 Sunrise Valley Dr., STE 110, Reston, VA 20191
   —*American Biology Teacher*
4. The National Science Teachers Association, 1840 Wilson Blvd., Arlington, VA 22201-3000
   —*Science Teacher, Science and Children, Science Scope,* and *Journal of College Science Teaching*
5. The School Science and Mathematics Association, Curriculum and Foundations, Bloomsburg University, 400 East Second Street, Bloomsburg, PA 17815-1301
   —*School Science and Mathematics*
6. The National Association for Research in Science Teaching, c/o Arthur L. White, The Ohio State University, 1929 Kenny Rd., Rm. 200E, Columbus, OH 43210
   —*Journal of Research in Science Teaching*
7. The American Association for the Advancement of Science, 1200 New York Ave., NW, Washington, DC 20005
   —*Science*
8. Council for Elementary Science, International, University of Nevada-Reno, College of Education, M/S 282, Reno, NV 89557
   —*Science Education*

Membership in a professional organization carries benefits proportional to the member's active participation in the organization. Attendance at periodic meetings contributes to a sense of cohesiveness and shared objectives, the stimulation of meeting professional coworkers, and the absorption of new ideas. Voluntary participation as a panel member or speaker at a discussion session is a highly beneficial experience. It is not necessarily true that a teacher must have many years of experience before being considered worthy of a presentation at a professional meeting. A young, enthusiastic science teacher with a fresh approach to a problem can make a definite contribution to a meeting of this type.

Professional journals provide another source of teaching ideas. A science teacher should personally subscribe to one or two and make it a habit to regularly read others that may be purchased by the school library. Occasional contribution of teaching ideas for publication in a professional journal is highly motivating and is encouraged. The professional benefits of such a practice are unlimited because it helps one to become known in science-teaching circles and to make valuable contacts.

Professional journals usually contain feature articles on subject-matter topics of current interest; ideas for improvement of classroom teaching techniques; information on professional meetings; book reviews; information on teaching materials, apparatus, and resource books; information on career opportunities for secondary school students in science; and information on scholarships and contests for students and teachers.

BECOMING A BETTER SCIENCE TEACHER

As discussed in the introduction to this text, part of being a science teacher is engaging in the process of becoming a better science teacher. In this chapter, we will use a self-evaluation inventory to examine immediate concerns of science teachers. (See Activity 22–6: Improving My Science Teaching, at the end of this chapter.) Although this activity concentrates on improving various aspects of science teaching, the feedback will also contribute to your becoming a better educator and a more fulfilled person.

Exchanging ideas with other teachers while participating in committee work stimulates professional growth.

Remember, you do not have to be a bad science teacher to become a better one. Science teachers want to improve, as is shown by their continued involvement in workshops, college courses, attendance at conventions, and so forth. The responsibility for improving is yours; moreover, the means of developing as a science teacher are unique to your preferences, problems, and potential. Based on the categories in the self-evaluation inventory, several possible means are suggested.

The *National Science Education Standards* outline several assumptions concerning the desired relationships between science teachers and their students. Among these are the following:

1. What people learn is greatly influenced by how they are taught.
2. The actions of teachers are deeply influenced by their visions of science as an enterprise and as a subject to be taught and learned in school.
3. Cognitive research indicates that knowledge is actively constructed by a student through a process that is individual and social.
4. Actions of teachers are deeply influenced by their understanding of their students and the relationships they have with them.
5. Teachers are continuous learners, inquiring into the understanding of science, their students, and their teaching practice (Bailey, 1978).

Scientific Knowledge

Consider these relatively easy ways to update and/or keep abreast of scientific developments:

1. Read an introductory textbook in an area in which you need improvement.
2. Enroll in science courses at a local college or university.
3. Contact the district or state science supervisor and see whether a workshop can be organized.
4. Join the American Association for the Advancement of Science and read their journal, *Science* (the figure changes with year of publication). The editorials will keep you up to date on social concerns and scientific developments.
5. Read *Scientific American* or purchase offprints of articles or the monographs of accumulated articles on important topics.
6. Join the National Science Teachers Association and read one of their journals: *Science and Children, Science Teacher, Science Scope,* or *Journal of College Science Teaching.*
7. Subscribe to and read *Science News* or *Science World.*
8. Attend local, state, regional, and national conventions of scientific societies, and academies of science, science teachers, and teachers.
9. Make a point of watching television programs on scientific issues. *Nova* is a science program sponsored by the National Science Foundation and is shown on the Public Broadcasting System.
10. Read the science sections of weekly magazines, such as *Time* or *Newsweek.*
11. Go to local museums and planetariums.

Planning and Organization

If planning and organization are concerns, part of the problem can be improved through personal effort toward better lesson planning and classroom organization. We suggest the following:

1. Read the chapters on planning in any teaching-methods textbook.
2. Find a colleague who is well organized and ask if the two of you could spend some time planning classes together.
3. Ask the science supervisor to look over your science program and suggest ways to improve the organization.
4. Have a colleague observe your teaching and make suggestions concerning your lesson plans and class management.

The *National Science Education Standards* give considerable help in the planning and organization responsibilities of science teachers. Foremost in their suggestions is that teachers of science should plan and execute an inquiry-based science program for their students. A further suggestion is that teachers develop strategies that support the development of student understanding and comprehension of science topics rather than mere memorization and rote learning. "Inquiry into real questions generated from student experiences is the central strategy for teaching science" (NRC, 1996).

Teaching Methods

Teachers often find it difficult to break old teaching habits and try new methods of teaching, but you can do it. Here are some suggestions:

1. Read chapters on different methods in any science-methods textbook and then imagine how the different approaches could work in your classroom.
2. Look over journals—such as *Science and Children, Science Teacher, American Biology Teacher, Physics Teacher,* and *Journal of Geological Education*—for new approaches to science teaching.
3. Take a professional day and observe several science teachers who use methods that you are interested in adopting.
4. Read professional books on science and education.

GUEST EDITORIAL ◆ MELINDA BELL

Student Teacher
Northfield Senior High School, Northfield, Minnesota

STUDENT TEACHING IN SCIENCE

"We never learn as much with a student teacher."

"The student teachers are always nervous, lack confidence, and can't keep the classes under control."

"The student teachers expect us to be like college students because that is what they are most familiar with."

These comments were generated by high school students in the school where I am doing my student teaching. I think it is important to take them seriously, although I will rapidly deny that they characterize each and every student teacher. Sure, we're all bound to be a little nervous and to be somewhat unsure of how to discipline or how to present material so it is clear, understandable, and interesting to the students. But that doesn't mean we have to be bogged down by those things!

There is so much else that we, as student teachers, have going for us. We are well armed with a knowledge of our subject and a delightful artillery of methods in which we can present our material. We are bright and enthusiastic and willing to try things in new, innovative ways. We have taken a science teaching methods course that has hopefully prepared us in some other ways. We even have students who will see advantages in our being there!

"Student teachers are young and don't seem as fuddy-duddy as the regular teacher."

"Student teachers are more on our level so they are easier to approach."

"Sometimes the student teacher can explain things in a different way than the regular teacher so more students understand it."

All of these things don't make student teaching easy; rather, they make it an exciting challenge and an opportunity for you to practice your skills—accepting the lesson plans that don't work, as well as feeling accomplishment and pride when your lesson goes over well, and the students get excited about something that you taught them! Not all of your students are going to enjoy you as a teacher, but some will welcome you openly, along with the fresh change and enthusiasm you bring to the classroom.

Some of my friends are amazed by the amount of enjoyment I get out of student teaching.

"Don't you get bored teaching the same material over and over?" is a question commonly asked. Once I've recovered from the shock of picturing myself bored, I reply that I can teach the same or similar materials in such a variety of ways that it remains interesting to me. In fact, the personalities of each class are generally so varied that the best way of presenting the material to one class might be the worst method for another. Gauging the class correctly and presenting the material in a suitable manner for that class is the challenge in making the lesson a successful one.

My friends also worry that teaching will not be intellectually satisfying enough for me. After all, it is only high school material! That is the least of my worries! I really learned about DNA when I had to understand it thoroughly enough to answer the students' questions on it, and when I had to be able to explain what newspaper articles meant when they talked about genetic engineering. To make DNA relevant, I had to ensure that it touched something that they are conscious of as happening in the world today. That holds for whether we are talking about DNA and test-tube babies or about photosynthesis and the greenhouse effect. If it doesn't make sense to them and if they don't find it relevant, it will be rapidly forgotten.

The intellectual challenge for me is to keep up on the recent advances in different areas of science and understand how these advances are applicable to the students' world today. Some people are curious as to why I am going into education when I could go on into research or a medical profession. Selfishly, it is because I hope that I will be an influence through teaching and other aspects of my life in helping people to understand that every decision they make is a reflection on how they look at the world. And science to me has an important message for everyone. Science is a way of looking at the world and dealing with the world on a physical level. Science gives us a method we can use for finding solutions to problems that come up in everyday life. It is unfortunate that science, for many people, is an object to be feared or held in mystified awe. Science is not magic. It is merely a way of putting curiosity and creativity together to come up with reasonable explanations for unanswered questions.

Not everyone has the capacity to become a nuclear physicist, but everyone can learn what processes a scientist goes through in his or her thinking and can apply these same methods to areas of his or her own life. If I can get that across to my students, I will feel that I have accomplished something.

Because I believe in science and because I am excited about the things we can learn from it, I want to share that with others. My own interest in it causes me to be enthusiastic and to remain involved myself.

5. Team-teach with another science teacher who uses different methods.
6. Request a student teacher—student teachers often have new and different approaches to science teaching.

Interpersonal Relations

Interpersonal relations is an area that is essential to effective science teaching, yet it is one that often is neglected in the education of science teachers. Some suggestions that may help include the following:

1. Practice active listening when students talk.
2. Use questions that encourage students to express their ideas on certain issues.
3. Attend a workshop or course on human relations.
4. Read and apply ideas from *Human Relations and Your Career: A Guide to Interpersonal Skills* by David Johnson.

Personal Enthusiasm

If you lack enthusiasm for teaching science, the problem is difficult, but not impossible, to resolve. The reason for the difficulty is that the problem involves a very personal dimension of your teaching. We can recommend an introspective route to improvement.

1. Think about your original interest and excitement in science and teaching. What made you choose science teaching? Now, think about what you know about yourself and teaching science. What is lacking? Where did the spark of enthusiasm go?
2. List your frustrations with teaching. What are the problems you have encountered as a science teacher? What caused a burnout or your change of interest in science teaching?
3. Attend meetings of science teachers such as NSTA or NABT. These meetings often can inspire enthusiasm through new ideas and new colleagues.
4. Form a group to improve teaching in your school. You will probably find others who share your problem, and the discussion and support can certainly assist you in developing your enthusiasm for teaching.
5. Take a professional day and visit other science teachers who are dynamic and enthusiastic.
6. Request a sabbatical.

BEING A PERSON, EDUCATOR, AND SCIENCE TEACHER

Young children are often surprised to find that their teacher does not live at school. Older students think it is funny to meet their teacher shopping or on a picnic. Students often perceive the science teacher and not the person. We are all, however, first and foremost, people. What does this mean? Being a person means we share qualities with all other people: We struggle with decisions, we are sad and happy, we succeed and fail, we make mistakes and get things right, we are frustrated and fulfilled. Too often, students do not see us as people. Students should understand that we belong to the community and have hobbies, interests, and ideas that go beyond science teaching.

As an educator, science teachers are in the helping profession. Their identity is with people more than objects. Their goal is to help people improve their health, education, and welfare. There are aspects of science teaching that are shared with other helping professionals, such as doctors, counselors, social workers, nurses, and psychologists. The shared qualities have to do primarily with the interpersonal relations—the personal dimension of science teaching, those qualities that contribute to effective interactions among people, and that eventually contribute to someone facilitating another's personal development.

The science teacher has elected to help others through a better understanding of the physical and biological world, the methods of gaining knowledge about this world, and the role of science in society. Here the qualities of the person, the educator, and the science teacher should unite to achieve the dual goal of furthering the personal development of students and society through science education.

Much time, money, and effort have been expended on improving the science curriculum. Most science curricula have carefully structured texts and materials so the science teacher will have the maximum opportunity for a good teaching experience. The contribution of new programs and textbooks has been invaluable. But although curriculum materials are necessary and can account for some success in the classroom, they are not sufficient; they cannot account for effective and successful science teaching. The science teacher is still the crucial variable and the one person who must pull all the pieces together for effective teaching.

A review of the research literature on good, ideal, effective, or successful teaching reveals that it is impossible to identify any particular set of variables that amounts to being a good teacher. Yet, we all have had good science teachers, we know good science teachers, and, most important, we want to be good science teachers. Rather than looking at the research and concluding that we can't identify the characteristics of good science teaching, perhaps we can take a different view and thus form a different conclusion. Perhaps good science teachers have developed their potential, their talents, and their attributes, all of which give them an identifying teaching style. It is understandable then that our research efforts cannot find common characteristics, for the answer is to be found in uniqueness, not commonality.

Being a science teacher means improving. Science teachers want to improve and can improve. Even an especially good science teacher can become a better one. Often science teachers complain, "I just didn't seem to be effective today; the students seemed confused and frustrated. I didn't get the concept across." However, they never finish the statement with, "and if you think I was bad today—wait until tomorrow. I'll really be much worse!" Unfortunately, just the desire to improve is not enough; there must be a commitment to becoming a better science teacher through changing or altering one's personal teaching style.

Critics of education have done much to point out the wrongs of education and little to give direction. One result of this critical confrontation has been defensiveness by many teachers and administrators. Displacing blame is one manifestation of this defensiveness, the "let's blame somebody or something else" syndrome: "We would if we had money." "I have thirty-five children in my class." "Well, what do you expect?" and "The home has more influence than the short time students are in my classroom." The "let's try something new" syndrome is another manifestation. Teaching machines, contract performance, accountability, competency-based programs, and the open classroom are examples of this approach. The ideas presented in this chapter center on the science teacher developing as a person and as an educator. Our theme might be "Let's get with it as

people and perform as professionals." You can be in any classroom, with any children, and with any curriculum to develop your competency as a science teacher. The ideas presented are not easy; for the most part, they deal with personal improvement and fulfillment.

Start being a science teacher by looking at your potential and not at your limitations. Becoming aware of the importance of the suggestions for improvement and translating them into actual practice can result in your development as a science teacher. The process of becoming a better science teacher is long, and it takes courage to overcome the many small barriers to personal and professional growth. It is not something that can occur through the purchase of a new set of science materials, a single workshop, or reading one methods textbook. Being a science teacher requires continuous personal development aimed toward the ideal of being a great educator; and for those who say, "I can't be a great science teacher," we reply, "If not you—then who?" We all have much more potential than we use. It is the actualization of this potential that will help you become a better science teacher, educator, and person.

SUMMARY

Student teaching is the most important phase of the prospective teacher's training. Entered into with enthusiasm and a willingness to learn, the experience will be a valuable culmination of college preparation for teaching.

The selection of subject, school, and supervising teacher is enhanced by visits to schools before the semester or quarter of student teaching. It is advisable to do one's student teaching in the major field of preparation to capitalize on one's strength of subject-matter competency.

The usual pattern of preparation is to spend several days or a week observing the class one is going to teach. Such observation can be done on a systematic basis and promotes real insight into the individual differences present in the class. Student teachers can be assistant teachers in the truest sense if they are alert to developing problems, anticipate future activities of the class, and prepare themselves accordingly.

Taking over the class to teach a lesson or a unit will be completely successful if student teachers plan adequately in consultation with their supervising teachers and make their preparations carefully. Advance rehearsal for the first day of teaching is an advisable procedure, particularly if the time budget is questionable or if class questions are anticipated. An immediate follow-up of a day of teaching with a brief conference with the supervising teacher is advisable. Necessary changes in lesson plans can be made at this time.

A desirable arrangement is to follow the student-teaching quarter with a final quarter on the college campus before graduation. At this time, seminars in special problems of teaching can be most profitable, and the student teacher can reflect on the teaching experience. This affords the opportunity to give maximum attention to the important choice of a first teaching position in the light of the recent experience in student teaching.

Being a science teacher has its professional frustrations and motivational needs: safety, security, love and belongingness, and self-esteem are ways of thinking about levels of fulfillment in your job. Some of the professional challenges of the new millenium are competency and accountability, facilities and equipment, curriculum and instruction, funding, disruptive students, and career education.

Today's science teacher is in a position of respect and responsibility. The demand for well-prepared science teachers has never been greater, and the rewards are exceptional.

Decision making is a crucial aspect of being a science teacher. The particular focus of decision making is on two seemingly paradoxical aspects of teaching—that one must maintain a direction and that one must demonstrate flexibility. The balance between these variables is set by the science teacher's decisions. A personal theory of instruction will help guide the science teacher's decisions and develop a consistent pattern of responses to the instantaneous demands of the classroom.

Proper education of the science teacher in this fast-moving scientific age is a matter of increasing concern. A suitable balance of general education, subject-matter preparation, and professional training must be achieved. The current trend is toward strengthening all of these areas, particularly subject-matter preparation. Attainment of a bachelor's degree does not end the science teacher's

education. More and more, graduate work, up to and beyond the master's level, is being demanded. From a financial standpoint, it is generally to the teacher's advantage to obtain this advanced training as soon as possible. Better-paying jobs with other attractive features frequently await the applicant who has additional training.

The science teacher can grow professionally in many ways. Graduate coursework, inservice institutes and workshops, summer institutes, committee involvement, membership in professional organizations, a program of reading, participation in meetings, and writing for professional journals are but a few possibilities. It is important to realize that continual growth and experience are necessary if one is to be an enthusiastic, productive science teacher.

Being a science teacher is more than signing your first contract or teaching your first class. It is more than your knowledge of science, capacity to plan, ability to use different methods, and your enthusiasm for teaching. Although these attributes are included, being a science teacher also means the following:

1. Courage to continue your professional growth
2. Commitment to doing a better job tomorrow
3. Competence to fulfill your professional duties
4. Compassion toward your students
5. Caring for your own dignity, integrity, and worth and for the dignity, integrity, and worth of those in your care.

The professional educator of today faces a challenging future. Investment in superior preparation and recognition of the need for continual professional growth can provide rich rewards: a citizenry better educated in the area of science.

INVESTIGATING SCIENCE TEACHING

ACTIVITY 22–1
INDIVIDUAL DIFFERENCES

1. In your observation of a science class, use a checklist such as on page 313 to discover the individual differences present in the class. At the end of a week, discuss your observations with the teacher. How does the student's achievement appear to correlate with your observations of study habits and classroom behavior?

2. List the traits you would like to see in the supervising teacher with whom you wish to do your practice teaching. Using this list as a guide, objectively analyze your own traits and compare them. Do you think similar or opposite traits are preferable, or that a judicious blend of both is preferable?

Activity 22–2
Being a Professional Science Teacher

1. Write to the department of education in your state and obtain a summary of the current salary schedule in the major cities. Compare the starting salaries for teachers with bachelor's degrees and master's degrees. Compare the annual salary increase and the number of years required to reach maximum salary.

2. Obtain a copy of *Guidelines for Preparation Programs of Teachers of Secondary School Science and Mathematics* from the American Association for the Advancement of Science, Washington, DC. Compare the training you have received with that recommended by this group.

3. Prepare a critical analysis of two professional journals, such as *Science Teacher, School Science and Mathematics, American Biology Teacher,* and *Physics Teacher.* Examine the feature articles, classroom teaching tips, articles contributed by teachers in the field, book reviews, and other parts of the publications.

4. Prepare a critical review of two research-oriented professional science teaching journals, such as *Science Education* and *Journal of Research for Science Teaching.* Report on the results of one research study published in each of the journals reviewed.

Activity 22–3
Fulfillments and Frustrations

Joan is approaching your desk. "Look, I solved the chemistry problem. It was easy after you explained the difference between ionic and covalent bonding." Then, with a warm smile, she said, "I really appreciate the extra time you spend helping me; you are a good teacher and I'm glad I decided to take chemistry." What would you do?

1. Ask her if she solved the other chemistry problems.
2. Say nothing, smile, and go on with your work.
3. Tell her that it is just part of your job.
4. Smile and thank her for the compliment.
5. Tell her you are glad she asked you about the problem.

You have just sat through one more insufferable faculty meeting. The results of the meeting: your clerical work will increase due to a new grading system; your budget has been reduced by 50 percent (and the price of science materials, equipment, and textbooks has gone up 25 percent); your new duty is to supervise the cafeteria; your new class will be a "difficult, but small" group of students; your salary increase for next year will be 3 percent below the present rate of inflation. What would you do?

1. Quit.
2. Go to the next NEA or AFT meeting and demand a change in contracts.
3. Ignore the situation because one-fourth of the problems will be changed in the next two weeks; one-fourth of the changes will never be implemented; you can ignore one-fourth of the problems, and the remaining one-fourth are "part of the territory."
4. Make an appointment with the principal and politely, but firmly, inform her that she has asked too much of you.
5. Talk over the problems with several colleagues.
6. Go to a psychotherapist to see if you or the school system is sick.

Once you have selected the option closest to what you think, you might discuss it with a partner. What else would you do?

ACTIVITY 22–4
DEVELOPING AN INSTRUCTIONAL THEORY

The idea of an instructional theory was introduced in Chapter 2. Now it might be a good idea to return to this idea. To help you develop your instructional theory, complete the following exercise.

1. What is the aim of your science teaching? What is the broad goal you would hope to achieve through your interaction with students in the science classroom?
   a. What is your primary goal?
   b. What are your secondary aims?

2. Based on your understanding of yourself, students, science, and society, what are your justifications for the goal and aims cited above?
   a. Why are these and not other aims to be the focus of science education?
   b. In a broad sense, what is to be done or not done to achieve these aims?

3. What are your conclusions about what to do, and how and when to achieve these aims?
   a. By what specific instructional methods or processes are the aims developed?
   b. What is your science curriculum?
   c. Is there any sequence in your instructional theory?

In sum, you should first state your aims, second, justify why these aims are important, and third, explain how you plan to achieve these aims through your science curriculum and instruction.

ACTIVITY 22–5
WHAT WOULD YOU DO NOW?

Based on your sense of direction and flexibility, what would you do as a science teacher in these situations?

1. You are introducing a biology lesson on predator–prey relationships. The chameleons and crickets you ordered for the students to observe have not arrived. What would you do?

2. You are teaching a physical science lesson on energy. The class was supposed to read the chapter on energy in the book. You suddenly realize that several of the students cannot read at the level of your textbook. What would you do?

3. During an earth science lesson on the planets, a student informs you that he has talked with a visitor from another planet—called Xerob. He describes the visitor in detail. The class is interested and starts asking the student questions. What would you do?

4. The unit is on health, the lesson on smoking. A student tells about a person she knows who is 85 years old and very healthy. This person has smoked two packages of cigarettes a day for over 60 years. In addition, the person drinks, eats candy, and does not watch his diet. What would you do?

ACTIVITY 22–6
IMPROVING MY SCIENCE TEACHING

What are your strengths and weaknesses? How do you think you should improve as a science teacher? Following is a self-evaluation inventory designed to provide answers to these questions. We don't know how you would like to become more effective as a science teacher. Of course, the answers to these questions vary from person to person. The inventory will provide you with insights concerning some of your own characteristics as a science teacher. The self-evaluation inventory is based on items used in a study of teacher effectiveness and later modified for the study of science teaching. Only selected items are used here.

The following statements are descriptions of various facets of science teaching. Read each of the statements carefully. Using the scale, indicate how each statement presently characterizes you as a science teacher.

1. Never characteristic of me. I really need to improve.
2. Seldom characteristic of me. I should improve this aspect of my science teaching.
3. Sometimes characteristic of me. I should evaluate this aspect of my science teaching.
4. Frequently characteristic of me. This is a good aspect of my science teaching.
5. Very characteristic of me. This is a real strength of my teaching.

As a science teacher, I

_____ 1. am well read in science.

_____ 2. have a well-organized science course.

_____ 3. adjust my teaching to the class situation.

_____ 4. have a good rapport with my science students.

_____ 5. enjoy teaching science to students.

_____ 6. have a thorough knowledge of science.

_____ 7. have always planned and am prepared for science class.

_____ 8. use a variety of techniques in teaching science.

_____ 9. recognize the unique needs of my science students.

_____ 10. am enthusiastic about teaching science.

_____ 11. present science concepts that are current and relevant.

_____ 12. recognize the need to modify daily and unit plans.

_____ 13. facilitate different types of student activities in science.

_____ 14. relate well with students on the individual and group level.

_____ 15. become excited when students learn science.

_____ 16. am well informed in science-related fields.

_____ 17. have thought about the long-range goals of my science class.

_____ 18. use different curriculum materials and instructional approaches to teach science.

_____ 19. am sincere while helping my science students.

_____ 20. make an extra effort to help students learn science.

_____ 21. am knowledgeable concerning science-related social issues.

_____ 22. have a continuity of course material in science.

_____ 23. provide adequate opportunity for active work by science students.

_____ 24. listen to student questions and ideas.

_____ 25. am excited and energetic when teaching science.

Now go back and add up your responses for the items listed below in the left column. Divide the total by 5. The result should be a number between 1 and 5 for each of the categories listed. Refer back to the five-point scale for your evaluation.

Items	Average		Category
1, 6, 11, 16, 21	÷ 5	_____	Knowledge of science
2, 7, 12, 17, 22	÷ 5	_____	Planning and organization
3, 8, 13, 18, 23	÷ 5	_____	Teaching methods
4, 9, 14, 19, 24	÷ 5	_____	Personal relations
5, 10, 15, 20, 25	÷ 5	_____	Enthusiasm

REFERENCES

Adams, B.J. (1968). A study of the retention of biological information by BSCS students and traditional biology students. Ed.D. dissertation, Colorado State College.

Adams, P.E., & Krockover, G.H. (1997). Concerns and perceptions of beginning secondary science and mathematics teachers. *Science Education, 81*(1): 29–50.

Adler, M. (1982). *The Paideia proposal: An educational manifesto.* New York: Macmillan.

Agin, M. (1974). Education for scientific literacy: A conceptual frame of reference and some applications. *Science Education, 58*: 3.

Aldridge, B., & Johnston, K. (1984). Trends and issues in science education. In R. Bybee, J. Carlson, & A. McCormack (Eds.), *Redesigning Science and Technology Education, 1984 NSTA Yearbook.* Washington, DC: National Science Teachers Association.

American Association for the Advancement of Science (AAAS). (1963). *The new school science: A report to school administrators on regional orientation conferences in science.* Publication no. 63-6 (p. 29), Washington, DC.

AAAS. (1989). *Science for all Americans: A project 2061 report on goals in science, mathematics, and technology.* Washington, DC: Author.

AAAS. (1993). *Benchmarks for science literacy.* Washington, DC: Author.

AAAS. (2001). *Designs for science literacy.* New York: Oxford University Press.

American Association of University Women Educational Foundation (AAUW). (1998). *Gender gaps: Where schools still fail our children.* Washington, DC: Author.

AAUW. (1991). Shortchanging girls, shortchanging America, executive summary. Washington, D.C.: AAUW Foundation.

AAUW. (2004). *Under the microscope: A decade of gender equity projects in the sciences.* Washington, DC: AAUW Foundation.

American Chemical Society. (1997). *Chemistry in the national science education standards: A reader and resource manual for high school teachers.* Washington, DC: American Chemical Society.

Anderson, C.W. (1987). Incorporating recent research on learning into the process of science curriculum development. Commissioned paper for IBM-supported design project. Colorado Springs, CO: Biological Sciences Curriculum Study.

Anderson, C.W. (1987). Strategic teaching in science. In B.F. Jones (Ed.), *Strategic Teaching and Learning: Cognitive Instruction in the Content Areas.* Alexandria, VA: Association for Supervision and Curriculum Development.

Anderson, C., & Smith, E. (1983). Teacher behavior associated with conceptual learning in science. Paper presented at the Annual Meeting of the American Educational Research Association, Montreal, Canada.

Anderson, R. (1983). Are yesterday's goals adequate for tomorrow? *Science Education, 67*(2): 171–176.

Anderson, R. (2002). Reforming science teaching: What research says about inquiry. *Journal of Science Teacher Education, 13*(1): 1–12.

Appleton, K. (1997). Analysis and description of students' learning during science classes using a constructivist-based model. *Journal of Research in Science Teaching, 34*(3): 303–318.

Appleton, K., & Asoko, H. (1996). A case study of a teacher's progress toward using a constructivist view of learning to improve teaching in elementary school. *Science Education, 80*(2): 165–180.

Armbruster, B. B., et al. (1991). Reading and questioning in content area lessons. *Journal of Reading Behavior, 23*(1): 35–39.

Armstrong, K., & Weber, K. (1991). Genetic engineering—A lesson on bioethics for the classroom. *American Biology Teacher, 53*: 294–297.

Atkin, J., & Karplus, R. (1962). Discovery or invention? *Science Teacher, 29*(5): 45–51.

Atwater, M.M. (1994). The multicultural science classroom. *The Science Teacher, 62*(2): 20–23.

Ausubel, D. (1963). *The psychology of meaningful verbal learning.* New York: Grune & Stratton.

Ausubel, D. (1968). *Educational psychology: A cognitive view.* New York: Academic Press.

Ausubel, D., Novak, J., & Hanesian, H. (1978). *Educational psychology: A cognitive view.* New York: Holt, Rinehart, and Winston.

Ayer, A.J. (1952). *Language, truth and logic.* New York: Dover Publications.

Bacon, F. (1960). *The new organon.* New York: Bobbs-Merrill.

Bacon, F. (1963). The importance of the experiment. In L.B. Young (Ed.), *Exploring the Universe* (p. 143). New York: McGraw-Hill.

Bailey, G.D. (1978). Teacher self-assessment: In search of a philosophical foundation. *National Association of Secondary School Principals Bulletin, 62*(422): 64–70.

Bakker, G., & Clark, C. (1988). *Explanation: An introduction to the philosophy of science.* Mountain View, CA: Mayfield.

Bangert-Downs, R., Kulik, C., Kulik, J., & Morgan, M. (1991). The instructional effect of feedback in testlike events. *Review of Education Research, 61*(2): 213–238.

Banks, J.A. (1993). Multicultural education: Development, dimensions, and challenges. *Phi Delta Kappan:* 22–28.

Banks, J.A. (1994). Transforming the mainstream curriculum. *Educational Leadership 51*(8): 4–8.

Barba, R., & Cardinale, L. (1991). Are females invisible students? An investigation of teacher–student questioning interactions. *School Science and Mathematics, 91*(7): 306–310.

Barbour, I.G. (1974). *Myths, models and paradigms.* New York: Harper & Row.

Belenky, M., Clinchy, B., Goldberger, N., & Tarule, J. (1986). *Women's ways of knowing: The development of self, voice, and mind.* New York: Basic Books.

Bell, L.I. (2002). Strategies that close the gap. *Educational Leadership, 60*(4): 32–34.

Berkheimer, G., & Anderson, C. (1989). The matter and molecules project: Curriculum development based on conceptual change research. Paper presented at the Annual Meeting of the National Association for Research in Science Teaching, San Francisco.

Berliner, D. (1984). The half-full glass: A review of research on teaching. In P. Hosford (Ed.), *Using What We Know about Teaching.* Alexandria, VA: Association for Supervision and Curriculum Development.

Berry, B. (2002). *What it means to be a "highly qualified teacher."* Chapel Hill, NC: Southeast Center for Teaching Quality.

Bert, C.R.G & Bert, M. (1992). *The Native American: An exceptionality in education and counseling.* ERIC Document Reproduction Service No. ED351, 168.

Bestor, A. (1953). *Educational wastelands: A retreat from learning in our public schools.* Urbana: University of Illinois Press.

Bingman, R.M. (Ed.) (1969). *Inquiry objectives in the teaching of biology.* Position paper 1(1). Kansas City, MO: Mid-Continent Regional Educational Laboratory and Biological Sciences Curriculum Study.

Biological Sciences Curriculum Study (BSCS). (1992, September). *Innovative science education.* Colorado College: Colorado Springs, CO.

BSCS. (2000). *Making sense of integrated science: A guide for high schools.* Colorado Springs, CO: Author.

BSCS. (2005). *BSCS science: An inquiry approach.* Dubuque, IA: Kendall/Hunt Publishing.

BSCS. (2006). *The BSCS 5E instructional model: Origins and effectiveness.* Colorado Springs, CO: Author.

BSCS. (2006). *Why does inquiry matter? Because that's what science is all about!* Dubuque, IA: Kendall/Hunt Publishing.

Birnie, H. (1982). *An introduction of the learning cycle.* Saskatoon, Canada: University of Kastachewan Press.

Black, P., & Wiliam, D. (1998a). Assessment and classroom learning. *Assessment in Education, 5*(1): 7–74.

Black, P., & Wiliam, D. (1998b). Inside the black box: raising standards through classroom assessment. *Phi Delta Kappan, 80*(2): 139–148.

Bloom, B., et al. (1950). *A taxonomy of educational objectives: Handbook 1, The cognitive domain.* New York: David McKay.

Blosser, P. (1983). The role of the laboratory in science teaching. *School Science and Mathematics, 83*(2).

Boraiko, A.A. (1982). The chip. *National Geographic, 162*(4): 420–457.

Bourque, M., Champagne, A., & Crissman, S. (1997). *1996 science performance standards: Achievement results for the nation and states.* Washington, DC: National Assessment Governing Board.

Brandwein, P. (1979). A general theory of instruction. *Science Education, 63*(3): 291.

Bransford, J., Pellegrino, M., & Donovan, W. (Eds.). (1999). *How people learn: Bridging research and practice.* Washington, DC: National Academy Press.

Bransford, J., Brown, A., & Cocking, R. (Eds.). (2000). *How people learn: Brain, mind, experience, and school.* Washington, DC: National Academy Press.

Brazelton, T.B., & Greenspan, S.I. (2000). *The irreducible needs of children: What every child must have to grow, learn, and flourish.* Boulder, CO: Perseus Book Group.

Bronowski, J. (1959). The values of science. In A. Maslow (Ed.), *New Knowledge in Human Values* (p. 55). Chicago: Henry Regnery Company.

Bronowski, J. (1965). *Science and human values.* New York: Harper & Row.

Bronowski, J. (1966). *The identity of man.* Garden City, NY: Doubleday/Natural History Press.

Bronowski, J. (1973, December). The principle of tolerance. *The Atlantic Monthly:* 60–66.

Brown, A.L. (1994). The advancement of learning. *Educational Researcher, 23*(8): 4–12.

Brown, K., & Obourn, E. (1961). *Offerings and enrollments in science and mathematics in public high schools, 1958.* Washington, DC: U.S. Government Printing Office.

Brown, L.M., & Gilligan, C. (1992). *Meeting at the crossroads: Women's psychology and girls' development.* Cambridge, MA: Harvard University Press.

Bruer, J. (1994). *Schools for thought.* Cambridge, MA: The MIT Press.

Bruner, J.S. (1960). *The process of education.* New York: Vintage.

Bruner, J.S. (1968). *Toward a theory of instruction.* New York: W.W. Norton.

Bryant, A., & Clark, E. (2000). How parents raise boys and girls. *Newsweek,* Fall/Winter: 64–65.

Butler, R., & Neuman, O. (1995). Effects of task and ego-achievement goals on help-seeking behaviors and attitudes. *Journal of Educational Psychology, 87*(2): 261–271.

Bybee, R.W. (1973). The teacher I like best: Perceptions of advantaged, average, and disadvantaged science students. *School Science and Mathematics, 73*(5): 384–390.

Bybee, R.W. (1975). The ideal elementary science teacher: Perceptions of children, pre-service and in-service elementary science teachers. *School Science and Mathematics, 75*(3): 229–235.

Bybee, R.W. (1978). Science educators' perceptions of the ideal science teacher. *School Science and Mathematics, 78*(1): 13–22.

Bybee, R.W. (1987). Science education and the science-technology-society (STS) theme. *Science Education, 71*(5): 667–783.

Bybee, R.W. (1997). *Achieving scientific literacy: From purposes to practices*. Portsmouth, NH: Heinemann.

Bybee, R.W. (Ed.). (2002). *Learning science and the science of learning*. Arlington, VA: NSTA Press.

Bybee, R.W., & Sund, R. (1982). *Piaget for educators*. Columbus, OH: Merrill.

Bybee, R.W., Buchwald, C.E., Crissman, S., Heil, D.R., Kuerbis, P.J., Matsumoto, C., & McInerney, J.D. (1990). *Science and technology education for the middle years: Frameworks for curriculum and instruction*. Washington, DC: The National Center for Improving Science Education.

Bybee, R.W., et al. (1991). Teaching history and nature of science: A rationale. *Science Education, 75*(1).

Bybee, R.W., & DeBoer, G.E. (1993). Goals and the science curriculum. In D. Gabel (Ed.), *A Handbook of Research on Science Teaching and Learning*. Washington, DC: National Science Teachers Association.

Bybee R.W., & DeBoer, G. (1994). Research on goals for the science curriciulum. In D. Gabel (Ed.), *Handbook of research on Science Teaching and Learning*. Washington, DC: National Science Teachers Association.

Caldwell, O. (1924). Report of the American Association for the Advancement of Science: Committee on the place of the sciences in education. *Science, 60*: 536.

Cameron, J., & Pierce, D. (1994). Reinforcement, reward, intrinsic motivation: A meta-analysis. *Review of Educational Research, 64*(3): 363–423.

Caramazza, A., McCloskey, M., & Green, B. (1981). Naïve beliefs. In 'Sophisticated' Subjects: Misconceptions about Trajectories of Objects. *Cognition, 9*: 117–123.

Carter, J.L., & Nakosteen, A.R. (1971, February). Summer: A BSCS evaluation study. *The Biological Sciences Curriculum Study*: 42.

Cawelti, G. (1968). Innovative practices in high schools: Who does what—and why—and how. *Nation's Schools, 79*: 36–41.

Central Association of Science and Mathematics Teachers. (1915). Report of the central association of science and mathematics teachers committee on the unified high school science course. *School Science and Mathematics, 15*(4): 334.

Chambers, J.A., & Sprecher, J.W. (1983). *Computer-assisted instruction*. Englewood Cliffs, NJ: Prentice Hall.

Champagne, A. (1987). The psychological basis for a model of science instruction. Commissioned paper for IBM-supported design project. Colorado Springs, CO: Biological Sciences Curriculum Study.

Champagne, A., et al. (1987, May/June). Middle school science texts: What's wrong that could be made right?

American Association for the Advancement of Science Books & Films.

Champagne, A.B., Klopfer, L.E., & Gunstone, R.F. (1982). Cognitive research and the design of science instruction. *Educational Psychologist, 17*(1): 31–53.

Chi, M.T.H., & Koeske, R.D. (1983). Network representation of child's dinosaur knowledge. *Development Psychology, 19*: 29–39.

Chiapetta, E.L. (1976). A review of Piagetian studies relevant to science instruction at the secondary and college level. *Science Education, 60*(2): 253–261.

Christensen, J. (1994). Integrated secondary science: The time is now. In *New Directions in Education*. Dubuque, IA: Kendall/Hunt Publishing.

Cobb, N. (Ed.). (1994). *The future of education: Perspectives on national standards in America*. New York: College Entrance Examination Board.

Collins, A. (1995). National science education standards in the United States: A process and a product. *Studies in Science Education, 26*(1): 7–37.

Combs, A.W., Avila, D.L., & Purkey, W.W. (1978). *Helping relationships: Basic/concepts for the helping professions*. Boston: Allyn and Bacon.

Commission on the Reorganization of Secondary Education. (1918). *Cardinal principles of secondary education*. Bulletin 1918, No. 35, pp. 12–13, Washington, DC: U.S. Bureau of Education.

Committee on Secondary School Studies. (1893). *Report of the committee of ten on secondary studies*. Washington, DC: National Education Association.

Conference Proceedings from the National Conference on the Revolution in Earth and Space Science Education, June 21–24, 2001, Snowmass, CO. *www.earthscienceedrevolution.org/recommend/technology.cfm*

Confrey, J. (1990). A review of the research on student conceptions in mathematics, science, and programming. In C.B. Cazden (Ed.), *Review of Research in Education* (pp. 3–56). Washington, DC: The American Educational Research Association.

Connelly, F.M., Finegold, M., Clipsham, J., & Wahlstrom, M.W. (1977). *Scientific enquiry and the teaching of science*. Toronto, Ontario: The Ontario Institute for Studies in Education.

Costenson, K., & Lawson, A. (1986). Why isn't inquiry used in more classrooms? *American Biology Teacher, 48*(3): 150–158.

Council of Chief State School Officers. (2000). *Key state education policies on K–12 education: 2000*. Washington, DC: Author.

Crismond, D. (2001). Learning and using science ideas when doing investigate-and-redesign tasks: A study of naïve, novice, and expert designers doing constrained and scaffolded design work. *Journal of Research in Science Teaching, 38*(7): 791–820.

Damon, W. (1999). The moral development of children. *Scientific American, 281*: 72–78.

Darder, A. (1995). Buscando America: The contributions of critical Latino educators to the academic development and empowerment of Latino students in the U.S. In C. E. Sleeter and P. L. McLaren (Eds.), *Multicultural Education,*

Critical Pedagogy, and the Politics of Difference. Albany, NY: SUNY.

DeBoer, G.E. (1991). *A history of ideas in science education.* New York: Teachers College Press.

Department of Secondary School Principals. (1946). *Planning for American youth.* Washington, DC: National Education Association.

Descartes, R. (1970). Discourse on the method of rightly conducting reason. In E. Haldone & F.R.T. Ross (Eds.), *The Philosophical Works of Descartes* (p. 91). New York: Cambridge University Press.

Deutsch, M. (1973). *The resolution of conflict.* New Haven, CT: Yale University Press.

Dewey, J. (1910). Science as subject matter and as method. *Science*: 121–127.

Dewey, J. (1938). *Logic: The theory of inquiry.* New York: MacMillan.

Diller, T. (1982). Do your questions promote or prevent thinking? *Learning, 11*: 56–57.

Donato, R., & Hernández, D. (1994). Metacognitive equity for Mexican American language-minority students. In R. Rodriquez (Ed.), *Compendium of Readings in Bilingual Education: Issues and Practices.* San Antonio, TX: Texas Association for Bilingual Education.

Donovan, M.S., & Bransford, J.D. (Eds.). (2005). *How students learn: Science in the classroom.* Washington, DC: The National Academies Press.

Driver, R., Guesne, E., & Tiberghien, A. (Eds.) (1985). *Children's ideas in science.* Philadelphia: Open University Press.

Driver, R., & Oldham, V. (1986). A constructivist approach to curriculum development in science. *Studies in Science Education, 13*: 105–122.

Driver, R., Squires, A., Rushworth, P., & Wood-Robinson, V. (1994). *Making sense of secondary science: Research into children's ideas.* New York: Routledge.

Druva, C., & Anderson, R. (1983). Science teachers' characteristics by teacher behavior and by student outcome: A meta-analysis of research. *Journal of Research in Science Teaching, 20*(5): 467–479.

Dublin, P., Pressman, H., & Vaughn, T. (1994). *Integrating computers in your classroom: Middle and secondary science.* New York: HarperCollins.

Duit, R. (1987). Research on students' alternative frameworks in science: Topics, theoretical frameworks, consequences for science teaching. *Proceedings of the Second International Seminar on Misconceptions and Educational Strategies in Science and Mathematics,* Ithaca, NY.

Duschl, R. (1994). Research on the history and philosophy of science. In D.H. Gabel (Ed.), *Handbook of Research on Science Teaching and Learning,* pp. 443–465. New York: Macmillan.

Duschl, R.A., Schweingruber, H.A., & Shouse, A. W. (Eds.). (2007.) *Taking science to school: Learning and teaching science in grades K–8.* Washington, DC: National Academy Press.

Education Development Center. (1968). *Introductory physical science—physical science II: A progress report.* Newton, MA: IPS Group.

Educational Policies Commission. (1952). *Education for all American youth: A further look.* Washington, DC: National Education Association and the American Association of School Administrators.

Fornoff, F.J. (1970). Survey of the teaching of chemistry in secondary schools. *School and Society, 98*: 242–243.

Frederiksen, J.R., & Collins, A. (1989). A systems approach to educational testing. *Educational Researcher, 18*(9): 27–32.

Friend, M., & Bursuck, W. (1996). *Including students with special needs: A practical guide for classroom teachers.* Boston: Allyn and Bacon.

Fullan, M. (2001). *The new meaning of educational change.* New York: Teachers College Press, Columbia University.

Gardner, A.L., Mason, C.L., & Matyas, M.L. (1989). Equity, excellence, and 'just plain good teaching.' *American Biology Teacher, 51*(2): 72–77.

Gardner, M., & Yager, R. (1983, October). How does the U.S. stack up? *Science Teacher*: 22–25.

Gazzetti, B.J., Snyder, T.E., Glass, G.V., & Gamas, W.S. (1993). Promoting conceptual change in science: A comparative meta-analysis of instructional interventions from reading education and science education. *Reading Research Quarterly, 28*(2): 117–158.

George, K.D. (1965). The effect of BSCS and conventional biology in critical thinking. *Journal of Research in Science Teaching, 3*: 293–299.

German, P., Haskins, S., & Avis, S. (1996). Analysis of nine high school biology laboratory manuals promoting scientific inquiry. *Journal of Research in Science Teaching, 33*(5): 475–500.

German, P., Aram, R., & Burke, G. (1996). Identifying patterns and relationships among the responses of seventh-grade students to the science process skills of designing experiments. *Journal of Research in Science Teaching, 33*(1): 78–99.

Gilligan, C. (1985). *In a different voice.* Boston: Harvard University Press.

Glatthorn, A. (1994). *Developing a quality curriculum.* Alexandria, VA: ASCD.

Golbeck, S.L. (1986). The role of physical content in Piagetian spatial tasks: Sex differences in spatial knowledge. *Journal of Research in Science Teaching, 23*: 321–333.

Gonzales, P., Calsyn, C., et al. (2000). *Highlights from the third international math and science study—repeat (TIMSS-R)* (NCES 2001-027). Washington, DC: National Center for Education Statistics.

Gould, S.J. (1988, January). The case of the creeping fox terrier clone, *Natural History.*

Granger, C.R., & Yager, R.E. (1970). Type of high school biology program and its effect on student attitude and achievement in college life science. *Journal of Research in Science Teaching, 7*: 383–389.

GREEN. (1996). Available at *http://mail.igc.apc.org/green/*

Grobman, A. (1963). Quoted in American Association for the Advancement of Science. *The new school science: A report to school administrators on regional orientation conferences in science.* Publication no. 63–6 (p. 27), Washington, DC.

Gronland, N. (1970). *Stating behavioral objectives for classroom instruction.* New York: Macmillan.

Gruhn, W.T., & Douglas, N.R. (1977). *The modern junior high school,* 3d ed. New York: The Ronald Press.

Guild, P. (1994). The culture/learning style connection. *Educational Leadership, 51*(8): 16–21.

Hackett, J. (1992). Constructivism: Hands on and minds on. In *Science Matters,* Staff Development Series. New York: Macmillan-McGraw Hill.

Hall, G.E. (1989). Changing practice in high school: A process not an event. In W.G. Rosen, (Ed.), *High School Biology: Today and Tomorrow.* Washington, DC: National Academy Press.

Harms, N., & Kohl, S. (1980). *Project synthesis.* Final report submitted to the National Science Foundation. Boulder, CO: University of Colorado.

Harms, N., & Yager, R. (Eds.) (1981). *What research says to the science teacher,* vol. 3. Washington, DC: National Science Teachers Association.

Harrison, A. (1982). Goals of science education. *Science, 217*(455): 109.

Harvard Project Physics. (1967). *Newsletter no. 1.* Cambridge: Harvard University Press.

Hatton, J., & Plouffe, P.B. (1997). *Science and its ways of knowing.* Upper Saddle River, NJ: Prentice Hall.

Hayes-Jacobs, H. (1989). *Interdisciplinary curriculum: Design and implementation.* Alexandria, VA: Association for Supervisors and Curriculum Development.

Hawkins, D. (1965). Messing about in science. *Science and Children, 2*(6): 5–9.

Helgeson, S.L., Blosser, P.E., & Howe, R.W. (1977). *The status of pre-college science, mathematics, and social science education: 1955–1975,* vol. 1, Science Education (SE 78-73 Vol. 1, Center for Science and Mathematics Education, Ohio State University, NSF Contract C762067). Washington, DC: U.S. Government Printing Office.

Hempel, C.G. (1966). *Philosophy of natural science.* Englewood Cliffs, NJ: Prentice Hall.

Hewson, M. (1984). The role of conceptual conflict in conceptual change and the design of science instruction. *Instructional Science, 13*: 1–13.

Hewson, P. (1981). A conceptual change approach to learning science. *European Journal of Science Education, 3*(4): 383–396.

Hewson, P., & Hewson, M. (1988). An appropriate conception of teaching science: A view from studies of science learning. *Science Education, 72*(5): 597–614.

Hewson, P., & Thorley, N.R. (1989). The conditions of conceptual change in the classroom. *International Journal of Science Education* (Special Issue), *11*: 541–653.

Hewson, P.W., et al. (1995). Determining the conceptions of teaching science held by experienced high school science teachers. *Journal of Research in Science Teaching, 32*(5): 503–520.

Hinerman, F. (1994). Multimedia labs. *Science Teacher, 61*(3): 38–41.

Hofstein, A., & Walberg, H.J. (1995). Insructional strategies. In B.J. Fraser & H.J. Walberg (Eds.), *Improving Science Education.* Chicago: University of Chicago Press.

Howard, B.C. (1989). *Learning to persist—persisting to learn.* ERIC Document Reproduction Service No. ED325, 592.

Howe, C.K. (1994). Improving the achievement of Hispanic students. *Educational Leadership, 51*(8): 42–44.

Hrabowski, F.A. (2002). Raising minority achievement in science and math. *Educational Leadership, 60*(4): 44–48.

Hume, D. (1955). An enquiry concerning human understanding. In C.W. Hendel (Ed.), *Hume: Selections* (p. 123). New York: Charles Scribner's & Sons.

Hunter, M. (1976). *Improved instruction.* El Segundo, CA: TIP Publications.

Hunter, M. (1982). *Mastery teaching.* El Segundo, CA: TIP Publications.

Hurd, P. (1978). The golden age of biological education: 1960–1975. In W. Mayer (Ed.), *Biology Teachers Handbook,* 3rd ed. New York: Wiley & Sons.

Hurd, P. (1983). State of precollege education in mathematics and science. *Science Education, 67*(1): 57–67.

Hurd, P. (1984). *Reforming science education: The search for a new vision* (p. 17). Washington, DC: Council for Basic Education.

Hurd, P., Bybee, R.W., Kahle, J.B., & Yager, R. (1980). Biology education in secondary schools of the United States. *The American Biology Teacher, 42*(7): 388–410.

Hurd, P., Robinson, J., McConnell, M., & Ross, N. (1981). *The status of middle school and junior high school science,* (p. 15). Center for Educational Research and Evaluation, Colorado Springs, CO: The Biological Sciences Curriculum Study.

Johnson, D., et al. (1981). Effects of cooperative, competitive and individualistic goal structures on achievement: A meta-analysis. *Psychological Bulletin, 89*: 47–62.

Johnson, D., Johnson, R., Johnson-Holubec, E., & Roy, P. (1986). *Circles of learning: Cooperation in the classroom.* Alexandria, VA: Association for Supervision and Curriculum Development.

Johnson, D., Johnson, R., Dudley, B., & Burnett, R. (1992). Teaching students to be peer mediators. *Educational Leadership*: 10–13.

Kahle, J. B. (1998). *Measuring progress toward equity in science and mathematics education.* Madison, WI: National Institute for Science Education.

Karplus, R. (1980). Teaching for the development of reasoning. In Association for the Education of Teachers of Science Yearbook, A.E. Lawson (Ed.), *The Psychology of Teaching for Thinking and Creativity.* Columbus, OH: ERIC Clearinghouse for Science, Mathematics, and Environmental Education.

Karplus, R., et al. (1977). *Teaching and the development of reasoning.* Berkeley: University of California Press.

Kibler, R., et al. (1970). *Behavioral objective and instruction.* Boston: Allyn & Bacon.

Kay, A. (1995). Computers, networks and education. *Scientific American, Special Issue: The Computer in the 21st Century*: 148–155.

Kibler, R. and others. (1970) *Behavioral objectives and instruction.* Boston: Allyn & Bacon.

Kimball, N. (1993). Essential elements of MBLs. In R. Ruopp, G. Shahaf, B. Drayton, & M. Pfister (Eds.), *LabNet: Toward a Community of Practice.* Hillsdale, NJ: Lawrence Erlbaum Associates.

King, A. (1994). Guiding knowledge construction in the classroom: Effects of teaching children how to question and how to explain. *American Educational Research Journal, 31*(2): 338–368.

Klapper, M.H. (1995). Beyond the scientific method. *The Science Teacher*: 36–40.

Klein, S., & Sherwood, R. (2005). Gender equitable curricula in high school science and engineering. In *Proceedings of the 2005 American Society for Engineering Education Annual Conference & Exposition*. American Society for Engineering Education.

Kliebard, H. (1992). *Forging the American curriculum: Essays in curriculum history and theory*. New York: National Academy Press.

Kluger, A.N., & deNisi, A. (1996). The effects of feedback interventions on performance: A historical review, A meta-analysis, and a preliminary feedback intervention theory. *Psychological Bulletin, 119*(2): 254–284.

Kohlberg, L. (1977, June). The cognitive-developmental approach to moral education. *Phi Delta Kappan*: 670–677.

Krathwohl, D., et al. (1965). *Taxonomy of educational objectives: Handbook 2, Affective domain*. New York: David McKay.

Kuhn, T. (1970). *The structure of scientific revolutions*. Chicago: University of Chicago Press.

Kyle, W., & Shymansky, J. (1989). Enhancing learning through conceptual change in teaching. In *Research Matters to the Science Teacher*, No. 21. University of Maryland, College Park, Maryland: National Association for Research in Science Teaching.

Layman, J., Ochoa, G., & Heikkinen, H. (1996). *Inquiry and learning: Realizing science standards in the classroom*. New York: College Entrance Examination Board.

Ladson-Billings, G. (1994). What we can learn from multicultural education research. *Educational Leadership, 51*(8): 22–27.

Lawson, A. (1988). A better way to teach biology. *American Biology Teacher, 50*(5): 266–278.

Lemke, M., Calsyn, C., Lippman, L., Jocelyn, L., Kastberg, D., Liu, Y.Y., Roey, S., Williams, T., Kruger, T., & Baisu, G. (2001). *Outcomes of learning: Results from the 2000 program for international student assessment of 15-year-olds in reading, mathematics, and science literacy* (NCES 2002-115). U.S. Department of Education, National Center for Educational Statistics Washington, DC: U.S. Government Printing Office.

Leonard, W. H. (1991). A recipe for uncookbooking laboratory investigations. *Journal of College Science Teaching, 21*: 84–87.

Linn, M.C., & Hyde, J.S. (1989). Gender, mathematics, and science. *Educational Researcher, 18*(8): 17–19, 22–27.

Lockard, J.D. (Ed.). (1970). *Seventh report of the international clearinghouse on science and mathematics curricular developments* (p. 305). College Park: Science Teaching Center, University of Maryland.

Losen, D. & Orfield, G. (Eds.) (2002). The Civil rights project. *Racial Inequity in Special Education*. Cambridge, MA: Harvard Education Press.

Lott, G.W. (1983). The effect of inquiry teaching and advanced organizers upon student outcomes in science education. *Journal of Research in Science Teaching, 20*(5): 434–438.

Loucks-Horsley, S., Hewson, P., Love, N., & Stiles, K. (2003). *Designing professional development for teachers of science and mathematics*. Thousand Oaks, CA: Corwin Press.

Luzner, E.A. (1986). Cognitive development: Learning and the development of change. In G.D. Phye & T. Andre (Eds.), *Cognitive Classroom Learning*. New York: Academic Press.

Madrazo, G., & Hounshell, P.B. (1993). Multicultural education: Implications for science education and supervision. *Science Educator, 2*(1): 17–20.

Mager, R. (1997). *Preparing instructional objectives: A critical tool in the development of effective instruction*. Atlanta: The Center for Effective Performance.

Maier, C.A. (2001). Building phylogenetic trees from DNA sequence data: Investigating polar bear and giant panda ancestry. *American Biology Teacher, 63*(9): 642–646.

Malcom, S.M. (1990). Who will do science in the next century? *Scientific American, 262*(2): 112.

Mallow, H.V. (1986). *Science Anxiety: The Fear of Science and How to Overcome It*. Clearwater, FL: H & H Publishing Co., Inc.

Mallow, J.V. (1991). Reading science. *Journal of Reading, 34*: 324–328.

Mallow, J.V., & Greenberg, S. (1983). Science Anxiety and Science Learning. *The Physics Teacher, 21*:95–99.

Marland, S. (1972). *Education of the gifted and talented*. Washington, DC: U.S. Government Printing Office.

Martin, M., Mullis, I., et al. (2000). *Executive summary: TIMSS 1999 international science report*. Chestnut Hill, MA: Boston College.

Marzano, R. J. (2003). *What works in schools: translating Research into action*. Association for Supervision & Curriculum Development.

Mayr, E. (1997). *This is biology: The science of the living world*. Cambridge, MA: The Belknap Press of Harvard University Press.

McGilly, K. (Ed.). (1995). *Classrom lessons*. Cambridge, MA: The MIT Press.

McInerney, J.D. (1986). Biology textbooks—whose business? *American Biology Teacher, 48*(7).

McInerney, J.D. (1987). Curriculum development at the Biological Sciences Curriculum Study. *Educational Leadership*: 24–28.

McLaren, A., & Gaskell, P.J. (1995). Now you see it, now you don't: Gender as an issue in school science. In J. Gaskell & J. Willinsky (Eds.), *Gender informs curriculum: From enrichment to transformation*. New York: Teachers College Press.

McTighe, J., & Ferrara, S. (1998). *Assessing learning in the classroom*. Washington, DC: National Education Association.

Means, B., Penuel, W.R., & Padilla, C. (2001). *The connected school: Technology and learning in high school*. New York: John Wiley.

Milne, M., & Ransome, W. (1993). Helping girls succeed. *Education Week, 13*(8): 23.

Minstrell, J.A. (1989). Teaching science for understanding. In L. Resnick & L. Klopfer (Eds.), *Toward the thinking curriculum: Current cognitive research, 1989 yearbook of the ASCD*. Alexandria, VA: Association for Supervision and Curriculum Development.

Minstrell, J., & van Zee, E. (Eds.). (2000). *Inquiring in inquiry learning and teaching in science*. Washington, DC: American Association for the Advancement of Science.

Mistler-Jackson, M. (2003). *The novice and the expert: How gender and experience influence student participation, interest and learning in an internet-based science project*. Ann Arbor, MI: UMI.

Mistler-Jackson, M., & Songer, N.B. (2000). Student motivation and internet technology: Are students empowered to learn science? *Journal of Research in Science Teaching, 37*(5): 459–479.

Moore, J.A. (1993). *Science as a way of knowing: The foundations of modern biology.* Cambridge, MA: Harvard University Press.

Muller, C., & Riegle-Crumb, C. (2006). No boys allowed. *http://www.utexas.edu/features/2005/friendship/*

Mullis, I.V., & Jenkins, L.B. (1988, September). *The science report card: Elements of risk and recovery.* Princeton, NJ: Education Testing Service.

Murnane, R., & Raizen, S. (Eds.). (1988). *Improving indicators of the quality of science and mathematics education in grades K–12.* Washington, DC: National Academy Press.

Murtadha, K. (1995). An African-centered pedagogy in dialog with liberatory multiculturalism. In C. E. Sleeter & P. L. McLaren (Eds.), *Multicultural Education, Critical Pedagogy, and the Politics of Difference.* Albany, NY: SUNY.

National Assessment of Educational Progress (NAEP). (2006). Executive Summary *http://nationsreportcard.gov/tuda_science/t0101.asp.*

National Assessment of Educational Progress, Science Achievement in the Schools. (1978a). *A summary of results from the 1976–1977 national assessment of science* (Science Report No. 08-01). Denver, CO: Education Commission of the States.

National Assessment of Educational Progress. (1978b). *Three national assessments of science: Changes in achievement, 1969–1977.* Denver, CO: Education Commission of the States.

National Assessment Governing Board (NAGB). (2006). *Science framework for the 2009 National Assessment of Educational Progress.* Developed by WestEd and the Council of Chief State School Officers, Prepublication Edition: NAEP.

National Center for Education Statistics (NCES), U.S.Department of Education, Office of Educational Research and Improvement. (2001). *The nation's report card: Science highlights 2000* (NCES 2002-452). Washington, DC: Author.

National Council of Teachers of Mathematics. (2000). *Curriculum and evaluation standards for school mathematics.* Reston, VA: Author.

National Research Council (NRC). (1996). *National science education standards.* Washington, DC: National Academy Press.

NRC. (1999). *Designing mathematics or science curriculum programs: A guide for using mathematics and science education standards.* Washington, DC: National Academy Press.

NRC. (2000). *Inquiry and the national science education standards: A guide for teaching and learning.* Washington, DC: National Academy Press.

NRC. (2001). *Classroom assessment and the national science education standards.* Washington, DC: National Academy Press.

NRC. (2002). *Investigating the influence of standards: A framework for research in mathematics, science, and technology education.* Washington, DC: National Academy Press.

NRC. (2006). *America's lab report: Investigations in high school science.* Washington, DC: National Academy Press.

National Science Board Commission on Precollege Education in Mathematics, Science and Technology. (1983). *Educating Americans for the 21st century.* Washington, DC: National Science Board.

National Science Teachers Association. (1963). Secondary school science and mathematics teachers. *NSF Bulletin* 63-10: 4. Washington, DC: U.S. Government Printing Office.

National Society for the Study of Education. (1932). *A program for science teaching.* Chicago: University of Chicago Press.

National Society for the Study of Education. (1947). *Science education in American schools.* Chicago: University of Chicago Press.

Neidorf, T.S., Binkley, M., Gattis, K., & Nohara, D. (2004). *A content comparison of the NAEP, TIMSS, and PISA 2003 mathematics assessments.* Washington, DC: U.S. Department of Education, National Center for Education Statistics.

Newmann, F.M. (1988). Can depth replace coverage in the high school curriculum? *Phi Delta Kappan, 69*(5): 345–348.

Noddings, N. (1992). The gender issue. *Educational Leadership, 49*(4): 65–70.

Novak, A. (1963). Scientific inquiry in the laboratory. *The American Biology Teacher:* 342–346.

Novak, J.D. (1988). Learning science and the science of learning. *Studies in Science Education, 15:* 77–101.

Oakes, J., & the Rand Corporation. (1990). Opportunities, achievement, and choice: Women and minority students in science and mathematics. In C.D. Cazden, (Ed.), *Review of Research in Education* (pp. 153–222). Washington, DC: The American Educational Research Association.

Obourn, E.S. (1961). Aids for teaching science observation—Basis for effective science learning. Office of Education Publication No. 29024. Washington, DC: U.S. Government Printing Office.

Olugbemiro, J., & Olajide, J. (1995). Wait-time, classroom discourse, and the influence of sociocultural factors in science teaching. *Science Education, 79*(3): 233–249.

Orenstein, P. (1994). *Schoolgirls: Young women, self-esteem, and the confidence gap.* New York: Bantam Doubleday Dell Publishing Group.

Organisation for Economic Co-operation and Development (PISA). (2003). *The PISA 2003 assessment framework: Mathematics, reading, science and problem solving knowledge and skills.* Paris, France: Author.

Osborne, R., & Freyberg, P. (Eds.). (1983). Concepts, misconceptions, and alternative conceptions: Changing perspectives in science education. *Studies in Science Education, 10:* 61–98.

Osbourn, J., Jones, B., & Stein, M. (1985, April). The case for improving textbooks. *Educational Leadership.*

Otto, P.B. (1991). What research says: Finding an answer in questioning strategies. *Science and Children, 28:* 44–47.

Pedersen, J.E. (1992). The effects of a cooperative controversy. Presented as an STS issue, on achievement and anxiety in secondary science. *School Science and Mathematics, 92*(7): 374–380.

Pella, M.O., O'Hearn, G.T., & Gale, C.W. (1966). Referrents to scientific literacy. *Journal of Research in Science Teaching, 4:* 199–208.

Pellegrino, J., Chudowsky, N., & Glaser, R. (Eds.). (2001). *Knowing what students know.* Washington, DC: National Academy Press.

Pipher, M. (1994). *Reviving Ophelia: Saving the selves of adolescent girls.* New York: Ballantine Books.

Pogrow, S. (1988). Teaching thinking to at-risk elementary students. *Educational Leadership:* 79–85.

Polanyi, M. (1959). *The study of man.* Chicago: University of Chicago Press.

Polanyi, M. (1964). *Personal knowledge: Toward a post-critical philosophy.* New York: Harper & Row.

Polanyi, M. (1967). *The tacit dimension.* Garden City, NY: Anchor Books.

Popper, K. (1965). *Conjectures and refutations: The growth of scientific knowledge.* New York: Harper & Row.

Popper, K. (1968). *The logic of scientific discovery.* New York: Harper & Row.

Porter, A., & Brophy, J. (1988, May). Synthesis of research on good teaching: Insights from the work of the Institute for Research on Teaching. *Educational Leadership*: 74–85.

Posner, G. (1994). *Analyzing the curriculum.* New York: McGraw-Hill.

Posner, G.J., Strike, K.A., Hewson, P.W., & Gerzog, W.A. (1982). Accommodation of a scientific conception: Toward a theory of conceptual change. *Science Education, 66*(2): 211–227.

Powell, J., Short, J., & Landes, N. (2002). Curriculum reform, professional development, and powerful learning. In R. W. Bybee (Ed.), *Learning Science and the Science of Learning* (pp. 121–136). Arlington, VA: NSTA Press.

Progressive Education Association. (1938). *Science in general education.* New York: Appleton-Century-Crofts.

Ravitch, D. (1995). *National standards in American education: A citizen's guide.* Washington, DC: The Brookings Institution.

Redfield, D.D., & Darrow, S.P. (1970, April). *Physics Teacher, 8*: 170–180.

Renner, J., Grant, R., & Sutherland, P. (1978). Content and concrete thought. *Science Education, 62*(2): 215–221.

Renner, J., Abraham, M., & Birnie, H. (1985). The importance of the FORM of student acquisition of data in physics learning cycles. *Journal of Research in Science Teaching, 22*(4): 303–326.

Renner, J., & Abraham, M. (1986). The sequence of learning cycle activities in high school chemistry. *Journal of Research in Science Teaching, 23*(2): 121–143.

Renner, J.W., Abraham, R.W., & Birnie, H.H. (1986). The importance of the form of student acquisition of data in physics learning cycles. *Journal of Research in Science Teaching, 23*(2): 121–143.

Rickover, H. (1970). *Education and freedom.* New York: Random House.

Roberts, D. (1982). Developing the concept of 'curriculum emphasis' in science education. *Science Education, 66*(2): 243–260.

Roberts, R., & Bazler, J. (1993). Adapting for disabilities. *The Science Teacher, 60*(1): 21–25.

Robertson, I. (2000). Imitative problem solving: Why transfer of learning often fails to occur. *Instructional Science, 28*(4): 263–289.

Rolón, C.A. (2002). Educating Latino students. *Educational Leadership, 60*(4): 40–43.

Roth, K. (1985). *Conceptual learning and student processing of science texts* (Research Series No. 167). East Lansing, MI: Institute for Research on Teaching, Michigan State University.

Roth, K. (1994). Second thoughts about interdisciplinary studies. *American Educator, 18*(1): 48.

Roth, K., & Anderson C. (1988). Promoting conceptual change learning from science textbooks. In P. Ramsden (Ed.), *Improving Learning: New Perspectives.* New York: Kogan Page Publishers.

Ruopp, R., & Pfister, M. (1993). An introduction to LabNet. In R. Ruopp, G. Shahaf, B. Drayton, & M. Pfister (Eds.), *LabNet: Toward a Community of Practice.* Hillsdale, NJ: Lawrence Erlbaum Associates.

Ruopp, R., & Haavind, S. (1993). From current practices to projects. In R. Ruopp, G. Shahaf, B. Drayton, & M. Pfister (Eds.), *LabNet: Toward a Community of Practice.* Hillsdale, NJ: Lawrence Erlbaum Associates.

Rowe, M. (1970). Wait-time and rewards as instructional variables: Influence on inquiry and sense of fate control. *New Science in the Inner City.* New York: Teachers College, Columbia University, Unpublished paper.

Rowe, M. (1974). Wait time and rewards as instructional variables: Their influence on language, logic, and fate control. Part One. Wait Time. *Journal of Research in Science Teaching, 11*: 81–94.

Rowe, M.B. (1979). *Teaching science by continuous inquiry.* New York: McGraw Hill.

Rutherford, F. J. (1964). The role of inquiry in science teaching. *Journal of Research in Science Teaching, 2*: 80–84.

Ruiz-Primo, M., Li, M., Ayala, C., & Shavelson, R. (2004). Evaluating student science notebooks as an assessment tool. *International Journal of Science Education, 26*(12): 1477–1506.

Rutherford, F. J., & Ahlgren, A. (1989). *Science for all Americans.* New York: Oxford University Press.

Sachse, T.P. (1989). Making science happen. *Educational Leadership, 47*(3): 18–21.

Sadker, M., & Sadker, D. (1994). *Failing at fairness: How our schools cheat girls.* New York: Macmillan.

Sadler, R. (1989). Formative assessment and the design of instructional systems. *Instructional Science, 18*: 119–144.

Saiz, D. (1994). PC possibilities. *Science Teacher, 61*(3): 28–31.

Salmon, W.C. (1973, May). Confirmation. *Scientific American*: 75–83.

Schmidt, W., et al. (1996). *Characterizing pedagogical flow: An investigation of mathematics and science teaching in six countries.* Dordrecht/Boston/London: Kluwer Academic Publishers.

Schmidt, W., McKnight, C., & Raizen, S. (1997). *A splintered vision: An investigation of U.S. science and mathematics education.* Dordrecht/Boston/London: Kluwer Academic Publishers.

Schmidt, W., et al. (1998). *Facing the consequences: Using TIMSS for a closer look at United States mathematics and science education.* Dordrecht/Boston/London: Kluwer Academic Publishers.

Schofield, J.W. (1995). *Computers and classroom culture.* New York: Cambridge University Press.

Schwab, J.J. (1958). The teaching of science as inquiry. *Bulletin of the Atomic Scientists, 14*: 374–379.

Schwab, J.J. (1960). Enquiry, the science teacher, and the educator. *The Science Teacher*: 6–11.

Schwab. J. (1966). *The teaching of science.* Cambridge, MA: Harvard University Press.

Seeman, M. (1959, December). The meaning of alienation. *American Sociological Review, 24*: 783–791.

Serrano, R.G. (1977, June). *The status of science, mathematics, and social science in Western City, USA, Case studies in science education* (Booklet 7: 10–13). Urbana-Champaign: University of Illinois.

Shavelson, R.J., Carey, N.B., & Webb, N.M. (1990). Indicators of science achievement: Options for a powerful policy instrument. *Phi Delta Kappan, 71*(9): 692–697.

Shepard, L.A. (2003). Reconsidering large-scale assessment to heighten its relevance to learning. In J.M. Atkin & J.E. Coffey, *Everyday Assessment in the Science Classroom* (pp. 121–126). Washington, DC: National Science Teachers Association.

Showalter, V. (1974). What is unified science education? Program objectives and scientific literacy. *Prism, 2*(2): 1–6.

Shulman, L.S. (1986). Those who understand: Knowledge growth in teaching. *Educational Researcher, 15*(2): 4–14.

Shymansky, J. (1984). BSCS programs; Just how effective were they? *The American Biology Teacher, 46*(1): 54–57.

Shymansky, J., Kyle, W., & Alport, J. (1983). The effects of new science curricula on student performance. *Journal of Research in Science Teaching, 20*(5): 387–404.

Smith, C., Carey, S., & Wiser, M. (1985). On differentiation: A case study of the development of the concepts of size, weight, and density. *Cognition*: 177–237.

Smith, M. L. (1977, May). *Teaching and science education in fall, river, case studies in science education.* (Booklet 2: 5–9). Urbana-Champaign: University of Illinois.

Snir, J., Smith, C., & Grosslight, L. (1995). Conceptually enhanced simulations: A computer tool for science teaching. In D.N. Perkins et al. (Eds.), *Software Goes to School: Teaching for Understanding with New Technologies.* New York: Oxford University Press.

Songer, N.B. (1996). Exploring learning opportunities in coordinated network-enhanced classrooms: A case of kids as global scientists. *The Journal of the Learning Sciences, 5*(4): 297–327.

Stake, R., & Easley, J. (1977). Case studies in science education. Project at the Center for Instructional Research and Curriculum Evaluation. Urbana-Champaign: University of Illinois.

Stake, R., Easley, J., et al. (1978). *Case studies in science education,* (SE 78–74 vol. 1 and SE 78–74 vol. 2). Center for Instructional Research and Curriculum Evaluation, University of Illinois at Urbana-Champaign (NSF Contract C7621134). Washington, DC: U.S. Government Printing Office.

Stanford Center for Development in Teaching. (1963). *Stanford teacher competence appraisal guide.* Stanford, CA: Author.

Stedman, C. H. (1987). Fortuitous strategies on inquiry in the good ole days. *Science Education, 71*(5): 657–665.

Stephenson, R. (1978). Relationships between the intellectual level of the learner and student achievement in high school chemistry. Ph.D. dissertation, University of Northern Colorado.

Stiggins, R.J. (2001). *Student-involved classroom assessment.* Columbus, OH: Merrill Prentice Hall.

Storey, R., & Carter, J. (1992). Why the scientific method? *The Science Teacher*: 18–21.

Taylor, D., & Lorimer, M. (2002). Helping boys succeed. *Educational Leadership, 60*(4): 68–71.

Taylor, K.L. (2002). Through the eyes of students. *Educational Leadership, 60*(4): 72–75.

Texley, J. Kwan, T., and Sammers, J. (2004). Investigating safely: A guide for high school teachers. Washington, D.C.: NSTA.

The Civil Rights Project. (2002). In D. Losen, & G. Orfield, (Eds.), *Racial Inequity in Special Education.* Cambridge, MA: Harvard Education Press.

Thompson, R. E. (1970). A survey of the teaching of physics in secondary schools. *School and Society, 98*: 243–244.

Tobin, K., Tippins, D., & Gallard, A. (1994). Research on instructional strategies for teaching science. In D. Gabel, (Ed.), *Handbook of Research on Science Teaching and Learning.* New York: MacMillan Publishing Company.

Trowbridge, D.E., & McDermott, L.C. (1981). Investigation of student understanding of the concept of acceleration in one dimension. *American Journal of Physics, 49*: 242–253.

Tyler, R. (1949). *Basic principles of curriculum and instruction.* Chicago: University of Chicago Press.

Underhill, O.E. (1941). *The origins and development of elementary-school science.* New York: Scott Foresman.

University of Maryland, College Park: Chemistry Department. (1973). *IAC Newsletter, 2*(1): 3.

U.S. Department of Education, National Center for Education Statistics. (1996). *Pursuing excellence.* Washington, DC: U.S. Government Printing Office.

U.S. Department of Education. (2004). *Toward a new golden age in American education: How the internet, the law and today's students are revolutionizing expectations.* Washington, DC: Office of Educational Technology.

U.S. Office of Education. (1951). *Life adjustment education for every youth.* Washington, DC: U.S. Government Printing Office.

Valverde, G., & Schmidt, W. (1997–1998). Refocusing U.S. math and science education. *Issues in Science and Technology, 2*: 60–66.

Veugelers, W. (2000). Different ways of teaching values. *Educational Review, 51*(1): 37–46.

Villegas, A.M. (1991). Culturally responsive teaching. In *Foundations for Tomorrow's Teachers #1.* Princeton, NJ: Educational Testing Service.

Vygotsky, L.S. (1968). *Thought and language.* A. Kozulin (Trans. and Ed.). Cambridge, MA: MIT Press.

Walker, R. (1977, April). *Case studies in science education: Boston* (Booklet 11: 6, 7, 15, 25). Urbana-Champaign: University of Illinois.

Wandersee, J.H. (1986). Can the history of science help science educators anticipate students' misconceptions? *Journal of Research in Science Teaching, 23*: 581–597.

Wandersee, J., Mintzes, J., & Novak, J. (1994). Research on alternative conceptions in science. In D. Gabel (Ed.), *Handbook of Research on Science Teaching and Learning.* New York: Macmillan.

Wang, A.Y. (1993). Cultural familial predicators predictors of children's metacognitive and academic performance. *Journal of Research in Childhood Education, 7*(2): 83–90.

Wasik, J.L. (1971). A comparison of cognitive performance of PSSC and non-PSSC students. *Journal of Research in Science Teaching,* 8(1): 85–90.

Watson, B., & Konicek, R. (1990). Teaching for conceptual change: Confronting children's experience. *Phi Delta Kappan,* 71(9): 680–685.

Wavering, M.J., Perry, B., & Bird, D. (1986). Performance of students in grades 6, 9, and 12 on five logical, spatial, and formal tasks. *Journal of Research in Science Teaching,* 23: 321–333.

Weiss, I. (1978). *Report of the 1977 national survey of science, mathematics, and social studies education* (SE 78–72). Center for Educational Research and Evaluation, Research Triangle Institute (NSF Contract C7619848). Washington, DC: U.S. Government Printing Office.

Weiss, I. (1987). *Report of the 1985–86 national survey of science and mathematics education.* Research Triangle Park, NC: Research Triangle Institute.

Weiss, I., Banilower, E., McMahon, K., & Smith, P. (2001). *Report of the 2000 national survey of science and mathematics education.* Chapel Hill, NC: Horizon Research Inc.

Welch W. (1969). Correlates of course satisfaction in high school physics. *Journal of Research in Science Teaching,* 6: 54–58.

Welch, W. (1977, April). *Science education in Urbanville: A case study, Case studies in science education* (Booklet 5: 4–5). Urbana-Champaign: University of Illinois.

Welch, W.W., Klopfer, L.E., Aikenhead, G.S., & Robinson, J.T. (1981). The role of inquiry in science education: Analysis and recommendations. *Science Education,* 5(1): 33–50.

Wells, J., & Lewis, L. (2006). *Internet access in U.S. public schools and classrooms: 1994–2005* (NCES 2007–020). U.S. Department of Education. Washington, DC: National Center for Education Statistics.

Wiggins, G., & McTighe, J. (2005). *Understanding by design.* Alexandria, VA: Association for Supervision and Curriculum Development.

Wilen, W. (1984). Implications of research on questioning for the teacher educator. *Journal of Research and Development in Education,* 2.

Yager, R. (Ed.). (1996). *Science/technology/society as reform in science education.* Albany: State University of New York Press.

Yore, L.D. (1991). Secondary science teachers attitudes toward and beliefs about science reading and science textbooks. *Journal of Research in Science Teaching,* 28(1): 55–72.

NAME INDEX

SUBJECT INDEX